PIRATES
MERCHANTS
DEVILS
AND
DARK DEEDS

PIRATES MERCHANTS DEVILS ᚠᚾᚦᚠᚱᛚᚷᛈᚾAND᛫ᛁᚦᛋᚲᚤᚺᛏᛒ DARK DEEDS

TRADE, EXPLORATION AND RELIGION FROM THE ICE AGE TO THE VIKING AGE

SHANI OATES

Thoth Publications

Copyright © 2025 Shani Oates
Thoth Publications Ltd, 2025.

Shani Oates has the moral right to be identified as the author of this work.

A CIP catalogue record for this book is available from the British Library

All rights reserved. No part of this publication may be reproduced, stored in a retrieval system, or transmitted, in any form or by any means, electronic, mechanical, photocopying, recording or otherwise, without the prior permission of the publishers.

Published by Thoth Publications
Whitwick Road, Markfield,
Leicestershire LE67 9QB

ISBN 978-1913660475
Web address: www.thothpublications.com
Email: enquiries@thoth.co.uk

CONTENTS

PART ONE: THE OLD WORLD – PEOPLES, ETHNICITY AND CULTURE

INTRODUCTION TO PART ONE: The Geocentric Politics of Migration: Ice Age to Viking Age … 9

Old World Cultures … 11
Remnants of a Material Culture … 22
Ethnogenesis (Ice-Age to Iron Age) … 25
Ethnicity … 34
Rock Art as a Neolithic Narrative Culture … 47
Sámi and Narrative Art … 58
Liminal Narratives and Ships of the Dead … 61
Maritime Trade and Traditions … 63
Sails Design, A Vanity of Prestige? … 69
The Deer Mother and The Mother of Animals … 75
Cultural Transitions … 87
Spirits of Fire and Hearth … 95
Earth Mother Archetypes … 99
Enarei – A Sacred Priesthood … 106
The Shamanic Landscape of the Arctic … 110

PART TWO: DEATH AND CREATION

INTRODUCTION TO PART TWO: Monumental Structures as Houses of the Dead … 123

Ancestral Markers – Cultic Sites … 126
Coffin Boats and Boat Burials … 136
Funerary Culture: Kurgans … 146
Khirigsuur … 148
Pazyryk Mummies … 156
Tamgas and Taltos … 159
Proto-Slavic Peoples: Their Idols, Beliefs and Origins … 163
Warrior Funerary Stelae … 170
Tengrism … 175
The Royal Scythians and the Steppe Peoples … 178
Warrior Peoples of the Sun … 184
Warrior Hero Cults of Stone and Iron … 193

Time and Eternity - The Cosmic Mill	198
Finnar	216
Sámi Culture in Scandinavia	225

Part Three: The Skin Trade, Slavic Gods and The Northern Crusades

Introduction to Part Three: Heritage and the Legacy: Being Vikingr — 232

Thule	237
The Skin Trade	240
Kievan Rus' – Early Trade in the East	251
Medieval Trade	258
Slavic Religion: The Natural Origins of Folkloric Belief	264
The Sacred Isle of Rügen and the 'Howling God'	269
Earth and Sky: An Eternal Harmony	277
Thunder Spirits	284
Gods of The Russian Primary Chronicle	291
The Zbruch Idol	310
The Continuity of Folk Culture	314
Baptism and Hell-Fire	319
Jómsborg?	325
The Wends	331
The Northern or Baltic Crusades	339

Appendices

Appendix I: Who is the Sky Father?	344
Appendix II: Influential Western-European Tribal Peoples	350
Appendix III: A Vital Chronology of Eastern Tribes Peoples and the Steppe Nations/Confederacies	351
Appendix IV: Early Slavic Expansion	356
Appendix V: Wars and Conquests of the Türkic Khaganates	359
Appendix VI: Háraldr – King of Norway	360
Appendix VII: Language	361

Glossary of cultures that have enriched and contributed to the Northern landscape.	363
Bibliography	370

Part One:
THE OLD WORLD – PEOPLES, BELIEFS, ETHNICITY AND CULTURE

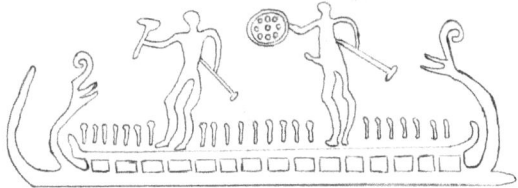

INTRODUCTION To Part One
The Geocentric Politics of Migration: Ice Age to Viking Age

THE HUMAN SPECIES is tenacious to say the least; its keen instinct for survival initiated a finely tuned (reciprocal) relationship with all things visible and invisible that explored and exploited all sensory experience. We do what we need to, we are adaptable, we adjust. Therefore, this book is primarily about how we interact with our environment in terms of that relationship with the divine, and how we interact with each other as we move around the landscape doing whatever we need to, to thrive and to evolve. Those two things are inexorably intertwined, and though ultimately managed by Orlog (Law of Destiny), they are each led by Wyrd (Fate). Nothing is static, and everything changes. Striving for balance, we fear chaos, and rightfully so. Mistrusting what we don't know, we developed the mechanics of superstition to protect ourselves from those things, and those things often include other people.

Traditionally speaking, borderlands and boundaries are areas of conflict that were historically besieged with pirates and bandits, and it is these threats that led to customs related to cautionary activities and rituals to stave off or neutralise those potentialities. Liminal spaces were no exception. In the old world, peoples of different cultures, languages and customs encountered one another with trepidation, encouraged only by necessity to engage. Those encounters celebrate all we have in common as a species, but more importantly, the remarkable diversity of humankind, our illuminating artistry, articulation and creativity, and the power of mind, of comprehension and enquiry. Above all, our capacity for invention is astonishing.

Our Northern history remains largely unsung, eclipsed by the glamour of the classical world and its colourful legacy of Romanised culture. But there is another world, no less vibrant and exciting, no less fascinating or challenging, and its impact is only now being finally

10 PIRATES, MERCHANTS, DEVILS & DARK DEEDS

acknowledged and investigated by western scholars, who previously snubbed its simple yet profound treasures for those iconic edifices of the Mediterranean and the Middle East. Here then is a very different history, yet it is one we can recognise ourselves in. Who we are, originates here. Culture is a journey of experiential discovery in an ever-changing landscape. Around a visual landscape and narrative texts, we construct a foundation based in archaeological artefacts that vie for our attention and interpretation. Each of us may see that differently. Amidst the cold hard science, we find an aesthetic that defies absolutes. In their own way, historians are poets of the past, their vision inspires us to look again at what we thought we knew. It is my hope this tome will unpick set patterns and reweave them into a more faithful explanation of a northern world we can better understand, better relate to, and better appreciate as the blood and bones of our ancestry. We begin when nature renewed herself at the end of the last Ice Age. This harsh environment ultimately generated the renaissance of northern culture.

OLD WORLD CULTURES

During the last glacial event, the whole of Scandinavia was under ice. Previous human occupation of the Arctic and subarctic Eurasia, dates to the last phase of the Upper Palaeolithic Period when the earliest Arctic settlers and their descendants were specialized hunters of the rich game resources on land and sea. Following the herds, they tracked into the northeastern tip of Siberia, becoming the first humans to cross into the vast territories of North America, though there is no agreement whether this occurred after the last Ice Age event which ended around 11050 BCE, or prior to it around, 28050 BCE. Either way, several waves of migration followed, and in both directions as the thawing ice caps flooded the land bridge to Asia. Climatic warming around 9700 BCE[1], led to the growth and rapid expansion of the vital taiga (boreal forest[2]). It is here our relationship with the wild 'Other' began.

Those swamp and bog marshes then gave way to arboreal forests that gradually dominated huge tracts of land. And, as the populace increased, so did the range of settlement sites throughout these rich, abundant landscapes.[3] Mesolithic pioneers of the Northernmost areas of Fennoscandia have left us the first signs of human and animal (re)habitation we recognise as the emergent (Komsa[4] and Fosna[5]) Stone Age hunter-gatherer (fisher-foraging) cultures. Though initially

---

1. This marked the transition from the Pleistocene to the Holocene Epoch. The mean annual temperature reached 2.5°C above that of today, allowing Neolithic people to advance forward across Europe and Asia. In the Canadian Arctic and in Manitoba, the mean temperature passed 4°C above present averages. **2.** Taiga is a subarctic (coniferous) forest of pines, spruces, and larches, a buffer zone between the northern tundra and the temperate forests of the southern regions. The ground of the Taiga is mostly permafrost. **3.** An extremely rich and abundant period for early humans over much of the world. In Europe it eventually facilitated the wealthy cultures that flourished during the Bronze Age. Bold navigators began using the seaways to trade between the eastern Mediterranean, the British Isles, and the Baltic. See: https://www.britannica.com/science/Holocene-Epoch/The-Pleistocene-Holocene-boundary **4.** Komsa is now an obsolete term for the archaeological culture of the nomadic hunters and gatherers of the late Palaeolithic and early Mesolithic. Early Mesolithic sites on the Kola peninsula resemble the Norwegian 'Komsa' Culture sites, though they also suffer from the lack of reliable dating. **5.** The nomadic Komsa Culture was followed by the semi-nomadic (maritime) Fosna culture, which existed in Northern Norway.

12 PIRATES, MERCHANTS, DEVILS & DARK DEEDS

distinct, these pioneering cultures merged together quite successfully. In the thousand years between 7500 and 6500 BCE., Norway roughly acquired its current recognisable coastline in contra-distinction to that ascribed to the lower lying regions of eastern Sweden, western and southern Finland, and most of Denmark, which look very different today.

This is because the former areas lay beneath the waters of a new and larger melt-water lake, while in the latter area the sea had not yet reached the level at which it stands today. In both instances, however, the cause was the same, for it was the now-largely vanished ice-sheet that was responsible. Indeed, only a few small masses of dead ice languished on the slopes of Lappland at the time. The disappearance of the Scandinavian ice-sheet had two very different results. In the first place, as it melted, the water that it had locked up for thousands of years (together with the continental ice-sheets that covered North America) flowed back into the ocean, ultimately raising sea levels by as much as 300 feet. At the same time, the crushing burden of its weight having been removed from the land, the depressed block of the earth's crust beneath the glacier's center began bouncing back to its former elevation – more slowly than the oceans rose, but continuing for a longer time. (In fact, the isostatic rebound of the Scandinavian peninsula has not yet been completed, for in the Oslofjord region the land continues to rise at the rate of about 1 foot per century and in the Umeå district of Sweden – in the immediate vicinity of the ice-sheet's center – at the rate of 3 feet per century).[6]

As the ice melted, the sea-level rose, allowing melt-waters to advance far up into the eastern valleys, dragging marine clay some 80 miles inland into Lake Mjösa. Another example of this shift occurred some 20-30 miles inland into central Norway, where we find the highest post-glacial marine limit of land that had risen from 400 to 600 feet. In fact, when the Fosna culture people arrived, the sea level (relative to the land) stood some 500 feet higher than it does today, making any settlement below that level, a physical impossibility. Conversely, between 5000 and 4000 BCE, the land rose in some

---

6. Vincent H. Malmström. "Norway Before the Vikings: Part I - From Glacial Times to the Stone Age." (Dartmouth College, 2012). https://web.archive.org/web/20120204235040/http://www.dartmouth.edu/~izapa/E-31.pdf.In Norway, the rise in ocean level had outpaced the isostatic rebound of the land, and most of the melting of the dead-ice tongues in the lower valleys of the southeast took place directly into the sea. The relationship between rising land mass and sea levels is incredibly complex and is subject to many regional variations. There is no generic equation for this, and I certainly advise those interested, to study all the good science relating to it, especially as it relates to the major stages in the human occupancy of the land, and many of the reasons for moving across it. See also: Melheim, 2020.

areas by approximately 300 feet, which explains the presence of the Nøstvet (forest-based hunting) culture (at a site approximately 12 miles southeast of Oslo), situated about 200 feet above the present sea level. "Both [the Nøstvet and the Fosna] were Mesolithic hunting societies whose artifacts continued to be fashioned from the only raw materials that were familiar to them − stone, bone, and horn."[7] With rising temperatures, the stage was set for the adoption of farming in Norway, circa 2500 BCE.[8] "Indeed, the climate in southeastern Norway at the time would have been directly comparable to that of northern France today, representing a latitudinal shift of nearly 10°!"[9]

Professing an ancient heritage from those various Ice Age hunter-gatherer populations, the Sámi people currently represent a Finnic-speaking, ethnic minority of numerous tribes throughout northern Scandinavia, Finland and parts of western Russia (known collectively as Fennoscandia).

Language, race and ethnicity combine in varying degrees to form a 'people,' who splinter into tribal units and thusly, generate further nuanced variations in those patterns of evolution and expansion. To avoid generalisations, we now look to new sciences for genetic markers (specifically haplogroups) for more precise indicators of shifting movement patterns. A popular theory in the past had suggested the Sámi represented an aboriginal population who were later displaced by Germanic-speaking migrants, however, recent intensive studies highlight a more complex settlement pattern. For example, the new science confirms that both the Germanic-speaking populations and the Finnic-speaking populations share lines of descent from the same groups of people who first emerged and then populated the northern regions after the last Ice Age event ocurred around 10000 years ago.[10]

Researchers who had long speculated that the Komsa people are the ancestors of the Sámi, whose mythic origins profess a two-part migration from the north (Ukraine), and the south (Iberia), now have validation for their model.[11] Modern skeletal and DNA analyses confirm two major waves of migration that reached Scandinavia after the ice

---

7. Malmström, 2012. **8.** At that time, temperatures averaged two to three degrees Celsius warmer than they are now. **9.** Malmstrom, 2012. **10.** See Appendix V
11. Northwest European hunter-gatherers from around 10000 BCE to 5000 BCE, exhibit high frequencies of DNA diversity similar to those of European hunter-gatherers from Iberia to Scandinavia, aligning neatly with the appearance of rock art glyphs found in Northern Scandinavia (Jamtland center of Sweden, Nord-Trondelag center of Norway and Nordland in Norway). Dated from around 7050 BCE to 4050 BCE, these early images focus mainly on hunting and fishing.

14   PIRATES, MERCHANTS, DEVILS & DARK DEEDS

sheets retreated. The first people to arrive from their southwestern Iberian Refuge, were formerly of Palaeo-European origin. They had blue eyes, mediterranean complexions, and darker hair, whereas the later peoples who had travelled northwards from the northeastern regions around the Black Sea and the Ukraine, had paler hair and skin with varied eye colours, which were mainly brown.[12]

The subsistence life-style of the European cave dwelling Gravettian hunter-gatherers[13] who'd endured the long frigid Ice Age[14] of Prehistoric Europe, contributed key genetic material to their descendants who became the north bound travellers from their Iberian and Ukrainian Refuges. When the northern peoples returned home after their long sojourn in the south during that Ice Age event, they carried with them a heritage celebrated through the vast scope of rock art features scattered across the northern hemisphere.[15] The aesthetic legacy of those Upper Palaeolithic artworks are reflected in the archaic enigmatic petroglyphs and engravings in France and Spain (dated to around 27050 BCE to 22050 BCE), and in the portable ivory and clay sculptures found in Czechoslovakian burials[16] (erroneously dubbed as 'Venus' or fertility figurines). These incredible artworks reveal a fabulous envisioning of a world burgeoning with life. Graves were generously furnished with purpose-built offerings, personal adornments and jewellery fashioned from shells.

The peoples of the Gravettian[17] culture also enjoyed the use of crude ceramics, blunt knives, pointed arrowheads, and most intriguing of all, boomerangs, a feature that no doubt contributed to the intrinsic magical qualities ascribed much later to Þórr's legendary Mjölnir, that like the boomerang, always returned to his hand.

After reaching the Baltic and southern area of Finland, many of those returning tribes faded into obscurity across northern Europe as they blended and merged with other peoples, equally dependent upon the now expansive movement of herds. Over the course of their two-

---

12. Eastern Hunter-gatherers who survived the last glacial maximum in the western Eurasian refuge have contributed some 75% Ancient North Eurasian DNA.   **13.** European Upper Palaeolithic, circa 31050 BCE.   **14.** During the Last Glacial Maximum, glaciers spread to 25% of the global landmass, and sea levels dropped more than 400 feet, exposing the land beneath the English Channel.   **15.** Both the Suomusjärvi and Komsa peoples (as seen in the paintings of Kapova Cave and Lascaux Caves, respectively) from the former regions of their ancestral refuge during the Glacial Event.   **16.** At Dolni Vestonice. See: https://www.nytimes.com/2023/03/01/science/dna-hunter-gatherers-europe.html (Retrieved 4th July 2024)   **17.** Western Gravettian, known mainly from cave sites in France, Spain, and England, and the other is the Eastern Gravettian of Central Europe and Russia. See: Glossary.

and-a-half millennium migration, needful interactions amongst this vast swathe of peoples (both economically and socially), led to the development of certain commonalities of culture and belief. In other words, their journey initiated a cosmology discernible in their later respective Finno-Ugric belief systems.[18] When the early remains of Stone Age peoples who had occupied the regions of Alta, Finnmark were found, certain artefacts (of slate and quartz) could be traced back to the Ural Mountains that span Northern Russia and north-west Fennoscandia.[19] Cultural continuity between these Stone Age people and the Sámi specifically, is assumed on evidential basis relating to artistic similarities in the decorative patterns found on archaeological bone objects favoured by the later Sámi. Although material culture evolved through interactions with other peoples, there is no archaeological evidence of displacement - one population did not replace another. They appeared to have lived side by side without incident. At this stage, they were not in competition, and food was abundant.[20]

Dating of rock art is based on their location's height above sea level, so is unfortunately subject to vastly complex associated dynamics that render general dating methods unreliable.[21] Remains of various Neolithic and Bronze Age artefacts found at Oleniy Ostrov, the Ural Mountains, the peat bogs of Finland (Gorbunovo) and Russia (Shigir), include wooden buckets and Mesolithic skis with elk and bird head terminals. As one of the newly emerging (material) cultures of the Mesolithic, the people of the *Suomusjärvi*[22] culture for example, represent the ancestors of the Finnish people, making the Diving-Bird myth common to many northern traditions, an important tenet of

---

18. Around 6000 BCE, the Proto-Uralic language began to split, forming the Proto-Finno-Ugric, and the Proto-Samoyed language groups. **19.** In fact, recent archaeological discoveries in Finnish Lapland and along the coast of Norway show distinctive similarities between the slightly older Suomusjärvi material culture (ca. 7000 BCE, being one of the first to spread into Finland from the east), with those of the Palaeo-European Komsa (material) culture (which originated in southern Europe). **20.** Red deer, bear, fox, wolf, hare, fish and birds are noted. **21.** The relationship between the flooding of meltwaters and glacial rebound is quite complex and very much region dependant. **22.** Proto-Finns developed a shamanic hunting-gathering-fisher-foraging culture similar to peoples across the sub-Arctic Eurasian regions (such as the Evenks of Siberia), probably through their links to the Suomusjärvi Culture, which was itself an earlier mix of post-Swiderian cultures formed of the various migrating peoples from the regions around Finland (namely, Estonia, Karelia, and the Volga). Being relatively close in terms of ethnic and linguistic ties, these groups enjoyed reciprocal cultural influences that were maintained through traditional marriage and kinship ties. See: Harold Alden, Shamanism and Sacred Arts in Finland – Part 2. https://www.spiritboat.ca/2014/06/shamanism-and-sacred-arts-in-finland.html (Accessed 19th September 2024).

their cosmology. It is therefore remarkable to discover in those early Cave Art images, the depiction of not just universal hunting scenes (involving horse, auroch, deer, bison, stags, bulls and a reindeer) but of an ithyphallic man with a bird's head whose facial features suggest a person in deep trance; beside him is a bird-headed staff and a spear. We cannot be certain of course, but this does appear to be an early image of a shaman.

Thusly, as the Proto-Sámi[23] people advanced northwards between 11000 and 10000 years ago, they clearly encountered others[24] who contributed to their genetic and linguistic characteristics. Benefitting from a flourishing trade of material industry, cultural enrichment (physical, material and spiritual), and inter-marriage, the resulting peoples settled across Norway, Finmark and the regions of Fennoscandia.[25] The Sámi hold a unique position amongst the numerous other peoples of the Arctic regions with whom they shared and developed shamanic traditions, though certain distinctions are apparent, namely the attribution of female shamans, for which we find no evidence of in Sámi tradition. Rock art and the erection of sacred structures is a highly significant feature of these early shamanic cultures[26] that collectively assert a strong, evolving spiritual belief system, reaching from the Black Sea to Brittany between 6050 BCE and 1050 BCE.

We are now able follow the trail of (Komsa) cultural artefacts (associated with the proto-Sámi) that is fully supported by linguistic (and genetic) evidence[27] across the northern landscapes that include the mountain regions of Alta Finnmark. Researchers speculate that the Komsa Culture people are therefore the main ancestors of the Sámi whose original mountainous location may also explain the importance

---

23. The Proto-Sami people thus sit alongside the Uralic, and later Finno-Ugric people. Even though the Komsa possibly spoke an ancient European language, by 7500 BCE, members of the Suomusjarvi Culture had travelled north to Komsa culture territory, so it seems likely that the early ancestors of the Sámi adopted the Proto-Uralic language from those visitors. **24.** Western European Post-Ahrensburgian cultures: Fosna-Hensbacka and Komsa and Eastern European (Polish) Post-Swiderian cultures, Kunda, Veretye, Suomusjärvi, respectively. See Glossary of Cultures. **25.** Indeed, fishing nets found on the Karelian Isthmus close to the Russia-Finland border, confirm evidence of human occupation in southern Finland around c 7340 BCE. **26.** Just as the Suomusjärvi people were heir to a Palaeolithic rock painting tradition (represented in the paintings in Kapova Cave), the Komsa culture people were descended from the sacred rock artists of Lascaux Caves, in France. **27.** Linguistic evidence lends more credence to this theory as Sámi languages and modern Uralic languages share a common ancestor.

of the sacred mountain in their cosmology. The subsistence foundation of the Komsa Culture (being almost exclusively sea-oriented, living mainly off seal hunting, fishing and boat-building) is particularly integral to the Fennoscandian rock art cultures, and indeed played a significant role in shaping the beliefs and ethnic cultures of northern peoples.

Around 8000 years ago, these ancestors of the Sámi people finally reached, and then settled across northern Scandinavia. When considering movements of people, it is important to remember that at this time, most of the European landscape was still arctic tundra, (similar to how we envision Siberia today). This means that overland travel was achieved on skis and sleds. And indeed, these are the images we see in the form of petroglyphs and pictograms that cover the towering rock formations in Norway, Sweden and Finland. Some of these near to coastal points depict early forms of shipping that may indicate later arrivals by boat, as traders or invaders.

Conditions in the arctic regions were gruelling, but with clever management, seasonal seal hunting with kayaks, and the dogsled for winter, the people here increased their subsistence options across a considerable geographic range. Kept for transportation and hunting, dogs have been pulling sleds across the Arctic (and almost certainly in Siberia too) for thousands of years.[28] In fact, sleds were pulled by people, dogs or reindeer,[29] depending upon location and era.[30] Hauled by man, rather than dog, a sled runner dated to around 8000 BCE., was recovered in Heinola (Finland), and is probably the oldest yet found.[31]

An artistic reconstruction of a sled runner found in eastern Finland at Lapinlahti,[32] exactly mirrors some of the vessels displayed on the Alta rock art, which offers greater clarity of recognition. Evidently, not all those images are boats or canoes, some are various types of sled[33] that have diverse functions and cargoes from furs to people, alive and dead, for transport and burial. Sled mobility was probably achieved by pushing from the rear and pulling at the sides with a rope at the

---

28. Archaeological features involving dog traction from the Siberian Neolithic (4000 BCE - 1200 BCE) have been documented in the Kamchatka Peninsula. **29.** Domestic reindeer herds were however relatively small before the 17th century CE. **30.** Radiocarbon dating of some sled runner fragments confirm dates of 6480 BCE to 6175 BCE. See: Emma Vitale; Jacob A. Rasmussen et al. "An Ethnographic Framework For Identifying Dog Sledding In The Archaeological Record." *Journal Of Archaeological Science* 159 (2023). https://doi.org/10.1016/j.jas.2023.105856 (Accessed 12th September 2024). **31.** Ibid. **32.** A radiocarbon date of the runner indicates that it was made between 4060 and 3950 BCE. **33.** As shown in a 17th century print reproduced in a book by N. Witsen (Antropova 1953).

front for steering. It is estimated that at least five men were needed to accomplish this manoeuvre.[34] This understanding does explain why not all the so-called carts or wagons have draft animals preceding them in the rock art images.

Remnants of ski runners similar to those used by the east Siberian Yakut were also used for winter transportation across the tundra and ice flows of a style in continuous use by the peoples of the northern Urals as described by a 12th-Century CE Arab traveller.[35] Other wooden artefacts unearthed in excavations at a Mesolithic marshland include many tools associated with a fishing subsistence,[36] along with pieces from the prow of a ship. Sled construction depended on very limited resources; materials were either upcycled or salvaged from driftwood.[37] As prey moved in line with ice flows, the various tribes' peoples followed it across northern Canada into Greenland, carrying with them the Inuit language to Greenland, and north-eastwards into Finnmark. Naturally, Finnmark is where we find the highest concentration of Sámi people.[38]

There is a popular (mis)conceptualization of the Sámi, identifying them as reindeer herders, despite the fact that only a very small minority of the Sámi are still involved in traditional reindeer herding today. Moreover, the Sámi were not always reindeer hunters, nor herders; their ancestors (like so many others of the northern regions) once revered and followed, the elk. Because traditional marriage and kinship ties bonded disparate peoples, this shared reverence and reliance upon the elk was preserved for millennia, until climatic changes shifted their mode of subsistence.

When we mention shamanism, we automatically imagine, as we should, the northern regions of Siberia and Central Asia. Yet as the historical 'homelands' of shamanism, the underlying cultures of those peoples are largely ignored, neglected in favour of the shamanisms of North and South Americas. Supporting a case for early forms of northern shamanism, ritual artefacts found in burial sites in the

---

34. Bernard Gramsch and Klaus Kloss. "Excavations near Friesack: an Early Mesolithic Marshland Site in the Northern Plain of Central Europe." *The Mesolithic in Europe: Papers Presented at the Third International Symposium Edinburgh 1985*. Edited by Clive Bonsall. (John Donald Publishers, 1990) **35.** Abu-Hamid describes small planks bound to the feet and guided with a long hand-held strap resembling a horse's bridle. **36.** Gramsch, 1990. Other items found here were tools and weapons for hunting and fishing: bows, arrows, spears, throwing-sticks, landing-nets, fish traps, a scraper, several, stakes, a fragment of a fishing basket or mat, a net made of sedge fibre, a pine bark float and a fish scarer (botalo). **37.** Vitale, et al, 2023. **38.** Similarly, Northern Sweden bears the name Lappmark.

OLD WORLD CULTURES 19

northern section of Lake Onega[39] in Karelia, Russia, near Finland, include sculpted images (in wood, clay and bone) of significant totemic animals (namely elk) that we know to be compatible with other items of the shamans' ritual paraphernalia. One artefact appears to be a bipedal elk figure that probably represents a shaman in ritual guise.[40] The presence of beaver mandibles in the grave may also indicate a shamanic (or Clan) totem. Holes in the elk head sculptures[41] found here, possibly served to mount a staff through, much like the later hobby horses of popular European folkloric celebration. Similar to the Siberian shaman's turu (a staff that provided a microcosmic link to the macrocosmic world tree that assists the shaman to communicate with an animal haltija[42]), this peripatetic totemic staff would literally become the shaman's ritual 'horse,' to be 'ridden' as he traverses the layers of being within and between the invisible and visible realms. Following many principles of magic, customs evolved taboo substitutes for the word for 'elk,' to avoid referring to it directly.

There are numerous images of ritual clothing, specialised attire supposedly worn by authentic shamans, but in reality, very few tribes subscribed to this. Many simply wore practical, traditional clothing. Across the broad spectrum of culturally assigned shamanism, specialised clothing (ritual dress) is the exception rather than the rule. Where it is worn, the detailing is intense and excessive. Bearing so much metal, tunics can weigh up several hundred pounds. Effigies, charms, amulets, talismans and symbols are formed into pendants, collarettes and breastplates that collectively represent a mythic cosmology. Sewn into the shaman's tunic of rough woolen cloth or hide (elk, deer or bear), the reinforced fabric creates a form of armour bearing its own narrative. In some rare cases, the design on the front

---

39. Across the region of Oleneostrovski mogilnik (Yuzhny Oleni – South Deer Island). Situated in the northwest part of the European portion of Russia, between Lake Ladoga and the White Sea, Lake Onega is the second largest lake in Europe. **40.** Anna Leena Siikala. "Finnish Rock Art, Animal Ceremonialism and Shamanism." *Temenos: studies in comparative religion, presented by scholars in Denmark, Finland, Norway and Sweden* 17. (Finnish Society for the study of Comparative Religion, 1981): 81-100 **41.** Dating from 7000 BCE - 6000 BCE, the Huittinen Head was found in southwest Finland (formerly settled by peoples of the Suomusjärvi culture). **42.** A *haltija* is a spirit helper in Finnish mythology that also guards or protects something or someone. The word is possibly derived from the Gothic *haltijar*, which referred to the original settler of a homestead. Similar to the Nisse or Tömte, *haltija* are principally associated with home and hearth. However, there are elemental and locational *haltijas*, of the rivers and forests for example. Gravesites also have their own *haltijas* (kalman väki - 'death folk'). In broader terms haltija refers to virtue or power.

and back represents the iron bones of the shaman's re-enforced spirit body, which is also that of his mentor and lineaged ancestors. This enrichment process occurs during the induction to shaman-hood, when the shaman undergoes metaphysical dismemberment and reassembly with renewed magical vigour.

1. Mesolithic Sled

Certain anomalies in the cardinal orientation of some burials and of the grave goods within them, suggest the occupancy of specific, distinct individuals, that given the information available to us, assert possible roles as ritual specialists. In the north sector of the grave site, four shaft graves (holding two males, a female and a youth), are uniquely oriented towards the west; furthermore, the bodies are placed in a seated or upright position, rather than being laid out horizontally. In many cultures of this region (circa 6500 BCE), west was sometimes considered to be the direction that provided access to the Underworld domain of spirit ancestors.[43]

Furthermore, it appears that two separate populations used this burial ground and ritual gathering place, each occupying different sectors of the site (at Oleneostrovski mogilnik). To the north, we find the remains of indigenous (Kunda) people, who exhibited northern European and Uralic features.[44] Elk artefacts found here represent the totemic aspects of native peoples for whom the elk was culturally (therefore spiritually) significant. They remain ethnically distinct from grave goods found in the southern sector of the Oleneostrovski mogilnik region that feature the afore-mentioned totemic snake sculptures, and which belong to people with southern European and Siberian features who were almost certainly newcomers to the area. Furthermore, the clan occupying the southern sector probably had links to the Komsa Culture of northern Norway, Sweden, Finland and the Kola Peninsula of Russia. As totemic icons, both elk and snake have immense significance in the developing cultures and ethnicity of

---

43. Marek Zvelebil. "The Agricultural Transition And The Origins Of Neolithic Society In Europe." *Documenta Praehistorica.* XXVIII (2001): 1-26. 10.4312/dp.28.1.https://www.researchgate.net/publication/291911861_The_agricultural_transition_and_the_origins_of_Neolithic_society_in_Europe (Accessed 19th October 2023).
44. Zvelebil, 2001.

OLD WORLD CULTURES 21

the various tribes' peoples of the northern regions, becoming core artistic features of later remains and artefacts, extending even to the decoration of clothing and of drums.

Agriculture arrived from the Balkans some 6000 years ago, but it was not widely adopted, nor quickly, at least not initially; instead, the nomads of the north clung doggedly to their hunter-gatherer fisher/forager lifestyle. Temporary hunting sites occupied high terraces where some pits and hearths were found with faunal remains that again indicate the dominance of elk and beaver. Across the northeast Eurasian area, the elk was the most significant beast (game animal) and principle messenger from the Otherworld of invisible ancestral spirits. So when a Mesolithic wooden boat prow in the likeness of an elk was found in Rovaniemi, Finland, it was not unexpected. In some Slavic traditions the European elk acquires cultic, mythological significance, and is even represented as a constellation.

REMNANTS OF A MATERIAL CULTURE

As the subsistence base in Finland shifted from elk and bear hunting to seal-hunting, it coincided with the introduction of pottery to this region (which possibly originated in China)[45]. This important innovation explains much about the engagement and movement of culture. Trading and marriage networks between the Upper Volga and Finland that may have existed as early as 7000 BCE, facilitated the diffusion of the material culture of pottery-making westwards. Understanding such shifts in material culture allow us to properly interpret the ethnic and linguistic cultural changes of peoples utilising them. For instance, spiritual beliefs develop in response to environment, fuelled by the economics of subsistence, be that foraging, herding, hunting, fishing, agriculture or trade.

For around 5000 years from the Mesolithic Age[46], and throughout the Neolithic Age, the Volga-Oka region of Russia served as a centralised trading hub, fusing cultures, ethnicities and languages within its cosmopolitan environment. As these influences leeched out into Finland/Karelia, potters became highly valued members of their communities. Because women were ever the movers and shakers of technology and material culture in much of the old world, their pre-existing role in the production of baskets for portable storage led to the widely accepted assumption that women were responsible for crafting and decorating pottery for domestic, ritual and funerary use. Women were certainly familiar with the processing and maintenance of hearths for cooking and warmth, so were ideally placed to advance the necessary knowledge of temperature control already in their hands. Nevertheless, there is a discernible ritual dimension to the making and decorating of

---

45. Archaeologists assert the arrival of pottery culture marked the end of the late Mesolithic Age and the beginning of the early Neolithic Age in Finland. See: Glossary.
46. That is, between 8500 BCE, until about 3100 BCE, being the end of the Comb Ware III period. See: Glossary.

pottery. Everything, from the choice of clay, the fixing medium, (dung, ash, crushed bones) to the colour of the wash and the incised lines, expressed ritualistic choices relating to invisible world of spirit. Firing the clay infused the vessels with elemental, animistic presences.

As animists, the ancient Finns believed everything in the world was alive with the spirit of the creator, and that stones, animals, trees, the wind and the rain had individual consciousness. They also believed human beings could communicate with them if we found the right language, and could master the operative technique. As a blank canvas, pottery styles became a medium for the experimentation with symbols and patterns that reflect the relational boundaries and pathways with, and to, all things 'Other.'[47] Embodying the cosmology of the populations producing it, pottery thus became another means of navigation into other worlds, as cremation urns for the dead, and as urns for the containment and distribution of sacrificial foods and beverages. Pots also provided domestic storage for seal fat (both for household use and for trade).[48]

It has been argued more recently that the narrative designs which decorate various pottery artefacts were not simply representing the world of the hunter-gatherer through fashioned symbols and metaphors as 'mental maps' of their cosmology and beliefs, but rather, that they literally embody it.[49] Their distinct mythopoeia manifests through the function of sacred art whence they become ritualised tools, not merely tools of ritual. At this point of sympathetic alignment with an imbued spiritual object, a state of 'reconciliation' occurs in their use: "The boundaries between person and place, between self and the landscape, dissolve altogether. It is at this point that, as the people say, they become their ancestors and discover the real meaning of things."[50]

Inspired by cosmological mythopoeia, communication with

---

47. The 19th century French anthropologist and ethnologist, Claude Lévi-Strauss, pioneered the context and explanation of this procedure. His work was instrumental in the development of structuralism, a discipline that focuses on shared unconscious mental structures. Levi-Strauss believed that beneath visible cultural differences, lie deep structures common to all human minds that shape how we organize our experiences and make sense of the world. **48.** Dr Kamil Adamczak. "Pots Full Of History.' In, Journal Proceedings of the National Academy of Sciences. (Nicolaus Copernicus University in Torun, 2023). DOI 10.1073/pnas.2310138120 (Accessed 28th July 2024). **49.** Tim Ingold. (Ed.) *Key Debates in Anthropology* (Routledge:1996). **50.** Ingold, 1996

ancestral spirits is facilitated through the inherent magics of ritual tools, enabling shamans to see, feel and know the minds and thoughts of their ancestors, and thus be guided by their wisdoms. In turn their experiences feed the expression of that synergy. Pottery thus became the sacred medium of an ever-shifting cosmology, to which the designs made upon them are representative of.[51] As both function and product of ritual, such artefacts demonstrate a very specific ritual code of practice that stand beside "the drum, mask, headdress, bag, and bones or images of ritually significant animals."[52]

Before the northern arctic and subarctic territories were named Fennoscandia, Sápmi, Norway, Sweden, or Finland, the nomads who populated these regions were first mentioned by Tacitus in 98 CE., who referred to them as Fenni. Others since have referred to them as Lapps. Both terms are incorrect.[53] The far northeastern region of Siberia is the home of the so-called Paleo-Siberian (Paleo-Asiatic, or Hyperborean) peoples, namely, the Chukchi, Koryak, Itelmen, and Yukaghir. Stretching from Norway to the region of the Ob River in Siberia and then southward into the Carpathian Basin in central Europe and the Ukraine, the area inhabited by the Finno-Ugric peoples is extensive. Because information relating to their culture and early movements is sketchy at best, the history of their geographic dispersion is now reliant on linguistic criteria, therefore, interpretations vary significantly.[54] When combined in new environments, the diaspora of culture and language generates adaptive ethnicities and spirituality that develop accordingly. Charting some of those movements will being clarity.

---

51. Major cultural changes that arose in Neolithic Finland influenced the cosmologies of hunter-gatherers, making pottery a 'marker' of social transformation.
52. Zvelebil, 2001. **53.** Lands currently occupied by the Sámi people are commonly referred to in homogenous terms such as 'Lapland,' which is also incorrect geographically and politically as this is considered to be an offensive term to modern Sámi people, who prefer the simple term: Sápmi. **54.** See Appendix VI

ETHNOGENESIS (ICE-AGE TO IRON AGE)

During the last Glacial Event (Ice Age), we have learned how some of the earliest ancestors of the Sámi people had evidently taken refuge in the Iberian Peninsula. As noted above, when the Scandinavian Ice Sheet receded, they followed the herds of elk streaming northwards, settling eventually in Norway, Sweden, Finland, and the Kola Peninsula of Russia.[55] Several hundred years later, a similar situation transpired from the Ukrainian Refuge, where former settlements of hunter gatherers (who would later be identified as Finno-Ugrian)[56] had similarly taken refuge across the southern Russian Plain. Dispersing westwards and northwards (via Poland), they left traces of their genetic signature as they shifted up along the Tamir Peninsula into the most northerly region of Eurasia and into arctic Russia (where the indigenous Nenets/Samoyeds[57] still live), Finland and into Norway's northern coast (Finnmark). In Fennoscandia, they merged with (indigenous) Proto-Finns (in the region of the Finnish/Russian boundary)[58] and other early ancestors of the Sámi from the Komsa Culture people, and possibly even others from the region we know today as Poland.[59] Proto Finns developed a shamanic hunting-gathering-fishing culture similar to peoples across sub-Arctic Eurasia, such as the shamanism of the Evenks of Siberia.

---

55. In Karelia, the North European Ahrensburghian archaeological culture was succeeded by the early Suomusjärvi culture. The Komsa culture found its way to the Kola peninsula. Post-Swiderian cultures swept through almost all of western Russia. See Glossary. **56.** Finno-Ugric is a traditional grouping of all languages in the Uralic language family with the exception of the Samoyedic languages. **57.** Genetic connections between Bol'shoy Oleni Ostrov (1550 BCE) and modern-day central Siberian Buryats, indicate an early eastern connection with the west. Genetic evidence extends further connections through west Siberia to the Altai regions. Nganasan peoples are thought to be the descendants of Paleo-Siberian peoples who were culturally assimilated by various Samoyedic indigenous peoples of Siberia. **58.** To where the comb-ware is dated to approximately 7600 years ago. **59.** See overleaf

Many language shifts occurred in prehistory, so while the origin of Sámi languages ultimately lies somewhere around and beyond Lake Onega, in genetic terms,[60] we may now recognise that the Sámi people are of ancient 'European' descent.[61] Anthropologists had (wrongly) assumed in centuries past, that the Sámi people were entirely distinct physically from other Europeans. However, genetics is a very complex science in that we may trace only the surviving lines of descent along the separate maternal and paternal lineages. Both male and female DNA lines are lost when males produce only females and vice versa, or, when there are no surviving children at all. Maternal DNA tracked in Iron Age Finland confirms it was home to separate and diverse populations. We may trace the mother-daughter lines (Mitochondrial DNA) among the Sámi population to their Iberian forebears. A very small percentage only, of Sámi Mitochondrial DNA, originates in Asia. Wandering eastwards from southwest Europe, these ancestral mothers then headed north through Finland and Russia.

Due to complex marriage patterns between groups, tracing the paternal Sámi lines is less easy, but we find that only around twenty percent of the direct father-son lines are derived from generic groups common to the Central and Eastern Europe regions (we now know as Bulgaria, Hungary, Avdeevo and the Ukraine). An even smaller percentage of men can be traced back to Iberia, which suggests that as women moved northwards, they intermarried with men from other tribes, and that almost all male siblings they had, possibly intermarried with women from nearby local tribes and stayed behind. By far the most common paternal lines amongst the Sámi occur from men descended from other Finnic/Uralic/Asian groups living in Siberia, Russia, and Finland, when the Sámi mothers (whose female ancestors had migrated from southwestern Europe), finally arrived in those regions.

---

59. Sámi DNA diversity presumably arose via a combination of multiple founder event(s) and reproductive isolation imposed by the challenging conditions of sub-arctic Europe. **60.** Mitochondrial DNA (mtDNA) as well as paternally inherited Y-chromosomal haplogroups variations were used in the study. See: Luigi Luca Cavalli-Sforza. Genes, Peoples, and Languages. (University of California Press, 2001):116. **61.** As obscure descendants of a narrow, yet distinctive subset of European peoples (related to the post-Last Glacial Maximum colonization of the northern parts of Europe), the Sámi people are nonetheless genetically diverse from other groups throughout Northern Europe. See: K. Tambets, et al. "The Western And Eastern Roots Of The Sámi-The Story Of Genetic 'Outliers' Told By Mitochondrial DNA And Y chromosomes." *Am J Hum Genet.* April. 74(4)(2004): 661-82. doi: 10.1086/383203. (Accessed 20th December 2024).

ETHNOGENESIS (ICE-AGE TO IRON-AGE)   27

Sharing beliefs anchored in the land and its resources that involved animistic, totemistic and shamanistic practises within a clan-based social structure, marital gene pooling and trading had occurred for many hundreds of years between the early peoples of Central and East Siberia, Eurasia, the Urals, and the Scandinavian and Baltic regions. These include the populations of Norwegians, Swedes, Finns, Ingrians, Karelians, and of course, the Sámi. Given their shared histories, it cannot be coincidence that both the Finns and the Sámi both developed similar traditions.

Summarising what we have learned thus far, the Sámi people demonstrate a mixed descent that began with the original Ice Age hunter-gatherers from a maternal gene-pool that later blended with lines of descent from peoples of Siberian and Mongolian ancestry in their paternal gene-pool. Minor traces from more recent (male) lines of agriculturalists supplement this formulation. Apparently, genes associated with ancient farming populations were more common in the east, whereas lineages inherited from hunter-gatherers were more prevalent in the west. "This indicates that the studied Iron Age populations have had an impact on the gene pool of contemporary Finns."[62] So it is evident that Sámi peoples have significantly higher proportions of a Siberian gene-pool (with less influences from the agricultural mothers from Old Europe and males from the last Caucasian migration) than Scandinavian peoples.[63] Moreover, parallel findings related to cultural developments suggest that northern Europeans spoke an early form of a Finno-Ugric language.[64]

Dispersed across the mountains, forests and tundra, other peoples shared this brutal landscape, namely, the Nenets, the Dolgan, the Even (Lamut) and the Nganasan.[65] However, the principal Indigenous population of the taiga stretching eastward from the Yenisey River to the Sea of Okhotsk, are the Evenk (formerly Tungus). The southern Evenk peoples were principally horse and cattle pastoralists, some were fishermen and hunters, while the more traditional forest-dwelling Evenk were wild reindeer hunters and trappers. These subsistence modalities are traditionally those that support shamanism. This is because it

---

62. https://yle.fi/uutiset/osasto/news/iron_age_dna_sheds_light_on_finns_genetic_origin/11072769i (Accessed 30th December 2024).   **63.** Ibid. See Appendix VI   **64.** Some researchers promote the probability that modern Sámi languages originate in a Proto-Sámi language (rooted in an Early Proto-Finnic stage), possibly reaching even further back to an Ur-Sprache (the so-called Proto-Uralic), from which it is believed all present-day Uralic languages developed.   **65.** Tim Ingold. https://www.britannica.com/place/Arctic/Political-and-environmental-issues (Retrieved 12th June 2024)

was thought that their survival depended upon the relationship and intervention of the shaman with all things 'Other.' Because agriculture and pastoralism developed slowly, the domestication of reindeer occurred at different periods across the arctic and subarctic regions, impacting the socio-religio-political aspects of culture indirectly through shifts in subsistence and economy.[66]

We should remember too how the Norway inhabited by the Fosna and Komsa (culture) peoples was much like Greenland is today. Unlike the Fosna culture, the Komsa culture was entirely sea-oriented, and the Komsa people were specialized seal hunters who lived in the inner fjords most of the year, with seasonal forays to their outer reaches in the summer to hunt and fish. The Komsa culture shows little affinity with any eastern group to the east, with the possible exception of the Askola culture identified near Helsinki in Finland. Farming and stock-raising innovations brought by Megalithic seafarers (who ultimately traced their origins to the eastern Mediterranean) moved northward along the coasts of Denmark and western Sweden, to reach southeastern Norway. [67]The early and extended phase of contact between forager and farmer communities in the fourth millennium BCE may have established enduring kinship ties, resulting in associated transferral of exchange from the inter-tribal to tribal context, i.e. from negative to generalised/balanced reciprocity. Such relations were also likely to result in intermarriage rather than loss of women to farming communities, and consequently in the blending of cultural traits and the genesis of a new archaeological culture.[68]

Because the agricultural needs of the Fosna (culture) peoples were so different from those of the hunter and the fisherman, they did not supplant the earlier subsistence's with their own but instead drifted in alongside of it, albeit only in the most geographically favourable regions. Nevertheless, as Norway's first agriculturalists, they found the environment so marginal that they depended far more on pastoralism than they did on tilling the soil for their sustenance. Moreover, in order to survive, they occasionally resorted to hunting and fishing, retaining a measure of semi-nomadism by practicing transhumance (the seasonal movement of livestock between the lowlands to the mountains). Although traces of the Fosna culture occur into historic times, the

---

66. Possibly influenced by early Finnish and later Scandinavian peasants, other areas of Sápmi began their domestication of reindeer herds that were managed for their milk, meat and for draft. **67.** Malstrom, 2012. **68.** Marek Zvelebi. The agricultural transition and the origins of Neolithic society in Europe. *Documenta Praehistorica XXVIII*

ETHNOGENESIS (ICE-AGE TO IRON-AGE)   29

Komsa culture seems to have disappeared about 2000 BCE. The shift into the Neolithic[69] had evinced innovations in so many areas of life across the Norwegian region, not confined to subsistence alone, but manifest in a wealth of artefacts relating to death and funerary cults. Within the large burial mounds, we find elaborate grave goods that indicate new beliefs in an after-life, fertility cults, the divine feminine, and a veneration of the sun. These were and remain vital tenets of the beliefs of not only the Sámi peoples, but those peoples who merged with them culturally and genetically during the multi-layered, multi-wave migrations of peoples and ideas over successive generations. Norway's rock art and megalithic sites present an unrelenting testament to that enduring cultural impact.

Other archaeological evidence suggests further correlations with the later arrival in Norway of very different groups of nomadic herdsmen (known historically as 'Aryans'[70]) moving overland in small numbers from the southeast regions of the Caspian Sea.[71] Mesolithic (Middle Stone Age) hunting and fishing continued alongside Neolithic (New Stone Age) farming and grazing, just as the use of stone tools continued long after the first introduction of metal into Norway.[72] As populations dwindled, technological innovations in metallurgy appeared that would ultimately revive those downward trends. Iron tool technology was slowly introduced from Western Europe into Scandinavia, but because the method of producing it from the upland bog ore did not become generally known for several centuries, the depopulation of Norway and the rise in poverty continued as people struggled against the elements. All former stability and prosperity that had characterized Norwegian agriculture during the Bronze Age disintegrated. Supplies of iron in Norway only began to meet local

---

69. In northern regions, terms such 'Stone Age,' 'Bronze Age,' and 'Iron Age,' carry little weight, and have little real meaning, because here, the dimensions of time and space simply overlap without distinction. **70.** Lacking the horse, this earlier notion is now in dispute. Nevertheless, by using linguistic and place-name evidence, the philologist Andreas Hansen builds a strong case for the agricultural settlement of Norway having been accomplished by the Aryans. See Melheim, 2020. **71.** As the post-glacial climate grew warmer, the increasing aridity of pasture land obliged them to abandon the Central Asian steppes. Some moved southward into India, while others retreated westward into the maritime margins of Europe. **72.** The Bronze Age in Norway is characterized by a relative paucity of finds, since the region lacked the copper and tin needed to make bronze, this meant that all of the 'raw materials' had to be imported, usually from a considerable distance. Rogaland and Lista on the southwest coast, emerged as the country's first and most important centres of metal culture.

demands for tools and weapons at the onset of the first century CE, which also coincided with climatic improvements that essentially reversed such ill-fortune amongst agriculturalists. Population boomed once again, and "for the first time the farmer could and did actively expand his domain at the direct expense of the hunter."[73]

Already we begin to see the shift in emphasis for the relationships with all things 'Other,' which by necessity changed to focus more on fertility and fecundity than on the hunt. As conflicts arose and defensive structures increased across frontier regions (between hunter and farmer) particularly, for some, that emphasis shifted again to one of military and war.

Furthermore, not only is there more than a ten-fold increase in the number of grave finds dating from the Roman Iron Age as opposed to the Celtic Iron Age, but they are also dominated by 'warrior graves,' revealing the presence of a strong military caste within Norwegian society at the time. That this warrior caste was in fairly intimate contact with the Roman Empire is shown by their faithful emulation of weapon styles then in use by the legionnaires, Older grave finds contain the short, broad, one-edged sword first developed by the Romans, while later ones contain the long, narrow, double-edged swords which superseded them. Indeed, contacts between Norway and the Roman Empire in the later Iron Age were not restricted to weapons, but demonstrate a lively trade involving bronze goods, jewellery, and glass as well. That this trade had rather well-defined hinterlands is seen from that fact that distinctive items seem to have had their own patterns of spatial distribution. [74]

Trade relationships flourished in spite of minor regional and inter-regional conflict, so we should see and understand the reality here of a network of rising complexity, and the exponential increase in the movements of trade goods and of people, both as slaves and traders. This ultimately led to exploitation and marginalization of the Sámi peoples, especially around the coastal regions, but for a while at least, the very different cultures thrived alongside one another, possibly reaching into the Viking Age.[75]

To pay for the imports of bronze, jewellery, and glass, however, Norway's agricultural and/or military elite were obliged to export the only surplus commodities their country possessed, namely items of the chase. Consequently, their struggle with

---

73. Ibid. **74.** Ibid. This also coincides with a number of place names that incorporate 'Finn.' Finn bore a similar connotation to 'barbarian,' as used by the Romans for the peoples outside the Limes It is often confused with Lapps, used interchangeably when in fact those latter peoples did not arrive in Norway until around 1000 CE.
75. Malmström, 2012.

ETHNOGENESIS (ICE-AGE TO IRON-AGE)   31

the hunting people of the mountains and northern coasts may have been as strongly motivated by the desire to forcibly incorporate them into a 'commercial' economy as it was by the wish to annex their lands for pastoral use.[76]

This economic drive led to the development of some of the earliest politicised (and defensive) farmsteads in Norway, whereby a clear demarcation between cultivated (farming) land and the pastureland which included hunting and fishing grounds the farms depended on for their subsidiary support. Boundaries around farmsteads, which became a salient feature of a protective enclosure, were delineated by four specially marked wooden posts, as reflected in the Scythian shrine to Ares, and in the structure of the later Icelandic hólmganga rites. At this time, we witness a remarkable evolution in the dynamic of the social unit, which in turn impacted modes of spirituality and belief.

Place-name evidence sheds considerable light on the political and religious significance attached to the earliest farms. Among the oldest of farm names are those referring to sacred meadows and fields (-vin, -vang, and -åker), a sacred grove of trees (- lund), or individual trees for which a special reverence was felt, as to the oak, ash, and spruce (-eik, -ask, and -gran, respectively). Similarly, many early farms were named for the stone altar (-horg), place, of sacrifice (-hov), or holy character (-ve) that was associated with a given deity. On the other hand, the name of many an early farm was inspired by more mundane considerations, some of the oldest being -heim (which originally meant 'world' and later became synonymous with 'home'), -gard (which first meant 'fence' and then 'farm'), and -bø, or -by (which meant simply 'a place of residence'). [77]

It is worth noting how those early settlers were probably "small groups of livestock drovers pushing their way up along the river valleys in search of clearings where they might pasture their animals and till the soil."[78] As people previously accustomed to coastal regions, fish, and other words relating to fishing are absent in their language. What is particularly interesting (and of some relevance here in the evolution of language from various cultural groups), is the root origin of certain words that clearly became readily standardised and widely applied. To the above list of IE words adopted into proto-Norse language, we may add similar terms associated with specific areas of the landscape. For example, "apart from their very oldest settlements – which usually carried monosyllabic names descriptive of topographic features such

---

76. Ibid.   **77.** Ibid.   **78.** Malstrom, 2012.

as Berg (mountain), Ås (ridge), Dal (valley), Nes (peninsula), etc. – their early settlements in Denmark have suffixes such as *-løv, -løse*, and *-inge*, all of which relate to grassy areas or meadows"[79] of southern and eastern climes.

The geographic spread of agricultural settlement is reflected in the sharp increase of farmsteads indicated by place name all bearing the suffix, -heim. (whose meaning evolved from 'world' to 'home" or 'residence'), and later by farmsteads with the suffix -stadir (meaning simply 'place,' or 'stopping-place' in a nomadic context)[80]. Of course, hundreds of years later, some of these terms were still in use by Snorre and other medieval authors where they had become romanticised in legend as the worlds or realms of the 'gods' in Norse mythology. Two excellent examples would be: Ås-gardr and Vana-heim; others such as ing and dal, found their way into names that describe higher spirits (or gods – *Ing* and *Heimdallr* – as they had come to be thought of through medieval literature) associated with their original meanings relating to the fertile landscapes upon which they depended for survival and protection.

As early settlers to these northern regions, the so-called Aryan[81] pastoralists and farmers referred to the people already inhabiting the coasts and uplands as 'Finns,' which should not be confused with 'Lapp,' being a term used in reference to people who arrived in Norway much later around 1000 CE., possibly even by Scandinavian people at that time, concerning the (non-Germanic) Finns. As farming and hunting cultures vied for territory, certain myths arose of exaggerated conflict that could feasibly have provided the foundational material for the cosmological battles found in Snorre's sagas. Because we know that as late as the 10th century CE., "both the Borgarting and Eidsivating laws (in southeastern Norway) had strong prohibitions against "travelling to the Finns to foretell the future,""[82] this correlation is made even more concrete when we consider that "similar provisions seem to have been lacking in the Gulating and Frostating laws, which applied to Vestlandet and Trøndelag respectively. As concomitants of the new economy came a new level of technology and a new religious faith."[83]

Throughout the later Middle Ages, trading and raiding expeditions entered Sápmi to plunder trade goods, principally of fur for the Danish, Swedish, and Russian crowns, who all at some point attempted to rule

---

79. Ibid. **80.** Ibid. **81.** Although the techniques of fashioning stone became more sophisticated, there seems to have been no knowledge of pottery, which supports a pastoral origin rather than an agricultural origin for the 'Aryans.' **82.** Ibid. **83.**Ibid.

ETHNOGENESIS (ICE-AGE TO IRON-AGE) 33

Sápmi.[84] The Sámi became subjected to harsh taxation for the privilege of free movement across the various areas of Sápmi for their own seasonal hunts. Unfortunately, because the region's conquest by Russian fur hunters eradicated many details of indigenous life before they could be thoroughly recorded,[85] any information on kinship patterns and social organization among the peoples of the Eurasian Arctic and subarctic is scant at best.[86] It is nonetheless curious to note, that with the significant exception of the Saka, all northern Eurasian peoples are politically egalitarian, and, despite individual differences in wealth and influence, there are no formal chiefly offices or institutionalized hierarchies. As for Arctic and subarctic peoples generally, a strong emphasis is placed on the value of personal autonomy. This contrasts markedly with the socio-political institutions of medieval Scandinavia and Europe. One of the greatest markers for such institutions is ethnicity.

---

84. By the mid-17th century, Cossacks and fur traders had crossed the entire breadth of Siberia, from the Urals to the Pacific coast. **85.** Ingold, 2024. **86.** Although the origins of the Clan system can be traced to the pastoral peoples of the southern Siberian Steppes, the climatic shift to Taiga and Tundra environments diminished in its importance.

ETHNICITY

Although we often refer to a specific era in the past as the 'Migration Period,'[87] this is an artificial construct for the purposes of categorisation and nothing else, it means nothing to the peoples involved, and does nothing to assist our understanding or identification of them in terms of 'ethnicity,' or as people. Derived from the Greek ethnos (and the Latin ethnicus), 'ethnic' is a term that perhaps best refers to people who share certain customs or traits by which they are identified. Since the Middle Ages until the mid-19th century, the popular equivalent English term 'folk' was used when referring to the supposed ethnicity of heathens and pagans.[88]

With regard to the origins of a people's culture in both material and socio-religious forms, a progressive theory now gaining traction asserts a curated view of migration as sequential leapfrog settlements.[89] As groups followed the northwards shifting herds over the lands freed from ice, some migrants settled, even as others within their group moved onwards, and so on. In this way, no one people, language, culture, or ethnicity occupied any one region exclusively, nor were they wholly colonised or supplanted by others; neither was this an homogenisation of people, but was instead, a fluid admixture of people and culture. Frontier mobility of populations occur naturally within contact zones between foragers and farmers, and along established social networks, such as trading partnerships, kinship lines and marriage alliances.[90] Together with 'Leapfrog colonisation' (traced by mitochondrial DNA and Y-chromosomal DNA and dated to 6550

---

87. The Migration Period (400 CE to 500 CE) on the southern coast of the Baltic Sea is partly characterized in part by Scandinavian objects, such as bracteates inscribed with runic inscriptions from Wapno near Pila, and Karlino. **88.** Henry George Liddell and Robert Scott. 'A Greek-English Lexicon.' https://www.perseus.tufts.edu/hopper/searchresults?q=ethnos (Retrieved 21st May 2024). **89.** Commonly referred to as 'Leapfrog colonisation.' **90.** Contact only through trade and exchange without interactive gene replacement is highly improbable. See: Lene Melheim and Anette Sand-Eriksen. "Rock Art and Trade Networks: From Scandinavia to the Italian Alps." Open Archaeology 6 (2020): 86-106. 10.1515/opar-2020-0101. (Retrieved 21st May 2024).

ETHNICITY

BCE to 3550 BCE), these models are currently accepted as being more realistic alternatives to other forms of movement previously considered in academia.[91] Ultimately, ideas and resources move, with or without people.

Because of the ambiguities surrounding ethnicity, it is often confused with nationality, an idea that is nothing less than an irrational oxymoron. It is the very opposite. Moreover, it cannot be assumed that language, material culture and gene pools are mutually coeval, nor their influences equitable in the determination of ethnicity. By contrast, religious beliefs historically linked to a presumed ethnic identity, were often passed down through generations in order to preserve cultural heritage (tradition and customs). Nevertheless, ethnic signatures within material (archaeological) cultures are unidentifiable, and as such, we are forced to accept that social tradition exists in constant flux - it bears no static markers. Concepts of ethnicity are therefore temporal and spatial to the extent that "historically, we cannot assume that notions of ethnicity, as we understand them today, can be projected into the past. Ethnic groups are subjective, constructed and situational, deeply embedded in economic and political relations."[92] All of this is true.

Where interactions between different groups generate social or economic stress, specific ethnic indicators may then arise and become amplified to the extent there may be visible traces evident in the material culture.[93] Ultimately though, there is no clear or identifiable relationship between the social culture of ethnic groupings and archaeological cultures. "We now know that archaeological cultures do not, as a rule, correlate with ethnic groups, although there are exceptions. The correlative nature of this relationship has now been evaluated and mostly discredited by anthropologists, archaeologists, and linguists."[94]

There is no way of knowing how ethnicity would have functioned in prehistoric societies; some argue that it is impossible for archaeologists to reach prehistoric peoples' self-definitions and self-understandings, and have expressed serious

---

91. Whereby small groups form an enclave settlement among native inhabitants causing gene replacement which creates regionally variable, genetic 'islands' that may be diffused in time through gene mixing with local population. See: Zvelebi, 2001. **92.** Carl-Gösta Ojala. "Sámi Prehistories, The Politics of Archaeology and Identity in Northernmost Europe." (Occasional Papers) *Archaeology* 47. (Institutionen För Arkeologi Och Antik Historia Uppsala Universitet, 2009): 30 **93.** Ibid **94.** Melheim and Sand-Eriksen, 2020. Neither archaeological nor genetic evidence alone shed any light on the linguistic identity or ethnicity of colonising populations.

doubts about the possibilities of tracing ethnic groups in the past. Another view is that ethnicity simply did not exist in prehistoric societies, as it is a phenomenon closely related to the general historical developments of the last centuries and more specifically to the development of modernism. Furthermore, the concept of ethnicity has been criticised because it is too easily misused by present-day groups for legitimizing political claims, and because it operates on a too abstract level to have any real analytical significance.[95]

Ethnic groups we know as Slavs, Franks or Balts are not named as, nor associated with, archaeological cultures, just as Komsa Culture does not represent a group of people with particular social commonalities, only the similarities of the pottery style it adopted. By way of further example, the unique Bell Beaker[96] (material) culture that came to dominate Europe, is now accepted as being a synergistic blend of two social cultures from Iberia and Asia. It seems the rich patterns of material culture indicate only the locus of use or popularity, not their agency of dispersal. This vital information revises our understanding of the recognition and processing of the human social, political and religious unit. Clearly, we must look to other means of recognising and assessing the nature and expression of ethnicity beyond the bewildering ambiguities highlighted in the analyses of archaeological (material) cultures, that is, if it even exists at all outside its conceptual construct.

Because the meaning of things is situational and dependent on social context, an object can be loaded with several meanings, whose significance will change with the context of use and with time. Artefacts are not merely used as tools or symbols, but are actively manipulated in the negotiation of identities, negotiation for status and power, negotiation for resources, and negotiation of the meaning of things and events (as, for example, in the representation of the past). It follows then that artefacts do not reveal the past in the way it was, but are 'meaningfully constituted' by a double process of interpretation, 'double hermeneutic.' The first occurred through the agency of human actors in antiquity in the specific context of the ideologies of the past, the second is imposed by the ideological codes and knowledge of the contemporary investigators.[97]

This firmly suggests that ethnicity is nothing more than a modern reactionary socio-political phenomenon, a source (and consequence)

---

95. Ojala, 2009: 30 **96.** The (Eurasian) Bell Beaker culture has an origin in the Iberian Peninsula (Spain and Portugal) (c. 2700 BCE), but also in Eastern Europe via the Yamna (or Yamnaya) culture. **97.** Ibid. This fluidity of boundaries of social identity is particularly true among hunter-gatherer societies and other groups with low population densities.

ETHNICITY

of conflict and division frequently used to justify discrimination and oppression, whereby "interest groups competing for economic and political resources and territory,"[98] become characterised in terms of their perceived identities as 'ethnic' groups. We can certainly see how easily it has become a much-abused tool in that field, yet as an abstract term, it is devoid of any real analytical significance. It is more about perception than reality. Although ethnicity may be construed as an inherited or societally imposed construct, ultimately, both are mutable and adaptable. Individuals or groups may shift over time from one ethnic group to another, through intermarriage, acculturation, tribal or clan adoption, and religious conversion.

Ethnicity implies a state of belonging to others who share a common social identity, because identity (as we have learned), is itself a fluid concept of culture based in either language or religion (sometimes both), all such defining markers can be adopted, altered, changed, and if wished, rejected. Therefore, the traditionally assumed genetic markers for 'ethnic' identity have now been replaced by the notion of a new collective identity determined by various sociological factors of class, gender, belief, age, or language, and is identified by time sensitive (social, political and religious) symbols that relate to them. [99] Anthropology is a much underestimated marker for identifying cultural identity, especially when applied through an analysis of a people's cosmology, which in turn, becomes a tool that allows us to make comparisons between the mythologies of seemingly disparate peoples in order to observe how readily the absorption, adoption and adaptation occurs between them. It is that structure of belief that offers us the most effective method of seeking origin and influence, and when aligned with the disciplines of linguistics and archaeology, it is remarkably accurate.

Linguistics may be the queen of Indo-European studies and archaeology may play its role, but we are not limited to those. (...) [For] example, the characteristics of a *Tiwaz among the Proto Germans, the Roman Jupiter, Greek Zeus Pater, and Vedic Dyaus Pitar tells us what sort of god the one whose name we can reconstruct through linguistics – *Dyeus Pter – was. Comparative mythology has great power, and like anything with great power must be used carefully. It is subject to the same rules as comparative linguistics. Using these three tools, we reconstruct our Proto-Indo-European culture. "Indo European" is a linguistic term, and from the belief that linguistic units may be correlated with cultural units, it has become a cultural term. What it is not is a racial term. "Indo-European" and "Proto-Indo-

---

98. Ojala, 2009: 30 **99.** Ibid.

European" are linguistic terms first and cultural terms second. Since both language and culture may be transferred from one genetic grouping to another, neither term may be used to refer to a race. No race is more Indo-European than another, except in the very limited sense that more of their ancestors spoke an Indo-European language. Still, since no language is superior to another, the postulating of any racial superiority on linguistic grounds is just plain silly. In case anyone has missed it, let me say it one more time: "Indo-European" is not a race.[100]

Such distinctions are imperative to my own exploration and explanations of tropes and ideologies that mask and distract, obscure and taint; so be aware, language is a media for persuasion. Misdirection actually becomes harder, not easier when each media is used in conjunction with others. Cohesion is the ideal we strive for. Where it occurs naturally, void of manipulation, it becomes the prize we all seek and the key to who we are, as a species – one race of many cultures. When used individually, these disciplines may guide us towards a solution, but because they often leave it unresolved, additional assistance from those other disciplines are needed further down the line. Working through various anomalies requires a holistic approach, and in every instant, people are the one constant. Where language is introduced into a geographical area or a tribe of people through trade, settlement or conquest, the speech patterns of the indigenous populations are significantly impacted. Around five thousand years ago, further changes to our language structure occurred with the introduction of the Indo-European language family to Europe and to the North from eastern Ukraine and the Caucasus region. Generating the formation of the Germanic and Old Nordic languages, that migration event coincided with the introduction of the 'tall' genome to the peoples of the lands in the regions of the north we know today as Scandinavia. A shared language family (i.e., Celtic) does not necessarily mean that all the speakers are ethnically or genetically related. In each era, the prevailing language is found primarily in trade, be that Akkadian, Greek, Latin, Arabic, or English.[101] Language reflects political and cultural power, something the

---

100. Ceisiwr Serith. *Deep Ancestors: Practising the Religion of the Proto Indo-Europeans.* (ADF Publishing, 2007).   **101.** Various languages have provided communication across cultural and linguistic barriers throughout recorded history, hence the term lingua franca (free language) for people not sharing a first language. English is the current dominant lingua franca of international diplomacy, business, science, popular culture, technology and aviation. Nevertheless, some language groups such as Finnish, Hungarian and Basque have retained their original languages despite massive cultural influence from other regions.

ETHNICITY

Sámi know all too well from the suppression of their own. Alongside the Finns, the Sámi had retained an older, native Finno-Ugric language form in contrast to the Indo-European language forms that came to dominate the various regions of Scandinavia.

This clarification broadens our understanding of the actual nature of ethnicity, while narrowing its application in the fields of technology and anthropology. When studying the behaviours, identities and beliefs of ancient peoples, these considerations are crucial to any comprehension we may glean from the limited or challenging sources open to us.[102] In turn, this rebounds onto how we perceive our social interactions today.

Networks of ethnicity involve not necessarily only people, but also for instance, material culture, places and landscapes, ancestors and animals. The past is often important, as a resource and a structure in the creation and re-creation of myths about group identity.[103]

As mentioned above, any individual is free to learn a language or social customs in order to assimilate into an ethnic group to form groups, clans or even tribes. Again, as noted, notions of ethnicity and race are not supported by genetics and cannot therefore be scientifically defined. Diversity is cosmetic only, and strangely, genetic differences are far greater between individuals than in groups of people.[104] Although no completely satisfactory scientific explanation is yet forthcoming with regard to our physical differences (skin colour, facial features, hair texture), the common explanation is that such things actually represent ancestral adaptations to different environments. Genome admixes several millennia ago ably dismiss any notion of any presumption of so-called 'racial purity' – which is another offensive and anachronistic oxymoron.

To be clear, there is no such thing as racial purity. Nor cultural purity, nor even ethnic purity. As human beings, we are in fact one race – that

---

102. An ethnicity or ethnic group is a social grouping or category of people who identify with each other on the basis of perceived shared attributes that distinguish them from other (often larger) social groups. Those attributes can include a common origin, or ancestry, tradition, language, history, myth, society, religion, kinship patterns, physical contiguity, or social treatment. What sets them apart is what defines them. In theory, this should mean that people of different origins, who speak different languages may yet share an ethnicity, that is, if they uphold the tenets of a shared principle, such as faith. In which case, Christians could then be considered an ethnic group, even though that seems improbable. **103**. A. Metraux, A. "United Nations Economic and Security Council Statement by Experts on Problems of Race," *American Anthropologist* 53(1) (1950): 142–145. **104**. Luigi Luca Cavalli-Sforza; Paolo Menozzi; Alberto Piazza. (Eds.) The History and Geography of Human Genes. (Princeton: Princeton University Press, 1994).

of 'humankind.' Outside of this single sweeping, all-encompassing definition, there is no such thing as 'race.' Attempts to impress this false notion as an evident truth, are rhetorical, politically divisive social constructs, and are deliberately engineered to induce prejudice and alter our perceptions of self and of others. 'Race' is an artificial imposition. Race is often explained subjectively as a matter of skin colour, of genetics, of supposed physical characteristics, of biology for example. These are all entirely false propositions.

National, religious, geographic, linguistic and cultural groups do not necessarily coincide with racial groups: and the cultural traits of such groups have no demonstrated genetic connection with racial traits. Because serious errors of this kind are habitually committed when the term 'race' is used in popular parlance, it would be better when speaking of human races to drop the term 'race altogether and speak of ethnic groups.[105]

This notion returns us to the dubious and historically unsupported notion of ethnicity. Ideas about the ethnic representations even within an ethnically diverse group, might not always be shared or supported by all its members. Because identity is not a fixed condition, but changes in response to external circumstances, relationships and beliefs thus change over time and the adherence and significance to perceived boundaries may be understood and regarded differently by the various individuals who supposedly exist within them.

It is perhaps prudent at this point to dispel another (politically motivated) offensive notion, that of nationalism – it never existed in the past, and it shouldn't now. Nation states are a relatively new mode of political engineering, historically speaking, that ironically serve only to fuel the debates that separate us further. The social anthropological view on current cultural identity is useful for understanding how cultural identity was falsely applied in the past. For instance, there seems to be an unwritten taboo in Scandinavian archaeology concerning the approach towards the barriers imposed by (perceived) ethnicity that compromises any genuine investigation, marking the results no less bias than the reports of our predecessors.[106] This has meant that research and scientific enquiry into the evolution of culture, made disparaging comparisons between the Sámi and Scandinavian peoples, which suggested the former stagnated, while the latter developed exponentially.[107]

---

105. Metraux, 1950: 142-145.   **106.** Inger Zachrisson. "The Sámi And Their Interaction With The Nordic Peoples." In, *The Viking World.* Edited by Stefan Brink and Neil Price. *Routledge, 2008): 32-9.

ETHNICITY 41

Ethnic groups often form a diverse cultural mosaic within larger societies. In the West, we recognise a certain perspective of ethnicity that, like the anachronistic notions of race and nation, developed in the context of European colonial expansion, when commerce and capitalism cast shadows over swathes of population movements, even as state boundaries were becoming ever more rigidly defined.[108] For example, during the Middle Ages there was a significant movement of Finns northwards into the areas of Sápmi known as Finnmark, where the (formerly named) Lapps historically had their main hunting and fishing grounds. "The Finns began to penetrate inland along the shores of the rivers and lakes, the Lapps either moved to hunting grounds further north or were assimilated by the Finns."[109] By 1758, the settlement of numerous Finish farmsteads across the whole of Kemi Lappmark, was a huge factor in the social formation and definition of (cultural) ethnicity applied to those peoples, jointly.

There is no doubt that through "Christian missionizing, social control and colonialization,"[110] the peoples of Sápmi experienced extensive cultural changes that decimated their lifestyle traditions, and ultimately their cultural beliefs which accompanied them. It is ironic then to observe how the Nordic peoples of Sweden and Norway viewed the Finns with some measure of fear and suspicion, when we learn that the Finns in turn, similarly viewed the magical beliefs (centred around shamanism) and related customs of the Sámi (who were themselves confusingly also known as Lapps). While "Sámi society was regarded as the very home of magic and devilry, the Sámi, from their side, feared with good reason the power of the state/church hierarchy, and its ability to sentence people to be burned because of their faith."[111]

Due to the extreme politicising of all terms relating to the cultural aspects of a given people, ethnicity is without doubt, an extremely loaded concept that defies adequate definition and application. Sensitivity is a key issue of this potentially incendiary subject.

Ethnicity is controversial as it is part of a long tradition of external categorization, arranging and ranking of people in the present and the past, within evolutionary, ethnocentric, colonialist and racist frameworks of interpretation. It is also controversial because it is so intimately connected with political issues and

---

107. Venke Olsen. "Northern Scandinavia: A Multi-Ethnic Society Seen from an Ethnological Point-of-View." In, *Northern Studies Volume 23*.1986 **108.** Eric Wolf. Europe and the People Without History. (University of California Press. 1982): 380-381. **109.** John L. Irwin. *The Finns and the Lapps: How they Live and Work* (David & Charles, 1973): 144. **110.** Ibid. **111.**Ibid..

agendas in the present, including nationalism, nationalism of previously colonized people, claims for indigenous and minority rights and self-determination, and, of course, because of the ethnic conflicts, ethnic cleansing and genocides that have drowned the word "ethnic" in blood. [112]

Ethnic identity is used to assert distinction amongst others whereby the notion of separation - between 'us' and 'them' becomes a defining principle. Therefore, "an ethnic group is described as any group of people who set themselves apart and/or are set apart by others with whom they interact, or co-exist, on the basis of their perceptions of cultural differentiation and/or common descent."[113] Even so, the level of speculation within this field of enquiry remains unnecessarily excessive. Thusly, "there is a sort of 'one-entity' syndrome in archaeological research, an urge for a single basic unit for categorizing people, a unit in which language, cultural identity, material culture and genetics are fused."[114]

One possible way forward through this mire, is the suggestion that we approach the matter of identity not through ethnicity (often the province of minority groups), but through culture (which largely concerns the majority group), where there is greater scope for contextual comparisons. In Sweden, only the Sámi are perceived of as an ethnic group, not the Swedish people themselves, even though recent DNA analyses confirm that Scandinavia has been a melting pot of cultures ever since the first people arrived after the last Ice Age. And yet the historicity of Scandinavia is rarely approached in the same context as that of Fennoscandia. Semantics contribute to the artificial boundaries created by terminology. For instance, the Arctic Stone Age suggests a separation or distinction from that of the Nordic Stone Age, which does not exist in reality.[115] It is a concept of categorisation only, a tool of convenience. Nothing more.

With regard to the challenging issue of ethnicity and indigeneity, literary sources from the 18th century muddy the waters yet further in their limited understanding of merging and emerging cultures of peoples affected by migration and settlement. "Because of the perceived similarities between the Sámi and the Finnish peoples, and the fact that they could both be referred to by the old ethnonym 'Finn' in the early textual sources, the hypothesis concerning Sámi and Finnish origins

---

112. Ojala, 2009 113. Ibid. 114. Ojala, 2009 115. The Nordic Stone Age is the Stone Age of Scandinavia. During the Weichselian glaciation (115000-11700 years ago), almost all of Scandinavia was permanently covered by a thick layer of ice.

ETHNICITY 43

often merged into one common theory about the Sámi and Finns as the aboriginal population in Scandinavia."[116] Politics is ever a grubby, self-serving business, and historical events remain contributary factors in modern claims of ownership and indeed even to the creation of the rock art (whether related to burials or independent of it) scattered across Finnmark and other northern landscapes.

Attempting to unravel this ethnic entanglement today, is a political minefield, particularly as these disputed issues gained significant traction since Finland's independence from both Sweden and Russia. In many ways, despite conflicting claims of ownership of the rock art (and possibly even because of it), both the Finns and the Sámi are re-discovering and retrieving their complex and intertwined cultural histories. Tracking language[117] and genetics[118] helps us to better understand the material culture we find in the archaeological record, which collectively inform the constructs we build for identifying ethnicity. Our subsequent understanding of cultural development is ultimately dependent upon an elusive premise. Ethnicity is fluid, amorphous; it will not yield to enforced classification. Being in a state of constant flux, it avoids homogeneity. The historical and contemporary overuse of the term 'ethnicity,' is clearly imprecise and inappropriate. Indeed, its consistent failure to assist our comprehension of all notions of identity, has compounded its specious and erroneous application.

In fact, even after this brief foray into the politically sensitive nature of the meaning of ethnicity, it is evident that attempts to determine the ethnohistory of the Sámi peoples of the Sápmi regions (in Sweden and Norway especially) with any degree of confidence is extremely problematic and remains without unanimous conclusion.[119] From whence the Sámi peoples originated, along with the origin and fusion of their appearance and language[120] all remain a specialist region of

---

116. Ojala, 2009: 119 **117.** Finno-Ugric languages moved westwards to Fennoscandia. **118.** From the northeast and southwest. **119.** The debate centres on them being a Stone Age culture and their 'magical' use of T-shaped slate tools and the speculation that they could be prototypes for the Y-shaped antler hammers we know were later used as beaters for the Sámi drums. See: Sonja Hukantaival. "The Goat and the Cathedral – Archaeology of Folk Religion in Medieval Turku." (*Mirator* 19(1) 2018) For discussions on the controversial issue of race, see: "The Race Biology of the Swedish Lapps": With the Collaboration of the Staff of the [Swedish State] Institute [for Race Biology] and of Professor K. B. Wiklund. General survey. Prehistory. Demography. Future of the Lapps, Part 1. Lundborg, Herman Bernhard; Wahlund, Sten Gösta William. (Eds.) (Almqvist & Wiksell: Uppsala 1932); Hans Hildebrand. *Svenska folket under hednatiden. Ethografisk avhandling.* (in Swedish) (Iwar Haeggström, 1866). **120.** See overleaf

intense research[121] involving disciplines that now incorporate not just language, but also genetics to trace the movement of peoples from the Stone Age to the Iron Age. Yet, if we can be objective and pragmatic, this may itself be a moot point, for "even if the owners of the rock paintings, settlements, and burial places were not the direct ancestors of contemporary Sámi, they were still ethnically close [whatever that actually means]. Sámi culture has to be identified as the remnants of the ancient culture of the people from Eastern-European forest shelterbelts."[122] Others are less cautious and state boldly that "no matter what we call the people who lived here during the Stone Age, they *are* the forefathers of today's Sámi."[123]

The perennial issue of the Sámi's aboriginality and original settlement across Scandinavia during the early postglacial period continue to be debated in the 21st century, and now, with the benefit of scientific methodologies, we may be moving towards a resolve. However, this is a slow and convoluted procedure, especially as Sweden remains unyielding on this issue.

The image of Sweden as mono-ethnic in history and prehistory [continues], along with the image of the Sámi as a homogeneous, traditional, unchanged, exotic 'primitive remnant or relic of the past' — which has often been the role assigned to the Sámi in Swedish cultural heritage scenarios and in particular in popular and touristic representations.[124]

As a new science, genetics is able to participate in, and to some extent, diffuse the heated debates centred on indigeneity. [125] We are now able to determine two major theories that dominate the highly sensitive matter of indigeneity; one stresses the non-Finno-Ugric origin of the Proto-Sámi, the other asserts a Finno-Ugric origin.[126]

The first theory posits the notion that the Sámi are the indigenous people of large areas throughout the Nordic countries and in northern Europe "who genetically descend, to a large extent, from those

---

120. The relationship between the Sámi and Finnish languages and those of the Finno-Ugric and Samoyed languages in present-day Russia, was already recognised in the early 18th century. 121. This is a very complex subject, and certainly beyond my remit here, far better to study the extensive and erudite treatises on the matters of ethnicity, origin, genetics and displacement v diffusion arguments at source. See: Ojala, 2009. 122. Ojala, 2009. 123. I. M. Mulk. "Laponia, Lapplands världsarv: ett natur- och kulturarv att förvaltas för framtiden." In, Volume 6 of Småskrifter. (Ájtte, Svenskt Fjäll- och Samemuseum 2000). 124. Ojala, 2009. 125. Neil Price. *The Viking Way. Religion and War in Late Iron Age Scandinavia.* (Uppsala University. 2002). See also: Zachrisson, 2008.

peoples who first colonized Sápmi at the end of the Last Ice Age some 11000 years ago."[127] And indeed, archaeological evidence supports an expansive movement and fusion sometime between 8000 BCE and 6000 BCE, when several different cultural groups (including Proto Sámi), made their way to their 'core' settlement areas. This contrasts with the Swedish version of Sámi ethnogenesis in the northern areas of Sápmi during the Iron Age, a premise which relates to the second theory that asserts the Sámi are relatively late immigrants to Scandinavia (possibly as late as 700 BCE to 400 BCE), whose slow migration, generation by generation,[128] placed them in their current homeland shortly after the beginning of the Common Era[129] as people who possibly merged with the chaotic diaspora of the Scythian peoples from the Pontic Steppe regions of central and eastern Russia.

Nevertheless, the debate continues in the 21st century, and more recently, the historical presence of the Sámi in the central region of Sweden, continues to raise controversy. "Some of the controversy involves the so-called 'insjögravar' lake graves from the Iron Age,[130] and the Viking Age and Early Medieval settlement site and burial

---

126. P. Santos; G. Gonzàlez-Fortes; E. Trucchi; A. Ceolin; G. Cordoni; C. Guardiano; G. Longobardi., and G. Barbujani G. (Eds.) "More Rule than Exception: Parallel Evidence of Ancient Migrations in Grammars and Genomes of Finno-Ugric Speakers." In, Genes (Basel). 11(12) (2020). doi: 10.3390/genes11121491. PMID: 33322364; PMCID: PMC7763979. See also: Elmer Bogarve. "An Analysis Of How The Political Legitimacy Of The Sámi Peoples Is Perceived By Actors In The Indigenous Community Itself." European Studies: Politics, Societies, and Cultures. Bachelor's Thesis. Spring 2022.https://www.divaportal.org/smash/get/diva2:1733289/FULLTEXT03 (Retrieved 12th January 2024) **127.** Francis Joy. Sámi Shamanism, Cosmology and Art as Systems of Embedded Knowledge. (University of Lapland. 2018) **128.** P. M. Dolukhanov. "The Pleistocene-Holocene transition in northern Eurasia: Environmental changes and human adaptations." *Quaternary International* Vols 41/42 (1997):181-191. doi:10.1016/S1040-6182(96)00051-1 **129.** Proto Sámi peoples journeyed along the ancient river routes of northern Russia. Some, who may have originally spoken the same western Uralic language, stayed in the regions between Karelia, Ladoga and Lake Ilmen, and even further to the east and to the southeast. Arriving at the Finnish lakes around 1600 to 1500 BCE, these peoples later assumed the Sámi moniker. **130.** Historians have regarded 6th century Scandinavia as a place from which waves of groups of people continuously immigrated to the European continent. See: M. Müller-Wille (Ed.) "Byzantine Presence in Viking Age Sweden – Archaeological Finds and their Interpretation." In, Rom und Byzanz im Norden: Mission und Glaubenswechsel im Ostseeraum während des 8.-14. Jahrhunderts; internationale Fachkonferenz der Deutschen Forschungsgemein- schaft in Verbindung mit der Akademie der Wissenschaften und der Literatur, Mainz, Kiel. 18-25th September. (Stuttgart, 1994): 291-311

site of Vivallen in Härjedalen."¹³¹ The absence of proper settlement sites near to where vast Iron Age and later Vendel Age grave fields have been discovered in Sweden especially, suggests they are hunting-ground graves, none of which are able to offer ethnic markers.

*It is no exaggeration to say that for many archaeologists in Sweden the lake-graves have become the most obvious symbol for the complex of problems concerning the relation between Sámi prehistory and Nordic or Germanic prehistory in the Iron Age. The discussions on the lake-graves have in much been based on different views on the modes of subsistence, and the economic relations, of the population in the interior of central and southern Norrland during the Iron Age. In a recent publication, Evert Baudou and Henrik von Stedingk have questioned the idea that a traditional hunter-gatherer culture existed in the interior of Central Norrland during the Iron Age.*¹³²

Other grave sites found near lakes and on mountains in Norway may be seen as variants of the same spiritual phenomenon that we may more confidently ascribe (mainly) to the Sámi. Therefore, given what we are finally realising concerning Sámi influences upon Norse peoples, it seems highly probable that peoples other than Sámi are buried at some of these sites. We might be looking at a synergistic culture deeply influenced by close contact and proximity necessitated by trade.

---

131. Zachrisson, 2008. 132. Ojala, 2009.

ROCK ART AS A NEOLITHIC NARRATIVE CULTURE

Because a people's history is recorded in art, be that sculptural, textual, on rock, fabric or parchment, the 'grande narrative' is the cultural expression of life and death and all that lies in between, so examples of such have much to tell us. . Scandinavian rock art falls into two timeframe categories (but also spans between them): The Nordic Stone Age: (in Norway) 8000 BCE to1800 BCE,[133] and the Nordic Bronze Age: 1700 BCE to 500 BCE. With over thirty thousand registered sites, Scandinavia has the largest concentration of Bronze Age rock art in Europe, most of which is abstract (cup marks and spirals for example) and non-figurative images from the early Neolithic. The most prolific, expressive rock art forms in Norway are the vast Helleristinger carvings that portray several thousand images of people, farm implements, ships and other sea-faring vessels, fish, game, and religious symbols[134] that collectively relate to the hunter-gatherer communities in the northernmost part of Europe.[135] Coincidently, the Nordic Bronze Age is when we see imported artefacts of gold and bronze, and the large stone burial monuments known as stone ships.

Around 5300 BCE, we see images of men (or 'mighty spirits') who are depicted in conflict, often with erect phalluses to demonstrate their vitality and fertility. As expressions of the Ertebølle Mesolithic industry[136] (which is a uniquely hunter-gatherer, forager and fisher, pottery-making culture amongst sedentary agriculturalists) in Southern Scandinavia (Denmark), these coastal peoples used red ochre and deer

---

133. T. Lødøen and G. Mandt. *The Rock Art of Norway*. (Windgather Press, 2010).
134. K. Kristiansen. "Seafaring Voyages And Rock Art Ships." In, *The Dover Boat in Context: Society and Water Transport in Prehistoric Europe*. Edited by P. Clark. (Oxbow Books. 2004): 111–21. **135.** Lødøen and Mandt, 2010. **136.** Ertebølle Culture is properly a tool industry of the coastal regions of northern Europe, circa 9000 BCE to 3500 BCE. See: Glossary.

antlers in their burials. Some necklaces and belts of animal teeth and shells were found in female graves.

More recent historical events relating to the eventual shift to reindeer herding and corralling are not recorded here amongst these ancient artworks. As a result, the images we see, record clashes with various armed warriors, scenes of hunting (bear and elk), the arrival of many people in boats, and their own nomadic wanderings in carts and sleds across the vast tundra and glacial areas that span the northern wastelands. In keeping with epic narratives, some heroic figures feature in many of the rock art pictographs. Their status is represented through their size; they appear as giants, so much larger than the figures that surround and support them. Renowned tribal chiefs and warriors are acknowledged (honoured) in celebratory ceremonies, so it is unsurprising that they should feature so prominently on the huge crags and rocks, where their vigour and virility is plain for all to see. Oral myths articulate their deeds, setting example for others to emulate. In later times, some of these heroic characters were associated with Christian saints.

Spanning many hundreds of years, from the Palaeolithic to the Iron Age, rock art imagery appears to have reached its peak popularity in the Bronze Age (in Norway circa 1800 BCE, until 400 CE). Rock art in the form of petroglyphs (carvings) and pictograms (painted images) is found in significant numbers throughout Fennoscandia. Overall, the varied images that occur in Bronze Age rock art across northern Europe incorporate a broad collection of varied tools, ranging from ships, wagons, carts and chariots, tools, weapons, ards (light ploughs), to crafted items of bronze, wood, stone, and textiles. Many of these objects relate to hunting, herding, farming, fishing, conflict and copulation. Anthropomorphic beings appear in various cameos as acrobats and lur-blowers, but mainly as warriors, armed with axe, spear or bow. In addition to abstract motifs and patterns (cross marks, cup marks, sun-wheels, and concentric circles), other images include domestic and wild animals, birds and zoomorphic figures, some with distorted human features and bodily anomalies such as wings, or a beaked face. Other curious glyphs depict what appear to be hunters or shamans challenging large serpents. These remarkable artworks collectively demonstrate notions of belief and magic that depict social events, celebration, propitiation, rites of passage and others, all of significance to the cosmologies of these peoples.[137] Some images appear to allude to significant historical events, especially those of a traumatic or profound nature.

Coastal rocks are covered in images of boats, ranging from small (fishing) coracles to long ships (up to four metres in length) for transporting people, cattle and goods. Most of these images can be reliably dated to around 10000 years ago and may therefore be the world's oldest depictions of sea vessels. The people of Fennoscandia believe these ancient boat sketches may represent spiritual journeys along the waterways towards the land of the dead, the mythical world of Sáiva for example. Though widely debated without clear conclusions, these bewildering images continue to attract countless opinions, varying considerably in their interpretation. After careful analysis of the history and context for the artworks, I believe they may compose an analogue of their journey, physically (from a point of origin), and spiritually (from engagements with, and petitions to, otherworldly spirits), representing as a whole, a history of their migration and settlement as hunter gatherers, to their later confrontations with initial colonisers.

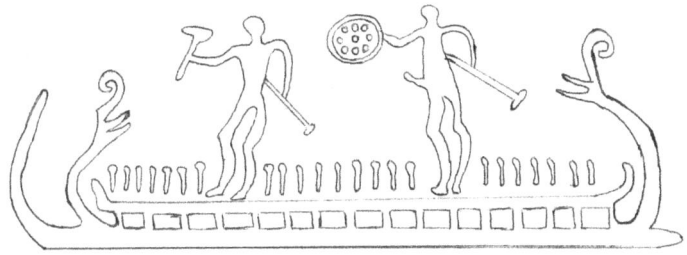

2. Svenebby Tanum Warriors

It is possible to date the later rock art ships from the Tanum area in northern Sweden chronologically. Ships with inward-turned prows dominated the Middle Bronze Age (c.1600 BCE to 1100 BCE), whereas ship images from the Late Bronze Age (1100 BCE to 500 BCE), are shown with outward-turned prows with animal head terminals. During the Early Iron Age, 500 BCE to 300 BCE, the ship images became more symmetrical in shape.[138] Images of ships depicted on rock art

---

137. Joakim Goldhahn. "Sagaholm: North European Bronze Age Rock Art and Burial Ritual." (Oxbow Books, 2016); Joakim Goldhahn and Johan Ling. "Bronze Age Rock Art in Northern Europe: Contexts and Interpretations." (2013) DOI:10.1093/OXFORDHB/9780199572861.013.0015 **138.** According to progressive studies of the shore displacement phenomena in the Tanum area in northern Bohuslän, Sweden, the sea level was even higher, estimated around 16-18 m higher at the beginning of the Middle Bronze Age (c. 1600 BCE), and about 10-12 m higher at its end (c. 500 BCE). See: See: Goldhahn and Ling, 2013.

thus assist our grasp of maritime history and the skill of maritime voyagers throughout the Nordic Bronze Age.[139] The Nordic Bronze Age rock art site at Lista contains numerous ship motifs that show typological similarities with other ship images found on the slates from Mjeltehaugen, a site speculated as originating in the Late Neolithic, when sea levels were metres higher than these shorelines today.[140] Overall, around 70 per cent of rock art is found within 100 metres of the sea.[141]

Even natural cyclical climatic events have devastating consequences for the planet. Indeed, we suffer still the consequences of many such past events. Nonetheless, we have much to learn from them. For example, it may be a surprise for some, to learn that just 6000 years ago, the sea level was actually higher than today, a fact that allows us to assume tentative dates for the rock art along northern shorelines by studying submergence levels. Because of the complex relationship between rising sea-levels due to deglaciation, and rising landmasses, due to glacial isostatic adjustment (glacial rebound), precise dating of rock art sites is not possible.[142] A good example of this can be seen in Denmark, where Stone Age coastlines and landmasses, tilted by powerful geological forces, have pushed up land in northern Jutland by 12 metres above sea level, a shift which has submerged the land in southern Jutland beneath 3 metres of water. Prior to the warming climate that led to the development of sea-faring craft further south, the most efficient mode of transport for early nomadic hunter-gatherer peoples in the north, was by vessels similar to the Heinola sled that has known parallels in the East Baltic and Northwest Russia.

---

139. Knut Ivar Austvoll. "The Emergence of Coercive Societies in Northwestern Scandinavia During the Late Neolithic–Early Bronze Age." *Open Archaeology*, 2020. doi:10.1515/opar-2020-0100; A. S. Sand-Eriksen. "Mjeltehaugen: Europe's northernmost Bell Beaker expression?" *New Perspectives on the Bronze Age. Proceedings of the 13th Nordic Bronze Age Symposium held in Gothenburg 9th to 13th June 2015* (7-18). Edited by S. Bergerbrant and A. Wessman. (Archaeopress, 2017). Approximately 125,000 years ago, the sea level was approximately 8 meters higher than it is today. See also: https://www.e-education.psu.edu/earth107/node/1496 (Retrieved 30th July 2024). **140.** Christopher Prescott; Anette Sand-Eriksen; Knut Ivar Austvoll. "The Sea and Bronze Age Transformations." In, Water and Power in Past Societies (177-197). Edited by E. Holt. (SUNY Press. 2018). **141.** Approximately 125,000 years ago, the sea level was approximately 8 meters higher than it is today. See: https://www.e-education.psu.edu/earth107/node/1496 (Retrieved 30th July 2024) **142.** I would advise any serious researcher of petroglyphs across the northern regions, to study the science noted here, as its effects refute the possibility of definitive dating for the Art works in question.

Shore displacement must be taken into consideration in all studies concerning northern European rock art, especially since the historical land mass beneath the vast ice sheet covering the Scandinavian Peninsula, once released from its immense pressure, subsequently inculcated a rapid rebound.[143] Areas of less ice density experienced less shore displacement than others.[144] Because numerous 20th century studies failed to factor this phenomenon into their findings when analysing, dating and interpreting the (mostly Bronze Age) rock art data, they present incorrect information and conclusions that are at best naively misleading, and which are at worst, deliberately specious.

The development of land and sea craft so essential to the subsistence of pre-historic peoples is a fascinating testament to the ingenuity and resilience of our ancestors. Their own homage to that chronology is preserved and celebrated across the northern regions; some fine examples can be seen on the high cliffs of Gobustan[145] on the edge of the Caspian Sea, in Azerbaijan.[146] Here we find an incredible display of mesmerizing images that depict prehistoric life in the Caucasus, of ancient populations travelling on reed boats, of men hunting (some with bows[147]) antelope and wild bulls, and of women dancing. Of greater interest for our purposes here, are the petroglyphs of what appear to be long boats in the style of the much later Viking Age ships, but which could be from the 12th century to the 8th century BCE, when rainfall was heavy, and waterways were abundant.

This suggests a continuity of boat-building skills preserved in the

---

143. Vincent H. Malmström. "Norway Before the Vikings." http://www.dartmouth.edu/~izapa/E-31.pdf (Retrieved 1st July 2024). **144.** Studies suggest that at the beginning of the Bronze Age, in some places, sea levels were between 3 to 15 metres higher than at present. By the end of the Bronze Age, these levels had dropped to around 3 to 1 metres above sea level. The diminishing height and placement of shoreline Rock Art indicates a correlation with those sea levels. See: K. Sognnes. "Symbols in a Changing World: Rock-Art and The Transition from Hunting to Farming in mid-Norway." In, *The Archaeology of Rock-Art*. Edited by C. Chippindale and P. S. C. Tacon. (Cambridge,1998): 146–162. **145.** Over 6,000 rock engravings bear witness to 40000 years of art displayed on this rocky plateau that rises out of the semi-desert in central Azerbaijan. This archaeological site of monumental history includes caves, settlements and burials that show intensive human habitation during the wet period which followed the last Ice Age, from the Upper Palaeolithic through to the Middle Ages. **146.** I. Caferzade. *Gobustan: Naskal'nye izobrazenija*, Akademija Nauk Azerbajdzanskoj SSR, (Institut istorii, 1973); T. Ibragimov. "Rock drawings of Gobustan. Archetypes of our artistic consciousness." (2012). archive.org, Open Source, ark:/13960/t85j46k15 (Accessed 30th October 2024). **147.** The oldest extant bows in one piece are the elm Holmegaard bows from Denmark, which were dated to 9000 BCE.

52 PIRATES, MERCHANTS, DEVILS & DARK DEEDS

movement of peoples over several thousand years. Using canoes and sleds to traverse the landscape, some of these peoples (of the Corded Ware Culture) who reached the regions we now know as Scandinavia no later than the Iron Age, inscribed the vast array of petroglyphs at Tunum Sweden. Rock art images there feature a wide array of animals including, boar, auroch, ibex goat, stickmen, and a horse with rider.[148] The petroglyphs of the Alta region of northern Norway may depict symbols later associated with the Sámi people, and indeed, the similarity to the pictograms of shamanic landscapes painted onto Sámi drums is striking. The Alta rock art spans over 5000 years, ending around the time the Sámi people properly emerged around 50 BCE.

Considerably older drawings, dating from around 6000 BCE, portray boats filled with both armed and unarmed oarsmen, with images of the sun on their bows. It is no coincidence that the Sámi's reverence of the sun is celebrated in the artworks that decorate their drums as well as the coastal crags and high cliffs. Overall, the rock art of Gobustan occupies a prominent place among the similar cultural monuments of Karelia, Siberia and Central Asia, with many of them sharing a number of common features with kindred rock drawings found in Scandinavia. Moreover, based on the archaeological finds and recent studies on the content of the petroglyphs, a possible connection between the Azeris[149] and the peoples of Scandinavia, is suggested, since some of the original habitants of the region, the Medes, were not a Türkic people, but an Indo-European people. Despite the convolutions, this plausibly ties in with recent research into Scandinavian DNA confirming migrations from and through this area. Culture, in all its forms, allows us to track the movements and influences of people and their ideas, their innovations, beliefs, social structures and language.

Ideas first posited decades ago by Gordon Childe (that had since fallen out of favour) regarding the direct impact on the development of Scandinavian peoples from movements of material culture across northern and eastern Europe during the Bronze Age, are now being re-visited.[150] Childe believed that the appearance of a strong warrior

---

148. Caferzade, 1973. 149. Old Azeri was the language of this region of Iran before it adopted the Türkic language of the same name. Historical research showed that Azeris were an Iranic people before the arrival of Seljuq Turks to the region. See: M. A. Jazayery and Ahmad Kasravi. (1890-1946), In, *Encyclopaedic Historiography of the Muslim World*. Edited by N .K. Singh and A. Samiuddin. (Global Vision Publishing House. 2003). 150. C. Prescott and E. Walderhaug. "The Last Frontier? Processes of Indo-Europeanization in Northern Europe. The Norwegian Case." *Journal of Indo-European Studies* 23 (1995): 257-280.

identity signified the origin of the individualizing chiefdoms in the Early Bronze Age who had endorsed (invested in and benefited from) the trade of metal ores. Traces of copper found in Danish metalwork dating from the 16th to the 14th centuries BCE, provides hard evidence of local and long-distance trade (and potential cultural exchanges) between Scandinavia, Wales and the South Tyrolean (Italian) Alps which continued throughout the second millennium BCE. Trade was supplemented by travelling metal prospectors, which again impacted the movement of peoples along with material (and social) culture, language and ethnicity, all to varying degrees. These innovative shifts in social patterns contributed significantly to the appearance of the first rock art ship motifs in this period, probably in celebration of a new technology that functioned as the foundation for the development of a new sociopolitical structure. The mapping of seaways enabled bold explorers to access foreign goods and nurture long-distance alliance ties.

This information offers us an opportunity to reconsider previous theories about the circulation of various metal ores (especially copper), and to the exchange mechanisms relating to trade, the connotations of which impact social obligations such as marriage and gift exchange, and cultural transmission, especially traditions relating to ritual and funerary practises. No-one survives in glorious isolation. Hubs were generated for this evolving network, with the Carpathian Basin forming a major crossroads between temperate Europe, the Eurasian steppes, and the Aegean world. Although Nordic culture is well known for its hospitality customs, it is by no means unique; its parallel system in Greece, known as xenia, places a similar emphasis on social obligations between guest and host, but is perhaps less renown. Deemed to be superior to all other obligations, xenia describes a diplomatic relationship honoured through gift giving or by the bestowing of an artefact. A xenos item represented the ratification of a guest-friendship dynamic, a manifest testament of protection which allowed safe travel across several regions and boundaries during the Bronze Age, ensuring that even in times of conflict, trade-routes remained open.[151] "By carrying an artefact deriving from xenia exchange, the artefact could function as a 'passport.'"[152]

There is an obvious correlation between the geographical location of the central hub for the collection and distribution of metals, and

---

151. Flemming Kaul. "Middle Bronze Age Long-Distance Exchange: Amber, Early Glass and Guest Friendship, Xenia." In, Trade before Civilization: Long Distance Exchange and the Rise of Social Complexity. Edited by J. Ling, R. J. Chacon and K. Kristiansen. (Cambridge University Press, 2022). 152. Melheim, and Sand-Eriksen, 2020.

the confluence of rock art images that demonstrate those cross-cultural style dynamics. Similarly, the overall maritime location of Scandinavian rock art has led to interpretations of the rock art sites as maritime ports, where such sites were a locus for trade and exchange. Celebration and festival would therefore naturally accompany "seasonal aggregations"[153] at trading hubs. It follows that centuries of trade and travel between the southeast and the northwest areas led to a synergistic fusion of compatible and complementary expressions of cultural correspondences from around 1000 BCE, and throughout the Iron Age. The Baltic Gundestrup Cauldron is a prime example of this level of prestigious gift exchange/obligation between significant persons of importance.

Sourced in the south Tyrolean copper mines, raw metals spread across Northern Europe, reaching up the west coast of the Scandinavian Peninsula, confirming that, regardless of style, after c. 1300 BCE, the Italian Alps became the dominant supplier of metal for Bronze Age swords in Scandinavia, Germany and Italy. This is unsurprising, since the presence of jadeite axes in the western Baltic area, affirms a trading network between northern Italy and Scandinavia as early as c. 4300 BCE to 3800 BCE. Finds of Nordic octagonal-hilted swords in southern Germany and the Alpine region[154] (and local imitations of them) are suggestive of xenia weapon exchange,[155] and may account for the discovery of prestigious artefacts in burials that are clearly decades old. Furthermore, "a gifted sword could be carried for generations as a token of a guest-friendship established between one's forefathers," before finding its way into the burial record.[156]

Interactions between cultures demonstrably generate substantial mutual influences that endure the shifting tides of affiliations and social bonding. It seems the trade in amber and salt was a factor in the dispersal of the face urn burial tradition across Northern Europe in the Nordic Late Bronze Age. Long-distance trade with Iberia is evident in the similarities of their rock art imagery.[157] The significance of this new understanding of Bronze Age rock art as a reflection of core themes relating to the maritime trading societies of northern peoples,

---

151. Flemming Kaul. "Middle Bronze Age Long-Distance Exchange: Amber, Early Glass and Guest Friendship, Xenia." In, Trade before Civilization: Long Distance Exchange and the Rise of Social Complexity. Edited by J. Ling, R. J. Chacon and K. Kristiansen. (Cambridge University Press, 2022). **152.** Melheim, and Sand-Eriksen, 2020. **153.** Ibid. **154.** Ibid. **155.** Obligatory gift exchange that form alliances and contracts between persons of authority, generating kinship ties through ritualised friendships. **156.** Ibid. **157.** Pan-European symbolism is an established feature of Scandinavian rock art.

affirms the high value attached to trade, that more importantly, does not diminish the spiritual aspects of belief attached to such activities, and does in fact, emphasise it.[158] Changes in social trends can be tracked quite reliably across continents through burial contexts providing persuasive evidence for close cultural connections between Scandinavia and the Continent. More importantly, recent studies profess evidence of a shared cult of the sun that relates primarily to the notion of maritime travel,[159] which also celebrates the sun's own movement. Consider here the role or function of the glorious Trondheim carriage artefact.

3. Trondheim Sun Carriage

Somewhat redolent of warrior stelae from the Iberian Peninsula, is the Kyrkje-Eide stela (from Stryn in the northern part of Vestland, dating to c. 1300 BCE); the bas relief image suggests a clothed figure with an axe, dagger, sickle, and various other tools, and is also an example of the influential contact between northern Scandinavia and Europe. A further parallel exists between the Kyrkje-Eide stela and the famous 'Egtvedgirl,' whose origins we may now confirm are not Jutish as previously supposed, but are very probably southeastern Sweden or Rogaland in

---

158. Ibid. Ship motifs have a mainly coastal distribution, with around 12,000 images of ships spread across 30,000 registered rock art sites in Scandinavia. **159.** E. Blanchard-Wrigglesworth; C. M. Bitz; M. M. Holland. "Influence of Initial Conditions and Climate Forcing On Predicting Arctic Sea Ice." Geophys. Res. Lett., 38 (2011): 203-204. L18503, doi:10.1029/2011GL048807 (2011): 203-204.

western Norway.[160] The resemblances between the artefact assemblage from the Kyrkje-Eide stela and those from the Egtved burial are striking. This young woman was buried around 1370 BCE, in an oak moss-lined and bark-covered coffin that was enclosed within the barrow. Preserved in acidic soil, her remains include arm-rings, an earring, a horn comb, a bronze awl, corded skirt and woven blouse; her disc-shaped "bronze belt-plate, symbolizing the sun, has led to the suggestions that the Egtved girl was a priestess of a sun worshipping cult."[161] While her belt-plate and comb are stylistically Scandinavian, certain other objects appear as common grave goods in both Scandinavian and European graves.[162]

Sámi rock art is stylistically very similar to art found in Italy. Important sites near to the northern alpine regions of Mont Bego and Val Camonica, preserve over 30000 petroglyphs, "consisting largely of horned and human figures, anthropomorphs, and weaponry, such as daggers, halberds and axes, that span a considerable time period, beginning around 12000 BCE, and ceasing only with the arrival of the Romans in 16 BCE."[163] Understanding rock art as a narrative perspective into the societal changes (economic, religious and political) affected by geographical trade and exchange patterns provides us with an incredibly vibrant resource.

Clear zoomorphic elements present in the rock art symbols may indicate shamanic trance-states or vision-quests. A popular interpretation of some of the images explores the possibility of them as representations of hunting magic specifically involving the sacred totemic beasts of each tribe or clan. In the earliest phases the rock art is heavily invested in hunting, sharing stylistic and thematic similarities with the Arctic rock art in northern Scandinavia. Over time, the focus shifts from animal or prey to humans, and the emergence of metallurgy viz, weaponry such as the aforementioned halberds, axes and daggers. Nevertheless, ships are continuously present and numerically dominant in Scandinavian rock art until the Iron Age transition occurred.

Other images at Val Camonica share remarkable similarities with

---

160. S. Sabatini and S. Bergerbrant. (Eds.) *The Textile Revolution in Bronze Age Europe: Production, Specialisation, Consumption*. (Cambridge University Press, 2019). See also: Sophie Bergerbrant. "Revisiting the 'Egtved Girl." (2019). https://www.researchgate.net/publication/333046418_Revisiting_the_'Egtved_Girl' (Retrieved 15th August 2024)   **161.** Melheim and Sand-Eriksen, 2020.   **162.** Bergerbrant, 2019: 30. It is believed that the transmission of the sun cult to northern Europe took place during the Nordic Bronze Age.   **163.** Melheim and Sand-Eriksen, 2020. Alpine rock art production came to an end when the Romans started to regulate (and control) the trade routes through here early in the 1st century CE.

ROCK ART AS A NEOLITHIC NARRATIVE CULTURE 57

Scandinavian rock art, particularly where they relate to warriors with weapons, whose mythological associations may therefore be less distinct than previously imagined. Over 1100 separate carvings (almost half of which are birds), can be found at Lake Onega, a central hub for expressing material and aesthetic culture. Anthropomorphic images feature here, along with several other symbols, including otter, fish, beavers, rods, trees, snakes, and an exceptionally rare demonic spirit. The White Sea rock art (located at the lower reaches of the Vyg River) features over 2000 realistic images of battle scenes, and also of sea and forest-animal hunting scenes (mainly of white-whale and elk) with figures on skis with bows and arrows, or with clubs on sleds.[164]

Other more obscure motifs appear to resemble ladders, making identification problematic. It has been suggested they could be bridges or fences, and that the lines are oars or dancing peoples, all as if seen from a bird's eye perspective.[165] My personal view is that the ladder-like motifs are more likely to be sleds, or canoes. This much is certainly evident in their appearance. Trade and the means of its transportation and distribution were primary considerations such that rivers and the coastal seas became the supply routes between ports and trading hubs. The movement (in trade and gift exchange) of copper, tin, gold, Baltic amber, glass beads, warriors and slaves, towards the end of the Middle Bronze Age emphasises the thriving trade relationships between northern Italy and Scandinavia.[166]

---

164. Melheim and Sand-Eriksen, 2020. **165.** Johan Ling, Peter Skoglund and Ulf Bertilsson (Eds.) "Picturing the Bronze Age." In, *Swedish Rock Art Research Series* (Oxbow Books. 2015): 473. See also: Johan Ling. "Elevated Rock Art." (2014): 257-68. doi:10.2307/J.CTVH1DPXR. (Accessed 2nd May 2024). **166.** . Kaul, 2022. Material evidence confirms cultural connections between Italy and the Baltic/Scandinavia during the Bronze Age. Trade connections peak c.1500 BCE to 1100 BCE with the importation of copper from the Italian Alps to Scandinavia.

SÁMI NARRATIVE ART

Early trade with external groups promoted cultural exchanges that inspired Bronze Age civilizations and their attendant technological evolutions. As fundamental issues relating to life, they are reflected in the monumental stone canvases across the northern regions, which offer insights into the concerns and celebrations of the Neolithic and Bronze Ages. For the Steppe nomads, compliance to a new worldview was a survival imperative. Rituals relating to life-style and funerary customs absorbed and expressed those cognitive shifts. Imitated behaviour often acquires shifts in symbolisms appropriate to the adopted status or changes in religious meaning, especially where supernatural agents are considered the direct guarantors of economic prosperity.

Even though the relationship between the Sámi and the Neolithic Petroglyphs found in (former) Lapland and Finnmark remains unproven, the evidence is hard to refute. That Sámi ancestors were the (Komsaculture) hunter-gatherers of the late Palaeolithic and early Mesolithic is widely known, and although the art is generally referred to as 'Finnish,' the rock-art is unmistakably of Sámi ancestry, it is their ethnic culture demonstrated here. Peppering the cliffsides that once hugged the rocky coastlines of western Sweden, artworks include animals (reindeer and horses), boats, humans, and various geometrical symbols (namely spirals and concentric circles). Which people painted them and why, continues to arouse speculative debate.

Although we have no evidence of who the actual persons were that created the prehistoric landscape art; namely rock carvings and paintings, the content of their work shows overwhelmingly how they have been ritual specialists and people with extraordinary skills and abilities and who made contact with unseen worlds and the spirits who dwell there. (...) Throughout the Nordic countries within the last several decades, in-depth historical research investigating the correlations linking symbols, figures, designs and patterns between prehistoric rock carvings, paintings and Sámi shaman drum motifs has determined how there are remarkable parallels and thereby, links between such documented art forms. As a result, much ambiguity has arisen in relation to the cultural context and ethnicity of the prehistoric art.[167]

SÁMI NARRATIVE ART 59

From all we have learned, it is evident that Finnish Rock art is justifiably associated with the cultural changes within Sámi history that are also repeated on the drum-heads of the Sámi noaidi.

Despite alterations through time, continuities [of culture] can be discerned with depictions on the Sámi drums used by shamans in Medieval Norway. Such long-term continuities in the nature and locus of ritual and art have major potential implications for our understanding of the formulation of contemporary European society.[168]

Images from the numerous rock art pictographs and petroglyphs confirm the use of drums since the Stone Age. Further studies will yield a deeper understanding of the spiritual beliefs of hunter/gatherer peoples where context is everything.[169] In terms of sources of oral histories and ethnicities in the north, rock art represents the earliest embedded language systems where knowledge has been recorded, and yet there are noticeable absences that offer significant clues relating to their understanding of the visible and invisible worlds they existed in.[170] Narrative traditions and artistic tropes preserve the ideologies of a people, and in this, the Sámi excel in both. Life reflects art and vice versa, both on the rock face and in the drum-head symbolisms. The same cosmological and yet equally narrative approach was also transferred from those huge edifices and monolithic constructions to the decoration of the shamans' drums in Norway, Sweden and Finland. From the 17th and 18th centuries, these drum images demonstrate discernible links between the Sámi and these early settlements located in the south-east of the country, albeit in lands the Sámi no longer occupy.

Throughout Scandinavia, prehistoric rock art depictions are characterised by the absence of domestic scenes – huts, interiors, food preparation and consumption in the home. The 'inside' possibly largely female roles, are 'denied' in the art. Rather it is 'outside' activities such as hunting, fishing and rituals, which are accorded importance. And, of course, the art itself occurs outside settlements and domestic pottery, and the domestic sphere in general, are often not the focus of decoration and symbolic

---

167. Francis Joy. "Sámi Shamanism Past and Present and the Desecration of the Sacred in Finland." In, *Philosophy of Law in the Arctic*. Edited by D. Bunikowski. (Lapin yliopisto, Arktinen keskus, 2016): 53-60 **168.** Knut Helskog. "Selective Depictions. A Study of 3,500 Years of Rock Carvings from Arctic Norway and Their Relationship to the Sámi Drums." In, *Archaeology as Long-Term History*. Edited by I. Hodder. (Cambridge Uni. Press, 1987): 17-30 **169.** Birgitta Berglund. "Recently Discovered Gievrie (South-Sámi Shaman Drums) – Contexts, Meanings and Narratives." *Act a Borealia: A Nordic Journal of Circumpolar Societies*, 22(2) (2005): 128-152. DOI: 10.1080/ 08003830500327689 (Accessed 1st February, 2013). **170.** Helskog, 1987: 17.

elaboration. Spatiality, the 'outside' realm is often associated with death (burial) and rituals (such as ritual hoardings). In the Neolithic in southern Scandinavia, it is the 'outside' world, which is particularly associated with symbolic elaboration and decoration. Through time, the boundary between inside and outside, domestic and wild, receives different emphasis in changing social contexts. [171]

Rock art demonstrates cognitive symbolisms profoundly connected to the Sámi consciousness. As a visual heritage, this complements and celebrates traditions of oral transmission that collectively serve the process of anamnesis, no matter how obscure the source.

Because hunters were living within the ice or caves, or perhaps travelling by boats in the summer and on skis in the winter, the absence of indoor domestic art scenes makes sense to me, reflecting as it does, their hunting, fishing and trapping culture. Albeit much diminished, these lifestyle practices can still be found within Sámi culture up until the present time. We also know that because of the volumes of glacial melt water, hunters spent more time living on boats, a factor which also supports the high occurrence of such vessels in the rock art of that period..[172]

Arguably then, evidence of human habitation along the coastal areas of the Arctic Ocean lends firm support to the notion that boats were used to navigate the coastlines and waterways, yet this is often overlooked, or overshadowed by a very different emphasis. This is because Sámi history has been largely recorded and interpreted by persons from outside Sámi culture, most of whom were religious missionaries or priests, from the 17th and 18th centuries, whose bias is palpable. More recently, however, research is directed towards gaining a wider understanding of Sámi culture and in particular, previous Sámi occupancy in the central and southern areas of Finland, which has helped to examine rock paintings (and drum symbolism) of both nomadic and sedentary peoples in a new light.

---

171. Joy, 2018. **172.** Ibid.

LIMINAL NARRATIVES AND SHIPS OF THE DEAD

Funerary traditions and customs were fluid, adaptive, and generally in step with the shifting social and ethnic patterns that linked the movements of people to the Tumulus culture as it evolved along the northwestern coast of Norway visible to other wayfarers who travelled by land and sea.[173] Rock art reflects and is governed by environment, society, particularly its needs and demands, this much we have established. There are over a hundred acknowledged examples of rock art in Finland, and almost all of them are located near water, specifically in the outer island areas, where rock art and burial monuments (in the form of cairns and stállo sites) indicate patterns of belief in the deliberate placement of the dead in liminal zones. There appears to be an observable relationship between death and rock art in the funerary landscape of Sweden and Norway, where many rock art sites are sited within metres of prehistoric burial structures. The Sagaholm Bronze Age barrow from Sweden is a striking example. Dated to around 1500 BCE to 1100 BCE, the huge mound (22–24 m in diameter and 4 m high), though damaged, consists of decorated slabs that housed a considerable haul of grave goods, including many horses and ships that accompanied the four human beings interred there.

Liminal boundaries betwixt land and water have provided sacred locations that have endured for many, many hundreds of years, in various forms throughout the Bronze Age, and later as Sámi Sieidi sites. Looking outwards to the liminal horizon of the sea, many Early Bronze Age cairns pepper the Baltic and the North Atlantic shorelines. Other funerary monuments built on small islands off the coast were obviously reached only by boat.[174] Empty vessels seem particularly

---

173. Melheim and Sand-Eriksen, 2020. **174.** Richard Bradley; Peter Skoglund; Joakim Wehlin. "Imaginary Vessels In The Late Bronze Age Of Gotland And South Scandinavia: Ship Settings, Rock Carvings And Decorated Metalwork." *Current Swedish Archaeology* Vol 18 (2010). **175.** R. Bradley. *Image and Audience. Rethinking Prehistoric Art.* (Oxford University Press, 2009).

suggestive of an association with the dead,[175] for instance, all but one of the ship carvings that decorate the Hjortekrog complex (outcrop and Late Bronze Age cairns) are void of people. Rock art works found at other burial sites (Kivik and Sagaholm) depict ships with 'people' travelling one way that return as empty vessels, a motif that may commemorate a body of ancestors sailing off to the land of the dead.[176] While some burial sites maintain a distinct connection between the land that sustains them and their immediate ancestors, it seems likely that maritime cairns indicate a relationship between the dead and the sea, a nod perhaps to their origins, and overseas ancestors.

As we shall see, there is an observable correlation between the ship motifs portrayed across rock art sites and the construction of sacred sites, either as animistic shrines to local spirits, or as funerary barrows and cairns at strategic locations along the coastal regions around 1600 BCE. This correlation perfectly demonstrates the rapid construction of dwellings at strategic locations along the coast during the Nordic Bronze Age that reflects this material expression of wealth, stratified power, kinship, alliance ties, elitism and property rights.[177] Celebrating the heroic qualities of the accumulation of abundance, these are the tropes that account for all commemorative burials and funerary monuments.

---

176. P. Skoglund. "Cosmology And Performance: Narrative Perspectives On Scandinavian Rock Art." In, *Changing Pictures: Rock Art Traditions and Visions in Northern Europe*. Edited by J. Goldhahn, I. Fuglestvedt, and A. Jones. (Oxford: Oxbow Books, 2010): 127–38. **177.** Melheim and Sand-Eriksen, 2020. Signifying rising wealth and status, cairns increased in size from the late Neolithic onwards through to the Early Bronze Age (c. 2350 BCE to 1100 BCE), emerging with additional interior coffins.

MARITIME TRADE AND TRADITIONS

Scandinavian rock art images depict thousands of water-faring vessels, mainly canoes, yet strangely, many experts presume the artists were farmers. I do not share this view, and though it is popular, I believe it needs serious revision. "It is, however, only recently that the predominance of ships has been understood as a key expression of genuinely maritime societies, rather than religious symbols related to agricultural fertility rituals." [178] These people were nothing if not pragmatic. Rock art motifs along the coastlines indicate distinct zones for the living and the dead. In fact, the areas of the living appear to focus on trade and industry, while those of the dead, offer funerary complexes in the liminal zones.

From canoes to warships, boat styles are not merely different by design, but seem to signify profound (and variable) purposes in ritual and narrative art. Early water craft were very simple in design, without masts or sails.[179] Many were little more than basic canoes constructed of stretched skin (hide); others were of rough sewn-plank boats.[180] The Hjortspring boat (canoe)[181] from Denmark, is an exceptional and rare example of a plank-built seafaring vessel from the Scandinavian Pre-Roman Iron Age (c.400 BCE to 300 BCE).[182] It is thought that a vessel of this size could transport around a dozen people.

Ship images in Scandinavian rock art are depicted in profile, emphasising the raised prow and stern. Indicating the direction of travel, some petroglyphs embellish the prow with a horse's head.[183] The

---

178. Melheim and Sand-Eriksen, 2020. **179.** There is no real evidence for the use of masts and sails in any of the rock art before the 6th century CE. See: Christer Westerdahl. The Ship as Symbol in Prehistoric and Medieval Scandinavia. (Copenhagen National Museum, 1995): 42 **180.** Bradley, Skoglund & Wehlin, 2010. **181.** Found in a bog in Hjortspring Mose, on the island of Als in Sønderjylland, Denmark, excavated in 1921-1922. **182.** Bradley, Skoglund & Wehlin, 2010. **183.** Later vessels have a symmetrical profile. Similar boats are depicted on the coasts of Norway, where most of the artworks date from the Neolithic and Bronze Age. See: Johan Ling. "War Canoes or Social Units? Human Representation in Rock-Art Ships." *European Journal of Archaeology* 15 (3) (2012): 465-485

vertical strokes may indicate the oars, and therefore crew. We have no way of knowing who the people are depicted on these boats, though it is generally thought they may represent ancestors, the dead, incoming traders, outgoing migrants, even, might I suggest, people taken away as slaves. Some images may therefore express a narrative lament, a record of the traumatic events of their world. Certainly, the trade in slaves during the Bronze Age was prolific and would be an event harrowing enough to be worthy of recording.

As a social demonstration of graphic artworks that depict impactful events, a plausible parallel is suggested in some Pictish sites across northern Scotland where images of Viking ships are etched onto slates. These dramatic motifs have been described as narrative graffiti produced by non-literate indigenous peoples, as a reaction to their contact with outsiders from a literate world, possibly during conflict with those outsiders.[184] Of course, more than one thing can be true; there may be manifold causes and reasons for such enigmatic rock art images. There is certainly a marked change in the subject matter of the motifs portrayed, which is a valid indicator of a paradigm shift in socio-religious culture.

On low ground, near to the (present) shoreline, ships and axes are the main iconic rock art features (tools, weapons may indicate martial activity) that support the notion of seasonal activity associated with a more economic, socio-political usage – trade and exchange for example.[185] Other areas further inland and on higher ground feature more abstract images such as concentric circles, sun symbols and humans (including the undersoles of feet), with very few water craft.[186] Processions, small craft, animals, and trees, collectively suggest settlement areas that relate to very different ritual spheres of praxis associated with agriculture of a pragmatic, but no less devout nature than hunting cameos.[187]

Excavations at some comparatively small and less complex coastal rock art sites (all located on higher ground), have yielded surprising features[188] that include hearths, postholes, heaps of fire-cracked stones and "traces of metallurgical activity, such as fragments of tuyères, furnace linings, crucibles, and moulds."[189] This distinguishes these social areas from rock

---

184 U. O'Meadhra. "Viking-Age Sketches And Motif-Pieces From The Northern Earldoms." In, *The Viking Age in Caithness, Orkney and the North Atlantic*. Edited by C. E. Batey and J. Jesch & C. D. Morris. (Edinburgh Uni Press. 1993): 423-440 **185.** Although rock art ships appear on the mainland of Scandinavia, there is a marked concentration on Gotland and which may bear a relationship with the decorated metalwork that is often found in burials. See: Kristiansen, 2004: 111–21 **186.** Melheim and Sand-Eriksen, 2020. **187.** Lødøen and Mandt, 2010. **188.** Radiocarbon dating of these finds demonstrate a clear chronological connection between the prehistoric activity and the rock art imagery, with dates that range from approximately 1500 BCE to 300 BCE. See: Ling, Skoglund and Bertilsson, 2015.

art shoreline sites that (generally) turn out to be more or less void of industry.[190] It seems plausible "that the centralized metal workshops in the Nordic region, often maritime sites, served as landing and market places."[191] Although the Mountain Sámi were clearly smelting iron early in the first millennium CE, for knives and arrow heads, they were also keen traders between Sweden and Norway, and attended the traditional seasonal markets evolving throughout the Viking Age (primarily held at Uppsala in Sweden and Grunnfjord in Norway) long established for this purpose.[192]

Recently discovered rock engravings found within the mountainous regions of northern Sweden, occur at former prehistoric settlement sites that were still a hive of activity when used by the nomadic Mountain Sámi as seasonal reindeer pasture and hunting grounds.[193] Many of these have cultural significance as 'stállo sites'[194] According to Sámi folklore, a Stállo (Stalo, or Staaloe; or Northern Sami Stállu) refers to an oversized, human-like but hostile creature, much akin to an ogre, who deems mortal flesh a delicacy. Numerous mountain shrines occur at the locations of their presumed habitation. Because later (Viking Age) 'stállo sites' coincide with such long-standing settlement sites, (maintained for the purposes of seasonal hunting), we may correlate such activity with the thriving fur trade of the late Iron Age, which continued through to the Nordic Medieval period, c. 500 BCE to 1400 CE.[195] Although the

---

189. L. Bengtsson and J. Ling. "Scandinavia's Most Finds Associated Rock Art Site." Adoranten 2007): 40-50. rockartscandinavia.se, 2008.; Ulf Bertilsson. "The Rock Carvings of Northern Bohuslän: Spatial Structures and Social Symbols." *Stockholm Studies in Archaeology* 7 (Stockholm University. 1987). **190.** Bengtsson, L. 'To Excavate Images: Some Results From The Tanum Rock Art project 1997–2004,' In, Representations and Communications: Creating an Archaeological Matrix of Late Prehistoric Rock Art. Edited by Å. Fredell, K. Kristiansen, and F. Criado Boado. (Oxbow Books, 2010): 116-131. **191.** Melheim and Sand-Eriksen, 2020 **192.** Håkan Rydving. *The End Of Drum-Time: Religious Change Among The Lule Sámi. 1670s–1740s.* (Almqvist & Wiksell International, 1993). **193.** I. M. Mulk. "Sacrificial Places And Their Meaning In Sámi Society." In, *Sacred sites, Sacred Places.* Edited by D. Carmichael, J. Hubert, B. Reeves & A. Schanche. (London, 1994): 121-131 **194.** Emilie Demant Hatt and Barbara Sjoholm. "Folktales." In, *By the Fire: Sami Folktales and Legends.* (Minneapolis; London: University of Minnesota Press, 2019): 58-67. doi:10.5749/j.ctvfjcx2d.9 (Accessed November 25th, 2024) See also: Lars Levi Laestadius and Juha Pentikäinen. (Eds). Fragments of Lappish Mythology. K. Börje Vähämäki. (Trans.) (Aspasia Books, 2002). **195.** Inga-Maria Mulk and Tim Bayliss-Smith. "Sámi Rock Engravings From The Mountains in Laponia, Northern Sweden." (1998). In, *Folklore,* (Estonian Literary Museum Scholarly Press, 1999) See also: I. M. Mulk. "The Role of The Sámi In Fur Trading During The Late Iron Age And Nordic Medieval Period In The Light Of The Sámi Sacrificial Sites in Lapland, Northern Sweden." *Acta Borealia* 13 (1996): 47-80.

trading of furs especially was already well established before the Viking Age, this had become an intensified process of cultural interchange around 1000 CE.[196]

The so-called stállo-foundations are the most prominent ancient monuments in the mountain areas of Sweden. On the basis of archaeological, historical and ethnological evidence, (...) [this] type of construction [is] likely to be associated with stállo-foundations dating to the Viking Age. It is argued, in contrast to most accepted ideas, that the stállo-foundations represent the remains of permanent hut dwellings. It is suggested that these huts were built from mountain birch and birch bark, on a bow-pole framework. The surrounding embankments and sunken floors, typical features of the foundations, allowed the construction of low-angled ceilings. This structural design would have enabled the buildings to withstand strong winds and the weight of lying snow, as well as increasing heat retention. (...) We also suggest that the stállo-foundations represent a system of reindeer herding in which the mountain ridges in the west and areas in Norway were used throughout the year.[197]

Sámi living on the Norwegian coast have demonstrated certain aspects of Nordic culture since the early Iron Age, including a substantial linguistic influence from the 4th century CE onwards.[198] Sámi hunting culture inherited a long tradition of watercraft,[199] as shown in their Stone Age and Bronze Age rock art, a technological skill they developed further during the Iron Age. The later Bårset (mastless), funerary boat from Nord-Kvaløy, Troms (of Sámi construction), dated

---

196. These invasive intrusions to all Sámi culture continued unabated for several more centuries, bringing total change to all areas of their socio-religious, and socio-political structure. The transition from hunting to herding brought with it a period of intense confrontation between Sámi and non-Sámi cultures on the frontiers of Swedish, Norwegian and Russian colonial expansion. See: Håkan Rydving. "The Sámi Drums And The Religious Encounter in The 17th And 18th Centuries." In, *The Sámi Shaman Drum. Aboensis* 14 (1988): 28-51. Scripta, Instituti Donneriani. Edited by Tore Ahlbäck and Jans Bergman. (Donner Institute, Åbo, Finland). https://doi.org/10.30674/scripta.67195 (1991). (Accessed 12th March 2023). **197.** L. Liedgren and I. Bergman. "Aspects of the Construction of Prehistoric Stálló-Foundations and Stálló-Buildings." *Acta Borealia*, 26(1) (2009): 3-26. https://doi.org/10.1080/08003830902951516 (Accessed November 25th, 2024). **198.** J. P. Mallory. *In Search of the Indo-Europeans: Language, Archaeology, and Myth*. (Thames & Hudson Ltd., 1989). **199.** S. Wickler. "Visualizing Sami Waterscapes In Northern Norway From An Archaeological Perspective." In, *A Circumpolar Reappraisal: The Legacy of Gutorm Gjessing (1906–1979)*. Edited by C. Westerdahl. (Brit Archaeol Rep, Int Series 2154., 2010): 349–61. For details of Sámi boatbuilding techniques, see: Christer Westerdahl. "Boats Apart. Building and Equipping an Iron-Age and Early-Medieval Ship in Northern Europe." *International Journal of Nautical Archaeology*, 37 (2007): 17-31. https://doi.org/10.1111/j.1095-9270.2007.00170.x (Accessed 23rd October 2023).

from around 700 CE, is a perfect example of a common shared theme that evolved between the Sámi and the Norse peoples. However, a great part of Sámi boat terminology is of primitive Norse origin, derived from their mutual interactions tentatively placed around north Norway (Helgeland) somewhere between 300 CE to 600 CE.

In addition to farming, some of the Norsemen were plundering, tax levying and trading with the Sámi population of hunters and fishers. These activities have been viewed by some historians as the means whereby rich farmers and Viking chiefs acquired their wealth. Alternatively, it can be argued that in fact the main form of interaction between Norsemen and Sámi was gift exchange, which provided a better means for both parties to establish stable and mutually beneficial relations, especially in the fur trade. [200]*During the Viking and Medieval periods (c. 800 CE to 1500 CE) there was an increase in long-distance sea trade and a growing assimilation of the Coastal Sámi in north Norway into a more sedentary lifestyle. Inland, however, the Mountain Sámi group associations (sijdda) continued to be engaged in reindeer hunting in connection with the fur trade. [...] The sijdda society that developed during the 1st millennium CE, was organised to achieve cooperation among specialised task groups, redistribution and satisfactory exchange relationships with outsiders. The evidence from the sacrificial sites suggests that the trade of the Mountain Sámi was eastwards with Finns, Karelians and Russians as well as westwards with the Norwegians.*[201]

This knowledge allows us to reconsider how we perceive images from the Padjelanta region of Sweden that depicts six boats in profile with double-ended hulls; one even has an inwards curve at both ends, similar to the shape of the hulls of the Viking Age funeral ships discovered at Oseberg[202] and Kvalsund. Four figures are vaguely recognisable, two of which seem to be human, while two other antlered forms, each have four legs. "There is a large human figure standing outside and to the right of Boat 3, carrying in one hand a bow or possibly a drum, and in the other hand a spear, paddle or net." [203]

Nordic influence amongst the Coastal Sámi is confirmed by

---

200. This fur trade connected the Mountain Sámi both with communities living far to the east and with Coastal Sámi and the Nordic settlers to the west. **201.** Mulk and Bayliss-Smith, 1999. **202.** Dated to about 800 CE, the Viking Age Oseberg Ship was discovered in Norway. It contained one of the most elaborate burial assemblages found in the northern hemisphere. Along with the interred remains of two women of high social status, were 13 horses, three ornately carved sleighs, dogs, an ox, an ornately carved wagon, collapsable bedsteads, an oak chest, a wooden bucket with brass fittings (possibly from Ireland), and many other treasures and household goods, including several textiles. **203.** Mulk and Bayliss-Smith, 1999.

archaeological evidence, and it seems the outer fjords were farmed for barley by early Norse farmers from at least 300 CE.[204] The adoption of certain maritime phrases into the Sámi language further supports external Norse influences upon the Sámi refinement of their watercraft.[205] "The inner coastal area [around Tysfjord] should be seen as a place of transaction between Mountain Sámi, Coastal Sámi, and the Nordic farming, fishing and trading communities of the outer coastal zone, interactions which seem to have intensified from about 600 CE onwards."[206] Despite their distinct life-styles, Sámi from different regions, traded and intermarried with each other, sharing their language, knowledge, and culture mutually, as noted above. In the post-Viking period, the Coastal Sámi embraced agriculture and animal husbandry which led to an increasingly sedentary lifestyle, while the Mountain Sámi continued their seasonal nomadic subsistence, fishing, wild reindeer hunting and fur trading. Trade generated such wealth that several hoards of silver objects dating from the late Viking Age were found in the outer coastal regions that formerly belonged to the Sámi.

The pre-dominance of boats in Sámi culture is preserved in the tenacious midwinter customs that endured conversion. One of these involved the setting aside of food and animal fat in hand-crafted birch bark boats, which hung on the trees outside for the landvaettir and ancestral spirits, and which resemble the older sacrificial offerings to the wind and water spirits by the Lule Sámi especially.[207] The relationship between boats and the dead, and to all invisible spirits, is undeniable. By extension, this has further connotations for shamanism as the spiritual core of the Sámi people, confirming again that there is no separation between the sacred and the mundane. The pragmatism of trade did not detract from the sacred significance of the boat as a vehicle for the dead.

---

204. The distribution of Nordic graves suggests that in the early Iron Age (before c. 400 CE), farming settlement was restricted to the outer coastal area. **205.** A. Nesheim. "Eastern and Western elements in Lapp culture." In, *Lapps and Norsemen in Olden Times*. Serie A, Nr. 26 (Instituttet for Sammenlignende Kulturforskning, Oslo, 1967):104-168 **206.** Mulk and Bayliss-Smith. 1999. **207.** P. Fjellström. Cultural and Traditional Ecological Perspectives on Sámi Religion. In, *Sámi Religion*. T. Ahlbäck (Ed.) (Åbo, Finland: Donner Institute for Research in Religious and Cultural History. 1987) 34-45

SAIL DESIGN, A VANITY OF PRESTIGE

Despite the obvious long-standing northern maritime tradition of water craft, sails and mast technology did not arrive in Scandinavia until sometime between around 700 CE to 800 CE, as an innovation that facilitated the Viking Age expansion eastwards across Europe to Russia, and westwards over the Atlantic to Iceland and Greenland. During the Vendel period (c. 500 CE to 800 CE), the first small rectangular sails can be seen on the 7th-Century Gotland picture stones. Fully rigged vessels such as those found at Oseberg (built c. 820 CE) and Gokstad (c. 890 CE), do not appear until almost two centuries later.[208] Vikingr activity is popularly linked with the signature term – 'longships' (karfar, Old Norse) particularly when raiding, (at least initially), but later the term became associated with trading and slaving). Rooted in the Celtic *longa, longships is in fact a term that does not refer to the length of the boat, but to the boat as a vessel bearing foreign travellers. Built with masts and sails in addition to oars, the longships did not require deep water anchorage, so could be beached easily.

Although the square sail was known and used in the Mediterranean Sea several thousand years BCE, its adoption by North Germanic peoples, was initially slow and unenthusiastic. Reasons proposed for this, suggest that during the Vendel Period (the Merovingian Iron Age in Europe and Sweden), certain pressing imperatives socially and politically delayed that uptake. Encounters with the Roman trappings of war, on both land and sea, ostensibly refute any Germanic ignorance of such technology. In fact, knowledge of it appears on a curious artefact found in the river Weser that displays a Roman sailing ship accompanied by a runic inscription. The sleek, low profile mastless boats were largely undetected at distance, a vital imperative when attacking vulnerable coastlines, hence the endurance of rowing ships.

---

208. Although the square sail was used in the 7th century on ships like Sutton Hoo (c. 625) and Kvalsund (c. 690), these were still essentially rowing boats. See: Mulk and Bayliss-Smith. 1999.

4. The Weser bone. Göttlicher 1989 (Bremen/ Bremerhaven).

Larger or grander vessels may have served in funerary contexts, but few if any would have been equipped with sails, nor deemed sea-worthy, certainly not the boat at Sutton Hoo, though it, and the later Oseberg ship were irrefutably prestigious vessels, built specifically for funerary purposes.[209]

During the earlier part of the Vendel Period, (Swedish Iron Age), the knarr served as both cargo trader[210] (people and goods), and warship,[211] a notion confirmed in contemporary skaldic verse which uses the same term. The purposeful decision taken at the onset of the Viking Age, which possibly initiated it, was to adopt sails and mast technology. That innovation was swift and decisive.[212] More importantly, it appears commensurate with the internal development of northern states across Scandinavia, thus replacing the outmoded petty fiefdoms aligned to

---

209. The Oseberg is a mast-bearing ship, albeit deemed too weak to bear full sail. **210.** A. E. Christensen. "Ship Graffiti: *The Ship As Symbol In Prehistoric And Medieval Scandinavia.*" In, A Collection of Essays: The Ship as Symbol in Prehistoric and Medieval Scandinavia. Papers from an International Research Seminar at the Danish National Museum, Copenhagen, 5th-7th May 1994. Edited by O. Crumlin-Pedersen and B.M. Thye. (National Museum of Copenhagen, 1995): 180-185. See also: K. Sognnes. "Symbols in a Changing World: Rock-Art and The Transition from Hunting to Farming in mid-Norway." In, *The Archaeology of Rock-Art.* Edited by C. Chippindale and P.S.C. Taco. (Cambridge,1998): 146-162   **211.** Äskekärr boat from southwest Sweden (c. 960), the Klåstad boat from south Norway (c. 980) from Roskilde in Denmark. See: Ole Crumlin-Pedersen; Inger M. Bojesen-Koefoed; Athena Trakadas. *Hjortspring: a Pre-Roman Iron Age Warship In Context.* Edited by Ole Crumlin-Pedersen and Athena Trakadas. (Roskilde: Viking Ship Museum, 2003). **212.** Christer Westerdahl. "Society and Sail. On Symbols As Specific Social Values And Ships As Catalysts Of Social Units." In, A Collection of Essays: *The Ship as Symbol in Prehistoric and Medieval Scandinavia.* Papers from an International Research Seminar at the Danish National Museum, Copenhagen, 5th-7th May 1994. Edited by O. Crumlin-Pedersen and B. M. Thye. (National Museum of Copenhagen, 1995): 41-50

SAILS DESIGN, A VANITY OF PRESTIGE 71

minor chieftains. Wealth and power became prime motivators in the push to exploit new lands, deepen old trading alliances, and forge new ones. The sail was a principle requisite of that ambition. As a wealthier land with good resources at its disposal, Denmark adopted it first, Sweden, Norway and Finland were forced to follow.

Viking Age ships were essentially rowing barges, and in medieval texts we find references to the "territorial concept of Roden in Uppland, Sweden, literally meaning 'the rowing districts,' later called Roslagen."[213] An early 11th century reference relates to this a phrase that appears on runic stones, written as "i Roð konungi, 'in the Rod of the King' (...) and personalized in the concept of Håkans Rod, (...) the personal name probably referring to the king himself."[214] To add to the intriguing list of possible meanings for the origin of the word Rus', it is even proposed that "the concept of roðr, 'rowing, rowing team,' must have been so characteristic of the system, that it has not only been the basis of the Finnish name of Sweden, Fi Ruotsi (Est Rootsi), but also the Russian Rus'."[215]

It is interesting that several popular terms relating to the martial aspects of the former Iron Age societies, including *rod*, eventually became associated with portions of land and the legal claims to them. Others are, *lið*, which refers "to the entourage (German: *Gefolgschaft*) of a local chieftain. Already in these times the ship was very probably a microcosm in the sense reflected by the later levy (*leding, leidang, ledung*) organisation. *Hå/hamna*, literally meaning rowlock and fastening for the oar, in the *ledung*, of the Medieval province laws, was the smallest unit, a couple of farmsteads, sometimes a hamlet."[216] Kudos was an alure, an appeal to vanity, the Achilles heel of all north men. Such esteem was pursued even into the grave: "The deceased leader of the *lið* or the *visi, styrir* or *styrimaðr* (captain) of the *lið* or of the *levy* fleet district has still his seat at the stern in the boat graves. His skeleton may even wield the metal handle of his steering rudder."[217] Being a member of this kind of military rowing crew for a chieftain's ship likewise offered considerable prestige in that highly competitive, male, hierarchical society.

The honour of being a bonde, a free man equipped with his own axe, sword and spear, may have been even less important than this permanent seat on a warship

---

213. Ibid. **214.** Ibid. The number of men in his employ, and the size and number of boats they man, indicate the wealth and power of individual chieftains **215.** Ibid. **216.** Ibid. **217.** Ibid. Acquisition and winning were so important to the Viking Age, that games of war and strategy, known as Hnefatafl, featured amongst the grave goods.

of one's master. (…) We may even find a remnant of this rowing society in two important and well-known concepts, viking and ledung (levy fleet organization).[218]

Many explanations have been suggested for the etymology of the term 'Víking(r),' which does not describe a pirate, so much as it does his actions when he goes 'a' pirating. It better refers to "a 'raid' or 'a sea journey' ('going a-viking' – Vikingr). I would here propose that it may have had something to do with the *vika*, the ancient Nordic rowing measure, in the sense that it means [one] half of a rowing crew."[219] It is suggested that the rhythmic sweeping motion of the oars as they rise and fall from the dragon-prowed galleys could be poetically seen and described as dragon's wings. This iconic imagery could easily have inspired the notion of a flying ship – the legendary S*kiðblaðnir*.[220]

Rowing ships have clear military advantages over sailing ships, but the obvious advantages of the latter won the day overall. To be observed, even far out at sea demonstrates power and a strong desire to be seen; it instils fear and inspires envy, particularly if a fleet of ships each display the same sail design (in the form of colour, symbols or animal totems) as the insignia, attributed to a single powerful warlord or trader. This notion would add further purpose as the precursor of clan heraldry and regalia. These are both psychological and social functions of the sail innovation. Sails also demonstrate legitimacy, a lack of deception, an essential trait for successful trading operations.

Archaeology has thus far not yielded evidence of decorated sails from Scandinavian Viking Age ships; for that we must look to the literary record. In the later 16th century *Historia (De forma et usu antiquarum nauium Septentrionalium, book* 10:2, 1976: 181), Olaus Magnus enigmatically refers to the distinguishing "signs, colours and names ('*signis, coloribus et nominibus/ distinctae*'),"[221] of each leader. So, it is not beyond the realms of possibility that such things were becoming a popular feature, centuries earlier.[222] Images of Viking Age ships appear as popular motifs as graffiti on church walls and water-mills; they even appear in former Neolithic, Bronze Age and early Iron Age tombs and cairns (Maes Howe for example, on Orkney). Many of these later sailing ships can be associated with the Sámi, whose relationship with, and contribution to, the boat-building technology is substantial and should not be overlooked. In addition to their value as trade ships,

---

218. Ibid. **219.** Ibid. The inference being a change of rowers as part of the full team. **220.** Ibid. **221.** Ibid. **222.** Westerdahl, 1995. This author provides other recorded examples from the Viking Age.

SAILS DESIGN, A VANITY OF PRESTIGE 73

Sámi water vessels bear an iconic status, rich with cultural and symbolic imagery.[223]

Sewn together with willow roots, the older, aforementioned plank and clinker boat method of construction, was a technique eagerly embraced by the Coastal Sámi who became renowned master boat-builders, a craft they were able to exploit due to "their control of the pine forests of the inner coastal area."[224] A reference to this type of vessel is found in Snorre's *Heimskringla*,[225] in *Inges saga*, where a Norse chief (living north of Tysfjord), commissioned Sámi boat-builders (living in Gljuvrafjord) to craft him two boats. Built without nails, the finished boats were big enough to bear twelve oarsmen on each side.[226] Craftsmen amongst the Coastal Sámi began manufacturing trading vessels in the fjords around 1000 CE, and it is possible the distinctive 'Nordland' boat was built in one of these sites. That such cultural innovation is apparent as a visual celebration etched into the very rock structures around and close to the major trading points of the Coastal Sámi, should not surprise us.

One of the essential human abilities is to acquire new skills and knowledge, either through direct teaching or by means of imitation. This ability developed as both a tool and product of human evolution. It is a well-known fact, that the evolutionary process is a matter of culture as well as biology.[227]

The adoption of new technologies, did not however, drastically alter the core tenets of that culture, at least initially. Some innovative, ambitious leaders recognised this increased yield as power, as currency, and as trade. Feeding a dedicated military elite became possible. Cults arose in the wake of a new generation of priestly prophets and men of might and means, displacing the former shamans whose relationship with the Other, mitigated rituals that secured successful hunting and fishing expeditions. Those new exceptions forced a re-defining of core beliefs, including humankind's relationships with the divine, with other human beings, and with the dead.[228] Such changes develop in both

---

223. Mulk and Bayliss Smith, 1999. **224.** Ibid. **225.** Written in Old Norse around 1230CE in Iceland, *Heimskringla* is a collection of sagas about Swedish and Norwegian kings, specifically the Swedish dynasty of the Ynglings, who claim a lineage reaching back to Freyr (Yngve) of the Vanaland people, and to Óðinn. The sagas also include mythological and historical accounts of Norwegian rulers that followed the legendary 9th century Harald Fairhair. **226.** Mulk and Bayliss-Smith, 1999. **227.** Michal Cigán. *Priest-king of The Warriors and Witch-Queen of The Others: Cargo Cult and Witch Hunt in Indo-European Myth and Reality*. (Brno: Masaryk University Press, [2016] 2019):17-27 **228.** M. Mead. *Continuities in Cultural Evolution*. (New Haven: Yale University Press. 1964): 193-194

individual and communal thinking, naturally and progressively.

Overall, we may conclude that as a means of communication, rock art, no matter the form or location, was clearly not random, but was used in very specific ways that reflect and celebrate all aspects of life, work, disaster, catastrophe and death, and such motifs tend to be zoned accordingly. In regions away from the coast, other forms of rock art reflect the beliefs and lives of nomadic peoples.

THE DEER MOTHER
AND THE
MOTHER OF ANIMALS

Art is the most impactful media for the preservation of culture, be that on a small scale (on drums and clothing for instance), or, on a grand scale, on the aforementioned cliffs, mountainsides, and other monumental media such as those found in funerary complexes. Having looked already at the rock art of the northern regions (concerned mainly with the sea and other waterways), there is a wealth of knowledge to be gleaned from the monoliths and megalithic structures further eastwards. It is in Eurasia that we find the origins of many customs and traditions relating to the spirituality and magics of the land that influenced the proto Sámi and proto Norse peoples initially, then the Scandinavian traditions noted in the later sagas and Eddas, albeit in remnant form. And though much altered by that circuitous route, they are still recognisable.

I am of the firm opinion that the beliefs expressed in art, laid the foundation of myths we popularly associate with northern peoples. The use of large scale grand narrative art relevant to this line of enquiry therefore occurs in other northern regions, namely the petroglyphs of the Altai mountains (in Eurasia). A popular motif present in almost all art of the ancient world centres around cervids. It is within the human nature to divinise that which sustains us, no matter the form. In this case, the deer was the beast that fed and clothed them. Its revered status should therefore be expected. Even when subsistence shifted from hunter-gathering to herding and farming, the deer never lost its divine status, it merely took a step back. Common images that appear in the petroglyphs of the Altai mountains illustrate the life of ancient hunters and herders in the steppes and deserts of Eurasia. Deer, goats, wild bulls, bears, anthropomorphic figures, camels, wolves, horses, chariots and fighting beasts. Composed in narrative motifs that relate to migration, hunting and war, these profound images form the basic themes of later heroic myths and legends associated with northern cosmologies.

In Old Icelandic tradition, the deer is the most common mythic horned animal, and is often associated with the second most common image of the ancient world – the Cosmic Tree. Together, these two icons appear in the myths and legends of all northern peoples. In the Eddas, the deer is called hjortr, and is similar to its early Germanic cognates OE heorot (Engl, hart) and OHG hiruz 'deer' (Ger. Hirsch), from a root meaning 'horn, antler; antlered animal.' Celtic languages also use a secondary term based on 'antler': Bret. *karo*, Corn. *carow* 'deer.'[229] Given that the trek to the Underworld was an arduous and potentially treacherous journey where assistance from otherworldly spirits was deemed essential, the vehicle for that journey was granted primarily in the form of a deer. Propitiated and ridden by shamans into the Otherworld realms, this psychopompic medium is known as the 'horse.' Over time, the 'horse' evolved (in form but not function) in ritual tradition to become the drum or even a riding pole within the various shamanic traditions of northern peoples.

Change is crucial to the evolution of humankind, though our progressions have not always served our best interests. Innovations are not always embraced, some are adopted slowly, others are ruthlessly rejected. Compromises during needful transitions are essential, and it is these regions of synergistic symbiosis we find the truly liminal boundaries of our society to be the most intriguing and fulfilling. Around 7000 years ago, we find archaeological evidence across the Pontic-Caspian Steppe regions that confirms the interaction between semi-nomadic Proto-Indo-European groups of hunter-gatherers, and the settled farmers of Afro-Asian origin. Inspired by their efficiency, the hunters improved their own stockbreeding techniques that had been preserved through many generations entirely for sacral and ritual purposes only.[230] The increased cattle yield had not diminished the sacrality of the beast, nor its ritual status and feasting function.[231]

Sacred cattle, perceived as a gift of divine providence continued to

---

229. From 'antlered': See: Walter Porzig. Die Gliederung des Indogermanischen Sprachgebiets [The Indo-European Languages]. Heidelberg: Universitätsverlag Winter, (1954). 251 Paper, DM 35. **230.** More than a way of life, cattle was an economy, a currency and a mode of worship. Nitrogen levels in the bones of the semi-nomadic hunters reveal a continued general marine diet. **231.** D.W. Anthony. *The Horse, The Wheel, and The Language: How Bronze-Age Riders from The Eurasian Steppes Shaped The Modern World*, (Princeton University Press. 2007): 153-161

THE DEER MOTHER

be celebrated. The people were not worshipping the beast as god, but as a gift *from* god. Within ritual, the beasts were not brutally slaughtered, but were killed mindfully, in dedication, with all due honour for that sacrificial principle. Feasting was a sacred rite of hospitality; it was not the gluttonous indulgence later clerics recorded of it. It was not sacrilegious. To impress this notion of sacredness relating to cattle, taboos and other superstitions developed around the killing and consumption of stock, especially cows, except for ritual purposes. Cattle and their consumption featured in several IE creation myths, and myths relating to the first sacrifice, *"for instance the key anthropogonic role of the primordial milk cow Auðumbla in Gylfaginning, the incident with sacred herds of Helios in Odyssey or generally the common PIE concept of Otherworld as a (cattle) pasture *uel-."*[232]

5. Mongolian Deer Stone Monolith

Language is one of the first cultural traits to become affected by social buffers. Loan words are drafted in, and other anachronistic anomalies remain as relics of a bygone era. The U rúne developed in this cattle economy of movable wealth. Several other words take precedence that strongly reflect the attributes of the natural source of this new economic wealth. PIE terms for cattle – **pek̂ u-*; cow – **guou-* and bull – **bouk*, attested mainly via Slavic and Celtic dialects, or the semitic root – *gud –*,[233] in later times, became elevated as epithets and even theonyms, first for zoomorphic deities,[234] then as humanoid, androcentric gods.

---

232. V. T. Gamkrelidze. V. V. and Ivanov. *Indo-European and the Indo-Europeans: reconstruction and historical analysis of a Proto-language and a proto V.V. culture. Part I: The text*, Nichols, J. (Trans.) Edited by W. Winter. (Mouton de Gruyter, 1995): 723   **233.** A. Dolgopolsky. *Nostraic Dictionary*, (Cambridge: McDonald Institute for Archaeological Research, 2008): 258. See Appendix I   **234.** The Pouka, Bouk and Buckka have survived as supernatural zoomorphic figures based on domestic beasts; the ram, bull, or goat, are thus celebrated in the modern guising traditions as folkloric variants of the medieval Charivari processions across Europe. In England, we recognise these folkloric forms as the horned Bucca and the mischievous spirit – Puck.

Nevertheless, in any orally transmitted narrative, despite all the obligatory pressures of universal cognitive patterns, together with general patterns of human social life, semantic details survive in the structure of language itself. Where written language is in the record, we often find a rich abundant tradition of aesthetic and narrative art. And no less fluid, those artworks have much to tell us about the nature of change.

During the early Bronze Age, the transformation from pre-existent matrilineal clanships to patrilineal clans is readily apparent in the narrative motifs that adorn the huge Deer Stone monoliths from an earlier age.[235] At this point the solar cults once associated with the divine female source became transposed to the newly rising solar cults of the male hero. The Mother of Animals who had once appeared in the late Neolithic petroglyphs as an antlerless female elk (indicating her status as the ever-renewing life-sustaining source), together with a boat or sled, to transport the dead to their final destination, disappears. In the Lake Baikal/Angara region of Siberia, the divine Elk Mother, known as Bugady Musun, is sometimes depicted as a curious (female) human/animal hybrid, though she later reappeared in the guise of a primal horned auroch.[236]

Since the early Neolithic, the (horned) female reindeer has been venerated by northern people across Scandinavia, Russia, and Siberia, as a spiritual figure associated with fertility, fecundity, motherhood, regeneration and the rebirth of the Sun. As nomads following the seasonal reindeer migrations, the very survival of the Sámi people depended upon the reindeer for milk, food, clothing and shelter. Across much of the northern world, the deer's seasonal migration indicated the shifts between the waning and waxing light of the Sun, whose warmth nourished the flora and fauna of these inclement regions. At midwinter, warm butter (a symbol of the Sun) was smeared on doorposts as a sacrificial offering to Beaivi (the Sun).[237] Although the following extract is rather fanciful, it does preserve an element of raw historical animism within its polished folkloric expression of indigenous customs related to the reindeer.

---

235. Esther Jacobson. "The Deer Goddess of Ancient Siberia: A Study in the Ecology of Belief." In, *Studies in the History of Religions, Volume LV:91*. (E. J. Brill, 1993). The great petroglyphic representations of elk, particular of female elk, date to the Serovo stage (fourth-third millennium). During the Kitoy (third-to early second millennium BCE), the monumental significance of this artwork diminished. This transition reflects a shift in subsistence culture that departs form a reliance on forest and river hunting and fishing, to pasture-based cattle farming. **236.** An early species of cattle now extinct. 237. Known to the Lithuanian and Latvian people as Saule.

THE DEER MOTHER

Long, long ago, a state of society existed in the Highlands, when woman was supreme; all women were supernatural and magical; (...) men were in the hunting stage of development and feared women, their spiritual mothers, all of whom were capable of guiding the destinies of men magically, either for their weal or woe, as they chose; the deer was a god; the ghosts of deer became fairy or supernatural women; and deer were the cattle of the fairies or of supernatural beings.[238]

Fantasy elements aside, this is a fine example that perfectly demonstrates a continuity of the natural reverence for a divine female spirit of creation, and one that is reflected in The Mothers, and The Fates in all their forms within all cultures. Moreover, while both male and female reindeer grow antlers in the summer each year, male reindeer shed their antlers quite early, around the onset of winter, usually in late November; female reindeer retain their antlers through gestation until they give birth in the spring.[239] In keeping with this view of the divine feminine, the Slavic Mother *Rohanitsa*, is often shown with antlers and gives birth to deer as well as children.

In unwrapping the layers that obscure the image of the deer of the early nomads, one finds that it was rooted in a symbolic system revolving around the Animal Mother: the Deer-Mother as Tree of Life and as source of life and death.[240]

Within the funerary mound complexes of the Central Eurasian Steppes, the heavily inscribed Deer Stones are characteristically flat, upright stone shards. Varying in style throughout the Bronze and Iron Ages, the tall, slender stelae often depict cervids in the distinctive Animal Style that recurs with considerable popularity in European artworks of the late Iron Age and into the Vendel period. Other animals such as wild cats, boars or horses are featured, albeit in far fewer numbers, though all collectively represent the animistic and transformative powers bestowed upon them by the Mother of Animals. Those virtues were inherited or appropriated by the shamans of later traditions. Relating to emergent life, fertility and human beneficence, the Mother of Animals was not however a totemic being, rather, she was the Source itself. Emphasising human dependency upon animals, hunting and the interaction between human beings and the spirits of Otherworld, cosmological narratives express an uncomplicated focus

---

238. J. G. McKay. "The Deer-Cult and the Deer-Goddess Cult of the Ancient Caledonians." In, *Folklore Journal* 43(2) (1932): 144-174 **239.** This means that in northern folklore, all of Santa's reindeer, including Rudolph, would be Female! **240.** Jacobson, 1993.

on survival within the rigorous and challenging cycle of life. Having no ambition beyond food, clothes and shelter, sustenance was primary.

Woman was also seen as the ultimate expression of Life. It was she who taught how to help birth the reindeer young, gather herbs and berries to feed in order to bring the milk, followed the estrus and gestation cycles of the reindeer cows and learned to fashion warm and nearly indestructible clothing from reindeer hide, bone and sinew. Reindeer, like the creative Feminine, were considered most sacred. Artefacts and funerary practices identified from thousands of years ago in Sámi and Siberian burial sites indicate that some of the most important spiritual guides were women. [241]

A principle expression of the reverence for the horned Deer Mother is found in the pre-historic kokoshnik, a horned head-dress traditionally worn by female shamans to reflect their connection to this primal spirit. Between the 14th and 19th centuries, the (Slavic) horned kichka (or kika/kichko) remained part of the folk costumes of central and southern Russia. In later times (post-conversion), these horns were sometimes turned downwards, or wrapped around each other to create an oval dome above the head in order to avoid offending the sensibilities

6. Kitchka

(condemnatory prejudices) of the Church. More recently, this totemic Russian two-horned headdress is preserved as a prized cultural piece that features in traditional bridal outfits as symbols demonstrative of female autonomy and power.

Several female images on the Deer Stones are described as 'birthing figures,'[242] though I personally consider these figures are perhaps better associated with the Sheela na Gigg whose apotropaic purposes are evident in their vulval exposure. Other images, referred to as 'skirted bird women,'[243] appear to be dancing, but should not be considered erotic or sexual.[244] With arms raised to the sky, they are probably more divine than human, though we cannot determine this for certain. Some are adorned with stag antlers, and so their presence on the threshold

---

241. Jacobson, 1993. 47 **242.** Jacobson Tepfer, 2015. 94 **243.** Ibid. **244.** Jacobson Tepfer, 2015.123

THE DEER MOTHER 81

between animals and humans, and between the living and the dead, appears significant. Drawn without facial features, it is their form that is emphasised. These are not portraits, but representations of mythic concepts where memory is fluid, and individuals are merely part of the chain in that process.

Petroglyphs in the taiga region of the Altai Mountains[245] similarly express themes centred upon the mythic and liminal aspects within the purview of the divine feminine, her role as the Guardian of the road to the land of the dead, and the heroic male figures she inspires or empowers. This theme is demonstrated in a magnificent textile recovered from the frozen burial of Pazyryk 5 in the Russian Altai region. Here, the small figure of a male rider stands before a much larger, imposing figure of an enthroned, crowned woman who bears a substantial tree branch resembling the curved horns of a stag[246] that also appears to be the Tree of Life. Appearing in so many examples of contextual art of the Bronze Age as the Mother of Animals (and therefore of life and death),[247] her comparative size next to the other smaller male figure, indicates her status as a divine being. Her other hand is raised perhaps in blessing (or warning) to the young warrior who faces west.

The Mother of Animals is portrayed as a huge cow, moose or reindeer in Evenk mythic tradition. Her body is the host for the sacred tree of the clan, a theme later echoed in the Scandinavian myths of Auðumbla and of Ymír. It is important that we recognise the role of therianthropic figures in all guises, especially as they are "frequently associated with rituals of transition and liminality, or with the intermediate stages of creation, when the world is neither its primal nor its finished state."[248] And so they were perfectly suited to the transient ambiguities of the androgynous priesthoods who ultimately became associated with them.

---

245. The word Altai refers to gold found in abundance in the rivers of the Altai region, also rich in iron, drawing much lightning to this region heavily mined by the Türkic speaking peoples. **246.** Joan Aruz, Ann Farkas, and Elisabetta Valtz Fino (Eds). "Filipovka and the Art of the Steppes, The Golden Deer of Eurasia." (Yale University Press, The Metropolitan Museum of Art, 2006): 3-17. **247.** Esther Jacobson-Tepfer challenges existing theories on Early Nomadic cosmology by examining the symbolic structures as they appear in the art and archaeological sources of the Early Nomads. **248.** Y. Ustinova. "6 Snake-Limbed and Tendril Limbed Goddesses in the Art and Mythology of the Mediterranean and Black Sea, Scythians and Greeks: Cultural Interactions in Scythia, Athens and the Early Roman Empire (6th century BCE. – 1st century CE.)." (University of Exeter Press, 2005): 64-79.

Deer iconography attributed to the early nomads of South Siberia and northern Central Asia clearly demonstrates a 'religion' which evolved around the Deer Mother and the high-status women who represented her. The deer was held sacred to numerous pre-historic peoples; the Hittites upheld it as a totem animal, an ancestor, and as the (mistress) mother of the clan or tribe associated with life and death. As such, the reindeer depicted on Mongolian Deer Stones are often shown leaping or flying through the air bearing birds, the sun, moon, and stars within her stylised antlers that depict the Tree of Life. Poetically speaking, it is the Deer Mother who carries the life-giving sun safely through winter's darkest, longest night in her horns. Persisting into the Bronze Age, the cosmic hunt myth centred around the sun cycle, reflecting the prevailing beliefs and concerns of humankind.

Prior to the later rise in popularity of the horse across Eurasia, horned animals such as the stag and the elk represented the forward movement in time, the eternal shift, symbolically manifest in the ship, the wheel and the sun itself.[249] In this respect, the peoples of Siberia shared a similar sun-centric cosmology with the peoples of Mongolia. "Siberian ethnographic materials show that the link of the elk-maral image with the sun, is one of the most ancient elements of the cosmological concepts of the peoples of Siberia."[250] Enduring as an artistic motif from the Siberian Steppe in the east, and Iberia in the west, the analogous association between tree branches and the elk's antlers, appears to have cognate representation reaching into northern Europe, and may therefore explain the alighting birds in the Irish poem *Buile Suibhne*.[251] Belonging to the Ulster Cycle of Irish mythology, this motif is yet another indication of this deep-rooted mythological theme. In this poem, the horned spirit Fer Benn[252] addresses the clan mother and mother of the herd as Siberians might have invoked their Animal Mother.[253] "Cidh iomdha dom dhamraidh-si / Though many are my stags,"[254] and again: "A mathair na groidhi-si / O mother of this herd."[255]

---

249. Peter Gelling and Hilda Ellis Davidson. *The Chariot of the Sun: and Other Rites And Symbols of the Northern Bronze Age*. (J. M. Dent & Sons. 1969): 94 **250.** A. F. Anisimov. "Cosmological concepts of the people of the North." In, *Studies in Siberian shamanism: Arctic Institute of North America anthropology of the North: Translations from Russian sources*, N°4. Edited by Henry N Michael. (University of Toronto Press. 1963): 163-176 **251.** A. P. Okladnikov. "Yakutia Before its Incorporation into the Russian State." In, *Studies in Siberian shamanism: Arctic Institute of North America anthropology of the North: Translations from Russian sources*, N°8. (University of Toronto Press, 1970): 156

THE DEER MOTHER 83

The rite shingkelavun *deserves mention here because the Evenki hunters, like the Palaeolithic sorcerers portrayed in the Trois Frères caves, wore ritual costumes, with caps made from the skulls of reindeer or elks, imitating the heads of these animals. The object was to perform ritual pantomimes, supposed to bring all the animals of the taiga to the clan's hunting grounds. This rite lasted many days, and was carried out by the entire clan near the rocks, cliffs, and trees sacred to it, the bugady. In essence, this ritual corresponded to the legend of the pursuit of the sun-animal by hunters, its killing and death, and then the sacrificial meal, with the subsequent solemn burial of the bones and the miraculous resurrection of the buried animal.*[256]

The miraculous resurrection of the animals killed and consumed in feasting mentioned here, is another theme we can recognise in the Norse myths of Þórr's goats, Tanngrisnir and Tanngnjóstr who co-incidentally pull his chariot (a symbol associated with the male, heroic solar cults). The goat's provision as meat for the hungry, is never diminished and renews each day[257] with Þórr's resurrection of them with his hammer, Mjölnir. Sæhrímnir, who also appears in Norse mythology, is consumed nightly by the einherjar and is similarly replenished through a magical procedure involving the enchanted cauldron Eldhrímnir. In both cases there are strict rules (and taboos) to ensure this procedure is not compromised.

A few images depict theriomorphic and zoomorphic figures whose ritual function is ambiguous, though they may represent an early tribal

---

252. Fer Benn: "Man of The Peaks," (Mountains), "The 'Horned/Pronged Man.'" See: Edward Gwynn. (Ed. & Trans.), "Carn Furbaide" *The Metrical Dindshenchas* Vol. 4. (Dublin Institute for Advanced Studies, 1906). This epithet could be a poetic reference to lightning, or a reference to the Dagda being horned, a not-uncommon feature in British and Gaulish iconography. Furbaide (Ferbend) is a character from the Ulster Cycle of Irish mythology, whose name derives from Old Irish *urbad*, meaning cutting. See also: Joseph O'Neill (Ed. & Trans.) "Cath Boinde." In, *Ériu* Vol.2 (1905): 173-185. The glossary *Cóir Anmann* states that the horns – two of silver and one of gold - were on his helmet. See also: Whitley Stokes. "Cóir Anmann." (Fitness of Names) In, *Irische Text mit Wörterbuch, Dritte Serie, 2 Heft*. (Verlag Von S. Hirzel. 1897): 200-111 **253.** Anisimov, 1963:163. **254.** For the adventures of Suibhne Geilt, a middle-Irish Romance, see: J. G. O'Keeffe. "Buile Suibhne." (The Frenzy of Suibhne) Intro. By Jospeh Falaky Nagy. (Irish Texts Society. [1913] 1996): 79 **255.** O'Keeffe, [1913] 1996: 79-81 **256.** Gilles Boucherit. "A Deer Cult in Buile Suibhne." In, XIV Comhdháil Idirnáisiúnta Sa Léann Ceilteach XIV International Congress of Celtic Studies, (Maynooth, Ireland, 2011). https://hal.archives-ouvertes.fr/hal-00621072v4 (Accessed 2nd May 2024). **257.** As attested in the *Poetic Edda*, compiled in the 13th century from earlier traditional sources, and the *Prose Edda*, supposedly composed by Snorre Sturlusson in the 13th century.

priesthood, seers, or shamans. Accompanied by raptorial birds, some of the figures wear tall, pointed hats reminiscent of the one worn by the Pazyryk Ice Maiden.[258] One deer stone bears an image that is very similar to the wooden bog figure which has a socketed vulva. We find other Bronze Age deer petroglyphs scattered across the Iberian Peninsula that later appear in Ireland and Scotland, where we know the deer was associated with funerary processes, possibly in connection with the beasts' iconic role as the mythic and totemic ancestors of several Germanic and Celtic speaking tribes.

An unusual type of monolith or balbal, features bejewelled, anthropomorphized figures depicted with a variety of weapons and tools, many of which hang from their belts. They are not posed wielding them and there are no indications of conflict or battle dating from the Bronze Age through to the Iron Age. Such stones are distributed throughout Mongolia, Tannu-Tuva, northern China, and the Altai across to the Black Sea, Georgia, and the Elbe basin. Many of the oldest stones erected in Mongolia have their obverse faces oriented to the east, towards the rising sun and the dawning (re-birthing) of new life. The Mongolian Deer Stones are much less artistic than those that appear on the Scythian Altai regions and appear to relate to smaller domestic family groups, indicating that perhaps they were not yet confederations or huge tribal concerns.

Some stones were boundary or possible guardian stones, and with that understanding, we may observe how several stones encircle or frame burial mounds (kurgans). Detailed art works depict hunting scenes, and several anthropomorphic images of what appear to be highly stylised tribal (ancestral) spirit masks. Other images portray the transport of the dead to their mounds on horse-drawn carts of four and then the two wheeled funerary carts that replaced them. Accompanied by other cattle, but mostly deer, humans in various ritual settings, together with two wheeled carts and four wheeled wagons also began to appear in South Siberian art.

With the exception of the high-status Pazyryk burial, no other wagons or carts have been discovered in the Altai regions from the Bronze or early Iron Age. Male riders sometimes accompany the carts. Brought by incoming cattle herders whose social structure and economy was very different, wheeled carts are not actually practical in battle and serve no viable military purpose, so appear to function only

---

258. Esther Jacobson-Tepfer. "The Hunter, the Stag, and the Mother of Animals: Image, Monument, and Landscape in Ancient North Asia." (Oxford Uni Press, 2015): 63.

as funerary vehicles. Moreover, the engineering and construction of the Pazyryk 5 burial carriage renders it unfit for rigorous or distance travelling, its design makes it suitable only for the short procession to the tomb, and its placement within, whence it serves as a vehicle to the Land of the Dead. As funerary traditions changed during the early Iron Age, images of horse riding gradually replaced those of carts and wagons. At the same time, we begin to see horse sacrifice as part of the rituals for the mound interments of the dead, irrespective of wealth or gender. Increased contact through trade and the movement of peoples in turn, provide clear indications of changes in culture.

Male and female figures wear stylised antlers in some rock art images; some horns are even draped with ritual streamers and sometimes a small vertical post or tree stands between the horns.[259] Their purpose is clearly protective and propitiatory. Representing the effective transition between the most archaic beliefs surrounding the animal mother and her gradual transformation during the Bronze Age, the dominant figures on the Karakol slabs wear horns with feather-like halos. A male figure with outstretched crescent moon shaped horns strongly resembles the Iron Age metal figure from Tissø. Some of the figures are striding and peripatetic, and long-haired women stand alongside the carts suggesting their presence at the burials is relevant, albeit beyond our kenning.

Former images of horned Stags were likewise replaced by those of stylised horses that resemble or represent stags. The famous Deer Stones of South Siberia and Mongolia depict many images of male warriors and hunters in addition to stylised stags. Depicting the horses as stags in this way may have appeased their ancestral spirits.[260] Other horned animals appear on the Deer Stones to a lesser degree, namely rams and goats; sometimes wolves and raptor birds on later stones. The importance of the stag and the symbolism of its relationship with death and the Otherworld, nevertheless lingered, and could be the reason why the horned cup fashioned from the sacred totemic animal, was used for funerary traditions, distinguishing it from man-made cups of clay and wood used for ordinary feasting occasions. Adding yet another mythic layer to the stags' complex symbolism, it inherited a solar aspect from the Indo-Iranian cosmological traditions. This in turn relates to later Siberian mythic tradition. Often associated

---

259. Jacobson-Tepfer, 2015: 83   260. Three principal theories regard the origins of the deer image in relation to the archaic Scytho-Siberian artistic style, either in the Near East, Central Asia or Siberia.

with lightning and therefore power and fecundity, horns remained a persistent element in all art forms.

As the stag antlered animals gradually transformed from stag bird to stag wolf, parallel changes ocurred in the Pazyryk culture that manifested in the dramatic surge and prominence of the wolf totem for the people of the Altai regions. These images and the beliefs associated with them, are far-removed from those of the mounted warrior who stands before the Primal Mother seeking her permission to enter the Land of the Dead. She who was once the earth figure there at the beginning and the end of life, as the full cycle and liminal pivot, fades from the art of the Altai nomads.[261] The Tree of Life that represents the embodiment of her spirit, sometimes depicted as the World Mountain, evolved into simplified images as stylised clan symbols that relate to the ancient, sacred homelands, the runic symbol oðel, is a prime example of this artistic shift. The purpose of the tree itself became preserved in memory as the sacred pole of the shaman's tent whence it became the vertical symbol of the linear transitional pattern that takes us from death to life, into death and the Otherworld. Perhaps in recognition of this deeply ingrained cultural tenet, we should remember that in much of northern culture, of the Sámi especially, the grandmother is the keeper of wisdom. Females were thus assigned the qualification of generation, a virtue later demonstrated in the roles, of seer, spæ and völva (that combine in Séiðr).

The Altai artists thus represent the very real phenomenal world and its preoccupation with a hunting economy, with appeals and appeasements to the land and its animal spirits. Artistic compositions demonstrate the emerging centrality of the human experience as traditions rooted in the spirit world, with the understanding that the spirit world is the source and sustenance of all human existence, reaching back to a supreme Creatrix of all life, despite cumulative cultural changes. As mentioned above, to be a successful hunter, various taboos, rituals and sacrifices to the spirit world were observed as imperatives. Of course, the hunter was always accompanied at a distance by the wolf, the predatory scavenger who was never fully domesticated, travelling with the herds and herders across the Steppe, bringing down the animals weakened by the chase. Their kills were no doubt confiscated by the hunters in times of need.

---

261. Jacobson-Tepfer, 2015: 312

CULTURAL TRANSITIONS

Matrilineal cults had flourished throughout the Neolithic until about 2400 BCE, in the Pontic-Caspian Steppes,[262] throughout the Yamnaya period until the evolutionary use of the horse changed everything. Bronze Age hunters merged cultures with Kurgan pastoralists of the Steppe during a continuous round of migrations in both directions changing forever the Steppe culture.[263] Nonetheless, deep-rooted mythic traditions within all cultural threads point back to an ancient worldview of the land and of the divine feminine, and to an original homeland in the mountains, where wild beasts of the planes roam, ripe for hunting. Traditionally each sacred mountain was associated with a particular lineage or tribe. The resulting sacralization of a mountain and by extension of the lineage, reflects a belief in indwelling spirits and their power to influence the well-being of people mediated by the shamans for a successful hunt, good pasture, good water and a safe journey.[264]

As Neolithic Western Steppe Herders,[265] the Yamnaya[266] people are a genetic admixture between two distinctive hunter-gatherer populations: various peoples of Siberia (known as the 'Eastern (European) Hunter-Gatherers') and the (proto-Scythian) people of Iran (known as the 'Caucasus hunter-gatherers').[267] Singularly focused on animal husbandry, they utilised Bronze and Iron Age metalworking technology in tandem with horse-drawn carts and other innovations to expand across Eurasia, which facilitated the spread of Indo-European and Uralic languages.

---

262. Anthony, 2007: 306-309 **263.** An earlier diffusion of the Yamnaya ventured across the Pontic-Caspian Steppes circa 3300 BCE, pausing only briefly before initiating a large migration stream two hundred years later up into the Danube valley and into the Carpathian basin during the Early Bronze Age. See: M. G. Levin and L. P. Potapov. The Peoples of Siberia, (The University of Chicago Press, 1964): 99. See: Glossary. **264.** See: forthcoming (unpublished) volume on Sámi Shamanism: "Song of The North," by Shani Oates. **265.** The Western Steppe extends from the grassy plains at the mouth of the Danube River along the north shore of the Black Sea, across the lower Volga, and eastward as far as the Altai Mountains. Also known as the Pontic-Caspian Steppe. Indo-European languages originated here. **266.** See Appendices II, III, IV and Glossary. **267.** See overleaf

Cosmological concepts of the people of the north initially based in animism, shifted the emphasis from a cosmic Mother to either the shepherd of her herd, or her favoured hunter, the sometime hero who was once the guardian of her sacred lands.[268] Among the Tungus (Evenks) of Siberia, this cosmic female spirit, the *bugady enintyn*, is accompanied by another, the *dunne mushunin* (musunin), or spirit of the land, who sits with her beneath the roots of their sacred, guardian clan tree.[269] As two female clan spirits that reside under that boundary tree as the liminal marker of the worlds of men and of spirits, their uncanny resemblance to the Teutonic Norns and the Nordic Nornir — of no listed number originally, but who became three, in myth by classical association with the Hellenic Moirae and the Roman Parcae - is quite remarkable. To the Evenk peoples, the mistress of the clan lands, was thought to be anthropomorphic, while the mythical cosmic mother of all people and animals,[270] was perceived as the zoomorphic elk or deer. With the decline of the matrilineal clan structure, the zoomorphic cosmic Mother was diminished into that of mistress to the shamanic figure, losing her role as Creatrix and her zoomorphic features. Thus transformed, she became a mediating spirit of the dead whose anthropomorphic features are reflected into the manifest wooden doll fetish that embodied the hearth spirit for the family or clan, held thereafter by the shamans under his or her domain.

In socio-religious terms, the 'Spirit of the Hunt' was ultimately replaced by the 'Spirit of the Animals,' coexisting only on the marginal peripheries of sedentary farmers and stock-breeders by the sedentary hunters along with the nomadic hunters. With the later decline of Scytho-Siberian culture, the deer was destined to endure only through the shamanistic traditions of Siberia and Central Asia.[271] Hunter-gatherers naturally require different means of subsistence to those of agriculturalists. Having limited contact with outsiders, hunter-gatherers were often highly mobile and migratory, living in temporary shelters[272] and in small tribal groups. Diet was seasonally dependent, with little

---

267. Martina Unterländer; Friso Palstra; Iosif Lazaridis; Aleksandr Pilipenko; Zuzana Hofmanová; Melanie Groß, et al. "Ancestry and Demography and Descendants of Iron Age Nomads of the Eurasian Steppe." Nature Communications 8 (2017) doi:10.1038/ncomms14615   **268.** As the heroic guardian figure, Fer Benn is very similar to one of the Evenk's spirit-ancestors who dwell in the nether world, linked within the clan tree or cosmic tree, guarding the life and well-being of the clan.   **269.** Anisimov, 1963: 176   **270.** Ibid.   **271.** Jacobson, 1993.   **272.** These seasonal mobile 'tent' structures were skins stretched over light wooden frames, placed in carts, not unlike the pioneer wagons of the wild west frontiers.

surplus. This contrasts significantly with farming, which focussed on surplus and storage that could support larger population groups. The agricultural division of labour gradually led to specialization of labour within complex societies, and to the subsequent development of trading networks to exchange their surplus commodities. These are patterns we see repeated throughout the northern regions of Fennoscandia and Scandinavia.

Resisting change, the Nenet people of Siberia subsist still in the traditional manner of their forebears. Ever close to death, their appeasement of the spirits of place, of the hunt and of the animals remains essential for their well-being. During the seasonal movements of nomadic tribes, the father was the hunter and guide for the whole household that would move to new pastures through wild landscapes, therefore in need of protection from predators and desirous of the bounty required to sustain them in their meanderings. Changes in material culture sometimes appear to have ocurred suddenly, though the fundamental issues that initiated them are not always easy to follow.[273] What is more certain, is that over time, the meanings and contexts of rituals relating to the living and the dead changed. We must not assume that beliefs remain constant and fossilized over several hundred years. Our only insight into how those changes developed is through studying the artworks and artefacts produced by the actual folk cultures concerned.

The Evenk[274] belonged to an indigenous cluster of animistic,[275] semi-nomadic, semi-shamanic northern peoples of the Tungus regions of Siberia who depended on reindeer herding, hunting and fishing. Included amongst them are the Samoyed, Nenet, Nanai, the Yakut and the (sun-arctic) Paleo-Siberian Ket. Pressure from the aggressive Xiongnu forced the Evenk people to move further north during the Bronze and Iron Ages.[276] Although they did not all share the same language or culture, Siberian ethnography is based in culture related objects myths, legends, folktales and songs relating to their migrations and subsistence into and within the brutal tundra of Siberia.[277] Many

---

273. For example, we now know that the Neolithic Revolution was not sudden and progressed over several hundred years. **274.** The ethnonym, Evenk, actually refers to a culture of reindeer husbandry. **275.** Holding to a belief in the indwelling spirit of natural objects and animals, the elements, rain wind, snow thunder etc. **276.** A pattern later repeated during the 16th century, when the native populations migrated further into the inhospitable regions of the north-east in order to escape the economic religious and cultural pressure from incoming Russian settlers. Because of this, they are the largest surviving Siberian indigenous population. **277.** See overeaf

other groups became extinct when their way of life became threatened by the pressures of industry and religion.[278]

Rituals were clan-based, designed to reinforce the notion of autonomy and of family structure within their challenging environments. Within this schema, it seems certain cultic tenets relating to the Clan Mother as the Earth Mother and animal Mother of Life and Death, were tenaciously adhered to in the farthest northly regions of Siberia. Cultic factions came to be managed by specific shamanic practitioners on behalf of the community, replacing the roles previously observed by the individual heads of each household.[279]

Although the obscure spirits of the herd, and of the dead continued to be mediated by the shamans, the nuanced rites relating to the animal spirits remained in the domain of the Mother of Animals, whose cults they subsumed. Nevertheless, it is because of those deeply rooted animisms, the rituals surrounding the construction of the shamans' drums must adhere to strictures of tribal lineage. To remain authentic, this means that everything from the wood to the skins used, must be culled from the clan's own land; this observance acknowledged the sacred landscape pertaining to the place of origin (mountains), but also to the spirits of the land that now nourish them. Without that blessing, the shamans have no legitimacy.

These landvættir traditions are strikingly similar to those of the Scandinavian and Fennoscandian countries. For instance, as noted earlier, the sacred female mother mountain is a theme central to all the myths and legends of these regions. Her indwelling spirit is often subject to intrusive male heroes whose presence acknowledges the virtue she possesses that they need access to, or dominion of. That social conflict over time is reflected in the mountains' identity as a naked female spirit with whom the hunter or male shaman sleeps, forming a propitious bond that will ensure success.[280] This theme endures, and is found in

---

277. "Social organization was based on moieties, patrilineal kinship, exogamy, and kin-regulated production, consumption, inheritance, and ideology [...] Women had real equality with men, and elderly women enjoyed high "male" status. Families desired numerous children and suffered high infant mortality. Children participated in domestic life from an early age. The small population, combined with strict adherence to exogamy, led to a high degree of interethnic marriage." See: Richard B. Lee and Richard Daly (Eds.) *The Cambridge Encyclopaedia of Hunters and Gatherers*. (Cambridge Uni. Press, 1999). **278.** In recent centuries, The Russian Orthodox Church impacted massively on the various nomadic and shamanistic peoples whose oral traditions are already consigned to the realm of legend. **279.** Jacobson-Tepfer, 2015: 323 **279.** Jacobson-Tepfer, 2015: 323 **280.** Jacobson-Tepfer, 2015: 323

the Scandinavian myth where Óðinn steals the mead from its female mountain guardian, Gunnlöð. Traditionally, women retained their dominion over the hearth spirits, sharing other elements reflective of the sacred and ancient male and female mysteries explored within and preserved by the taboos and customs of mediation with the 'Other' that jointly serve the family, the clan, the tribe, the community, and the whole people.

Many heroic legends involve not only sacred mother mountains or caves, but notions of treasure, guardian spirits and a measure of fate and magic. Hearth spirits were deemed to be far less challenging or dangerous, and therefore required different rituals of propitiation and appeasement. On the other hand, both hunters and herders were vulnerable and needed protection from the wild things that roam abroad. Bear cults are related to shamanic traditions, and invariably perceive of a male heaven, a weather-oriented sky father invoked by men seeking power and prowess in all forms of battle – the hunt or in the field. Conversely, women's power is generally based in the land or earth made fecund by the natural rivers and replenished by the rain that falls down from the sky father upon and into them.

The Mother gifts the virtues of tribal animal totems to her people for their beneficence and protection (mainly wolf, bear and stag), so for their protection, there are many taboos surrounding the killing and consumption of these totemic animals. Numerous myths and further taboos surround the intermarriage between bears and human girls, for example – heroic figures are said to derive from such unions. Animal skins are said to possess great magic and power that is imparted to the wearer. Mythic traditions of arctic (and subarctic) peoples demonstrate various strands of superstitious belief associated with certain animals. For instance, the Ket see the bear as the animal reflex of womankind, and as a rebirthing catalyst, a dualistic construct that closely parallels how the Evenk relate to the giant Mother Goose, whom they believed consumed her people in death, in order to replenish the souls of the living.[281]

A strong duality pervaded the Ket world-view. Their myths reflect upon the origin of the world and its structure, the actions both of culture heroes of the distant past, and of more recent humans. The supreme being, Es' (sky, god), was identified with the sky and the phenomena of nature. He was opposed by the evil mistress of both the north and the land of the dead: Khosedam. The south was the realm of the mistress of birds of passage: Tomem. The earth, water, and fire

---

281. Lee & Daly, 1999.

were "mothers." *Success in hunting depended on the support of the master/mistress of the forest animals, 'Kaigus'. Intensive hunting and fishing were accompanied by ceremonies intended to assist the regeneration of the species taken. The ritual cycle, closely connected with the bear hunt, stressed the "bear feast," as bears were identified with deceased relatives.*[282]

The sky and the earth are two major elements pertaining to the lower and upper worlds that exist within the divine, invisible body of the Earth Mother (manifest through all her animals). As the Universal Creatrix, she is at once imminent and transcendent, without form beyond that of her creations. She is sometimes referred to as Umai, (my mother) which is not a name but an epithet that means, "she who carries off the dead."[283] She has a dark counterpart (Kara) who brings sickness and harm.

All elements of the natural world, celestial and terrestrial (the earth, water, sun, moon, Venus, and the north star) were personified by the Ket as female. For ritual purposes, the regions linked to renewal were placed in the south and east, while death has dominion in the North and West. Entranced shamans journey along one of seven roads to the other realms. In Ket tradition, shamans enter into a relationship with the bear (woman) spirit (Kaigus) that mates with and awards those shamans who serve her, hunting success for their tribal communities in turn. The Kaigus is not dissimilar to the *dis-*, the *Ides*, and the *Hamingja*, of Scandinavian tradition. As noted above, small female wooden dolls (similar to the 'death dolls' made by Nenet shamans) embody the protective household spirits that could be dressed, fed and propitiated by the male shamans or other ritual specialists, who inherit them from their male predecessors. Similarly, Ket children were protected by the household *alel* spirit. These were made from fashioned pieces of larch that were dressed in cloth and fur and decorated with beads and copper. Used in popular forms of divination, these spirit 'dolls' were thrown up into the air as a question was posed, if the fetish landed faceup, the answer was deemed to be positive.[284]

Affirming the antiquity of clan lineage, this tradition asserts a male heritage for the continued transmission of protective roles for which he is dependent upon arcane female spirits of nurture centred in the hearth. Under the domain and province of the hearth matriarch, the household (fire) spirits, called Bokam, guard the hearth and in return, receive hearth offerings of meat and tea. As nomads, the hearth was

---

282. Ibid.   283. Jacobson-Tepfer, 2015: 328   284. Ibid.

a mobile element of the camp, and after reassembly at any new site, new fires were kindled from the embers carried from the hearth of the previous encampment. The fire embers were carefully transported in a special box so they could be redistributed amongst kin to ensure they were granted the aegis of warmth and light – the manifest virtues of the Sun, encapsulated within each domicile, for succour and protection.

Several Siberian groups (including the Ket and Evenk peoples), perceived fire as a female element, which demonstrates a strange dynamic between the patriarchal nature of ancestry within family cults (that look to the past), and the older matriarchal cult of the hearth fire, often addressed as grandmother or eneke (that look to the generations yet to come).[285] This brings to mind the Scandinavian tales and legends surrounding Rigr's appearance at the hearths of three women that led to the generation not just of all people, but specifically of their distinct crafts suited to their roles within a functioning society. It was the role and office of the clan mother, or mistress of the chum tent, to maintain the cultic rituals surrounding the eneke, as the protective household spirit for her family and clan. The hearth provides the spiritual link that travels down through future generations, binding souls to the passage of time, symbolised by the rising smoke from the hearth-fire, escaping through the smoke-hole atop the tent pole, the vertical representation of all worlds, stemming from its base within the earth as the belly of the Clan Mother.[286]

As a matriarchal tradition, the sacred grandmother spirit of the hearth fire could not be given away to an outsider of the clan. It remained always within that family, passed from mother to daughter, reflecting an ancient belief in the divine feminine as the creator and protector of all things. This affirms the primary significance of this cult prior to the supplementary ancestral cult of the male line that eventually superseded it, through the role of the shaman. The hearth cults focussed on the cycle of life and death and the relationship with the spirits of all living things within those cycles – animal or human. Shamanic rituals diverged from this, concentrating more on the harmful or negative effects emanating from the dead, that affected or afflicted the living, in mind and body. The dead were deemed to be malignant or vengeful, requiring appeasement or banishment. The realm of the dead was the domain of the shaman, who journeyed there to make appeals to the ancestors. The spirits in the mothers' narrative

285. Ibid.   **286.** Ibid.

motifs were zoomorphic, whereas in those of the shaman, the spirits are anthropomorphic.

Like many Siberian peoples, the oral traditions of the Ket can be roughly separated into three general types: those that centre on clan and household protective deities considered essential to the well-being of the social unit: those that refer to the mythic figures whose powers transcend concerns for daily well-being and instead affect the tribal lands in the tribal well-being: and those that centre on shamanic figures and interweave the heroic exploits with shamanic function. All three oral traditions are constantly interwoven within the song's stories and aphorisms handed down from generation to generation, the Ket universe reaffirms the interconnection between individual human well-being and significant world.[287]

---

287. Ibid.

SPIRITS OF FIRE
AND HEARTH

Herodotus compiled a report that contained mainly Greek names for the principal Scythian spirits he'd observed. In addition to Zeus, a storm spirit (akin to the Sky Father whom Herodotus compared to Papaios) there is Hestia,[288] a hearth and fire spirit (akin to Mother Earth). Here, the Sarmatians diverged from the Scythians in their veneration of fire rather than of nature.[289] As a proto-Iranian people, fire was central to the spirituality of both the Saka (Sakas) and to Scythians; it was an element Tabiti fully embodied. Herodotos' Hellenization of her name is related to several Eurasian variants of a root word signifying heat and warmth, and was thus perfectly suited to his association of her with Hestia. Moreover, because fire was central to the cosmological beliefs of many Eurasian peoples, evidence of solar and fire cults are attested in Sarmatian funerary rites where pieces of chalk and realgar, symbolising the element of fire, were found alongside weapons and horse harnesses in pit graves, or in tumuli.[290]

As a typical Proto-Indo-European archetype, Tabiti shares a solar affiliation with Irish Brighid to the Baltic Gabija, a tenet retained in Slavic and much northern mythology. The solar female archetype sometimes appeared as the mother of the heroic warrior sun god, a guise in which she is given less emphasis. Despite her strong association with the sun (fire and heat), Tabiti is also connected to the earth, namely the chthonic elements of funerary constructions – the death mounds or kurgans bearing ochre painted solar discs. These bear a spiritual affinity with the radial sun disc kurgans of the Mongolian

---

288. The concept of fire as the primeval substance upon which the universe is based is deeply embedded in the Indo-Iranian belief systems. **289.** Lauren J. Barnhart. *The Totemic Significance Of The Deer In Iron Age Scythian And Sarmatian Cultures In Eastern Europe And Central Asia*. A Thesis Submitted To Johns Hopkins University In Conformity With Requirements For The Degree Of Master Of Liberal Arts Baltimore, Maryland October 2022. **290.** Yulia Ustinova. The Supreme Gods of the Bosporan Kingdom: Celestial Aphrodite and the Most High God. (Brill, 1999): 255-283

plains. Aptly named 'sun graves,' these are known from various early Indo-European cultures such as the aforementioned Afanasievo and Andronovo,[291] suggesting that even in death, the sun was important to the afterlife beliefs of these people. The Sun is of course the presence of the divine.

Not all deities associated with fire that feature in Indo-European mythologies are necessarily directly solar in nature, and while Tabiti's name is not cognate to most words for sun, which in Indo-European languages stems from the root *sóh2wll/*seh2ul, there are sufficient overlaps with similar figures present in Eurasian mythologies who are linked through a shared element in fire, for Tabiti to retain those firm connections. Brighid for example, blurs with Sulis/Grian. The relationship is implicit to the point there is an understated feminine connection to all aspects of the sun, especially the dawn: *h2éwsos, a potency Tabitu shares with Argimpasa.

The binding vows of loyalty undertaken by Scythians involved blood-letting into a communal bowl that was mixed with wine and partaken of by all witnesses, sometimes jointly, from the same cup, but let's not forget, they also regularly drank mare's blood and milk (koumiss) for sustenance. All weapons were then dipped into this mixture as pledges of blood-brotherhood were made by one and all to each other in this most sacred ceremony. Each brother would swear to defend another with their own life. The mightiest vows were sworn by the king's own hearth. Broken vows were believed to impair the king's health, which would not improve until the culprit was found. In such cases, a sorcerous priesthood known as the Enarei were tasked with discovering who that was.

Strong connections between the solar or fire deities and oath-taking appears to be a ubiquitous tenet throughout Indo-European mythologies, forging direct links between law making, oath taking and the hearth spirit. In the western world, this has perhaps survived through the mechanism of old laws,[292] possibly inherited from the Roman superstition attached to fire as a visible symbol of the right to occupy the land the fire/hearth resides upon. Hence its perpetual flame was of extreme importance in temples, places of government and in domiciles. According to Herodotos, Tabiti punished broken oaths by death. In

---

291. Christoph Baumer. *The History of Central Asia: The Age of the Steppe Warriors* (Volume 1) (I.B. Tauris, 2012).   **292.** Claims to land ownership and its occupation often rest on the presence of an active hearth.   See: Ceisiwr Serith. *Deep Ancestors: Practising the Religion of the Proto Indo-Europeans.* (ADF Publishing, 2007).

this, she is perhaps the forerunner of Týr (Tiw, Deus), aligned in the role of moral and ethical behaviour as lawful and binding ties. Some, like Tabiti, are further associated with the vows undertaken in marriage, often dramatized in Heiros Gamos rites that celebrate the relationship between the divine spirit of the sun or dawn and the divine twins.[293] Objects made of gold (which symbolizes the sun) may symbolize the celestial element of Tabiti.

As the supreme female hearth spirit, Tabiti embodied the abstract notion of life and creation as primordial fire (just as the central sun is represented to the Sámi through the reindeer), therefore there are no physical representations of her. All other spirits descend from Tabiti, namely Api (the Earth) and Papaios (Heaven, in the form of Air or Wind),[294] giving the three levels that represent their Cosmology.[295] The Vulture, Stallion and Kara fish similarly represent each of these levels, similar to the traits exhibited in Sámi Cosmology in the form of a bird, an elk and a fish, so we can immediately see the parallels with the Sámi and their own belief system reflected here. Furthermore, as a hearth spirit, Tabiti was the patron of society and of families, and she thus protected the family and the clan, hence she was a symbol of supreme authority connected with the king's royal power. Tabiti bears a sacred connection to the deer (and the sun) through the hearth fire. Deer are an abundant presence in Scythian art, clearly attesting to the animal's symbolic importance; stags in particular were sacrificed to Tabiti.[296]

In myth and visual representation, the deer is often associated with the sun as a symbol of male potency, yet the deer is an atypical solar symbol among Indo-European cultures, which typically prefer horses as the heroic steeds of the sun in symbiosis with humankind, especially

---

293. Hinds, [1962] 2010. **294.** Existing initially as an inseparable unity, Api was the consort of Papaios. Their conjoining of opposing principles (eg. above and below, male and female, warmth and moisture), parallels the union between Ahura Mazda (Heaven) and Armaiti (Earth) in the Avesta, and thus reflects the Indo-Iranic cosmological tradition of a sacred 'marriage' between Heaven and Earth that first created and then sustains the world. See: Bruce Lincoln, 2014. "Once again 'the Scythian' Myth Of Origins." (Herodotus 4.5-10). In, Nordlit, 19. 10.7557/13.3188. https://www.researchgate.net/publication/285316455_Once_again_the_Scythian_myth_of_origins_Herodotus_45-10 (Retrieved 6th June 2024). **295.** There are no anthropomorphic representations of Tabiti, Papaios and Api. See: Barry Cunliffe. *The Scythians – Nomad Warriors of the Steppe*. (Oxford Uni Press. 2019): 265-290 **296.** Jacobson, 1993. The Hittite sun goddess was also associated with deer sacrifices which appears to be an original Proto-Indo-European feature as found in cultures as early as the Andronovo, who were possibly influenced by northern Eurasian cultures.

under the dominion of male heroic figures. In this, they depart from traditions and beliefs of early northern peoples. In many shamanistic societies and indigenous cultures in North Eurasia, the hearth and the herd were inter-related such that the hearth is deemed central to all well-being. We should not forget that for Northern peoples, the hearth is also associated with Dhéghom Matr – The Damp Mother Earth (Mati syra zemlja). The hearth is literally, "the center of the world and acted as an axis connection where the dead passed through to the lower world." This otherworldly portal was perceived as a possible means by which evil spirits could find their way into the visible world of the living, whence the luck and good fortune fades from that family/clan, leading the herd to stray far from the camp. Their successful seasonal return was therefore always met with great celebration.

When in the fall the weather begins to turn cold once more the men return with the herds… At the first approach of the herds the fires in the houses are extinguished and new sacred fires are lighted outside containing a spark from the sacred fire-board… Some said that 'the herd is met with fire in the same manner as relatives and guests are welcomed; while, according to others, the fire signifies the source whence the reindeer originated.[297]

---

297. W. W. Malandra. "The Concept of Movement in History of Religions: A Religio-Historical Study of Reindeer in the Spiritual Life of North Eurasian Peoples." Numen 14, no. 1 (1967): 23-69 https://doi.org/10.2307/3269697 (Accessed 2nd December 2023).

EARTH MOTHER ARCHETYPES

Through the Mistress of Animals, we have a marked connection between the Saka (Sakas), the Pazyryks, the peoples of the Altai, Mongols, and the peoples of Fennoscandia and Scandinavia. Having power over life and death, the divine Matriarch is celebrated in all artistic media; perhaps it was hoped her iconic imagery would allow them to bask in her reflected glory. One beast above all others is portrayed over and over again, to the degree that it is almost impossible to ignore her true significance.

Due largely to their nomadic lifestyle that brought them into contact with others, Indo-European peoples frequently adopted the higher spirits that personified the lands they dominated, abandoning old ones, or layering them up to create hybrid forms that are difficult to trace. Therefore, a continuity of the earth 'goddess' archetype does not exist beyond the basic characteristics of being female and an association with fertility. Unlike the sky father, the earth mother does not have a consistent Proto-Indo-European reconstruction in literature, although the damp earth is personified in almost all Indo-European religions, especially Slavic and northern religious traditions. Linked to the root *h₂ep, meaning 'water," the female chthonic Scythian spirit known as 'Api' is often depicted with phytomorphic (i.e. plant-like) or serpent feet, as noted in the wonderful figurine taken from the Kul-Oba kurgan. Equated by Herodotos to Gaia, Api is often paired with Papaios, however, because of a tenuous syncretism with Aphrodite Ourania (based on oracular virtue, oath-taking and her ubiquitous presence as moisture[298]) by classical authors, Api is also linked to Artimpasa. The moist fecund earth in most Indo-European religions is associated with motherhood, though we should remember an older, primeval, amoral ambivalent, power, who births monsters, gods and men, hence her pre-historic association with chaos. Across much of the ancient world,

---

298. As noted in Greek, Irish and Slavic myth.

this chthonic figure is depicted in serpentine form. Artimpasa is no exception.

Of lesser importance than Tabiti, winged female figures (such as the one found in the Bolshaia Bliznitsa kurgan) are generally assumed to be depictions of Artimpasa who is often depicted in a more accessible as an anthropomorphised spirit. It is possible that such highly stylised figures may also relate to Api, a vegetal fertility spirit who seems to be a facet of Artimpasa. This Mistress of Animals relates to the deer as a (sacrificial) giver of life; as a representative of the Tree of Life, she shares its symbolic embodiment. Creation is sustained out of the sacrifice of death (a trait commonly associated with the first sacrifice of the Creator to initiate life itself). Artimpasa was a complex (and some believe androgynous) divine spirit of fertility who possessed the gifts of sovereignty, authority and divine rule (hence her connection to oaths). In this role, she was guardian of laws representing material wealth (itself a divine form of mana, sometimes explained as a priestly force), manifest in gold, but also wealth in all its various forms, including domestic animals, precious objects, and fecundity. In her capacity as the people's guardian, Artimpasa oversaw success in warfare. Argimpasa is a scribal corruption of Artimpasa.[299]

7. Artimpasa

The Pontic Olbian Greeks identified the wild, chaotic force of nature (personified as the Mistress of Animals) with a bifurcate limbed figure, a form they believed was cognate with Cybele, Demeter, Pantikapaion, Aphrodite Apatura or Medusa, the Etruscan Cel (Mother of the gods), Persephone and even Hecate.[300] In the 5th century BCE, Herodotus refers to a therianthrope who closely resembles the Hesiodic Echidna, a 'she-viper' (being half woman and half snake) and

---

299. Ustinova, 1999.   **300.** David Braund. "Greater Olbia: Ethnic, Religious, Economic, and Political Interactions in the Region of Olbia, c.600-100 BCE." In, Classical Olbia and the Scythian World: From the Sixth Century BCE to the Second Century CE. Edited by David Braund and S. D. Kryzhintskiy. [in Russian] (Oxford University Press. (2007): 33-77

who lived in a cave and was known as the progenitor of the Scythian people. [301]"In the Mediterranean world and its environs, the earliest examples of the tendril or snake-limbed creature appear in Italy, South Russia and the northern Balkans. Only later, in the fourth century, are they attested in Lycia and Cyprus."[302]

Several representations of this therianthropic female tendrilled figure[303] (Rankenfrau) were found in Chersonesos Taurica, in the 4th-Century BCE Hellenic funerary complex (of a possible Scythian king) within the Kul-Oba burial-mound and also in a burial-mound near the village of Ivanovskaya.[304] She is bearing what appears to be a severed head and according to some, a (supposed) scimitar.[305] The small gold relief plates bearing images related to The Mistress of Animals as a winged female figure with vegetal or zoomorphic extremities, can be traced back to the zoomorphic iconographic type of the Potnia Theron (North Pontic region), and may be found as a common decoration of the Classical period.

Bearing the surname of the Furies, the Mixoparthenos ('half-maiden') was a zoomorphic figure of Greek mythology, whose origins reside in the region of the Black sea. Somewhat akin to the Sirens, this beautiful female form generally resembles a strange double-terminated fish or snake. Sometimes, her lower

8. Mixoparthenos

---

301. A collection of closely related ancient Iranic peoples who inhabited Central Asia and the Pontic–Caspian steppe in Eastern Europe throughout Classical Antiquity. **302.** Ustinova, 2005: 75. **303.** I believe the androgyny ascribed to her form by some to be misplaced, and I refute the identification of her supposed 'beard' used to validate that claim. Even a cursory glance at this golden artefact readily confirms a complete absence of a 'beard.' There is only her own neck. **304.** Fragments of bronze cauldrons, the terminal of a rhyton, and plates bearing the depiction of a horse's head found here, are typical of funerary complexes in contact zones of Greek and barbarian culture. See: Roman V. Stoyanov. "On the Iconography of the Potnia Theron in the North Pontic Region." Ancient Civilizations from Scythia to Siberia 27 no. 1 (2021): 1-10 doi:10.1163/15700577-12341386. (Accessed 17th April 2024). **305.** Although the sword/scimitar is disputed, when seen from reverse side, the curve of a small hand-held sickle in her right hand is discernible, offering a more credible alternative.

limbs become splayed tendrils of exotic plants. "To this day, there is no generally agreed opinion among scholars as to how the various depictions of the tendril goddess should be interpreted."[306] On the Kul-Oba variant, the tiny plates are best utilised as decorative pieces for sewing on to a specialised garment, specifically the kalathos (stylised basket crown) as depicted by this figure, who also wears a peplos (Greek dress). Behind her back, emanating from her shoulders, are the stylised bestial heads of horned lions. The bearded head in her left hand is best identified with a satyr mask used in the mysteries associated with the chthonic cult of Artemis Orphia. In her temple in Sparta, fragments of several hundred masks have been found, which are too small to wear and were probably carried in processions. This male image is possibly associated with Pan, but this is again an assumption posed by some academics. Herodotus[307] records the legend of a Mixoparthenos whose sexual encounter with Heracles produced three sons, one of whom was the apical ancestor of the Scythian peoples, in much the same way that the Melusine birthed the Merovingians.

Artimpasa[308] was the Scythian variant of the divine Iranian entity 'Arti/AsI, who was similarly a patron of fertility, marriage and wealth. Artimpasa exhibits compound influences from the Thracian populations of the western Pontic Steppe conquered by the Scythians. During the Scythians' sojourn in Western Asia, they absorbed influences from the Iranic, Greek, Mesopotamian and Canaanite religions,[309] notably in the form of several figures, including Anahita, Ištar-'Aštart, Aphrodite Urania and Bendis. This is to be anticipated since the Scythian religion is assumed to have been related to the earlier Proto-Indo-Iranic religion as well as to contemporary Eastern Iranic and Ossetian traditions that influenced later Slavic, Hungarian and Türkic mythologies.[310]

In like manner of Anahita, Artimpasa grants the power of

---

306. Stoyanov, 2021. **307**. Histories, (4.9.2) **308**. The first element of Artimpasa's name, 'Arti' is derived from the Iranian Goddess, (Arti); the second element is related to two terms that share a common root: 'paya,' (meaning pasture) and 'pati,' (meaning lord). **309.** Ustinova, 1999. **310**. Barnhart, 2022. After the complete defeat and displacement/absorption of the Scythians by first century Goths and Sarmatians, the Sarmatians continued to live in Central Asia and Eastern Europe before being dispersed in turn, by the Altaic Huns in the 4th century, whence they were partially driven to Spain and North Africa. Various Sarmatian splinter groups survived into the Middle Ages living in the Caucasus. Known as the Ossetians (who continue to speak a form of their ancient Iranian language), they are the only direct surviving descendants of the Scythians and Sarmatian Alans. "From that point, Turkic languages replaced Iranian as the dominant idiom spoken in Eurasia."

life and rulership to the youthful heroes via offering the rhyton to them. Rhyta are specific, ceremonial vessels used for drinking sacred beverages consumed or libated in all religious rituals. Zoomorphic vessels in the shape of various animals (often carved from animal horns) are inexorably linked with the performative cultic practice of 'god-drinking' – a direct imbibement of mana or divine essence popular in the ancient world comparable to the Eucharist of Christian mystics. "Zoomorphic (animal-shaped vessels) and anthropomorphic (decorated with a human face in relief) ritual vessels were common throughout the 2nd millennium BCE and were used in the Hittite cult in relation to a god serving and/or drinking."[311]

Flanked by her symbol, the Tree of Life,[312] the Great Mother appears seated (enthroned) before the male hero, demi-god, or priest king to be. He stands (or kneels) awaiting her authorisation of his divine power to rule through her. She alone may legitimise his rule and status through her divine benediction, a custom and tradition that became a ceremonial investiture, or sacred marriage. Additional ornamentation typically consists of vegetal and solar imagery. Variations of this popular motif appear in several frescoes that decorate the tombs of Scythian nobility.[313] As a striking motif, we should not be surprised to discover it may feature in one of the Nag Hammadi texts titled "On the Origin of the World," where Adam kneels before Eve, calling her the Mother of all living, announcing it was She who gave him life.

Elsewhere, a seated Artimpasa holding a mirror[314] and a branch-like sceptre appears on the signet ring of (the Scythian) King Scyles, an heirloom artefact inherited from generation to generation of the Scythian royal dynasty as a token of the royal power invested in them, through being her Consort. This reflects a clear Levantine influence on the role of Artimpasa, since her Mesopotamian equivalents all assumed this intimate dominance. "In the early common era, the Huns and Mongols worshipped an identical goddess whom they referred to as 'the Shamaness.'"[315] Traditional religious belief and practice

---

311. Y. Heffron. "The Material Culture of Hittite 'God-drinking.'" *Journal of Ancient Near Eastern Religions* 14. (2014): 164-185. 10.1163/15692124-12341261 (Accessed 19th December, 2024).   **312.** A universal metaphoric construct within which all realms and living creatures, seen and unseen, reside. The 'World Tree' or 'Tree of Life,' is often an epithet for the Creatrix itself that nourishes and protects its creation. **313.** Ustinova, 1999: 67-128. **314.** Sarmatians buried their priestesses with mirrors, which are attested symbols of feminine principle, eroticism and fertility that also played a significant role in the wedding rites of Iranic peoples. Indeed, their magical efficacy inculcated their use in prophetic and shamanic rites. **315.** Barnhart, 2022

throughout the Eurasian north was shamanistic in form (indeed, the term 'shaman' is of Evenk derivation).

Within the early stages of prehistory, it is possible that only deities were thought to enact the role of the shaman; or that the deer embodied shamanistic travel along the axis of the World Tree. As witnessed within ancient literature, the deer may have been a feminine deity with exceptional speed of movement, suggesting omnipresence. The next step would have been for the hero to embark on this journey. In the Sumerian epic, Gilgamesh descends to the underworld to then make his way back to the earth again. The earliest cuneiform record of this narrative is dated to the 3rd millennium BCE, which makes this epic one of the most ancient pieces of literature. Perhaps these heroic activities were then transferred to the role of the practitioner, such as the Enarei who [believed they] learned their practice from Argimpasa. Esther Jacobson clarifies that shamanism is generally practiced by a group of people who are set apart, who travel between this world and the other worlds. They act as guides for souls who have lost their way in the struggles between life and death. This differs from the religious practice among household members and group leaders that involves the protection of livestock, family members, and the hearth fire on the earthly plane of existence.[316]

In Scythian and Sarmatian art, women are associated with either mythical or wild, fearful animals such as lions and snakes,[317] or birds of prey.[318] Beyond that, "women are only present under supernatural circumstances, while men are depicted in daily activities, such as milking livestock, stringing a bow, sealing a pact of blood brotherhood, or engaging in warfare."[319] Accompanied by wild animals, some obscure depictions of the anthropomorphic Mistress of Animals include wings or plant-like features (tendrils, branches). Her importance is observed even amongst the beliefs of the Evenks of Siberia:

> … *the [clan] mistress governs the clan land and her abode is usually thought to be located under the sacred cosmic tree of the clan where her husband and other herdsmen tend vast numbers of animals of all kinds. Commencing the séance the shaman declares the purpose of his mission, rallies his spirits, and 'departs for the world where*

---

316. Ibid. **317.** In Slavic mythology, snakes are companions of Veles who sometimes assumes a form of a snake or fire-breathing dragon. Because snakes hibernate underground, they are connected to the Underworld realm of Ancestors, and know the past, the present, and the future. Also, they were often envisioned as the guardians of the underground treasure. In some legends, a child born from a woman and a dragon becomes a mighty hero "bogatyr" that eventually slays the very dragon that produced him. Garbled form of the mythic conception of an ancestral figure in Sami lore. **318.** Esther Jacobson. The Art of the Scythians – The Interpretation of Cultures at the Edge of the Hellenic World. (Brill, 1995): 60 **319.** Barnhart, 2022.

EARTH MOTHER ARCHETYPES

dunne mushun, the mistress of the clan land, lives, by penetrating under the roots of the sacred clan-tree.'[320]

Before any hunt was undertaken, the shaman needed permission from this primal Matriarch, who granted her beneficence only once she was convinced the number of animals they planned to slaughter were necessary. No more no less. The origins of the concept of the Primal Mother as the Mistress of Animals are in dispute, some scholars place her in the Ancient Near East, while others favour Eastern Europe. Most importantly, the early deer related art of the Pontic Steppe Scythians, originates in the Bronze Age[321] culture of the Altai-Sayan Mountains and is most likely to be a manifestation of a deeply rooted shamanistic belief system. A petroglyph carved on a rock at Georgievskaya is of a shamanic figure holding a drum and beater that has items attached to it, as does his clothing. [322]Human migration and cross-cultural contact maintained the narratives of a divine feminine deer spirit throughout many regions and eras as witnessed in the much later folkloric traditions of Scotland, Ireland and even Germany (and other areas of Europe) that demonstrate deep-rooted inherited beliefs associated with hunting deer.

In the folklore of the Scottish Highlands, for example, supernatural female figures were able to transform themselves into the red deer. An Irish divine spirit of the deer known as the 'Old Woman of Beare,' was a psychopomp for those who were traveling to the Land of the Dead.[323] Deer cults originate in the eras when people subsisted from hunting wild reindeer, and not the later herding cultures dependant upon domesticated reindeer. In celebration of similar life-sustaining concepts, stag dances were performed in Germany during the Middle Ages by men dressed as women, which is reminiscent of the female dress of the Enarei priesthood among the Scythians. The Enarei are fundamental to northern magical traditions.

---

320. Malandra, 1967: 23-69 **321.** Deer imagery found in the Bronze Age deer stones of Siberia and Mongolia, circa 1300-700 BCE, places it at the dawn of the Scythian age. **322.** Cunliffe, 2019: 92-93 **323.** J. G. McKay, 1932: 144-145 Widely revered across northern Europe, the cult of the deer mother was a figure that McKay sought to promote in Scotland as a traditional feminine spirit of the 'Other.' His book explores the sacred significance of the deer and reindeer in northern shamanic traditions – which he understood as being essentially female and associated with the Tree of Life, fertility, motherhood, birth and the rebirth of the sun.

ENAREI: A SACRED PRIESTHOOD

Artimpasa is highlighted by Herodotus as ruling a particular class of Scythian clerics, the Enarei. The cult of Artimpasa was performed by the Enarei, who were powerful (and allegedly transvestite) priests garnered from the most noble families affiliated to an orgiastic aspect of her chthonic cult,[324] but more exclusively to her bifurcate totemic form often loosely described as the 'Snake-Legged Goddess.'[325] The Enarei (singular Enaree), were "Scythian androgynous/effeminate priests and shamanistic soothsayers who played an important role in the Scythian religion."[326] At this point it is worth a deeper investigation into this cult, as the explanation holds considerable relevance to the charge of *ergi* amongst the much later Scandinavian *séiðmenn*. The association will become absolutely transparent as I proceed.

Herodotus tells us the Enarei claimed that 'Aphrodite' (Artimpasa) gave them the art of divination. Unlike traditional Scythian soothsayers who used willow rods for divining by laying them out in rows upon the ground, gathering them up and repeating the process until an answer is achieved, the Enarei were professional seers who performed their divinations with the inner bark of the linden tree, which they cut into three strips (withies) to weave into plaits around their fingers to obtain answers to pertinent questions.[327] The Greek world was more than familiar with cults and rites of prophecy and divination.

---

324. Safaee Yazdan. "Scythian and Zoroastrian Earth Goddesses: A Comparative Study on Api and Armaiti." In, *Archaeology of Iran in the Historical Period*. University of Tehran Science and Humanities Series. Edited by Kamal-Aldin Niknami and Ali Hozhabri. (Springer International Publishing. 2020): 65-75 doi:10.1007/978-3-030-41776-5_6 **325.** I believe this generic identification to be in error. Her lower limbs, that are supposedly snakes may be something else entirely. Given that the 'snakes' appear over her peplos rather than under it, I believe them to be stylised animal terminals formed from the trailing folds of her peplos. Careful comparative study shows several variations of vegetal tendrils, stylised bird heads (typically griffins), and mythical creatures such as dragons, that are only sometimes reptilian. The griffin was a primary symbol associated with the Proto Iranic peoples. **326.** Barnhart, 2022.

ENAREI: A SACRED PRIESTHOOD 107

The Greek term 'Enarei' is derived from the Scythian term Anarya, meaning 'unmanly.'[328] The term 'anarya' is composed of, *a–*, meaning non –, and *narya*, which was derived from *nar–*, meaning man.[329] The Enarei's affiliation to an orgiastic (chthonic) cult is clearly influenced by Near Eastern fertility goddesses, and its rites thus combined indigenous Scythian religious practices of a shamanistic nature, which appear to be related in kind to those of indigenous Siberian peoples, in addition to those imported from Levantine religions.[330] The Enarei consumed cannabis (probably in vapour form)[331] in their religious rituals, and may therefore be amongst the earliest (recorded) spiritual practitioners to have used mind-altering substances. It has also been suggested this usage implies a controversial connection between gender non-conforming spiritual practitioners and the use of mind-altering substances.[332] It is unclear if Scythian and Sarmatian groups used fly agaric in their religious practice, however, according to Herodotus and archaeological evidence, Scythians used hemp seeds to hallucinate after burial rituals as a source of purification. A copper pot with burned hemp seeds and a small steam tent were found in a Pazyryk burial mound among the Scytho-Siberians. While this is not a shamanic practice, the use of hallucinogens was central to their traditions.[333]

The Enarei were all men of an elite class, possibly chosen for their androgynous features, which were believed to be a sign of their unique connection to divinity. Believed by the Scythians to be inherently different from other males, they wore clothing that closely resembled

---

327. I have to admit my disappointment in learning that this priesthood was in every sense as corrupt as many others of the ancient world, (from the Pythia to Scandinavian Lawspeakers, to the Witchfinder Generals, to name but 3 of so many) subject as they were to bribes and greed (beneficiaries all of the wealth of those accused whom their 'visions' proved to be guilty. **328.** Askold I. Ivantchik "Scythians." In, *Encyclopædia Iranica.* Encyclopædia Iranica Foundation (Brill Publishers, 2018). **329.** Askold I. Ivantchik. "L'idéologie royale des Scythes et son expression dans la littérature et l'iconographie grecques: l'apport de la numismatique." [The Royal Ideology of the Scythians and its Expression in Greek Literature and Iconography: the Contribution of Numismatics]. Dialogues d'histoire ancienne [Dialogues of Ancient History]. 42 (1) (2016): 305-329 **330.** Ustinova, 2005; 64-79 **331.** Attested archaeologically in Saka tombs from Siberia, which contained tripods, braziers, pelts, and charcoal containing remains of cannabis leaves and fruits, with one of the Pazyryk burials containing a pot, inside of which were cannabis fruits, as well as a copper censer used to burn cannabis. See: Randy P. Conner. "Enaree." *Cassell's Encyclopaedia of Queer Myth, Symbol, and Spirit: Gay, Lesbian, Bisexual, and Transgender Lore.* (Cassell, 1997). **332.** Conner, 1997. **333.** Zaur Hasanov. "A Reflection of the Cimmerian and Scythian Religious Rites in Archaeology," Proceedings of the 8th International Congress on the Archaeology of the Ancient Near East., Volume 3 (University of Warsaw, 2012): 527-540

the attire worn by women. We should remember that many late modern indigenous groups viewed the Underworld as an inversion of this world, in which everything in the Underworld is the opposite, and therefore more powerful, and more directly connected to the invisible, divine world. This perspective might help explain a contributing factor in the deliberate selection of transvestite and transexual persons in the practise of shamanism. Or, it might simply be that by sidestepping any form of rigid gender identification, embracing instead all aspects of their neutral existence at the point of conception (remember that according to their cosmological beliefs, some of these peoples believed they could persuade their deities to manipulate a neutral embryo into a male foetus) both psychological and physiological, they became effectively limitless in the Otherworld.

The Enarei priesthood were certainly deemed to be extraordinarily powerful shamans, who inspired fear and were thus accordingly given special respect in Scythian society. As exemplary exponents of chthonic cults of ecstasy associated with a female creatrix and Mistress of Animals, the Enarei appear to have lived their early lives as men. Their adoption of transvestitism occurring only later in their lives (which they believed was a 7th century BCE curse resulting from the Scythian sack of a temple in Ascalon to Aštart) when they found themselves incapable of sexual intercourse.[334] It remains unknown if the Enarei practised ritual castration (similar to the adherents of Cult of Kybele), or merely refrained from heterosexual intercourse, although it is thought they were not celibate. In fact, the writings of Pseudo-Hippocrates suggest that they adopted the receptive role during anal intercourse with men.[335] Despite all these possible explanations for the use and application of this form of priesthood, it is worth bearing in mind that excessive use of cannabis induces impotency (both performatively and reproductively). Science is often a mirror to the curses of the natural world.

Sceptres used by the Enarei as symbols of authority were capped with ornate pole tops (some of which included metal or beaded rattles). Discovered throughout the steppe from Mongolia to the Great Hungarian Plain, they were not indistinct from those used by the Völur. The oldest pole sceptres (from Tuva and the Minusinsk Basin) date from the 8th century BCE, and are topped by a stag or ibex standing with its feet together as if perched on a rocky eminence (redolent perhaps of the Royal Sutton Hoo Whetstone sceptre). Some

---

334. Ustinova, 1999: 67-128 **335.** Conner, 1997: 129-131

ENAREI: A SACRED PRIESTHOOD 109

recent pole tops are even more elaborate in design, molded as tree branches with bells, birds and other animals hanging from them. The Enarei (Anarya) may have used small drums in their rituals and worn shamanic antlered headdresses similar to those found in Saka (Sakas) horse burials and those worn in more recent times by Siberian shamans.[336]

---

336. Cunliffe, 2019: 265-290

THE SHAMANIC LANDSCAPE OF THE ARCTIC

Many arctic peoples are patrilineal, though the Sámi kinship unusually awards equal significance to both maternal and paternal family.

The origins of the clan system may lie with the pastoral peoples of the southern Siberian Steppes, but with the transition to taiga and tundra environments the significance of clans appears to fade out. With the significant exception of the Saka (Sakas), all northern Eurasian peoples are politically egalitarian, and, despite individual differences in wealth and influence, there are no formal chiefly offices or institutionalized hierarchies. As for Arctic and subarctic peoples generally, a strong emphasis is placed on the value of personal autonomy.[337]

These characteristics apply to the many peoples of the northern regions, who all look to the east to find their origins through numerous (over layering) stages of migration by the Finno-Ugric populations westward from the Ural Mountains toward the Baltic regions[338] Settlement was ever sparse amongst hunting cultures, so traditions were often slow to change, at least initially, until language played its part in the gradual shift for many of these peoples to sedentary agriculture.[339] Each of the Finno-Ugric peoples has its own cultural history, habitat, and phases of modernity, and of all the Finno-Ugric peoples, the Sámi cherished their hunting and nomadic culture the longest, moving slowly toward the northern regions away from Lakes Ladoga and Onega (northeast of St. Petersburg) to the northern parts of Fennoscandia and the Kola Peninsula (far northern Russia).

Northern peoples of the arctic and subarctic regions all hold to the notion of totem animals[340] for each tribe or clan, recognised as apical

---

337. D. E. Dumond; Moira Dunbar.,et al. "Arctic." In, *Encyclopedia Britannica*, 2025. https://www.britannica.com/place/Arctic. (Accessed 120th January 2025). **338.** The latest possible date would be about 1500 BCE (the evidence being the Baltic loanwords in proto-Finnic). **339.** Most of Finland was converted to Christianity by way of Sweden, beginning in the 12th century, and the country remained Roman Catholic until Lutheranism was established in the 16th century. **340.** This subject is also dealt with in depth in the forthcoming as yet unpublished ms., "Song of The North," by Shani Oates.

spirits, and the taboos associated with them. The nature of exogamic patrilineal clans (involving marriage outside a particular blood related kinship group) of numerous Ob Ugrian peoples forbids marriages within each totemic group, so a healthy people is comprised of a balanced mix from other totemic groups. Men of the bear clan may take wives from the dog clan for example.

Creation myths therefore vary accordingly, though some share certain aspects that can be traced through time. In Finland we find a common trope shared by many other northern peoples that describes a mythic account of the anthropogonic (origin of man) which begins with a tree stump (or pole that holds up the sky) on a mound that rises from the sea, and splitting open, the first human couple steps forth from the broken stump. Indeed the Nordic eschatological myth of Lif and Lifasa, is strongly redolent of this motif. In other Finno-Ugric cosmographic (world-describing) scenarios we find other well-known motifs and concepts that involve bodies of water (or seas) encircling the world beneath a canopy of the heavens, the central point of which is the North Star likened to a nail to which the sky is tethered as it rotates day through night, ad finitum.

The Otherworld is not divided from our own, it is not separate, rather, it is of invisible spirits entwined with the visible, material world on this middle realm of earth. Below, is the Underworld of the dead, which exists as a real location near to the village, and another, distant metaphysical realm, far to the north behind the burning stream, known in Norse cosmology as Hvergelmir. As noted above, the pillar (the axis mundi) being central to several cosmologies, was celebrated as the focus of order and fecundity in the form of the Irminsul, Yggdrasil, and possibly even Sampo. This mythic view is in accord with the shamanistic worldview, wherein the cosmos is divided into many layers, and the shamans traverse between them, aided or hindered by various spirits for the benefit of their people, seeking cures for illness and the location of game for the hunters.

Animism was the prevailing belief of such communities. Everything is imbued with spirit, and a healthy spirit feeds a healthy body, and vice versa, and so it was often the shamans' role to ensure the health and welfare of the people in their community. Human souls were deemed to be especially vulnerable, and soul loss could lead to illness or even death. Amulets and talismans were carried by ordinary people, connecting them to the spirit world during mundane activities. Some folk even practised basic forms of divination for their families, independent of the ritual specialist or shaman. As a form of human reincarnation, the names of honoured ancestors are awarded to the newly born to provide protection and good fortune for them. Such a naming adoption is first approached through propitiation to the appropriate female higher spirits, by which the name of a deceased person was given to a child who 'becomes' that person by being addressed with kinship terms appropriate to the deceased.

Within long-cherished folk magic practises, including those previously of Mongolia, it was again common for the rituals to be conducted by the head of each family, who as laymen, acted on behalf of their family with the spirits of the land and hearth. Like those of the Sámi, this role was later assumed (in some areas) by the shamans and later still, by Lamaist monks, removing control into that of a dedicated priesthood. All forms of worship and ritual came under their strict control. Mediation, divination, healing and propitiation from thereon in, came under the domain of the specialist practitioner – folk magic and ritual practises were removed from the direct domain of the folk.

The use of incense, incantatory prayers, and sacrificial offerings became major features of shamanistic practises. The Secret History of the Mongols recalls a religious practise prior to the development of shamanistic practises within it, inferring that development was relatively recent, most probably after the millennium, perhaps even as late as the 12th century.[341] Additional prayers and invocations were offered to the great spirits of armoured men on horseback – *Sülde Tngri, Dayicin Tngri* and *Geser* – and to the White Old Man (*Cayan Ebügen*). As a work contemporary with the earliest sections of the *Eddas, The Secret History of the Mongols* bears many interesting shared associations and concepts, emphasising the significance of heroic ancestry, battle leaders, a pantheon of lesser gods, an overruling higher god, elemental factions, the role of fate, and most curious of all, the wisest of all gods who in both instances is referred to by the curious usage of white as a description of his extreme hoary age and translucency as a nebulous spirit (*tngrii*).

As a figure of high rank at the time of Cinggis Khan, Cayan Ebügen's robe would also have been perceived as white, the colour of the priesthood in Mongolia at that time.[342] According to Mongolian folklore, Cayan Ebügen tngrii – the White Old Man – descended from his high mountain domain only to meter punishments to transgressors

---

341. Even so, Tengrism was subject to considerable external influence from Christianity and Islam. **342.** Walther Heissig. *The Religions of Mongolia*. Translated by Geoffrey Samuel. (Routledge & Kegan-Paul, 1970): 77

THE SHAMANIC LANDSCAPE OF THE ARTIC 113

of societal law. This suggests he was perceived in the role of judge. He thus bears similar but not identical traits to Heimdallr, a contemporary figure of Norse tradition found in the Eddas. Many sorcerous or shamanic mythic traditions throughout the world are related to the visionary arts of the seer,[343] initiated by a variety of ecstatic or frenzied activities, ranging from battle to prophecy, popular to both east and western folkloric romance. *"The most interesting figure in Norse mantic tradition of the God Óðinn, whose most obvious affinities are with the Siberian shamans whom he resembles in a remarkable degree."*[344] Setting aside the terminology here that relates the Óðinic figure with a god, the frenzied psychology of the Siberian shaman is a most excellent fit and compares favourably with several central mythic figures East and West, aligning the shamanistic and Geilt traditions[345] as parallel literary motifs.[346]

It is tempting to suppose that they may have formed a link in early times between the ancient mantic systems of the southern portion of Eurasia, as the cult of Óðinn and other features of Norse religion bear witness to an ancient link between Teutonic and Celtic manticism on the one hand and the shamanism of northern Asia on the other. [347]

Rituals staged by Sámi shaman take place in and around the shaman's tent (chum) that represents the world tree and the Sámi clan lands connected to it. In some instances, a great furious river flows and winds around and through these worlds. On the plains, where water flows are limited and mild, great winding, sandy trackways connect these worlds. It is hard not to see Hvergelmir and Níðhöggr in the boiling, surging rivers and dusty choking trackways noted here. Close to the chum, wooden idols were erected to represent the shaman's male and female spirit helpers that evolved into revered ancestors, then ultimately, into tribal deities. Animal spirits that aided the shaman, were chosen for their relevance to the economy and subsistence that tribe depended upon, which varied according to location, so were very region specific.

Redolent perhaps of this winding trail between the worlds, rows of stones led off from burial mounds to nearby rivers, guiding the dead on their way. It was believed that even the spirit of the dead could be brought back from the land of the dead by the spirit of a shaman

---

343. N. K. Chadwick. *Poetry & Prophecy*. (Cambridge University Press, 1952): 50
344. Chadwick, 1952. 10 **345.** A figure of Irish myth and legend, the geilt are both possessed by and possessor of, supernatural inspiration and power, a practitioner of archaic techniques of ecstasy. **346.** Boucherit, 2011. **347.** Chadwick, 1952: 12

traversing the river in a larch bark boat. It is immensely significant that the shaman must first acquire permission from the 'mistress of the land of the dead' to enter her realms to retrieve the spirit of the dead person into the land of the living. Within this, we may easily discern several descent myths, including Óðinn's mission to retrieve Balðr. Appearing on the magnificent Pazyryk textile, these customs are also portrayed on many of the painted images and pictographs on the rocks above the *Lena, Angara, Upper Yenisei* and *Toms* rivers.[348]

Under animism, the divine laws of time and space are reflected through all levels of existence upon the axial pole of life and death. All realms are filled with spirit entities, all of which emanate from or exist within a supreme spirit, generally of the heavens or sky. This is how the *tngrii* (spirits) are perceived. In the Ket tradition, the supreme spirit to whom all people give thanks for their fecund existence is the *Buga*, perceived as both male and female. The *Buga* may share the same route as the Boga (tyr) of the Slavic tradition. Everything is beholden to the law of *Buga*, as the divine spirit source whose literal blessings are essential for survival. From her form as a giant moose, reindeer or wild cow, all physical beings derive their own existence. Her role as Creatrix and spiritual presence within all worlds, is distinct from the totemic beasts assumed for each clan or family, and from whom they take their identity and protection. This suggests the human aspects relating to ancient sacred figures emerged only later as the concept of clan origins separated from the primary image of the animal mother and clan animal mother. Her afore mentioned dwelling beneath the root of the sacred clan tree, confirms her arcane role as guardian. Each clan or family had its own tree, clan mother and guardian, that were mythically all part of the one Tree, Mother and Guardian. It is entirely possible that the absolute supremacy *Buga* came to represent was influenced by Russian orthodox notions of godhead. Once again, it is impossible to separate pre-shamanic mythic traditions from post-shamanic practise.

Mythic tradition evidently became so entangled within the ensuing shamanic cults designed to interact with them, it is now impossible to separate their rituals and functions, or determine at what point one merged into the other. Many shamanic traditions are survivals from former cults centred around the original Creatrix along with the Animal Mother spirit all shamans serve, albeit individually through various animal totems. The introduction of shamanism evidently required certain rituals of its own to facilitate the anthropomorphic nature of the work,

---

348. Jacobson-Tepfer, 2015: 340

THE SHAMANIC LANDSCAPE OF THE ARTIC 115

that is, to access the animistic world effectively and safely. Therefore, the soul of a future shaman was required to journey down into the Underworld accompanied by his or her predecessor, as a spirit ancestor.

As a matter of historical ethnology, shamanism is not a vocation, a shaman is elected by spirits who guide the apprentice through incredibly brutal and challenging ordeals. This involves pushing the mind and body beyond their natural boundaries. During this process, shamans are figuratively dismembered while in an unconscious state, prostrate within their tent (chum). Afterwards, the spirits restore them to wholeness, sewn with iron wire, rendering them capable of incredible feats and in communion with those spirits as a mediator for the rest of their people.

9. Shamans

In other traditions, the apprentice shaman is first taken to the guardian tree, generally a sacred larch *turu*, the would-be shaman was required to bond with the ancestral spirit guardian of the tree. Once achieved, the shaman would be suspended from the tree in an iron cage from which his or her spirit must break free of and descend to the Underworld of the dead. In that place, after the clan mother had consumed the shaman's anthropomorphic soul, the shaman would then birth their own animal soul double, known as the *Khargi*. Small iron fetish figures that embody the *Khargi* animal souls, hang from the tunics and aprons worn by Ket and Evenk shaman, ready to be employed in their journeying works through the transformative power of the Evenk *bugady enintyn* — "*the mistress-mother of the clan*,"[349] from whose body the Axis Mundi grows.

Shamanic selection and rebirth through the evisceration by the 'Old Woman' reduced her function to that of totemic cult object and transformed the animal spirit source to an anthropomorphic form. Her association with all antlered and horned animals and raptorial birds is echoed within the narrative images painted onto the shaman's

---

349. Jacobson, 1993.

drum and the back boards of the Ket sleds, a tradition we witness reflected in the monumental rock art, and which continued well into the Soviet period.

In addition to healing people when living, and guiding the soul to the after-world when dead, shamans are responsible for following the game, for knowing where the hunt must take place. They alone retrieve this information from the spirits. For that, a state of ecstasy is required, induced by chanting, drumming, breath control and fasting. While journeying, hostile spirits may attack or delay the shamans from their task.

Shamans were also expected to contact a few more strongly personified spirit-beings, such as the female being (whose name and attributes varied from group to group) who governed important land or sea mammals; when game was scarce, the shaman might cajole her into providing more bounty. In Greenland the shaman was also an entertainer whose séances, escape tricks, and noisy spirit helpers could enliven a long winter's night in the communal house. Later shamans even hosted séances in the communal building during the long, dark nights of the Greenland winter.[350]

As an interesting aside, it is apt to note here that the traditional ceremonial clothing worn by medicine women and female shamans of Siberia and Lapland was green and white, and included a red peaked hat, curled-toed boots, reindeer mittens with fur lining and trim, which colours aside, is all very reminiscent of the clothing ascribed to Þorbjörg lítilvölva (the 'little volva') whose predictions were well met in 10th-Century Greenland.[351]

Sámi women were known to wander, travelling as seers (Völur) across Fennoscandia, and ultimately, Iceland and Greenland, conducting rites recognised in Norse culture as Varðlokkur and Séiðr. Conversely, customs adhered to by the Suebians whom Tacitus encountered, sound very much like the certain rites held by the hereditary guardian priests of the Votyaks and Zyryans at the Luds,[352] which forbade women and children to be present; the stricture on men was that they must first bathe before entering. The hides of animals sacrificed hung in the trees, and its meat was consumed there. Each people developed cultural songs, epic poems, myths and legends around their seasonal activities, the spirits and specific heroic people (including named shamans) involved and the places relevant to them.

---

350. D. E. Dumond; Moira Dunbar., et al. "Arctic." In, *Encyclopedia Britannica*, 2025. https://www.britannica.com/place/Arctic. (Accessed 120th January 2025). **351.** It is also curious that such outfits consequently became associated with the mythical elves in folklore. **352.** The Finnish and Estonian peoples had comparable groves, though we know little of the rituals undertaken there.

THE SHAMANIC LANDSCAPE OF THE ARTIC 117

Although referred to already, it is worth reiterating here how shamanic culture defines the worlds in terms of realms above, below and of the visible, material world itself. Significant features of the Proto-Uralic cosmology maintain this layered (non-hierarchical) view of the cosmos where higher spirits, animals and animal spirits, human beings and human spirits reside alongside each other in the visible and the invisible realms. Both the drum (covered with the hides of totem animals), and drumstick, are the 'horse' ridden by the shamans through those realms; three main worlds in all. Sometimes, with sub-domains totalling seven, nine, or more, up to unknown numbers, were layered up and held together upon the world pillar running through the centre of the whole system, and crowned by the nowl that fixes this great pole to the rotating heavens. The Ob Ugrians and the Nenets favour a myth of seven or nine heavenly realms. A communication network exists from this tiered universe – again depicted mythically as a tree – extending from the Underworld of the dead to the celestial regions of the higher spirits, in which birds (mainly swans, geese and ducks) traverse at the whim of the shamans commanding them. It is a notable feature of arctic and subarctic cosmologies that higher female spirits, known as the (old) women of the north and south, preside over all matters of life and death.

Many temple structures are also modelled on this archaic tiered construct, observed by the temple priests of the Sabaean and Sumerian peoples, but also of China, India, Iran, Arabia, Egypt, Tibet, Cambodia, and Mesoamerica. Complex astronomical events were calculated and observed from these high towers – the celestial ladders to the heavens – a primary tenet of all ancient civilisations.[353] The stars above form patterns recognised by the shamans, that also guide the traveller on land and sea.

Time, rhythm and motion. These are the keys to those mysteries, pulsed by the Great Mill. Connected to this, the celestial blacksmith is perceived as the legitimate heir to the grand architect and creator. The Smith and The Shaman are brothers, both feeding and serving the Anvil and the Mill.[354] The celestial Smith generates meteoric iron from which the terrestrial shaman may mold his tokens, sewn into his costume of totemic hides that bond him in spirit to his discarnate teachers. Sadly, there is much we still do not know of these remarkable activities, since Christendom was so very successful in its destruction of all non-Christian traditions and their attendant beliefs and rituals. Remnants only remain, fractured and incomplete, surviving as seeds in

---

353. Giorgio de Santillana and Hertha von Dechend. *Hamlets Mill* (David R. Godine Inc. 1977): 121-124   **354.** Ibid.

the Siberian and Finnish folktales. That knowledge awaits only our willingness to grasp it.

Humboldt said that when people encounter new knowledge that challenges the status quo, they will first deny a thing, then they will belittle it, then they will decide that it had been known all along.[355] *"He that will have a cake out of the wheat must needs tarry the grinding."* [356] Piercing through the symbology that enshrouds the minds and thought patterns of those remote ancestors of ours, often appears as a Sisyphus task. All gods must perish. That is to say, the Titans, followed by the Olympian gods. The younger gods are the new heroes of each age or era. Time demands new people to fulfil the heroic roles needful to foster hope and garner strength as chaos overwhelms each age as it draws to a close. Of course, tradition and custom changes with each era, and the heroes must step up to meet them accordingly.

Taking into account the rather later introduction of shamanistic, ancestral cults into the Siberian early Iron Age cultures, than had been previously imagined,[357] the belief systems it subsumed, offer an intriguing key to animistic cognitive processes. A challenge to conventional thought asserts that our assumption of certain figures portrayed in several key examples of Neolithic Petroglyphs as shaman, is premature, and that the masked or horned figures are primary animistic spirits.[358] As a mediating traveller between the three realms of the world tree or pole as the axis mundi – by means of a spirit steed or drum, aided by the spirit doubles embodied in the iron and organic figures woven in the shamans' carefully constructed attire - this role clearly indicates a displacement of societal power around the beginning of the Iron Age. Furthermore, these changes reflect the shift in lifestyle and economy of these peoples, factors vital to the evolution of mythic tradition, belief and ritual practises. In this shift, at this time, I see the formation and rise of a figure of poesis and ecstatic frenzy, whose later name would reflect those traits, and who would become a mediator for

---

355. Wilhelm von Humboldt. 18th C. Prussian philosopher. **356.** Pandarus. Scene 1. William Shakespeare. "Troilus and Cressida." In, The Globe Shakespeare. Edited by W. G. Clark and W. Aldis Wright. (Nelson Doubleday Inc. 1960).https://www.litcharts.com/shakescleare/shakespeare-translations/troilus-and-cressida/act-1-scene-1 **357.** The appearance of the role of shaman within the Siberian communities arose much later than had been previously imagined, sometime in the second part of the first millennium BCE. See: Nikolaï D Mironov and S. M. Shirokogoroff,. "Sramana-Shaman: Etymology Of The Word Shaman." *In, Journal of the North China Branch of the Royal Asiatic Society. Vol. LV,* (Royal Asiatic Society. 1924): 105-130. **358.** Jacobson-Tepfer, 2015: 328

those of his cult. Birthed in the early Iron Age, this figure embodied the very essence of shamanism, recognisable still in the much later Vendel period, remaining without name and form until Christianity homogenised all the disparate variable virtues attributable to him as a named deity they could then demonise and diminish.

Like the devil, he had to first be constructed before he could be defeated. An idea cannot be crushed, but a 'god' can. This mantic, turbulent figure thus had many names and faces, all garnered under his one title, and qualified as epithets or heiti - an all-inclusive solution to eradicate a nebulous figure that had long defied direct identification. By placing an emphasis on the totemic, ancestral elements of lineage and initiation or adoption, the shaman became the effective voice for and of his people. Dreams, visions, seership and sorcery ceased to be a democratic practise, shifting to the cultic specialist, a core elitism eagerly embraced by male-oriented martial cults particularly.[359] Animistic spirits of the land or elements had no need of names, the words we know them by are merely descriptors of virtue or function, and were propitiated by myriad variations dependent upon native tongue and cultural perception. Thunder serves well enough as an example of how this elemental force is perceived through that cultural titling: *Þórr, Þunar, Teshoub, Rimmon*, and *Perkunas*. Curious Bronze Age thunderstones found in Viking Age burials attest to their significance as amulets or talismans that may be related to Þórr as the legendary spirit of this powerful elemental force.

Many Finno-Ugric peoples place an emphasis on the sky spirit as sky father; to the Nenets, he is *Num*; to the Khanty, he is *Num-Turom* and *Sängke*; to the Mansi, he is *Num-Tarom*; and to the various Sámi, he is known as *Tiermes, Horagalles*, and *Radien*, to name but a few. Amongst the Arctic Finno-Ugric peoples is a common belief in a host of invisible spirits, ranging from elementals to genii loci (landvættir), and the guardian spirits of hearth and home, not as a strict hierarchy as all spirits were deemed equally important, be they ancestral or weather related. Spirits above, of the sky, were no more important than those below, of the Underworld. It was more about their role. Everything had its place and purpose, and every area of life was safe-guarded. Pragmatism and need alone guided ritual practise, directed by seasons and circumstance.

---

359. From the nebulous mantic spirit of the Pontic Steppe, the anthropomorphic representation of frenzied possession would manifest in the now famous artworks discovered at Sutton Hoo and elsewhere, who centuries later would become immortalised in (Eddaic) poetic fiction as Óðinn.

These entities were not worshipped, but they were propitiated, and as part of the reciprocal relationship with them, certain obligations and duties were undertaken to maintain their goodwill in hunting or fishing, or their expertise in facing down crises. An overall, though distant Creatrix (often imagined as a nebulous entity who was manifest in the sacred reindeer, or elk) is also acknowledged, but in general, it was the spirits who governed their day to day needs that were most popular. Although this belief system falls under the purview of animism, which immediately democratises everyone's relationship with spirit, the northern peoples very much relied upon the services of ritual specialists, who were typically but not always, the shamans.[360]

As a reflection of this animistic yet pragmatic understanding of the Nenet world, language perfectly describes the nature, gender, and role of such spirits. For instance, the compound names of guardian spirits are formed of two elements, the first indicates the sphere of action and the second relates to gender: while Vu-murt refers to Water-man, Cheremis Pört-kuguza, means the Old Man of the House, and Pört-kuwa, is the Old Woman of the House. Herr der Tiere, is Master of Animals. Because their world was filled with only visible and invisible spirits, everything was considered alive in the truest sense of animism, a relationship with those who had passed on, was continued in spirit. Death does not bring separation. Ancestors are instantly approachable and reproachable for that matter, as judges, advisors, and guardians in matters relating to family. Ancestors are also venerated in diverse ways across the arctic and subarctic regions, in folk customs and in the form of shrines and effigies,[361] all developed purposefully to maintain these relationships associated with death itself, its preparation and burial, and to its commemoration and celebration.

Nevertheless, the Finno-Ugric peoples have had to be adaptive; acculturation and conversion (to Christianity and Islam) have shifted them from their origins considerably. Over time they have observed cumulative layers of traditional cyclic rites involving specific rites of passage, divination, staving of disasters, and issues of subsistence. Rites related to life, honoured the spirits of the South, while those related to death, focussed on the North.

---

360. See forthcoming unpublished ms., "Song of The North," by Shani Oates, which focusses on the shamanic practises of the Sámi and other northern peoples. **361**. Death effigies made by Nenet shamans are cherished, clothed and fed for up to three years, in rare cases, this could be extended for decades.

Part Two:
DEATH AND CREATION

INTRODUCTION to Part Two
Monumental Structures as Houses of the Dead

WHEN SEEKING to better understand a people's beliefs and culture, we look to the dead. The rituals surrounding transitions of souls into the next world reflect the complex nuances of the societies of the living. Sacred sites the world over, have monumental structures that commemorate the dead, reflecting how life and death become inexorably entwined, etched into the very fabric of the landscape that nurtures and sustains them in both the visible and the invisible realms. Accumulated layers of belief spanning many hundreds of years became embedded in the North Asian sacred sites and rock art of the Mongolian horse dependent cultures that dominated the regions of present-day Kazakhstan and southern Europe.[1] Rocky outcrops and boulders were carefully chosen for their size and shape as templates for the narratives of their folk history regarding totemic animals and the construction of sacred mounds.[2] Mountain shrines, composed of stones and sticks, were the locus of cultic attention, receiving dedications and offerings of food and drink for the genii loci (landvættir). These were established at specific wayfaring points of danger – on ridges and on passes and entrances to canyons - where travellers may encounter danger and would therefore require the assistance of indwelling spirits.

Ultimately, the rituals and beliefs of a people centred on the customs of life and death are hard to interpret from the archaeological record, where remnant objects and material remains often pose more questions than they solve. Material objects found within a remarkable series of burial mounds include astonishing ritual attire for people and for the animals buried alongside them.

---

[1]. During the Iron Age, early nomads from the Saiyan and Altai region encountered imperial expansion by Turk and Mongol tribes. [2]. Ovoo, also spelled Oboo.

124   PIRATES, MERCHANTS, DEVILS & DARK DEEDS

Rituals are the actions that can formalize religious beliefs. Rituals can also be a direct result of legitimizing a belief system, reinforcing a new, or altered, view of the world which also impacts political and economic interactions within a culture. Rituals can be representative of cosmological beliefs but also the "daily patterns of everyday life" and it is impossible to separate the two concepts.[3]

Every item in a tomb may indicate ritual activity, spiritual belief, cultural custom, or more typically, the simple pragmatisms of daily life. Naturally, these are again not mutually exclusive, and we are ill-equipped to qualify their exact purpose, placement and function in their societies. At best, we may recognise certain traits and motifs that may superficially appear to resemble those discovered elsewhere, mindful it does not mean their purpose was equal. By way of example, an embalming procedure undertaken for the body of the chieftain or king is strikingly similar to the treatment described of Mímir's skull in the Eddas, whereby it is cut open, cleaned out and packed with various herbs: "chopped marsh plants, incense, and parsley seed and anise" and then sewn back together.[4] The body was then placed on a wagon, which transported the embalmed body to another region in the east, prepared as the tomb for his eternal rest. Another similar ritual procedure is described by Herodotus following the death of an Issedonian tribal chieftain: "The dead man's head was then "laid bare," cleaned out, gilded and afterwards honoured as a "sacred image."[5] Comparable rituals were conducted in the Altai regions and across the Mongolian plains where:

> *(...) The king was placed in a "great four-cornered pit" on a bed with spears placed on either side of the body. The burial was closed with planks of wood and "plaited rushes" and before the final seal was put in place, a concubine was strangled and thrown in as well.*[6]

I believe these striking motifs may have sourced the tales composed by later travellers such as Ibn Fadlan, whose now famous description of a Rus' funeral has acquired its own legend.[7] Herodotus also refers

---

3. Kathryn Macfarland. Religion, Ritual Behaviour and Landscapes In Iron Age Central Eurasia. (The University of Arizona. 2010) Https://Www.Academia.Edu/8210983/Religion_Ritual_Behavior_And_Landscapes_In_Iron_Age_Central_Eurasia (Accessed 16th May 2021   **4.** Macfarland, 2010.   **5.** Ibid.   **6.** Ibid.   **7.** Ibn Fadlan's account is not that of an eye-witness. He was not privy to these events. Moreover, the translation of many Greek texts by Muslim Arabic scholars from the 8th century should not be overlooked here. Islamic scholars were more than familiar with the works of Herodotus and other historians, mathematicians and philosophers, long before they reached the western world, when Christian kings and clerics finally had access to them and commissioned their translation into Latin in later centuries.

INTRODUCTION TO PART TWO 125

to other funerary rituals involving wagons, this time undertaken by the Scythian peoples. Prior to burial, the closest relative transported the body on a wagon in a circular procession as they visited kith and kin for forty days, each of whom must receive and entertain all who follow in that train, being mindful to offer a portion of food to the deceased. Hospitality was a sacred tenet of old-world traditions. This process signified a rite of passage for the dead, of transit to another realm of spirits. Once the body was interred in the eastern regions of the landscape, all participants in the procession purified themselves by "anointing and washing their heads"[8] and their bodies in a sauna style sweat-lodge. A fire pit was dug out and filled with red-hot stones, over which hempseeds were cast. The ensuing vapour caused the Scythians to howl atavistically.

Censers and tripods found in the Pazyryk burials located in the Altai Mountains may corroborate this account. "The purification of the surviving family and friends could have been a way to allow the deceased to pass onto their next life, unhindered by ties to the living. It is also possible that these rites of passage were preventing the defilement of the living by the dead."[9] Many of the discovered artefacts better relate to household and land spirits similar in function to the Roman Lares, who are amongst the numerous unnamed figures found in abundance at the domestic level. These are distinct from the state gods of the imperial pantheon, which are equally distinct from what are commonly perceived of as similar or cognate forms within other cultures. For instance, it is very difficult to dissociate reality from the hyperbolic media associations that unabashedly list deific forms as Þórr, Týr, Freyr and Óðinn, and worse, the images of various artefacts they are automatically identified with, without any provenance whatsoever. This problem of misappropriation is rooted in our over familiarity with myths composed hundreds of years after all of them (with the exception of Þórr) that ceased to be relevant to actual pagans and heathens.

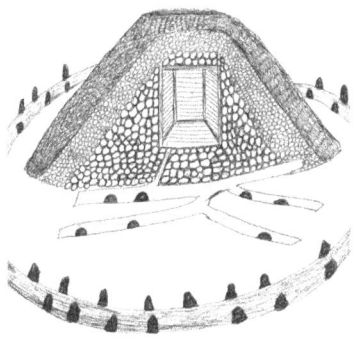

1. Houses of the dead – Kurgan Mound

---

8. Macfarland, 2010. **9.** Ibid.

ANCESTRAL MARKERS – CULTIC SITES

A group of native (Türkic speaking) people from Western Siberia (Oblast, Russia), known as the Teleuts (historically considered as part of the Kazak nationality), lived near the inhospitable Altai mountains in conic yurts made out of bark wood.[10] Following a semi – nomadic ancestral cult, their cosmogonical beliefs were typically animistic, incorporating a cosmological shamanic practise that perceives a flat earth above which, 16 layers exist, each featuring its own guardian spirit.[11] Peaking above these, a 'higher' divine female spirit rules all. Like many others native and non-native to these regions, the Teleuts of Siberia and the Altai have long been hunters and livestock herders of horses, goats, cattle, and sheep.

This relationship with horses would appear to be of long-standing. Reaching across from the east of the southern Ural Mountains to the northern Eurasian steppe (north Kazakhstan), the Bronze Age Sintashta culture (named after the fortified site in this same region of Chelyabinsk Oblast, in Russia), indicates an eastward migration of peoples from the Corded Ware culture, whose main industry here was copper-mining for metalworking. Animal sacrifice (mainly horse) is evident in over three-quarters of the burials in this region. Horse-drawn carts were found alongside the sacrificed beasts in high-status kurgans, claimed by some as the earliest recorded in the world. Should this be proven, it suggests progressive development from the wagon burials of the earlier Yamnaya culture.

Other traditions from the arctic regions of Siberia which may have sourced the myths that influenced the authors of the Eddas, reside with

---

10. Their language is classified as a southern dialect of the Altay language, though the Teleuts consider themselves to be a distinct people and many don't accept being labelled as Altaian. The Teleuts emerged from the intermarriages between the Kipchaks and Mongols. See: *Encyclopaedia of the World's Minorities.* Edited by Carl Skutsch and Martin Ryle. (Routledge, 2005): 82-83 **11.** Many of these traditional nomadic, shamanic societies were gradually lost in the process of the enforced Christianization of the population towards the end of the 19th century, lingering longer in peripheral regions.

the Khanty people of the former USSR, in Western Siberia. Like those mentioned by Snorre, their universe is also composed around three vertical tiers: the upper (sky) world, the middle (earth) world, and an Underworld beneath it. When transposed onto a horizontal plane, the Underworld is equated with the cold north and the upper world with the south. The dead are interred in dug-out canoes (a common theme it would seem), whose souls travel northwards down the river to the Underworld. It is worth noting here the marked similarity to a concept referred to in Norse mythology regarding Niflheimr,[12] particularly as archaeological evidence suggests this western Siberian practice may be roughly dated to around 700 CE.

Supernatural beings inhabit all realms, appearing in all forms and genders, anthropomorphic or zoomorphic, many of which are deemed fairly generic, except for the genii loci. Spirits of place were approached and propitiated in much the same way as the Germanic land-wights and the Scandinavian landvættir, with gifts, offerings, sacrifice and prayers. In daily life, the most influential of these spirits are the local or clan spirits.[13] In accordance with the North/South axial cosmology noted above, sacred sites where the local land guardian spirits live, are always upstream of Khanty settlements; conversely, the tombs of the dead are always located downstream. Communication with the spirit world was later mediated through the shamans, whose role among the Khanty is primarily to restore order, and to banish chaos through its manifestations within the tribe as sickness and ill-luck.

Shamans and other ritual specialists were called upon to conduct rites for the community, while the male and female heads of each family were generally responsible for conducting simple but distinct rites for their own purposes. Among the Sámi Cultic sites (Sieidi) were zoned accordingly for men, women, or community. As nomadic

---

12. The word *Niflheimr* – meaning land of mist and cloud – is only found in the Gylfaginning and the much-debated Hrafnagaldur Óðins, and is often used interchangeably with Niflhel, a poetic embellishment of Hel (the realm of the dead) found in Old Norse poems that are much older than those two works. Niflheimr is almost certainly an invention of the author of those two works, normally credited to Snorre. See: Rudolf Simek. *Dictionary of Northern Mythology*. Translated by Angela Hall (D. S. Brewer. [1993] 2000): 232. *nebh- Proto-Indo-European root meaning cloud. It forms all or part of: nebula; nebular; nebulosity; nebulous; Neptune; Nibelungenlied; Niflheimr; nimbus. The hypothetical source of/evidence for its existence is provided by: Sanskrit nabhas- vapor, cloud, mists, fog, sky; Greek nephele, nephos cloud; Latin nebula mist, vapor, fog, smoke, exhalation; German Nebel fog; Old English nifol dark, gloomy; Welsh niwl cloud, fog; Slavic nebo: https://www.etymonline.com/search?q=nifol (Accessed 18th July 2021)   13. Peter Jordan. *Material Culture and Sacred Landscape: The Anthropology of the Siberian Khanty*, (AltaMira Press, 2003): 137

peoples, Ob Ugrian dwellings and shrines were transported with them on their seasonal expeditions on special sledges. Nomadic peoples maintain a very unique relationship with the land that is seasonal and cyclical. In many respects it is no less intense, nor expressive than how peoples rooted to fixed locations relate to their environment. Moving between specific areas or regions renders the landscape no less sacred, and indeed, sharing stories and memories linked to them, affirms a significant relationship with, and reverence for, the land itself, and the spirits housed within and upon it. Over time, as people in some regions (in the north-east especially),[14] became more sedentary, ritual specialists evolved their roles to elevate their importance as officiating 'priests,' whose exclusive skills came at a premium. Seasonal, outdoor sanctuaries or Luds (sacred groves) and Sieidi sites were developed as open temple-like structures,[15] or were eventually abandoned in favour of enclosed hofs and cultic buildings. Carved images on wood and stone were reported present in the groves by the earliest travellers to these regions, not of gods, as was incorrectly assumed, but of ancestral spirits. The eastern Finns and the Ugrians similarly venerated their ancestral dead, sometimes representing them as polycephalic (multiple-headed) wooden posts.[16]

Far to the north, beyond the Steppe, beyond the taiga, beyond even the tundra, there is an Island sanctuary that bears many cairns raised for the dead, a frozen necropolis void of trees and the living. This holy Vaygach Island was once a sacred funerary complex for the Nenets people living there; Vaygach appropriately means 'territory of death.' Scandinavian skalds imagined these remote Northerly islands were inhabited by strange spirits and otherworldly creatures. They composed sagas and songs about these islands (Vaygach and Yugoria), as Jötunheimr.

Other similar cultic sites existed in the Central, Northern and Polar Urals are associated with wooden idols. Using descriptions and logs composed by travellers and ethnographers, we are able to gain some insight into the beliefs of the circumpolar peoples,[17] and to form an idea of the ritual practises that might have taken place on this sacred Island, which was taboo to both women and outsiders. Of some relevance to this

---

14. The Volga Finns and the Permians for example. **15.** Leszek Słupecki."West Slavic Pagan Ritual As Described At The Beginning Of The Eleventh Century.' In, Old Norse Religion In Long-Term Perspectives: Origins, Changes, and Interactions: An international Conference in Lund, Sweden, June 3-7. 2004. Edited by A. Andrén; K. Jennbert; C. Raudvere. (Nordic Academic Press, 2006): 224-28 **16.** Bente Magnus, *Men, Gods and Masks-in Nordic Iron Age Art, Ten thousand years of folk art in the North*; Nordic Iron Age Art 1, (Cologne: König, 2006).

ANCESTRAL MARKERS - CULTIC SITESS

region and to this display of ancestral cultic markers, is the giant Shigir pre-historic sculpture. Found in a Russian bog, it is some 12000 years old, making it the oldest wooden effigy or totem[18] in the world. This smooth iconic piece is covered with human faces and hands that may represent ancestral figures. Standing over five metres high, it bears comparison to the 10500 years old stone balbal totem found at Gobleki Tepi in Turkey.[19]

Thousands of years later, animistic tribal societies continued to revere totems in the form of poles, pillars or plank-like sculptures that are comparable to the sacred Irminsul structure that has otherwise evaded satisfactory explanation. Several Iron Age cultic images discovered in peat bogs across Central and Northern Europe, affirm a long-standing function of belief amongst Celtic speaking peoples.[20] This trend extends further northwards and eastwards. Other wooden anthropomorphic figures were also found in the West Slavic settlement areas around the Elbe.[21] Saxo Grammaticus describes the Temple at Arkona as containing a great four-headed idol, far taller than a man.[22] Although there is evidence to suggest that some wooden pole idols may originate in the Mesolithic through to the Bronze Age, the influential trend to anthropomorphise wooden idols and pole figures[23] did not reach the Eastern Slavic regions until the much later 10th century.[24]

Sacred trees such as the Geismar Oak and the

2. Shigir

---

17. Archaeological context determined by descriptions and analysis of materials from the pagan shrine Bolvanskii Nos I on Vaygach Island. **18.** The Ojibwe word for clan (doodem) was borrowed into English as totem. A totem is a spirit being or sacred object that serves as a cultic focus for a specific group of people, such as a family, clan, lineage, or tribe. See: Shani Oates. *The Search for Odinn, From Pontic Steppe to Sutton Hoo.* (Anathema Publishing. 2022). **19.** See: https://tepetelegrams.wordpress.com/2017/03/01/the-gobekli-tepe-totem-pole/ (Retrieved 12 April 2021).
20. Miranda J. Aldhouse Green. *An Archaeology of Images: Iconology and Cosmology in Iron Age and Roman Europe.* (Routledge, 2004): 60 **21.** For example, the temple finds from Groß Raden (now part of Sternberg) and Ralswiek and those from Neubrandenburg, all in Mecklenburg-Vorpommern, and Altfriesack (now part of Fehrbellin, Brandenburg).
22. Saxo Grammaticus, Gesta Danorum 14.39. See: Saxo Grammaticus: Gesta Danorum: *The History of the Danes,* Vol. 1. Edited by Karsten Friis-Jensen. (Oxford University Press; Oxford Medieval Texts, 2015). **23.** Rudolf Simek. "Pole gods." *Dictionary of Northern Mythology.* (D. S. Brewer, 2000): 258 **24.** Sebastian Brather. *Archeology of the Western Slavs: Siedlung, Wirtschaft and Gesellschaft in early and high medieval Eastern Mediterranean Europe,* 2nd ed., Reallexikon der Germanischen Altertumskunde, Ergänzungsband 61 (De Gruyter, 2008): 320-325 (in German).

Donnar's Oak, are mentioned in chronicles and penitentials as crude tree trunks erected in the open air. Other significant wooden Idols, or rather, totems, include the ithyphallic wooden figure found in Broddenbjerg, Jutland, (535 BCE to 520 BCE); the pair of female figures from Oberdoria, Thuringia, Germany, the very different flat stake panel male and female pairs found at Wittemoor Timber Trackway, Berne, Lower Saxony. Other similar ancestral wooden post images are the Braak (forked stick) bog effigies[25] found in Bavaria (Suevi territory) dated to the 3rd to 2nd century BCE.[26] An oakwood figure known as the 'Ballachulish Goddess,' dated around 520 CE to 730 CE, was found in Argyll, Scotland. Despite spanning a period of two to three thousand years, I believe that in principle, symbolism and function, these wooden totems are not dissimilar to the ancestral polycephalic posts of the Nenets (Samoyed) peoples of Siberia.

Looking again at the information relating to the Volga Vikingr as relayed in Ibn Fadlan's early 10th-Century account, we are told of the curious ritual conducted by alighting seamen upon their successful return to harbour involving offerings of food and alcohol, to a roughly carved pole effigy. "This piece of wood has a face like the face of a man and is surrounded by small figurines behind which are long pieces of wood set up in the ground."[27]

Fadlan's description sounds remarkably similar to a fine example of a sieidi shrine,[28] observed in the form of the seven-faced wooden effigy of Vesako, and recorded along with other cultic structures (khekhe), [29] by a 16th century English navigator while exploring the region. On behalf of the Muscovy Company,[30] Steven Borough visited Russia in 1556 CE, seeking a northern passage to India. Borough described them as "the worst and the most unartificial worke that ever I saw." [31] He further recorded how: "the eyes and mouthes of sundrie of them were bloodie, they had the shape of men, women and children, very

---

25. Similar to the nine- foot wooden stick figure from Foerlev Nymölle, Denmark, and the later post figure at Rebild, Skovhuse, Denmark, both female. **26.** Most of the figures which have been preserved are of oak, which was probably preferred for its endurance in the mostly wet locations where they were deposited. **27.** James E. Montgomery. "Ibn Fadlan and the Rusiyyah." Journal of Arabic and Islamic Studies 3, 2000. DOI: https://doi.org/10.5617/jais.4553 **28.** A principal spirit crudely carved from natural materials, namely, wood or even stone. **29.** According to the Brockhaus and Efron dictionary, the wooden Vesako stood surrounded by 20 medium-sized idols, 400 smaller wooden ones, and 20 varied stone idols stood 50 'sazhens' from the main idol. https://tourism.arctic-russia.ru/en/sights/vaygach-state-nature-reserve/ (Retrieved 10th August 2024). **30.** See: https://www.rbth.com/history/331675-how-siberia-was-once-separate-country (Retrieved 12th August 2024).

ANCESTRAL MARKERS – CULTIC SITES

grosly wrought, and that with they had made for other parts, was also sprinckled with blood."[32]

Three hundred years later, 19th-century missionaries described this ancestral totem and polycephalic figure as an ancient wooden god accompanied by his demonic horde. Equally horrified by the sight of fresh reindeer blood amongst the piles of stones, skulls (of bear and deer), bones and driftwood, the missionaries destroyed almost all of them.[33] These cultic structures (khekhe) were the Arctic equivalents of the Ovoo cairns of Mongolia. According to local history records, Vesako originally stood on Vaygach, the Island of the Dead. It now stands on the smaller satellite island – Bolshoi Tsinkovy, where it and several replica cairns are maintained by the Nenets people who believe that its removal here brought a curse upon those involved.

Before their enforced and difficult conversion in the 19th century, Vaygach was once the sacred cultic centre for Nenet hunters who honoured their sacred ancestral sites (khebidia ia) in seasonal rites of pilgrimage centred on survival and sacrifice while eking out a grim existence on these bleak Islands. For many centuries, the Nenet people of Siberia had believed in a benevolent male creator, a great spirit of the sky named Num, commonly known as the 'Old Man.' His son, Nga, was lord of the Underworld, a chthonic domain of the dead (and later, of chaos and strife).[34]

As supreme spirits, Num and Nga are comparable to the Tengri and Erlik spirits of the peoples in the regions further to the south where the Khanty and Mansi peoples resided. However, there were signs that two main shrines received sacrificial offerings; in addition to Vesako, on the southern point of the island, another shrine existed in the north to Hadako (Khadako). It should be noted that in keeping with many animistic peoples, descriptive titles or functional epithets are awarded their spirits, who are not otherwise named. Vesako, simply means Old man (of the south); Khadako means Old Woman (of the north), the Mother of Animals to whom they offered sacrifices for successful hunting or fishing.

---

31. See: Nenets: https://www.arcticrussiatravel.com/nenets-autonomous-okrug/ (Accessed 11th June 2021). **32.** Ibid. **33.** Nenets transported smaller totems around with them on sleds that were kept in their chums (tents), and were subject to strict taboos. Believed to have too much powerful energy already, post-pubescent women could not approach them. These ancestral totems wore clothing which was replaced each year. **34.** Post conversion, these two spirits were placed in opposition as dualistic entities.

"The main female deity is represented not by hand-made idols, but by a work of nature: an elongated stone at the top of a rock."[35]

After the wanton destruction of their major tribal totems and ancestral cairns on Vaygach, the Nenet peoples were converted to Christianity, initiating a massive cultural shift that led to the wholesale abandonment of their former existence here. Until the Soviet era, Vaygach remained uninhabited. Russians still refer to these Islands as the Midnight Lands.

Since the end of the Viking Age in the 11thcentury CE, the Nenets (Samoyds) have traded furs (mainly sable) with Russians for metal objects they otherwise had no access to. Towards the end of the 15th century, Russian sailors founded an early trading post in Siberia on the Taz estuary across from the Yamal Peninsula. Towns and fortresses soon followed during the 16th century, encroaching upon the previous solitude enjoyed by the nomadic Nenets (Samoyed), who lived only in tents (chums). After these invasive settlements, all former peaceful trading ceased, as the Russians implemented aggressive demands for heavy tribute in sable, arctic fox, polar bear and wolf pelts. Forced into meeting brutal levies, the peoples of Siberia began witnessing their hunter/gatherer life-style and cultural identity slowly disappearing as they struggled to make their quotas. Hunting became mass slaughter. There was no reciprocity, no spirituality, no relationship with the land in this rape of resources.

Since at least the 14th century, and possibly earlier, they had domesticated the reindeer for sled pulling and hunting. Nomadic reindeer herding became an increasing necessity in the 17th century; some tribes broke away and headed further north into the arctic tundra to escape this erosion of culture, following the decreasing herds on their natural migration routes. Russian trading posts and settlements did not reach the Yamal Peninsula until the 1920s, at which point, conversions were almost completed.[36] Those who had travelled the farthest north into the Yamal Peninsula, held out the longest, and there are some Nenets today who fiercely declare themselves to be non-Christian. Nonetheless, because of the dissolution of their former way of life and the invasive actions by Russians into Nenets lands, the Nenets believe the Russians are the children of Nga.[37]

---

35. https://tourism.arctic-russia.ru/en/sights/vaygach-state-nature-reserve/ (Retrieved 10th August 2024) **36.** See: Nenets: https://www.yamalpeninsulatravel.com/who-are-the-nenets/ (Accessed 12th June 2021). **37.** Ibid. "Under Soviet collectivisation, nearly all the reindeer were confiscated, and Nenets were forced to work for state camps. Today, most have returned to their traditional way of life while those who remain in state camps favour them for the security offered."

ANCESTRAL MARKERS – CULTIC SITES   133

It seems the proto-Samoyed (Nenet) people had migrated to the arctic during the 1st millennium BCE, from the Altai-Sayan region near Mongolia, merging through inter-marriage with the Sikhirtya, an aboriginal people of the Yamal region, renowned for their short stature and extraordinary appearance. According to legend, the Sikhirtya became marginalised, shunted into liminal regions, mainly caves and deep fissures, inducing many tales of their otherworldly existence. The superstitious Nenets still believe those brutal, subterranean places maintain traces of the region's oldest inhabitants – the Sikhirtya (also as Sirtya). Known as 'little people,' whose distinctive speech pattern evinced a slight stutter, they are the "supernatural beings who were also skilled blacksmiths,[38] jewellers, fishers, and hunters [...] emerging [only] at night or under fog,"[39] to practise their magics. These photophobic, pale-skinned, fair-haired, white(blue)-eyed dwarvish people, were also famed for their beautiful clothing and a passion for metal jewellery.

The existence of such curious folk is supported by archaeological traces of fishers and smiths in the remote tundra of Siberia, via a name that "comes from the 'sipyr' – a people who lived in the Nenets tundra beyond the polar circle. [...] better known as the 'Sikhirtya.'"[40] Unlike the reindeer herding Nenets, it is believed that the Sikhirtya herded 'earth deer'– or mammoths." Again, this folklore was not without its influences that clearly reached the Norse peoples through trade and patterns of migration.

In the circumpolar north, parallels can be made between the Siberian Sikhirtya and the Inuit Inuralaat, mischievous little people of whom stories are passed down through oral culture. Like Sikhirtya, Inuralaat were derived from a real culture – the Thule people – smaller statured humans who lived in the Canadian Arctic thousands of years ago preceding Inuit.[41]

Extraordinary encounters with such alluring and seductive folk appear similar to the myths of the beautiful *Huldufölk*, a mysterious (and in some accounts, dark-haired) hidden people believed to be the elves

---

38. Artefacts of bronze castings of animals (bear, wolf, eagle, boar) are unearthed in the sacred sanctuaries of the Khanty, Mansi, and Nenets. **39.** See: https://feheleyfinearts.com/sikhirtya-figures-from-siberia/ (Retrieved 12th August 2024) **40.** Since the Bronze Age, consecutive waves of peoples migrated and settled in Siberia. The Siberian Tatars evolved from the merging of Iranian, Türkic and native Ugric tribal peoples who were all subjugated at the beginning of the 13th century by Genghis Khan's Mongol Empire. The Khanate he established controlled the trade routes from Asia to Europe. See: https://www.rbth.com/history/331675-how-siberia-was-once-separate-country (Retrieved 12th August 2022). **41.** Ibid.

of Icelandic and Faroese folklore. "Oral tales concerning Icelandic elves and Trölls no doubt served as warning fables. They prevented many children from wandering away from human habitations, taught Iceland's topographical history, and instilled fear and respect for the harsh powers of nature."[42] Norse folklore is of course replete with tales of various peoples of the Otherworld, all of whom share similar attributes and abilities relating to magics, spells and other beliefs discouraged and disparaged by Christianity. In some Nenets legends, seeing a Sirtya by chance could bring intense joy, but also suffering. Sirtya were capable of both. It is said they often stole children and were always ready with a curse, and yet, they were often a friend (and spirit guide) to many shamans. Academic and popular opinion vary quite dramatically regarding these denizens of the Otherworld, ranging from ancestral to nature spirits, and from distinct races of people to witches; historically speaking, however, these beings are essentially alike. Politics, religion and ethnicity mark the variables. "It is the trope of our times to locate the question of culture in the realm of the beyond," and yet, "A boundary is not that at which something stops but, as the Greeks recognized, the boundary is that from which something begins its presencing,"[43] therefore all inexplicable things exist on that liminal bridge.

Artefacts recovered from Bronze Age sites across the arctic regions have filled Siberian museums with archaic pottery, beautiful metal pendants and carved bone tools by peoples as yet unidentified, but whose profiles strongly resemble those of the Sirtya. A 15th-Century journal belonging to French explorers of the Arctic regions of Russia, records their encounters with a strange, non-Samoyed race, short in stature, attired in white polar bear fur, whose dwellings are imaginatively described as composed of moss and fishbones. Caves discovered in the tundra naturally reveal signs of ancient habitation. Nenet artists continue to immortalise these ethereal beings in their wistful etchings on antler bone, portraying the Sirtya residing in their chums, adorned with intricate jewellery, guarding their mounds or herding their hoary mammoths. Unsurprisingly, in the cosmology of the Sirtya folk, we encounter again the three worlds of Nenet shamans – upper, middle, and lower –[44] that in turn reflect a similar cosmological template ascribed to the three worlds of Proto-Indo-European myth: *Bhudhnon*

---

42. Ólína Thorvarðardóttir. "Spirits of the Land: A Tool for Social Education." *Bookbird* 37 (4) 1999: 34 **43.** Martin Heidegger, quoted by Homi Bhabha, in *The Location of Culture*, (Routledge,1994). **44.** See: https://inuit.com/pages/sirtya-mysterious-race (Retrieved 12th February 2025)

ANCESTRAL MARKERS – CULTIC SITES 135

("Bottom"), *Médhyom* ("Middle"), and *Weis* ("Air").[45] Médhyom, or Middle- Earth is cognate with the Norse Midgarðr.

Nenet reindeer bone carvings of the small white arctic dwarves are almost identical in appearance to the Dagenheim idol, England, 2459 BCE to 2110 BCE, and to the Bronze Age female figurines from Skåne, Blekinge and Våstergötland, Sweden. It can be observed how they all bear the strange, hooped rings about them, very similar to those that decorate some early bracteates.[46] There are very clear patterns of association between these elements of belief across Scandinavia, Fennoscandia and Eurasia that should not be ignored when constructing origins for the myths we see in the Eddas.

---

45. Gamkrelidze and Ivanov, 1994; 405, 408-409   **46.** See: Oates, 2022.

COFFIN BOATS AND BOAT BURIALS

During the last part of the Mesolithic period, dugout boats (crude canoes) were sometimes used as coffins or even lids in certain burials. At the early underwater burial site at Møllegabet, in the Funen archipelago, a boat was discovered that contained the skeletal remains of a young adult male who was covered with a layer of birch bark shavings before he was buried under water, close by his settlement.[47] This process may demonstrate early boat burials in Scandinavia, and is remarkably similar to some Sámi tree trunk dug out burials. Recent archaeology is now realising that more and more Viking Age sites are exhibiting traits that identify them as Sámi, and not Scandinavian. Nonetheless, other issues add to problems of identification.

Normally, differences in location, morphology, body treatment, and funerary objects separate Old Norse graves from Sámi graves. The former generally date from the pre-Roman Iron-Age period to the mid-11th century CE, and mostly comprise prominently placed stone-constructed burial mounds (ie cairns). From the Viking period, male graves contain weapons and tools while female graves contain jewellery and housewares, but there are gender variations and status differences. Collectively, funerary objects demonstrate wide contacts between Hálogaland and the Continent, the British Isles, and Eastern Europe, as well as the Old Norse Finnmark and other Fennoscandian regions.[48]

A boat-burial mound in a shallow bog on Skogøya Island (Nordland, Norway) that contained an Old Norse Viking Age axe, also shows traces of birch bark under the boat. The boat itself exhibits seam sewing comparable to that of verified Sámi boat burials, making this burial's ethnicity somewhat ambiguous.[49] Whether this burial is

---

47. The remains of dugout boats are typically found at excavations in waterlogged, environments, often pet-bogs where wood is easily preserved. **48.** A. Svestad. "Buried in Between: Re-interpreting the Skjoldehamn Medieval Bog Burial of Arctic Norway." Medieval Archaeology, 65(2) (2021): 286-321. https://doi.org/10.1080/00766097.20 21.1997202 (2021) (Retrieved 24th July 2024). **49.** Svestad, 2021. Has several more examples of both Sámi and Old Norse graves that exhibit similar customs to each other

COFFIN BOATS AND BOAT BURIALS 137

Old Norse, displaying Sámi influences or vice versa, those influences show irrevocable proof of the extent of their social interactions. These customs diverged considerably in the Middle Ages when Christianity introduced new customs associated with Scandinavian burial rites.[50] Other Viking and pre-Viking Age Boat burials (some of which are cremations) at Lindholm Høje in Denmark, feature amongst the 700 burial mounds, that include numerous 'stone ships.' As symbolic structures they perhaps signify the deceased's voyage to the afterlife and indicate the importance of sea-faring continuously through to the Viking Age.

Certain features noted here clearly influenced the development of the much later Birka burials in Sweden and the boat burials of the Rus', made famous by the later accounts of the Islamic traveller, ambassador and information gatherer, Ibn Fadlan whose account of a Rus' boat burial has entered into legend. As a very specific cultural trait of Northern European peoples observed in their migrations and travels across Northern Europe, Asia and Russia, ship burials endured for many hundreds of years. Movement and migration were major factors in the early development of European peoples to the extent that many of them acquired their names in association with this movement. For example, the Langobard eponym for Germanic peoples simply means foreign travellers (note, not 'long beards'). Early Germanic exiles or travellers in Ireland were often identified by the term loinges, preserved in the name of Ireland's former national airline, Aer Lingus, meaning an – airborne – vessel of foreign travellers. A person who operates a ship (a mariner) is Loingseach, from which we get lynch and the lynch pins – the long nails used to join the boards for the hull.

Sharing a predilection for stone constructions, the burials of both Old Norse and Sámi peoples are nonetheless placed differently within the landscape. For instance, Sámi graves generally make use of natural features that are often concealed under slabs or wall cavities near to large bodies of water, a feature which differentiates Sámi burial customs from Old Norse burials, in that the latter typically expressed a preferential use of cairns or shallow inhumation graves. Of course, there are exceptions in each case, and we are more certain of the "unique burial features [that] include the shrouding or winding of the corpse in birch bark sewn with reindeer-sinew thread, and/ or placement in a pulka (North Sámi: geres)" – a sled.[51] I find this immensely significant given that we know that traditions and customs

---

50. Ibid. wooden coffins slowly replaced boat and birch bark burials. 51. Svestad, 2021.

surrounding Sámi funerary rites continued almost unchanged for over 2500 years (900 BCE to 1600/1700CE).[52] So, while it is stated that the use of sleds is "only known for certain since the Viking period," the fact that sleds are depicted in the reems of pre-historic Fennoscandian rock art suggests otherwise. Sleds were of course a versatile form of transport and would have been used for transporting many things other than providing burials for bodies.

Birch bark appears in burial contexts of various and/or mixed ethnic affiliations from the Merovingian period to the High Middle Ages. Other intriguing finds are recorded in several of the prominent Swedish Merovingian-period to Viking-Age ship burials of Vendel and Valsgärde (both of which have parallels to the Sutton Hoo ship burial), where birch-bark 'rugs' or 'shrouding' were sewn with sinew-threads. This indicates Sámi interactions with the uppermost Old Norse elite in southern Scandinavia. It is worth remembering that birch-bark shrouding sewn with sinew-thread is probably the most distinct feature of Sámi burial customs.[53]

Excavations at a huge grave field site,[54] have revealed an individual shrouded in birch-bark, which (as noted above) is a typical Sámi burial custom in historical times. Bone analysis of the 12th century skeletal remains found in a richly furnished grave (no 9) has determined it to be biologically male, and despite this, "the Vivallen individual has been interpreted as a gender-mixing shaman, possibly belonging to Sámi culture."[55] His grave "contained several female objects in addition to male objects, such as a necklace of 36 pearls, a silver brooch, a needle case, and a linen tunic similar to those found in female graves at the Swedish Birka cemetery of the Viking period. Another skeletally determined male grave at Vivallen also contained mixed-gender objects."[56] There are rare cases where biological males found in Scandinavian graves have been purposefully buried with feminine clothing and jewellery in order to humiliate them in death. These individuals could be strangers, outcasts, magic-workers, etc.[57]

Moreover, in another very similar grave site known as the Suontaka burial, the grave goods of this individual who was originally cast as an

---

52. Ibid 53. Ibid. 54. The Vivallen cemetery in Härjedalen is a medieval province of Norway, though now in mid-Sweden. 55. See: Ulla Moilanen; Tuija Kirkinen; Saari Nelli-Johanna; Adam Rohrlach; Johannes Krause; Päivi Onkamo and Elina Salmela,. (Eds.) "A Woman with a Sword? – Weapon Grave at Suontaka Vesitorninmäki, Finland." European Journal of Archaeology 25 (2021).10.1017/eaa.2021.30. https://www.researchgate.net/publication/353260449_A_Woman_with_a_Sword_-_Weapon_Grave_at_Suontaka_Vesitorninmaki_Finland. 56. Svestad, 2021. 57. Moilanen et al, 2021.

elderly woman, contains both female and male artefacts (sword and jewellery).[58] This person was certainly wealthy and well connected. Furs and other fine grave goods and the manner of care taken in the burial confirm their high (and possibly revered) status. "Jewellery, particularly of Finnish, Karelian and East-Baltic origin, appears in graves from the Viking Age to the Late Middle Ages, which again indicates the Sámi's close contact with these regions."[59]

Boundaries between burial sites are not always clear. Mixed grave sites occur where we find heathen and Christian, Sámi and Norse people in very similar burials with little to differentiate between them. This hybridization may resolve certain anomalies of transition and of interrelational influences, which is an important feature of culture to realise, but it should not remove the distinctions between them that formulate their cultural and ethnic identities. Cultural hybridity is not unique to the northern regions, but occurs across supposed geographical boundaries, that in the old world, were considerably more fluid. "When inter-ethnic involvements become significant, they would probably result in a conspicuous blend of features, especially if boundaries and power structures were under pressure of dissolution or demolition."[60]

Clothing tends to indicate sex and certain cultural traits, but again, nothing is rigid and a considerable amount of flexibility is evident amongst both Scandinavian (Nordic) and Sámi traditions. However, certain colours, patterns, embroideries and braids "indicate a distinct ethnic and possibly Sámi affiliation."[61] During the Middle Ages, Sámi clothing for men and women were likewise very similar and were markedly comparable to the tunics and baggy trousers worn by men in Denmark and the southern regions of Scandinavia. Disputes concerning ethnic and gender identities have generated questions regarding the 20th century methods used to determine the sex, cultural and possible ethnic origin of bodies found in curious localities, and have led to the re-examination of many once initially determined as Swedish (Old Norse).

Refinements and advancements in the DNA analysis of the human remains are able to overturn some former borderline assumptions; dating techniques are similarly being re-evaluated. Indeed, the controversial 11th-Century Skjoldehamn body is exemplary in this. Discovered in Arctic Norway the Skjoldehamn grave "contained a fully

---

58. The Suontaka individual may exhibit symptoms of Klinefelter syndrome. See: Moilanen et al, 2021. **59.** Svestad, 2021. **60.** Svestad, 2021. **61.** Ibid.

clothed skeleton wrapped in a wool blanket, lashed with leather straps and tin ring-ornamented woven bands. The body was laid on a reindeer pelt, which in turn was placed on sticks of birch."[62] Great care was obviously given to the person in this burial, and although it was initially suggested this body was "non-Sámi and possibly an Old Norse / Norwegian woman,"[63] needful "re-examinations of the [Skjoldehamn] grave finds suggest a blend of Old Norse and Sámi features, as well as pagan and possible Christian features"[64] in the Viking and Early Middle Ages.

Certainly, the intriguing "blend of Old Norse and Sámi burial features, including aspects such as orientation, body position, furnishing, and proximity to Old Norse burial mounds, rather indicates a transitional hybrid burial." This new knowledge now offers a better perspective for understanding such overlapping complexities and better "challenges previous mono-cultural interpretations."[65] Cultural hybridisation is also evident in "graves from other regions of Fennoscandia in both its northern and southern parts, as well as in relation to changes in religion and cultural landscapes." The dating has been reassessed "at the point of transition between the [heathen] Viking period and the [Christian]Nordic early medieval period, with dates ranging from 890 CE to 1224 CE."[66] With regard to the Skjoldehamn grave, and others mentioned here like it, we must fully appreciate the socio/political and religious context for its deposition. It was an era of transition, of flux, on all levels. The world began to shrink as latent nation states slowly emerged.

According to the written records, there are possible indications of small pockets of Christianised Sámi present in eastern Norway in the Early Middle Ages, which ties in very well with some examples of birch-bark shrouding (albeit without sinew-thread) that were excavated in some of the oldest 10th to 12th century graves at St Clemens churchyard in Oslo, and of several 11th to 12th century graves found at Bø in Telemark (southern Norway). Along with the ambiguous finds at the Haug cemetery, this demonstrates very well the ambiguity of many grave sites across Scandinavia and Fennoscandia, which may represent Norwegian, Sámi, or hybrid burials customs from heathen, or Christian Sámi admixtures. As Christianisation took a firm hold in Norway (and Fennoscandia), there is an observable decline in the use

---

62. Ibid.   **63**. Ibid.   **64**. Ibid.   **65**. Ibid.   **66**. According to Svestad, "There is little indication that the grave is directly related to the late Bronze-Age (1100 BCE to 500 BCE) Scandinavian or north-western European bog-burial tradition." See: Svestad, 2021.

of birch bark in burial contexts that remained only in Sámi graves. Attempts to unify Norway through Christianity as a monolithic religion evidently generated a new dynamic of faith that contributed to the curious anomalies and inconsistencies discovered in the burial record. The puzzling features of the Skjoldehamn burial are almost certainly a product of cultural hybridisation. While this view does not dismiss possibilities of cross-gendered grave occupants, it does challenge them, suggesting perhaps that such views might better reflect a 21st century paradigm being projected backwards. However, the possibility that some of the more prominent burials might be of noaidi, ritual practitioners or shamans, remains undiminished.

In Old Norse society both non-Sámi and Sámi wore 'magical' clothes. The magic tunic of the Háleygir chieftain Tore Hund from Bjarkøy Island, yet another neighbour to Andøya Island, is notable. It appears from Sigvat the Skald's poem Erfidrápa that the Sámi made the tunic that protected Tore in the famous battle with King Óláf Haroldsson at Stiklestad in Trønderlag in 1030 CE, the incident that ostensibly led to the final breakthrough of Christianity in Norway. The poem underlines the relationships between the Háleygir and the Sámi, as well as the significance of sorcery in their mutual struggle against Christianisation and the unification of Norway.[67]

Magic and sorcery are attributes of Old Norse and Sámi cultures, and both exhibit known instances of boundary transgression, which may include gender expression, though there is no way of knowing if this was incidental or requisite. Sagas that were written hundreds of years after the events are so heavily biased, they cannot be used to determine the veracity or speculation of such matters. Certain features of the Vivallen grave no. 9 for example, indicate the burial of a Sámi shaman, though not conclusively. Similarly, in Norse society, Séiðr, which has significant shamanistic features, is primarily a female activity, even though we know that powerful seiðmenn (male sorcerers) were also practitioners. Among their number were Óðinn and Loki, who are both accused of ergi, a term linked to notions of alleged 'unmanliness,' which has many interpretations, but may in part relate to the style of clothing worn by such practitioners.[68]

Clothing styles are often cited as indicators of gender-crossing, which I have shown to be unreliable, and often presumptuous. This is not to say that ritual costume is not stylised for magical practitioners,

---

[67]. Svestad, 2021. [68]. My own thoughts on this are expressed elsewhere. See: the chapter on Enarei

indeed, I do advocate for this premise, but more in terms of a 'Uni' sex, that transcends both contemporary male and female clothing, rather than being 'cross-gendered clothing,' where men might wear women's clothing, and vice versa. In fact, from what has been gleaned from the archaeological record, Sámi noaidi were unusual in that they do not appear to have worn specialist clothing. As noted above, although both Sámi men and women naturally wore similar clothing, this was not generally the case across Scandinavia. Any male (or female for that matter) in Norse society adopting clothing typically worn by their opposite gender, would make them distinct, and attract attention that may not have always been understood or fully accepted, particularly in the conversion period.

There is a wonderful description of the clothing worn by a female shaman who features in the Norse sagas, whose ethnicity eludes us, yet is in some ways suggested by her clothing, which is distinctly hybrid, neither Norse, nor Sámi, and neither typical of a shaman, nor of a Völva, except for her staff. That she was a seer and Séiðkona is not in dispute. That her clothing determines a specific gender bias is however, unlikely.

Particular attention is given to the Séiðr-woman Thorbjorg at Herjolfsnes (Greenland), called Litilvolva (Little Sibyl), in Eiríks saga rauða (the Saga of Eirik the Red). Notably, her 'magical' outfit is described in detail, which includes a blue (or black) cloak with bands and inlaid gems, a black hood of lambskin lined with white cat skin, shaggy calf-skin shoes attached with long thongs with tin buttons at the end, and a pouch around her waist with talismans. Among her equipment is mentioned a spoon of brass and an edgeless knife with an ivory shaft. As remarked by Brit Solli, the blue-coloured cloak is a familiar attribute of Óðinn, and the knife with a broken edge is considered healing in Old Norse sources. The metals (including tin buttons) may thus be sorcerer or shaman characteristics, as commented on by Neil Price.[69]

Old Norse settlements in Norway were principally located in the outer coastal areas that corresponds with the region of Hålogaland (above the arctic circle), which appears in Old Norse written sources. Although considered distinct from "the Sámi settlements found mainly to the north and east of this region, and in interior areas, recent archaeological research suggests that boundaries were less fixed than hitherto known,"[70] and furthermore, that "boundaries were also blurred in the Vesterålen region, traditionally perceived as an Old

---

69. Svestad, 2021.

Norse or Norwegian settlement area and referred to as Omð in the Old Norse sources."[71]

Early interactions between the two groups, which nevertheless seem to have increased over the course of the Iron Age, and particularly the Viking period and the Early Middle Ages. This interaction probably implied exchange of goods and services, as well as alliances and inter-ethnic marriages; the latter, for instance, may be indicated by female Old Norse graves with furnishings associated with the Sámi.[72]

With the exception of heathens in Hålogaland,[73] in Arctic Norway (who held out the longest), the Old Norse people were Christianised quite early, and quickly (around two hundred years from the 9th to the 11th centuries) with little resistance. Some early conversion amongst the Sámi also occurred, adding further ambiguities in transitional burials across regions of known interactions. Sámi graves are generally egalitarian, with little variation in grave goods between genders. As noted above, cultural hybridity further muddies the waters (even in the Haug cemetery). Generally speaking, W/E grave orientations indicate Christian burials, just as N/S grave orientations indicate Sámi burials, but not always. In the Early Middle Ages, social identity was dependent upon, and directly related to, group identity. As personal status became more individualised towards the twelfth century, social boundaries tightened and a shift ocurred in burial customs that began to emphasize more personal aspects such as gender or age. Social status in life was generally (but not always) dependent upon gender. To reflect this societal development, burial customs became more homogeneous by the Late Middle Ages, whence female burials became less distinct. It is possible this occurred in direct relation to the gradual imposition of new religious beliefs and ecclesiastical restrictions that led to the diminishment (and displacement) of women in medieval society. Thankfully, there were highly acclaimed exceptions, without which, we would never know the true value of Viking Age women on the cusp of conversion.

The transition to Christian burial practice also seems to vary in function and chronology between various Fennoscandian regions, creating a disjointed picture overall. As an example, the co-existence of Christian rune stones and pagan burials in Svealand (Sweden proper) indicates that pagans and Christians lived alongside each other until the 12th century CE, while burial customs in Västergötland (SW

---

70. Svestad, 2021. **71.** Svestad, 2021. **72.** Svestad, 2021. **73.** Also a cemetery at Haug, in the Vesterålen region, which is one of Norway's oldest Christian cemeteries, dated 950 CE to 1250 CE.

Gothland, part of SW Sweden) indicate a swift Christianisation during the mid-10th century CE. In Arctic Norway, pagan burial customs seem to endure well into the 11th century CE, and sometimes even later, as is evident at the late 13th century burial mound or cenotaph at the Haugnesodden promontory on Arnøya Island in Troms and Finnmark county. This is notable for its location in the borderland between the Háleygir of Hålogaland and the Sámi of Finnmark.[74]

In the following example, four stone-covered rectangular hearths arranged in a row discovered at a Viking Age settlement site close by the Lake Aursjøen[75] each had a single large stone placed at one end, the boaššu-stones found in traditional Sámi dwellings. Moreover, because those traits have no parallel in the Norse tradition, this discovery suggests that pre-historic Sámi settlements were larger than previously imagined, and more importantly, that extensive (trading and marriage) contacts existed in the Viking Age between the Norse and the Sámi groups, again, far greater than previously imagined.

As excavations continue, so do the debates on how, and even if, it is possible to determine ethnicity from grave deposits. Having established that ethnicity is a dynamic and fluid phenomenon, our interpretations must reflect that, it can no longer be restricted to either 'Sámi' or 'Germanic/Norse.' There is evidently a considerable level of hybridization resulting from the level of contact and exchange between them, especially when farming settlements were established in the area, and the south Sámi people of Norway became more dependent on the reindeer for their livelihoods.[76] Culture is not linear however. It is suggested that "a differentiated Sámi society had existed already in the Late Iron Age, which was in contrast to the then dominant view that the Sámi had lived as egalitarian hunters, fishers and gatherers until the emergence of reindeer pastoralism in historical times."[77] Historical developments in the Sámi communities are complex and heterogeneous. Peoples, like their remains, are neither monolithic nor

---

74. Svestad, 2021. Despite contrary claims of complete early conversion of the people of Hålogaland in the saga of Óláf Tryggvason in Heimskringla (the history of the kings of Norway), conversion was in fact very sparce and sporadic. See note above.   **75.** In Norway, in 2006. Obviously, that one such Sámi site exists this far south in Norway, indicates with certainty the existence of other similar sites across this region   **76.** It is suggested that Sámi became reindeer pastoralists with the introduction of domesticated reindeer herding in the Viking Age. See: A. .K. Salmi. "The Archaeology of Reindeer Domestication and Herding Practices in Northern Fennoscandia." In, *The Archaeology of Reindeer Domestication and Herding Practices in Northern Fennoscandia* 31 (2023): 617-660 https://doi.org/10.1007/s10814-022-09182-8 (Accessed 27th October 2024)

homogeneous with regard to their cultural or ethnic identities. Stállo foundations (religious sites) found in the mountains could be remains from early reindeer pastoralism, or Sámi hunters, who utilized the mountain areas for hunting wild reindeer in order to engage in the flourishing and profitable international fur trade.[78]

[It is important that we must not] over-simplify the social, cultural and economic processes involved in the development of Sámi societies in the Iron Age, Middle Ages and Early Modern Time, and to create an illusion that the history is only about a transition from one mode of "traditional hunting society" to another mode of "reindeer husbandry society." It becomes more and more clear that the hunting society itself was not homogeneous and undifferentiated (Hansen 1996), and that, therefore, there is a need for more focus on the regional and temporal variation in the study of the evolving social, cultural and economic forms in the Sámi societies.[79]

Reindeer husbandry has functioned in the past as a powerful ethnic symbol for the Sámi people, yet we must shift our gaze from this stereotypical view of them in our time as an identity marker, as so few Sámi are reliant upon it. Ultimately, as discussed earlier, there is no single agreement among scholars on the ethnogenesis of the Sámi people, diaspora and early settlement boundaries of the Sámi.[80]

---

77. Carl-Gösta Ojala. "Sámi Prehistories, The Politics of Archaeology and Identity in Northernmost Europe Occasional Papers," In, Archaeology 47. (Institutionen För Arkeologi Och Antik Historia Uppsala Universitet, 2009). **78.** I. M. Mulk and T. P. Bayliss-Smith. "The Representation of Sámi Cultural Identity In The Cultural Landscapes Of Northern Sweden: The Use And Misuse Of Archaeological Evidence." In, *The Archaeology and Anthropology of landscape*. Edited by P. J. Ucko and J. Layton. (Routledge, 1998): 358-396. **79.** Ojala, 2009. **80.** Ibid. The Iron Age was the time of the maximum distribution of the Sámi people, whose numbers decreased gradually from the 1st millennium CE. as other ethnic groups, such as the Baltic Finns, Germans and Slavs expanded.

FUNERARY CULTURE: KURGANS

Early nomadic peoples left significant markers in character traits that would undisputedly come to represent the cultural identity of North European peoples. These people also share an inspiring heritage that includes the creation of the wheel and the domestication and celebration of the horse. Research has placed less emphasis on other factors of certain traditions, such as burial customs – noted by Dr. Marija Gimbutas as Kurgan or Mound culture – and the erection of commemorative, sometimes ancestral stelae to denote territorial dominance.

Gimbutas maintained that Europeans and their culture originated in the Pontic Steppe, shifting over the north coastline of the Black Sea, expanding outwards into Northern Europe circa 4000 BCE, transported by nomads associated with Kurgan cultural traditions.[81] Not everyone agrees with this view, so an alternative and more popular theory, is that Proto Indo-Europeans spread outwards from eastern Anatolia, circa 5000 BCE, following the route of agriculture.[82] Neither premise is entirely supported by linguistic, agricultural or genetic evidence. Linguistics especially

3. Khirigusur

---

81. Marija Gimbutas. *The Slavs*. Edited by Dr. Glyn Daniel. (Thames and Hudson. 1971); Marija Gimbutas. "Slavic Religion." *The Encyclopaedia of Religion. Volume 13*. Edited by Mircea Eliade. (Collier Macmillan Publishing Company, 1987). **82.** The north and eastern regions of Anatolia were originally inhabited by non-Indo-European speakers. Indo-Europeans entered Anatolia sometime later between 2000 BCE -1800 BCE.

FUNERARY CULTURE: KURGANS 147

propose a non-Indo-European (I-E) origin, a notion given much traction by supportive archaeology. However, this may be an issue of semantics, as the evidence for the origin of North European culture persuades us to look beyond the Black Sea region into Anatolia and the Caucasus in successive, but increasing waves since the late Neolithic period through to the Bronze Age. And because culture is transported by people and by goods, all that remains uncertain, is the manner of acculturation.

These origins are vital for understanding the commonalities of culture shared by the Sámi and Nordic peoples whose ancestors span the vast arctic Tundra of the Siberian plains, down into Mongolia, and who were invested in a major cultural tradition centred on the reverence of spirit inhabited stones, generally large monolithic specimens, or grouped megalithic structures. These are propitiated with prayers and animal sacrifices, milk, cheeses and alcohol. In Finland, stones that are very similar (in function) to the Sieidi stone structures of the Sámi, but visually more akin to the balbals of Mongolia, are known as a Napakivi (pole/navel stone). Another, smaller standing stone is known as a tonttukivi (elf stone), which is propitiated for matters dealing with fertility, protection or death. Like the balbals, these are sometimes found near to burial mounds. Such stones have also been found in the Sámi regions of Norway.

Kurgan stelae depict symbols and stylistic motifs that would later be associated with Nordic and Pictish artistry. Culture specific birds and beasts such as raptors (birds of prey), wolves, deer, boar and goat, find pertinent representation across this wide geographic region and its attendant demography of people. Metal smithing techniques acquired from the Hittites facilitated rapid expansion during the European Iron Age, which led to the establishment of elite centres of industry that were monopolised by specific tribes associated with that craft. Traditional symbols of the warrior class, including the labrys and the horned helmet, were later attributed to sea-faring travellers; later still, the Vikingr.

KHIRIGSUUR

Often compared to the Central Eurasian Kurgans, the Mongolian khirigsuur are amongst the most striking stone funerary monuments of the ancient world. From above they appear as solar mandalas, radiating out to the cardinal points from a central mound. Dependent upon location, khirigsuur (c. 1300 BCE to 800 BCE) have altars placed on those cardinal points (north, west, east and south), for offerings and ritual celebration. Complex patterns formed of rocks and slabs add further intriguing detail to the funerary mounds, though not all of them contain burials. Those that do, have very few grave goods, and are therefore a perplexing contrast to the rich and elaborate Pazyryk Kurgans that followed them. Both cultures present an additional feature that surrounds the mound in the form of a square, the corners of which were aligned to cardinal points and contained smaller mound burials.

Some of these contain the skulls and hooves of horses.[83] The square may represent the four corners of the earth in a nuanced mythic system.[84] Iron Age Eurasian Kurgans and the Bronze Age khirigsuur complexes that preceded them, evince a hoary spirituality anchored in sacred landscapes, which collectively present a narrative, cosmological map relating to the lives of settled, semi-nomadic and nomadic peoples.[85]

Generally conflated as the 'Deer Stone-Khirgisuur Complex,' the Bronze Age Mongolian Khirigsuurs were in fact frequently appropriated by the later Iron Age Deer Stone builders throughout the Mongolian Altai region. In turn, the Pazyryk burial sites were later plundered and quarried for Scythian burials,[86] leaving us with layers of funerary

---

83. Esther Jacobson-Tepfer. "Deer Stones." Monumental Archaeology in the Mongolian Altai. (Brill, 2023): 155-191 doi:10.1163/9789004541306_008 (Retrieved 3rd August 2024). **84.** These enclosures vary considerably, ranging from tens to thousands of square meters. Individual mounds within these vast complexes range from two to forty meters in diameter, and four to eight meters in height. **85.** Macfarland, 2010. **86.** Jacobson-Tepfer, 2023. Early Bronze Age groups in the northern Altai region were followed by the Iron Age Pazyryks, who were quickly replaced by the Sauromatians and the Sarmations from the middle of the first millennium BCE, all of whom are most commonly referred to as Scytho - Siberian cultures, particularly around the Black Sea regions.

KHIRIGSUUR 149

artefacts and grave sites. These provide a rich source of information from which we may construct insightful impressions of their cultures and how they merged and evolved. The elite horse dependant cultures accrued fabulous wealth and status, which incontrovertibly altered the whole character of the nomadic lifestyle, to the extent that warriors and warfare became a notable feature of the Iron Age world. Their spirituality incorporates a strong relationship with totemism, which manifests in the bronze pole tops forged as rams, stags, moose, even large horned agali (sheep).

Their elaborate graves also contain other artefacts that typically reflect the distinct roles allotted to men and women. We may view things differently now, but this was the reality of their world, and we should try to understand that, rather than rewrite it to suit our modern sensibilities. After all, they were pragmatic rather than sexist. Primarily, the graves are about status and reputation, hence the items found within them, relate to that premise. Male burials of this type exhibit a vast array of weapons (bows, arrows, quivers, pole-axes (halberds), knives, swords, and whetstones), some of which are clearly ceremonial. Richly gilded in gold with regional Animal Style decorative motifs of real and fantasy beasts, the artistry and craftsmanship is extraordinary. A four-wheeled wooden chariot, wagon fragments and a Yurt[87] were amongst the other finds from these regions.

"Hierarchy among women seems to be expressed by the exotic or local nature of pottery, the amount of jewellery they possessed, and the inclusion of a horse or horse tack in their burial or kurgan."[88] Horses and weapons included in both male and female burial tableaus are primarily an indication of their noble, elite status, rather than of any presumed warriorhood: that would certainly be a mistake. In this context they indicate prestige (though nobles were of course warriors and leaders).[89] Similarly, elaborate clothing, head-dresses, mirrors, fine ceramics and a stunning array of jewellery appear in

4. Mongolian deer stone

---

87. Felted yurts were popular amongst Asian nomads. **88.** Macfarland, 2010. **89.** Macfarland, 2010. The early domestication of the horse occurred here in the Altai regions of Central Asia, and quickly became popular with the Persians, Assyrians and Greeks, providing a basis for the birth of the hero in mythic literature.

male and female burials. Wooden chariots, carts and wagons are a key feature of kurgan burials. Images of two-or four-wheeled carts occur in European, Eurasian and southern Scandinavian rock art: "Motifs are mostly depicted from a bird's eye perspective; however, there are some exceptions where the image is in profile."[90] Interpretations vary, though most tend to ally them to solar cults, or to Bronze Age cattle-herding,[91] but mainly to the newly emerging cults of warriors and warfare. But there is far more to it. I believe that some of these carts and waggons were also used by nomadic peoples as funerary vehicles, thus demonstrating a continuity of important cultural traditions relating to the transport of the dead. The precedents established in these mound burials in Mongolian (and Scythian) culture, undoubtedly contributed to that of the emerging Sámi.

Horse riding was slowly adopted by the people of South Siberia in the 7th to the 6th century BCE, around the time the early Iron Age rock art of the (south Siberian) mountain Steppe region (spanning Mongolia, and eastern Kazakhstan, across to the northern shores of the Black Sea) declined. The hunting culture of the Mongolian Steppe nomads had initially depended upon the seasonal herding of animals for furs and food, but gradually shifted into one that became fully horse dependent as a semi-nomadic lifestyle.[92] This meant the horse gradually replaced the stag as the principle beast revered, along with the wolf and the eagle. "By the early Iron Age when the early nomadic world was shifting to a new social order, expanding across the Eurasian Steppe, the Mother of Animals disappeared with the stag to be replaced by the body of its predator, showing the rise of the warrior culture and tribal dominance."[93]

Sacrificed and interred alongside their owners within the (kurgans) mounds, horses were generally buried whole. Each horse was adorned with elaborate ornaments that gave the appearance of otherworldly creatures, and the illusion of a beast transformed. Such elaborate

---

90. Lene Melheim and Anette Sand-Eriksen. "Rock Art and Trade Networks: From Scandinavia to the Italian Alps." Open Archaeology 6 (2020): 86-106. 10.1515/opar-2020-0101   **91.** Esther Jacobson Tepfer. The Hunter, the Stag, and the Mother of Animals: Image, Monument, and Landscape in Ancient North Asia. (Oxford University Press, 2015).   **92.** Ibid. Several nomadic groups, including the Xiongnu were confederated under this young new horse culture of Mongolia.   **93.** For an in-depth exploration of this as a locus of sacred tradition amongst the early Bronze-Age peoples of the Altai, Steppe and Mongolian plains. See: Esther Jacobson. "The Deer Goddess of Ancient Siberia: A Study in the Ecology of Belief." In, *Studies in the History of Religions*, Volume LV: 91. Leiden: E. J. Brill, 1993; Jacobson, 2015.

horse masks found amongst the rich grave finds used for funerary rites, offer a clear acknowledgment of the Elk spirit, the ancestral totem of these peoples in a time when they were hunters rather than herders. As we have already discussed, the significance of the stag was not lost however, but achieved an iconic status. Heavily ornamented horses deliberately mimicked the zoomorphic stags motifs of the cultic warrior elite.[94] Horses were morphed into fantastic stags (ibex, elk or reindeer) with antlered points that terminated in fabulous exotic birds such as the peacock and cockerel, both sacred to the later Iranic peoples, most especially to the later Yezidis.

Thanks to these grave gifts, the horse acquired the attributes of the deer and its regenerative power, or that of the ibex, which was venerated as an 'inhabitant of heaven' and a symbol of fertility. It appears that the horse, symbolically transformed into a deer or ibex, served as guide and mount for the deceased in entering the afterlife.[95]

Many of these exotic images appear on the later bracteates and sceattas of the Germanic Migration Age, typically described as horses, and ruthlessly (mis)attributed to Sleipnir and Óðinn.[96] Despite this, I strongly believe the Iron Age artefacts and ritual regalia from these and other grave sites mentioned below contributed significantly to the mythic culture of the later Scandinavian and Fennoscandian peoples.

With regard to the importance of the horse, Herodotus (4.68, 127) informs us of the solemn oath of duty taken by the chieftain to serve his people. Horses feature in an Ossete legend as the means of transport, (possibly as spirit animals) to the Otherworld in dreams where heroes retrieve treasure that will benefit their kin. This motif very much resembles the tale of Arthur's Raid on the Underworld as recorded in the 15th-Century *Tri Thlws ar Ddeg Ynys Prydain*,

5. Bracteate

which appears to be an elegant re-telling of the 9th-Century Welsh poem, *Preiddeu Annfwyn*,[97] ascribed to the 6th-Century poet and shaman

---

94. Jacobson Tepfer, 2015: 274 **95.** Cristoph Baumer. *The History of Central Asia: The Age of the Steppe Warriors* (Volume I). I.B. Tauris, 2012: 163 **96.** Oates, 2022. **97.** Annwfn is the Underworld of Celtic speaking peoples invariably described as a Castle or Fortress. See: Sarah Higley (Trans.) Preiddeu Annwn: The Spoils of Annwn. The Camelot Project 2007. https://d.lib.rochester.edu/camelot/text/preiddeu-annwn (Accessed 20th March 2022)

152   PIRATES, MERCHANTS, DEVILS & DARK DEEDS

Taliesin. In the *Tri Thlws ar Ddeg Ynys Prydain*, [98] we learn of the 13 magical treasures of Britain Arthur hunted down in the northern regions of Britain (referred to as Hen Ogledd which is possibly Scotland, or Northern Ireland; ships were certainly ships needed to get them there). The treasure comprised of clothing, weapons, food and various vessels for food and drink, items related to transportation, and other high-status items such as jewellery and gaming pieces.

To all intents and purposes, this adventure describes the plunder of a burial mound, possibly of a former king or high Chieftain. I share Higley's belief that an earlier common source inspired the later Welsh and Irish accounts.[99] Legends of heroes and their exploits furnish literary tradition over millennia with countless adaptations interpreted culturally. This tale would be no exception. Moreover, scholars have long ruminated on the possibility that these Otherworld fables are actually detailed records of very real attacks on Ireland (Wales and Scotland) that involved (mainly cattle) raids on early settlers. In Welsh lore, an island to the west provides an explanation of the Irish name for the fortress, Caer Sidi, and of the difficulty of conversing with the watchmen on the wall as recorded in the Historia Brittonum. Many such places are often guarded by a host of deities, demi-gods, heroes and arcane titans, the fey and elven folk. Some of these fantastic entities appear as mythical and zoomorphic beings in the artworks found as grave goods, carved, etched or molded on pottery and precious metalworks. The deer motif is unequivocally sacred, serving as guardians, guides and benefactors of all tribal descendants. The Mother of Animals features on the glorious Pazyryk felt-hanging, enthroned (in Persian style) before the visiting hero. Bearing some mysterious meaning, the tree branch she raises before him is styled as intricate deer antlers.

Alongside weaponry, Scythian art utilises supernatural bird and stag motifs extensively, typified by the finds in the Filippovka tomb. As a symbol of (divine) kingship, the composite bow brought significant advantage to the nomadic peoples using them. A mounted Steppe warrior armed with such, was indeed formidable. They were heirloom legacy pieces passed from one king to another, no doubt accompanied by attendant tales of heroism and marvellous feats. An image on the magnificent gold vessel retrieved from the Kul' Oba tumulus (a

98. *Tri Thlws ar Ddeg Ynys Prydain*, ed. and tr. Rachel Bromwich, Trioedd Ynys Prydein. Cardiff: University of Wales Press, 1978; revised ed. 1991 (Critical edition of the trioedd texts with notes, first published in 1961). Appendix III. Edited from Cardiff MS. 17, pp. 95–6, and other variants.   **99.** Higley, 2007.

5th-Century BCE Scythian royal barrow discovered in the Crimea). Resembling a Scythian tent, the canopied timber ceiling of this tomb is decorated with dramatic gilding. Furnished with numerous items of gold and precious stones, the king and the woman who accompanied him, were housed here for eternity.

We may never solve the mysterious origins of the Saka peoples, a broad term encompassing peoples of Asian and proto-European ancestry in varying degrees of genetic admixtures. Their complex migration and settlement patterns generated an intricate ethnohistory, rich in influences east and west from their long 1000 year presence in the steppe regions. The 4th-century BCE high-status burial in kurgan 1 at Filippovka is almost certainly of a Sarmatian chieftain or king, himself a member of the tribal confederation that encompassed a wide array of cultures reaching across Eurasia, to Siberia, China and Thrace. The narrative animal art style typical of the steppe nomads evidently has deeply symbolic significance, both ambiguous and elusive to our modern eye. They were steeped in tradition and culture in ways we cannot begin to imagine.

Seventeen kurgans were excavated here, unearthing several human remains whose skulls were mainly brachycranial broad-faced Caucasoids.[100] Several exhibited varying admixtures of proto-European (of the Bronze Age, possibly Andronovo cultures)[101] and Asiatic morphology (of the 7th- 5th centuries BCE, possibly originating in the Altai regions.).

6. Scythian warriors on a dagger from Filippovka

Commonly cited as Sarmatian, or sometimes as Sauromatian, the skull and facial feature analysis of the various specimens found at Filippovka, reveal morphologies distinct from those of Scythians and Sarmatians of the Lower Volga River regions. This suggests that peoples buried in the Filippovka (and other similar sites) of this region belonged to a nomadic culture independent of both, of possible kindred to the Saka Massagetaes (Indo/Iranians) who lived on the Central Steppes of Kazakhstan. If this could be proven, it would connect nomadic cultures of the eastern tribes of

---

100. Egor Kitov. "Revisiting the Issue of Connections Among the Nomads Social Elite from the Southern Urals According to Craniology Data from the Filippovka Kurgans." Nižnevolžskij Arheologičeskij Vestnik, 2024. DOI: https://doi.org/10.15688/nav.jvolsu.2024.1.2 (Retrieved 19th February 2025). **101**. See Appendices and Glossary.

the Saka with those of the southern Urals; in other words, genetic divergencies did not inhibit a shared ethnic culture. In addition to this shared culture and ideology, the archaeological data supports a strong economic relationship primarily based on trade. Greek and Achaemenid artefacts alongside numerous luxury goods from Persia and Asia were found in the Altai tombs, even Chinese silk in later burials of Pazyryk 3 and 5.

Despite this thriving economy, Herodotus claims strife and intertribal warfare eventually destroyed their mutual way of life, and the supremacy of their presence across the steppe regions. We are informed by him that throughout the 5th century BCE, the Scythians were forced westwards into the north Pontic region by warring tribal factions of the Massagetae, the Issedones, the Saka and others under that umbrella (namely remote, obscure, unknown ancestral or mythical tribes), and some of 'Iranian' origin. As legendary warriors, they were known to the 7th-Century BCE Assyrians who refer to them as Ishkuzai.

This level of ethnic diversity presents problems of identification for the various historical peoples of in the Royal tombs at Chertomlyk and Solokha (north of the Black Sea) and in the Pazyryk and Tuekta kurgans of the Altai regions. Similar to the Einherjar of Norse mythology, certain warriors of the Gerrhi were considered by the Scythians to be ancestors who now reside in the Otherworld plains above the burial sites of Scythian kings. In fact, according to their own dynamic mythology, the Scythians claim dramatic descent from Zeus through Targitäus (a son borne by a daughter of the Dnepr), the first man to occupy Scythian territory. Fathering three sons of his own, they became the leaders of the three main Scythian tribes. In compliance with their creation myth, the meaning of their names (Lipoxaïs, Arpoxaïs and Colaxaïs), announces them as kings of the Mountain, Water and Sun – the three planes of being, and the elements of air, water/earth and fire.

It is notable that monumental rock-art narratives occurred in these main areas of conflict and migration – the Altai and Kazakhstan. It is entirely possible that the regions of Tanum (Sweden) and Alta (Norway)[102] encountered similar incidences that initially led to their grand narrative art motifs, and then ultimately, to their decline.

Between the Volga and Don rivers, a new wave of nomads

---

102. Rock art petroglyphs and paintings of the Alta Fjord near the arctic circle span mainly from the Neolithic to the Bronze Age, with some later images from around 500 BCE. It is the only (listed) prehistoric monument site in Norway.

KHIRIGSUUR 155

swept over the steppes in the 4th century BCE, merging with the Sauromatians, effecting a discernible cultural shift towards influences from the Greek colonies of the Pontic regions. This confederation of Eurasian nomads dominated these regions for the next few centuries. Gradually the incompatibility of the superstructure of sedentary lifestyles (Of the major civilizations of Greece, Assyria, Iran and China) compromised that of the Scythian nomads, causing a shift in their own social order. Forced to accommodate the new hierarchy, there is a marked rise in the number of smaller tombs erected here, accompanied by a brief resurgence of high-status Kurgan building during the 6th century BCE, built as the funerary preserve of chieftains and their retainers (kurgan 2 for example). Simultaneously, the erection of deer-stones and other similar rock-art styles begin to disappear from the funerary complexes.[103]

---

103. *The Golden Deer of Eurasia: Scythian and Sarmatian Treasures from the Russian Steppes.* Edited by Joan Aruz, with Ann Farkas, Andrei Alekseev, and Elena Korolkova (Yale Uni Press, 2000).

PAZYRYK MUMMIES

Across the Altai regions, many Pazyryk tombs were robbed in antiquity. Those that remain demonstrate an unparalleled and continued reverence for the dead. Permafrost conditions preserved the bodies (already stuffed with embalming herbs) of several high-status folk interred in the kurgans of the Eurasian Steppe nomads,[104] along with organic materials (cloth and wood) that would normally perish.[105] From these extraordinary, rare, mummified remains discovered in the Altai Mountains,[106] we have learned much about their previously elusive culture.

A warrior-chief buried in the fourth century was so well preserved that his tattoos were still vivid: a fish on his right shin, deer and a mountain goat on his left arm, a winged monster and an eagle-beaked deer on his right arm, a griffin twining from his chest around

7. Altai Funerary Cart.

to his back, and many more. Numerous horses were found in the Pazyryk tombs, too, with saddles and bridles still in place. One kurgan had ten fine reddish-furred horses wearing colourful felt saddlecloths decorated with images of real and fantastic creatures.[107]

Horses clearly held tremendous spiritual meaning for many Indo-Europeans, in life and in death, yet antlered stags were also held in great reverence, hence their elaborate treatment in funerary motifs. Fabulous zoomorphic (winged and horned) masks made of gold,

---

104. As noted above, this region was peopled by the Pazyryk, Altai, Scythian and Sarmatian peoples between the 5th and 3rd centuries BCE, all of whom share strikingly similar burial traditions in kurgans with rich grave goods and horse sacrifices. **105.** Colourful woollen rugs and hangings, silk garments, musical instruments, pottery items, all of which reveal a wealth in wide-ranging trade goods, even mirrors from China. **106.** The Ukok plateau of the Eurasian Steppes borders China, Kazakhstan and Mongolia. **107.** Jacobson Tepfer, 2015: 274

leather, felt, feathers and fur, adorn the skulls of the horses buried with a Pazyryk chieftain, in grand imitation of great stags and elk. One grave that has grabbed considerable attention is perhaps that of the Ice Maiden,[108] whose tattooed, mummified remains forms part of a wider complex known as the (east-facing) Pazyryk burials.[109] Preserved in a subterranean burial chamber (kurgan), this 5th-Century BCE Scytho-Siberian woman[110] was clothed in fine embroidered (Indian) silks, wool and fur. Upon her head, she wears a wig and an extraordinary headdress that stands almost a metre high, and which is almost identical to the one worn by a petroglyph figure that depicts the Tree of Life beneath which deer graze. She lay in a coffin carved from a larch tree log, decorated with leather appliqués of deer figures. Her grave goods include tables, a cup, food, drink, a mirror and several horses.

All the burials in this kurgan complex contain wide-ranging and far-reaching luxury crafted trade goods, particularly in the mound of the chieftain in Pazyryk 5 c. 241 BCE, with its extraordinary, unique carpet depicting the seated 'giantess' (named as) Tabiti and the mounted rider before her. From the more sedentary regions of China, India, Persia, Greece and Sogdiana, these trade goods were carried by the nomadic warriors in ox-carts or camel back through the Steppe. Other items chosen for internment with the bodies in the tombs and kurgans, are varied; some were produced by local artisans imitating foreign aesthetics, yet altered sufficiently to align more closely to their own cultural ethos regarding zoomorphic imagery, specifically of animal hybridity. As a mythical beast that was possibly an adaptation of the vulture or eagle, griffins were a popular motif of the Scythians, and clearly find favour amongst the Pazyryk peoples, feature here. Revered for their intelligence, ferocity and ruthless ability to hunt their prey, raptors were evidently a prestigious creature.

---

108. Ak-Alakha-3 (Mound 1, burial 2). Also known as the Princess of Ukok or the Altai Princess, the Ice Maiden was a representative of the Iron Age Pazyryk culture of the Siberian Steppe. Her preservation is due to water that froze when grave robbers undermined the sealed coverings while plundering the male burial above her. See: T. A. Chikisheva; N. V. Polosmak; Alisa Zubova. "The Burial at Ak-Alakha-3 Mound 1, Gorny Altai: New Findings1." *Archaeology Ethnology and Anthropology of Eurasia* 43(1) (2015):144-154. DOI:10.1016/j.aeae.2015.07.016   https://www.researchgate.net/publication/283858350_The_Burial_at_Ak-Alakha-3_Mound_1_Gorny_Altai_New_Findings1 (Accessed 1st January. 2022).   109. The Pazyryk Culture is related to the Central Asian Scythian cultures. See: Chikisheva, Polosmak, and Zubova, 2015.   110. Her ethnography is currently a matter of contention between China and Russia. The dead were buried in coffins carved out of the trunks of larch trees. It was a traditional custom shared with the emerging proto-Sámi and other northern peoples.

158 PIRATES, MERCHANTS, DEVILS & DARK DEEDS

Of mixed ethnicity, the Pazyryk people observed a strict hierarchy in life and in their funerary traditions, yet, somewhat unusually, Pazyryk culture supported a non-dynastic leadership. Chosen entirely on merit,[111] it is a premise similar to the Tanist system of later Northern traditions, where only the strongest and wisest warrior would be chosen as leader and clan chieftain. Although it was short-lived, the Pazyryk culture and its close kindred nomadic groups evidently shared ancestral animistic cosmologies involving shamanistic and totemic practises. Their heterogeneous use of symbolic animal fetishes and Tamgas demonstrates a profound awareness of harmonious environmental symbiosis. Theirs was a spirituality of completion and unification across all realms of being, where each virtue is indistinct from another – of complex layers bound together.

---

111. Ibid. The burial above the Ice Princess contained a male who is unrelated to her but is also of high status. His obvious physical deformities meant he was unable to take his place in this equine centred people as a warrior. His diminished value suggests he was a likely candidate for sacrifice.

TAMGAS AND TALTOS

Tamgas and Taltos are individual clan emblems developed from a shared ancestry that proudly bears an affinity with the flora and fauna of the earth. Tamgas indicate those symbolic identities in artistic formats in non-literate societies where information is conveyed through spoken language, or through visual and physical means amongst agro-pastoral communities. Strictly speaking, 'Tamga' would not be appropriate to describe the pre-Türkic marks of the ancient Iranian peoples; instead, the term nishan is more suitable.[112] Nonetheless, Türkic peoples may have developed the ideograms further, extending their use for trade and accounting purposes, much as cuneiform functioned in Mesopotamia. They also appear in Mongolia, Kazakhstan and even some Slavic nations.

Particular marks in the form of signs and symbols are a primitive, though very efficient way to convey information on identity. As mnemonic devices, they may be depicted on a variety of objects – seals, pottery, bricks and stones, head-gear, carpets, dress and even skin – that are immediately recognisable and understandable to literate and non-literate people.[113] Not all symbols are necessarily sacred; some were developed purely for mundane administrative purposes, albeit rooted in a cultural legacy. Even so, Tamgas slowly change through generational shifts where the dynamic and significance is determined by socio-political and religious relationships and advances. There is a hierarchy in the application of Tamgas which has been retained by the Polish nobility. Note the stacked tree twig Tamgas on the Taltos drums, rúnic inscriptions and on ancestral figures. The Tamga that signifies the Ash?nà People is a graphic image very similar to the iconic wolf etched into the stone at the Maeshowe chambered cairn on Orkney.

---

112. The word Tamga possibly originates in the Alanic language, which is itself directly descended from the earlier Scytho-Sarmatian language. It therefore belongs to the family of the Eastern Iranian languages. 113. Manassero, Niccolò. "Tamgas, A Code of The Steppes." In, *Identity Marks and Writing Among The Ancient Iranians*. (The Silkroad Foundation, 2013). http://www.silkroadfoundation.org/newsletter/vol11/SilkRoad_11_2013_manassero.pdf (2013). (Accessed 23rd December 2022)

160 PIRATES, MERCHANTS, DEVILS & DARK DEEDS

Other images that appear on the Taltos drums also appear on Siberian and Altai petroglyphs, kurgan stones, deer stones and balbals. Most common are the comet, dots, stars, squares, horses, deer, hunters and dancing women that suggest a cultural commonality or cross-cultural influences.[114]

Several rúnic inscriptions found in North-eastern Bulgaria and parts of Romania appear to be adapted from very similar graphemes discovered in Old Türkic and Sogdian alphabets based in the Hunnic/ Oghur Türkic language. Because of this, some scholars have proposed the possibility that rúnes arrived in Europe via the Huns of Central Asia. As stone-engraving customs cognate with those of Rome, they closely resemble the works of Sasanian and Türkic reliefs.[115] The Göktürks were the first Türkic people to write Old Türkic in a rúnic script, the Orkhon script that imparts the story of an empire of the 'kök türk' (translated as Celestial Türks) and of its first Kagan (Khan, King, Shah).

These people were composed of a multi-layered tribal ethnicity entitled 'A-shih-na.'[116] The Göktürk Khaganate[117] operated under a democratic regime, Khagans from the Ashinà clan were subordinate to a sovereign authority controlled by a council of tribal chiefs.[118]

As the ancestors of the Türkic (Týrk) peoples, the Türkü A-Shih-na, are known later as 'Ashinà,' a term rooted in the Saka (Sakas) languages of central Asia that bears an association with the colour blue (gök in Turkic). Legend claims the blue it refers to is the blue eye of the white raven, as sourced in the mythic folklore assigned to the Ashinà.[119] Türkic peoples refer to blue eyes through the term, *Gök baký°*, which means 'Sky/Heaven Look, or , alternatively as, *gök göz,*

---

114. Note the Teleut sled figure in relation to this descriptive list. **115.** The Sasanian Madara Rider is a badly eroded altar stone that mentions 'Tengri' in a Greek inscription deciphered as "Khan sybigi Omurtag, ruler from god...was...and made sacrifice to god Tangra...itchurgu boila...gold." An Ottoman manuscript noted that the Bulgarian God was named 'Tängri.'See: Florin Curta. Southeastern Europe in the Middle Ages, 500-1250. (Cambridge University Press, 2006) **116.** As constructed from Yenisey rúne forms, and the later Uygur alphabet. **117.** The Khaganate was the first state known as Türk, which eventually collapsed due to a series of dynastic conflicts, but many states and peoples later retained the name Türk. **118.** Türk is ultimately derived from the proto-Türkic migration-term ᚱᛏᚷᚻ, the Old Türkic *türi-/tori, means foundation, tribal root, lineage, (mythic) ancestry; take shape, to be born, created, arise, spring up). The first recorded use of Türk as a political name appears in a 6th-Century CE Chinese text that mentioned trade between Türkic tribes and the Sogdians along the Silk Road. There is a textual support for the ancient rúnic inscriptions of the Türks. See: Appendices III and IV. **119.** Arab chronicles refer to the Ashinà people as Shane. This (etymological) root is shared by the Sanskrit form 'Shani,' which signifies the once baneful deity Saturn, whose totemic beast is also the raven.

meaning, 'Heaven/Sky Eye.' Because the word turquoise comes from the French word meaning Türkic,[120] the colour blue is now strongly identified with the east.[121] Mythical, ancestral totems of the Türkic peoples naturally relate to the wolf [122] and raven, primarily, but also to horses and other raptorial birds such as the eagle. In fact, the Tamga for Ashinà actually means 'raven.'

It is strikingly apparent that these central and eastern European artistic signs and symbols significantly influenced the construction of not just Scandinavian rúnes, but also fundamental aspects of their mythology and cosmology. Other reasons are proposed for the sacrality of blue eyes that focus more on the wolf, a beast so hallowed, its name must never be spoken. Instead, the peoples of Azerbaijan refer to the wolf as arziðara, meaning 'the black mouth.' In Yakut, wolf is rendered as either *Uhun kuturuk*, 'the long tail,' or, *Hallan uolla-Göðün oðlu*, meaning, 'the son of heaven.' Similarly, in Kyrgyz, *Gök uul*, also means 'the son of heaven,' while in Chuvash, *Tanaran uolla*, translates to 'The holy dog.' It is, I think, pertinent to the evolving mythology of the Nordic peoples of Scandinavia that in the Kyrgyz mythology, the hero adopts the form of a wolf in combat, and that the Gagauz believe wolves are able to 'see' and 'hear' everything (like Heimdallr and All father). The blue wolf's eye charms evoke this sacred tribal totemism in order to dispel the 'evil eye' cast by maleficent persons.[123]

As part of a larger tribal Türkic confederacy, the Ashinà clan was formed from Post-Hunnish and local Iranian tribes in the modern region of Eastern Turkestan from the 3rd century BCE, to around the middle of the 5th century CE. One of the major contributors to the Ashinà[124] clan's ethnicity, especially in terms of economics, politics, religion along with diplomatic trade practises, was another closely related Türkic people, the Sogdians, who shared their ancestral myths.[125] As famed artisans and metalsmiths, they settled briefly near a mountain quarry in the Altai mountains that took on the appearance of a helmet, from which they derived their name: tuju – Türk. Altai means gold

---

120. This blue/green colour of the stone turquoise is still used in Turkish jewellery as a protection against the evil eye. **121.** Hence Göktürk meant the 'Turks of the East,' possibly concerns an elite, noble, even royal family or clan of Saka origin. The term bori, used to identify the ruler's retinue as wolves, probably also derived from one of the Iranian languages, possibly Scythian. **122.** The Teleuts revere the wolf as their forefather. **123.** Mirlan Namatov. "The Wolf Totem." In, *Journal of Eurasian Studies*. Volume II., Issue 2. April-June 2010 https://tinyurl.com/y929om8h **124.** 'Ashlnà' derives from an Iranian dialect. According to Saka etymology, ashina (<asseina ~ assena) refers to the value awarded to the (sky) blue colour. **125.** See overleaf.

mountain, so it is fitting that the migrant Ashinà, integrated well with the settled (non-nomadic) Sogdian and Uygur[126] peoples, all of whom were noted for their fine gold jewellery, as were the Scythian peoples collectively. Göktürk funeral rites described in The Old Book of Tang confirm the tremendous ceremony attached to the cremations, horse burials, and cairn building, noting especially, the circumambulations around the tent by horse riders and of the telling of stories that commemorate the feats and deeds of the deceased warrior or chieftain, particularly his battles. These funeral rites probably evolved from various influences absorbed from the ruling noble tribes of the Ashinà, especially the cremation element, and are indeed similar to those discovered in Southern Siberia in the Türkic time period. Almost all the factors of the Ashinà funeral rites have cognate elements within those of Indo-Europe. In the Slavic funerary rites especially, we may note comparative feasting and horse-riding events.

125. "Eurasia encompassed much of Central Asia up to the Tarim Basin. [...] (present-day southern Xinjiang, China). Dominant ethnic groups among the Scythian-speakers were nomadic pastoralists of Central Asia and the Pontic-Caspian Steppe. Traces of their language are found in the works of ancient classical authors, in Hittite and in inscriptions as far east as the Ukraine, down into Carpathian Basin and the Greek Colonies of the Black Sea." https://languagelog.ldc.upenn.edu/nll/?p=63123 (Retrieved 2nd September 2024). 126. For whom the (IE) Tocharian language, was initially predominant (now extinct). It is related to Sogdian and Scythian Saka languages.

PROTO-SLAVIC PEOPLES: THEIR IDOLS, BELIEFS AND ORIGINS

Understanding the movements, trade and settlement of diverse peoples across northern Europe allows us to build a clearer perspective regarding the spiritual nature of their cultural approaches to life and death, specifically what areas were commonalities, or idiosyncratic - what were unique or generic. With this knowledge, we may discover certain traits, names or forms we now recognise in the figure we came to know as Óðinn, and of the activities associated with this dramatic figure.

We find numerous origin legends recounted in poetry, a narrative device Snorre and other Scandinavian medieval poets made good use of in their manipulations of historical sources, both oral and written. For instance, both English and Frankish legends claim a distinctive heritage whereby the elite or ruling peoples of north-west Europe and Scandinavia can trace their ancestors back to Óðinn, whom it is said, arrived from the East with six sons, and further, that he and his sons founded dynasties in those regions.

During the long and fruitful occupation of the Ukraine by humankind, one of their most impactful advances was in the domestication of the horse somewhere between the late Neolithic (c. 4000 BCE) and the Bronze Age (c. 2000 BCE). By the 8th century BCE, the Scythians (Scoloti) had settled amongst the Eastern Slavs[127] in the Ukraine, making it the centre of their expansive influences, culturally and politically.

Germanic cultural origins, its people and beliefs can be traced to these regions from the proto-historic period through to the Bronze and Iron Ages. From the Eurasian Steppes around 4000 years BCE, the movement of these peoples first occurred, continuing in pulsing

---

127. Ancestors to the modern Ukrainians, modern Belarusians and Russians. See: Philip Longsworth. "*Russia: The Once and Future Empire from Pre-History to Putin.*" (St. Martin's Press, 2006): 38

migrations up until around 2300 BCE. They remained a semi-nomadic, pastoralist, patriarchal, patrilinear people[128] focussed on horse-breeding, which gave them exceptional mobility and allowed them to infiltrate and dominate the regions that surrounded them in later centuries. In common with many other peoples of this vast region across the east, horses were held in great reverence. As discussed previously, a central tenet in the ethnicity of these peoples, the horse (in both principle and symbol), massively influenced the cultures of Iran (Scythian) Sarmatian and Germanic peoples to the west. We know that the repeated incursions into the proto-Slavic agricultural and pastoralist regions, first by peoples of the Iranian language groups, then by the Germanic Goths,[129] induced a cultural shift throughout the ancestral Slavic lands of the western Ukraine and into adjacent lands, during the Migration Age. That Slavic tribes had not perished under the Goths is evidenced by historical records. Slavs and Germanic peoples were inexorably entwined since the Bronze Age, continuing close interactions through custom and lore and culture.

Many Germanic loan words remain in Slavic language for – house, stall, stable, grave, loaf, dish, kettle debt, interest, profit, loan, raid, warrior, deceive, sword, metal for money, tribute, knight, hero, priest, trumpet, wine, fig, garment, letter, writing, book, armed troop, penalty tax, property, cattle, church, helmet, hill, animals, wall, fence - indicating a commonality of culture. Goths exerted strong influences of spirituality over their Slavic subjects. The Gothic interlude was ultimately terminated by the unrelenting hostilities of the Hunnic horde who decimated these regions before their own advances came to an abrupt end with the death of Atilla in 453 CE.[130]

Prior to these dramatic Iron Age events, the peoples of the north

---

128. Note, not misogynist. Unlike the Roman patriarchy, the women of these tribal peoples were highly regarded and enjoyed significant freedoms not afforded their illustrious Roman sisters. **129.** The Gothic migrations began in 166 CE. Ostragoths reached the Black Sea c. 214 CE, clashing with the Dacians on the Roman frontier. These states flourished until the Hunnic invasion 375 CE. **130.** Atilla's last wife seems to have had a Germanic name form, Ildico, which may be a diminutive form of the noun *hildaz, meaning battle, and given to Hildr, a Valkyrja. Hildr is a common element in Germanic female names, as found in *Grímhild or *Kremhild, Svanhildr, Brynhildr and Gunnhildr. Her name is often reconstructed as *Hildiko ('little Hildr'). See: George T. Gillespie. *Catalogue of Persons Named in German Heroic Literature, 700-1600: Including Named Animals and Objects and Ethnic Names.* (Oxford University, 1973): 21. See also: Katherine Marie Olley. "The Icelandic Hogni: The Re-imagining of a Nibelung Hero in the Eddic Tradition." *Scandinavian Studies.* 90 (2) (2018): 237-264. doi:10.5406/scanstud.90.2.0237. (Accessed 15th March 2022).

PROTO-SLAVIC PEOPLES 165

Pontic Steppe assimilated the dominant culture of the husbandmen of the east (during the Chalcolithic Copper Age), which then tracked across into the Balkans, and central Europe (passing through Bulgaria, Macedonia, Romania, and Bosnia), shifting down into the Danube along trade routes. The Steppe peoples brought agriculture, hill forts and sophisticated burials involving house-like timber structures erected within low mounds, filled with simple unpainted pottery of cord-ware impressions.[131] This denotes a marked departure from the collective passage graves (noted in European Stone Age) into the chieftain and elite burial mounds or Kurgans of the much wealthier Bronze Age.

Migrations of eastern Germanic peoples began in the wake of the aggressive incursions from peoples of this Kurgan mound culture. Southern Scandinavia experienced a similar immense cultural change as an era of competing chieftains and of a warrior elite. Barrow cemeteries with inhumation cists were arranged near settlements, along the riverbanks or shores, persisting in the proto-Slavic regions. Cremations and flat cemeteries developed very slowly, overlapping with the newer round barrows constructed with timber roofs, that sound very similar to the early description of the mythical halls and realms of the Scandinavian gods – Valhöll, and Ásgarðr. Tumuli with very different artefacts are found within eastern Slovakia and south-east Poland, north-west Ukraine (Moldavia and Kiev).

Around 1200 BCE, the people of the Steppe moved west from the lower Volga, north of the Black Sea into the Dniester river basin and the north Carpathian regions, bringing metallurgy to the Proto Slavic peoples. Trade from the west, initiated further cultural changes. Bronze Age trade however, was in ornamental metalwork rather than weaponry.[132] The archaeological remains of several gold smithies and jewellery workshops confirm a developed trade. This quickly changed as the demand for weapons increased, at which point, Iron bars were then used as currency. Delineated by the Steppe belt and the Carpathians, this probable nucleus of the Slavic peoples was retained by the Polabian Slavs, close to where the Germanic peoples emerged, and with whom they were later in considerable conflict, particularly during the 6th to 7th centuries CE. Distinct from the Carpathian regions of the Slavs, the Proto-Germanic regions include Holland,

---

131. Mounds, grave goods - originally simple jewellery and pottery, flint knives to bronze, from stone spear heads to bronze. Flint sickles, animal bones confirm their agriculture and animal domestication. North Pontic peoples favoured stone cist graves in round barrows with timber roofs. **132.** Proto Slavs made very few weapons compared to Europe, Germany and Iran. Iron was not introduced until later.

166 PIRATES, MERCHANTS, DEVILS & DARK DEEDS

Denmark, Sweden and western Germany. By the Bronze Age however, the Proto-Slavic peoples had begun to form greater distinctions from their Germanic neighbours through influences into Germany from central Europe.[133]

Over time, the Proto-Slavs absorbed the ethnicities of surrounding peoples who entered and settled in their homeland. In fact, the north Pontic area became a melting pot of peoples who survived the Scythian encroachments, the expansion of Greek cities,[134] the settlement of Roman provinces, and more latterly, the infiltration of Sarmatians and Germanic tribes. c.400 BCE to 200 BCE. West of the Black Sea, between the Finno-Ugric tribes of the north and the Roman borders to the south, the Vandals moved into the regions between the Oder and the Elbe, previously occupied by ancient Slavic peoples. Due to the movements of Vandals and Goths, Przeworsk culture[135] appeared in southern Poland (eastern Slovakia). Their ethnic decor, pottery and jewellery design is similar to Moldavian and Prague work, and to culture established as the Romanised Celtic tradition of 2nd to the 4th century. The East Slavs of the Ukraine (approximately present-day Romania) lived alongside Hellenised Sarmatians, Romanised Greeks, Dacians and Getae, together with the new Germanic/Gothic occupants, sharing an extensive network of trade, commerce and cultural exchange. This is evidenced in the richer grave goods of this period that includes many items of Slavic influence: glass beads, ornate combs, Scythian bows, trapezoidal fibulae with the pointelle decoration that so enamoured the Germanic bracteate and weapon manufacturers, clay figurines and pottery decorated with the very popular swastika, similar to that noted on the Spong Hill artefact found in the UK.

Beloved by the Scythians, the griffin was a recurring motif, particularly on metal-work. Other items that appear in these cross-cultural burials include: barbed arrow heads, Roman fibulae and bracteates, Scythian and Sarmatian belt clasps, rare Avar Silver spurs

---

133. A unity existed between the Balts and Slavs who were separated from Europe and who shared a common language root. **134.** Contact with Greek culture significantly affected Sarmatian culture and art which therefore influenced Slavic culture in turn. In time the Sarmatian lost its distinctive Greek traits and the north Pontic region became synthesised in a more uniform material culture. **135.** The Przeworsk culture is part of an Iron Age archaeological complex that dates from the 3rd century BCE to the 5th century CE. It ran concurrent with that of Hallstatt (Upper Austria, linked to Proto-Celtic and early Celtic people of the Early Iron Age in Europe, c. 800 to 450 BCE) and La Tène (Switzerland, European Iron Age, site dates to about 450 BCE to the 1st century BCE and extends from Ireland to Anatolia and from Portugal to Czechia).

PROTO-SLAVIC PEOPLES 167

and wooden buckets with bronze pointille decoration. At this time, many of the graves are still largely of timber construction, styled as small huts within low mounds.[136] Slavic and Germanic elements continued to merge through their farming communities as the Slavs absorbed the former Germanic peoples in the 6th century, when they entered the middle and upper Elbe valley, shortly after settling in Bohemia c. 500 CE to 550 CE. They drank mead and barley wine, made boats from hollowed trees, and spoke a barbaric language, but also Hunnic, Gothic and Latin, characteristics shared by all Slavic peoples. Their culture is that which many might typically think of as Germanic/Scandinavian, yet the ethnicity is clearly Slavic, differing substantially however from the Germanic Franks, the Merovingians, whose later conversion to Catholicism, inevitably changed the expression of their beliefs through culture.

From around 700 BCE to 400 CE, Iranian, Sarmatian and Scythian influences from the North Pontic, is strongly present in this region, being especially notable in language structure. Rivers north of the Black Sea also carry Iranian names. Certain Iranian words drafted into the Slavic languages, notably – *Bogu* for a generic divine spirit, *ragi* for paradise, and *svetu* for a specific divine quality – establish the spiritual core of a relationship with all things Other, as virtues later developed into localised 'god-forms.' This was of course, a universal tendency, and not unique to these regions. Common Germanic names for Indo-European trees such as oak, ash, hornbeam birch, alder, aspen elm, and maple, were adopted into the proto-Slavic language, suggesting a Slavic homeland location devoid of those deciduous trees in the forest Steppe belt northeast of the Carpathian Mountains. For example, the word *buk*, for beech, is adapted from Germanic language groups. Around the first century CE, in Bello Gallica 6, 10., it appears as *baca,* as in the expression *silva bacenis*.[137] The analytical disciplines that linguistics and archaeology provide greatly advance our understanding of the development of culture for these peoples, enabling us to look beyond literary sources, which taken in isolation, are wholly unreliable.

Though of vague location, somewhere north of the Black Sea, the whole northern region stretching to the Ural Mountains was inhabited by Scythians, Sarmatians, and Alans, the Souveni and the Alanorsi. Historical records do not generally name the Slavic tribes prior to the first centuries CE., by which time, the Slavic lands had already been

---

136. Cremations and inhumations also continue. **137.** Caesar provides further examples for other trees such as larch, yew etc. Beech larch and yew grew to the west of the original Slavic homeland. The Balts, the Indo-Iranians, the Illyrians, and Germanic speakers all shame similar linguistics.

invaded by Sarmatians and Germanic tribes. Ptolemy (100 CE to 178 CE), had referred to the Slovani, which he wrote as Soubenoi (Suevian perhaps?), a name that vanished from the record, surfacing as Sklavenoi[138] centuries later in an account of the Gothic Wars (c.536-7 CE) by the 6th -Century Byzantine historian, Procopius.[139] Slav is an elusive term, often described inaccurately as meaning slave. However, Slava means glory; Slovo, meaning word or speech, and could imply a people who share a similar tongue (like the Celts), unlike their Germanic neighbours to the west, who did not. It is also a term that may relate to the Polish word for flax – slowien in the Ukraine – slovien. As a healing plant, its Indo-European root means to be clean and pure. Themes of abundance and purification permeate Slavic culture, being particularly relevant to their belief structure. To that end certain taboos were prescribed alongside the deeply rooted traditional customs that maintained ritual purity.[140]

Culture is dependent upon environment, and is a product of it. Centuries of Slavic colonisation from their homeland nucleus, created a wide dispersal of culture and language, forming a deeper tribal identity distinct between the alpine and Czech regions and those of the Ukraine and Russian Steppe and plains peoples, which were fundamentally Asiatic.[141] Clan and kindred groups reflect Slavic culture.

Jordanes' descriptions of Columbanus' experiences with the Slavs very much reflects what the material record confirms of the structure and organisation of domestic and ritual space arranged to effect a harmony with their cosmology. Feasting and hospitality were imperatives of this society. The focus on the hearth as a shrine as a core-centred family unit is highly significant; that nuclear hearth when extended to a larger family is called an 'otdel,'[142] meaning a sharing of foundation, a communal place of nurture (very similar to Oðel). A house father and house mother were head-kinsmen for their family unit. Natural ethnicity dissipated however, the further from the Steppe the people moved. A military aristocracy, mounted as cavalry was named vitiez, a Slavic term derived from Germanic Vikingr or hvitvingr, which appears to signify mercenary warriors. Graves containing mounted warriors appear in the

---

138. This was possibly the Slavic peoples of the lower Danube region, making the Sklavenoi, the south Slavs the first to be mentioned as such historically. **139.** Jordanes, a contemporary of Procopius, discusses the Sclavini in his history of 551 CE, locating them between Carpathian Mountains and the Urals, somewhat east of Dniester river. They dispersed from their original homeland outwards into Slovakia, Czechoslovakia, Pomerania and Novgorod. **140.** These fundamental priorities survived in folklore as various customs noted and recorded in the 19th century. **141.** See Appendix IV. **142.** Marija Gimbutas. *The Slavs*. Edited by Dr. Glyn Daniel. (Thames and Hudson, 1971): 137

Avar period. Stirrups were introduced by the Avars; horse trapping and masks for the horses too. Swords were an insignia of rank.

Ukraine's true political power originated with the establishment of a state known as the Kievan Rus' (6th to the 13th century CE). Although the origins of the word Rus' remain uncertain, a possibility arises in 'Rhos,' a term applied to the Swedes associated with a founding dynasty based in Kyiv, a city that in the ensuing centuries became a pivotal trading hub for both the Christian Byzantine Europe and the Islamic East. The Rus' are rumoured to have been formed of early Swedish migrants and traders who by the 10th century, were assimilated into the native Slavic culture. Major trade routes flowed down the three main rivers of the Eurasian Steppe: The Volga, The Kama and The Vyatka. Battles for domination of regional pastureland and trading networks were a constant tribulation for the peoples who settled there. Kazan Tatars formed the main population along that route.

Other peoples of these regions scattered across the Pontic-Caspian Steppe and Siberia in smaller groups, include the nomadic horse archers, the Kipchak (QıpCaq) people contribute substantially to this fascinating, evolving history. This is especially notable in their expansion outwards from the Altai region over the following centuries as part of a confederation with the Cumans with whom they fused, culturally and ethnically, exchanging weaponry and language skills. As part of the Türkic Khaganate of the Altai region of the Eurasian Steppe, the Kipchak (QıpCaq) people are first mentioned in the 8th century. According to Kipchak (QıpCaq) folk etymology, their name means hollow tree, being the place in myth, where their original human ancestress gave birth to her son.[143] The term offers intriguing possibilities associated with Hela, whose form is typically a hollow tree, especially her back (side) that is always hidden from view. Cumans had shamans who were required to communicate with the spirit world to forecast the outcome of certain actions and events, to heal, and to deal with the spirits of the dead.[144] The Cumans referred to their shamans as Kam (female: kam katun); their activities were referred to as qamlyqet, meaning 'to prophesy.'[145]

---

143. János Eckmann. "The Mamluk-Kipchak Literature." In, Central Asiatic Journal, Vol. 8 (no. 4) (Harrassowitz Verlag, 1963): 304-319. https://www.jstor.org/stable/i40089557 (Accessed 8th July 2024). **144.** Peter Linehan; Janet Laughland Nelson; Marios Costambeys. (Eds.) The Medieval World Routledge Worlds Series 10, 82-83 (Routledge. 2003). **145.** Ibid.

WARRIOR FUNERARY STELAE

Khazar, Uygur, Ashlnà, Kipchak and Cuman peoples shared funerary and Kurgan burial practises for housing the cremated or inhumed bodies, along with grave goods. Cuman and Bulgar nobles were typically buried in full warrior gear, seated on a chair, with their prized horse, weapons and most trusted or honoured retainer, or servant while alive.[146] Anthropomorphic stone stelae were erected upon the top and around the kurgans (i.e. tumuli). Spanning five millennia[147] – across Anatolia, Eurasia and throughout Russia, from the Crimea to the Ukraine particularly - these rough-cut obelisks are multi-ethnic, representing various cultures and peoples as testaments to eternity. Two stelae contain female figures, depicted without limb definition, dated sometime between the 15th and the 11th centuries BCE, perhaps derived from a Eurasian Steppe culture that had infiltrated into the Near East.[148]

The very earliest are associated with the Pit Grave culture of the Pontic-Caspian Steppe (and therefore with the Proto-Indo-Europeans).[149] Iron Age specimens are identified with the Scythians, while medieval examples are identified with Türkic peoples, as memorials to the honoured dead. Known as babas (Kyrgyz - balbal), a term rooted in a Türkic word meaning ancestor or grandfather,[150] the

---

146. Julian Baldick. *Animal and Shaman: Ancient Religions of Central Asia* (I.B. Tauris, 2012): 53 147. The earliest anthropomorphic stelae date to the 4th millennium BCE, and are associated with the early Bronze Age Yamna Horizon, in particular with the Kemi Oba culture of the Crimea and adjacent Steppe region. See: J. P. Mallory and D. Q. Adams. "Kemi Oba Culture," In, *Encyclopaedia of Indo-European Culture,* 327-8 (Taylor Francis, 1997a). 148. Veli Sevin. "Mystery Stelae." In, *Archaeology* Volume 53, Number 4, (July/August 2000) https://www.jstor.org/stable/41779470 (Accessed 16th June 2024). See also Antonio Sagona *The Heritage of Eastern Turkey:* from earliest settlements to Islam (Macmillan Art Publishing. 2006): 68-71 149. Similar stelae are found in large numbers in Southern Russia, Ukraine, Prussia, southern Siberia, Central Asia, Turkey and Mongolia. See: D.W. Anthony. *The Horse, The Wheel, and The Language: How Bronze-Age Riders from The Eurasian Steppes Shaped The Modern World.* Princeton University Press, 2007.

impression is one of fond commemoration. As markers of prestige amongst the peoples of the Altai regions, some represented a less benign purpose. The many that once formed circular boundaries around the kurgans and causeways, and the rows to them, featured as peoples subjugated in conquest, or of enemies overcome in battle.[151] Many tombs have no balbals. Apparently, there are buried ashes of women and children.

Balbals have two clearly distinct forms: conical (The Steppe-dwellers) and flat, with shaved tops (Altaians). These curious conical and flat shapes also appear as 8th-century headdresses.[152] Amongst the oldest balbals found are the several hundred primitive Slavic examples situated in the Ukraine,[153] most of which are crude, rough-hewn slabs with simple protruding heads bearing basic facial features; some trunks give the impression of limbs or breasts. Others specimens are considerably more complex, featuring ornaments, weapons, human or animal figures.[154] The simple, early type of anthropomorphic stelae are also found in the Alpine region of Italy, southern France and Portugal.[155] Further examples have also been found in Bulgaria.

Some obelisks are found still standing on kurgans, others were found buried in the slopes. Many have been destroyed or removed from the perimeters of the mounds that encircled them. Whether present as guardians or as symbols of conquest is hard to determine. The contemporary relationship between the mounds, the obelisks on the top, and those around them, remains uncertain, as is the matter of their status. Thankfully, various European and Russian antiquarians and travellers of the 13th to the 19th centuries,[156] noted the appearance

---

150. Stone babas (rock figures) found across southern Ukraine and other areas of the Russian Steppes, were associated with Cuman shamanism. Because the Cumans tolerated all religions, conversions to Islam and Christianity ocurred quickly. See: Forostyuk, O. D. Luhansk Religious Region Lugansk: Svitlytsia, 2004. **151.** L. N. Gumilev. Ancient Türks (Ayris Press [1993] 2007): 261 **152.** Ibid. **153.** Anthony, 2007: 339 **154.** Mallory and Adams, 1997a.: 544-546. **155.** The Cimmerians of the early 1st millennium BCE left around ten distinctive stone stelae. Another four or five deer stones dating to the same time period are known from the northern Caucasus. See: John Robb. "People of Stone: Stelae, Personhood And Society In Prehistoric Europe." In, Journal of Archaeological Method and Theory, Vol. 16, no. 3 (2009):162-183 DOI 10.1007/s10816-009-9066-z (Accessed 18th June 2024). **156.** Kurgan obelisks are quarried from sandstone, limestone or granite, averaging around 3.5 m to 0.7 m in height, but many reach 1.5-2 m. Most are simple stone columns of indeterminate sex. Men have moustaches (sometimes with beard) with metal breastplates and belts, sometimes with a sword or other weapons.; women are with bared breasts, wearing peculiar headdresses, with girdles or necklaces on the neck.

and location of kurgan obelisks complete with illustrations, preserving to some extent our scant knowledge of these people and their customs. Shortly after a mass baptism of Cumans in Moldavia in 1277 CE, a Franciscan traveller who visited the Mongols provides a striking account of Cuman customs.

Cumans built statues for dead notables, facing east and holding a cup (these statues are not to be confused with the balbals, which represent the enemies that were killed by him). He also notes that for richer notables, the Cumans built tombs in the form of houses. Rubruk gives an eyewitness account about a man who had recently died: the Cumans had hung up sixteen horses' hides, in groups of four, between high poles, facing the four points of the compass. The mourners then also placed koumis (a fermented mares' milk drink widely drunk in Inner Asia) for the dead man to consume. Other graves had plenty of stones statues placed around them (balbals), with four tall ones placed to face the points of the compass.[157]

The reference to the four taller posts, situated to face the cardinal points brings to mind the enigmatic Zbruch obelisk, the Khirigsuur, and the equally mysterious polycephalic tools found in various graves. That these objects are linked to their cultural beliefs is unequivocal. Overseeing, or the ability to see in all directions, is evidently a significant imperative of guardianship. That principle is carried through into Scandinavian mythology in the figures of Heimdallr and Óðinn whose ubiquitous sight is legendary. Animism is the single prominent unifying feature of the Steppe peoples of Eurasia and the Artic regions, enduring from the Neolithic - through the Bronze Age into the Migration and Iron Ages.

There were groups of Kipchaks in the Pontic-Caspian Steppe, Syr Darya and Siberia. The Cuman-Kipchak confederation was eventually conquered by the Mongols in the early 13th century. The Kipchaks practiced Shamanism, although Muslim conversion occurred near Islamic centres.[158] Medieval Kipchaks possessed blue or green eyes

---

157. The Cumans [Kipchak] were known by the Germans as Valans and their province Valania, which stretched from the Danube as far as the Don, being the borderline of Asia and Europe. The Cuman Kipchaks lived and pastured their sheep on that land between the Don and the Volga. See: W. W. Rockhill. "The Journey of William of Rubruck To The Eastern Parts of The World, 1253-55, As Narrated By Himself, With Two Accounts of The Earlier Journey of John of Pian de Carpine." (London: Hakluyt Society, 1900).
158. Some Kipchaks and Cumans converted to Islam, joining the Golden Horde; others converted to Christianity in the 11th century to repel the Horde's dominance. See: Timothy May. "The Mongol Empire." In, A Historical Encyclopaedia [2 Volumes]. (ABC-CLIO, 2016).Sources and y-dna Studies with Regard to the Early and Medieval Türkic Peoples." In, Inner Asia, 19 (2) (2017):197-239. DOI:10.1163/22105018-12340089 (Accessed 17th July 2023).

and red hair,[159] causing the Chinese to mistake them for the newly arrived Russians. Similarly, the Cumans were reported to be handsome people with blond hair, fair skin and blue eyes,[160] often mistaken for Scandinavians by other traders and travellers, especially by Arabs.

The Cuman-Kipchaks operated via marital alliances. The fundamental unit of Cuman society was the family, made up of blood relatives. A group of families formed a clan, led by a chief; a group of clans formed a tribe, led by a khan. Cuman ancestors were celebrated, and provided status for the living. The dead received objects whose lavishness indicated the recipient's social rank. Like other nomadic nations, the Cuman-Kipchaks initiated binding blood oaths (with the purpose of symbolically cementing a bond) by the drinking or mixing of each other's blood.

Cuman divination practices used sacred animals, especially the wolf and dog. Individual, tribes and clans were also named after the various types of wolf and dog, or sometimes a leader of the clan. Clans lived together in movable settlements on carts named 'Cuman towers' by Kievan Rus' chroniclers. The Cumans were fierce and formidable nomadic warriors of the Eurasian Steppe, culturally sophisticated, and militarily powerful, who exerted an enduring influence on the medieval Balkans, wielded mainly through its grip on trade along the Volga river and to the Orient. The Cumans were thus active in commerce with traders from Central Asia to Venice, having a commercial interest in Crimea, where they also took tribute from Crimean cities. The Cumans entered the grasslands of the present-day southern Russian Steppe in the 11th century CE and went on to assault the Byzantine Empire, the Kingdom of Hungary, and the Kievan Rus'.

The Cumans imposed strict rules (taboos) against theft and other transgressions, so the law of blood vengeance was very common among the Cuman-Kipchaks. Cuman-Kipchak women fought alongside their fellow male warriors. Women were shown great respect and would often ride on a horse or wagon while the men walked.161 Cuman men wore elaborate 'spirit' masks in battle. To that end, the Cuman people practiced a curious belief system that blended animistic and shamanistic

---

159. Their characteristic phenotype links them to the Pecheneg nomads found in the kurgans in eastern Ukraine. See: Joo-Yup Lee and Shuntu Kuang. "A Comparative Analysis of Chinese Historical Sources and y-dna Studies with Regard to the Early and Medieval Türkic Peoples." In, *Inner Asia*, 19 (2) (2017): 197-239. DOI:10.1163/22105018-12340089 (Accessed 17th July 2023). **160.** Ion Grumeza. *The Roots of Balkanization: Eastern Europe C.E. 500–1500*. (University Press of America. 2010). **161.** Cumans: Encyclopediaofukraine.com. (Accessed 10th May 2020).

174 PIRATES, MERCHANTS, DEVILS & DARK DEEDS

elements, known as Tengrism. As external observers of the rituals and beliefs of the Türks and Mongols, Western anthropologists first applied 'shamanism' as a term that focuses primarily upon the rituals of the neighbouring[162] Tungusic and Samoyedic-speaking peoples.[163] As one of the major non-Christian forms of religious belief widely practiced in Central Eurasia, Tngriism, or Tengriism,[164] is a complex Proto-Indo-European religion that formalised an overlay of insular animisms with pastoral shamanic practices from the western Steppe.[165] "The structure of the reconstructed Proto-Indo-European religion is actually closer to that of the early Türks than to the religion of any people of Neolithic European, Near Eastern or Mediterranean antiquity."[166] Possessing a diverse number of deities, spirits and gods (tngrii), Tengrism successfully syncretised the various disparate Türkic and Mongolic folk religions.[167]

---

162. Being similar to various other religious traditions of Siberia, Central Asia and Northeast Asia. See: Raffaele Pettazzoni. "Turco-Mongols and Related Peoples. The All-Knowing God." In, Researches into Early Religion and Culture. Translated by H. J. Rose. (Methuen and Co. [1955] 1956): 261 **163.** In theory, core shamanism applies only to subsistence level nomads of the Tungus regions. However, reflex shamanism is a broader more inclusive term for semi-nomadic peoples of the Altai regions of Southern Siberia. **164.** Tengrism is a 19th century term that refers to a folk religion originating in Central Asia and the Eurasian Steppes that relates to an Iron Age religion. Also known as Tengriism, Tengerism, or Tengrianism. **165.** See: "Song of the North," a forthcoming unpublished ms, by Shani Oates. **166.** Andrei A. Znamensky. "Az osiség szépsége: altáji török sámánok a szibériai regionális gondolkodásban (1860-1920)." In, Csodaszarvas. Ostörténet, vallás és néphagyomány. Vol. I, 128 (in Hungarian). Edited by Adam Molnár. (Molnár Kiadó, 2005). **167.** Pettazzoni, [1955] 1956. The term folk religion refers to the variable domestic beliefs and practises of the people as opposed to either that of the state (where appropriate) or of elite cultic practices.

TENGRISM

Within the broad spectrum of belief concerning the unseen spirits of the Otherworld, various, similar shamanic traditions developed during the early Iron Age,[168] built upon the concepts founded in the animistic principles of the terrestrial and extra-terrestrial worlds known as Tengrism, a belief predominantly of the heavens as the holy motivating force within the Universe, but also of the earth. The Türkic supreme spirit of the heavens (as sky, light and the Sun) is represented by the oldest known Türko-Mongolian word that may have originated on the frontiers of China in the 2nd century BCE. Tengri/Tangra (Tengeri/Tangara)[169] was first recorded in Chinese chronicles in the 4th century BCE as the divine figure worshipped by the Asiatic Huns who later formed the Xiongnu Empire (c. 209 BCE).

"There is no doubt that between the 6th and 9th centuries, Tengrism was the religion among the nomads of the steppes."[170]

A 9th-Century manuscript, 'Irk Bitig,' known as the 'Book of Omens,' refers to Tengri as Türük Tängrisi (God of Turks).[171] Although the chief tngri is Köke Mongke Tngri (Eternal Blue Heaven[172]), his dualistic counterpart is Etügen Eke (Earth-Mother). Between them exists a multiplicity of elemental and lesser spirits of the Otherworld. Some have suggested that Tngri (the Sky) is derived from Old Türkic: Tenk (daybreak) or Tan (dawn).[173]

Of the numerous tngrii (spirits) mentioned in the Secret History

168. See: "Song of the North," a forthcoming unpublished ms, by Shani Oates for further information relating to Sámi Shamanism. **169.** Both possess pre-Turkic and pre-Mongolian ethnic elements. **170.** According to Hungarian archaeological research, the religion of the Magyars (Hungarians) until the end of the 10th C. (before Christianity) was a form of Tengrism and Shamanism. See: Yazar András Róna-Tas, *Hungarians and Europe in the early Middle Ages: an introduction to early Hungarian history.* (Yayıncı Central European University Press, 1999). **171.** Talât Tekin and Irk Bitig. "The Book of Omens." In, *Turcologica* 18. (Harrassowitz Verlag, 1993). **172.** Tngri (Heaven) is considered cognate with the Indo-European *Dyeus, meaning divine, and the East Asian Tian (Chinese: Sky; Heaven). **173.** Tanyu Hikmet. *İslâmlıktan Önce Türkler'de Tek Tanrı İnancı* [The Belief of Monotheism among Pre-Islamic Turks] (in Turkish) (Ankara Universitesi Basimevi Ankara, 1980): 11-13

of the Mongols that exist in various forms and groups across a wide-ranging area geographically, each according to function,[174] most notable of these are the tngrii of the four corners, whose presence in the funerary khirigsuur are again evident as guardians of the cardinal directions, reflecting those of the aforementioned burial that influenced Ibn Fadlan.[175]

As a religious practise, Tengrism rose in popularity to become the official religion of several medieval states,[176] developing to meet the needs of a more complex society by the 12th to the 13th centuries. This elevated Tngri to a monistic overarching holy force of nature witnessed through the sacred glory (light, fire, elements, wind etc) of the heavens above, who encompasses a range of animistic presences and spirts to fulfil the various roles and tasks asked of him. The lesser elemental tngrii spirits, however, are split unevenly between benevolent spirits of light and malevolent, terrifying spirits of the dark. All tngrii were called upon only by leaders and great shamans belonging to all the clans and responsible for their welfare. Three groups of ancestral tngrii[177] command attention: those of former chieftains or leaders, whose souls could be propitiated by any family or clan member, or petitioned for help; the Protector-Spirits that include the souls of great shamans; and as Guardian-Spirits made up of the souls of lesser shamans and land spirits associated with a specific locality assigned to each clan. By living a respectful life that does not violate the laws of nature, humankind may continue to exist in harmony in a balanced world, free from chaos, enabling them to perfect their personal (wind-horse) spirit.

Horses were central to Cuman culture and semi-nomadic way of life, and their main activity was animal husbandry,[178] raising horses,

---

174. Klaus Hesse. "On the History of Mongolian Shamanism in Anthropological Perspective." In, *Anthropos* 82, no. 4/6 (1987): 403-13 http://www.jstor.org/stable/40463470. 49 (Accessed 11th June 2021). See also: Walther Heissig. *The Religions of Mongolia*, Translated by Geoffrey Samuel. (Routledge & Kegan-Paul, 1970).
175. By 1000 CE, there was a differentiation between the western and eastern parts of the Mongolian landscape. Heissig, 1970: 70   **176.** Göktürk Khaganate, Western Türkic Khaganate, Eastern Turkic Khaganate, Old Great Bulgaria, Danube Bulgaria, Volga Bulgaria, and Eastern Tourkia (Khazaria). Among Türkic peoples Tengrism was radically supplanted by Islam, while in Mongolia it survives as a synthesis with Tibetan Buddhism. See Appendix V   **177.** Marlene Laruelle. "Tengrism: In Search For Central Asia's Spiritual Roots." In, *Central Asia-Caucasus Analyst Bi-Weekly Briefing* Vol. 8, no. 5, (Kennan Institute, 2006).   **178.** Justin Dragosani-Brantingham. "An Illustrated Introduction to the Kipchak Turks." ([1999] 2011) (PDF). www.kipchak.com. (Accessed 29th October 2020)

sheep, goats, camels, and cattle. They moved north with their herds in summer and returned south in winter. Some Cumans began trading and farming, as well as blacksmithing, some were involved in furriery, shoe making, saddle making, bow making, and textiles. They mainly sold and exported animals, mostly horses, and animal products. Cuman names were descriptive and represented a personal trait or an idea. As they were close to the Kievan Rus' principalities, Cuman khans and important families began to slavicize their names. Ukrainian princely families were often connected by marriage with Cuman khans, lessening wars and conflicts.

The Codex Cumanicus was initially written by Italian merchants c.1294 CE.[179] It was later combined with Cuman riddles, religious texts and some Italian verses from German missionaries, c.1356,[180] as a linguistic manual for the Türkic Cuman language of the Middle Ages, designed to help Catholic missionaries communicate with the Cumans. It consisted of a Latin-Persian-Cuman glossary, grammar observations, lists of consumer goods and Cuman riddles. Trade between Italian merchants and Crimean traders along the Black Sea had developed in the 13th century and these manuals advised on the religion, culture and customs of the peoples they would likely encounter on trading missions, much as a modern travel guide might offer, including translations, key words and a gazetteer.[181] Within them, the Cuman Riddles are a crucial source for the study of early Türkic folklore. The Cumans' language was a form of Kipchak Türkic that appears to have possessed a stylised rúnic script found in a Cuman grave.[182] Iranian words designate certain religious concepts.

---

179. Some parts are older, dating to the 11th Century. **180.** Éva Kincses-Nagy. *A Disappeared People and a Disappeared Language: The Cumans and the Cuman language of Hungary*, (Szeged University Press, 2013): 17 **181.** Joseph F Stanley. "Negotiating Trade: Merchant Manuals and Cross-Cultural Exchange in the Medieval Mediterranean." *The Interdisciplinary Journal of Study Abroad Volume XXX, Issue 1*, Winter (Simmons College, 2018) https://files.eric.ed.gov/fulltext/EJ1168964.pdf (Accessed 27th July 2021) **182.** Kincses-Nagy, 2013: 176

THE ROYAL SCYTHIANS AND THE STEPPE PEOPLES

Other peoples from these regions whose remarkable cultures have augmented our vast historical legacy and whose funerary traditions as mentioned by Herodotus, may originate in similar or shared practises amongst Siberian indigenous groups, particularly their sacred relationship with horses and stags. Norse culture was certainly enriched by it, ultimately, as was that of the Sámi. Petroglyphs are not merely decorative art; they offer a narrative history of the beliefs of a people, in their society, but most of all, the reverence for a universal Mother, and though her iconic importance may have waned in later cultures, her presence never did. Although many of the images on the earlier Bronze Age Mongolian Deer Stones are abstract, some likewise refer to the hunt and to the warrior horde, but mainly to the importance of the Stag throughout the Bronze Age.

Herodotus crucially identified the Scythian presence along the northern coast of the Black Sea regions east into the Altai Mountains. Providing valuable ethnohistoric contexts for those contemporary peoples and their wide-ranging influences across Eurasia, Herodotus informs us that Scythian ancestors were buried far from the Black Sea, an indication perhaps that this part of Central Asia was more appropriate for burying people of high status. Royal Scythians oriented their burials in the far eastern, remote regions of their territory, in kurgan structures that vary considerably in size.[183] Located most commonly in forest and forest-Steppe regions, or near rivers, they are generally found in groups of surface structures that comprise of a large kurgan, surrounded by several smaller satellite mounds. These often radiate out from the larger tumuli or earthen mounds, and are covered over with further stones.[184]

---

183. The interior wooden structures vary in diameter from 3-120 meters, and in height, from 2-15 meters.   **184.** The Iron Age Central Eurasian landscape is dotted with burial tumuli typically termed Kurgans or khirigsuurs (also khereksurs) in Mongolia. Kurgans are structures that vary in composition based on geographic location and materials available.

THE ROYAL SCYTHIANS

From the 7th century BCE, Scythian tribes began their short-lived domination of the Pontic Steppe. They were in turn, displaced by the Sarmatians from the 2nd century BCE, except in the Crimea, where they held out for a few centuries longer. Their monumental funerary structures were the carefully crafted stone stelae we know as balbals, [185] which featured motifs in deep relief, of naked warriors with daggers, spears, and axes, holding drinking vessels (rhytons). Similar images proved popular with the later Kipchak/Cuman balbals that likewise depict warriors holding drinking horns in their upraised right hands. Many also show a sword or dagger suspended from a warrior's belt. Amongst the many stone monuments we may find on the Mongolian plane, are several balbals that again depict moustached bearded and belted male figures holding cups, raised in greeting or blessing.

The Kipchak balbals display women with necklaces, girdles and bared breasts. Some hold a rhyton. A remarkable female figurine of obvious high status holds a ring.[186] Facing east along the river trails, the balbals could represent revered individuals - tribal elders perhaps - who were most certainly important ancestors. These are not gods nor idols of gods, and should not be considered as such. Many of them are guardians and way markers of certain tombs that no doubt served as pilgrimages for current leaders and chieftains of tribes that lived and worked on these lands.

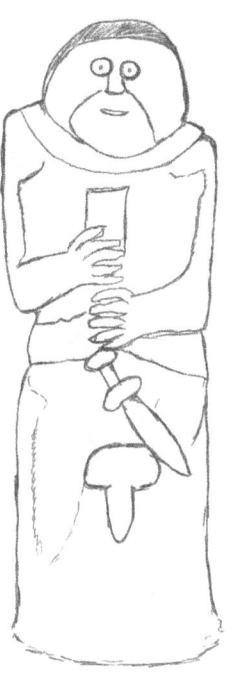

8. balbal [A Kurgan stelae (statue) of a Scythian at Khortytsia, Ukraine

Warrior culture was celebrated above all other traits. One of the artefacts discovered in this tomb depict two Scythian men drinking together from the same drinking horn in a declaration that celebrates their profound bond of brotherhood. As blood brothers, they were bound to support and defend each other to the death. Like those of the Cumans, the oath was sealed by drinking wine mixed with their

---

185. Commemorative stone stelae found in funerary contexts. **186.** L. N. Gumilev. Ancient Türks, (Moscow: Ayris Press [1993] 2007): 32

blood within a cup, from which they were expected to drink together. The highest vows were made by the king's or chieftain's hearth, the place of the sacred and the holy – being the residence of ancestry (who bear witness to such acts), and the locus of authority and law for each clan, tribe or family. Found in the Crimean Kul Oba burial mound, this tiny gold plaque is only a two-inch-high cameo, and is one of several that appears on a five-inch high vase made of gold and silver depicting warriors in various other activities. Several of these images would not be out of place on a Norse artefact.

After the 5th century BCE, Central Asian Kurgan structures (Scythian, Sarmatian, or Sauromatian[187]), were modified by the addition of a series of subterranean, inter-connected rooms where the valued belongings were buried along with the embalmed bodies of the dead. For information on Scythian funerary customs, we turn again to Herodotus, whose description of a Scythian royal funeral seems utterly incredible. Herodotus records elements of human sacrifice alongside that of horses, and of their placement as figures in staged cameos within the tombs. Stakes were apparently placed through the embalmed figures to keep them upright and together.[188]

He describes the initial erection of a massive square mound, after which the king is embalmed and processed in an open waggon around his territories amongst his lamenting subjects before he is finally buried with all his horses, treasures, weapons, armour, chattels, wine, grain, servants, wives and concubines.[189] This entire procedure takes a year to complete; the tomb is finally sealed when the dead warriors accompanying the royal chieftain are raised upon their dead horses and arranged upright in a circle around the mound, as guardians in the after world.

---

187. Labelling material culture associated with Iron Age Central Eurasian equestrians, utilizes the names Scythian, Sarmatian, Sauromatian, Saka, Xiongnu and Yuezhi by default. In reality, these terms should depend on geographic location and dating (based on stylistic chronologies) of the site and materials. All names are laden with preconceptions relating to appropriate time period, geographic location, and the type of material culture that is most associated with that label. For clarity, the Iron Age roughly concerns the 800 years between c.900 BCE -100 BCE. The term Scythian is associated with all mobile peoples of the Altai Mountains and to the west, including later sites associated with the historical terms Sarmatian and Sauromatian. Saka identifies the sites of mobile people in modern-day Kazakhstan. Xiongnu (Asiatic Huns) identifies the sites of mobile people in modern-day Mongolia and Northern China. See: Macfarland, 2010. **188.** Herodotus, Histories 2.60. See: G. C. Macaulay, G. C. (Barnes & Noble Classics, 2004). **189.** Over subsequent centuries, many of these fabulous 6th century BCE to 4th century BCE tombs (kurgans) have been robbed of their fabulous opulence; the smaller ones were ploughed over, but some remained (mainly in the Ukraine), and the excavations fully support Herodotos' account. See: David Asheri, Alan Lloyd and Aldo Corcella. A Commentary on Herodotus, Books I-IV. (Oxford University Press. 2007).

THE ROYAL SCYTHIANS 181

IV. 71. *The body of the dead king is laid in the grave prepared for it, stretched upon a mattress; spears are fixed in the ground on either side of the corpse, and beams stretched across above it to form a roof, which is covered with a thatching of osier twigs. In the open space around the body of the king they bury one of his concubines, first killing her by strangling, and also his cup-bearer, his cook, his groom, his lackey, his messenger, some of his horses, firstlings of all his other possessions, and some golden cups; for they use neither silver nor brass. After this they set to work, and raise a vast mound above the grave, all of them vying with each other and seeking to make it as tall as possible.*

IV.72. When a year is gone by, further ceremonies take place. Fifty of the best of the late king's attendants are taken, all native Scythians (for, as bought slaves are unknown in the country, the

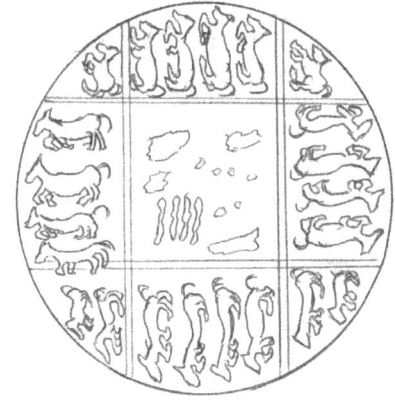

9. Scythian burial with many horses

Scythian kings choose any of their subjects that they like, to wait on them) fifty of these are taken and strangled, with fifty of the most beautiful horses. When they are dead, their bowels are taken out, and the cavity cleaned, filled full of chaff, and straightway sewn up again. This done, a number of posts are driven into the ground, in sets of two pairs each, and on every pair half the felly of a wheel is placed archwise; then strong stakes are run lengthways through the bodies of the horses from tail to neck, and they are mounted up upon the fellies, so that the felly in front supports the shoulders of the horse, while that behind sustains the belly and quarters, the legs dangling in mid-air; each horse is furnished with a bit and bridle, which latter is stretched out in front of the horse, and fastened to a peg. The fifty strangled youths are then mounted severally on the fifty horses. To effect this, a second stake is passed through their bodies along the course of the spine to the neck; the lower end of which projects from the body, and is fixed into a socket, made in the stake that runs lengthwise down the horse. The fifty riders are thus ranged in a circle round the tomb, and so left.[190]

---

190. George Rawlinson. *The History of Herodotus*, 4 vols. Edited by Jessalynn Bird, Brittany Blagburn, Anna Noone, and Marirose Osborne. (Tandy-Thomas Co, 1909). The prose has been modernized at points for the benefit of twenty-first century readers. https://human.libretexts.org/Courses/Saint_Mary's_College_(Notre_Dame_IN)/Humanistic_Studies/Supplemental_Modules/Herodotus%3A _Racist_ or_Ethnographer%3F (Accessed 10th January 2025).

Herodotus' explanation that the riders were left as unburied guardians of the dead, is a notion we find reflected in a 4th-Century BCE burial site at Chertomlÿk (in the Northern Pontic region of the Ukraine), where ground level outriders are placed as guardians to those within, corroborates Herodotus's account.[191] This grizzly tradition is well attested in European funerary contexts: "In research literature, death riders are referred to in German as 'totenreiter.'"[192] It is more probable however that Herodotus was describing a Pazyryk burial. Furthermore, "embalmed bodies have been excavated at many other sites, including the Pazyryk kurgans in the Altai region of Siberia, dated from the 5th to the 3rd centuries BCE. The Yüeh-chih culture buried at Pazyryk shares many similarities with Scythian and Sarmatian cultures."[193] Herodotus also refers to the high caps worn by the Saka in their funerary cameos that tapered to a point, topped with fixed zoomorphic wooden sculptures.

Houses for the dead were constructed of wooden logs and covered with layers of birch bark and moss, which entombed the (often embalmed) bodies placed in larch log coffins together with personal and treasured items needed in the next world. Nevertheless, Scythian funeral customs are variable, and the Royal tombs are especially unique. Petroglyphs carved by Pre-Scythian Neolithic peoples portray various tree antler styles including coniferous and deciduous representations,[194] a theme centred on The Tree of Life that was a fundamental tenet in their cosmology.

It is perhaps pertinent to recall here how the funerary traditions prevalent amongst indigenous peoples of the northern regions, invariably relate to the deer, suggesting that in times past, the deer may have acted as a (psychopompic) guide to the Underworld. A ritual conducted by the Chukchee people (without the aid of a shaman) engage four reindeer that pull the funeral sled in a procession to the burial site. Upon arrival at the site, the sled is turned and positioned so that the head of the corpse was pointed "toward 'midnight," that is to say, north. Once the reindeer are unhitched, they are killed outright,

---

191. Askold I. Ivantchick. "The Funeral of Scythian Kings." In, The Barbarians of Ancient Europe – Realities and Interactions (Cambridge University Press, 2011): 88
192. Lauren J. Barnhart. "The Totemic Significance Of The Deer In Iron Age Scythian And Sarmatian Cultures In Eastern Europe And Central Asia." Masters Degree. (Johns Hopkins University, Maryland, 2022). **193.** Ibid. **194.** Anatoli I. Martynov. "The Solar Cult and the Tree of Life," In, Arctic Anthropology, Volume 25, Number 2 (University of Wisconsin Press, 1988): 16 https://www.jstor.org/stable/i40013071 (Accessed 1st August 2023).

THE ROYAL SCYTHIANS 183

stabbed from both sides simultaneously by funerary attendants. The reins and harness are immediately put back onto the fallen reindeer, albeit in reverse of the usual placement. Within the Underworld, everything is reversed. To ensure they will be restored the right way round in the land of the dead, all items, from mirrors to bows are therefore found broken in the burial mounds. At this point, when all else is completed, "The chief of the cortège, sitting in his place astride the corpse, jerks the reins violently, and urges the reindeer with the whip, pretending that he is going fast to the country of the dead."[195]

---

195. W.W. Malandra, W. W. "The Concept of Movement in History of Religions: A Religio-Historical Study of Reindeer in the Spiritual Life of North Eurasian Peoples." *Numen* 14, no. 1 (1967): 23–69. https://doi.org/10.2307/3269697

WARRIOR PEOPLES
OF THE SUN

By the 8th century BCE, the Royal Scythians (Scoloti) had established a cultural and political heartland in the Ukraine region. Having driven out the Cimmerians, migrating groups of Scythians[196] occupied the Central Eurasian Steppe and the Forest Steppe.[197] Land to the north of the Black Sea was primarily agricultural. Migrations to these regions by strong, efficient military people, and the suppression of the agrarian population already subsisting there, was an expected pattern for these regions. The Saka (Sakas) peoples[198] gradually switched from a hunting subsistence to mainly herding sheep, cattle, and horses, a shift that led to their annexation of pastureland across the eastern Steppes, Tien Shan, and the Altai Mountains, reaching the Siberian border by the 4th century BCE.[199] Other groups from the Black Sea area of the Ukraine[200] that influenced the admixture of genetic and cultural material of the northern peoples and their cosmologies, can be found in central Europe, in whose origins lay the nomadic pastoralists of Central Asia and the Pontic-Caspian Steppe (specifically the dominant ethnic groups among the Scythian-speakers). Fragments of the Scythian (and Ossetian) language garnered from inscriptions

---

196. During the 9th century BCE, domesticated reindeer first appear east of the Ural Mountains in Siberia, spreading outwards from that region. There remains some uncertainty as to whether or not the ancestors of the Scythian peoples were reindeer herders, but the reindeer was certainly important culturally, and absolutely essential to their hunting subsistence. This and the deer's totemic reverence indicate a strong shamanic trait. Life was completely organised around herd movements. **197.** Barry Cunliffe. *The Scythians - Nomad Warriors of the Steppe* (Oxford Uni. Press, 2019).
198. Between the 9th century BCE to the 5th century CE, these nomadic Eastern Iranian peoples lived in the Eurasian Steppe and the Tarim Basin. They can be distinguished from the Scythian nomadic peoples who mainly occupied the western Steppe (of the Pontic-Caspian region of southern Russia and western Kazakhstan).
199. Kathryn Hinds. *Scythians and Sarmatians.* (Marshall Cavendish Benchmark New York, [1962] 2010). **200.** Scythia included today's Central Ukraine, South-Eastern Ukraine, Southern Russia, Russian Volga and South-Ural regions, also to a smaller extent north-eastern Balkans and around Moldova

and names quoted in ancient Greek works indicate that it was an Indo-European language. As non-literate speakers of Iranian languages, Scythian culture was maintained through oral tradition.

Although the historically attested inhabitants of these regions have been uncritically labelled as nomads, namely the Scythians, Sarmatians, Sauromatians, Saka, and Xiongnu, it is an imprecise term. In fact, there are five different Greek words that translate as nomad, but which infer nuanced distinctions, ranging from those who tend sheep, who subsist in poverty, who are without wealth, who roam, to those who thrive on pastoralism. Strabo blithely refers to the peoples of this region as nomadic wagon-dwellers. These terms are not mutually exclusive, and problems of translation and interpretation make them difficult to define. Certainly, their very complexity makes understanding the relationship with the land, and its various spirits, with all nomadic people, who maintained the seasonal herd movements across the Steppe, a problematic undertaking. Where in the past, fortified settlements were not associated with nomadic groups (even when discovered near to burial sites of nomadic peoples), recent research has initiated a re-thinking of this outmoded perspective.

Of course, as noted above, we now know that several semi-nomadic and nomadic tribes of the Iron Age (8th century BCE to the 1st century BCE) subsisting in the North Caucasus Scythian/Sarmatian sites were farmers of wheat, barley, and millet, and breeders of cattle, sheep, horses, and pigs.[201] They had a strong social structure, a ruling elite, a bonded workforce who tended the land, militias, and later, a priesthood of sorts, whom we would better understand as shamans. They produced their own pottery, examples of which have surfaced in kurgan burials contemporary with certain, selective sedentary settlements, proving the non-universal application of the term nomad.[202] Once the historical, archaeological, and ethnographic evidence is studied, certain patterns emerge for our consideration relating to cosmological factors.[203]

The Altai (Tian Shan) mountains were rich in gold and ore which required defence, giving rise to myths of strange hybrid winged beasts such as griffins,[204] a beast the Iron Age Scythians held sacred. The griffin is not dissimilar in function to the folkloric dragon, a beast also noted

---

201. Macfarland, 2010. Pastoral nomadism, a form of agriculture itself, would have been practiced in areas not conducive to other types of agriculture, and subsistence would depend entirely on the herding of animals across a large landscape constantly in search of fodder and water to keep the animals alive. **202.** Anatoly M. Khazanov. *Nomads and the Outside World*. (University of Wisconsin Press. 1994): 21 **203.** Macfarland, 2010. **204.** Adrienne Mayor. "What Were the Griffins?" *Folklore* 104 (1&2). (Taylor & Francis Group LLC, 1993): 40-53

for their fierce guardianship of gold and treasure hoards.[205] Mythical and zoomorphic themes evident in their fantastic artistry articulate a very specific Animal Style on objects associated with the Scythian, Saka, and Xiongnu peoples[206] (particularly from their burial grounds), that may assist in the location of the metallurgical processing sites of their related kurgan groups. Cultural transitions had clearly shifted from a dependence on hunting and fishing in the forests and rivers, to dependence on raising livestock in the rich pastures on the plains, to trading and manufacturing metal objects.

Large, fortified settlements throughout the Royal Scythian territories were probably constructed to protect their network of metallurgical workshops, an indication of a complex economy concerned with more than seasonal agriculture and herding animals. Around the year 450 BCE, when Herodotus visited Olbia, a Greek colony and major trading hub on the north coast of the Black Sea, he confirms the prosperity of Scythians who had become (partially) sedentary and adopted agriculture. In addition to grain, the Scythians also supplied the Greeks with slaves, livestock, and animal products such as furs and leather.[207] This made them very wealthy. Make no mistake, these were flourishing trading economies, emphasising precisely the premise I wish to convey throughout this book, of a non-static culture that is adaptive and constantly evolving. Belief systems are inexorably linked to trade, economy and subsistence, and change accordingly.

So great was the prestige attached to the Scythian peoples, many later European origin legends claim some connection to them, including the

---

205. Macfarland, 2010. Protoceratops' Skeletons found in close proximity to gold deposits, could have contributed to the idea that fabulous beasts such as the griffins guarded the "approaches to gold in the Altai foothills." **206.** "The Xiongnu, otherwise known as the Asiatic Huns, created a powerful alliance of cattle-breeding tribes in the late third to early second century BCE and then dominated the eastern part of Central Asia for four centuries." See: Sergei S. Miniaev and L. M. Sakharovskaia. Investigation of a Xiongnu Royal Tomb Complex in the Tsaraam Valley Institute for the History of Material Culture, Russian Academy of Sciences, St. Petersburg. https://edspace.american.edu/silkroadjournal/wp-content/uploads/sites/984/2017/09/Foreign-Tribes-in-the-Xiongnu-Confederation.pdf (Accessed 19th October 2023). **207.** Ateas, the last king of Scythia's golden age, died in 339 BCE fighting Philip of Macedonia. This led to the capture and enslavement of thousands of Scythian women and children; their wealth and livestock were plundered as booty. This was a period of massive upheaval for the Steppe nomads. During the 4th to the 3rd centuries BCE, the Sarmatians migrated into Sauromatian lands between the Volga and the Don. By around 200 BCE, the center of Scythian power had shifted south to the Black Sea region of the Crimea. The Scythian kingdom gradually declined, falling finally with the later invasions of the Goths in the 3rd century CE, and the Huns in the 4th century CE.

WARRIOR PEOPLES OF THE SUN 187

Poles, Picts, Gaels, Scots, Hungarians, Medes, Franks, Angles, Saxons, Celtic speaking peoples and even Caucasian Albania. Scythian peoples are also related to the Sarmatians, a large Iranian confederation that existed in classical antiquity.[208] All bear the ethnonym Saka (Sakas) (which corresponds with the Chinese name Sai,) that derives either from skuoa (northern Iranian term for archer), or from the Iranian root sag, which means deer in Ossetian.

The term Skythai for Scythian was assigned by the Greeks, while the Iranians referred to the nomads along their borders as the Saka (Sakas).[209] This historical etymology again stresses the cultural relationship between archery and the deer that implies its totemic association for the Saka (Sakas) people. Deer imagery appears everywhere [210] in Scythian artworks (from tattoos, clothing, weapons and hand mirrors to horse's tack and wagons) where it is a living embodiment of a culture where "... the human being stands in nature, not over nature."[211] As a source of power in life and death, the deer was central to the spiritual belief system of the Scythians and Sarmatians whose ancestors were the first to domesticate and train the horse for riding and trading. [212] Within the animal style motif of Scythian and Sarmatian cultures, [213] a trinity of animals represented the three different localities of the World Tree: birds for the celestial sphere, herd animals for the earth, and predators or mythical creatures for the Underworld. This division of the universe is also attested in a passage of the Avesta, where Vohu Manah shows to Zarathuštra, the vision of a vulture in the sky, a stallion on the earth, and the Kara fish in the water.[214] As an example of a hoofed animal

---

208. Thriving from the 5th century BCE to the 4th century CE, the highly successful Sarmatians spoke an Iranian language, from a family group that includes Persian (or Farsi), Pashtun (a language of Afghanistan), and Ossetic (a descendant of the Alans' language, now spoken in parts of Georgia and southern Russia). **209.** The Saka[s] were a group of nomadic Eastern Iranian peoples (related to the Scythians) who historically inhabited the northern and eastern Eurasian Steppe and the Tarim Basin. **210.** The deer was of immense significance to the Eurasian peoples of the Steppe. I strongly recommend interested researchers to read Esther Jacobson's seminal work on this subject, beginning with: The Deer Goddess of Ancient Siberia - A Study in the Ecology of Belief (E.J. Brill, 1993). **211.** Baumer, 2012): 110. **212.** The first horses were domesticated in this region, first in the Volga region, and then in Northern Kazakhstan between 4800 BCE to 3700 BCE. **213.** The Altai Mountains of Eurasia are where Kazakhstan, West Siberia, Mongolia, and China meet, and where this animal style originates. **214.** Askold I. Vantchik. "Une légende sur l'origine des Scythes (HDT. IV 5-7) et le problème des sources du Scythicos logos d'Hérodote" [A Legend on the Origin of the Scythians (Hdt. IV 5-7) and the problems of the sources of Herodotus's Scythicos logos]. In, *Revue des Études Grecques* [Review of Greek Studies] (in French). 112 (1) (1999): 141-192 doi:10.3406/reg.1999.4355. JSTOR 4426001I.

of middle earth, the deer was vested with the supernatural power to fly through the celestial sphere. In this exceptional capacity, the sacred deer may have served as a psychopomp in the Underworld.[215]

Originating in the central parts of the Eurasian Steppe, the Sarmatians,[216] like the Saka (Sakas), were also part of the Indo-Iranian Steppe peoples. Archaeological finds support suggestions that these groups of peoples (Scythians, Saka (Sakas) and Sarmatians)[217] were collectively descended from the earlier Timber-grave and Andronovo cultures. The Andronovo culture people exhibited pronounced Caucasoid features. Considered a beautiful people with fierce eyes, Sarmatian[218] noblemen were tall and of graceful stature. Their fair or reddish hair was worn long, as were their beards. It was also said of them how: "danger and war are a pleasure to the Alani, and among them that man is called happy who has lost his life in battle. (. . .) They have no idea of slavery, inasmuch as they themselves are all born of noble families; and those whom even now they appoint to be judges are always men of proved experience and skill in war."[219] However, the Sarmatian warrior nomads extorted tribute from other Steppe nomads in the form of materials (wood and metals), grain (and other foodstuffs). Sometimes they would trade with livestock, leather, and other animal products, but more often than not, they used their warrior skills to raid instead. Settlements filled with ordinary farmers and craftspeople on or near the Steppe were vulnerable to such raids.

Certain aspects of their culture (related to horsemanship particularly) share considerable commonality with Mongolian peoples, specifically a liberal lifestyle, and the enrolment of both men and women as warriors.[220] "Among the Sauromatians, there was a law that no woman could marry until she had killed in battle, and therefore

---

215. Barnhart, 2022. **216.** By 200 BCE, the Scythians had overwhelmed the closely related Sarmatians whose territorial conquests three centuries later stretched from the Vistula River to the mouth of the Danube (in Germany), and eastward to the Volga, bordering the shores of the Black and Caspian seas (bordering Russia), as well as the Caucasus to the south (Eurasian border). They were eventually assimilated by the Proto-Slavic population of Eastern Europe. **217.** In the 3rd century CE, the dominance of the Pontic Steppe by these peoples was broken by the Germanic Goths, whom the Sarmatians joined a century later along with other Germanic tribes (Vandals) in the settlement squabbles of the collapsing Western Roman Empire. **218.** As a 4th century retired roman soldier, Ammianus Marcellinus began his history of the Roman Empire, covering the period from the 1st to the 4th centuries, in which he refers to the Alani directly as a people within the Sarmatian confederacy. **219.** Hinds, 2010. **220.** Archaeology confirms that one out of three or four nomad women of the Steppes was an active warrior buried with her weapons. **221.** Barnhart, 2022.

some women never married. The rich female graves among this early group of Sarmatians reflect their egalitarian social structure."[221] In this, the Sarmatians diverged from the Scythians, and the former's prominence of their women in warfare, may have provided inspiration for the Greek legends of warrior women referred to as Amazons by Herodotus. The graves of armed female warriors found in southern Ukraine and Russia have yielded archaeological evidence that support Herodotus' report that the athletic women of this region ride, shoot, and throw the javelin while mounted on horse-back, albeit of the Sarmatian peoples rather than the Scythians. Herodotus was not the first nor the only historian to confuse (or conflate) the two. [222]

More than forty of the kurgans explored by archaeologists in Scythian territory contained the graves of women warriors. The oldest of these dates to the fourth century BCE. The dead woman was buried not only with jewellery, pottery, a bronze mirror, and a spindle (a tool for spinning wool into thread), but also two long iron spear points and a quiver filled with forty-seven arrows. At her feet lay the skeleton of a young man, who took only an iron ring and two small bells into the afterlife with him. A woman in another kurgan had similar grave goods and weapons, as well as a belt reinforced with iron strips (a common piece of Scythian armour). [223]

Out of fifty-three kurgans investigated at Chertomlyk, six of them were for women. Elsewhere, up to twenty percent of Sauromatian warrior burials of the 5th and 4th centuries BCE, were also women, confirming that such splendour was not confined to men alone. Indeed, some kurgans reveal the extraordinary reverence given to high status women. Furthermore, according to the 1st-Century BCE historian Diodorus Siculus, "there came in Scythia a period of revolutions, in which the sovereigns were women endowed with exceptional valour. For among these peoples the women train for war just as do the men."[224]

Warrior clothing was sewn from plain-weave wool, hemp cloth, silk fabrics, felt, leather and hides, often embroidered, and adorned with felt applique work, or metal (golden) plaques as decorative armour. Herodotus claimed that "The women of the Sauromatæ have continued from that day to the present to observe their ancient customs, frequently hunting on horseback with their husbands, sometimes even unaccompanied; in war taking the field; and wearing the very same dress as the men ."[225] in the form of practical tunics and

---

222. Archaeologists have found evidence to support Herodotus's story at a site now known as Belsk, on a tributary of the Dnieper River. **223.** Hinds, 2010. **224.** Ibid. **225.** Herodotus. The History IV.116. Rawlinson, 1909.

loose trousers - perfect for horse riding. Nonetheless, it was generally believed that female warriors were merely legends. Recent discoveries are now able to prove the existence of female warriors, albeit restricted to some areas, and in some eras only. So, despite the caveat that so much remains fantasy and wishful thinking with regard to female warriors, what is particularly interesting is that the items[226] found in female burials suggest a sacral element to their roles, indicating that these warrior women also functioned as battle priestesses.

> *These ladies of prestige surely dominated the Steppes from Pazyryk and Ukok in the Gorny Altai region of southern Siberia (Russia) to Issyk in southern Kazakstan, further south in the neighbouring Xinjiang province of western China (old Turkestan); and northwest beyond Pokrovka to a more recently re-excavated kurgans at Prokhorovska, Russia.*[227]

Despite their love of gold and bronze adornments, the Sarmatians (and Scythians by default), lacked available iron, which meant their weapons were largely fashioned of bone and wood, as was the bulk of their armour. They honed their killing skills with whips and lassos, and were legendary archers, able to fire rapidly, raining arrows upon their foes, left and right. The warriors' coup de grâce was their ability to control their horses completely with knees and calves while at full gallop which left their upper bodies free to twist around (stirrup-free) to shoot at enemies behind them. The recurve bow was held away from the body, and the Steppe rider was known to shoot backwards while riding away from their pursuers,

10. Parthian shot – female mounted warrior with composite bow

---

226. Hinds, 2010. Small portable altars, carved bone spoons, bronze mirrors, and amulets in the shape of animals. Pieces of coloured minerals ground into powders may have been used as inks to draw symbolic designs on their bodies. The mirrors, too, were probably for symbolic, religious purposes, most particularly for divination and healing. "These were among the priestesses' main duties, along with making regular offerings—of milk, koumiss, cheese, and meat— to the gods and other spirits."**227.** https://www.labrys.net.br/labrys22/archeo/jeannine_daviskimball.htm (Retrieved 10th August 2024).

using the flow of the wind to aid in the shot (a mirror was possibly sometimes used for this). This manoeuvre was referred to as the Parthian shot.[228] Steppe nomads were trained to ride before they could walk; adult warriors were so accomplished on horseback, they appeared as one with the horse, hence the Greek myth of such people as centaurs.

Across Eurasia and indeed, the northern subarctic regions, the bow was a powerful weapon that contributed to the dominance of Steppe riders. "Modern parallels suggest that a Scythian archer could shoot about 15-20 arrows a minute, probably averaging a distance of about 500-600 feet and achieving accuracy at about 200 feet."[229] Scythian (and Sarmatian) arrowheads typically sported three barbs that ripped flesh when attempts were made to extract them from wounds, a futile enterprise, as their tips were often dipped in a poisonous mix of snake venom, blood, and dung. The poison, named specifically as 'scythicon' by Greek writers, or, as Ovid put it, "the flying metal [that] promised a double death,"[230] is exemplary in its representation of the 'flying venom' (mentioned in Anglo-Saxon Herbals) that northern peoples were so fearful of, and that shamans were always in combat with.

Scythian customs related to warfare, though extremely brutal, are indicative of barbarous times. There are many incredulous tales of drinking the blood of the first victim slain, of scalping, and even of making drinking cups from the skull caps of a prized opponent. Around 700 CE, [231] Hesiod highlights the nomads' dependence on their horses for transportation and food in his reference to them as "mare-milking Scythians."[232] Their staple drink was koumiss, a fermented, slightly alcoholic mares' milk, rich in vitamin C and other nutrients. They also ate horsemeat, especially at funeral and religious feasts. It is reported of them, that before battle and during food shortages, they would drink horse blood (from a small nick to the animal's neck, which did not seriously harm the horse). They also depended on horses for raw materials such as horsehide, horsehair, hoofs (for fashioning armour), and bone, as noted above.

Herodotus wrote of the customs and attire of certain other 'Saka

---

228. Baumer, 2012: 86. See also: Cristoph Baumer. The History of Central Asia: The History of Central Asia: The Age of Islam and the Mongols (Volume 3). (London and New York: I.B. Tauris. 2016). **229.** Adrienne Mayor. The Amazons –Lives & Legends of Warrior Women Across the Ancient World. (Princeton University Press, 2014.) **230.** Hinds, [1962] 2010. **231.** It is thought that Greek traders probably came into contact with the Scythians near the Black Sea in the late 8th century BCE. **232.** Hinds, [1962] 2010

(Sakas)s' groups, and there is one in particular of some interest here in tracing the origins of the genetic, ethnic and cultural influences on the Sámi and other northern peoples of the Arctic and sub-arctic regions. East of the Caspian Sea, the Massagetae's customs were apparently very similar to those of the Scythians, except they carried battle-axes, used bronze spear-points and arrowheads, and adorned themselves and their mounts with excessive amounts of gold.[233] Of particular interest here, is a reference made by the Persians to the 'pointed hat Sakas,' especially when we consider that, according to Herodotus, the (Saka) queen Tomyris reigned over the Massagetae (an Iranian speaking people of Central Asia.) and led a defensive manoeuvre against an attack by Cyrus the Great of the Achaemenid (Persian) Empire, defeating and killing him in 530 BCE.[234]

---

233. Adrienne Mayor. "Amazons In The Iranian World." (2017) In, *Encyclopædia Iranica*. https://www.iranicaonline.org/articles/amazons-ii ; Robert Rollinger. (2003). "Herodotus iv. Cyrus According To Herodotus." In, *Encyclopædia Iranica* https://www.iranicaonline.org/articles/herodotus-iv   See also: Rüdiger Schmitt. "Massagetae." (2018). In,   *Encyclopædia Iranica*. https://www.iranicaonline.org/articles/massagetae (All retrieved 7th July, 2024)   **234.** Mayor, [2017] 2003.

WARRIOR HERO CULTS OF STONE AND IRON

As semi-nomadic, animistic people, the Scythians had previously shied away from the creation of altars, temples, or statues of their deities,[235] yet Scythian funerary stelae of the 6th and 5th centuries BCE, depict warriors who represent the deceased buried in the kurgans. Holding drinking horns (rhytons) in their right hands, this is an image we are accustomed to seeing in relation to Norse myth and legend as written in the sagas, and on funerary stelae mentioned above.

The Scythians also revered a form of Ares, represented by an ever increasing (square) pile of brushwood upon which an ancient iron scimitar in an upright position was placed, relating to his lesser known, but older attribution as an agricultural deity.[236] This exceptional altar is believed to be a cosmological model of the universe with its central

---

235. According to Herodotus (who was perhaps viewing the Scythians through a Greek pantheonic perspective), they revered seven higher spirits (led by the highest –Thagimasadas, who was really only worshipped by the Royal Scythians), as did the Sarmatian tribe of the Alans and the Ossetians. This heptatheism was a typical feature of Indo-Iranic tradition. Note the later development of the seven Ameša Spenta (Bounteous Immortals) led by Ahura Mazda (the Uncreated Creator from whom they emanated), worshipped in the Zoroastrian religion of the (southern) Iranic peoples, which had significantly transformed the concepts of the Indo-Iranic religion while also inheriting several features of it. The leading deities of the Indic Vedic pantheon, the Aditya, were also seven in number. See: Safaee Yazdan. "Scythian and Zoroastrian Earth Goddesses: A Comparative Study on Api and Armaiti." In, *Archaeology of Iran in the Historical Period*. (University of Tehran Science and Humanities Series. Edited by Kamal-Aldin Niknami and Ali Hozhabri. Springer International Publishing, 2020): 65-75. doi:10.1007/978-3-030-41776-5_6 See Also: Esther Jacobson. *The Art of the Scythians: The Interpenetration of Cultures at the Edge of the Hellenic World*. (Brill Publishers, 1995).
236. Ibid. See also: Herodotus, The Histories, 258-259. This tradition may be reflected in Jordanes's assertion that Attila had obtained the sacred Scythian sword which had fallen from the sky that he called the "Sword of Mars," and which he believed made him powerful in war and made of him the "prince of the entire world." See also: Patrick J. Geary. "Germanic Tradition and Royal Ideology in the Ninth Century: The Visio Karoli Magni." In, *Living with the Dead in the Middle Ages*. (Cornell University Press, 1994) 63. doi:10.7591/9781501721632-005. (Accessed 13th August 2022).

zone representing the air space above the enclosed brushwood mound symbolising the world mountain (of origin).[237] The iron sword is a symbol of 'Ares' the manifest spirit of fertility and vigour. Herodotos observed this rather curious reverence for a war/fertility deity whom he equates with Ares, a probable analogue of Hercules, but again, does not name.[238] Herodotus provides a description of a complex wooden temple with its centrepiece of an iron sword. No other Scythian figure was revered with shrines and icons representing them, though we can place the described construction type and reverence for such a deific figure with the Alans.

The Roman state machine sent several thousand Eurasian peoples to northern Britain to garrison Hadrian's Wall, including the Sarmatians, who by sheer force of number must have left their mark on the folklore and beliefs of the general populace around those regions. It is therefore remarkable that just a few hundred years later, the historian Ammianus Marcellinus, when remarking upon the beliefs of the Sarmatians, claimed a parallel veneration for the sword.

In their country is neither temple nor shrine, nor even thatched hut; only a naked sword stuck into the soil, which they worship with due reverence. Such is the war god who presides over the lands on which they wander.[239]

Given that a warrior caste is speculated for Proto-Indo-European culture, the sword – commonly, but falsely associated with Óðinn – represented this anonymous figure in much the same way that it did Tiew in Germanic religion, and Týr in Norse. These tenacious beliefs preserved for centuries by northern peoples have led some scholars to draw parallels with the myths around King Arthur and his enchanted sword, and to actively promote Arthur as a Sarmatian commander. Of course, some of the earliest legends about King Arthur and his knights do feature in the borderlands of northern Britain.

Although Herodotus did not name this figure, a possible name occurs earlier, in his description of the origin of the Scythians where he claims that the Scythians are descendants of the three sons of Targitaos (Targitaios), a son of Zeus and "the daughter of the river Borysthenes."[240] Herodotos generally used Greek theonyms, but here, he specifically addressed Targitaos differently. Very few studies have examined the etymological origin of Targitaos, though it is assumed it

---

237. Cunliffe, 2019. **238.** Strabo, Pliny the Elder, Claudius Ptolemy and Stephanus of Byzantium all describe the worship of 'Ares' in the Scythian regions. **239.** Hinds, [1962] 2010. **240.** Geary, 1994.

shares various theonyms derived from the root *(s)tenh₂ ("thunder"), namely Hittite Tarhunt, Armenian Torks, Celtic Taranis, Latin Tonans and of course, Norse Þör. This obscure theonym appears to have been an alternate name of *Perkwunos, the Proto-Indo-European storm deity and predecessor to all the above thunder deities in addition to the Indo-Iranian Indra, Roman Mars, Lithuanian *Perkunas*, Slavic *Perun* and countless others, including Hercules.[241]

As a Proto-Indo-European cultural hero, Targitaos is typically associated with storms and the aversion of chaos, thus implying a fundamental relationship with the oak tree, which represents the axis mundi, and possibly even the world tree. As such, Targitaos could be a possible reflex of *Perkwunos* (making his parents Papaios and possibly Api.) In fact, many similar thunder figures considered to be *Perkwunos reflexes, are presented in a pantheon, where they are the children of either a sky father (i.e. Hercules), or an earth mother (i.e. Þör) or both (i.e. Indra). Although Ares is often equated with Mars, the two gods have distinct origins and roles, at least initially. Ares was associated with fertility and fecund weather, while Mars embodied warfare. Furthermore, while Mars is accepted as a reflex of the storm deity, Zeus, Ares is evidently not, here the *Perkwunos* reflex is Hercules.[242] Scythians are cited in several sources as partakers of ritualistic drinks which appear to be analogous to those of other Indo-European cultures that personify the deity Soma/Haoma in Hinduism and Zoroastrianism respectively. The consumption of these beverages increased combat stamina and sexual potency. It would therefore be surprising if the 'Scythian Ares' was not likewise the embodiment of this same potent spirit.

Scythian art styles reveal much about their culture, especially its progression under Greek influence. Papaios was perceived of as a divine ancestor who sired the hero Targitaos, who latter sired the ancestors of the Scythians. The identification of Papaios with Zeus marks him as an elemental of the skies (though not specifically a 'sky father,') a Scythian reflex of the Proto-Indo-European *Dyeus Ph2ter, the much-fabled patriarchal figure, whose numerous reflexes appear in virtually all Indo-European languages.[243] Depictions of Papaios are

---

241. Edgar C Polomé. "The Slavic Gods and the Indo-European Heritage" In, Festschrift für Nikola R. Pribic. Edited by Wolfgang Gesemann and Helmut Schaller. (Hieronymus Verlag Neuried, 1983): 545-555 **242.** Ibid. **243.** The *dyeus/*dyeus/*dyew/*deiwos root may be preserved in the last syllable of Papaios, and also the Thracian Sabazios likewise; equally, it could simply be a calque. Etymologies may include the Proto-Indo-European root *peh, – 'to protect.' See: Appendix I

generally rare, but figurines flanked by griffins or birds of prey seem to be a depiction of him. One image of a Scythian kurgan figurine (artist unknown) appears to be of Papaios. Its presentation is in a pompous heroic style that is now very often associated (incorrectly) with Óðinn. Stylistically, the powerful front-facing figure with glazed, staring eyes, flanked with eagles, stands proudly, a style that certainly influenced Iron Age art forms in Eurasia and Northern Europe. The Sutton Hoo complex and later Nordic stone stele, demonstrate this art style most effectively. The strong and instinctive tendency to pair a sky deity with an earth deity (that appears in almost all northern cosmologies) is not actually typical of most Indo-European religions, though all the indications suggest this original relationship was possibly lost when "the *Dyeus reflexes shifted from personifications of the sky to societal or abstract gods."[244] Clearly, the emphasis is on his elemental potency.

Death, malevolence and hunger are the greatest combatants of the ancient world. The endurance of the animal world would have been an inspiration to humankind. There is absence of theology but an abundance of culture to plumb here. Status power, prestige and elitism developed among a dominant class whose superior authority was enabled in its control and factionalisation. Manipulation has ever been a tool of those able to recognise and wield it. Monuments and artworks are a testament to their endurance of belief, the features of which relinquish only a fraction of the secrets embedded there, patterns that now narrate the mythic histories only to those with the customary keys of culture to interpret them. For those of us outside those cultures we can at best offer only theories and we have no way of gauging their authenticity or veracity. These cultures were sophisticated in ways we cannot begin to imagine, and also, ordered and efficient in ways we cannot begin to appreciate. Their spatial and conceptual awareness, cosmology and environment have become so utterly divergent from our own. The world of spirit is much diluted in the western worldview, where only what is manifest is considered real and tangible. I believe this leads to loss and despair, frustration and disaffection from within and without. There is a pressing need, an urgency to rebuild these associations and pathways through between and around the Otherworld, a view our ancestors and their forebears knew and understood only too well. It is not enough to pay lip-service to an icon or idol we have no means of interaction with, in the spirit world.

Many images are hard to decipher and interpret. This is sometimes

---

244. Hinds, [1962] 2010.

due to the errors made in the initial transference from the actual stone to paper, which sometimes occurs from the direct tracings or even lines drawn over the grooves in the stone perceived by the viewer as original, when others, perhaps worn away or obscured are in fact original. Initial errors often compound over time, changing the images substantially, and our understanding of them by default. A prime example of this, occurs in the paddles of a boat that neither depict a boat nor paddles but are, I believe, a sled and ski-prongs on Scandinavian rock art. Prudence and pragmatism demand that we broaden our perceptions to other possibilities more pertinent to the time, place and culture of the peoples they represent and who created them. As puzzles far removed from our time, our world and our land, our own eyes transmit messages to our brains hardwired to perceive and interpret images according to our current worldview. This is an embedded bias we are hard pushed to side-line, still, we are duty bound to try. Cognitive archaeology is a specialist field as is anthropology, two disciplines we must strive to draw from if we are to ever have any hope of even scratching the surface of these grand narratives.

TIME AND ETERNITY – THE COSMIC MILL

Creation and well-being are unequivocally linked to the divine feminine, themes that recur in all cultures, and so often veiled in allegory and mythopoesis. Everything returns us to the vital premise of her role in death and in creation. Throughout the Siberian and the Altai regions, certain features from Indo-Iranian[245] mythic tradition relating to this remarkable relationship were similarly woven into Scythian and Arctic cosmology (and eschatology).

Mythic tropes regarding divine ancestral beings that relate indirectly to the Deer Goddess as the Creatrix and divine Mother of all (who also has the power of death), offer us a possible explanation for her curious association with the foaming waters of the sea.[246] Rígr is also linked to this mythic motif of the Cosmic Mill through Heimdallr's relationship with the nine daughters of the sea, but also with the glorious heavens connected to the Mill.[247] Mundilfæri (the father of the sun and moon) signifies the mill-like device that turns the heavens by means of a 'handle'– mondull. This turning of the cosmos, pictured as a mill, is the diurnal and yearly movement of the heavens, giving us the fertile and cyclical seasons intrinsic to humankind's survival.[248] As the mondull

---

245. In Vedic mythology, the churning of the Milky Ocean also represents a parallel instance of the fertile milling of vast bodies of water. See: Clive Tolley. "Evidence for The Existence of a Cosmic Mill in Germanic Mythology. An Excerpt from 'The Mill In Norse And Finnish Mythology.'" In, Saga-Book for the Viking Society of Northern Research, 24 (1994-97): 63-82. https://www.jstor.org/stable/48611731. (Accessed 26th October 2022). **246.** As a land-locked deity, her association with the sea is artistically portrayed through the stylised deer antlers that curl and flow as ocean waves. **247.** According to Hyndluljóð (*Voluspá* in skamma 9), Heimdallr's nine giant-mothers are named: *Gjálp, Greip, Eistla, Eyrgjafa, Úlfrún, Angeyja, Imdur, Atla, and Járnsaxa*. The first two, are also cited as daughters of the fire-giant Geirroð (*Skáldskaparmál*, 26). Another *Imdur*, from *ím*, meanings embers – also refers to fire. Járnsaxa, '*she who crushes the iron*,' produces the grist – iron as the mineral product of the sea and swampy waters mixed with sand and clay, laid down in time.

TIME AND ETERNITY – THE COSMIC MILL 199

(handle of the heavens), Sol and Mani's fixed paths are the points of departure and arrival, described by kenningar as 'horse-doors,'[249] hung on the eastern and western mountain-walls of Midgarðr. Mundilfæri regulates the starry firmament through whom Mani regulates the rising and sinking of the sea's flow and ebb tides. Mundilfæri is thus one of the vís regin, wise rulers who generate order in the seeming chaos of creation, under whose aegis, all natural and eternal phenomena occur. Mundilfæri is perhaps one of the most neglected and underestimated primary forces of Germanic mythology.

At this point it is worth while spending extra time to savour a traditional Ket folktale that tells of two giant female figures who turn the wheel of the year and of human lives[250] – thus of time – a tale that parallels that of the giant mill, Grotti,[251] turned by two sisters, Jotnar maidens of Norse tradition, named Fenja and Menja. No human could budge this great Mill, so the task fell to them, with instructions to grind out gold, peace and happiness. When the quernstones that made Grotti were first pulled from the earth, the tremors cracked and fractured the land and seabed, creating even then, the landscapes we now recognise. Because the Mill was enchanted, Grotti produced whatever the grinder bade of it. Several references made to this great Mill are found in *Skáldskaparmál*, where it is associated with certain riches and provisions. Hengikjøptr, a Jotunn, had long ago gifted Grotti to Fróði whose name is an alias of Freyr, the heroic titan of Norse legend, and provider for his people in the mythic Golden Age.

Singing out the Grottasøngr as they worked,[252] the roar of industry articulated by the grinding Mill, banished the virtue of silence and peace from Fróði's court forever.

The sound of their voices is the sound of the mill: þulu þyt. By using the verb þylja to describe the vocalization of their power, the girls become implicated in the

---

248. *Vafþrúðnismál*, 21 and *Grímnismál*, 40 tell us that the earth was made out of Ymir's flesh, the rocks out of his bones, and the sea from his blood. Earth is distinguished from rocks, means soil or sand that covers the solid ground. See: Tolley, 1994-1997.
249. Known as jódyr, as found in *Vǫluspá* 5, *Hauksbók*. **250.** Jacobson-Tepfer, 2015: 334 **251.** A brief extract from *Grottasøngr* appears only within *Skáldskaparmál* (SnE 135-38), where it is the preserved within the 14th century Prose Edda, a vellum manuscript, GKS 2367 4° (known since the 17th C. as the Codex Regius) and in a later paper manuscript (Utrecht, University Library Ms. 1374, known as the Codex Trajectinus), which appears to have stemmed from the same exemplar as GKS 2367 4°. Another 14th C. manuscript of *Skáldskaparmál*, AM 748 II 4°, quotes only the first stanza of the poem, which contains one of the numerous kenningar for gold in the legend of King Fróði who enslaved two Jotnar maids to drive the Mill. **252.** Tolley, 1994-1997.

well-attested but still mysterious tradition of declamations by þulir (figures who recited highly valued knowledge) and, within the Eddaic context, the authoritative enunciation of mythological verities.[253]

In his greed for gold, Fróði drove them hard, day and night, until Menga – weary from her relentless toil – withdrew herself from the mill's incessant grinding, and began to chant her curse upon it, grinding out an army that ousted him from power.

In this saga, the prophecy of doom is revealed where peace and plenty, turned to war and famine; chaos ground by the mill threatened death for all. Grinding out bitter, arid salt, the mill filled the oceans and the seas, grinding yet further all the rocks upon the seabed until a great whirlpool engulfed all vessels and marine life that traversed too closely.[254] This maelstrom appeared from the hole in the sunken millstone that caused the tides to breach all land masses, sucking in and swallowing ships like a huge sea-monster.[255] Embedded at the bottom of the ocean, the Mill is a permanent fixture attached to the mill of the heavens, grinding time and matter, marking the roles of chaos and law and order in equal measure. All the spirits and beings of all realms are suspended between these immense forces. One astute study examines the allegorical perspective of the poem:[256]

The mythological motivation of the plot and, in particular, the way in which the morphing of the supernatural female speakers among giantesses, Valkyrja, Völva, and Norn can be understood as the protean personification of fate deployed in the poem in order to expose the unworthiness of Fróði to continue in his role as king. In the theatrically contrived space of a day and a night, the king's fate is revised in

---

253. Judy Quinn. "Mythological Motivation in Eddic Heroic Poetry: Interpreting Grottasöngr." In, Revisiting the Poetic Edda. Essays on Old Norse Heroic Legend. Edited by Paul Acker and Carolyne Larrington. (Routledge, 2013): 159-182 **254.** Tolly, 1994-1997. Similar tales occur in the Odyssey of a giant mill and of the toiling to grind the barley meal, and in mythic histories of the biblical worlds – Egypt, Mesopotamia, India, Turkey and Slavic Russia. **255.** Another legend claims that Stroma, an island off the northern coast of the mainland of Scotland, which has a dangerous whirlpool known by a Norse name: Swelki ('sea mill') is powered still by the two giant women, Grotti-Fenni and Grotti-Meni, who live beneath the seafloor and cause dangerous whirlpools, causing damage to local shipping. See: A. Sutherland – AncientPages.com https://www.ancientpages.com/2020/02/15/fenja-and-menja-sisters/ (retrieved 13th August 2024). **256.** Numerous other kenningar for gold are attested in poems from the 10th to the 13th centuries, including the poet's guide, the Háttatal (st. 43), being the final section of the Prose Edda. Opinions vary concerning the dating of the poem's composition, typically estimated around 1200 CE. A few boldly assert an earlier date contemporary with or close to Eyvindr Skáldaspillir timeline in the 10th century, a view I uphold.

TIME AND ETERNITY – THE COSMIC MILL   201

view of his impolitic exploitation of the giantesses who might otherwise have greatly benefited his kingdom with the natural resources they are portrayed as controlling.[257]

Fróði – the wise one, failed utterly to recognise the song of Grotti (The Mill) as an expression of supernatural power. Sung by Fenja and Menja, the millstone's song is an invocation invested with fateful consequence for the foolish greed of a king who failed to secure the patronage of the primal giants he sought to exploit. Names are clearly awarded with a sense of irony. The poem exposes Fróði's lack of wisdom and his acute failure to recognise the primacy of the ancient race of beings, whose bounty is to be propitiated rather than exploited, paralleling King Geirrøðr's significant error in Grímnismál. "In terms of mytho-political etiquette: Fróði denies sleep to his exceptionally strong (though incognito) slaves [just as elsewhere in the Norse sagas], Geirrøðr denies the visiting (albeit disguised) god hospitality."[258] Fróði's lack of prudence was further compounded. Dramatic staging reveals the grim fate that befalls the errant kings, as just sentence and punishment is meted upon them. As a popular motif, similar trials emerge in other Eddaic encounters between mythological speakers and human figures, one such is the trial of the aforementioned folly of Geirrøðr regarding his lack of hospitality in Grímnismál; another is Álvíss, whose boastful arrogance is called to account in Álvíssmál.

Without exception, their ability to hold positions of power as worthy rulers is the nub of exposure here. It also clearly emphasises the mythic premise of fecundity as a gift from the Other, and the expected reciprocation and duty to them. A mutually beneficent state is achievable and indeed should be desirable – this much is the moral tone here. Greed, ignorance and a lack of respect for that Otherworld are conversely met with loss and retribution. Hence, the hubris of a false king is the ruin of his people. The poem engages the crucial motif of the powers of darkness associated with the Otherworld to effect their release, and Fróði's punishment. Deliberately aligned with the prophetic Völur, Fenja and Menja disclose in their judicial narration, how for nine winters of their youth, they created this spectre of industry – quarrying Grotti from the chthonic realms of the earth – a technological feat of engineering designed as a utopian resource for humankind.[259] "Unlike other resources belonging to the giants - such as the mead of poetry – the millstone has not been transmuted into a product by dwarfs or Æsir, and it apparently still needs giant strength

---

257. Quinn, 2013.   **258.** Quinn, 2013.   **259.** See overleaf

to make it productive."²⁶⁰ Most importantly, their anger signifies a just contempt for humankind's ignorance of this incredible gift.

> *The infinite prosperity that the mighty stone has the potential to produce stands as an emblem of what human culture, working in harmony with the natural world (through its female agents), might achieve. This, like so much else, the king has not understood.* ²⁶¹

Fenja and Menja continue to recount other crucial interventions they have made in the lives of kings, asserting their prescient role in the fateful trials they established for humankind. The role of fate and supernaturally disposed women in the petty squabbles of humankind, is witnessed in *Darraðarljóð*, an Eddaic poem quoted within *Njáls Saga*.

> *While Fenja and Menja are not explicitly identified as Valkyrjur in Grottasǫngr, the parallel with the discourse of Darraðarljóð brings definition to their role: when speakers like these choose to follow a king, they either promote him as a ruler of lands (and protect him in battle) or destroy his life. In both poems, the activity of the Valkyrjur is unconnected with Óðinn's project of stocking Valhöl with the best fighters in preparation for Ragnarök and more closely resembles the behaviour of Valkyrjur in the Helgi poems, where they turn their attention to selecting paragons of manhood out of the mêlée of battle and consigning to death those who do not impress them. While the Valkyrjur's capacity to choose the best is inflected by love in the Helgi poems, in Darraðarljóð and Grottasǫngr, it appears to be driven by the social ideal of a king worthy of ruling lands and people.* ²⁶²

Like the Irish kings' fragile relationship with the land spirit of sovereignty, a principle at the heart of the Fisher King's demise in the grail legends, failure to acknowledge that divine female spirit invites doom. Through Galðr magics, the songs of enchantment ring out, mercilessly weaving and milling the doom of humankind. In his lust for power and wealth, Fróði is oblivious to the signs unfurling before him; he neither hears nor sees them. A keen intuition and powers of observation (particularly with regard to omens and portents) were requisite virtues for kingship. "Fenja and Menja are portrayed as

---

259. "According to some old stories, the two unhappy girls still work at the mill. One version of the myth says that the two sisters, no longer oppressed and humiliated by any man, happily returned to Jötunheim with Grotte, which they used to grind out gold dust and export to many places worldwide. Their house - covered in gold dust - was often visited by people who wanted to steal the magical mill or the sisters' wealth. None of those visitors have yet survived to tell the story." See: A. Sutherland - AncientPages.com https://www.ancientpages.com/2020/02/15/fenja-and-menja-sisters/ (Retrieved 13th August 2024) **260.** Quinn, 2013. **261.** Ibid. **262.** Ibid.

political power brokers, able to choose the best kings, not, as already mentioned, for marriage or for death and further fighting in Valhöl, but for political success." [263]

> Song is the conceit in both Darraðarljóð and Grottasǫngr, the death sentences the Valkyrjur chant realized through the blast of fighting in which the doomed warriors are slain. Behind the unequivocal lyrics, however, the workings of fate are imagined in Darraðarljóð as the complex interweaving of spear paths: once the Valkyrjur have determined warriors' fates, the missiles hit their marks and blood is let on the battlefield. In Grottasǫngr, a different metaphor is used, the executors of fate expressing their industry not in terms of gory weaving, but of milling. Whereas the Valkyrjur of Darraðarljóð declare their warp is woven once the king's fate is sealed, Fenja and Menja toy with Fróði throughout the poem in their drawn-out sequence of references to the milling they will eventually finish. Just as the temporal perspective shifts during the course of the song, so the manner in which the giantesses turn the tables on Fróði is signalled in a number of ways. By describing their vanquishing of other kings in the past as a lack of quietness (vara kyrrseta), a hint is dropped about the significance of the racket they now make.[264]

Their (enchanted) songs then fall silent, a judicial statement of their disapproval, a withdrawal of their gift of beneficence through an unworthy king. The expression of so much power within the remit of supernatural women is an unusual motif for literary works of the 14th century, where generally, such women are portrayed only as evil sorceresses or as vehicles for mischief. This is not their role in Grottasǫngr. However, Grottasöngr draws on the Eddaic tradition of the trial, which again aligns their purpose to that of the Valkyrjur described in Darraðarljóð. Divine female figures are inexorably associated with Fate and with kingship in northern mythology. They guard and guide them, but also punish and defame them, as merit or unworthiness accords. Their judicial role is crystal clear.

> All three supernatural female figures, the Völva, the Norn, and the Valkyrja, are fundamentally personifications of Fate, yet the Valkyrja's role in choosing the moment of a hero's death seems to have invited the possibility of direct interaction, at a crucial moment, between the decreeing subject and the powerless object of destiny. In the minds of those who pondered the workings of fate in Eddaic poetry, it seems to have been a short step from a warrior's death being mortgaged on the battlefield by a princess-Valkyrja to the length of a king's reign being re-negotiated by an unimpressed Valkyrja-giantess -though in these difficult-to-date traditions, the move might, of course, have been in the opposite direction. [my emphasis] What

---

263. Quinn, 2023 **264.** Ibid

is shared by both kinds of Eddaic encounter is the notion that fate, once animated, is invested with a personality that is responsive to a hero's behaviour and that the assessment made of his merit (or lack of it) is, in broad terms, in line with cultural ideals of masculinity in general and kingship in particular. The Valkyrja activity of Fenja and Menja is therefore foundational to the conception of the interaction between the king and his Fate. [265]

Grottasøngr is therefore a sophisticated exploration of the mythological relationship between mortal kings and supernatural women, revealing the latter's power to continue to manipulate the Fate of kings, initiated, but not set by the Nornir at birth. That destiny is achievable, but only if the kings work and operate in the rightness of things, that is to say, if they fulfil their obligations to the people they serve. This reflects a high moral tone and underlying ethic of the reciprocity of oath-bound societies, where survival (of all) is dependent upon a certain altruism and cooperation. The neglect of any element can have devastating consequences. This is explored time and again within the sagas. Whereas later mythic motifs are concerned with the natural resources coveted by the 'gods,' which they steal from the arcane giants and convert into cultural resources - such as the cauldrons they use as brewing vessels - here, instead, the giantesses who appear in Grottasøngr, award those natural resources to mortal men, rather than as treasures solely for the 'gods.' This suggests the theme may be much older even than the extant remnants of the original poem used to draft the Eddaic tale upon.

Fróði's Mill is a myth that reiterates the corruption of creative abilities and resources at the hands of the greedy few that dominate society. It also expresses tropes associated with the basic cosmogonical tenets of animism relating to creation itself: how the frost giants came into being, how many were tragically destroyed, and how the sons of Borr slew the giant Ymir[266](from whose blood, dismembered body, bones and upturned skull plate were used to form the world, its heavens, mountains, plains and waters)- all of which are enmeshed within the purpose and events concerned with the giant Mill relating to the beginning and end of all things. An Arctic adventurer named Snæbjörn

---

265. Quinn, 2023. **266.** Cognate with Yemós, the twin of Mónus or Mánnus who are both the protagonists of the Proto Indo-European creation myth, involving the notion of primeval Chaos (Ghanos), the universal principle of Order (Ártus), a cosmic egg, (Olyowyóm), and the primeval cow (Ammadheinús) who nourished the twins. The PIE *Yemós* is the template for the Vedic *Yama*, the Iranian *Yima*, the Norse *Ymir*, and possibly the Roman *Remus*.

Hólmsteinsson of the late 10th century mentioned in Landnámabók, also alludes to a mighty water-mill turned by nine primeval women, the brides of the sea, which is a kenning for the dramatic tidal and whirlpooling waves in a lausavísa (Skj B I 201) attributed to him.[267] The paralleling of certain shared factors here regarding the Mill, the churning of the ocean, the nine waves - as daughters or brides - driven by female forces of creation, are not coincidental. Overtime, a possible confusion occurred that merged the myths of Græðir,[268] a greater Mill linked to the starry heavens (turned by nine maidens of the sea, who also appear as the nine mothers of Heimdallr), with the lesser Grotte - Fróði's Mill - turned by the giantesses Fenja and Menja, as told in the Grottasøngr, since its grist is the mold in which all life and vegetation grows. The remnants preserved in skaldic and Eddaic poetry thus appear contradictory at times as to which attributes are original to which Mill, particularly as only the latter myth was popularised.

The axial nail of the celestial realms is the North (Pole) star, around which all other realms revolve. Perceived as a glorious, divine Mill, it makes a significant appearance in the Finnish epic poem *Kalevala*, as Sampo, forged by the divine smith Ilmarinen. "Its structure is tripartite: one side grinds out corn, another produces salt, and coins come from the third,"[269] grinding out abundance and good fortune for barter and storage. Secured with nine locks and taken to the Mount of Copper, "Sampo puts out three roots, one deep into the earth, one into a mountain, while the third reaches out to the sea."[270] Comprised of three great roots anchored in water, on land and in the clouds, this strange structure closely resembles the mythic Yggdrasil; certainly as a cosmic pillar their parallel association is clear.[271]

Medieval saga literature of the 13th and 14th centuries thus preserves the significant core themes around which the legendary stories (based on these earlier oral traditions) express the common, shared beliefs of northern peoples. Recorded mainly in late medieval Iceland (with very little from Norway), these popular narratives are packed with representations of characters that conform to classic (if somewhat banal) stereotypes, be that the hero, villain, anti-hero, or

---

267. For more on this theme of a cosmic Mill, see: *The World-Mill at the Bottom of the Sea. The Meginwerk of the Ancient Germanic Cosmos* http://www.germanicmythology.com/original/cosmology5.html (Accessed 19th July 2021) **268.** *Skáldskaparmál*, 33. **269.** Alby Stone. The Cosmic Mill. https://www.indigogroup.co.uk/edge/cmill.htm (Retrieved 16th August 2024). **270.** Ibid. **271.** For a discussion of their similarities and differences, see: https://www.germanicmythology.com/original/cosmology5.html (Retrieved 15th August 2024)

monster. Although we should never approve the indiscriminate use of stereotypes, we must equally recognise their application in reality, especially historically; "group identities and group boundaries are maintained through stereotypes."[272] When reading these tales, we are directed towards certain patterns of medieval ideological thought, where perception is filtered through considered manipulation of the facts. Along with the carnivalesque and grotesque, comedic, "images depicting various figures of low social status, including peasants, actors and fools, seem to have been particularly popular in late medieval times,"[273] and became a commonplace feature of Icelandic manuscript illumination.

Scribes included them in the marginalia of sacred texts, creating a sub-culture that provided a visual commentary on the ethics and morals of the time, "where the world was sometimes turned upside-down in order to demote the sublime, and elevate the everyday."[274] Beyond the superficial burlesque imagery, the presentation of the 'Other' in such an oblique manner reminds the reader of the perils of the flesh, of the animal within; that monsters do not dwell only in the invisible realms.

One of the main representations of this culture was the grotesque body, with focus on the "lower" and inferior body parts and bodily needs, making these explicit. Comic figures, such as jugglers, fools, giants and dwarfs, were highlighted. Therefore, 'monsters' and other fabulous creatures of art and literature are usually grotesque in nature, and are found along with certain animals in realms that are outside the human and are consequently depicted in the margins.[275]

If we examine Old Norse literature, we find that Nordic women were modestly covered as it was deemed inappropriate to exhibit naked flesh.[276] This was very much the norm, and perfectly in accordance with moral principles demonstrated in other European communities during the Middle Ages. Conversely, a lascivious nature is popularly linked

---

272. Sirpa Aalto and Veli-Pekka Lehtola. "The Sámi Representations Reflecting The Multi-Ethnic North of The Saga Literature." *Journal of Northern Studies* 11 no. 2 (2017): 7-30 See also: Hermann Pálsson. "Úr landnorðri. Samar og ystu rætur íslenkrar menningar" [From the North-East. Sámi and the outermost roots of Icelandic culture] Studia Islandica 54, Reykjavík: Bókmenntafræðistofnun Háskóla Íslands,1997: 61 See also: Hermann Pálsson. "Searching For The Sámi In Early Icelandic Sources." (*Dieðut* I 1998): 75–83 **273.** Aðalheiður Guðmundsdóttir. "Behind the cloak, between the lines: Trölls and the symbolism of their clothing in Old Norse tradition.' In, European Journal of Scandinavian Studies 47, no. 2 (2017): 327-350. https://doi.org/10.1515/ejss-2017-0022 (Accessed 21st January 2022) **274.** Ibid. **275.** Ibid. **276.** Jenny M. Jochens. "Before The Male Gaze: The Absence Of The Female Body In Old Norse." In, Sex in the Middle Ages. A book of essays. Edited by Joyce E. Salisbury. (Garland, 1991): 3-29

to dark associations with magic and the supernatural, as something unnatural to 'good folk.'[277]

Nonetheless, there are numerous instances described in the *Fornaldarsögur* of sexual encounters between male protagonists (especially Þórr) with 'tröll-women,' or giantesses. Some contradictions occur, whereby the female 'trölls' are bearded or bald, scrawny or stout, fair or dark, large or small, though almost always as semi-human, ugly and loathsome. In *Sturlaugs saga starfsama*, for example, we are told of male heroes who are unable to discern the gender of three tröllkonur they encounter. Descriptions are intentionally unflattering. Tröll women are noted for their bizarre headdresses and wild, straggly (unkempt) hair, though often, their horrific form was a metaphor for their morose and irascible nature, but mainly for their skills as manipulators of phenomena. As workers of magic, the tröllkonur[278] are described as very amorous.[279] Tröll women are described as wearing tunics of coarse, shrivelled leather,[280] so short in some instances, their genitalia was barely concealed.[281] The depth of bawdy detail is not spared and is surprisingly crude in places. In fact, an Old Norse tale (translated from French literature), the 13th-Century *Möttuls saga*, likewise tells of a magic mantle or a cloak that literally, exposes adulterous women. By rising up at the back to reveal their sex, they are shown to be potentially adulterous or promiscuous.

In *Ketils saga hængs*, the protagonist Ketill (of possible Sámi origin) meets the 'dark as pitch' tröllkona Forað, as she came out of the 'myrky' sea. Similar beings are described in *Örvar-Odds saga*, where Oddr and his companions meet a female kvikindi (unnatural creature) who was also wearing a leather/skin tunic, and later, others within a cave seated around a fire. Another saga (*Hálfdanar saga Brönufóstra*), typically features three sisters, all flagðkonur, though sometimes, nine are noted. In some instances, however, the descriptions are sheer fantasy, especially where they are presented as deformed with hooked/beaked noses, enormous

---

277. See: S. Matthew and Kathryn A. Hain. (Eds.) Concubines and Courtesans: Women and Slavery in Islamic History. (Oxford: Oxford University Press, 2017): 124-42 **278.** (sing. tröllkona), flagðkonur (sing. flagðkona), skessur (sing. skessa) or gýgjar (sing. gýgur). See: Illuga saga Gríðarfóstra and Gríms saga loðinkinna **279.** A crude tröllkona named Ýma expresses her desire for Hjálmþér quite freely in Hjálmþérs saga ok Ölvés. **280.** By wearing nothing but animal skin, the inhabitants of the Northern realms are de-humanised, and represented as belonging somewhere between humankind and animals. **281.** In Egils saga einhenda ok Ásmundar berserkjabana, the two protagonists, Egill and Ásmundr experience such an encounter in this strange tale of lust, power, fate and magical treasure. See: Hermann Pálsson. *Seven Viking Romances*. Translated by Paul Edwards. (Penguin Classics, 1985).

teeth, or with ears that hung down their necks, with hands that were nothing less than claws of iron; one-eyed (cyclops) are borrowed from Greek myth. "Finally, in Norna-Gests þáttr, mention is made of a gýgr that the heroine Brynhildr Buðladóttir, better known from the heroic poems of *The Poetic Edda* and *Völsunga saga*, met on her way to Hel."[282] Fear often induces mistrust, which escalates into the irrational marginalization of other peoples simply because they are different to ourselves. We instinctively align ourselves to those who look and act as we do, having an automatic (negative) response to outsiders – in this instance the 'Trölls' represent the 'ethnic Other.'[283]

We must always be mindful that medieval authors and the recorders of history were mainly men, Christian monks and laymen, who would have been seriously challenged by promiscuity and alternative beliefs, particularly heathenism. Ascribing unpleasant attributes to them is therefore hardly surprising.[284] Ultimately, it was startling for even ordinary men travelling up into these lands to find Sámi women enjoying the same active freedoms as men, which were (generally) denied Scandinavian women.[285] Skilled with bows, they often joined the men on fishing and hunting expeditions. A few noted traders married Sámi women, many others took them as concubines. (With the exception of forced labour in the silver mines there is no record of the Sámi being slaves).

The prejudice applied to the Sámi in past centuries has led to inaccurate accounts of their role in the histories of Scandinavia, in particular their contribution to the settlement of Iceland and to trade relationships between the Icelanders and the Sámi of Finnmark. Where the Sámi do feature in the Icelandic sagas, they are presented as a remote people, with strange customs, almost semi-mythical, but mainly as beings endowed with sorcerous skills obsessed with witchcraft

---

282. Guðmundsdóttir, 2017. The same story is told in the Eddaic poem, *Helreið Brynhildar*, albeit with no mention of the appearance of the gýgr. Some Trölls give assistance to the heroes, some even behave as foster-mothers would. Some are known for their wisdom, having the ability to compose verse, which runs contra to the motif that suggests they are unintelligent. **283.** Ármann Jakobsson. "Beast and Man: Realism and the Occult in 'Egils Saga'" *Scandinavian Studies* 83, no. 1 (2011): 29-44 http://www.jstor.org/stable/23075433 (Accessed 27th October, 2023). Often, but not always, the appellations þurs, jötunn or tröll, inferred a Sámi background. **284.** In 1555, the archbishop Olaus Magnus described the inhabitants of northern Scandinavia in his Historia de Gentibus Septentrionalibus, making sure to emphasise their magic skills and dark natures. **285.** Else Mundal. "The Relationship between Sámi and Nordic Peoples Expressed in Terms of Family Associations." Journal of Northern Studies 3. (2010): 25-37 DOI:10.36368/jns.v3i2.600

TIME AND ETERNITY – THE COSMIC MILL 209

and the supernatural. It is for this reason that early Norwegian law placed bans on consulting them in matters related to soothsaying and divination. There are four types of magic workers listed in the poem Hyndlujóð, these are: Völur (prophetesses); Jötnar (warlocks); Vitkar (wizards) and Séiðberendr (sorceresses).

Because of how the Sámi were presented in the Old Norse Sagas, unfavourable comparisons were frequently made (by some scholars in the past) between them, as people living in the polar regions, and all things 'other,' most notably with the dvärgar ('dwarfs'). Often, the criteria for such assumptions, are based on the derogatory descriptions found in old literary sources. These include associations with various crafts, a love of treasure, their short stature, their disinterest in being warriors, and their extreme northern locality. Political complications added another dimension to the factionalising politics of land dominance.

Within saga literature, Trölls are the antithesis of what was believed to be normal for human women, both in appearance and behaviour. In *Eyrbyggja saga*, the magical performer Geirríðr is referred to as a Tröll, though the term as used here, concerns her magical powers rather than her appearance, or hint of promiscuity. A very good example of this occurs where the 9th-Century figure of Hallbjörn hálftröll refers to his daughter-in-law, a Sámi woman named Hrafnhildr, as a Tröll. As a term, Tröll is generally used disparagingly in the sagas to suggest or refer to a supernatural phenomenon, or to a sorcerous person. In the northern regions of Scandinavia, magic and shape-shifting were invariably associated with the semi-mythical Sámi.[286]

Tröll may also refer to malicious spirits or ghosts, or simply to the strength and intimidating presence of a particular liminal character connected with magical tendencies that by implication suggest heathenism, rather than any presumed racial slur. Hallbjörn's disapproval of Hrafnhildr relates to her suspected bewitchment of his son, nothing more.[287] Hallbjörn was also one of the very earliest settlers on the Island of Ramsta. Because his mother was a Sámi concubine, the hero of *Gríms saga loðinkinna*, is named as a half-tröll, like his paternal grandfather. Mentioned in the *Ketils saga hængs*, *Egils saga Skalla-Grímssonar*, and the *Landnámabók*, Hallbjorn hálftröll (also known as Hallbjörn Ulfsson), was the father of Ketil Trout of Hrafnista, and a prolific ancestor of some of the settlers of Iceland, including Skalla-Grimr Kveldulfsson.[288] In fact, according to the *Landnámabók* (Book of Settlements), at least nine of the original settlers had Sámi ancestry.[289]

---

286. Guðmundsdóttir, 2017; Jakobsson, 2011. 287. Aalto and Lehtola, 2017: 7-30

The Shetland Islands were already settled by Norwegians in the 8th century. There is an encounter with a Sámi sorceress named Grímhildr, who happens to be the sister of Hrímnir, a cave-dwelling giant near the White Sea who is also an extremely powerful sorcerer. It is pertinent that *Heiðreks saga* sites *Jötunheimr* near the White Sea, and it is no coincidence that the region of *Jötunheimr* is situated North-East of the Scandinavian peninsula, described as a sparsely populated area, of small 'Tröll' family units who live in caves or seasonal shacks/tents (gammar). Describing the Sámi as Trölls, effectively dehumanises them. Trölls therefore often appear as creatures with very exaggerated features and characteristics of semi-human, semi-'other' beings.[290]

References to the Sámi people as Trölls places an emphasis on their supposed barbarisms that may in some cases represent notions of Nordic superiority as the more civilized inhabitants of the Scandinavian peninsula, a view adopted commonly amongst tribes of disparate cultures, often for socio-political benefits. In Norse society, Trölls were perceived as primitive and monstrous, and as creatures steeped in magic, possessing the ability to shape-shift. According to the central thematic narrative of the Fornaldarsögur, the task of the Scandinavian hero[291] is to slay as many 'Trölls' as possible, removing the threat of chaos they represent to their own communities. This presents a typical example of how people from other tribes and cultures are demonised and vilified as outsiders, mistrusted and sometimes even abused for differences not fully understood. In Norse mythology, the Jötnar – the creatures of *Jötunheimr* – were seen as opposers of their old gods, hence it was Þórr's role to defend Ásgarðr against their presence in the homeland of the Æsir.

Giants in particular (Jötnar) are often presented as the enemies of the Æsir gods in Scandinavian mythology, yet the term literally refers to ambivalent characters, who could be wise, cunning, or completely lacking in such skills. "The fact that the Æsir gods could marry giants'

---

288. Hermann Pálsson. "The Sámi People in Old Norse Literature." In, Nordlit 5 (1999): 29-53. https://doi.org/10.7557/13.2143. (Accessed 11th May 2024). **289.** As recorded in the Landnámabók. Several other convincing examples can be found here. See: Pálsson, 1997: 62–84. **290.** Folkloric history has preserved such ideas in Fornaldarsögur, and which correlate with information found in other Old Norse literature, especially where the customs of the (Lapp) inhabitants of these regions relate to their fur goods and skin tents. Indeed, the Trölls' characteristic features are described in (often) disparaging terms that infer the Sámi people (Finnar). **291.** Ánn, the hero of *Áns saga bogsveigis*, is known for fighting with the Trölls in the North.

womenfolk, while a giant could not have an Æsir goddess as a wife,"[292] parallels a trend where Norse men (especially wealthy chieftains and traders) were perfectly comfortable taking Sámi women as wives and concubines.[293] Heroes and anti-heroes were often the result of such unions, whose significant adventures are often central, even crucial to the saga story.

The *Fornaldarsögur* (folktales) of Scandinavia commemorate the legendary (Iron Age) heroes of the past, from a time before the settlement of Iceland in the 9th century. In some of these sagas, the heroes take long journeys or quests to the north and east of Norway, into the regions populated by the Permians and the Sámi, who are often described as Finnar or Lappar Trölls, but sometimes with derogatory intent as flögð, risar (a giant), or Jötnar.[294] Quite often, these heroic figures ventured forth to plunder, to exact tribute from the nomadic peoples of those remote regions; sometimes for less nefarious reasons, to seek access to better hunting and fishing grounds, or in some cases to trade. Descriptive terms imply a sense of 'otherness,' suggesting a cultural relationship with the supernatural realms,[295] and with baneful beings and magics. The (typically) shorter stature of the Sámi people, their darker skin and very different facial and physical features all represented beings assimilated into that curious and enigmatic non-human world of Old Norse/Germanic mythology and folklore.

Perhaps the most notorious Sámi mentioned in the sagas is an early 9th-Century Norwegian trader and chieftain Hjor who regularly travelled to western Siberia to Bjarmland; he returned with a dark-skinned wife[296] named Ljufvina. Their son, born in Rogaland, had notable Eurasian features, and was known as Geirmund Heljarskinn, an epithet often translated as Hel-Hide/Skin or Dark-Skin; it can also mean Deathskin, a possible reference to his fiercesome reputation as a ruthless warrior. Born in Rogaland, he became one of the first men to settle Iceland with his Siberian wife Illþurrka. As a pioneer in international hunting economy, Geirmund Heljarskinn amassed

---

292 ..Aalto and Lehtola, 2017. **293**. However, the sources are silent on possible cases where Norse women may have taken Sámi men as partners. **294**. Singular: Tröll, flagð, risi, Jötunn, respectively. Sámi are often disparagingly associated with dwarfs, giants, witches, sorcerers and trölls. **295**. Jakobsson, 2011. **296**. Or concubine, the sources are unclear. Siberian people are typically of Mongol origin, with darker hair and skin than most north Europeans. Mitochondrial DNA (motherline) tests of Geirmund´s living descendants in Iceland, suggest a Sámi/Asian/Mongol ancestral mother. One of these descendants, Bergsveinn Birgisson, has written a book about his ancestor, entitled somewhat sensationally as "Den svarte vikingen" (The Black Viking.)

incredible wealth through his slave trading networks. He also possessed many slaves himself, some of whom were Christian men and women captured from Ireland and Scotland on raiding expeditions.

The original story of Geirmund Hel-Hide can be found in a short story in the *Landnámabók* called '*Geirmundar þáttr heljarskinns*'[297] and tells the strange story of how Geirmund and his twin brother Hámund were raised, first by slaves as young children (which was in fact, quite commonplace), then under full patronage from their father.[298] As adults they went aVikingr, and in turn won great riches and a reputation for being amongst the greatest Sea-Kings (pirates) of their time.[299] As a long-distance trader, Geirmund even came to the British Isles. During his prolonged absence, things changed in Norway. The legendary king Háraldr Finehair (850-60 CE to 931-40 CE.[300]) conquered rival Norwegian kings and, by the end of the 9th century, allegedly became the first monarch to unify Norway under a single political and religious banner. This induced many, including Geirmund, to escape Háraldr's tyranny by migrating to Iceland where he used his wealth and influence to found several farmsteads. He also secured a personal army of mercenaries, which he used to ruthlessly acquire (not always legally) tracts of land by force. Legend claims that when Geirmund eventually died, he received a ship burial fit for a king.[301]

The tale of Geirmund the Hel-skinned (*Geirmundar þáttr heljarskinns*) is a 13th-Century settlement narrative similar to others found in the Book of Icelanders (*Íslendingabók*), the Book of Settlements (*Landnámabók*), and numerous Sagas of Icelanders (*Íslendingasögur*). Its inclusion establishes a counterpoint to Iceland's integration into the Norwegian kingdom at the end of *The Saga of the Sturlungs*.[302] There is

---

297. Much is made today of the boys being of mixed race, particularly their skin colour, but in the saga period, while it was not commonplace, it was certainly not unusual to see mixed race children born to concubines of chieftains and their retainers. Others include the berserker/poet lineage of Kveldulf, Skallagrim and Egill Skallagrimsson and their descendant Illugi Tagldarbani. **298.** As with all matters of lineage, the formal acceptance of one's heirs is a point of law, and of custom, its traits are not racially motivated. There are numerous historical examples of western kings acknowledging their bastard sons born of their mistresses. **299.** Politics and power are embedded in class, not race. **300.** These dates vary depending on sources. Háraldr hárfagri -'Hårfagreætta'was also known as 'fairhair.' **301.** *The Book of Settlements* (Sturlubók version). Translated by Hermann Pálsson and Paul Edwards. (University of Manitoba Press, 1972, 2006). *Heimskringla*, by Snorre Sturlusson. Translated by Lee Hollander (Trans.) (University of Texas Press, 1964). *The Prose Edda* by Snorre Sturlusson. Translated by Jesse Byock. (Penguin Books, 2005). https://avaldsnes.info/en/informasjon/hjor/ (Retrieved 11th May 2023).

TIME AND ETERNITY – THE COSMIC MILL 213

certainly a marked bias in the legends about the first settlers, the authors of which follow the politics of migrants such as Geirmund to Iceland, but focus specifically upon how the Icelandic experiment in a stateless society failed so catastrophically. During this period, élite Icelanders engaged in ever-escalating private warfare to the point where they were forced to eventually cede sovereignty to the Norwegian king in the years 1262-64 CE. It is important however, to remember that although the Icelandic sagas are written in Old Norse,[303] they concern only the events, politics and beliefs of the people who shaped Iceland; the sagas do not reflect those of Norway, Sweden or Finland, other than to highlight Norway's hold over Iceland. Nonetheless, the ordinary folk do not appear to have shared in the very evident clerical bias.

Several sagas preserved legends and skaldic poems of mythological significance, others relate to social events, while some contain elements of both. Sometimes, advantageous marriages occurred between Scandinavian chieftains and Sámi women, whose occult abilities enhanced the politics of ambition and rulership.

The number of royal marriages with Sámi witches or their daughters is so high in the saga literature that, according to Kusmenko's ironic comment, one might conclude that the Sámi are the ancestors of the royal families of Norway, Sweden and Denmark. He suggests that when Heimskringla and Gesta Danorum were written in the 1200s, it was still possible to imagine that a Scandinavian king had a Sámi wife. However, as Kusmenko also proves, similar marriages are common between royals and giants in mythology. Mundal notes that the mixing of giants and the Sámi is typical evidence of the unreliability of the sagas as an historical source. Yet, she notes that, among the ancient Norse people, the kinship of the Sámi with Norwegian kings reflects a certain sense of unity with the Sámi, or even appreciation of them. A common family background bound the king of Norway to the Sámi and gave him the legitimacy to rule over them. This could be viewed as the construction of the legend of a state formed by two peoples. Gro Steinsland assumes that, according to the ancient Norse perspective, a king had to be a descendant of

---

302. This compilation survives in two medieval manuscripts: *The Book of Króksfjord* (*Króksfjarðarbók*) and *The Book of Reykjafjord* (*Reykjafjarðarbók*), as well as a plethora of post-medieval copies. **303.** A language spoken in the regions now known as Sweden, Norway, Denmark, Iceland (who continued to speak it after Scandinavia adopted Germanic based languages), the Orkneys and the Faroe Islands between ca. 600-1400 CE. Derived from Old Nordic, which was derived from Proto-Nordic, it was also spoken in the same areas, belonging to the Germanic branch of the Indo-European language family. See: E. Haugen and Jan Terje Faarlund. "Scandinavian languages." In, *Encyclopedia Britannica*, January 24, 2025. https://www.britannica.com/topic/Scandinavian-languages. (Accessed 28th March 2023).

giants or gods, the result of a marriage between two opposite sides, a Norwegian chieftain and a mythical character. When the sagas moved from the mythical to the historical level, people in the real world, such as the Sámi, could stand in for the giants. The key point was that the marriage was between high-ranking individuals, which is why the wives of kings were almost without exception daughters of "Sámi kings" – Finnakonungar.[304]

Because, it was deemed to be almost an imperative that legitimate lineage demonstrated a significant inclusion of a few otherworldly beings, one such high profile tale refers to the supposed marriage between the Norwegian King Háraldr Fairhair, and Snæfríðr (Snow-peace), the daughter of the Sámi chieftain Svási (also known as 'king' Svási), and through this union, a northern trading network was secured.[305] Although their marriage suggests the recognition of Sámi hierarchy and authority, and an affirmation of shared landscapes, at least in more southerly regions, it is interpreted by Snorre (writing as a Christian author), as the consequence of Sámi magic, an enchantment cast by Snæfríðr upon a jar of mead consumed by Háraldr Fairhair.[306] In fact, his desire for her, utterly consumed him to distraction, leading him to neglect his duties. It was said that even her death did not sever the ties spun by her spell, and that Háraldr sat by her corpse, lamenting her death for three winters, as his people lamented his madness – "Still, the Lappish girl drove Háraldr out of his mind."[307]

Secured thusly by the saga authors' own world view, the image of the Sámi in the sagas is anything but simple, and not always as straightforward to analyse as is often assumed. Indeed, not all their magics were presented negatively; myth blurs easily with history in the records of such relationships, particularly in the *Landnámabók* and *Flateyjarbók*. It seems that initial descriptions of the Sámi people, and indeed any information relating to them, however colourful, were taken up voraciously by various subjective writers of the saga material, and having read it, embellished it before repeating it themselves, thus generating a circular bias for the Sámi from that reductive resource.[308]

---

304. Aalto and Lehtola, 2017. **305.** It was not uncommon for Sámi chieftains to be referred to by the moniker, *Finnakonungr*, meaning 'king,' and similar marriages all proved to be mutually beneficial. To this day, several thousand Scandinavian loan words can be detected in the Sámi languages. **306.** To many scholars, the distinction between description of the Sámi people before and after conversion is transparently evident. **307.** This is the refrain from the anonymous early 13th century skaldic proverb poem, which appears in the Flateyjarbók. See: Roberta Frank. *Sex Lies And Málsháttakvaeæði: A Norse Poem From Medieval Orkney*. Edited by Judith Jesch. (Centre for the Study of the Viking Age. Uni of Notts. 2004).

TIME AND ETERNITY – THE COSMIC MILL 215

In *Heimskringla*, for example, Snorre Sturlusson repeats the legend of King Háraldr Fairhair and Snæfríðr in almost the same words as those found in *Ágrip af Noregs konungasogum*, an earlier account written around 1200 CE by an unknown author. This literary practice has not abated in recent centuries.

308. Else Mundal. "The Perception of the Sámis and Their Religion in Old Norse Sources." In, *Shamanism and Northern Ecology* 36. Edited by Juha Pentikäinen. (Mouton de Gruyter, 1996): 97-116

FINNAR

In many tales, we also encounter several other seemingly supernatural characters, whose roles appear indistinct from each other. Because there are so few direct references to finnar in the Landnámabók, it is very often assumed that the ambiguous appellations, Þurs, Jötunn or Tröll, all relate to the Sámi. For instance, Þurs is used interchangeably with a Tröll, sorcerer, or witch, often to imply an 'otherness' in a negative sense that mostly (but not always) refers to Sámi, to emphasise an engineered distinction from the (good) people of Scandinavia, while simultaneously presenting the Sámi as a strange, anti-social, even hostile people. "The Prose Edda, 5 which describes Scandinavian mythology, mentions giants and þursar, more specifically hrímþursar, which can be translated as 'frost giants,' for example."[309]

> The term *Tröll*, which in the sagas means a supernatural phenomenon, or a person who deals with the supernatural, can be connected with the Sámi. The term is used as a metaphor for anything beyond the limits of normality, to indicate the strength or size of a character, for example. The word can also refer to malicious spirits or ghosts. It is even associated with the Berserks, who metamorphose in battle, turning from a human into a bear or wolf. A metamorphosis naturally involves magic. Tröll is often translated into English as 'troll,' but it does not mean a troll as such, but rather a sorcerer. Jötunn literally means a giant, but in Scandinavian mythology giants are not only large in size, but form a diverse group and are ambivalent characters. [...] Giants were seen as Übergangscharakteren, as they were human-like characters who lived in a zone between the human world and that of the monstrous races. This connotation suited well the image of the finnar in the sagas, who lived somewhere between the known civilized world and the unknown periphery. The Sámi are comparable to giants in Scandinavian mythology, since similar characteristics are associated with them: they live outside the "centre," on the edge of the world and often in the north; snow is their element (as it is for

---

309. Ármann Jakobsson. "The Trollish Acts Of Þorgrímr The Witch: The Meanings Of Troll And Ergi In Medieval Iceland." In, *Saga-Book 32* (2008): 39–68. Https://Www.Jstor.Org/Stable/48610768 (Accessed 26th September 2023). See also: Jakobsson, 2011; Aalto and Lehtola, 2017.

the northern giants) and they know how to ski, shoot with a bow, predict the future and perform magic. Although Christianity and its negative attitude towards pagan magic are clearly visible in the sagas, magic and its use are not always depicted as negative. According to Gro Steinsland, the Scandinavian kings' marriages with the women of the finnar, as described in the sagas, repeat the literary topos found in mythology: Æsir kings marry the womenfolk of giants. Although these unions often ended unhappily, they resulted in a hero: the union of opposing forces created something new and unprecedented.[310]

Sámi presence is generally inferred by crude epithets, including the ancient Germanic term finn, in its Norse form finni, finnr, or finnar (pl).[311] As unnamed characters, the finnar share many attributes of the Sámi, having the ability to control natural phenomena, raise storms, shape-shift into birds, use magic to heal and to curse, perform divinations and even acts of prophecy. Perceived ethnic similarities between the Sámi and the Finnish peoples, led to both peoples being referred to by the old ethnonym 'Finn' in many similar early textual sources.[312]

In several of the Old Norse sagas, 'Finn' and 'Finnland' are mentioned, in what would seem to be present-day Jämtland and Härjedalen and also further to the south. Furthermore, the Ynglingasaga *mentions that several of the mythical Uppsala kings of the Ynglinga dynasty had sons with Finn women. [...] The contents of the Old Norse sources imply that the Sámi were a natural part of society and that the border between Sámi and Germanic peoples was not very sharp in Scandinavia.*[313]

Moreover, until recently, the word Finn was used in the Old Norse sources for the people of (former) Lapland and for non-Norwegians, who were probably a Sámi population. Ptolemy (d.165 CE), the Greek astronomer, geographer and mathematician, mentioned the 'Phinnoi' in his work *Geographia*, locating them on the northern part of the island 'Skandia.' Somewhat later, in the 6th century, Procopius, described a tribe inhabiting Thule as the 'Skrithiphinoi' (often interpreted as 'skiing Finns') in very derogatory terms as beast-like and uncivilised.[314] Amongst his other colourful observations,[315] Procopius also informs

---

310. Aalto and Lehtola, 2017. **311.** Ibid., The Old Norse word for Sámi was finni or finnr (jinna for women). **312.** The Norse referred to the Sámi as Finns and saw no significant difference between them and the people of Finland, since they all spoke Finnic languages. **313.** Ojala, 2009. **314.** Clive Tolley. Shamanism in Norse Myth and Magic, I-II. (Academia Scientiarum Fennica, 2009): 47 **315.** Hardly any of the historians describing the features, manners and customs of the arctic and sub-arctic peoples ever actually witnessed what they describe, but typically copied the assumptions cultivated by previous historians. Their accounts are substantially embellished.

us how the women also engage in the hunt (which better suggests a tribe of arctic peoples other than the Sámi).

Jordanes also refers to the island of Scandza (interpreted as the Scandinavian Peninsula), in his 6th century Gothic history, to the Screrefennae, in similar terms. In his *Historia Langobardorum* (History of the Lombards), Paulus Diaconus comments on the Winter and Summer Nights solstice phenomena of these regions, and also refers to the Scritofini (or Scritobini) as the snow-laden neighbours of Germania. From other 9th century accounts by travellers to these regions, namely Ohthere[316] and Wulfstan, we learn of the seasonally nomadic lifestyle of the 'Finnas'[317] peoples. Ohthere travelled from his home farm in Northern Norway to England around the year 890 CE, to the court of King Alfred the Great where he regaled him with tales of trade and exploration.

According to Ohthere's (Norwegian: Ottar) account, the (Mountain) Sámi remained primarily "fishers and bird-catchers and hunters."[318] Ohthere is a prime example of the new rising elite in Scandinavia. This powerful Norwegian chief gleaned considerable wealth in tribute[319] (gafole) paid to him by the Sámi in furs (seal, pine-marten, reindeer, bear, otter etc.), skins, hides, whetstones, soapstone, ropes and walrus tusks.[320] There is some debate how the word gafole should be interpreted. It can be linked to the Proto-Germanic word *gabula which means 'tribute,' as a type of tax or levy. The comparable Norse term gofga, meaning: 'to give, to sacrifice, to honour,' bears a subtle nod towards the reciprocal bonded relationship between a chieftain and the farmers in Norse society. Although the bonds appear to be economic transactions, the chieftain is obligated to provide political and martial protection in exchange for his farmers' resources.[321]

---

316. The 'terfinna land,' mentioned in Ohthere's account, has been compared with the Terskij bereg, the Ter Shore, the southern shore of the Kola Peninsula, which has been known from the 13th century as the Novgorodian administrative area, volost, of Tre. **317.** The name 'Finnas' is also referred to in the Old English poems, Beowulf and Widsith. **318.** N. Lund. (Ed.) C .E. Fell (Trans.). *Two Voyagers At The Court Of King Alfred. The Ventures Of Ohthere And Wulfstan Together With The Description Of Northern Europe From The Old English Orosius.* (William Sessions Limited, 1984). **319.** The Sámi were forced to abandon reindeer hunting and take up reindeer herding in order to produce the sizeable tribute demanded by the Norwegians. As other groups began to spread throughout Scandinavia, the Sámi were too scattered and disorganized to resist the intrusion by other, which led to their eventual marginalisation. **320.** Lund, 1984. **321.** The resources provided by the Sámi were the productions from hunting and trapping of great land and sea mammals, such as precious furs, walrus teeth, down and feathers, marine oil, and more. These goods were considered very valuable and were highly sought-after trade commodities and prestige goods.

This deeply symbolic relationship was built on strong, mutual loyalty and inter-dependence at its core, and embedded with many rules of conduct and mutual respect. It is this sense of gafole, Ohthere refers to. Increased contact between diverse peoples can often lead to a mutual sharing and absorption of culture, and simultaneously, a deepening expression that conversely emphasises distinctions between them; the use of signs, ornamentation, and dress style has for each people, a specific, symbolic and cultural meaning. Language provides an effective platform for mediation, hence the appearance of disparate loan words amongst northern peoples.

Farmsteads ultimately served their communities as religious centres, whereby the chieftains (as the farmer-noble) acted as both temporal and spiritual leader of the people within his clan as kith and kin.[322] As their liege lord, he was obliged to provide food and shelter for them. From this social and religious institution, legends were founded around heroes and (petty) kings whose names became immortalised in later sagas, some of whom achieved god-like status. Similarly, the regions they marshalled (indicated by the suffixes cited above) above achieved sacred, legendary and cultic status in later literature. Ultimately, tribal loyalties served to weld the individual farms and farming districts (*bygd*) into small kingdoms, leading to the pre-dominance of just a few named families who by their successes, established substantial lineages, also immortalised in the later sagas. Each chief was also known as a *hirse* a term that referred to his position as overseer of a particular ward. Because this embodied both physical and spiritual authority, law and the implementation of law, became a matter of consensus, (theoretically at least, in reality they were far from democratic), and thus we see the development of the law assemblies (ting) and law speakers.[323] Difficulties in accessibility through mountainous regions or dense tracts of forests, meant that other regions held their own annual assemblies for all legislative and judicial matters: the coastal districts established the *Borgarting*, and the interior districts, the *Eidsivating*.

Both the Borgarting and Eidsivating laws had strong prohibitions against

322. Finns were amongst the lowest thralls (the subservient class) within a growing three-tiered society, headed by the Jarls (farmer-nobles). Karls were the farm workers.
323. For landowners, these were commonly known as heimsting or heradsting. In Norway, the next higher level of official administration was the fylkesting or provincial assembly (similar perhaps to a modern-day the county council). Twenty-nine such bodies existed at the beginning of the Viking Age, with each having its own dedicated arena in the form of a valley or fjord. Above this, the Gulating, which first convened about the year 900 CE. at Gulen, was the regional assembly for western Norway.

"travelling to the Finns to fortell the future." This fact is doubly interesting because it reveals that the Finns were not only regarded as having supernatural powers, but that they also were very much in evidence in southeastern Norway, where the two laws applied, as late as the tenth century of the Christian era. On the other hand, similar provisions seem to have been lacking in the Gulating and Frostating laws, which applied to Vestlandet and Trøndelag respectively.[324]

Thusly named for the assembly site located on a peninsula jutting into the middle of Trondheimsfjord, central Norway was governed by the Frostating Law. Nonetheless, "executive power remained diffused through the individual valleys and fjords in the persons of district chiefs or petty kings."[325] Over time, these were each consumed by others with greater martial presence.

The association of temporal power with religion was seen in the mysticism attached to 'literacy' and the knowledge of runes. Persons who knew how to read and write in the runic alphabet were called erilaR, a word that eventually evolved into jarl, or English earl, The unification of Norway on a national scale is historically attributed to Harald Hårfagre ('the Fair-Haired') who defeated a coalition of petty kings at the battle of Hafursfjord, near Stavanger, in 872 CE. However, many western farmer-nobles preferred to forsake Norway rather than give their allegiance to Harald, thereby giving rise to an exodus that initiated the Norse settlement of Iceland c.874. There, accompanied by their retinues, they could continue to serve as the political and religious leaders of each of their respective districts.[326]

Overall conversion to Christianity by the 1100s inculcated a substantial shift in power, both in temporal and religious terms. It is ironic that the unification of Norwegian society, (as a model for so many others of this era) under one king, simultaneously witnessed the loss by that king of his spiritual authority and leadership.[327]

Conversion of the Scandinavian regions meant that matters of clairvoyance or magic (particularly witchcraft), became the preserve of the Sámi whose beliefs were assumed to be very similar to those of the formerly heathen Norse.[328] It is even claimed how a Sámi sorcerer assisted women to conceive "immaculately" with the help of a spirit conjured into them.[329] The most renowned of all female sorcerers mentioned in the sagas, was Gunnhilðr, who married Eirik Bloodaxe,

---

324. Malmström, 2012). **325.** Ibid. **326.** Ibid. **327.** Whence Olav Haraldsson (the son of Harald Hårfagre) achieved the status of saint at the Battle of Stiklestad in 1030 CE, Norway finally acquired its singular faith status. **328.** Mundal 1996; Mundal 2004. **329.** Pálsson, 1999: 29-53. Snorre Sturlusson. *Noregs konunga sögur* ['*Heimskringla*. The Kings' sagas of Norway'] Edited by Finnur Jónsson. København: Gad, 1911.

and according to Snorre Sturlasson, was not only wicked, but hailed from Hålogaland (Sámi territory in the Arctic circle), an inference that again connects the Sámi with sorcery.[330] Norwegians frequently travelled to Finnmark to consult the Sámi on matters of divination. Even the first Christian Norwegian King Olaf Tryggvason (d. 1000) visited a Sámi to hear prophecies about his future after his arrival in Norway (*Flateyjarbók* 1, 231).

Landnámabók *also mentions other people originating in Hålogaland or northern Norway, and the ability to perform magic is associated with many of them. Numerous references to "otherness" especially in the designations Jötunn, Tröll and Þurs do not, as such, prove the individuals' links to the Sámi in the way that the word Finnar would. It is noteworthy, however, that Pálsson could identify even a small concentration of place-names in Iceland possibly referring to the Sámi, including a region called Finnmark. Moreover, Pálsson mentioned local traditions involving wizards and sorcerers. (…) [Still, we should] always remember that the author/s of* Landnámabók *were members of the Icelandic-Norwegian elite, whose interpretations of Icelandic history reflected the need of the aristocracy to legitimise its claims on the land and privileges. Hence, in their works, literate men belonging to the social elite modified ideals related to the backgrounds of Icelanders—particularly the upper class. The 'better side' was emphasised, while the background of the Sámi, associated with witchcraft, was not necessarily a subject of pride.*[331]

Indeed, the Icelandic people have purposefully constructed a history for themselves that excludes or minimises the impact of other cultural influences on the establishment of Iceland as an independent nation. And this extends from the Sámi to Celtic[332] speaking peoples of whom we hear almost nothing; in fact, without genetic and archaeological evidence, we would remain unaware of their signature in this multi-cultural settlement.[333] We should certainly recognize the embedded bias of 13th-Century Icelandic saga writers towards immigrants bereft of noble birth, or of Christian heritage. Interactions "with heathens was (seen as) bad. Again, the purpose of the stereotypes in the sagas was to show what the proper Scandinavian was not: heathen."[334] The

---

330. Ibid. **331.** Aalto and Lehtola, 2017. **332.** Please note, Celtic is not a race or ethnicity, it is a language group **333.** Aalto and Lehtola, 2017. Scientists have estimated that up to 40 per cent of Iceland's first immigrants would have been Celtic speaking peoples of northern Europe, even though only around two per cent of the names mentioned in Landnámabók are of Celtic origin. More recent archaeological studies confirm considerable interactions between the Sámi and Norwegians, on many levels -sacred and mundane. **334.** Ibid.

Church in Norway was certainly nervous about continued contact with the so-called heathen Sámi, and subsequently navigated law codes to prevent it, hence associations of the Sámi with Witches, Trölls and Jötnar, as beings capable of sorcery and magic, all deliberately curated to instil fear, mistrust and even resentment. These negative and unsavoury views crept into Icelandic folklore and subsequently, all literature associated with it.

Now we can clearly see how all sagas are revisions or enhancements of earlier stories, retold as mythical legends or as object lessons against a pseudo-historical back-drop. Scandinavian peoples found the Sámi's prophetic capabilities very important, to the extent that several Sámi appear as advisers to prominent Scandinavian personalities, both mythological and historical. For instance, we are informed by Saxo that Othinus (Óðinn) sought out Finnish fortune-tellers and priests for advice on how to avenge the death of his son Baldrus (Baldr).

Sources such as the Latin *Historia Norwegiæ* (c. 1170 CE to 1190 CE), *Ágrip af Noregs konungasogum* and *Heimskringla*, refer to Sámi settlements across Norway throughout the Viking Age (and into the early Middle Ages), and to the 13th-Century provincial laws of eastern Norway (noted above) that forbade Norwegians from consulting the Sámi for predictions. The Borgarþingslog[335] declared it unlawful for anyone to travel to the Sámi to seek divination. Similarly, the law for the Eiðsifaþing outlawed any person who believed in the heathen Sámi's sorcerous abilities (by drum, sacrifice or enchanted herbal magics, or who even consulted them regarding such magics. No such provision existed in the *Gulaþing* (law) of western Norway, where the Sámi did not live.[336]

Even if Old Norse and Sámi constituted structurally different societies or dichotomous worlds in the Viking period and the Early and High Middle Ages, both written and archaeological sources indicate extensive relationships. As already mentioned, their relations seem to have started far earlier, as evidenced, for example, by the study of primeval Nordic loan-words in Sámi dialects and Old Norse and Sámi place names, which suggests significant interactions since the Roman Iron Age. The Old Norse written sources comprise important information for the Viking period and the Middle Ages, even if they contain fictional and anachronistic

---

335. One can read that it was forbidden "to go to Sámi" (fara till finna, gera finnfarar), "to believe in Sámi," (trúa á finna), "to go to Finnmark to ask for a prophesy" (at fara á Finnmerkr at spyrja spá), which indicates that in the 13th century this custom was widespread in eastern Norway. **336.** This affirms the joint occupation by the Sámi and the Norwegians within a long zone from the Tromsø region to the Oppland area in central Norway.

elements (the sagas in particular), and are written from an Old Norse or non-Sámi perspective. A number of stories and poems, however, mention Sámi interaction with the Old Norse peoples. While there are examples of the mistreatment of the Sámi, cooperation, confidence and mutual respect characterise relationships between them, of which the Sámi's magical skills are particularly valued.[337]

In this regard, certain traits and motifs can be easily recognised; for instance, witchcraft (raising storms especially), tracking, hunting, the winter cold, and travelling on skis (finnr skríðr), are typically associated with the Sámi.[338] There is much to suggest that the blacksmith Völunðr (whose father was a *finnakonungr*), was a Sámi shaman. In the *Völundarkviða*, Völunðr's brother Slagfiðr is described in terms commonly applied to the finnar which focus on them being adept skiers and hunters.[339]

There is much evidence to suggest that the two groups shared fundamental religious ideas, indicated by beliefs in some of the same gods and similar witchcraft or sorcery. For instance, sorcerers or 'shamans' of both groups were able to transform themselves into new shapes, cause bad weather, foretell the future, and use magic to heal or harm. These premises probably constituted mutual resistance against Christianisation, further suggested in the sources by instances in which the Sámi supported the Old Norse by sorcery and fighting on the pagan side. As previously noted, the opposition against Christianisation appears most substantial in Arctic Norway among the Háleygir. The well-known story of the great sorcerer and Háleygir chieftain Raud the Strong in Salten (mid-Nordland), who had a large group of Sámi at his disposal, is apparently symptomatic.[340]

Several further instances of witchcraft and shape-shifting occur in Olaf Tryggvason's saga (in *Heimskringla*), involving a Sámi shaman (kunnigr maðr - a 'knowing man') sent to scout Iceland in the shape of a whale at the behest of the Danish King Harald 'Bluetooth' Gormsson. Provoked by the unruly behaviour of the Icelanders, Harald decided he needed to learn of Iceland's defensive weaknesses for his retaliatory attack. Within the same saga, we also learn how the Sámi manufactured twelve enchanted reindeer skin hauberks for Þórrir (Tore Hund), that were impervious to the Vikingr's iron spears. (*Heimskringla* II).[341]

It is important to stress here that the Saga literature is not an

---

337. Svestad, 2021. **338.** Personal names of the Sámi often refer to coldness, snow or skiing. See: Sirpa Aalto. "Categorizing Otherness in the King's Sagas" In, Volume 10 of Publications of the University of Eastern Finland, Dissertations in social sciences. University of Eastern Finland, (2010): 169 **339.** Aalto and Lehtola, 2017. **340.** Svestad, 2021. **341.** Aalto and Lehtola, 2017.

accurate depiction of history, nor its events, it was never meant to be, that was not its purpose. In much the same way that Shakespeare's plays were composed as fantastical dramas, these works are devised as fictional entertainment, even where they bore historical elements. As socio-religio-political commentary, they are engineered to steer and guide the observers in object lessons, in morality, and on the perils of being out of sync with the system. This complex relationship between the Norse and Sami peoples reveals medieval prejudices and the tendency to revise the events of previous centuries through a Christian filter. Nonetheless, the texts remain a rich source of information concerning customs and traditions relating to trade, marriage, medicine, healing, politics and religion. All literature inadvertently presents the phenomena of mind, that is, the thinking dynamic of the time of record, and so, the presentation of the Sámi within such a framework, must be understood in that context if any real sense of who they were is to be achieved; otherwise it will be lost. Indeed, the multi-ethnic nature of Middle Age societies must be fully understood and realised.[342]

---

342. Ibid.

SÁMI CULTURE IN SCANDINAVIA

The Sámi people do not form an homogenous entity, neither in the present nor in the past. As a people rooted in the culture of (old) Northern Eurasia, the Sámi's influence upon the heathen culture of Scandinavia, in particular its mythology, should not be underestimated, though of course, amongst current Scandinavians anxious to preserve an autonomous version of their history, this is not a popular notion.

When we look at the relation between the Sámi and Scandinavians in the Viking Age without being prejudiced, we can conclude that the traditional opinion that Sámi cultural influence on the Scandinavians was impossible or minor, is false. On the contrary there are many elements in Scandinavian heathen culture and in Scandinavian languages which were borrowed by the Scandinavians from their northern neighbours before and during the Viking Age. We can even suppose that the formation of the Scandinavian culture and of the Common Scandinavian language in the period between the 6th and the 11th centuries was conditioned by Sámi-Scandinavian contacts to a very high degree.[343]

Later (medieval) prejudices against the Sámi were clearly not apparent before and during the Viking Age, quite the contrary. The cross-pollination of language is a testament to the considerable influences evident in the Scandinavian languages of that period. That this would naturally extend to culture too as a significant function of language is assured. Although the Nordic and the Sámi populations mutually influenced each other over many hundreds of years through their evolving shared cultures in matters of land, trade and intermarriage, it is clear that languages evolved along a very different course as their life-styles (being a product of regional subsistence) and subsequent beliefs, ultimately diverged considerably. Nonetheless, the shared roots are there, and quite apparent in subtle ways, particularly

---

343. Jurij K. Kusmenko. "Sámi and Scandinavians in the Viking Age." In, *Scandinavistica Vilnensis*. 65-94. 10.15388/ScandinavisticaVilnensis.2009.2.5. (Institute of Linguistic Studies, St.-Petersburg, Russian Academy of Sciences, 2009)

with regard to folk magic practises, though these were the first casualties of conversion. The inevitable process of Christianisation impacted both societies greatly, first in Nordic regions, between the 9th and the 11th centuries, and then later throughout Sápmi in the 17th century. Fortunately, there are sufficient clues in language especially that relate to the continued interactions between the Sámi and the Norse peoples in the saga literature spanning the 13th to the 16th centuries – mainly where magics are encountered – such that the Norse terms fjolkyngi and Séiðr infer Sámi sorcery. Despite the impact of the *Borgarþingslog*, Séiðr is undoubtedly the legacy of the Sámi people, yet the significance of this is minimised in its negligible inclusion in Icelandic literary material. Ironically however, as we have learned, it was in that 'distinct' capacity, the Sámi were consulted on matters of divination and the interpretation of dreams.

The substantial similarities between Norse *Séiðr* and Sámi *noaidevuohta* generated an identifiable overlap. It is now recognised that because Sámi wives were presumed to bring with them their native skills, which naturally included specific approaches to magic and ancestral cultic practises, divinatory consultations continued somewhat discretely in post conversion Scandinavia. Because Sámi practitioners mainly lived outside of the Christian world, at least initially, they were exempt from the law, and therefore, when there was a need for magic, conjuring, healing or spirit-summoning, it was the Sámi people who were approached. This is why such inclusions are presented in the saga literature and in such condemnatory terms – it is not heathenism that is being referred to here, but the strange and curious practices and beliefs of the Sámi peoples.

Nonetheless, the archaeological and written source material from the coastal region of Northern Norway, underline the frequent and close contact between the Norse and Sámi groups, via bonds secured through marriage and kinship ties, and through trade alliances. In fact, the Sámi were integral to the economic trading network of the Norse chieftains. Safe sea routes, maps and water worthy vessels were an essential part of this industry, which in part was achieved by building alliances along the coast. The development of those coastal allied networks of alliances generated conditions for safe long-distance travels and (more) direct trade routes.[344]

Norse settlements are thusly found spread along the outer coastlines, while the Sámi settlements are found further inland, in mountain

---

344. Ibid.

areas, valleys and marshlands.[345] The wealth of archaeological material from Northern Norway is testament to the diverse range of goods traded and exchanged across vast territories. Riches garnered from successful trading expeditions across the north, were fundamentally imperative in structuring the power hubs that sustained the chieftaincies needed for gift-exchange. The pressure for supply became a burdensome demand on the Sámi, especially in the Late Iron Age, when resource utilisation peaked. This development went hand in hand with increased social stratification, centralisation of power and expansion under the control of regional Earls.

During the Viking Age, the Sámi territory of Sápmi reached much further south than has been previously assumed up to now. The standard view that the southern Sámi did not appear in central Norway and central Sweden until the 16th-17th centuries, is no longer tenable; a revision is long overdue.[346] Archaeologists and historians continue to debate the location of the original southern border of the Sámi on the Scandinavian peninsula without resolution, even though the cultural contact between the Norse and the Sámi is clearly evident, and certainly occurred long before the Viking Age, continuing through it (possibly between 550 CE to 1050 CE.

In the Southern region of Sápmi, higher spirits that originated in the Scandinavian tradition, are named by Swedish and Norwegian missionaries as *Veralden Olmai* (Veraldar goð – Freyr); *Ruona* (Rana) (Rán); *Horagalles* (Þórrkarl), and *Ruotta* (Rota). These Scandinavian cognates are not found amongst the Lule Sámi, with the exception of *Storjunkare* (big ruler) and *Lilljunkare* (small ruler).[347] Traces of Sámi influence are evidenced in other characters from Norse mythology, namely, Thjazi, Skaði[348] and Ull, three Jötnar, who, as notable figures, all exhibit traits associated with the Sámi spirits of winter hunting and fishing. Skaði's mountain abode hints at the Sámi landscape of Arctic Norway. Skaði came to Ásgarðr to marry Njörd, but chose Óðinn instead, who fathered her sons, "of whom Sæmingr (whose name probably derives from a Sámi word for the Sámi people), became the ancestor of the Háleygir and the mighty Lade earls [including Hakon Jarl] who aspired to the throne of Norway,"[349] This is again an

---

345. Kusmenko, 2009. **346.** Ibid. **347.** There are around three thousand loanwords from the Scandinavian languages within the Sámi languages; many were borrowed during this common period. **348.** Skaði: Goth. *skadus* and the Old English: *sceadu*, both mean 'shadow.' See: E.O.G. Turville-Petre. *Myth and Religion of the North: The Religion of Ancient Scandinavia*. (Greenwood Press, 1964): 164 See: Ásgeir Blöndal Magnússon. Íslensk orðsifjabók. [Icelandic etymological dictionary] (Orðabók Háskólans, 1989). **349.** Svestad, 2021.

example of a high-ranking Sámi woman marrying a prestigious figure in Scandinavian myth and history. Exhibiting traits typically associated with Sámi women, Skaði excels at skiing, hunting (while on skis) and archery.

Marriage functioned as a mechanism for making peace and solving conflicts between peoples in Old Norse society, and to make or maintain alliances as well. Regardless of whether Skaði was exclusively Sámi and Snæfríðr was a real or fictional person, we should see these marriages as symbolic expressions of intimate relationships between Old Norse and the Sámi. Interestingly, proto-Scandinavian loan words in Sámi related to marriage and in-laws that apparently date to the Roman Iron Age may support the occurrence of mixed marriages, as do female graves with mixed ethnic features, such as the Hagbartholmen grave 1/1954.[350]

Furthermore, Skaði's father, Thjazi, is well-known for his adoption in the form of an eagle and his abduction of Iðunna from Ásgarðr in order to steal her apples of immortality and rejuvenation.[351] This motif has parallels in the Indo-Aryan tradition where the eagle Garuda steals the drink of immortality from the gods, showing the universality of a myth that may have reached Scandinavia from Indo-Aryans through the Siberian people. The Sámi word *bassi* (holy) as found in *Stoura Bassi Sieidi*, meaning 'the great spirit,' is an Indo-Aryan loan word (one of several) found in Finno-Ugric languages. A possible connection has been made between Thjazi and the (southern) Sámi word for water – *tjaehtsi*,[352] and thus by default, to the Sámi elemental spirit – Tjatsiolmai ('water man').[353] At the Sieidi sites dedicated to Tjatsiolmai, it has not gone unnoticed that some of these great stones take on the form of a birdlike-man or a giant bird.[354]

Very little is known of Ull, and as a possible Bronze Age spirit associated with (returning) light, possibly of the Sun,[355] Ull's gender is uncertain, ambiguous, and often, prejudicially determined. While Ull presents an enigma, even in Scandinavian mythology, this arcane spirit is associated with wild places, particularly with large bodies of water, and like Skaði, with winter snows, hunting and skiing, activities that when mentioned in the sagas, assume an identification with the Sámi. Living on the peripheral boundaries, that is, to the north, on the edge of the supposedly civilised world, the Sámi revel in the snow,

---

350. Ibid. **351.** Unsurprisingly, this huge bird-like man exists in the mythology of many northern Asiatic people from the Mongols to the Samoyeds. See: D. Katz. *The Image of the Netherworld in the Sumerian Sources* (CDL Press. 2003). **352.** Rasmus Rask. "En Udsigt over de lappiske og finiske Stammers Historie." In, Rasmus Rask: Ausgewählte Abhandlungen 2. (Kopenhagen. 1932-33): 285–320. **353.** Kusmenko, 2009. **354.** Ibid **355** Ull: Goth. wulþus 'glory, shine.' See: Magnússon, 1989. See: Aalto and Lehtola, 2017.

an unyielding element over which their mastery was legendary. Both Skaði and Ull appear to have connections with theophoric place names across middle Sweden and eastern Norway associated with winter hunting and skiing: Skadevi, Skädvi, Skädharg, and Ullevi, Ulleraker etc.[356] Skaði and her brothers are described as avid skiers and hunters, though they are not actually named as Sámi.

In addition to being proficient skiers, the Sámi were of course, renowned hunters and sorcerers. Coincidently, the cults of two Sámi spirit figures similarly associated with the winter hunt, namely *Juxakka* (bow woman) and *Leibolmai* (fisher-man/hunter) feature in the same regions, reinforcing the notion of intercultural fusion within their joint mythologies.[357] As an independent researcher into predominantly Indigenous cultures, I am of the opinion that the presence (through trade and marriage) of Sámi, Kven, and the Forest Finns throughout Fennoscandia,[358] confirms a long-standing trading and multi-cultural society.

Inevitable cultural exchanges that occurred between the Norse, Finns and Sámi peoples in language, clothing, beliefs, magics, folklore, and even aspects of religious practises, should be factored into Scandinavian studies in order to avoid the common error of a presumption of absolute distinctions.[359] Although saga literature attempts to conceal a multi-ethnic North, we find certain clues relating to the Sámi that reveal their complex relationship with the Norse peoples. During the Middle Ages, Fennoscandia was considerably more diverse culturally than we may imagine. Often, what we read is the version of history that best reflects the highly subjective mind and viewpoint of the (often clerical) author, rather than actual social reality.

---

356. Kusmenko, 2009. **357.** Ibid., The Sámi languages belong to the Finno-Ugric language family and are both structurally as well as etymologically different from the Nordic languages. See: Kusmenko, 2009, for a well-constructed and detailed exploration of the etymology of root words and how this relates to linguistic dispersal across the northern regions. **358.** 'Fennoscandia' is a geographical term used when referring to the Scandinavian and Kola peninsulas, mainland Finland, and Karelia. Across this region, there is great cultural and historical diversity amongst its peoples. **359.** Discerning ethnicities and the levels of conversion (ie: Christians and non-Christians), from the Landnámabók, Íslendingabók and Íslendingasögur, is almost impossible, as the description of the settlers extends only as far as the actual peoples, in most cases, their deeds only. See: Aalto and Lehtola, 2017.

Part Three:
THE SKIN TRADE, SLAVIC GODS AND THE NORTHERN CRUSADES

INTRODUCTION to Part Three
Heritage and the legacy:
Being Vikingr

SCANDINAVIAN PEOPLES circa 800-1050, whether Danish, Swedish or Norwegian in origin, are popularly referred to as 'Vikings.' However, this indiscriminate term and its application are incorrect. We should instead use the more accurate Old Norse word Vikingr that properly describes those engaged in the marauding activity of a person of the fjords, (vik), who navigated the small, narrow inlets advantageous to those pirates and raiders trading in slaves and plunder, often nefariously. For almost three hundred years they cut an unrivalled swathe across the northern hemisphere, east and west, acquiring a reputation for aggressive privateering that earned them the blood-chilling descriptor – Vikingr. Unfortunately, the title is misused when referring to other common settlers and farmers of this era.

Whether trader or warrior, their weapons are also inaccurately referred to as 'Viking' swords or 'Viking' axes for example, when in fact they should be regarded as Viking Age weapons. Swords especially were produced along the southern part of the Rhineland in the heart of the Frankish / Ottonian /German empires. Viking Age warriors coveted these prized objects and went to great lengths to acquire them, by theft or trade. The sight of their long-ships on the horizon inspired dread and awe, and if raiding, that fear was amplified by the monstrous dragon-like beasts that adorned their prows. The history of that beast and how it came to be identified synonymously with the Vikingr, is a fascinating and incredibly complex journey along The Silk Road. It is no coincidence that the Scandinavian longboat is practically identical in construction and appearance to the contemporaneous Chinese junks. Extensive early trade dramatically influenced many aspects of culture we automatically presume is native Scandinavian. Here, I aim to show this is to vastly underestimate the movement of ideas and of people.

Initial trading contacts between the Scandinavians and Britons ocurred sporadically before the early raids on Lindisfarne and Jarrow, reaching even into Wessex, as the incident that witnessed the killing (by Vikingr raiders) of a royal reeve named Beaduhard when expecting peaceful traders to those shores in 789. Desperation drove those with nothing to trade, to raid and plunder for captives who could be sold as slaves, and for goods with which to trade. Thus began the decades of fear as the Vikingr raided across Britain and Europe. Trading networks were slowly established, reaching into Russia, the Middle East and north Africa, and westwards into Iceland, Greenland and Vinland.

The free trade enjoyed throughout the 8th-Century Baltic regions between Scandinavians, Frisians, Slavs and Arabic merchants, with only a sporadic raid to mar relations, had deteriorated by the 9th century, as Vikingr raids gradually increased in frequency. We should remember that at this time, Norway, Denmark, and Sweden were not yet nation states. Social identity was kinship based and dependent only upon allegiances formed between clans. Crews gathered for Vikingr expeditions were not ethnically exclusive, as testified in the several non-ethnic terms used by others to describe Vikingr: rus -wicing, magi, gennti, pagani and pirati. Another term, danar (Danes) first appears in English as a political label used to describe peoples of various ethnicities under Scandinavian control. Everywhere across the world, in all eras, the mobilisation of trade spread cultural influences in myriad ways. Over the wide breadth of their expeditions, reaching from Newfoundland to Russia, down into the Mediterranean and Morocco, the Scandinavian peoples were no exception.

Norse peoples began settling the edges of the world, especially the Northern Isles of Orkney, Shetland, the Hebrides, the north western coasts of Scotland (Caithness and Sutherland) and Ireland, and many small islands around those extreme coastlines. These landscapes were not dissimilar to those of Norway, Denmark and Sweden. Generally speaking, the Danes generally settled further down the eastern regions of what would be Northumberland and Yorkshire. The Svear, (Swedes) travelled east, towards Russia. The vital histories, both east and west concerning this important period, covering the Viking Age and the immediate centuries after, were recorded only later, in the form of sagas and epic poetry.

He knows alone who has wandered wide,
and far has fared on the way,
what manner of mind a man doth own
who is wise of head and heart ~Hávamál[1]

Preserved as myth and legend, they reveal much about the beliefs and culture of the northern peoples, and more importantly, how these peoples perceived their world and how they interacted with each other based on those beliefs. Within these remarkable tales, we find glimpses of history that allow us to better understand a way of life that often appears alien to our own. Understanding the movement of people and goods is crucial to our correct apprehension of a world that is essentially worlds apart from our own, and indeed, worlds apart from what is generally presented or described in relation to the Viking Age. Norse culture was enriched substantially through their explorations, most notable in their fervent adoption of trade. As a typical feature of Viking Age finds, cultural eclecticism is evident in the Staffordshire and Galloway Hoards that include artefacts gathered from Scandinavia, Britain, Ireland, Continental Europe and Turkey. The acquisitive nature of the Scandinavian peoples is similarly reflected in the diverse and exotic grave-goods evident from the 9th to the 10th centuries. Because trade is not the first activity we typically associate with the Norse peoples, we have a tendency to view them only through acts of violence, carnage and turmoil. This makes their histories hard to navigate.

We are often directed towards an underlying premise that medieval warfare was initiated by religion. This is not strictly true. In order to properly understand the real motivation behind the brutal crusades and medieval warring factions, we need to explore instead, the reality of a world entirely motivated by profit and gain. Many misconceptions will be exposed here, the first of which involves the supposed conflicts of faith. I aim to show how trade was the real motivation behind wealth production, enslavements and wars in the developing worlds, both east and west of Scandinavia. It is also my intention to demonstrate how the beliefs of both Slavic and Germanic peoples found similar expression through various animistic cultural forms, whose virtues are remarkably cognate, how those forms informed their practises, and how they became distinguished almost universally in medieval literature, compounded as so-called 'heathen gods.' Our modern understanding is very much based on cumulative misrepresentations that need exposure and clarity in order to fully appreciate the real heathenisms of our northern ancestors.

---

1. Hávamál. The Words of Odin the High One from the Elder or Poetic Edda (Sæmund's Edda) translated by and edited by Olive Bray. https://sites.pitt.edu/~dash/havamal.html (Accessed 16th May 2022)

INTRODUCTION TO PART THREE 235

To uphold those claims, I must first focus on certain people and their movements in an earlier history of the Vikingr that returns us to the Bronze Age cultures that founded the Germanic and Scandinavian peoples from whom the Vikingr sprang. It is likely, that Proto Sámi, Fenno, and Kven people populated Scandinavia before the Proto-Germanic peoples arrived there (as speakers of a Proto-Indo-European language group) who migrated into Scandinavia, circa 3000 BCE, settling in southern Sweden, and along the coast of southern Norway.[2] Other significant contributors to the multi-cultural northern arena were the people known as the Tsjuder[3] (Chudes) whose ancestors were amongst the first people to resettle the northern regions of Scandinavia in the wake of the last Ice Age event. The Chudes had walked from the Baltic regions, over Karelia and Finnmark northwards into the lands of the Proto-Lapps (Northern Norway) whence in addition to being hunters, they became accomplished fishermen and seafarers. Adaptation was key to survival. Known in Swedish and Norse as Tsjuderfolket (an historically term applied in the early Russian annals to several Finnic peoples throughout what is now Estonia, Karelia and Northwestern Russia), the Chudes encompass other Baltic Finns who are also called volok, a term that may refer to the Karelians. Driven by the needs of an expansive fur trade, their presence possibly affected the movements of other peoples around them, not to mention the dynamics between them.

According to Icelandic chronicles, Kvens were raiding in northern Norway as late as 1271. Saxo Grammaticus writes in his *Gesta Danorum*, of the early 9th century conflict between the Finnish king Matul and Danish king Ragnarr Loðbrók.[4] Moreover, according to the 14th century *Norna-Gests þáttr saga*, a group of raiders referred to as Kvens (who were probably Finns) had been active in Sweden since the mid-8th century, confirming snippets of information found elsewhere in similar chronicles relating to the Finnish conflict with Sweden and Norway.[5]

Old East Slavic chronicles claim the Chudes were amongst those who founded the early Rus' state, along with the Slavs and the

---

2. Thousands of years later during the Iron Age, various Germanic tribes migrated from Scandinavia to East-Central Europe. This included the Rugii, Goths, Gepids, Vandals, Burgundians and others. **3.** Chud or Chude: Tsjuderfolket in Swedish and Norse. Folk etymology derives the word from Old East Slavic language (*chuzhoi*, 'foreign;' or *chudnoi* –'odd;' or *chud* -'weird'), or alternatively from *chudnyi*, meaning wonderful, miraculous, excellent, attractive. **4.** http://mcllibrary.org/DanishHistory/book9.html (Retrieved, 25th June 2024). **5.** The oldest historical traces of conflicts in Finland are runestones GS 13 and U 582 which are dated to the early 11th century.

(Swedish) Varangians. Depicted as exalted and beautiful in Russian folk legends, the Chudes were described as 'white-eyed,' a term that refers to pale (probably blue or green) eye colours.[6] Appraisals aside, the Chudes traditionally feature as generic villains in some Sámi legends, possibly because the Chudes behaved in much the same way as the later Vikingr, in other words, as violent invaders and pirates.[7] Evidently, not all contact was amicable. It's all about perspective, and who records the histories. Sorrowful Russian folk songs reminisce about the destruction of the Chudes when the Slavs occupied their territories. When a Chude township was attacked, it was claimed that Chude women drowned themselves in the river along with their jewels and children, rather than be raped and raided. This unrelenting sovereignty of selfhood would ultimately generate friction and further tragic consequences for these and other peoples who fell victim to the paradigms of their eras.

Since the beginning of the Viking Age, Scandinavian traders travelled westwards, eastwards and southwards, reaching Newfoundland, the Volga River, and Constantinople respectively, but not just to go raiding, looting and pillaging. Many were focussed upon the discovery and establishment of trade routes as needful sources of income for themselves and their descendants who would eventually populate Ireland, Scotland, England, France and the New World.[8] During this period of intense exploration, Iceland was visited and settled by Irish monks (the 'Papas')[9] in the 8th and 9th centuries CE, and then later still by various peoples of Fennoscandia. After settling Iceland in the 9th century, Norwegian Vikingr began exploring further afield. A century later, under the leadership of 'Eiríkur Rauði'[10] they reached the coast of North America, where Eiríkur founded a small Norse colony on Greenland (Kalaallit Nunaat) in 982-6. Reaching Svalbard and Novaya Zemlya, Eiríkr then established trade routes to the White Sea, competing with Russian merchant seafarers who had colonized the White Sea coasts in the 9th century. By the 11th century, the Russians had reached the mouth of the Ob River.[11]

---

6. Comments very similar to those of the Alani peoples. **7.** The Chudes suffered in turn when the Slavs were occupied their territories. **8.** Norwegian archaeologists have discovered a 9th century fishing and agricultural centre in the north of Norway amidst the dramatic mountains surrounding the power centres on the islands of Lofoten, an archipelago and a traditional district in the county of Nordland, in northern Norway. **9.** Norwegians referred to the Papas, or Irish priests, found also in Orkney and Shetland, and in the north of Scotland. **10.** Erik the Red, also known as Erik Thorvaldsson. **11.** Ingold, 2024.

THULE

Reports from the early explorations to the northern regions of the arctic and sub-arctic, are largely vague, filled with uncertain locations and ambiguous commentary. Sometime in antiquity, 'Thule' was a title assigned to a supposed archipelago far to the north of the Scandinavian seas.[12] As a seasoned navigator, geographer and astronomer, Pytheas, a Greek scientist and merchant of the 4th century BCE, ventured into many of the regions along the north Atlantic coast including the northern British Isles. Pytheas gave us a strange account of his own travels northwards in search of the source of amber as he voyaged from the Mediterranean, around Britain, to a place he called Thule, a remote place generally identified as either England, Iceland, the Shetlands, or Norway.[13] His detailed descriptions of the phenomena of those distant lands (Hyperborea) shrouded in mist, amaze us still, while leaving us equally perplexed. We can but imagine how he must have marvelled at the vista of the Midnight Sun and the Polar nights. Thule[14] is collectively described by others as a barren, unwelcome, inhospitable island, of extreme weather and light conditions that cannot support or sustain cereals, grains or livestock; its natives lived on fish, roots and millet. Information relating to Thule is particularly problematic and early medieval maps are often inaccurate and unhelpful; so the consensus is that Pytheas was referring to Iceland. In later poetry, the obscure, mythic landscape of Iceland became 'Ultima Thule,' meaning the 'farthest Thule,' signifying a distant northern place. As the frontiers of man's exploration gradually expanded, the legendary Ultima Thule acquired a more northerly location, shifting with the Viking Age explorers from the Faroe Islands to Iceland, and, when Iceland was colonized in the 9th century CE, Greenland became (Ultima) Thule in folklore.

---

12. Terence Edward Armstrong. "Study and exploration." https://www.britannica.com/place/Arctic/Political-and-environmental-issues (Retrieved 12th August 2024)
13. Richard F. Burton. Ultima Thule vol. 1(2), or, A Summer in Iceland. [1875]. [EBook #59584]. 2019 https://www.gutenberg.org/files/59584/59584-h/59584-h.htm (Retrieved, 12th August 2024). **14.** There are a number of derivations assigned to Thule; among these are the Gothic Tiel, or Tiule, meaning a goal or limit. Latin: Thule also spelled as Thyle, which represents the most northerly habitable location cited in Roman and Greek literature and cartography

238 PIRATES, MERCHANTS, DEVILS & DARK DEEDS

In these early centuries of the common era, the ability to hunt (whale and walrus) in the open seas of the arctic regions around the Bering Strait, led to the development of the Northern Maritime 'Thule Culture.' Characterised by harpoons and an open skin boat, 'Thule Culture' had already spread along the northern coast of Alaska and Canada to Greenland by 900. Thule Culture was concerned with trade. However, literature relating to the whaling Thule Culture of Greenland and the Polar Arctic, should not be confused with the mythic Thule landscapes of Norse and other Northern peoples.

A Norse explorer from Iceland named Leiv Eiriksson (c.970to c.1020), established a settlement at Vinland (coastal North America)

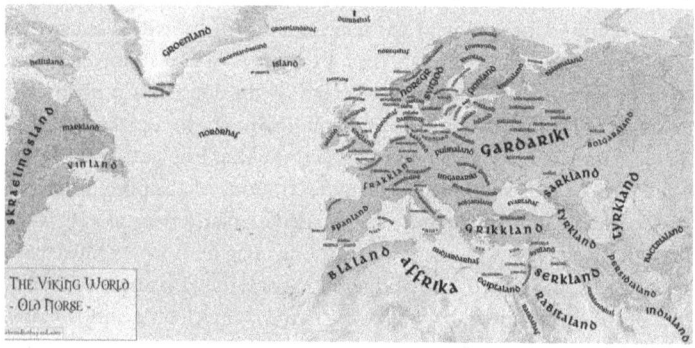

1. Map of Viking Age Exploration

around 1000, which may be the site discovered in Newfoundland known as L'Anse aux Meadows. As the son of Eiríkur the Rauði,[15] the founder of the first Norse settlement in Greenland, Leiv Eiriksson was among the first Europeans to land on continental North America (excluding Greenland). Arriving a few hundred years later in the Americas, Christopher Columbus claimed (in a letter) to have visited Iceland in 1477, when he would have become aware of the previous Norse voyage to those lands. The trade routes the settlers collectively established in Vinland, Greenland and across the North Americas, were known and recorded across Europe, especially by several clerical writers. One in particular was the medieval chronicler Adam of Bremen (c.1075) who based his account upon Danish reports.[16] The knowledge of Vinland could also have reached Christopher

---

15. Leiv's mother, Thjóðhildr (Þjóðhildur), was also of Norwegian origin.   16. Adam mentions the vines of Vinland (Winland) and the Danish travellers in Chapter 39 of Book IV of Adam von Bremen's *Gesta Danorum*. In, *Hamburgische Kirchengeschichte*, 275-276 [Hamburg's Church History] (in Latin and German). Edited by Bernard Schmeidler. (Hahnsche, 1917).

THULE

Columbus this way, giving him the impetus for his own voyages. The first apparent contact between the Norse and the indigenous people (referred to as skrælingjar by later Norse people) was made by Leiv's brother Thorvald, and resulted in detrimental conflict. Following the capture and execution of several natives in this skirmish, the Norse were attacked near to their beached ships, which they ably defended. This set-back to amicable relationships was endured and overcome; trade was re-established, and indeed, flourished. Oceanic traders shipped furs, amber, iron, walrus tusks, beeswax, coins, silver and slaves from the New World.

According to the Icelandic sagas, Leiv Eiriksson's eventual conversion to Roman Catholicism was at the behest of the Christian King of Norway, Olaf Tryggvason, who also endorsed Leiv's return to Greenland on a proselytising mission to the indigenous peoples there. As one of the first converts, Eiriksson's mother Thjóðhild, established a church in Greenland which was named after her. Leiv's father, Eirikur, remained hostile to the suggestion that he should abandon his pagan beliefs. Nothing is known of Eirikur after 1025, though one source claims the chieftaincy of Eiríksfjorðr supposedly passed to his son Thorvald. However, Eirikur's death is not mentioned in the sagas, so it is presumed he died in Greenland within a couple of years of Leiv's death, leaving us with no further information about this remarkable family. Unable to endure the harsh conditions in Vinland, almost all the settlers left. Those who remained maintained the successful trading route for furs and timber for several more centuries until Vinland was eventually colonised.[17] Despite having lived alongside the 'Thule Culture' people for almost three hundred years, there is little evidence of interaction between the Norse people of 'Thule' and the 'Thule Culture' peoples until the 13th century. Transport of trade goods or supplies during the harsh winters was by sled, pulled by dogs and/ or people, again reflecting the images of rock art elsewhere in the arctic regions. A period of increasing cold around 1400, caused the peoples of northern Canada to abandon their permanent winter settlements, forcing them to adapt to a nomadic seasonal pattern.[18] Meanwhile, the Vikingr had turned their eyes eastwards to the legendary riches of the Orient.

---

17. Patricia Sutherland. "The Norse and Native Norse Americans." In, Vikings: The North Atlantic Saga, 238-247. Edited by William W Fitzhugh and Elisabeth I Ward. (The Smithsonian Institution. 2000). **18.** Farming became untenable even in Greenland, and the Norse colony was also abandoned in the early 15th century. European fishermen built seasonal base camps on Greenland's southern coasts during the 16th and 17th centuries, and in 1721, a permanent Danish-Norwegian colony was founded on Greenland to convert them and to trade with all settlers. Ingold, 2024.

THE SKIN TRADE

In 10 CE, the Greek geographer Strabo lists human slaves as the commodities plundered by Rome alongside, metals, grain and cattle. After the Romans retreated from Britain and Europe, the Celts, Angles, Saxons and Jutes continued the trade in slaves to Europe largely unabated or altered until the arrival of the Vikingr, who ventured further afield into Africa and the Middle East. Only very rarely were black slaves from Africa brought to Europe, it did not become commonplace until after Columbus ' voyage to the New World. Slave traffic between the two continents of Europe and Africa did not begin in earnest until after the 8th century, at which point, and somewhat surprisingly, it was white Europeans who were taken into Africa and other Arab controlled regions. By the time European explorers and colonisers arrived in Africa in later centuries, slavery had already become a commonly accepted and widely practised way of life, and was not seen as anything startling or new, nor discriminatory. Even in more recent times when Britain and other European nations outlawed this abhorrent practice, many Africans continued keeping and trading in slaves. Grim as this is, this brutal fact reveals the darker side of human nature.

During the 7th-century, the newly created religion of Islam continued Arabia's lucrative trade in human trafficking albeit under the new and questionably moral directive to exclude one's fellow compatriots. Prior to Islam, most 'nations' would not enslave or trade their own people. Under Islam, faith overrode 'nationality', meaning that no Muslim could enslave another Muslim of the same 'faith,' irrespective of 'nationality'. Under Islamic law, slaves must be born of slaves, acquired in war, or traded. Trading became the most lucrative option. The Vikingr became their main suppliers, and many of their raids were undertaken to capture slaves or people that could be traded as slaves, which is why, despite current media hyperbolic misrepresentation, killing was kept to a minimum; only those who presented immediate threat were slaughtered. Anyone learned, such as monks and priests, commanded a high-value and were not often killed.[19] As a means of trade and wealth, slavery showed no signs of diminishment in the Vendel and Viking Ages.

THE SKIN TRADE 241

The Byzantines and Muslim Caliphates rose to power on the skin trade. For over four centuries, between the ninth to the twelfth centuries, the trail of human suffering was borne along the rivers of the Danube, Dniester, and Volga to the Mediterranean and Eastern markets. Concepts of race raised today against such vile practises are built on an entirely fabricated premise. Conversely, faith, nationality, culture and ethnicity are valid, legitimate descriptors relating to a person's identity, and are not mutually exclusive. People are merely commodities to be bought and exchanged, no more, no less.

Slave markets were found across the whole of the Silk Road, from Dublin on the shores of the Atlantic to Shandong on the Pacific. And while much of the trade was by private merchants, governments also profited by imposing taxes both on the movement and on the sale of slaves. As with many other 'things' traded along the Silk Road, there was both local and regional trade, as well as trade over longer distances. Dublin, for example, probably the largest slave market in western Europe, was convenient for the Irish, Vikings, and others who had seized captives in raids and battles.[20]

Traders from the north were no exception to this detestable practise. During the 8th century, the Vikingr began their raiding campaigns around the British Isles and western Frankia. Pushing south, they reached the southern coast of Spain, and possibly even northern Morocco. Raids continued across those regions until the end of the Viking Age. Archaeologists have discovered the beached anchors of longboats in Galicia near what appears to be a longphort[21] or Vikingr encampment. Built there during the early Viking Age for over wintering, these mounds are similar to motte-and-bailey constructions but are not generally found outside Ireland.

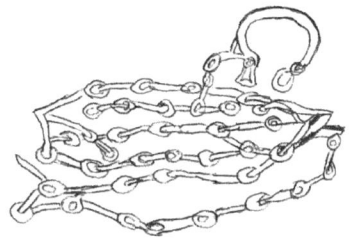

2. Viking Age slave collar and chains

As various people were lost along the way in these great expeditions, others were sometimes gathered from the regions where pauses in the

---

19. Webb, 2020. **20.** Susan Whitfield. *Silk, Slaves, and Stupas: Material Culture of the Silk Road.* (University of California Press, 2018). **21.** The term 'longphort' literally translates to 'ship camp.' See: Gareth Williams. *Viking Camps Case Studies and Comparisons.* Edited by Charlotte Hedenstierna-Jonson and Irene García Losquiño. (Routledge, Taylor & Francis Group, 2013). DOI: 10.4324/9781003347682-3

journey were required for restocking of supplies, retrieving ransoms or tribute, or to repair damage to their ships sustained during storms.[22] It was not uncommon for Scandinavian traders to gather and exchange slaves from all regions they travelled to, including Asia, Africa, the Mediterranean, and the British Isles. Vikingr, like the Romans before them, drafted in slaves from all regions with whom they traded, or conquered (sometimes these were one and the same). For example, countless Irish slaves, especially women, were traded as wives to populate Iceland. Of those slaves who made their way to serve in households across Norway and Sweden, some rose to become concubines or free folk, acquiring land, property and slaves of their own, though this was a very rare occurrence.

Pushing ever eastwards in their trading expeditions in search of great wealth, slave traffic typically travelled from back and forth, from north to south, through other Viking Age trading centres across Norway and Europe, ever eastwards. Arabic coins, pieces of silver used for payment, along with Asian jewellery and many objects imported from the British Isles and Finland, have been found at prime sites. A 6th-century woman's grave at Sleaford (Lincolnshire) had within it, an amber necklace from the Baltic. Six miles east of Sleaford, right on the edge of the Fens, there is a spur of high ground called Garwick, an Old English name, first recorded in the 13th century, which probably means 'trading-place of triangular shape.' It was active up until the 8th century, when it fell into decline. While the movement of goods was considerable, nothing matched the skin-trade for profit. From a business perspective, human beings were simply a more lucrative option.

Following former Roman Imperial trade routes that had extended over much of the Mediterranean and the regions of North Africa, stretching from Egypt to Morocco, Byzantine gold and bronze objects were traded during the early medieval era. North Africa was rapidly colonised and established as Muslim territory during the 7th century, retaining to this day Arabic cultural influences. Libyans, for example, have a mixed Berber (and Arab) heritage. Some south African regions – namely Zimbabwe — traded gold and ivory with Arabia and with the North African regions. The Barbary (North African) pirates were active slavers from the 8th century, peaking in the 16th and 17th centuries. Operating mainly around their own coast, they occasionally had slaving forays around Ireland and Britain.[23] From their trading base

---

22. Research of skeletal remains at various sited associated with Viking Age expeditions reveals sporadic incidents of graves containing non-Scandinavian peoples.

on Lundy island, the North African Barbary Pirates raided countless fishing villages & towns along the coastal fringes of England, reaching as far north west as the Faroe Islands, and stretching as far south east as the Mediterranean. It is estimated they captured more than a million English men, women and children (sometimes entire villages) into slavery across the Islamic world. Viking Age merchants traded many slaves to Russia brokered through the Middle Eastern Abbasid Caliphate (750-1258). The vast majority of peoples transported in the much later transatlantic slave trade, were captured from Central and West Africa by West African slave traders, who then sold them to European slave traders, many of whom were dispersed throughout the Ottoman Empire (14th -20th centuries).[24]

Clarity is essential when using the term African. Historical chroniclers from Bede to Helmold considered the former Romanised (and briefly Christian) regions of Libya, Tunisia, Morocco, Algiers, Egypt, and Carthage, as African, yet even today, very few, if any of these would identify as such. The continent may be Africa, but the people of the north African Mediterranean coastlines, typically do not identify as African, especially historically. As a term, African generally refers to the many countries that make up the Sub-Saharan regions of the continent of Africa. Understanding this is key to the issues of trade across and through these regions. Control of those trading routes was (and remains) of prime importance.

One of the earliest recorded instances of exchange between Europe and the New World, occurred in 1420, and refers to the capture of Inuit who were taken to Scandinavia as slaves.[25] This was the beginning of the transatlantic slave trade, when trade turned its acquisitive eye to the New World; it is not however *the* slave trade. What is startling is that it ocurred in a time when we should have been evolving away from such practises involving the misery and subjugation of human beings by other human beings, not embracing them. It is estimated that between the 15th and 18th centuries, around 8 to 12 million black slaves became a transatlantic commodity. While these figures describe an unimaginable horror, they pale by comparison to the industrial level figures we can now attribute to the Roman Empire alone. Empires were built on the back of slavery. It was a tragic but common policy

---

23. See: https://www.historic-uk.com/.../Barbary-Pirates-English.../ (Accessed 2nd July 2021). **24.** Henry Louis Gates, Jr. "Opinion – How to End the Slavery Blame-Game." (The New York Times, 2010). **25.** Jace Weaver "The Red Atlantic." *American Indian Quarterly*, 35, no. 3. (2011): 418-463, 477

in the ancient world, and it continued unabated through to the Bronze and Iron Ages. Africans enslaved and exported to the colonies endured a life expectancy double that of slaves taken by Rome to service its decadent hedonisms. Conservative estimates place the Roman slave trade in Europe at least 10 times that of the later transatlantic slave trade and that an equivalent figure of 12 million trafficked souls was reachable in a mere 25 years.[26] Slavery is not new, it has existed in many forms over the course of human existence and its abhorrent practice continues still.

At the time of the Norman Conquest, it is suggested that at least 10% of England's population were recorded as slaves. Slavery was not evenly observed throughout Britain, while some regions endorsed it liberally, others exhibited a very different approach to the social hierarchy of peoples jostling for survival in a brutal, unforgiving environment. Recorded by Norman, not English officials, the Domesday census reveals an extraordinary rejection of slavery by Danes who'd settled across Yorkshire and Lincolnshire, where Danelaw (Old English Dena lagu) was established. As Danish influence lessened further southwards, the pattern of slavery is witnessed, with a notable increase too in its percentage ratio to the general populace, rising from 1% in Nottingham and Derbyshire, to 24% in Gloucestershire, and almost as many in Cornwall. "These conditions of tenure were introduced by the Danes, and became so firmly established that the names given to such freeholders as "statesmen" in Cumberland, "freemen" and "yeomen" in Yorkshire, Westmorland and North Lancashire still exist at the present day."[27] In England, the practise of slavery was generally insular – one tribe to another.

Freedom from slavery, could be acquired in several ways, and this process of manumission was often celebrated with solemnized ceremony, in the presence of witnesses, and with supportive legal documentation. One such recorded case is worthy of a little deviation here, made rather more interesting by the Christian curse used in its declaration: "Here it is made known in this gospel that Godwig the Buck has bought Leofgifu the dairymaid at North Stoke and her offspring from Abbot Ælfsige for half a pound, to eternal freedom, in the witness of all the community at Bath. Christ blind him who

---

26. Simon Webb. *The Forgotten Slave Trade*. (Pen and Sword Books Ltd. 2020) **27.** S. W. Partington. *The Danes in Lancashire and Yorkshire* (Sherratt & Hughes, 1909) https://www.gutenberg.org/files/43910/43910-h/43910-h.htm (Accessed 8th March 2025)

ever perverts this."[28] Even more intriguing is that the location chosen for this unusual ceremony of liberation was often a church, but more frequently, an outdoor site – a crossroads, symbolic perhaps of the new options opening up for the person concerned. More probably, this location was chosen because of its connotation with the curious customs relating to pacts and covenants with the world of spirits who inhabit such sites.

Obsessed by fairness and a duty to impose a just law system, King Ælfred the Great was not opposed to slavery, only its abuses. When drawing up his written treaty with his Scandinavian adversaries, he composed a clause prohibiting Danes from arming and freeing former slaves. Danish settlers in the north-eastern and central regions of England clearly left an indelible imprint upon local custom, place names and local DNA. One major sphere of influence was in the treatment of land and its approach to cultivation that was very different to that of the former Saxon laws regarding land ownership. "In the areas of intensive Danish settlement, there were an unusually high number of sokemen, a class of personally free peasants attached to a lord rather than to the land."[29] This maintained traditional relationships between a lord and his people, built on suzerainty rather than sovereignty. In fact, a complex range of laws existed in the northern world surrounding the responsibilities, duties and obligations of slave ownership, and the subject is a broad study worthy of time.

Much seems dependent upon the variant application of categorisation and terminology, which, due to a lack of coherent standardisation means that the percentages relating to slavery could be as high as 30% in some areas. Distinctions were virtually non-existent, slave men, women and children were known as a theow or thrall in Old English, and a caeth in the Brythonic tongue, although the Norman terms as found in the Domesday Book that refer to servi and ancillae appear to indicate male and female slaves, respectively.[30] In Iron Age Britain, descendants of the native population under the yoke first of Roman, then waves of Germanic peoples, were referred to in native terms for Briton, and used interchangeably for "slave." Language contributes significantly to the confusion of the lack of clear

---

28. Dorothy Whitelock. *The Beginnings of English Society* (Penguin Books, 1963) **29.** The Editors of Encyclopaedia Britannica. "Danelaw." *Encyclopedia Britannica*, January 30, 2025. https://www.britannica.com/place/Danelaw. **30.** "Anglo-Norman Studies XI Proceedings of the Battle Conference 1988" (Boydell & Brewer, 1989): 191 – 220. DOI: https://doi.org/10.1017/9781846151934.011 (Accessed 8th March 2025)

definitions of those in 'servitude,' an oppressive and morally repugnant state not always acquired in the same way.

Generally, it applies to those who worked the land, labourers who toiled in the service of food production for those who'd bought or stole the land from others, and those workers along with it. Anglo-Saxon and Vikingr economy thrived on the maintenance of slaves, tasking men and women to gruelling labour-intensive work. Mercantile trade was so prolific that the renowned 10th-Century Muslim chronicler and scholar, Ibn Rustah referred to England as an island of seven kingdoms, and to London as a mighty port, a hub of exchange with all the world. Wool and slaves traded for Arab gold and silver contributed to a significant rise in the Saxon charters of land purchased (by coin) from the 8th century onwards.

Weakened by a spate of invasions, warfare and a rapid succession of foreign rulers, Norman rule crippled England's economy, and the famines caused by William's scorched earth policies are well documented. This led to the voluntary subjugation of many families into slavery in order to survive the unprecedented levels of poverty and starvation. Penal slavery was even a tactic of social justice, a means of dealing with the burdens on the public purse generated by criminal activities. Punishments placed people as indentured servants for varying terms. Men were put to hard work in the fields, or as soldiers for the king's wars in Europe. Women were assigned to the church parishes, fulfilling a number of socially demeaning and no less gruelling duties.

William the Conqueror's ban on the sale and export of Englishmen to France and overseas, though needful, did little in reality to stem the flow of bodies from Britain to Europe and beyond. Medieval society had inherited this literal stock in trade on an industrial level from the ancient world. Everything from a piece of wood to a person was an exploitable commodity and all nations in all eras condoned it as the means of acquiring wealth and status. It was an entirely non-partisan enterprise. While it is true that the majority of people were captured in war and sold as slaves, traded for money and goods, not everyone fell into such gravid misfortune this way. Many slaves were captured in battle, though as society became wealthier, many more were traded, bought and sold at the main trading centres and slave markets across Europe. These were mainly situated in Dublin, Bristol, York, Birka, Wolin, Verdun, Lisbon and Prague. Not all medieval kings condoned slavery, King Cnut was atypically opposed to it.

Conversely, an early 12th-century Pomeranian Count raided and captured the entire population of a Norwegian town as slaves.

As fewer battles ensued, many more poor folk were forced into slavery as punishment for minor crimes, or simply because they were destitute. Throughout England and across Europe, heathens, infidels and apostate Christians were especially prone to such brutalities. A 12th-Century doge of Venice, Enrico Dandolo, chronicled such events, commenting how "They come pale as the moon, their faces shadowed by fear, their wrists bloodied by iron."[31] Transported far afield, east and west, they became the sex workers and labourers of the rapidly expanding mercantile world. At least three 15th-Century popes banned the sale of Christians to Muslims, but this did little to resolve the matter, as Jewish traders were often used as brokers. For many centuries, Irish people were traded as far as the Russias and the Middle East. (If destined for Muslim owners, all men were first castrated, in fact, men already castrated for rape crimes were ideally placed for this service). We know that an apparent religious restriction imposed upon Christians and Muslims, essentially banned the enslavement of people sharing their stated faiths, however, the specificities of this opposed Catholics enslaving other Catholics, though other Christians were under no such stricture. Similarly, Shia Muslims, could enslave Sunni Muslims (and vice versa), but not their own, so egregious solutions remained permissible. Heathens and pagans were entirely without rights, and were consequently freely plundered by everyone.

Christianity long preached the moral high ground on slavery, but did little to prevent it, and often endorsed it privately, albeit in other forms. Once Catholicisim successfully supplanted alternative forms of Christianity, it had little recourse but to abandon its previous endorsement of non-Catholic Christian slavery, so alternative formats that established the feudal practices of serfdom and villeinage, did nothing to resolve the plight of the poor wretches, who through no fault of their own, were born at the wrong end of the social hierarchy and therefore chattels at the whim of the highest bidder. These new developments tied people to land, making ownership a tricky semantic legality. Capitalism will always find a way. Change the name, the practice continues.

Although England's involvement in the slave trade became illegal in 1807, slavery within the colonies laboured on until 1838, when it finally became illegal, or at least it appeared to. Nevertheless, in England,

---

31. Dandalo's promotion of the Fourth Crusade led to the overthrow of the Greek Byzantine Empire. See: A. Lombardo. "Enrico Dandolo." In, *Encyclopedia Britannica*, January 1, 2025. https://www.britannica.com/biography/Enrico-Dandolo. (Accessed 19th January 2025).

until 1844, a man could still sell his wife at the local market and draft his children into indentured service. From the biblical Joshua, to St Patrick, through to Cervantes in the 16th century, millennia of pirates have captured all manner of souls to service this foul industry centred on human trafficking. Throughout Victorian Britain, and even as late as the 1950s, the Church was responsible for rounding up children from workhouses and orphanages across the UK, who were then shipped out to various colonies across the Empire and sold to farmers as cheap slave labour.

The inhumane practise of slavery had never been an enterprise undertaken on the basis of skin-colour, rather, it was concerned with power and the subjugation of anyone who could be exploited. This was and remains an issue of social status, or class as some refer to it. Ill-conceived notions of racism developed across the western world as a social trend/perspective under the socio-political issues inherent within the process of colonialism, which led to a correlation between skin colour and the (false) evaluation of culture. Remember, all non-Christians were the only people not regulated or protected by the ban on the enslavement of those sharing the same faith. This meant the choice to take (non-Christian) Africans was based not in notions of racism, but in pragmatism; business practises thrive on it. Human beings are born with an inherent trust of outsiders, of anyone not of our tribe, or is alien to it. As part of our deep animal nature, we are naturally cautious, fearful even of anything dissimilar to ourselves, it is both regressive and negative. Yet survival depends upon that basic primal instinct. It is despicable that a natural fear has been exploited by governments who benefit from their divisive policies, and who have, through gross manipulation, turned that fear into an unnatural and unwarranted racism.

Hindu Caste systems and centuries of embedded 'racism' throughout Asia against the peoples of the African continent had compounded the impact of Darwin's (flawed) theory of evolution. This ultimately generated the abhorrent notion that darker skin is an indicator of presumed primitivisms and therefore deemed to be inferior. In the ancient world, everyone had slaves, everyone traded slaves. Slavery was and continues to be a worldwide economic and societal system that has endured for thousands of years, regardless of culture and religion. No matter the colour of one's skin, nor one's religious beliefs, slavery is a business enterprise controlled by wealth and power. Those with both, exploited those without either. Poor people everywhere remain exploitable commodities. Throughout our long history as people on this planet, black people enslaved white people, who enslaved brown people, who enslaved everyone in a vicious and unending circle in the jostle for wealth and power. Continued sexual activity with those enslaved over countless millennia renders the very notion of 'racial' purity an oxymoronic nonsense; it exists only in the warped ideology of disturbed cults seeking an implausible (and frankly) detestable social hierarchy. Race is a contrived discrimination, and the belief in any people's genetic purity an impossible absurdity. Multi-ethnic/cultural societies are nothing new.

Too few people are aware just how multicultural the Vikingr were. Their trading and raiding had brought them into contact with a kaleidoscope of peoples whose cultures impacted quite intensely upon theirs. Following the old Silk Roads via the Danube and its tributaries into Russia, through Byzantium and into the Mediterranean, their sphere of influence was considerable as they reseeded the beliefs and customs of northern Europeans along the way.

Almost all of what we know about the Viking raids comes from accounts written mainly by Arab historians, who referred to the Scandinavians as majus, a term meaning heathen, or worshipper of many gods. For example, the 11th-Century Cordoban historian Ibn Hayyan provides additional accounts of 10th-Century Vikingr raiders in Galicia, al-Andalus and Lisbon. According to Ibn Hawqal, an Arab geographer, the 10th-Century Viking slave trade moved south from Britain and Ireland, extending across the Mediterranean from Spain, across North Africa to Egypt, Byzantium, Baghdad and Russia. It was mainly the Eastern Scandinavians who traded in the western Baltic, penetrating Russia down into the Volga, Danube and Black Sea region, where they established further trade in amber and furs. Terrorizing the Baltic regions, the Vikingr reached Constantinople (Istanbul) along The Silk Road trade routes where they encountered other Slavic, Byzantine, Greek and Arabic traders.

The extent to which Arabic coins (dating 745-900) are discovered in Northern Russia, suggests that the basis of commerce and trade was largely biased towards coin.[32] "Türkic male slaves for the caliphate's army were taken from the borders of the Steppe in Central Asia to Nishapur, which sent thousands of slaves westward to Baghdad each

---

32. At Bolgar (capital city of the Volga Bulgarians), the Rus' traded slaves, sable, ermine, marten, squirrel, and other furs. See: Frederick S. Starr. *Lost Enlightenment: Central Asia's Golden Age from the Arab Conquest to Tamerlane.* (Princeton University Press, 2013).

year."[33] The oldest Arabian Middle Age coin located in Europe was found near the Lake Ladoga settlement in Russia. Other relics of Arabic commerce in Northern Russia in the provinces at the headwaters of the Volga, have emerged with notable discoveries made in districts where Scandinavian colonists were most active,[34] confirming a longstanding familiarity between them.[35] Byzantine coins and other objects of oriental origin are found in Scandinavia only after the 9th century, while specifically Russian objects do not appear in Scandinavia before the 11th century. Survivals of rúnic inscriptions mentioning Russia are comparatively rare, but do confirm Norse presence in Holmgarðr (Novgorod).

Through their interactions with such peoples, particularly those of Slavic origin, some Vikingr acquired other titles and reputations as the Rus' or as Varangians that distinguish them from their western associates. Initial outposts established by the first traders gradually expanded in the 9th century, developing into the cities of Kiev (Kyiv) and Novgorod. Some sources alternatively suggest the Varangian Rus' conquered and expanded earlier (Slavic) settlements in those regions. Due to the political implications generated by an acknowledgement of that version of events, it is not a popular proposition.[36] Who those people might be, and from whence they originated is another fundamental factor in the cultural disposition and ethnicity of the Central Eurasian peoples of the Bronze Age who so enriched the Scandinavian and Germanic peoples. Early Rus'[37] rulers sought political power and alliances through marriage, wives were chosen from amongst other Steppe peoples, forging new kinship ties.

---

33. Whitfield, 2018. **34.** Archaeological evidence of Scandinavian contact with Arabic traders via the Russian watercourses is corroborated by the Arab and Persian geographers, who refer to the Scandinavian centres of colonization in northern Russia. Arabic interest in geographical science developed rapidly between the 9th to the 11th-centuries **35.** Marek Jankowiak. "Dirhams for Slaves: Investigating the Slavic Slave Trade in the Tenth Century." Paper presented at the Medieval Seminar, All Souls, Oxford, February. 2012. https://www.academia.edu/1764468/Dirhams_for_slaves._Investigating_the_Slavic_slave_trade_in_the_tenth_century. (Accessed 26th January 2025). **36.** The 12th century *Kievan Primary Chronicle*, states that a group of Varangians known as the Rus,' and their leader Rurik, settled in Novgorod in 862 Kiev (Kiyv), which was later conquered by Oleg (a relative of Rurik, possibly a brother) in 882. Absorbed into Slavic culture, they were significant in the development of key states into Mother Russia. **37.** Pavel Dolukhanov. *The Early Slavs: Eastern Europe from the Initial Settlement to the Kievan Rus.'* (Routledge, 2014):182

KIEVAN RUS' - EARLY TRADE IN THE EAST

Seventh century Scandinavian merchant graves discovered at Grobin and Elblag have yielded artefacts that indicate signs of settlement in the Baltic regions far earlier than previously imagined. Fur trading was the main resource at this time, yet less than a century later, they'd added amber and slaves – all for Arabic silver (dirhems). Over the course of the 9th century, Scandinavian traders began settling in earnest in key locations, ripe for expansion. Koenungagard (Kiev) quickly followed by Holmgarðr (Novgorod), became centralised and militarised fortified towns, forming early states, if somewhat provincial. The Scandinavians were, after all a minority amidst the Slavic peoples already living there.

Predating the foundation of Moscow[38] as the capital of Russia by several centuries, the establishment of Novgorod and Kiev (Kyiv) played a significant role in the founding of the future Russian state. According to legends recorded in the East Slavic Chronicles, Kiev (Kyiv) was established first, sometime in the 7th century, namely by the Slavic prince Kyi, supported by three other siblings,

(Shchek, Khoryv, and a sister, named Lybid). Kyiv was the cultural and economic centre of the Slavic regions, reaching its influential peak in the 11th century. Bearing close ties to the Norse Varangians of the 9th century, Kyiv's major ruling dynasty, the Rurikids, controlled Belarus, Finland, Russia, and the Ukraine. Some heroic names involved in the rulership of Kyiv include Sviatoslav the Brave, Yaroslav the Wise, Mstislav the Great, Yuri Long Arm, St Olga, and Vladmir the Great, of whom we shall learn, initiated the mass conversion of the East Slavs to Eastern Orthodox Christianity in a controversial event known as the Baptism of Kyiv in the late 10th century, changing forever, the socio-religious, political landscape of Russia.

Cultural interactions were visible between the 'West Balts' region and Scandinavia from the early 5th century that endured until the

---

38. Moscow's later political prominence arose parallel to Kyiv's decline in the 13th century following a devastating sacking by the Mongols.

7th century, coming to a halt only with the earliest settlement phase in Truso.[39] Early Ports of Trade from the 8th to the 9th centuries, provided key connections through the cities of Dvina, Ladoga and Volga (a route also known as the 'Viking Road'), for the interplay of economy and trade between Scandinavia and Kiev. A prime example of this is Wolin, an island situated at the mouth of the river Oder. According to Wulfstan, the earliest commercial and workshop center was Ribe in Denmark, and Wolin in northwestern Poland (later the largest town in this region), and Janów Pomorski near the lake Druzno (probably Truso).[40] Infused by wealth from trading enterprise, Wolin expanded rapidly, shifting from a simple fishing port to a market town with harbour ramparts and palisades by 800. It had thriving communities of craftspeople working in textiles, metallurgy, and even shipbuilding. Building on the trade established in the Iron Age[41] around the Caspian Sea and the Don River, the Baltic Sea became the main trading route throughout the course of the 9th century, serving the numerous workshops in *Truso, Birka, Staraja Ladoga, Novgorod-Gorodischche* and *Wiskiauten*.

3. Scythian warrior

Prior to the establishment of Novgorod (meaning Newtown), on lake Ilmen, an older sea-port outpost[42] known as Aldeigjuborg in the early Viking Age, existed on the right bank of the Volkhov river. This prosperous Slavic trading outpost known to them as Ladoga, was later dominated by (Scandinavian) Rus', and renamed as Staraja Ladoga. The Rus' (Rhos) feature among the entourage of the Byzantine Emperor in 839, as mentioned in the Frankish Annals of St Bertin.

---

39. Sławomir Mozdzioch; Błażej Stanisławski; Przemysław Wiszewski. (Eds.) "Scandinavian culture in Medieval Poland." In, *Interdisciplinary Medieval Studies Volume I*. (Institute of Archaeology and Ethnology of the Polish Academy of Sciences. Wrocław, 2013). **40.** The terms *Truso, Drus, Trus, Druzno*, common in the Baltic territories mean 'salt.' That a huge concentration of imported Scandinavian objects occur across the Baltic regions rich in salt deposits, is not con-incidental. **41.** Indicated by boat graves in Vendel, Valsgärde and Helgö. **42.** Renamed *Staraya Ladoga*, this location has sourced numerous artefacts and principle burials connected with Scandinavian traders. Following the conversion of Vladimir in the 10th century, trade patterns shifted significantly as Novgorod's importance rapidly declined in favour of Kiev.

THE KIEVAN RUS'

Centred on Constantinople, Byzantium's orientation towards Greek culture (as characterised by Eastern (Greek) Orthodox Christianity), distinguished it from ancient Rome and its Latin culture. The earliest Byzantine record of the activities of the Swedish Rus', specifically the Paphlagonian raid, appears in the Greek Life of St. George of Amastris, a chronicle that was probably written prior to 842. Trade between the Rus' and the Greek Orthodox Byzantines was initially fruitful and peaceful, although sporadic raids on the Caspian Sea by the Rus' were recorded by Arab authors throughout the late 9th century and into the 10th century.

According to the Rus' Chronicles, Oleg advanced from Staraja Ladoga (Old Norse: Aldeigjuborg), to seize Kiev (Kyiv)[43] from his brothers (Askold and Dir), and other close male relatives. He is therefore credited with founding the mighty state of the Kievan Rus',[44] which he ruled from 879-912.[45] His deeds are legendary, although his supposed attack on Constantinople, the capital of the Byzantine Empire is however, in dispute. Certain dates and events attributed to Oleg are challenged by some historians, who point out certain inconsistencies with other sources of the East Slavs and the Khazars, namely, the Schechter Letter, a document that raises additional doubts surrounding Oleg's death and his succession. The accounts of Arab historians such as Ibn Miskawayh provide further support for those dissenting voices.

Serving as an outlet from the Baltic, Staraja Ladoga "was a very important port for the Vikings on their trade route from Scandinavia to the South and East, to the Arab Caliphate and Byzantine empire."[46] Here, "the Vikings sold [bees]wax, furs, most of all slaves, and in exchange received silver coins, the dirhems as the main profit of their long expeditions. They also bought stone and glass beads, which were sold to Finnic tribes in exchange for furs."[47] Scandinavian warrior-merchants began extending their raids southward along the Dnieper

---

43. The main East European trade route used by the Greeks and the Scandinavians, was the River Dnieper. That route was guarded by the hillside fortress city of Kiev (Kyiv). **44.** The modern states of Belarus, Russia, and the Ukraine were created from the devastation that occurred when the Kievan Rus' fell to the Mongols between 1237-1242. **45.** His resting place remains in dispute. The Russian Primary Chronicle and other Kievan sources claim that Kiev (Kyiv) is where Oleg's mortal remains reside. This is contested by other Novgorodian sources, that conversely claim his grave is a funerary barrow in Ladoga. His death is recorded in The Novgorod First Chronicle, a decade later in 922. **46.** https://feefhs.org/resource/russia-asrnh-staraia-ladoga (Accessed 9/10/2024) **47.** See overleaf

during the 9th century as they sought commercial contacts with the Orient and with Byzantium.

Beginning from the 9th century, the route from the Baltic Sea to the Black Sea became particularly profitable and important to the Slavs. One of Constantinople's most powerful trading partners was Ancient Russia. An important revival in relations between Russia and Constantinople happened in the 9th century.[48]

Combined literary and archaeological evidence acknowledges this flourishing 8th – 9th century commercial trading network between Russia, the Orient and Scandinavia.[49] From the trading towns of Birka and Gotland, Scandinavian traders sailed in their merchant vessels across the Baltic Sea, following the northern route along the Silk Road (through Ladoga) via the East European and Russian rivers, into the Black Sea regions. Under the firm grip of the hostile and belligerent Khazars living at the mouth of the Volga, tribute was extracted from the southern Slavic tribes trading there.

It seems certain that a Rus' Khaganate modelled on the Khazarian state developed in the eastern region, and that the Varangian chieftain of a tribal coalition had appropriated the title of qagan (khagan) as early as the 830s. The title, albeit possibly ideological only, survived to denote the early princes of the Kievan Rus,' whose capital, Kyiv (Kiev), is demonstrably associated with a Khazarian foundation.[50] Ibn Rustah's [51] account of a temporary site for the Rus' on a marshy island in a northern lake (at the head-waters of the Volga) supports this early location and the displacement of the Slavs previously settled there.[52] Ibn Rustah states that the Rus' could not originally speak Slavic.[53]

---

47. "There is archaeological evidence of intense craft and trade activities in Ladoga. One of the first workshops produced glass beads following the Arab method. The most famous belonged to the blacksmiths, whose abandoned tools were preserved extremely well due to the high moisture in the soil." https://feefhs.org/resource/russia-asrnh-staraia-ladoga (Accessed 9/10/2024) **48.** Konstantinos Thodis. "The Great Route 'From the Varangians to the Greeks.'"https://www.academia.edu/30094727/The_Great_Route_From_the_Varangians_to_the_Greeks_ (Accessed 29th December 2024) **49.** Swedish influence diminished so drastically throughout the 10th century, it had vanished by the 11th century. **50.** Thomas S. Noonan. "The Khazar Qaghanate and its impact on the early Rus' state: the Translatio Imperii from Itil to Kiev." In, Nomads in the Sedentary World. Curzon-IIAS Asian studies series. Edited by Anatoly M. Khazanov and André Wink. (Routledge, 2001): 76-102 **51.** The varying accounts of various Steppe nomads relating to the northern races and to the contentious identity of the Rus', appear within the works of Ibn Rustah (10th Century), Al Bakri (11th Century), and Gurdizi (11th Century) following interactions with those nomadic tribes encountered across Russia. **52.** An island where the river Volkhov flows out of Lake Il'men.'

THE KIEVAN RUS'

Practising no agriculture, the Rus' initially thrived on tribute customs, via the farming produce of Slavic labour, and the capture and sale of the Slavic people to the Khazars, Bulgars and Arabic merchants.[54] He also refers to the chief of the Rus' as their khagan, and to the collection of tithes from the merchants under his authority. When the three Varangian[55] 'brothers' Rurik, Sineus and Truvor[56] settled as distinct regional rulers of these lands in the 9th century, the exploitative tax tributes were supposedly brought to an abrupt end. Perhaps the now famous tricephalic totemic pillars were erected by Rus' princes to honour the three ancestral lines generated by those legendary founding figures[57] who established the Rus' as a dominant factor in the creation of the Northern Russian State.[58] One of the more curious epithets applied to Russia is 'Ruotsi,' a term initially used by the Finns, for the Svear (Swedes) initially hunting for pelts, who then established staged trading posts as afar as Birka and Hedeby. Ideas proffered for the meaning of Ruotsi intimate a possible origin in 'rodr,' a term of reference for a crew of oarsmen, or, 'rusioi,' being an adaptation of the Greek 'Rosomones,' a title given to the Heruli based on their auburn hair (red or ginger). For three centuries, the Heruli were a tribe of Scandinavian mercenaries operating in the Eastern Roman Empire (3rd-6th century).

Other Arabic writers describe the Rus' as warriors and pirates

---

53. Ironically, it was the Slavic tongue, culture and customs, that dominated the formation of the medieval Russian state. The adoption of Eastern Orthodox Christianity finally separated Russia from its Northern European development, returning it to its Slavic roots. **54.** Some Slavs became mercenaries for the Rus.' See: Hazzard Cross and Sherbowitz-Wetzor,1953: 42-5 **55.** Varangian is used in the earlier sections of the Chronicle as a generic term for the Germanic nations on the coasts of the Baltic, including Swedes, Gotlanders, the English, and the Rus. **56.** This Normanists' view, which accepts a Norse origin for the Rurikid Dynasty, is challenged by Anti-Normanists who argue for a Slavic origin of Russia and the other states. "The Normanist claims are currently deemed more valid, so it is generally accepted that the Norse leader Rurik (r. 862-879) founded an enduring dynasty, reaching to the reign of Ivan IV, first Tsar of Russia (r. 1547-1584) also known as Ivan the Terrible." See: Joshua J. Mark, 2018. https://www.worldhistory.org/Kievan_Rus/ (Accessed 29th December 2024). **57.** In myth, several sets of three brothers or sons, fought and established various aspects of the Rus' monopoly of the Russian State. In another legend referred to in the Primary Chronicle, the founders of the Kievan Rus' in Kiev (modern Kyiv) in Ukraine, were three brothers who are mentioned along with an obscure sister named Lybed. For an image of the three brothers, see: https://commons.wikimedia.org/wiki/File:Kyi,_Czech,_Khoryv_and_Lubed_in_der_Radziwi%C5%82%C5%82chronik.jpg **58.** See: *The Russian Primary Chronicle: Laurentian Text*. Samuel Hazzard Cross and Olgerd P. Sherbowitz-Wetzor. (Trans. & Eds.) (Mediaeval Academy of America, 1953): 42-5

(Vikingr) who voyaged with their merchandise to Spain, Italy, Constantinople, and Khazaria. At this time, *The Russian Primary Chronicle* [59] states that in the middle of the 9th century (specifically 859), Novgorod and its surrounding territories also became known as the land of the Rus', a term of possible Finnish origin relating to the Scandinavian Vikingr who subjugated the Finno-Ugric and Slavic traders settled there. Their insular colony Novgorod is readily identifiable as the Norse Holmgarðr. The Varangian Rus' very quickly developed a powerful warrior-merchant system, that challenged, then compromised the hegemony of the Khazar controlled[60] waterways in pursuit of Arab silver[61] (which flowed north through the Khazarian-Volga Bulgarian trading zones), and to trade in furs and ironwork. A significant factor in the formation of a Rus' state had been the tithes extracted by the Khazarian regime on all mercantile vessels. Again politics driven by profit meant they could acquire the source of tribute and power for itself.[62] The Khazar qagan had initially allowed the Rus' to use the trade route along the Volga River, and raid southwards into the Caspian on the condition that the Rus' share the booty equally with him. This amity was severed in 913, when a violent Varangian incursion through Arab lands breached a recent peace treaty between the Rus' and Byzantium, leading to an appeal by the Islamic guard to the Khazar qagan for permission to retaliate against the Rus' who were then massacred on their homeward journey.

Khazar rulers were forced to bar the Rus' from further passage down the Volga, ultimately sparking a war between them.[63] The Khazar alliance with the Byzantine Empire began to collapse in the early 10th century after their forces clashed in the Crimea. Seeking to convert the Rus,' Byzantium encouraged the Alans to attack this buffer state to

---

59. Possibly compiled in the 12th century and credited to the monk, Nestor. However, the earliest surviving manuscript is dated to the end of the 14th Century. Sections indicate copying from earlier documents. Although the Chronicle is regularly alluded to as a historical narrative, this is now challenged due to its inclusion of notable mythic or legendary aspects. In this it shares an ambiguous status in historical literature shared by the Eddas. **60.** The Khazars were initially protected by the Volga Bulgarians who converted to Islam in the 10th century, wresting their liberty from their Khazarian suzerains. See: Jonathan Shepard. "Closer Encounters with the Byzantine World: the Rus at the Straits of Kerch." In, Pre-Modern Russia and Its World: Essays in Honor of Thomas S. Noonan. Edited by Kathryn L. Reyerson, Theofanis G. Stavrou and James D. Tracy. Harrassowitz Verlag, 2006: 15-77. **61.** Over 520 separate hoards of this silver have been uncovered in Sweden and Gotland. **62.** Shepard, 2006: 19 **63.** Atil fell to Sviatoslav I c.968. See: Elli Kohen, History of the Byzantine Jews: A Microcosmos in the Thousand Year Empire, (University Press of America, 2007): 107

THE KIEVAN RUS'   257

weaken its hold on Crimea and the Caucasus in order to allow greater power to the Rus' in the north.[64] The eventual decline of the Khazar power monopoly throughout these territories, allowed the expansion of Arabic commerce along alternative trading routes to Byzantium via the Volga and other arterial rivers of Russia. Between 965 and 969, the Kievan Rus' ruler, Sviatoslav I of Kiev, and his allies, conquered the capital, Atil, ending Khazar independence in a period of shifting stabilities and ethnicities and the fluidity of faith and conversion.

Norway and Denmark were quite exposed to external influences from the English and Irish material cultures; Sweden was not, though all were influenced by the Finnish culture to varying degrees. Sweden continued to demonstrate the deepest ties to Russia, and Swedish communities travelled along the Russian watercourses during the 9th to the 10th centuries, parallel to the Norwegian migration westwards to Iceland, Greenland and North America.

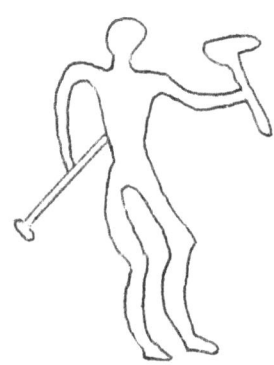

---

64. Thomas S. Noonan. "European Russia c.500 CE to c.1050 CE." In, The New Cambridge Medieval History: Volume 3, C.900-c.1024 C.E. Volume 3:485-534. Edited by T. Reuter and R. McKitterick. (Cambridge University Press, 1999): 499, 502-03

MEDIEVAL TRADE

Some scholars claim that a curious amulet found amongst other Swedish objects in Courland - where the Vikingr established their early domination in Russia - portrays the face of Óðinn.[65] However, I believe this is unlikely, as it does not follow that similarities in the aesthetic style of various cultural artefacts will demonstrate similar meanings amongst different people acquiring them through gift, theft or trade. Designs were emulated and copied, but were ultimately reinterpreted through the lens of the recipient culture. These artefacts, no matter the cultural context of their deposition, will always be later analysed and reinterpreted again by historians and anthropologists looking for significant meaning in the material remains discovered by archaeologists.[66]

In addition to the long-standing trade of furs, other trade goods were mostly, salt, coins, amber, glass and antler handicraft, some of which were modelled into tools or ornamentation. Amber and bone pendants in the shape of axes and hammers dedicated to Þórr, and hnefli gaming pieces (for playing Hnefatafl), were known both in Scandinavia and in the West Slavonic region of the Baltic Sea. Bone skates, skis and iron picks were crafted for walking on ice. This multidimensional range of material culture is a promising indication of the long-distance trade and interactive contacts in the Baltic Sea region between Scandinavian, North Russian, Slavonic, and West Baltic societies. The major cosmopolitan trading towns noted above, were surprisingly densely populated, and exhibited a polyethnic (and multi-faith) character in the same way as the oldest West Pomeranian centre.[67] At this time, (8th to the 10th centuries) Wolin was one of the

---

65. Cited as Thomas S. Noonan. See: Peter Sawyer. *The Oxford Illustrated History of the Vikings.* (Oxford University Press, 2001): 141-2 **66.** Oates, 22. **67.** Andrzej Buko. "Between Wolin and Truso: the Southern part of the Baltic Rim at the time of Rise of the Polish State (an archaeological perspective)." In, *The Image of the Baltic.* Edited by Michael F. Scholz, Robert Bohn and Carina Johansson. (Gotland University Press, 2012). See also: Natalia Radziwillowicz. "Considering the Connections Between Scandinavia and the Southern Baltic Coast in the 10th -11th Centuries." Innervate Volume X (2016-2017): XXXX

greatest port and trade centre; its 10th century wooden temple later became famous for its presumed dedications to *Svjatovit (Sventovit)*, an alleged pagan figure commonly depicted as the Wolin idol bearing four heads.[68]

Yet despite the archaeological and historical material evidence, it is not possible to reconcile the finds with the *ethnicity* of crafters and traders. Items denoting faith too can be problematic. Nevertheless, it was (in previous decades) deemed politic to identify archaeological finds (from tools to settlements) from the southern area of the Baltic Sea, as 'Scandinavian.' The possibility that ethnic groups other than Swedes or Norwegians may have created them, is too often omitted. Items from West Europe (glass vessels and weapons) or from the Orient (textiles, dirhams and beads), were exchanged for 'authentic Scandinavian objects': brooches, trefoil fibulae, rectangular strap mounts, posaments of fine silver thread, drinking horns, slate objects, soapstone, bone/antler combs, pottery[69] and the aforementioned gaming pieces.[70] Once objects are traded, the archaeological contexts they end up in often reveal drastically altered usage at some variance with their original intent or purpose. Many items were also not subject to the same conservative gender strictures as those applied in Scandinavia. For instance, oval brooches[71] and other ornaments discovered in Poland, Russia and the Baltic region, do not of themselves, reliably represent gender, so appear in both male and female graves. In the Scandinavian region such brooches appear only in female graves. Similarly, rectangular strap (belt) mounts and luxury silver posaments that in Scandinavia, generally occur only in male burials, have been found in high-status female graves in Swielubie and Birka.[72] The population here clearly

---

68. Bozena Werbart. "Khazars or Saltovo-Majaki Culture? Prejudices about Archaeology and Ethnicity." (Current Swedish Archaeology Vol. 4, 1996). **69.** Slavonic pottery occurs in the trade centres on Gotland, in Birka, Sigtuna, and Lund, serving as crude packaging and storage. **70.** Inga Hägg. "Die Textilfunde aus dem Hafen von Haithabu. Berichte über die ausgrabungen in Haithabu, Bericht 20. Neumünster." [The Textile Finds from the Port of Haithabu. Reports on the excavations at Haithabu, Report 20. Newspaper] (Karl Wachholz Verlag, 1984). Shelagh Lewins has made available an English summary of pages 38-42 and 168-170 at https://www.shelaghlewins.com/reenactment/hedeby_apron/hedeby_apron.htm. See also Inga Hagg, "Die Tracht." In, Birka II:2 Systematische Analysen der Graberfunde. Edited by Greta Arwidsson. [Systematic Analysis of the Graves Findings] Birka, Kungliga Vitterhets Historie och Antikvitets Akademien: II:2 (Birka, Kungliga Vitterhets Historie och Antikvitets Akademien, 1986). **71.** Oval brooches in male burials, as in barrow 21 in Swielubie. **72.** Inga Hägg, 1984; I. Gustin; D. T. Price; C. Arcini; L. Drenzel; S Kalmring. (2017). "Isotopes and Human Burials at Viking Age Birka and the Mälaren Region, East Central Sweden." Journal of Anthropological Archaeology 49 (2018): 19-38. https://doi.org/10.1016/j.jaa.2017.10.002

observed Scandinavian traditions relating to life and death, albeit with considerably more flair, and overlaid with an element of the exotic east, as noted in their fine clothing and exquisitely ornamental pieces.

Both men and women were active traders in the international markets, in southern Scandinavia, the southern Baltic Sea, Kiev, and in the eastern Volga region in Russia during the 8th to the 9th centuries. Women traders were not common-place, but the presence of weights in a few female burial records, is evidence enough that some women achieved this status. In this rich multi-cultural region, the staid traditions of their homelands were significantly relaxed.[73] However, this very much remained a man's world, and we know that certain proscriptions evidently applied to female traders. It would appear from the burial records that Scandinavian tradeswomen did not travel to the Islamic countries, since only male graves containing weights and scales (used in the silver markets) were found in Volga-Bulgaria, unlike the Kiev area.[74] Furthermore, and unsurprisingly, the sources (written by Christian and Muslim men) are silent on the subject of female traders.

Geographical position provides significant advantage. Russian territories formed the crossroads between the Christian and Muslim worlds, therefore exerted a considerable impact upon their cultural, economic and political advancement, while being susceptible to influences from both in return. Trade routes were the key factor in these developments - particularly along the Baltic that reached into the Black Sea regions - enabling profitable commercial relations to develop between northern Europe and the Byzantine Empire. This commercial route followed the Volkhov and Dnieper rivers, alongside areas inhabited by the East Slavs who also profited sufficiently to establish their own flourishing commercial, political and cultural centres. For some time, Kiev (Kyiv) in the South and Novgorod in the North, dominated trade and their collective expansion rapidly absorbed the East Slavs.

To clarify these events in their historical context, we should consider the social and political landscape as it was set across these regions at this time. The now legendary diplomatic mission of the Arab traveller Ahmad Ibn Fadlan of 921. (fl. 920s) into what is now Russia – as mentioned in The Risala, was ongoing. As an eager missionary for the Muslim faith, Ibn Fadlan had travelled on the behest

---

73. Anne Stalsberg. "Women As Actors In North European Viking Age Trade." In, *Social approaches to Viking Studies*. Edited by Ross Samson. Cruithne Press, 1991. **74.** In fact, there are no Scandinavian female grave finds in Volga-Bulgaria.

of the Abbasid caliphate, the imperial dynastic leaders who possessed religious and political authority throughout the east of the Byzantine Empire, stretching to the west of China until the 13th century. Fadlan's purpose was to explain Islamic law to the recently converted Volga Bulgars[75] who had migrated into Eastern Europe from the frontiers of China during the sixth and seventh centuries that brought various Türkic peoples westward from the far eastern reaches of Central Asia. We may credit the Türkic peoples with the earliest writing found thus far in North Asia. Their inscriptions during the 8th century refer to the heroic exploits of twin brothers, paralleling the Alci in the northern Germanic traditions.

An awareness of these factors regarding trade in these conflict zones, offers a completely different perspective on the purposes for the journeys made by Ibn Fadlan and other Arabic geographers to these regions, and of their encounters with the Rus' and of other Scandinavian peoples whose commerce through Russia was initially facilitated along the trans-Caspian Orient. Familiarity between the Arabic and Scandinavian peoples at the time of Fadlan's writings, was considerable. The need to trade forged an uneasy truce, strained further by intermittent conflicts. Ibn Fadlan's account of the various peoples he'd met on the Volga trading route, just a few decades ago, focussed upon the strange aforementioned fair-haired, blue-eyed people who had settled in the region as the main traders with the Bulgars. This group of Vikingr were known as the Varangians,[76] but also as the Rus'.[77] Others included various Türkic peoples, among them the Khazars, one of the few groups in history outside of Israel to adopt Judaism.[78] Nonetheless, other Arabic writers similarly provide markedly confused testimonies of the peoples they encountered, albeit hampered by a lack of genuine first-hand information, and a propensity to mistake

---

75. One group of Bulgars had continued moving to the western shores of the Black Sea, becoming Christianized and settling in the land that today bears their name. By contrast, the Volga Bulgars had settled along the eastern shores of the Volga River in what is now Russia. **76.** Varangians were Vikingr lured by stories of fantastic wealth. Around 862 CE, they sailed out of their homeland in Sweden, eastward across the Baltic Sea and up the rivers of Eastern Europe, working their way further inland, where they founded the great city of Novgorod. They eventually established control over Kiev, wrested from the Slavs who had founded it. A chieftain named Rurik (d. c. 879) emerged as their leader, founding an influential dynasty well into the late 16th century across Russia. **77.** Slavs used this term for the Varangians. **78.** Known as the Khazar Khanate, the Khazars occupied the southern end of the Volga as a Semitic state. Khazaria flourished until its destruction by the Kievan Rus' in the 11th century.

one fair-skinned tribe for another; in particular, the Slavs were not distinguished from those of Scandinavian origin. The term ~aqliib (fair-complexion) was used indiscriminately for the Volga Bulgarians,[79] the Germans, Saxons, Hungarians and the Varangians.[80]

Occupied by foreign merchants and emissaries, Birka was the centre of international trade, world-wide contacts, commerce and diplomacy. Of the chambered graves found in Birka housing women and children, around 20 include horses, often on platforms. Filled with eastern (or oriental) objects, including bird-of-prey mountings, Khazaric pottery, Khazar (heart-shaped silver) amulets from Saltovo, and a Khazar metal disc with an engraving of the Star of David, it seems several of these could be the high-status graves of foreigners (possibly Khazar or Kievan Rus). "The Birka and Kievan chamber graves (like in Sezdovitsy in Chernigov) yielded very similar objects of Khazar character. The older official interpretation was that the Chernigov chamber graves were of Scythian, Magyar or Alan origin."[81]

Sceattas (interpreted as Scandinavian imitations of Germano-Roman coins) displaying images of horses, a yurt, sun symbols and Viking Age ships (common grave goods in this region), were identified as Khazaric burials in at least two of the graves excavated at Birka. Within other 9th to the 10th-Century graves found here, belt mounts decorated with stylized plant ornaments, animal and human figures, have also been identified as Khazarian or Saltovo-Majaki. Yet this does not help us identify the occupants, who are generally classed as "easterners,' living among other foreigners in Birka, wearing eastern clothing, and using eastern burial customs."[82] Although archaeologists in the past have often suggested that these graves could be the burial of a "merchant-warrior clan of Swedish nobles," this makes little practical sense as those 'nobles' "were not located in Birka, but in the area of King Court on Adelsö, the island across the water, opposite the island of Björkö."[83] Today, this view is less pointed, and it is now suggested that "the chamber graves are the burial of foreigners, containing a large number of eastern objects, both Khazar and Kievan Rus."[84]

Because ethnicity or cultural identity is a subjective and variable phenomenon, ethnic prejudice within the field of archaeology continues to be subject to propagandistic falsifying. Discoveries

---

79. The Volga Bulgaria became an Islamic state in 922 CE, influencing, then controlling the region's trading networks and routes. 80. Hazzard Cross and Sherbowitz-Wetzor, 1953: 40-1 81. Werbart, 1996. 82. Werbart, 1996. 83. Ibid. 84. Ibid. See Appendix V and Glossary.

relating to the historical movement and settlement of trade and people under certain regimes[85] during the modern era, has been quite problematic. It seems it was deemed to be politically expedient (when recording the finds following excavation, and when writing them up in the archaeological literature), to omit, neglect or treat with prejudice, other ethnicities or religious beliefs.

The search for the treasures, objects and traces of this lost culture has been deliberately blocked in many countries, haunted by the spectre of the Khazars as skeletons in their national closets. There is still a certain neglect of Khazars in the early history of Russia, the focus being on the [Rus'] Viking-perspective; the situation in the former Soviet Union was an extreme example of that. The western archaeologists, on the other hand, regarded certain objects as 'Khazar, Magyar or Alan'. The south to north interpretation of the trade and 'colonization' of Viking Age Russia, in the light of the new dating of chamber graves in Birka and Russia of the 9th and 10th centuries, is not only one of the possible factors. According to these new ways of looking at Birka material, most of the chamber graves with ornaments (about 120), dated to the 10th century, can be interpreted as pagan Rus' with Khazar objects or, as pagan Khazar with Rus' features, and often interpreted as eastern ornaments. But where and how far is the East? Staraja Ladoga? Kiev? Khazaria?[86]

Changes in the material culture remind us that people constantly renew and improve their knowledge and personal circumstances; therefore, material culture contributes to our understanding of the redefining of cultural identities, and of the need to adjust our approaches accordingly when viewing and interpreting the evidence. We must carefully monitor the relationship between material culture and cultural identity, to ensure ideas of 'ethnicity' and 'ethnic identity' do not become perceived as hereditary, permanent, and unalterable, but remain instead, natural and fluid forms of identity. Other forms of identity are linked to belief, faith and custom; when combined, these form our cultural identity. What exists beyond that, is belief.

---

85. For example, due to Stalinist doctrine, the Khazars deliberately hid certain facts about their conversion to Judaism. **86.** Werbart, 1996.

SLAVIC RELIGION: THE NATURAL ORIGINS OF FOLKLORIC BELIEF

Having previously explored the cultural origins of the Slavic people, particular aspects of belief are reflected in the folkloric traditions that developed from them. Therefore, I feel there is a driving imperative to expose the collective roots of layered belief and influences that ultimately syncretised in the Vikingr culture, much of which has been erroneously attributed to an Óðinic Cultus. A people is more than the sum of its parts. Belief is not separatist unless it becomes fundamentalist. Belief is fluid, adaptive, evolving and ever shifting in its interpretations and manifestations. In the following section, the underlying threads of pre-Christian and non-Christian beliefs that formed the customs heavily disguised in the medieval sagas - appearing only in remnant form - are explored here to show beyond doubt how far we have strayed in our understanding of indigenous culture and insular belief.[87] Just how influential culture is to even an overarching, universal religion such as Christianity is evident in the way the latter is absorbed and expressed by the former. The threads of the old and new worlds, and the regions of east, west, north and south, were woven together to formulate a new means of expression.

It becomes obvious the spirits central to northern religious practises changed little (even after conversion), and could on no account be properly perceived of as 'gods.' Slavic paganism had not developed its own literary history, there had been no reason to do so. Investigations into the actual beliefs of the Slavs is therefore constrained; all the information concerning them comes via external and theoretical reconstructions founded upon assumed similarities

---

87. Particular attention is given to the animistic and totemic source and true nature of the Elder Gods introduced in book III of the Óðinn Trilogy (See: Shani Oates, *The Search for Óðinn*. Anathema Publishing Ltd., 2022), before moving through that early heroic period, forwards in time to reveal a final Continuity of Cult in the shamanisms that were plumbed to create the composite figure we have come to know as Óðinn.

SLAVIC RELIGION 265

or correspondences with deities and ritual practises of neighbouring peoples (Iranian and Balts for example).[88] We should therefore be mindful that all matters relating to former beliefs, possible temple construction, and the supposed nature of their practises, were recorded by the very Bishops who opposed and destroyed them.[89] Records of the conversion of the Polabian Slavs during the 12th century are found in extremely hostile sources only.[90] The Southern Slavs were among the first to succumb to conversion. For this reason, lateral and inclusive studies involving historical sources, folklore, and linguistic data must always be supported and accompanied by archaeological evidence. Slavic (and Baltic) religion and mythology are more conservative and closer to an original model of Proto-Indo-European religion.

Helmold's remarkable *Chronica Slavorum* preserves a record of Slavic beliefs and customs, for which we have no surviving Scandinavian or Germanic parallel. Beneath the glosses, it reveals a common but vital animistic apprehension of the divine as a nebulous presence within the sky that encompasses the atmosphere, air, wind, rain, snow, clouds, thunder and lightning. An exploration of Slavic beliefs provides us with a clearer perspective on those of the Norse, with whom they should be irrevocably associated. The West, East and South Slavs shared a deep reverence for all things celestial, including the (male) moon (Russian: Mesyats), the (female) sun (Solntse), and the stars. The movement of, and relationship between these celestial giants, provided a framework for many occult orders, craft guilds and groups, who have observed them closely, incorporating lore appropriate to them in their praxes and cosmologies.[91] As the benefactors of health and abundance, life and well-being, the celestial orbs were celebrated by dances in the round, fire and feasting, often at the turning of the seasons. Calendrical rituals were often determined by the agrarian fertility cycle, in this, the

---

88. Literary records were the province of missionaries waging against paganism. Moravia was Christianised by 863; Bulgaria by 885; Poland 966, Russia by 988. See: Gimbutas, 1987. **89.** Otto, a 12th century bishop from Bamberg, employed three biographers to record his campaigns against the pagan Slavs. Another source of information of Wendish paganism of the 9th to the 10th centuries, is provided by Bishop Thietmar of Merseburg. See also: Mark R. Munzinger. "The Profits of the Cross: Merchant Involvement In The Baltic Crusade (c. 1180 – 1230)." In, Journal of Medieval History, 32 (2006). **90.** Namely, by Ahmed Ibn Rustah, John Malalas, Bishop Thietmar of Merseburg, Adam of Bremen, Archbishop of Rheims Ebbo, Bishop Herbord, Saxo Grammaticus and Helmold of Bosau, all of whom deliver scathing polemics on the West and East Slavs. See also: The Russian Primary Chronicle, sometimes referred to as The Chronicle of Nestor or Tale of Bygone Years. **91.** Close to this author's heart, the CTC tradition follows this modus operandi.

active, masculine divine force, personified by thunder and lightning, invariably penetrated the earth as light and fire, stimulating fecundity and fructification.[92]

Early medieval sources that focus primarily upon the Baltic (Western) and Eastern Slavs refer to their pre-Christian beliefs as being founded in an unsophisticated mythology.[93] This suggests non-centralised cultic practises and dedications to life-giving forces known as bereginy; present in the land, rivers, and the elements.[94] Medieval Russian sermons and missives imparted to the lower clergy now provide us with interesting information regarding the differences between what they believed was the official paganism of the fledgling Kievan state (which it deemed to be a threat), and the folk religion practised beyond the main city states. Slavic folk religion was principally concerned with the spirit of life itself, with fertility, propitiated by rites celebrating death and the renewal of life. Theirs was an ingrained cultural saturation of animism, that even conversion only superficially overlaid. Their uncomplicated approach to the divine and to natural cycles was largely based in native custom, but was also strongly influenced by the Proto-Iranian shift in its perception of the supreme and nebulous god of Heaven (*$Dyeus$), that became defined by alternative terms for Sky.[95]

In all cases of change and transference, the possibility of contamination is most feared and therefore particular rituals that engage protection were primary actions. The sanctity of life deemed present mainly in the ground and in the sky are indisputable. Earth is protective and purificatory. For example, vows and oaths were followed by swallowing a mouthful of soil. Sins are breathed into furrows in the ground, and clods of earth are placed over cattle to protect them.

The influence of malignant sorcery on the psyche of the Russian peasant was overwhelming; if something went wrong in a family, be it crop failure, damage to livestock, drought, family discord, infertility, epidemics, or illness – it was attributed to the external agency of sorcerers and witches. At all times, rituals were enacted to avert chaos and to maintain order. One of the main purificatory elements was fire, used to expel spirits from house, land, beast and harvest. Mock battles and the burning of effigies often of straw, were intended to prevent penetration of evil spirits and illness. Torches carried on horseback, along with

92. Written sources refer to this force engaged by The West Slavs, as *Svetovit*, and for the East Slavs as *Perun*, a name related to the Prussian *Perkunos*, though it is not quite an absolute etymological derivation. **93.** This includes Thracians, Phrygians and Indo-Iranians. **94.** Gimbutas, 1987: 353-361 **95.** See Appendices.

great wheels and flaming poles were pushed in torchlit ceremonious to and from the cemeteries. Water drawn before sunrise and fumigation by juniper smoke, together with salt, were all used to circumambulate farmsteads, cattle, even people, for curative and prophylactic purposes. Midsummer centred around bonfires and water in the belief that the sun imbued the water with special rejuvenating essences; therefore, bathing was a primary activity in these celebrations. The destruction and burning or drowning of a tree effigy or scarecrow occurs only during the waxing tide of the year and never during the waning parts of the year in which harvesting was the primary activity. Eggs are the seeds of life, renewal, and rebirth. Loaves and eggs were blessed before being fed to cattle and people as part of the celebration to prevent the succumbing to infection and disease.

The Christian perspective elevated many spirits it deemed benign, or not in conflict with its tenets, to personages that achieved the status of Sainthood, namely St Nicholas, St George and St. Michael. Other Óðinic figures were demonised, and in some cases conflated with the devil (chert, bes), able to adopt any malignant form he chose, to beguile, mystify and deceive the unwitting. In Slavic tradition, a host of benign, if somewhat capricious spirits inhabit the world of man. The domovoi, (a house spirit, is the benevolent protector of the family. Conversely, the wild forests and huge bodies of water, filled people with foreboding and dread, the hostile spirits there (the leshii and vodianoi, respectively), were wild and unpredictable, ambivalent, and prone to malevolence. The field spirit (paulvoi), protector of the crops, resided somewhere in-between. Many of these virtue terms are familiar to us, found in the folk tales of past centuries, albeit written up there as actual names of deities rather than elemental spirits. Other Indo-European divine figures such as Rod, Iarilo, and Lada/o, are drafted into the Chronicles from various mediaeval sources.

What can be understood from the medieval literature and the folklore that developed since, is an overwhelming sense of the animistic spirit within the growth and life patterns that become lost or transferred in death and revived again as new life. But these cycles are not to be seen in the Frazerian sense of dying and resurrected gods, but simply a profound expression of the cycle of life. Based in those animisms, these beliefs only superficially appear to contrast with the higher mythology of the early Kievan Rus', whose veneration of Rod [96] and Rozhanitsy

---

96. Ivanits, 1989: 17-18. Other name forms for this deific figure are: Dievas (Lithuanian); Rid (Ukrainian); Rodu (Old East Slavic); Sud (South Slavic); Prabog, Praboh (Slovak)

was thoroughly misrepresented in medieval sources where they are described in comparable terms to other arcane pantheons, making Rod cognate with the ancient Egyptian god Osiris, as the genetrix of life.[97] However, the root *rod, refers to origin, kinship, tribe and destiny. Sud, which means judge, is a South Slavic name for the supreme divine driving force of the Universe, especially when conceived of as the interweaving of destiny.[98]

Rod (singular) and Rozanica (plural), literally (those) 'who give birth,' are properly the collective representation of the divine entities that manipulate Fate. As such, they refer to a complex array of elemental and totemic spirits, implying the union of the supreme god with matter, in order to shape reality. In kinships, Rod represents patrilineal ancestry; Rozanica, matrilineal ancestry,[99] the latter being akin to the Norse Dísir, the female ancestral spirits of female lineages who guided the Fate of their descendants. These cultic beliefs indicate the presence at the hearth, of very specific, personal, ancestral family spirits. The ancient Slavs offered bread, cheese, honey, porridge and mead to Rod and Rozanica,[100] the favoured food still, for all ancestral forms including the otherworldly landvættir, lares, and the fey. Due to the cultic reverence for ancestral forms, the defining line between them and purely animistic spirits, is irrevocably blurred. Popular in the Eastern Slavic regions, Rod merged with Svetovit of western regions.

---

97. Ivanits, 1989: 15 19th century scholars of Slavic religion corrected this misconception, referring to them instead as ancestral figures. **98.** Ivanits, 1989: 19-20. **99.** She has been compared to the Greek Aphrodite and the Indic Lakshmi, but especially to the Roman Juno, female consort of the supreme God. See: Jan Máchal. "Slavic Mythology." In, *The Mythology of all Races. III, Celtic and Slavic Mythology.* Edited by L. H. Gray. (Marshall Jones Company, 1918): 217-389 **100.** Ibid., 249

THE SACRED ISLE OF RÜGEN AND THE 'HOWLING GOD'

Some of the more martial aspects of enduring folk beliefs may also be sourced in the medieval period. For instance, in his *Gesta Danorum* of 1208, Saxo Grammaticus provides a description of the campaign that took place on the Island of Rügen several decades earlier in 1168, when the Slavs surrendered their stronghold treasury at Karentia[101] to the Danish troops of King Valdemar I. Saxo refers to a series of Slavic shrines that featured within this fortified area of Rügen (Karentia). One structure housed a large oak pillar, which he refers to as Rügievit,[102] claiming it meant god of Rügen, or Lord of Rügia,[103] which is closer, but still inaccurate. Composed of the Old Slavic rjuti, to roar or howl, and vit, meaning spirit, Rügievit is the Roaring/Howling spirit, a description that asserts the possibility of a tutelary (named) ancestral chieftain, known for that fierce protective quality, and also, equally appropriate, a guardian spirit of place; these are not necessarily always mutually exclusive. This conforms to a pattern whereby local spirits are named by others (generally outsiders) in terms that reflect the location and possibly even the social situation (occupation, status, culture) of people who dwell there. Spirit forms are generally molded in response to the relative needs of those who depend on them. We should remember that Rügen was home to various Slavic and Germanic tribes including, Pomeranians, Rügiians, Obodrites and Liuticians.

We may take this as representative of the various totems (in the form of wooden posts) placed not just in Rügen, but across the Slavic lands, extending into those of Germany and Scandinavia, to better

---

101. Karenz, Korantiza, later also Gharense, a medieval Slavic gord or burgwall on the island of Rügen in the Baltic Sea. It was the fortified administrative centre of the Rani tribe and of the Principality of Rugia.   102. Rügievit – (West Slavs and Baltic Slavs). Variants include: Rugiewit, Rujevit, Rugiwit, Ruevit, Riuvit, Rinvit.   103. Mathieu-Colas, 2017

appreciate the significance of these wooden posts as protective spirits, often the genii loci, sometimes an ancestral or tutelary figure, both of which are well attested cultural tenets of these peoples (as noted above). Saxo's description of the Rügievit oak pillar, having seven heads or seven faces (the text isn't clear), which converged at the top in a single crown,[104] bearing seven swords hanging from his girdle with one more in his hand, is startling, but very reminiscent of the wooden grave markers that are erected upon ancestral family mounds even today in the circumpolar and arctic regions of the Samoyed and Teleuts. Saxo states that other temples stood beside this one dedicated to similar warring deities – *Ruevit*,[105] Porenut and another variant – *Porevit*,[106] bearing shield and a lance, who is depicted with five faces, one of which is on his chest.[107] This title embodies the root *per defining the masculine virile force of generation. The triple-headed 'god' may simply reflect the afore-mentioned Slavic tradition of three (ancestral) leaders, often brothers or close kin.

4. Polycephalic *Svetovit*

Polycephalic wooden figures from the Baltic Sea area date from the 9th or 10th century and are popularly believed to represent *Svetovit/Svantevit*, a title reconstructed by Christian monks from the following forms: *svetb* meaning, saint, holy or sacred;[108] and *vit*, meaning divine, spirit, lord, leader, and ruler, possibly related to wise or wisdom. *Svantev/svitanje* is a form that contains the term zvar, which is associated with the rising or dawning light, possibly the sun as the morning star. As The Dawning One, Svetovit, bears the same miraculous attributes awarded to *Xors Dazhbog*, qualities that manifest in other heroic figures (namely Widukind and Óðinn), and in the sun symbols used to represent them. In Lithuanian:

---

104. Pettazzoni, 1967. **105.** They had or acquired calendrical significance. Jarovit, Ruevit, Parovit and other variants later developed into the names of saints with seasonal feast-days. **106.** Porevit – (West Slavs and Baltic Slavs) – had a cult centre in Garz in Rügen. Variants include: Porewit, Porevith, Porovit, Puruvit, Porenut (Germanisation as Proven or Prove). He appears to be an aspect or other name of Perun. He is attested as the tutelary deity of Oldenburg, also regarded as an aspect of Svetovit. **107.** Mathieu-Colas, 2017. **108.** Kroonen, 2003.

Šventavydis, relates to all things known as being holy: *Šventa* meaning holy,[109] *Vydis* meaning knowledge or seeing.[110] Based on the claim that his temple historically housed a horse used in prophecy, Svetovit is represented in modern imagery riding his white horse named Jary (the bright one).[111] Only the high priest rode the horse so that its behaviour was observed in order to forecast the outcome of battle as it walked over crossed spears. Horse oracles have a long history in this region, as attested by Tacitus.

The root **vid* [112] or **vit* refers to sight or vision (of a ruler – victory lord). *Vid*, as highlighted by the name variant Sutvid, may be identified as Svetovit, a term also found in *Rodiva*,[113] through her manifestation as *Vida*, the celestial and rainy aspect of a female divine spirit associated with light. The **vid/vit* root is significant to the relationship between the Slavic verb **voditi*, to lead, and the *Vohda-Woda-Wota*[114] connection to the Germanic *Wotan/Wodan*, a tutelary spirit form hailed in association with wisdom and prophecy. As the inspiring motivational force,[115] Wotan/Wodan and Svetovit are naturally associated with rúnes and rúnic wisdom. West Slavs referred to rúnes as *vitha*, from **vid* or **vit*, which refers to the sentience of "the multi-faceted essence of the supreme God."[116] As late medieval sources of the 13th and 14th centuries, the works of Saxo and Helmold, not to mention the *Knýtlinga Saga*, mention Svetovit, referring to him retrospectively as the patron protector of Rügen. Neither Svetovit nor any of its variants were in contemporary use by the peoples who observed his rites. Folk beliefs have their origin in the prevailing animistic reverence for elemental focus – primarily of thunder, that survived conversion. Needless to say, the use of such titles by peoples of the pre-Christian era remains unqualified. Repetition of the same interpretation of that non-Christian world by these eminent bishops, and others that followed them, presumes that almost all Slavic deities are variant forms of *Svetovit*.[117] As a fecund

---

109. Several Slavic, Lithuanian and Germanic variants relate to sacred waters, lakes and springs. Sacred Islands, are often deemed so, because of the holy waters that surround them.   110. Rick Derksen. Etymological Dictionary of the Slavic Inherited Lexicon. (Brill, 2007)   111. Dynda, 2014: 59   112. Vid, Vida, Wid, Vit, Wit, Sutvid, Wida, Vita, Wita — South Slavs, Serbs/Croats. The supreme polarity as male–female is documented among South Slavs also as Vid–Vida.   113. Marjanic, 2015: 181-204   114. Jan Hanuš Ignác. *Die Wissenschaft des slawischen Mythus im Weitesten, den altpreussisch-lithauischen Mythus mitumfassenden sinne: Nach Quellen bearbeitet, sammt der Literatur der slawisch-preussisch-lithauischen Archäologie und Mythologie.* (Stanislawów und Tarnow, J. Millikowski, 1842): 381   115. Marjanc, 2015:192   116. Ignác, 1842: 381   117. See overleaf

spirit, *Svetovit* represented bountiful harvests, the warming light of Summer, and even divination.

Elsewhere in these medieval source documents, we encounter mention of Svarog/ Zvarog[118] the divine spirit of smithcraft, also spirit of the wind who clears away all obstacles or obstruction. Knives were thrown into a whirlwind for protection, and people would cast themselves face downwards before all such cyclones to ward off the illness or misfortune the wind carried with it, crying out "belt around your neck."[119] This diminished its power, strangling the demon within its elemental dragon force. If we witness the appearance and behaviour of elemental vortices of wind, water and fire, we can see the gaping maw spiralling into a whipping tail.[120] There was some degree of continuity between the beliefs of the East, West Slavs and South Slavs, as exampled in another ritual shrine dedicated to a possible pan-Slavic deity of the sun and fire, referred to as Svarozhich/ Svarožic by the East Slavs, and Zuarasici /Zuarasiz, by the West Slavs.[121] Remembering that the Slavs lived side-by-side with the Scythians for many years, these are Iranian etymological terms that mean Son of Heaven, also known as Svarog, identified as the tutelary deity of the Baltic Slavs.[122] Fire is essential for life, especially the hearth fire and was highly revered in its elemental forms as lightening or from the celestial fire of the Sun

Khors and Dažbog were spirits of the sun, and its divine beneficence. Lado/a, an underworld spirit or of marriage, or the hunt, may possibly even be a simple poetic refrain and not a spirit at all. Lel and Polel are cognate with the Slavic Castor and Pollux. Linguistics suggest that Volos/Veles, functioned as a god of wealth (in cattle) and was connected to the dead. His Indo-European parallel could be the Vedic Varuna, a god of oaths and world order.[123]

High places such as tree lines and mountain tops are the locus of

---

117. The numerous rivers and lakes named for this spirit of place across the Slavic regions reflect the minor name variations: Svitovyd, Svyentovit, Svyatovit and Svetovid (Ukrainian); Svetovid, Svantevid, Svantovid, Suvid), Sutvid, Svevid, (Serbian, Croatian, Slovenian, Macedonian, Bosnian, and Bulgarian), Svantevit (Wendish, possibly the original proto-Slavic name), Svantovit, Svantovit (Czech and Slovak); Swantovít, Sventovit, Zvantevith (Latin and alternative name in Serbian and Croatian), Swietowit (Polish) and Lithuanian: Šventavydis. **118.** Iranian prefix - xvar =sun; Iranian suffix - og = divine spirit. **119.** Linda J. Ivanits. Russian Folk Belief. (M.E. Sharpe, 1989): 15 **120.** The fetters that restrained Fenris express a similar idea - staving chaos manifest in the whirlwind etc. **121.** Pettazzoni, 1967:155. A term also linked to Reidegost. Note the similar Russian term Zsarovitch, meaning leader, used right up the 1917 Revolution. **122.** Another variant is Xors Dazhbog – The Sun as the victor over darkness and the one who meters justice. **123.** Ivanits, 1989: 6-9

THE SACRED ISLE OF RÜGEN 273

elemental power, as are horizons. Where the land and sky meet and touch, life is generated from that contact. Preserved in legend, this arcane belief is articulated through Bogatyr the heroic god who rides above the treeline, bringing bandits or pirates to justice. Natural forces are great repositories of power, finding popular representation in the horse, a beast highly significant to both Slavs and Russians as a symbol of time. An ox, reindeer or horse, attached to the pole star, forever turns the mill of heavens above, shifting the seasons upon the earth beneath it. Hence the importance of Sampo and Grotte in mythological literary traditions. The horse superbly epitomises this otherworldly quality of time in all realms, of the living and the dead. The golden Sun chariot of Trundholm[124] is a fine example of this principle, of the movement of celestial objects representing the passage of time. War and winter herald the season of prophecy, of the spirits. Many localised deities had generic and taboo names, sacred noa names that remain unknown to us, presenting another mystery locked in time.

As Eurasian people leaning into an Iranian perspective, the Slavic world is enriched by elemental deities of the celestial regions who abide above them, represented by a reverence for an overall sky deity. The earth they occupy is represented by its ritual community (khorovod), inhabited with animals who thrive amongst the plants, trees, forests, and rivers, and shared by other manifest elementals and lesser spirits of this plane.[125] The Underworld beneath them is where the souls of dead ancestors dwell; this realm holds all the chthonic powers of life and death, moisture and generation. All three levels here relate to the axis mundi, a sacred pillar often in the form of a world tree or mountain. As deities of all worlds, they represent the vertical embodiment and mediation of the three worlds (Heaven, Earth and the Underworld), that in turn reflect the three social functions studied by Dumézil – sacerdotal (priests), martial (warriors) and economic (farmers). A clear parallel certainly occurs within a popular Scandinavian cosmology as relayed in *Rígsþula* or *Rígsmál*,[126] where an

---

124. Nordic Bronze Age (c. 1700 BCE to 500 BCE) possibly c.1400 BCE, though more conservative estimates place it around 900 BCE. Found in a peat bog on the island of Zealand, Denmark. 125. Including those of waters (*mavka* and *rusalka*), forests (*lisovyk*), fields (*polyovyk*), of households (*domovoi*), those of illnesses, luck and human ancestors. For example, *Leshii* is an important woodland spirit who distributed food to the hungry and assigns prey to hunters, but was later regarded as a deity of flocks and herds. 126. The *Lay of Rígr* is an Eddaic poem, preserved in a 14th-century manuscript (AM 242 fol., the *Codex Wormianus*). The identification of *Rígr* with *Heimdallr* is based on the first two lines of the Eddaic poem *Völuspá*. As an ancestor, or kinsman of humankind, this role is perhaps more appropriate for Óðinn, in which case, it is possible that the prose introduction was added by the compiler to conform it to the opening of *Völuspá*. See Appendices I and II.

Óðinic figure, named as Heimdallr (meaning spirit of all worlds) generates three human orders through a character named *Rígr*.

Slavic spirituality eventually merged Indo-European patriarchal themes with pre-Indo-European (Old European) matrifocal themes, as attested through a widespread and enduring devotion to *Mati syra zemlya /Mata syra zjemlja* (Damp Mother Earth). *Mokoš*,[127] an East Slavic fertility spirit of the marshlands, widely revered in the regions immediately north of the Black Sea, appears cognate with the Finno-Ugric, *Moksha*. Both *Moksha* and *Mokoš*, share qualities that suggest a close correlation with *Mati syra zeml'a/ Mata syra zjemlja*. Mokoš originates in mokosi, mokryi, meaning moist, so is well suited to her domain in the rich marshlands and bogs. She is the wet, strong, spotless one, the damp mother of the mound. The earth nourishes the living, and receives the dead. Female breast-shaped stones found in the earth are revered in her honour. Her significance is less keenly felt in the comparative mythology of Scandinavia, but is fully appreciated throughout Fennoscandia. Germanic peoples maintained an affinity with Nerthus and the Mothers. If we look beneath the surface, we will find the characteristics attributed to the Eddaic constructions of a Norse pantheon.

In fact, encouraged by this long-standing association between the supreme Proto-Slavic goddess *Mokoš*, and *Mati syra zeml'a*, the recent discovery of two roughly hewn figurative stones in Croatia, have been tentatively identified as 'Baba' stones. Baba has long been associated with *Mokoš* in Slavic folklore, but this would make these stones part of only a handful of actual representations of this otherwise elusive figure of pre-Christian Slavic Cosmology. A 16th-Century map from the Vienna Archives depicts one Baba drawn as a pillar and a monolith.[128] Votive offerings of fruit, wheat and oil were left upon these stones as a gift for the Baba to procure "good pasture, [and the] fertility of earth, livestock and infertile women."[129] In all cases, these stones are

---

127. *Mokoš* was the only female deity whose idol was erected by Vladimir the Great in his sanctuary at Kiev (Kyiv), along with statues named by others as *Perun, Simar'gl, Khors, Dažbog* and *Stri'bog*. The latter three represent the Iranian element in the ancient Slavic pantheon. See: Ivanits, 1989: 19 **128.** Jelka Vince Pallua. "A Newly Discovered Figurative Representation of the Mythical Baba – "Old Baba Vukoša" in St. Mary's Church of Gracišce in Istria." In Sacralization of Landscape and Sacred Places. (Proceedings of the 3rd International Scientific Conference of Mediaeval Archaeology of the Institute of Archaeology Zagreb, 2nd and 3rd June 2016). Edited by Juraj Belaj, Marijana Belaj, Siniša Krznar, Tajana Sekelj Ivancan and Tatjana Tkalcec. (Zbornik Institutaza, Arheologiju, Serta Instituti Archaeologici, Knjiga Volume 10, 2018): 105-115 **129.** Ibid.

THE SACRED ISLE OF RÜGEN 275

true shrines, sited near to, or around sacred water sources that sprang from holes in the damp earth. Folkloric remnants assert that bad luck befell those who moved shrines erected for her offerings. Due to their environment, many of the stones are slimy to the touch, so we must not forget that both water and humidity establish the perfect precondition for fertility.

As the primal mother, *Mokoš* is "'Mistress at the Gates' who stands at the crossing point from one area to another, from the celestial to the chthonic world, from life to death, summer to winter."[130] Her liminality adds to her ubiquitous virtue. Until the middle of the 20th century, these stones were still the focus of clandestine rituals, undertaken by women anxious about their own fertility. Again, it is interesting that all these epithets are finally being acknowledged as descriptors for those virtues, and not actual names. She is literally, the old, damp, fecund mother earth. Digging and ploughing was forbidden on certain times of the year to honour her. The earth was called upon to witness oaths, marriages, resolve disputes, and declare land rights (boundary marking). At such events portions of earth were again consumed to show the sincerity of all participants in oath taking ceremonies, as noted above. Flower garlands attached to poles, link the sky to the earth. Mokoš, the Damp (Mother) Earth and *Dažbog*, the bright sky (Father) appear to be genuine Slavic spirits. Mokoš is typically represented in the company of the Simurgh, a mythical creature of Iranian origin, adding further support to her origins there. In Novgorod, she was revered as the patron of spinners, childbirth, animals, the moon, and rain. Her basic forms shift with the needs of each geographical location, environment and cultural needs of the people revering her.

The (damp) 'Mother Earth' is the figure given the highest acclaim in surviving folk customs, celebrated near rivers and streams, where her effigies in revivalist traditions are often rolled into the water during the Spring Rites. The legend of *Mokoš* survived into the 20th century as the protector of women and sheep, from birth, and through their own birthing processes. As a minor female household spirit (domovoi) she punished women for violating prohibitions on spinning. The Church admonished women who asked for her help in household chores, accusing them saying: *"Did you not go to Mokoš?"*[131] Her head is disproportionately large, as are her long arms, the better to spin flax, which she does by night as the household sleeps. Her strange image is

---

130. Ibid. **131.** Joanna Hubbs. Mother Russia: The Feminine Myth in Russian Culture. (Indiana University Press, 1993). **132.** Hubbs, 1993.

preserved in embroidery, represented as a woman with uplifted hands, and flanked by two plough horses. Sometimes, Mokoš is shown with male sexual organs, [132] not as an hermaphrodite, but to emphasise her ability (in nature and in spirit) to possess, command, and control male potency. Male virility is very much in her gift. Rusalka, a female spirit whose mythology is of heterogeneous origin, was first welcomed, then banished from the fields and forests, by making a doll which at the end of the festivities was ritually torn apart in the green fields after the harvest.

EARTH AND SKY:
AN ETERNAL HARMONY

The Early Christian denial of the divinisation of the Mother Earth spirit was due to St. Aurelius Augustin's refutation of Varro's symbolic-naturalistic interpretation of Mother Earth. Augustin was keen to attribute such reverence to the fructifying and creative aspects of the earth, pointing out how these functions generated the diverse names 'Mother Earth' is known by.[133] In the contrivance of a Southern Slavic Pantheon, Helmold's *Chronica Slavorum*, c.1170, cites the celestial Siwa (Živa) as the divine female element for Polabian Slavs. However, the (Russian) *Chronicle of Nestor*, composed at least a century later, favours the terrestrial *Mokoš*.[134] The archaic relationship enjoined between *Mokoš*, as the moist (mother) earth, and the divine sky spirit (of thunder and lightning), is exemplary, appearing consistently across the northern regions of Europe, the Altai, Siberia and the Arctic.[135]

Unsurprisingly, her role became fully absorbed by the Cult of Mary, as mother of god, as intermediary, and as confessor for each and every one of her children – the human race. Given that the people of the Balkan regions and of Russia still hold a particular devotion to the Theotokos – divine Mother, it is not insignificant that the Pope (re)dedicated these regions to Mary. Throughout the Balkans, Vid

---

133. Augustin's body of work, The City of God [De civitate Dei], Book VII, 24 (Concerning the Surnames of Tellus and their Significations), contains his response to claims made by Varro concerning correspondences between various deities and their virtues. Amongst Varro's views is an error relating to the etymology of the last theonym: Lat. Vesta, Grk. Hestia, which actually means hearth, not fire directly. In this instance, this sacred aspect of fire has its roots in the Indo-European root ves, to burn. See: Marjana Marjanic. "The Dyadic Goddess and Duotheism in Nodilo's The Ancient Faith of the Serbs and the Croats." In, Studia Mythologica Slavica 6 (2015):181 DOI:10.3986/sms.v6i0.1783 See also: Saint Augustine. The City of God Against The Pagans. 2-3 (Loeb Classical Library, 1957). **134.** Marjanic, 2015. **135.** Roman Jakobson. "Slavic Mythology." In, Funk & Wagnalls Standard Dictionary of Folklore, Mythology and Legend, Volume Two J-Z. Edited by Maria Leach. (Funk & Wagnalls, 1950): 1025-1028

(Vit)¹³⁶ appears in the alternative name Ivan/Ive in the Midsummer carols that honour the Young (*Božić*)/Sun. As the waxing January Sun peaks at Midsummer, *Božic* asserts full strength in his theriomorphosis of the wolf provider (vuk hranitelj), celebrated in the customs of the wolfmen (vucari or carojicari), who carry an effigy of him along with his mother (the hag), the damp mother earth.

*Vid is the epicentral protagonist of the great divine theophany throughout the calendrical year, the androcentric focus, shifting all emphasis of her purpose to the subsidiary position. A perspective heavily ingrained in all Christian and male academia ever since.*¹³⁷

There is an evident dichotomy here where the pre-Christian Slavic beliefs preserved in the archaeology, reveal an ancient pre-Indo-European image of agriculture, and of creation. Being both matrifocal and matrilinear in culture, it is a notion that runs contra to ideas relating to Slavic paganism, as testified in the chronicles by Christian missionaries that assert masculine, androcentric deities of Indo-European origin.¹³⁸ A careful study of the early Slavic personification of the divine female entity as the dormant, winter earth, confirms her primary status suffered no diminishment or degradation, much as she did under transitional faiths that promulgated a male genetrix, wherein the female element became the locus of all sin, evil and the creatrix of monsters. This negative quality is paralleled in *The Eddas* where the destructive offspring of Loki (in female form) echoes the titanic progeny of Gaia and Tiamat who inculcate apocalyptic events.¹³⁹ Formed within subsequent literary traditions based in those misogynist chronicles of the medieval clergy, these perceptions are so ingrained in our modern culture, many accept without question, a hierarchical male pantheon of god-forms in historical paganism.

According to Tacitus the (Germanic) Mother Earth/ Nertha (Nerthum, id est, Terram mater)¹⁴⁰ was revered as the moving force behind all things, whose Island shrine is analogous to that of Svetovit on the Island of Rügen, and may even refer to it, as per the Suevian peoples. Among the Germanic peoples, the reverence for Nerthus¹⁴¹

---

136. A version of Svetovit. **137.** Christian priests and missionaries' woeful lack of knowledgeable motherhood and obstetrics, led them to condemn all polymorphic fertility cults. See: Marjanic, 2015. **138.** Gimbutas, 1971: 354 **139.** Diverse and multiple names exist for the Vedic feminine spiritual force to convey her supremacy in all things, and each name refers only to an aspect of her innumerable virtues, from the terrible to the benign. **140.** Tacitus, Germania. Translated by J.G.C. Anderson. (Bristol Classical Press, 1998).

as the damp Mother Earth may later have translated to The Cult of the Matrones under Roman influences, and is therefore relative to the Slavic appreciation and reverence for the (damp) Earth Mother. Her dynamic synergy with the sky father informs the basis of Indo-European cosmologies upon which the Germanic and Scandinavian beliefs were structured.[142] In the framework of Scandinavian and Germanic mythology, a confusing triad of theonymic dualities exists in Wodan, Óðinn and his associated spouses: Frau Gode-Wode/Freja, Freyja/ Frea, respectively, where all female roles relate empathically to Jord and Fjorgyn as the damp (mother) Earth, conflating with several 'male' earth figures in: Njorðr/ Yngve/Freyr and Fjorgynn who each bear the attributes of a fructifying earth.[143] Gender changes according to culture and interpretation. To this bewildering array of variances, we find that Perun is[144] sometimes associated with Zvarog/Svarog.[145] As poetic synonyms for land or the earth, the Norse Fjorgyn,[146] Fjorgynn and the Old Norse Jorð, are used in skaldic poems that feature in *The Eddas*. The first, Fjorgyn,[147] is described as the mother of Þórr;[148] a second and separate occurrence presents a masculine form, Fjorgynn, who is described as the father of Frigg, the wife of Óðinn. While some scholars believe Fjorgyn and Fjorgynn may have represented a

---

141. Angrboða may be a composite of *angw- water (cf. Lat. aqua) and boða - abode, therefore a cognate of Moksha and Nerthus? 142. See: Appendix I 143. Fru Gode-Wode (Vida) and Jord (the Earth appear in the Edda. There is another wife – Rind (Rindr), whose name means bark, that may parallel the Southern Slavic (Croatian) Grozda, another possible version of the (black fertile) Mother Earth. Since Rind is also the wife of Óðinn (the universal father), she can be regarded as the universal mother. See: Marjanic, 2015: 181-204 144. It is claimed that Perun and Svarog are two different names of the same tutelary figure, though some East Slavic tribes perceived Svarog as heaven's fire and of fire in general, rather than of war and thunder. 145. Svarog is associated with the military, smithcraft, and with fire (of the household) through Ognebog, and of the sun as Xors Dazhbog. The Indo-European root of the name is *swer, to speak, is related to *wer, to close, defend and protect. These may be various forms - tribal, metaphysical, or geographical - of the same tutelary figure, or avatars through sons or brothers.' 146. Guus Kroonen. Etymological Dictionary of Proto-Germanic. (Brill, 2013):136 Fjorgyn stems from Proto-Germanic *fergunja, meaning mountain, in the sense of a raised wooded area or escarpment. Alternatively, It may represent the feminine equivalent of *ferga - god. This latter term may be related to the PIE *per-kwun-iy (the realm of Perkwunos, i.e., the wooden mountains). Fjorgyn is cognate with the Gothic fairguni, the Old English firgen, both meaning mountain, and with the Old High German Firgunnea (the Ore Mountains). These terms infer the Ironwoods as the primal lands inhabited by female Jotnar. 147. Mallory, 1989: 129. Suggests a linguistic connection between Norse Fjorgynn, the Lithuanian god Perkinas, the Slavic god Perun and, perhaps, the Vedic rain god Parjanya, through IEP fergunja. 148. See: Völuspá and Hárbarðsljóð 56.

divine pair of which little information has survived, along with figures such as the theorized Ull/r and Ullin, Njorðr and Nerthus, and Freyr and Freyja,[149] this popular view nonetheless remains subjectively speculative, and not a little contrived.

Cosmological dualisms concerning the opposing qualities of day with night, and summer with winter, light and heat are often defined as male, where the dark and cold are invariably female, sterile, malevolent and annihilating.

These themes are reflected in the folkloric customs of modern-day revivalists who utilise the psychological re-evaluation of conditioned duality to ferment and conclude the passing of the seasons in relation to the rhythms of the earth and of man. Since Augustine, female cycles are ethically categorised as evil, in constant opposition to the benevolence of the male cycle of the (sun/son).'This polarisation denies the natural duality of both.[150] [my emphasis]

A remarkably detailed and unique example of a female monolith in Grobnik near Rijeka, of a grotesque female figure with broad hips and hypertrophied breasts, is described as a stone hag, possibly linked to the 'steatopygous Palaeolithic Venuses,' and thus linked indirectly to the damp *Mokoš*.[151] However, although I do not doubt a continuity of cult regarding the damp mother earth through the Palaeolithic to the Bronze Age and beyond, I believe this stone figure, like several others better relates to the belief in anasyrma, that is, apotropaic magics as represented by western folkloric figures known as 'Sheela na Gigs.' They no doubt merged in Christian chronicles and in folklore based in those misrepresentations of them.

Island sanctuaries were the ideal sites for ritual activity and celebration. And this is where the original bonded forms of sky and earth, once unified in the waters, became separated, then divided, then completely polarised. A Manichean influence is introduced through the Vandals, as noted by Helmold, who interprets their dualist philosophy in demonic terms. The Earth Mother, in various forms of *Mokoš*, too strong to eradicate, retained her role, albeit much diminished and sandwiched between the extremes of a supreme male spirit of the sky, and a now tangential male of the chthonic regions, who like *Zembog*, the earth giver associated with war, fertility, divination and abundance, appears to be a form of Veles.[152] These three forms were represented

---

149. H. R. Ellis Davidson. *Gods and Myths of Northern Europe* (Penguin Books, 1990): 106, 109, 111. **150.** Marjanic, 2015: 181-204. **151.** Jelka Vince-Pallua. "History and Legend in Stone – to Kiss the Baba." *Studia ethnologica Croatica* 7/8 No. 1 (1995/1996): 281-292

on the sacred tribal totems, the wooden posts erected in numerous outdoor regional shrines. Sharing similar concepts as the Norse and Balts, Slavs developed a cosmology that imagined the world as a giant oak tree (a World Tree), within which everything existed. In later centuries, the sacred pillar, or axis mundi, the mill shaft or pole that turns the universe, was represented by a three-headed figure, where the chthonic Veles, sustains the entire structure.[153] What is evident in this extension of the pillar into an anthropomorphic representation is the stamp of human authority upon a (Universal) celestial symbol. At this point that it became woven into all notions of kingship (as a divine attribution), an imposition of rulership, a manifest expression of the right of ownership and the right to rule its surrounding territory. This significator takes cultural form in other sacred trees and columns: bile tree, gardh tree, Irminsul, Yggdrasil, even Frodi's Mill – the Grotte. Oak trees were a sacred representation of this status, often serving as the original meeting place for assemblies and inaugurations.

A key tenet of Slavic mythology is the dynamic relationship between the thunderous spirit of the sky and his chthonic counterpart, who are depicted in folktales as bound in an eternal battle in the forms of a raptorial bird and a serpent/snake/dragon, respectively – essentially himself as the ouroboros. Originally a forest spirit and protector of wild animals, who appeared almost exclusively as a bear, the horned Veles was deemed capable of shape shifting into other types of animals, namely domestic cattle,[154] revealing the merging of traditions associated with hunting, herding and pastoralism. "The Slavic Veles is a compound name: Vel-es. The second part relates to Asura as well as to the Old Celtic god Esus, portrayed with a bull's head."[155] Certain traits link him to the Norse Ullr, and to the Vedic Varuna especially, who as a cattle god, shares Veles' propensity to punish miscreants and abjurers with disease.

---

152. The earliest known reference to Veles appears in the Rus'-Byzantine Treaty of 971, as the name the signatories make their vow to.   153. Adrian Ivakhiv. "The Revival of Ukrainian Native Faith." In, Modern Paganism in World Cultures: Comparative Perspectives. Edited by Michael F. Strmiska (ABC-Clio. 2005): 209-239
154. Veles, East Slavs, Rus' – Veless, Weless, Voloss, Woloss, Woles, Wlacie, Wel, and Walgino (Polish) though Weles is now more commonplace. The Book of Veles is dedicated to him. See: Michel Mathieu-Colas. "Dieux slaves et baltes." (PDF) In, Dictionnaire des noms des divinités, (Archive ouverte des Sciences de l'Homme et de la Société, Centre national de la recherche scientifique, 2017) https://web.archive.org/web/20170804140911/http://www.mathieu-colas.fr/michel/Classes/Dieux_slaves_et_baltes.pdf (Accessed 14th August 2021)   155. https://www.gornahoor.net/library/mcclain/BA_EPIC.pdf (Accessed 29th December 2024).

Having a strong cult base around Novgorod, Veles, or Volos is first mentioned in 10th century treaties. He is also the spirit of poetic inspiration and oracular or second sight, as highlighted by his name which comes from the Indo-European root *wel, which implies vision and magical ability. Walgino (Weles) is the name of the patron protector of cattle in Polish tradition.[156] Another name attributed to the animal spirit associated with Veles is Skotibog, which literally means Cattle Giver,[157] the patron of commerce, that is, of wealth and trade, oaths and contracts. Veles is linguistically related to vel – the unseen shades or spirits of the dead. Sorcerers and necromancers adopt names prefixed by this term, the oracular priestess *Veleda* – of the Germanic Bructeri people – is an excellent example of this use. South Slavs regarded Veles specifically as the *Lord of All Wolves*.[158] In the Nart Saga, he is named Tutyr, which is not too far removed from Týr, a figure who has their own association with this remarkable beast. As the king of the animals, the wolf is a divine being, particularly the white wolf. Some tribes considered the wolf to be a distant ancestor. A Türkic ethnogonic myth speaks of an ancestral cave in which the Ashinà were conceived from the mating of their human ancestor with a wolf ancestress.[159]

Though a foe to shepherds and pastoralists, among Eurasian grain farmers and animal husbandmen, wolves were highly revered. Shrines were erected on the land boundaries, where food and offerings were left to encourage the wolves to prowl and repel deer and wild boar who devastated their crops. Wolves were also greatly respected by the *Cuman–Kipchaks*, and they would sometimes howl along with them in commune. The personal bodyguard coterie of the khan were known as the Bori (wolf in Türkic).[160] Several of these early traits were further developed and refined into the features recognisable in the figure we know today as Óðinn, whose attributes closely parallel those of the chthonic Veles. However, attempts to ally Veles to seemingly similar classical forms, would yield a contradictory, inclusive, yet overlapping list of hosts in *Mars, Mercury, Pluto, Hermes and Mercurius*, all no-less problematic than their cognate forms presumed in Óðinn.

Helmold is the first to mention a dark god of ill fate or fortune in the form of Chernobog,[161] who is apparently similar to Zembog.

---

156. Mathieu-Colas, 2017. **157.** Mathieu-Colas, 2017. **158.** Dixon-Kennedy, 1998.
159. Peter Benjamin Golden. "The Conversion of the Khazars to Judaism." In, *The World of the Khazars: New Perspectives. Handbook of Oriental Studies.* Vol. 17. Edited by Peter B Golden, Haggai Ben-Shammai and András Róna-Tas. (Brill, 2007): 123–161
160. Ivanits, 1989: 13-17

EARTH AND SKY 283

Chernobog has a presumed counterpart in a theoretical cosmic duality, represented by Belobog, who does not appear until the 16th century, and then only as a possible hypostasis of good and evil.[162] Figures we imagine as arcane deities or gods, were actually elemental forces that articulated the waxing and waning virtues of light, harmonising the forces of order and chaos by default. Within all planes of being, a host of numinous and holy spirits guide and inform the people who revere them. In both the old and new worlds, ancestors[163] and the spirits of place[164] – both outside and inside the domestic dwellings – maintained their central importance in the seasonal and calendrical devotions of the people throughout the agrarian and herding cycles.

Among Slavic peoples, the Vila (of the same root as Veles[165] pertaining to the forest) are woodland maidens who accompany bogatyr-bogu,[166] bringing abundance and good-fortune. Thirteenth century records describe offerings to these beautiful, strong, naked maidens bearing bows, who could also appear as wolves, horses, falcons, snakes and whirlwinds. Folkloric legends of these battle maidens describe them as the companions of heroes, who dance upon the mountaintops, shooting all who approach them, or engaging them in a dance to the death. They may possibly relate to the mythic forms of Valkyrjur; at the very least, they may have informed or influenced those myths. Various spirits believed to manifest in certain places were revered as numinous and holy; they included springs, rivers, groves, rounded tops of hills and flat cliffs overlooking rivers. These traits reveal the underlying animistic, totemic and shamanic elements of a mythology shared by the peoples of these regions prior to their conversions to the major competing monotheisms of the first millennia.

---

161. An alternative name used by Baltic Slavs for Chernobog, is Tjarnaglofi (Black Head). See: Mathieu-Colas, 2017.   162. In 1538, the Pomeranian chronicler Thomas Kantzow mentioned him in his *Chronicle of Pomerania* in terms of good and bad fate (Order and Chaos). See: Yaroslav Gorbachov. "What Do We Know about *Chernobog and *Belo Bog." In, *Russian History* 44 (2-3)(2017): 209-242 doi: https://doi.org/10.1163/18763316-04402011 (Accessed 29th December 2024).   163. Slavs did not keep genealogical records, kindred was a matter of ethnicity, it could be adopted or married into.   164. These spirits included those of waters (*mavka and rusalka*), forests (*lisovyk*), fields (*polyovyk*), those of households (*domovoi*). See: Evel Gasparini. "Communal-banquets-and-related-practices#ref533502" In, *Encyclopedia Britannica*, December 27, 2024. https://www.britannica.com/topic/Slavic-religion (2024). (Accessed 27th December 2024).   165. *Volos (Veles)* the deific spirit of flocks also possessed an element of justice for the abjuration of oaths.   166. Referring to the divine Other, 'bogatyr' is a term of Buryat origin.

THUNDER SPIRITS

Early in the 6th century, the Byzantine historian Procopius referred to a storm spirit of thunder (*(s)tenh₂) and lightning revered among the ancient pagan Slavs,[167] whose cultic rites were performed in oak groves.[168] Like Tiw (Týr) this great elemental force shared a duty as the overseer of justice, a figure who ensured the maintenance of the right order of things. An awareness of the presence of this spirit was sensed in the atmospheric ions, witnessed in the thunderbolt, heard in the rattle of stones or the bellow of the bull, or the rumbling bleat of the he-goat, and felt in the scoring axe blade. Procopius refers to a certain South Slavic tribe, in De Bello Gothico, noting unwittingly perhaps, that the Slavs maintained no pantheon of gods, but held a singular reverence for the thunder and lightning spirit, seen as the overarching sky father, Deivos, the lord of all, to whom they dedicated the animals killed for celebratory feasts held in his honour, especially the ox.[169]

Helmold (c.1120-1177) attests to this belief in his Chronica Slavorum, whence he describes the Slavic cosmology of a single heavenly lord, supreme over all the lesser (elemental) spirits that govern nature. Represented by the lightning wheel symbols known as thunder marks, (gromovoi znak),[170] they remain popular in Christian Slavic folk crafts, appearing in embroideries, distaffs, jewellery, furniture and roof

---

167. Procopius and Jordanes in the 6th century, sparsely documented some Slavic concepts and practices. **168.** Perun is mentioned in addendums to *The Russian Primary Chronicle*, cited there as having been invoked in two 10th century treaties. Known as Perŭndan in the Polabian language. Known to Western Slavs as Prone, which also appears in Helmold's *Chronica Slavorum*. Polish piorun and Slovak parom denote thunder or lightning. Danish historian Saxo Grammaticus refers to Porenut as Perun's son in his early 13th century account. Perun became St. Elijah (Russian Iliya) post conversion. Communal feasts held on July 20th in honour of Perun or Iliya in modern times. **169.** In Slavic mythology, the highest spirit force is the sky, manifest in the thunder, lightning, storms, rain, law, war, fertility, fire, wind, mountains and oak trees. His attributes are horses, carts, and weapons, first of stone and later with those of metal, specifically the hammer or axe, a bow and arrows. See: Mike Dixon-Kennedy. Encyclopaedia of Russian & Slavic Myth and Legend (USA: ABC-CLIO,1998). **170.** Ivanits, 1989: 17

THUNDER SPIRITS

beams, along with the six petalled (rose) thunder wheel attributed to Rod, and other apotropaic symbols and staves for protection against malefic activity, be it sorcerous or elemental. Cognate with the Russian Rod,[171] this supreme male potency shares the virtues of all variations and manifestations of *Dyeus[172] that relate to a supreme divine spirit, particularly as the celestial (sky), amongst the Balts, Thracians, Phrygians and Indo-Iranians.[173] This figure is the means of wealth, and also the giver of wealth, suggesting a shared concept of the (Germanic) Drihten Lord and of Providence. These are of course, the traits funnelled into the construction of Wodan and Óðinn.

Although no name is attributed to the supreme celestial spirit by Procopius, numerous modern sources repeatedly cite it as Perun, whose name appears only later in medieval curses invoking the pure force of lightning and thunder, to be struck, or taken by that force. Symbolised by the axe, Perun is cognate with the Lithuanian Perkinas, a spirit of thunder. Perun's position as a principal, tutelary figure of the 10th-Century Rus', is considered cognate with many other spirits of thunder and lightning including Zeus, Indra and Þórr. It was believed that thunder bolts passed through the earth, grounding the beneficent force, fertilising and purifying the earth as it penetrated, removing all vestiges of death and barrenness. Iron balls and other shapes, including octagonal stones that initiated the creative designs of the gromovoi znak thunder marks, were lightly buried on the surface of the ground to purposely draw this propitious potency to it (and away from dwellings, animals, livestock and people). This draws a closer parallel between Þórr and Perun, lessening the association between thunder and Óðinn.

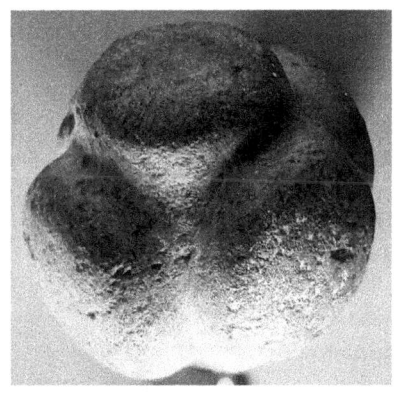

5. Thunder Stones

Drawing thunder naturally, oak trees became a symbol of the god's

---

171. Ivanits, 1989: 18-19 172. The supreme 'celestial' deity, Deivos, is cognate with Sanskrit Deva, Latin Deus, Old High German Ziu and Lithuanian Dievas. Avestan daeva, Old Church Slavonic div; Proto-Indo-European *deiwos (similar to Dyeus). See: Appendix I 173. The stars moon and sun were markers for the seasons; the moon was regarded as male, the sun – female.

manifest force, thus inducing a ban forbidding (Christian) people to sing before oak trees. We may now better understand Helmold's description of the fenced off area surrounding a sacred oak tree that clearly represented a hallowed area where the first spring thunder awakened the earth into productivity, an act so auspicious, that in some places, it was forbidden to place any metal implement into the earth until after this celestial 'marriage' event had occurred, so as not to lessen the force of this awakening. Prudent counsel set this Spring awakening to the later calendrical date of March 25th, better known as Lady Day. Before that time, the damp earth was considered to be pregnant. The grass and plants are then birthed, grow, flower and offer up their potency in their seeds. This expresses a wonderful cyclical relationship between the elements, a purpose linked in folklore that assists an understanding not contradicted by science. Though simplistic, it suggests a more honest and natural propitiatory reverence than the supposed later worship of idols, idols that were later still, anthropomorphised. Animals given or dedicated to the elemental forces, killed for the communal celebratory feasts, were deemed to be full of sacred manna (spiritually present divine blessings). This notion challenges the (all too common) dismissive charge which claims that certain descriptive terms used when relating to such profound actions, are merely a matter of semantics: god/divine spirit; sacrifice/offering; worship/reverence. The actual difference between these semantic terms is an entire opus of theology.[174]

One thunderous vitality was ultimately anthropomorphised in popular belief who has endured centuries of folklore. Depicted in Nordic regions as a mature, red-bearded warrior, a giant almost, who rides a two-wheeled iron chariot harnessed with goats. This iconic image demonstrates certain commonalities with other similar beings, yet cultural distinctions are also apparent. For instance, the Slavic thunder god, rides a fiery horse or sits upon a fiery chariot drawn by swift horses across the skies. The imperative of a popular divine spirit of thunder continued through into the 20th century, overlaid without compromise by Russian Orthodoxy. Slavic custom preserved this 'giant' figure in folklore and tradition. While Jötnar could be enormous, size was not an essential characteristic, equally, some Jötnar are described as bright and beautiful beings, while others are horrifyingly ghoulish. Indeed, the Jötnar are diverse creatures of an older time. As primal beings of

---

174. That these spirits become known and named as gods in later centuries is not in question, only that they were known and named as such prior to conversion.

elemental form, they haunted the vivid imagination of the Viking Age and beyond it, often immersed in romantic metaphor and allegory. The legendary accounts of Þórr's wrestling matches with numerous Jötnar are echoed in the Spring and Midsummer celebrations that honour the Mighty Mace (hammer) and the power of thunder. These customs were remarked upon as late as the 16th century.

Even now it happens from time to time on certain days of the year, that this voice of Perun [a special Novgorodian name for battle-cry] may be heard, and on these occasions the citizen suddenly run together and lash each other with ropes, and such a tumult arises therefrom, that all the effort of the governor can scarcely assuage it.[175]

Other folk customs relate to the Scandinavian legends of Þórr; for example, a mid-19th-century Russian writer recorded a superstitious custom shared with him by a Novgorodian fisherman concerning the protections granted by the patron spirit of thunder, from the treacherous serpents of the deep waters.[176] The traditions surrounding Ran are very similar to this. According to the Icelandic sagas of the late Middle Ages, Ran retrieves the drowned within her hall at the bottom of the Sea, where they are welcomed and fed, providing she was given coin at the onset of their sea-faring ventures. Because her realm is merely an antechamber to Hel's realm, the drowned are thereafter dispersed accordingly – given up to the ancestral spirits who claim them. The observance of the Russian legend is evident even into the 20th century, whereby coins were dropped into the river Volhov while navigating the Peryn peninsula by boat.[177] Naturally, the names of many rivers of the Slavic regions of Russia share the same root as those of northern Europe that found their way into Celtic legends and myth as spirits of the lands and waterways, often as regenerative forces under the guise of mother or father. In many cases, the sun, sky and day are adopted into the range of the thunderer, just as the waters and night are absorbed by the land. This belief stretches from the Tungus of Siberia to the Celtic speaking people of Ireland.[178]

Since Neolithic times, the squared off, bolt-like hammer/axe is

---

175. Sigmund Freiherr von Herberstein. Notes upon Russia: Being a translation of the earliest account of that country, entitled Rerum Moscoviticarum Commentarii. 2 [1549] (the original document, translated). (London: Hakluyt Society, 1852): 26 **176.** Þórr's legend is that he wrestles with all forms of Jotnar; here, this legend is akin to that of Þórr wrestling with the Midgarðr serpent. **177.** Vsevolod Miller. "Materialy dla istorii bylinnyh suzhetov." *Etnograficeskoe Obozrenie* 4 (Wydawnictwo Uniwersytetu Marii Curie-Skłodowskiej, 1891):129-31 (in Russian). **178.** See overlesf

identified with the thunderbolt, not dissimilar in fact to Indra's vajra. Axes were called strela, meaning arrow, inferring the force of the thunder bolt (akin to the Saxon elf bolts). Lightning bolts manifested as stones and stone arrows. According to folk beliefs, fulgurites, belemnites and other prehistoric stone, bone and flint tools found in the ground, are remains of the manifest weapons of the thunder spirit of the sky, referred to in modern folklore by a variety of names including: thunderstones, Perun's arrow, firestones, devil's finger and god's finger. If found, they were used in apotropaic magics to repel lightning strikes (as noted above), upon dwellings, people and cattle, but also against disease and blight in the crops. In addition, the strela repelled ill-fortune, bringing good fortune to babies and newlyweds. The popularity of a thunder cult is also widely attested through the artefacts, traditions and toponyms found amongst the Slavic, Baltic and Finno-Ugric peoples.

Þórr was known to the Finns as *Ukko* and to the Sámi as: *Thora Galles* – (T)*Horagalles*, meaning thunder spirit. Other names include: 'Thor-man,' *Grandfather, Bajanolmmai, Dierpmis/Tiermis, Pajonn Tordöm.*). Rather than Mjölnir (generally perceived as a mace, or hammer), the Sámi know this 'thunder weapon' as *Wetschera* or *Ajeke veccera*, which means 'grandfather's hammer.' Tiermes has another hammer, the first induces thunder and lightning, the second neutralises it. The Lithuanian *Perkunas*,[179] like *Þórr* and *Taranis*, is armed with arrows and an axe or hammer which behaves very much in the same manner as Þórr's Mjölnir, in that if thrown at evil spirits or people, it returns to his hand. Þórr's virtue to bless or curse is attributed to the magical virtue of Mjölnir. Like *Perun*, the Indo-European Latvian Perkun bears a similar weapon named Milna. Both weapons seem to be cognate with several other Eurasian and Slavic terms for thunder and lightning rooted in archaic Anatolian and Luwian forms. Over time, these became the numerous names we now use in association with the various mythic

---

178. The very name of the Dagda, Celtic *Dago-dewos* means good spirit, but also good day since día is rooted in *deiwo-s, meaning the light of day and beneficence. See: John T. Koch, Raimund Karl, Antone Minard, and Simon Ó Faoláin. (Eds.) "An Atlas for Celtic Studies:Aarchaeology And Names In Ancient Europe And Early Medieval Ireland, Britain and Brittany." Celtic Studies Publications 12. (Oxbow Books, 2007): 553   **179.** Perkwunos (Baltic), Perkunas (Lithuanian), and other similar cognates amongst the Slavic peoples are reconstructed titles that may share a common derivative in the PIE. term for thunder, i.e., the root *perkwu is associated with the spirit of the oak tree, possibly through lightning strikes, but in Proto-Slavic per-, acquired the literal meaning –to strike or slay. See: Gimbutas, 1971: 376

THUNDER SPIRITS 289

gods of thunder who possess magical weapons that destroy and create, revive and slaughter at the will of the divine spirit wielding them. These include: Taranis, Indra, Zeus, Rimmon and Teshoub. The ability to vanquish hostile forces of this and the Otherworld and conversely, to bring the fructifying rains, to clear the stormy skies and awaken the dormant earth with thunderbolts, made this spirit a popular favourite for farmers, but also fishermen, surprisingly. Therefore, we may now better appreciate why Þórr is revered by both fishermen and farmers, and why each craft developed the basic wedge (hammer) amulet into stylised anchors and plough frogs accordingly.

In addition to the wolf and certain birds of prey, Ob-Ugrian peoples of Siberia exhibit distinctive and anthropomorphic traits in their beliefs relating to the bear, who is both totem animal and guardian spirit. Perceived of as not only an animal, but also as human in reverted form, he is a bogatyr or 'son' of a divine spirit, maintaining at all times the special relationship the bear shares with humankind.[180] The volkash and bogatyr were divinely imbued shamans known for their ability to become animals and winds. Although a strong Iranian influence is suggested in the Avestan term for divine spirit - baga, which translated as the Slavic bog, there was a marked overlay across Europe in this period of a patriarchal presence, with its attendant warrior ethic. Steppe shamans of the Ukraine adopted the zoomorphic figure of a man-like dragon, the Zmei-bogatyr or serpent hero who appears in the heroic literature of the Kievan Rus' to combat the various elemental Zmei, for example, the polycephalic Zmey Gorynych that typically had three to twelve heads.[181] For the Türkic peoples of the Mongolian Steppe, a similar heroic figure, was known as the Tugarin Zmeyevich. The Bulgarian Lamia dwells in the marshy, muddy beds of the seas and lakes, or sometimes in mountainous caverns, or tree holes, and can stop the supply of water to the human population, demanding sacrificial offerings to undo its deed. The serpentine Lamia, bringer of drought, was considered the adversary of St. Ilya (Elijah) or a benevolent Zmei.[182] Benevolent Zmei are the land guardians, who also protect its peoples against intruders, foreign adversaries and attack, from elemental and other spirit forces of the Otherworld. Chudo Yudo is one of the guardians of the Water of Life and Death whose name was traditionally invoked in times of drought. Able to ride a

---

180. Anisimov, 1963. **181.** Joseph A. McCullough. *Dragon-slayers: From Béowulf to St. George.* (Osprey Publishing, 2013): 67 **182.** Mercia MacDermott. Bulgarian Folk Customs. (Jessica Kingsley Publishers, 1998): 63-4

horse and assume human-like forms, this spirit also has the ability to re-grow missing heads lost in combat, echoing the virtues of several classical and eastern mythic monsters.[183] From these spirits, the Slavic gods took form, and from those influences, the pagan deities of Russia entered the realm of folklore as supposed historical figures worshipped by the Rus' princes.

Influences from the Rus' impacted the beliefs and culture of Norway and Sweden especially. A primary example of this is Týr, whom I believe is neither Norse, nor Germanic in origin, despite common associations with Tiw/Twi/Tig and all other medieval Germanic derivatives. It is my view that Týr as a name/word/title, is initially of Slavic origin and sourced by the Rus'. Viking trade and admixture would have brought this word and its significance to Norway and Sweden as early as the 8th century. Hundreds of years later, Snorre appears to have merged the Slavic, Turkic (Hittie and Luwian) and Germanic titles, names and meanings to construct a 'Norse' deity he refers to as Týr.

183. The term may not be a name for a specific type of dragon at all, but rather a fanciful term for a generic monster, similar in fact, to the Þurz or Jotnar challenged by Þunar/Þórr.

GODS OF THE PRIMARY RUSSIAN CHRONICLE

In much the same way that the ancient titular rulers of Rome were all hailed as Ceasar, the pagan monarch-priests of Rus', Igor and other kings may have claimed the hereditary title of helgu, (ON). Some have therefore proposed that the 'Helgu' (meaning holy), who waged war in the 940s on Byzantium, as a nebulous and indeterminate figure, could be one of the archons of the Rus' cited in *De administrando imperio*, and possibly even one of the "fair and great princes" referred to in the two Russo-Byzantine treaties of 911 and 944. It is even possible that Oleg is not only this warring prince, but is also the Old Norse chieftain known as Helgi (who in true literary form, may be a figure based on Oleg). Helgu is an ambiguous title may mask the true religious affiliations of its bearer.[184] In fact, Oleg and Igor may have been nominal Christians. Although the names, Rurik, Oleg and Igor are attested amongst the late 10th-Century and 11th-Century Rurikids, it was uncommon for specific blood relationships between early minor Rurikid princes of the Rus' to be recorded in The Russian Primary Chronicle. Moreover, only the first four princes ruling Ancient Rus' had Scandinavian names: Riurik †879 (Hrørikr), Oleg †912 (Helgi), Igor´†945 (Ingvarr), Olga †969 (Helga).[185] From the second part of the 10th century (from the son of Igor and Olga Svyatoslav), the Russian princes had either Slavic, or later Christian names (being a requisite of baptism). Scandinavian ethnicity is confirmed in Eastern Europe by the consistent appearance of a variety of domestic implements inscribed with rúna during the Viking Age. In some locations, their sojourns were no doubt temporary, but in others, more permanent, as traders, merchants or mercenaries.

To assert his authority over the East Slavic areas, prince Vladimir proclaimed Kyiv a political and religious centre of uncompromising

---

184. Georgy Vernadsky. *Kievan Rus'*. (Yale University Press, 1977): 41 **185.** K. Düwel. "Runic Inscriptions In Eastern Europe." In, *Biblioteka Nauki*. https://bibliotekanauki.pl 2013. (Accessed 12th December 2023)

strength and consolidation.[186] After wresting the rulership of the Rus,' in Kyiv, Vladimir's first centralising reform was to unify the disparate idiosyncratic folk practises of a polyethnic population. This was as much shrewd as it was politic. Throughout his subsequent marches and campaigns to secure his kingdom, Prince Vladimir the Great erected pagan shrines to honour local land spirits. *The Russian Primary Chronicle* claims that the prince supposedly erected wooden statues of 'pagan gods' in Kyiv to mirror a shrine to his own tutelary patron at Peryn Hill at Novgorod, a sacred peninsula near Veliky[187] in 980. The Christian author of *The Russian Primary Chronicle* claims that during the eight years Vladimir the Great observed his reformed pagan cult, offerings and sacrifices were made beside the bases of many wooden idols, that supposedly included men,[188] some of whom were said to be Roman Catholic members of the Varangian guards he'd captured. Local spirits were observed by the common people, notably Veles who had a shrine in the merchant's district. Placing items of armoury and weaponry was however, a commonplace practise amongst Slavs. This form of tribute is not dissimilar to that of the Roman *spolia opima* tradition.[189]

Remembering that this Chronicle wrote about events that supposedly happened three to four hundred years earlier, it refers to the so-called idols by the following contrived (compound) Slavic names: Stri'bog,[190] *Khors, Dažbog*,[191] *Simar'gl*,[192] and *Mokoš*.[193] The Chronicle adds that *Perun* was the tallest and most beautiful of all the pagan idols, bearing a silver face mask with a golden moustache; a description that sounds like an actual mask, or possibly a masked helm. The Chronicle

---

186. A nomadic Turko-Tartar tribe known as Pechenegs (Patzinaks) moved onto the Steppe from the area between the Volga and the Yaik, driving the Magyars from the Don into the Danube basin by 860. In the decades following the Pechenegs' first contact with the princes of Kyiv in 915, they became a significant threat to the Kievan principality. **187.** Noted for its medieval pagan shrine complex, and for its well-preserved monastery. **188.** An idol to Perun was set beside the Volkhov river where the people of Novgorod presented their sacrifices. See: Hazzard Cross and Sherbowitz-Wetzor, 1953: 94   **189.** Oates, 2022   **190.** Of the East Slavs and Rus'. Strybog/Strzybog (Polish), also *Stribogu/ Stribog*, which literally means – Wealth Spreader. Spirit of winds and storms.   **191.** The Sun – *Xors Dazhbog*, was sometimes separated as related deities - *Khors* and *Dažbog*. (Old East Slavic, East Slavs, Rus') Iranian mythology placed great emphasis on the cult of the Sun, influencing how the Slavs perceived their own generic solar deity, Gerovit (modern-day Yarilo), whose heroic images were placed in every village shrine.   **192.** *Semargl, Simarg, Simargle, Simarigl, Simariglu* – Old East Slavic; *Sinnargual, Simnarguel* – East Slavs, Rus'. This draconian figure was influenced by the Persian *Simurgh*, the winged griffin, an image borrowed from 1st century Scytho-Sarmatian overlords. Semargl identifies as an aspect of *Perun*, but is also related to sailors as a figure of fortune and drinking. See: Gimbutas, 1971: 164-166   **193.** East Slavic earth mother. See: Ivanits, 1989): 13

seems in error here however. In the cases of the archeologically attested Slavic pagan shrines at Arkona, Garz, and Stettin, only one image was found in each shrine. This fact is intimated in Vladimir's mission, stated above, that all spirits and manifestations of thunder, lightning and the sky, would henceforth be known only in the singular form, to the exclusion of all other variants, named by the Chronicle's redactor as Perun, revealing yet another example of retrospective identification.

However, Perun is not mentioned directly in any of the records of Western Slavic traditional religion, merely a reference to an over-arching belief in a god of the heavens, mentioned by Helmold in his *Chronica Slavorum*, writing six centuries after Procopius, who'd observed the same proclivities amongst the Slavs. Rod, meaning heaven, had been the earliest supreme deific figure reflecting a simpler cosmology of earth and sky in union. Localised variants remained unnamed, possibly even forbidden amongst themselves. It would seem that the cult of Perun ironically superseded that of Rod, becoming popular only after prince Vladimir centralised former beliefs and ritual practises around a supposed pantheon of five icons to extend his power, authority and tribute in 980, displacing Rod completely. Just eight years later in 988, Prince Vladimir chose a new direction for the Rus' in Kiev. Remember, in the process of his religious reforms, he'd consolidated the contrived hierarchy of Russian pagan 'gods,' into a single deity, presumed by many to be Perun. A kapishche (pagan temple/shrine) was built to house his effigy near Lake Ilmen.

Evidence of Vladimir's staged religious reforms were discovered in 1951-2, when an archaeological expedition revealed the remains of a well-preserved sacred site complex beneath Vladimir's later 10th -century temple shrine that had clearly displaced a former pagan shrine on that site.[194] A large circular shrine located on the peak of Peryn Hill[195] (in the centre of Peryn Islet), was encompassed by a shallow ditch which had eight recessed bulges (apses) aligned to the points of the compass.[196] In the circle's centre, a 65cm hole provided a sizable socket slot for the wooden idol that was once erected there. Pieces of putrefied wood were found inside the hole.[197] The shrine's octagonal shape reflects a generic conformity to sacred site construction, where 8 represents the divine order. This overall plan suggests a symbolic

---

194. For Rod, See: Rybakov, 1987: 257   **195.** Vladimir Sedov. *Tserkov Rozhdestva Bogorodicy v Peryni: novgorodskiy variant bašneobraznogo hrama*, (in Russian). (Severny Palomnik, 2009): 93-8   **196.** Rybakov, 1987: 427   **197.** Sedov, 2009: 98-99 According to the *Novgorod First Chronicle,* the idol was hacked down, leaving only the base of the idol inside the hole.

association with the number nine. Indeed, in subsequent folklore, Perun, is said to be one of nine brothers, or the father of eight sons, making nine versions of Perkunas.

The excavations confirm the descriptions found in the chronicle that refers to several bonfires set around a central totemic post/pillar. Charcoal heaps reveal that fires were lit at all eight compass points and that the wood burned was oak. The charcoal heap in the eastern section, is significantly larger, indicating that fires burned here for longer, possibly at sunrise every day, rather than the weekly, or monthly ceremonial events the other fires related to. There is a clear celestial event here, marking lunar, solar or stellar risings. The excavations showed that the bonfires and the ditch were buried when the shrine was ravaged in ancient times. According to folklore, Perun's spouse was the sun, whom he shared with the chthonic Veles each night as she sank below the horizon. Again, this depicts the displacement of a female to a male for the earth's elemental virtue. Slavic peoples fused the personified Sun with the risen Christ, reserved in custom in modern times as a greeting to the rising sun, even in church.

In the elemental sense of the male generative force that manifests as thunder, Perun is related to the Germanic *Þórr* (Thunar) and to other Indo-European thunder deities.[198] Unfortunately, despite the habitual reference to *Perun* as the pagan East Slavic god of thunder and lightning, and a cognate of the Norse *Þórr* – imported by the Varangians – there is actually no evidence for a native Slavic deity of this name. Everything points to that title being a constructed term/name, created by one of the three authors who composed *The Russian Primary Chronicle*, or of one of several editing scribes for a universal spirit of thunder, derived from the Indo-European root[199] *'per- and *perkw (to strike or splinter), signifying both the splintering thunder and the splintered tree, especially the oak, with which *Perun* is associated.[200] Regarding the artificial construction of the name *Perun* used in the Chronicle, there are pertinent factors to consider. At the confluence of Lake Ilmen and the River Volhov, the

Peryn peninsula stands as the sacred landscape that served the region of Novgorod. Because the Slavic root -*per, originally referred to the spirits that inhabited oak trees, this veritable Island of oak groves

---

198. *Perkunos*: An Indo-European theonym related to thunder, concatenate with the epithets of Þunraz (Thor), Taranis (Celtic), and Tonans (Latin) Perun (Slavic), Ukko: (Finnish), Taranis (Celtic). **199.** And to the Vedic *Parjanya*, and the Greek *Keraunós* (thunderbolt, a rhymic form of *Peraunós*, used as an epithet of Zeus). **200.** The Latin name of the oak tree, quercus, comes from the same root.

would articulate the absolute sense of the sacred place. *Peryn* and *Perun* – where spirit is tangibly manifest.[201] This root word form also gave rise to the Baltic *Perkunas*, the Albanian *Perëndi*. Slavic people had their own, similar terms for the elemental, land and ancestral spirits, who again, were not considered gods in the classical sense, at least, not before the end of the first millennium. Prominent individual oaks were revered as guardian trees for each tribe or village, receiving offerings and occasional sacrifices, similar in form to Vladimir's original single tutelary shrine excavated at Peryn Hill, and possibly to others that were also erected in Kyiv. All the evidence supports the conclusion that many of the so-called god forms were later shaped and some even developed by Christian writers seeking to consolidate the veneration of animistic and totemic spirits in order to demonise and condemn them in more accessible forms.[202] After the Wendish Crusades and the Mongol invasions, Kyiv irrevocably lost its high status.[203]

According to the post-conversion legends that built up around the thunder spirit, Perkunas bears an axe, sword or hammer, lightning bolts or stones, and curiously, a bow with arrows, which suggests a firm continuity with old hunting traditions as observed in the huge rock art figures of bowman. Typical of all deific figures that came to be associated with the sky, he is mainly allied to the fructifying rains via the seasonal storms, tempests, but also with war/battle, law and order, fertility, oak trees and mountains. Other similar figures (not entirely cognate) are figures the Indo-European *Perkunos, the Slavic *Perun*, Finnish *Ukko*, the Norse *Þór* and the Celtic Taranis.[204]

No stranger to the nuances of cultural forms, the 15th-Century Polish astronomer Nicolaus Copernicus knew the Pole star as Perun's Eye.[205] Under such influences of Christian folklore, thunder as an elemental force, gradually came to be seen very differently – as a

---

201. The prefix per- may share links with Perun as the tutelary or totemic spirit that protected the Peryn region of Novgorod. Perun is celebrated on Thursday, suggested a correlation with the Germanic Þórr and the Vedic Indra, among others. **202.** Nonetheless, from fleeting descriptions, the impression is that older sacred areas were actually void of idolatry, except for an ancestral polycephalic wooden grave marker that denoted the location of a mound, near to water, or an oak grove, that possessed the requisite animistic presence. **203.** Kievan Rus' disintegrated as a state due to the Mongol invasions of 1237-1240. **204.** For an image of Perun bearing a lightning bolt. See: Society for the Protection of Monuments and Local History of the Lithuanian SSR(Lietuvos TSR paminklu apsaugos ir kraštotyros draugijos) - https://www.kernave.lt/kernaves-muziejui-90-metu/, Public Domain, https://commons.wikimedia.org/w/index.php?curid=151975270 (Accessed 27th February 2025) **205.** Rybakov, 1987: 237

literal 'god' of thunder. Other nebulous spirits similarly became anthropomorphic in appearance, receiving worship as divine (non-human) beings. Often belonging to an official state pantheon (a set, overarching family), each figure had supernatural abilities, or possessed the power of creation. Compare this with the wild, formless, animistic spirits of the land, of place and even of the domestic hearth, who are not grand, unless they are of the elements, and are often attached to individual families, and who, like them, are part of creation. Those spirits were revered, even venerated, but not worshipped. Tutelary figures are slightly more complex. They could on occasion, be ancestral figures, apical human or zoomorphic and totemic.

As mentioned above, there are no written sources by which the Slavic peoples described their beliefs or ritual practises. We have only those of their detractors that appear later, after the former paganisms had been subject to considerable reforms. For example, *Dažbog*, the gift-giving spirit, or beneficent one, became widely known as the generic Slavic sun-god, but only post conversion. Similarly, *Stri'bog* is often interpreted or described as the 'god' of the whistling winds, but prior to conversion, he was perceived of as a vegetation spirit. *Khors* has never been satisfactorily explained and *Simar'gl* seems to be a copyist's combination of *Sim*, a household spirit, and *Rogl*, a spirit of the harvest. *Mokoš* appears in connection with the moist earth, a genetrix later identified by classicists with Astarte, whose cult may have reached the Dnieper valley through oriental channels. *Volos (Veles)* was originally the guardian and guide of the dead; his attribute as god of flocks results only from a late assimilation to St.Blasius.[206] Taking over from the function of various tutelary entities and many of their shrines, the saints acted as intermediaries, between the petitioner and the new Christian God.

People continued to visit shrines to seek advice or assistance, interpretation of dreams or visions, and to celebrate at similar times of the year, significant to the growth and cultivation of cereals and cattle.[207] In this sense, very little changed. Behind the continuity of certain necessary actions, the teachings shifted dramatically as the clergy increasingly adopted very specific doctrinal distinctions. The cult of Saints developed to address the needful replacement of the numerous feral and domestic spirits as intermediaries between 'god'

---

206. Hazzard Cross and Sherbowitz-Wetzor, 1953: 227 **207.** Robert Bartlett. "Why Can the Dead Do Such Great Things?" In, *Saints and Worshippers From The Martyrs To The Reformation*, (Princeton University Press, 2013): 609

and humankind to discourage the propitiation of those spirits. Nonetheless, Vladimir's first religio-political reform was largely ineffectual. While Perun's cult had allegedly been observed by the Prince and his retainers, the peoples of Kievan Russia continued to regard their natural spirits and clan centred tutelary figures.

Written so long after the events it refers to, and by biased clerics, *The Russian Primary Chronicle* is viewed by many scholars today as a non-credible source on all counts, ranging from its representation of political events to those of religion. As a phenomenon of Christianity relating retrospectively to an imagined pagan era, the names, functions and roles of these and other similar idols were wholly misrepresented by the new clergy. It is very much a testament to the propaganda of its time. It served its purpose well. Slavic paganism presented very differently in reality. Idols per se, were not a typical feature of the indigenous Slavs, who opted either for natural shrines, or simple, often crude, rough hewn wooden ancestral posts. Tutelary[208] spirits of place, were equally important; markers were erected to signify their cultic presence enshrined within a sacred landscape. Ancestral shrines and sacred ritual sites on islands form a recurrent theme amongst the mythologies and histories of the Scandinavian and Germanic peoples, such that we find subtle references to them in the writings and chronicles of various historians, from Tacitus to the author of *The Eddas*.

Literature and oral folklore are different modes of communication. And moreover, their exchange - most theory, methodology and interpretation often the general replacement of oral tradition by literature - was usually related to the process of complex cultural change. This implies possible transformations of the texts which had successfully penetrated the boundary between both media. New spokesmen of elites, the emerging men of letters were often deeply engaged in political and economic aspects of an ongoing process. Their confrontation with obsolete oral texts took the wide range of possible forms, with positive as well as negative attitudes towards the old tradition. It would be naïve to imagine them as a priori neutral and scientifically objective anthropologists who tend to record 'original' mythological texts.[20]

In fact, with regard to the expression and format of mythic culture, "*Myth is far from being only a passive reflection of social reality. As any human utterance, it is a biased, manipulative and ideological entity, which*

---

208. A Tutelary spirit is a divine figure, though not a god, who is a patron, guide, guard, or protector of a particular area, geographic feature, person or people, nation, lineage, or occupation.   **209**. Cigán, 2019.

mainly reflects the interests and intentions of its creator." [210] In other words, it demonstrates the symbiotic relationship between the politics of state, the ruling elite, and the beliefs and customs of its people, created, assessed and manipulated through the medium of narratives constructed via the poets and storytellers, whose own professional roles are dependent upon the sponsorship of that state. Social norms and cultural constraints are at the mercy and behest of this hierarchical mechanism. The chroniclers of these cultural changes have written the histories we have absorbed, often without question. One of the men instrumental in that process, was Adam of Bremen (1050-1085), cleric and theologian, who composed a history of the Hamburgian Church to reveal and condemn the former heathen practises in Sweden.

Adam's mission was to present and preserve the superiority and domain of the Roman Catholic Church. This also meant editing out any details unfavourable to the Catholic directive. An early northern Germanic monasterial church previously established at Uppsala, was considered a threat to the expansive ambitions of the bishopric of Uppsala. The ensuing hostilities induced the propagandic references to a 'heathen' temple and fanciful descriptions based on the Slavic shrines that were dedicated to ancestral, land, totemic and tutelary spirits, often in the form of wooden poles, some of which were polycephalic.[211] Adam of Bremen's report was primarily concerned with discrediting an opposing version of his faith as heathen, insinuating a barbaric paganism, where in fact, the rites and beliefs, though Christian, were not Catholic. Moreover, his descriptions match those relating to the so-called (and supposedly pagan) temples of Eastern Europe. Recent studies now challenge even the location of such constructions based on the disparities between the writings of various chroniclers whose Christian bias predisposed them to refer to certain named figures as 'gods.'

Unfortunately, the priests and clerics recording this information misrepresented it, failing to comprehend the significance of the titles, which were not the names of deities, but descriptors of spirits of place, that over time became conflated as names for the indwelling protective spirits (which by and large, were not addressed by, or given direct names). Alternatively, it was deliberate, as suggested above – a carefully orchestrated propaganda. A perfect example of such errors relating to a spirit of place is cited by Thietmar of Merseburg[212] (VI, 23) who refers to Redigost, a figure both Adam of Bremen (II, 21;

---

210. Cigán, 2019. **211.** As previously noted of the arctic nomads, where the totems were not known to them as 'gods' in the modern, western sense of that term.

III, 51) and Helmold (I, 2),[213] claimed were worshiped in the form of Zuarasici (Swarozyc).[214] According to the Slavic grammatical rules, where the suffix -yc, -ic, -wicz, or -vic is added to a personal name, a patronym (meaning offspring or descendant relative to the titular name) is generated. This means that Svarožic, or Swarozyc is actually part of a family of divine spirits believed to inhabit that place, in this case, relating to Xvar/Svar.[215] Thietmar provides the earliest description of Redigost,[216] which is essentially a fortified site on a high mound, or gord, in 1014. This means that a guardian spirit of place, Redigost/Radegast (named for that place) became drafted into a hypothetical, reconstructed Slavic pantheon, and later, as the overseer of hospitality. A possible etymology may combine the Slavic rada – high council, and goscic – host, as the place of community. This principal attribute is superficially cognate with Mercury and in the 11th to the 12th centuries, would help correlate an Óðinic identity already formulated in that earlier time. Armed with a spear and helmet, Redigost, the guardian spirit of the West Slavic peoples, could also draw upon the qualities of war, fire, and the (dark) evening sky.

As a derivative or variation of the archaic spirit *Rod* (found also in *Radegast*), pertaining to all things of the sky or heaven, the ritual site on high ground is therefore significantly appropriate. Sites dedicated to a tutelary or ancestral figure are named for them specifically, becoming true toponyms over time. The three heads[217] later attributed to this figure are said to have derived from the three gates or ramparts to

---

212. Prince-Bishop of Merseburg from 1009 CE until his death in 1018 CE, Thietmar was an important chronicler of the reigns of German kings and Holy Roman Emperors of the Ottonian (Saxon) dynasty. Two of Thietmar's great-grandfathers, were Saxon nobles. Lothar II was killed fighting the Slavs at the Battle of Lenzen. **213.** Helmold cited Redigost as a deity of the Liutician (West Slavic Tribes) people in his 12th century *Chronica Slavorum*. Adam of Bremen refers to Redigost in his Gesta Hammaburgensis Ecclesiae Pontificum as the deity worshipped in the Liutician city of Radgosc. Thietmar of Merseburg claimed in his Chronicon that Radegast was the name of the holy city of the pagan Liuticians, a worshiper of many gods, specifically Zuarasici. According to Adam of Bremen, the Bishop of Mecklenburg, Johannes Scotus, was sacrificed to this god in 1066 CE during a pagan Wendish rebellion against Christianity. See: Leszek Slupecki. "West Slavic Pagan Ritual As Described At The Beginning Of The Eleventh Century.' In, Old Norse religion in long-term perspectives., Andrén, et al. 2004: 224-7 **214.** Containing the Iranian root xvar, meaning divine spirit of the sun/sky. **215.** Slavic grammar rules replace g with z, or ž. It is not impossible that Svar (here) could be related to Svear, the original term for the Swedish people, which would then imply a Swedish spirit of place. **216.** Variants forms: Radigast, Redigast, Riedegost, Radegaste, Radhost, all relative to the spirit of place or genius loci, rather than a titular god. Mathieu-Colas, 2017 **217.** Thietmar cites three, (tricornis), but Adam of Bremen lists nine..

the fort they later represented. Looking at this laterally, as guardian spirits, this would make sense. It is interesting here to note that the etymological origin for the figure of Thor, is assigned the meaning of 'gate'. Made of timber, the outside of the shrine was adorned with sculptures to which animal horns were attached. It contained armour, flags and several smaller idols. Built c.1000, but destroyed by fire in 1068, the wooden construction followed the square pattern of other similar sacred structures of Slavic regions and of Eurasia. Thietmar remarked that people paid homage here before going to war and again when they returned, offering their war booty, a custom that is again, not unlike the mars spolia observed in Rome, and like those temple shrines, horse and dice oracles were also utilised here.

Elsewhere, another similar shrine housed a sacred spear, another housed a huge shield – covered in gold leaf – dedicated to Gerovit (*Jarovit*),[218] the warrior (*Jaro*) spirit (*vit*), who appears cognate with *Wolgast* – the spirit of place associated with the martial and chthonic *Volos/Veles*. Herbord, one of the biographers of Bishop Otto, equates this martial spirit with Mars. Bishop Otto's mission was to destroy all heathen shrines and to plunder their riches. To that end, Helmold informs us, in 1124 CE, how these priceless treasures were removed as tribute, along with the three heads of an unnamed idol. Some scholars now believe this figure is a (modern) god-form named *Triglav*.[219] I dispute this deific attribution, on the more probable grounds that it represents the polycephalic totemic staves associated with those ancestral shrines that evolved/developed into the multi-headed idols of the medieval period. My estimation is not only culturally contextual, but compares favourably with numerous contemporary examples, discussed throughout these pages where deemed appropriate.

Early settlements known as gords,[220] founded on strategic sites

---

218. *Yarylo, Jarilo, Jarylo, Jaryla* = *Gerowit, Gierovit:* possessing strength and fertility. Derived from Gerovit or Jarovit, which literally means Strong/Wroth Lord (from the root *ger or *jar, strong, mighty, furious) or Bright Lord (Russian jaryj, bright - bright lord, popular in modern Russia as *Yarilo*, a bright, but powerful spirit of renewal) relating to the rising buoyancy of spring (madness). See: Mathieu-Colas, 2017. **219.** Jiří Dynda. "The Three-Headed One at the Crossroad: A Comparative Study of the Slavic God Triglav." In, *Studia mythologica Slavica*. Institute of Slovenian Ethnology 17 (2014):57-82. This author explores a hypothetical, metaphysical approach to this enigma. **220.** Peoples of the Lusatian culture (c. 1300–500 BCE) built gords during the late Bronze and early Iron Ages, reaching into the 7th to the 8th centuries CE, and beyond by other cultures, throughout (what is now) Poland, the Czech Republic, Hungary, Slovakia, eastern Germany, Romania, Moldova, Belarus, Serbia, Croatia, Bosnia and western Ukraine.

such as hills, lake islands, or stark peninsulas, were later developed as defensive structures, such as castles or citadels, and sometimes temples. Both terminology and usage here suggests a relative connection between the Scandinavian term 'garð '(of Holmgarðr for example), meaning a protected (often sacred) enclosure, and gord. Because gord[221] is related to the gard(hr) and to the gar(dh) tree (the single guardian tree on farmsteads imbued with an ancestral spirit protector) by default, the connection to that protective spirit is further enhanced. Moreover, that Novgorod, contains the suffix 'rod"– the spirit of place, is clearly no coincidence. It was fitting then, that Oleg of Novgorod (Holmgarðr), a Varangian prince (konung) who ruled the Rus' from the late 9th century to the early 10th century, took some of his men to a hilltop shrine to ratify a treaty by vowing upon their weapons before their local tutelary spirit patrons.

Writing in 1134, Helmold refers to this consecration during his mission in the Slavic lands, making a significant observation of another sacred plot he said was dedicated to the 'god' Proven (variant of *per), that was fenced off without idol or image. His description of a sacred area surrounding a thunder tree, perfectly fits the description of a guardian tree (a gar(dh) tree),[222] just like the great thunder oak referred to by Helmold in the previous section. Inconspicuous in their natural form, the space around them would thusly seem void of idol or image. Other myths focussing upon the virtues of cultural traits have become folk customs relating to sacred hospitality, in the manner attributed to *Radegast*, as mentioned above, especially of feasting with guests. As such, these rites that are invariably presided over by a localized spirit of place, or hearth, are valued by all Indo-European peoples.

Items of faith, like spirits of place, are equally prone to misidentification or misrepresentation. A fine example of this occurs in the pillared remains of the early 6th -century wooden temple structures found beneath Trondheim medieval church, and again at Uppsala, the royal seat of the Svear. Both are claimed as pagan, a notion possibly inspired by Bede's reference to the burning of a wooden temple enclosure to 'pagan gods' by a converted priest. Conversion was never that straightforward, nor its path that certain. With the possible exception of a description in the 13th-Century *Eyrbyggja Saga* that refers to an earlier Icelandic temple sanctuary supposedly dedicated to Þórr,

---

221. Issac Taylor. *Names and Their Histories: A Handbook of Historical Geography and Topographical Nomenclature*. (University of Michigan: Rivingtons, 1898). Gord is reconstructed from the Proto-Indo-European root ghortós – enclosure/enclosed land.
222. The single guardian tree on farmsteads imbued with an ancestral spirit protector.

the (literary and largely mythic) associations with pagan figures tend to post-date conversion. The alleged association of such temples with pagan gods remains unattested. Furthermore, the appearance of male and sometimes female sculpted or painted figures do not represent the remnants of a dying pagan culture. In fact, the ambiguity of that culture is considerably more pronounced than popular literature and media falsely assert, and indeed the supposed endurance of a pagan faith is less than tenuous.

Mythological artworks that adorn the numerous stave churches erected during the 11th century flurry of conversions across Norway,[223] depict a folkloric attachment to an already imagined heroic past they believed pre-dated the Christian era. Displacement is however, easy to achieve. It takes but one generation to disconnect from the beliefs of previous generations, and one generation to wholly embrace alternatives to them. The old die, and what the young thought preceded them, is often, the constructs of conquerors, be that of land or faith. Suggestions are readily absorbed in the desperation to cling to the comfort that faith offers. Irish Romanesque churches were architectural descendants of earlier wooden churches similar to 11th-Century Norwegian stave churches. In the Stave church of Hegge in Valdres, c.1200, carved wooden and stone facial masks are a common feature, evoking ancestral, totemic and Otherworld entities. Today, in our world, several of these images are typically identified as Óðinn, even by some scholars;[224] one in particular bears similarity to a facial rock-art glyph from the Ust-Taseyevsky Ritual Site.[225] This curious graffiti image also appears on a migration era plank fetish/icon. However, the latter clearly post-dates the stave pillar and is not contemporary with the late Iron Age carvings in this cultic complex. The original anthropomorphic idol was probably carved during the Scythian period of occupation. Alternative explanations for many of these buildings and the artefacts housed within them should be sought. Viable options do exist. As ever, context is everything.

Amongst West Slavs, temples were referred to by Chroniclers as

---

223. Michael F. Reed. "Norwegian Stave Churches and Their Pagan Antecedents." In, *RACAR: Revue D'art Canadienne / Canadian Art Review* 24, no. 2:3-13 (1997) http://www.jstor.org/stable/42631152. (Accessed June 21, 2021). **224.** Reed, 1997: 3-13. **225.** The so-called Ust-Taseyevsky Idol (or Taseyevsky) is on the left bank of the Taseyeva River, some 4 km from its confluence with the Angara, and 10 km from the village of Pervomaisk, some 300 km north from regional capital Krasnoyarsk. See: https://www.ancientpages.com/2021/01/18/why-was-the-face-of-mysterious-ust-taseyevsky-stone-idol-suddenly-changed/ (Accessed 17th June 2021).

continae (dwellings), as noted in Otto of Bamberg's (1060/1061-1139) biographies, wherein he asserts the view they were to be distinctly regarded as houses of the gods.[226] It should be stressed here, how the system of idolatry of the Baltic area was essentially manistic (pertaining to worship of ancestors). Rough wooden buildings each had an inner cell in which stood a figure or effigy, located within wider walled enclosures or fortifications that held up to four continae.[227] Different continae were owned by different kins-ship clans, and were used for ritual feasts and celebrations held in honour of their own ancestral figures, providing a typical layout similar to that described by Jordanes that had so offended Columbanus in the Slavic regions during the 6th to the 7th centuries. It is therefore, completely wrong to refer to these totemic effigies, possibly of ancestors, as gods, especially not in the sense of the classical state pantheons. Even the land spirits, lares or landvættir, were not worshiped as 'gods.' Offerings were also left for them at open shrines near to sacred elemental way-markers, where they were engaged as influential intermediaries with the greater elemental spirits. Elaborate rituals involving fire and water were constructed around the removal, handling and reburial of ancestral bones. Some of these customs have endured the centuries since, though not all who hold to them, may fully understand their true purpose or origin.

It is not irrelevant that until the 19th century there survived here and there throughout the Danubian-Balkan region the custom of reopening graves three, five, or seven years after interment, taking out the bones of the corpses, washing them, wrapping them in new linen, and reinterring them. [...] [sometimes] corpses would then be reinterred with the newly deceased. In protohistoric times the tumuli (mounds) of the mortuaries of the Krivichi, a populous tribe of the East Slavs of the northwest, the so-called long kurgans (burial mounds), contained cinerary urns buried in the tumulus together and all at one time. [...]. The cremations by the Krivichi are of exhumed bones. In the Volga region today the Mordvins still burn the disinterred bones of the dead in the flames of a "living fire" ignited by friction. [...] Seasonal festivals of the Slavs turn out to be almost entirely dedicated to the dead, very often without the participants realizing it, as in the case of the Koljada (Latin Kalendae)—the annual visit made by the spirits of the dead, under the disguise of beggars, to all the houses in the village. It is possible that the bones of the disinterred were kept for a long period inside the dwellings, as is still sometimes done in the Tyrol of Austria, and that the sacred corner – now occupied by the icon – was the place where they were kept.

---

226. Dynda, 2014. **227.** Ivakhiv, 2005: 21-212 **228.** See overleaf.

It seems that the temples were originally maintained by a dedicated priesthood, whose priests (volkhvs) also organised and led the rituals and festivals for the people, a duty that afforded them prestige, privilege, tribute, and a share of the military booty from the kins' chiefs.[229] Post-conversion, ancestral totems, and tutelary spirits were largely replaced with Christian patron saints, but not completely. Shrines of this kind were still being observed in 1331,[230] even by Christians. That such ingrained (folk) customs are based in culture, cannot be emphasised enough. Religion is simply an overlaid imposition that replaces and demonises prior beliefs and practises. Centuries pass and we are left with the strange, discombobulated remnants of those former beliefs in the form of fairy tales and horror stories. Our emotional responses to these are based in the psychology of those cultural foundations. It is part of who we are as people.[231]

Nevertheless, with regard to the past however, Arkona is often described as the last bastion of Slavic heathenism. Yet outside the fortified region of Karentia, further along the peninsula at the highest point of the Arkona headland, stood the main sanctuary on Rügen Island; a very different temple structure and one that is widely speculated upon.[232] This rather grand temple once housed a large idol we've already met – named by Saxo as *Svetovit* – that occupied a central sunken base in an inner room. Its highly decorated roof was supported by four columns, between which hung purple rugs in lieu of walls. Contrasting markedly with the very basic wooden shrines at Karentia, Saxo's elaborate description appears not unlike the early Orthodox churches established sporadically in these regions since the 9th century. The true religious orientation of this particular 'temple,' remains ambiguous, and needful of further consideration.[233] It is worth

---

228. Evel Gasparini. https://www.britannica.com/topic/Slavic-religion/Communal-banquets-and-related-practices#ref533502 (Accessed 29th December 2024). The custom of assigning a dedicated corner in domestic dwellings to site a sacred icon is one we may also recognise in Sámi tradition. **229.** None of which they relinquished easily. The common population remained attached to the volkhvs, the priests, who periodically, over centuries, led popular rebellions against the central power and the church. **230.** Raffaele Pettazzoni. "West Slav Paganism." In, *Essays on the History of Religions*, (Brill Archive, 1967). **231.** Remnants of these former belief survive in tales of the undead, monsters and vampires. See: Gasparini, 2024. **232.** The oracle was officiated over by the chief priest who predicted the future of his tribe by observing the behaviour of a white horse as it moved over spears upon the ground and the casting of die. **233.** It is worth noting, that conversion (Orthodox) did not alter iconography stylistically until the medieval period, that is after the influence of the Roman Catholic Baptismal mission.

remembering that the Roman Catholic Church labelled all non-Catholics as "heathens," a prejudicial term that applied not just to pagans, but to anyone who followed alternative "heretical" forms of Christianity. In the Baltic regions, the Bogomils were primary amongst them.

Archaeological materials found in the Slavic regions spanning the 9th to the 13th centuries, confirm that polycephalic figures appeared in different areas of the Baltic coast as items of trade and settlement. The tiny 9th-Century stone Wolin figure,[234] of unknown dedication,[235] is named after its location in Poland (Pomerania), and bears a striking stylistic resemblance to the 7th-Century Sutton Hoo whetstone, which is also noted for the four terminate heads under a strange domed hat. In pre-Roman and Roman Age Denmark, certain polycephalic cultic objects, such as whetstones,[236] and the four-faced metal fittings for suspending them,[237] were often discovered amongst the grave goods pertaining to early medieval English and Germanic kingship. Because these and other similar figurines appear to symbolize sacral power authorised by ancestral figures, and are associated with tribe, clan, or even the land spirits of the regions occupied, they would have held considerable appeal to the Vikingr who acquired them as trade or plunder. They were certainly wielded as items of legitimacy, by pagans and Christians alike. The small four-sided Wolin appear could therefore just as easily represent the four evangelists.[238] The point is, Christianity overlaid pre-existing beliefs, modifying the basic pagan template. The discoveries from Wolin and Szczecin have led some scholars to speculate that Wolin (inhabited by both Slavs and Scandinavians), may have been the basis for the semi-legendary settlements Jómsborg and Vineta. The size of the town was certainly exaggerated in contemporary sources, specifically by Adam of Bremen who claimed that Wolin/Jómsborg (of modern-day Poland) was the largest Viking Age town in Europe after Hedeby. The legendary Vikingr stronghold of Jómsborg is found

---

234. Excavated in Wolin (Western Pomerania, Northern Poland), this tiny artefact (a mere 9.3 cm high) was discovered beneath the floor of an 11th century house that stood near to another building interpreted as a kacina (pagan temple). **235.** But has nonetheless been named by its excavators as the ubiquitous Svetovit. **236.** Irene Baug; Filipowiak Wojciech; James Jansen; Sørlie RØhr Torkil. "Norse Whetstones in Slavic Areas – Indicators of Long-Distance Networks During the Viking Age and the Middle Ages," *Medieval Archaeology* 68 (1) (2024): 48-71 DOI:10.1080/00766097. 2024.2347751 (Accessed 4th January 2025). **237.** Wladyslaw Duczko. *Viking Rus: Studies on the Presence of Scandinavians in Eastern Europe* (Brill Academic Publishers. 2004): 5. **238.** This region of modern-day Poland was converted to Catholicism in the 12th century. Prior to this, the Wends and Slavs were largely followers of Arianism, an heretical unorthodox form of early Christianity.

on a 10th-century golden coin in conjunction with the name of Harald Bluetooth Gormsson. Known as the Curmsun Disc, this testament to the early conversion of many Norwegians eager to advance their trading alliances, bears a Latin inscription on one side. On the reverse, there is a Latin cross with four dots surrounded by an octagonal ridge.

The inscription reads as follows: "+ARALDCVRMSVN+REXADTANER+SCON+JVMN+CIV ALDIN+" and translates as: *"Harald Gormsson king of Danes, Scania, Jómsborg, town Aldinburg"* CVRMSVN is a transliteration from spoken Old Norse via rúnes into the Medieval Latin alphabet.[239]

The notion of small anthropomorphic or zoomorphic objects associated with the sphere of military or economic activities of early medieval societies still remains problematic. (...) In the majority of cases, anthropomorphic or zoomorphic artefacts are interpreted as being associated with a religion or cult, or with the practical spheres of everyday life and perceived as toys.

However, a closer analysis of all such artefacts reveals that their nature is much more complex and requires a wider study.[240]

Crucially, it must here be reiterated that the presence of polycephalic deific figures in modern Slavic mythology is entirely dependent upon the written accounts by non-native Christian propagandists who had long rejected all forms of ancestral based cults, and who had additionally rejected all unorthodox versions of Christianity. Interestingly, polycephalic beings do not occur at all in the Baltic or Germanic (Old Norse) mythologies, thereby suggesting that we reconsider this outdated perspective and seek contextual and cultural alternatives that are typically ancestral, totemic or tutelary. Their association with Vikingr culture is otherwise unsubstantiated and entirely misplaced. At least two lays of *The Poetic Edda* refer to polycephalic Jötnar, namely the six-headed son, begotten by Aurgelmir's feet in the Old Norse poem: *The Lay of Vafþrúðnir* (Vafþrúðnismál, 33),[241] and to the three-headed þurs or þursar in the Old Norse poem *The Lay of Skírnir (Skírnismál)*, both 10th century.[242] In keeping with Germanic tradition, three and

239. S. Rosborn. *A unique object from Harald Bluetooth's time?* (Malmö: Pilemedia. Academia,2015)https://www.academia.edu/9647410/A_unique_object_from_Harald_Bluetooth_s_time_2015_ (Accessed 10th October 2021). **240.** Kamil Kajkowski and Pawel Szczepanik. "The multi-faced so-called miniature idols from the Baltic Sea area." *Studia Mythologica Slavica* XVI, (Institute of Slovenian Ethnology, 2013): 55-86. http://sms.zrc-sazu.si/pdf/16/04-sms16-kajkowski_szczepanik.pdf (Accessed 12th February 2021). **241.** *The Poetic Edda.* Translated by Carolyne Larrington. (Oxford University Press. 1999). **242.** The poems are preserved in 13th century Codex Regius GKS 2365 4°, an Icelandic codex and partially in 14th century AM 748 I 4to.

its multiples apply here; so although there are no four-headed Jötnar in Germanic or Scandinavian mythology, their presence as three and six-headed mythic monsters reveals either cross-cultural absorption, which is highly improbable, as this trait does not present itself in Scandinavian nor Germanic artefacts; or, it was a concept drafted into literary traditions based upon the chronicles of learned clerics, which are then transmitted orally, through poetry and tale. Poetry was a medium for social commentary, criticism and moralising. Polycephalic imagery, formerly related to ancestral cults, became utilised as a primary expression of the monstrous, but also of anything unruly, unsavoury, or immoral. Anything deemed undesirable to the expanding force of Christianity became subject to non-too subtle polemics that condemns those traits.

An analogous example of social conditioning is conveyed further through the literature that occurs in *Skírnismál*, where Gerðr's refusal to marry the love-sick Freyr, results in his messenger Skírnir threatening her with a curse involving a loveless and abusive marriage to Hrímgrímnir (ON frost-masked) in Hel. Similarly, in *Lokásenná*, Loki casts harsh judgement upon Freyja for her promiscuity, yet his behaviour "only makes sense if judged by human social criteria - for as a fertility goddess Freyja is surely bound to engage in a large number of sexual encounters – so the sexual politics of *Skírnismál* are meaningful primarily as representations of human behaviour."[243] Gerðr was threatened first with a sword, that would remove her head from her neck, and secondly with a Gambanteinn, a wand to tame her, and thirdly with incarceration, madness and despair. Thirteenth-century Norwegians evidently believed that cursing obstinate women with social exile and shame, even with threats of rape and death, was an acceptable method to enforce compliance. Already the status of women had diminished markedly in the post-conversion world. *"Skírnir's strategies, it seems, were imitated in the human world at the time that Skírnismál was being written into the Codex Regius."*[244] Both Freyja and Gerðr's inability to make their own choices without inducing stigma was an object lesson to the very human audience it was intended

---

243. Because the condemnation of female promiscuity is the subject emphasised in this lay, the issue of the forceful sexual coercion applied by the supposed hero that is not condemned, exposes a worrying subtext. See: Carolyne Larrington. ([1992]1993). "What Does Woman Want?' Mær and munr in *Skírnismál*." Alvíssmál 1: 3-16 **244.** Ibid., The poem suppresses women's desire to exercise autonomy over their bodies and their lives, a theme championed in the Romance tale of *Gawain and the Loathly Lady* and in *Chaucer's Wife of Bath*.

for.[245] Loki's condemnation of Freyr for buying his bride with gold, is a similar moral relating to the price of desire, specifically, his lack of unmanly discipline, thus tainting the family line of the Ynglings.[246]

Social politics and propaganda of the 13th century aside, we return to the consideration of polycephalic artefacts where they do exist, being clearly significant in the mythical and otherworldly reality of the Slavs and Scandinavians, although the four-faced figures are better associated only within a Slavic cultural context. Slavs were present in the Baltic lands of Riga in Latvia at the beginning of the 13th century. This is attested in the contemporary *Chronicle of Henry of Livonia*, which describes a peculiar and tragic fate of a society that lived in the Lithuanian-Latvian border-zone, regarding a tribe known as Vindi, who are probably the Slavic Veneti, living by the Baltic coast.[247] Wooden and bone figures with phallic-shaped stems or handles, probably served as ritual fetishes relating to a particular sacral, and possibly ancestral or totemic power. The common and rather popular supposition that these objects are 'god idols' is not something I consider to be likely, and in my opinion, does not reflect their cultural beliefs. These curious items may even have been utilised in various fertility or love magic rituals similar to those ascribed to Þórr's Mjolnir, a particularly well-attested hand-held ritual object. Some scholars associate the name of the east-Slavic Wołos (Veles) with the Old Norse volsi – a desiccated horse phallus and cultic object used by women in very obscure ritual practices associated with fertility, but also, possibly related to certain Völur practises. We have much to learn from that world, a world that demands closer contextual study.

Parallels between similar artefacts relating to aesthetics, functionality and purpose, are neither coincidental, nor unique, as confirmed by further explorations into the roots and origins of Woden and Óðinn. As mythic figures of the northern world, everything discovered is indiscriminately associated with Woden and Óðinn. For example,

---

245. One version of the ms has notes on the margin that indicate the poem might have been performed as ritual drama. Ignoring the demonstrative content and context for this enforced relationship, this possible performance drama has been seized upon and interpreted somewhat romantically as a hieros gamos, where Gerðr and Freyr are seen as "the divine coupling of sky and earth or at least fertility god and representative of the soil." See: John Lindow. *Norse Mythology: A Guide to the Gods, Heroes, Rituals, and Beliefs.* (Oxford University Press, 2001): 139 See also: H. R. Ellis Davidson. *Roles of the Northern Goddess.* (Routledge. 1999): 86 **246.** Gerðr and Freyr are commonly seen as the divine coupling of sky and earth, or at the very least, as fertility spirits of the soil and sky. **247.** Kajkowski and Szczepanik, 2013: 55-86. The multi-faced so-called miniature idols from the Baltic Sea area.

during the 1958 excavations of Staraja Ladoga in Russia, a wooden cultic object, dated to the 9th to the 10th centuries, missing its hands and one leg, depicts a male figure with a moustache and beard, wearing a conical helmet. Another example from Veliky Novgorod dated to the 12th century (some two hundred years after Vladimir toppled a huge effigy that once stood here, into the river), concerns a short metal-worked sceptre with a single faced image believed to represent a thunder spirit. These votive figures are automatically posited as deific, and almost always as 'Óðinic,' yet, as shown here, their actual status as either local tribal spirits, or ancestral figures (sometimes one and the same) often in the form of crude carvings, is almost never considered. The tendency to relate these finds to major figures found in myths composed much later, is all too common.[248] That they do relate to (localised) elemental spirits is in no doubt.

---

248. See forthcoming unpublished ms, "Song of the North" by Shani Oates for an extensive exploration into this proposition.

THE ZBRUCH IDOL

Bishop Ebbo (c.775-851) claimed that the Slavic thunder/sky spirit was perceived as the embodiment of an axis mundi, being a summus deus (a sum of all things). Helmold later applied a similar term – deus deorum – god of all gods, associated with war, who (amongst northern Slavs[249]), was sometimes depicted with four-heads.[250] An urban settlement at Husiatyn on the west bank of the Zbruch River in the Ukraine, became the focus of considerable attention in 1848, when an unusual stone statue was discovered, partially submerged during a drought. Amidst this rocky terrain, famous for its caves, this enigmatic 10th century[251] four-sided sculpture remains at the centre of speculation and controversy. Claimed by its discoverer as a pre-Christian representation of *Svetovit* that also portrays the Underworld, the mortal world and the heavenly gods above, others believe 'The Zbruch Idol' – as it has been dubbed – to be a very clever fake. If genuine, however, it is more probably a refined example of a bałwan, created by the Kipchak - Cumans, known for their enigmatic ancestral stone sculptures. Former pagan shrines and various Slavic idols in Kiev and Novgorod, were typically crude and made of wood in the form of pillars or posts.[252] By comparison, bałwan (bolvan) is a pan-Slavic archaism for a cult image of non-Slavic origin, generally as monolithic stelae erected in honour of a guardian land spirit, or an heroic ancestor. The latter often feature as grave markers or effigies, originally placed upon cairns, a typical custom noted on the kurgan mounds, possibly adopted by the Slavs through their historical interactions with Türkic and Iranian peoples.[253]

Konstanty Zaborowski, who owned the village, donated the statue

---

249. Also known as the Polabian Slavs, and the Wends. 250. What each head represents is unknown, though suggestions range from the cardinal points and calendrical markers of the seasons, to elements, winds, and even to more philosophical inclinations similar to the four heads of Brahma. 251. Based on the fact that many stelae were abandoned when Poland was Christianised in 966. **252.** Henryk Łowmianski. Religia Słowian i jej upadek. (The Religion of Slavs and its Fall) (in Polish) Edited by Adam Mickiewicz. (Panstwowe Wydawnictwa Naukowe, 1979).

THE ZBRUCH IDOL 311

to the Polish Count Mieczysław Potocki, who reported it to the Kraków Scientific Society in 1850. Possibly swept up in the romantic nationalism of his time,[254] Potocki identified the figure as *Svetovit*, a deity primarily associated with the Island of Rügen. However, the circumstances of its discovery are nonetheless suspicious, therefore another view is posited that asserts the sculpture is a fake, a nationalist hoax produced by Zaborowski's brother Tymon (a famous poet), whose estate was located near the village where the statue was found.[255] The four faces of The Zbruch Idol[256] are more recently interpreted as markers for the four cardinal directions, where each is possibly a different colour that may relate to the elements.[257] Other stone idols have been discovered in this region, one of them, possibly female, holds a drinking horn (rhyton); a horse is engraved on the back side on the rather flat stelae. Depicted on huge rúne-stones and bracteates, with eagles and large birds of prey, this Slavic figure appears bearing very specific traditional symbols that include a white stallion, a horn of plenty and a sword. Svantovit is mentioned in the *Chronica Slavorum*, *Gesta Danorum*, and the *Knýtlinga saga*. An alternative proposal suggests that *Svetovit* is a later name, re-constructed from the name St. Vitus. It was common practice to assign the names of saints to older deific forms. Re-claiming is therefore not unusual, particularly if the former name was either unknown or forgotten, presuming that names had ever been applied. Many deific figures were originally unnamed. Like the small Wolin artefact,[258] the Zbruch Idol also bears a striking resemblance to the Sutton Hoo Whetstone discovered in a ship burial within the mound[259] of the 7th-Century Saxon chieftain, believed by many to be Rædwald.

---

253. Similar etymology is found in the Slavic word for god - bóg, a cognate of Sanskrit bhaga/Iranian or Persian bag. A cognate Vedic term is bhagvan, also transcribed as bhagwan. See: Aleksander Gieysztor. Mitologia Słowian. (Warsaw University, 1980): 186 **254.** The village and its region of Galicia was at that time in the Austrian Empire, but is now in part of Ukraine. **255.** Judith Kalik and Alexander Uchitel. Slavic Gods and Heroes. (Routledge; 2018): 56 **256.** Found in the Ukraine, the Zbruch Idol is on display at the Krakow Archaeological Museum. See image here: https://commons.wikimedia.org/w/index.php?curid=30940172 **257.** Rybakov asserts that the male with the horse and sword is Perun, the female bearing the horn of plenty is Mokoš, the female holding the ring is Lada, and the male deity with the solar symbol is Dažbog. He cites Veles an Underworld deity. Rybakov imaginatively suggests that all the smaller figures on the idol are aspects of a single over-arching 'god' - Rod, an epithet that simply means divine, and that the phallic shape of the artefact represents his all-encompassing virtue. See: Boris Rybakov. Yazycestvo drevney Rusi Moscow. (The Academy of Sciences of the USSR, 1987). **258.** See: https://en.wikipedia.org/wiki/Wolin_Svetovit#/media/File:Swietowit_wolinski.jpg **259.** The Sutton Hoo sites include settlements of the Neolithic, Beaker period, Bronze Age and Iron Age. (approx.18 mounds.)

312 PIRATES, MERCHANTS, DEVILS & DARK DEEDS

Very little is known about the religious beliefs of the pagan Anglo-Saxons of the 5th to the 7th-centuries. There is very little convincing evidence for shrines, temples or cult centres, but there is a great deal of investment in the burial rite which was probably of a highly charged and symbolic nature.[260]

Stylistically, the form of the proto-Indo-European stelae of the 3-2nd millennium BCE, are strikingly similar to those of the later Slavic period, crudely fashioned of wood, rarely of stone. Located on hills or mounds, and sometimes within hill-forts and elevated temples, where they existed at all, were very basic wooden structures; more generally, a sacred area was denoted by simple parallel wooden posts that acted as 'gateways.' Even in the later Christian era, statues of Christ and nobleman followed the Slavic cultural style now primarily associated with pre-Christian imagery; yet another bias that colours our perspective of the past. A continuous tradition of offerings placed at sacred sites, often in the form of grains and pots, are evident in the geographical strata covering several hundred years of activity.[261]

6. *Ancient Nordic Sami people offering to Diermes or Thor by Picart 1724*

Polycephalic iconography certainly featured throughout the Slavic regions, as mentioned by Helmold, though many of them are simply the rough-hewn wooden posts, pillars or Stapols described by clerics and bishops as 'idols of pagan gods,' displaying their inability to articulate past their inherent theological bias. As ancestral markers, the

---

260. Jezz Meredith. "Barber's Point: a Saxon settlement in the Alde Estuary." Saxon 61 (2011). **261.** In some places, such customs were observed by the Slavs until the 20th century. Deposits of dog and horse bones and skulls at such sites from historic and pre-historic periods are invariably associated with sacrifice.

wooden posts were frequently erected in sanctuaries dedicated to local land spirits. This enlightening perspective invites a reassessment of the former descriptions of the alleged temples at Uppsala described by Saxo and Adam of Bremen centuries later. Their generic accounts of how they imagined former pagan ritual space, were composed after the establishment of churches at Uppsala that had long replaced former shrines and ritual arenas. Influences from the Sámi Sieidi sites and the Slavic regions of the east - Arkona and Rügen - no doubt entered their vivid elaborations.

Christian missionaries in Denmark were overwhelmed by the entrenched animism of the Danish people. Their reverence for the divine in nature manifested through the elements and unseen spirits of the land. They erected no statues or idols to these spirits, just woodland shrines to honour them. Known as landstings, we find the remains of simple wooden structures at Lund, Odense, Viborg and Lejre that in many cases formed the foundations of the remarkable Stave Churches erected over them centuries later, such as those in Hemse, Gotland. This is often described as the stamp of dominion over the former landvætter (land-spirits), though I prefer to think of it as an absorption, an inclusion that allowed the ordinary folk to continue attending their natural places of reverence, with no diminishment in the notion of sacrality. Post conversion Danes continued to revere the sacred springs (kilder) and groves continued to be venerated as saints within their new faith. This custom survives in the well-dressing ceremonies in the regions once occupied by Danes.

Indeed, within that shift, it is evident that early cross designs closely resemble the amulet dedicated to Þórr. Norse chieftains were responsible for the religious rites undertaken for the welfare of their clans. As community leaders, their farmsteads became the place of assembly set aside for sacred rites. Cultic sites took two forms, the temple construction known as hofs, in which (later) idols were briefly housed and venerated, and rough-hewn external altars known as horgrs. All farmers working land leased from their Chieftains paid a toll to the temple, often in the form of animals that provided the means of sacrifice by the Goði needed for the celebratory feasting rites, a duty he was accountable for. The skalds in attendance at such events, ensured the lives and events of these people were woven into song long before they entered the written record.

THE CONTINUITY OF FOLK CULTURE

The lingering presence of a natural relationship with the land and its ancestral lore is evident in the endurance of Kurgan mound burials, which were not unusual in Russia, and persisted into the 1530s. Chronicles from that period, such as the Pskov Chronicle, and other archaeological data, confirm that even at that time, there were "no rural churches for the general use of the populace; churches existed only at the courts of boyars and princes."[262] Christianization of the countryside was the work, not of the 11th or 12th centuries, but of the 15th and 16th or even 17th century. This does not mean the rural people were not Christian, only that their understanding was not processed or universal, nor particularly dogmatic beyond clerical confines - it sat outside the official praxis, a superficial gloss overlaying deep-rooted cultural mores. Not until the 16th century was the Russian Orthodox Church strong enough to assume a powerful, centralising institution based on the model of the Catholic Church of Rome. They launched a concerted effort to eradicate the strong influence of apocryphal literature that had entered Russia between the 11th to the 15th centuries, through the rising cult of the Bogomils, especially strong amongst the southern Slavs. Nevertheless, Bogomil dualism influenced Slavic folk religion more deeply than the tenets of the Russian Orthodox Church. These merged with entrenched beliefs that preserve Indo-European and early Slavic ideas relating to an "holistic vision of a divine cosmos" and practices involving the veneration of fire as a channel to the divine world, the symbolism of the colour red and ultimately, the search for a glorious death.[263]

Sacred waterways are evident in the origin of the archaic word stem dun/don, which existed before the crystallization of linguistic

---

262. V. G. Vlasov. "The Christianization of Russian Peasants." In, Russian Traditional Culture: Religion, Gender and Customary Law. Edited by Marjorie Balzar Mandelstam, Ronald Radzai. (Routledge, 1992): 16-33 **263.** N. N. Veletskaya. "Forms of Transformation of Pagan Symbolism in the Old Believer Tradition." In, Russian Traditional Culture: Religion, Gender and Customary Law. Edited by Marjorie Mandelstam Balzer and Ronald Radzai. (Routledge, 1992): 48-60

root stocks. In Sanskrit the word for river is dhuni, a word introduced into the Slavic languages from the east where it appears as Don and Danube, Dniepr, and Dniestr. These are all borrowed from the Scythian *danu.[264] The Welsh Donwy confirms links between Celtic and Iranian traditions, that manifest further in their shared reverence for antlered beasts. Again, the Scytho-Sarmatian influence spread east and west to Iberia and Siberia.[265] And it cannot be overlooked that the Norse people considered themselves to be Þórr's children, a belief they imparted to those who settled in Iceland, continuing and preserving Þórr's popularity and cult. In Iceland, the Christ and his mother Mary were compared with Þórr and his (Earth) mother[266] at the Alþingi when the change to Christianity was agreed upon. Combining further the traditions of Þórr and his mother Fjorgyn with those of Christianity, a legend somewhat redolent of Mary's refuge in Provence, says that Mary in the guise of St. Sunniva, drifted across the North Sea from Ireland in a boat, taking refuge in a cave, thus establishing the hallowed setting for the first stave church in Norway.

Tribal peoples are invariably bound by occupation,[267] language and a sense of common origin, but customs varied, often following the traditional lore and law of their forefathers. As to religious practises, the pronounced absence in the 14th-Century *Russian Primary Chronicle* of any detailed information relating to the beliefs of the early Slavs, suggests an absence of any coherent official religion or structure. *"There is also very little evidence that anything like a systematic Slavic pantheon ever existed."* [268] Infact, the first reference to any Slavic deity occurs,

---

264. Note the similarity to danu of the Irish folkloric cosmology, who may share an origin in, or influence from, the Scythian peoples. **265.** Jacobson, 1993. **266** Fjorgyn (f) remains an unattested name; some scholars have proposed that it could be related to the Old English fruh, Old High German furuh, and Latin porca, all of which mean furrow or ridge. This meaning would support the persistent reverence in the Old English prayer to "Erce, mother of earth (Erce, eorþan modor"), recited when the plough cut the first furrow of the growing season, and milk, honey, flour, and water were poured into the soil as an offering to the land-wights. **267.** For example - farmers, or on the peripheries as nomads and cattle herders, traders and merchants along the Dnieper trade-route. **268.** Taking an oath before a Perun Idol, appears repeated in the Chronicle, mentioned again at the ratification of another later treaty of 945. When signing the Russo-Byzantine Treaty, the Christian Rus' swore their oath in the Church, before a statue of Christ, while the ruling prince and his men made invocations upon the mountain, according to 'heathen' custom. As noted already, this remains an ambiguous term. And though widely accepted, this tale is far from being an accurate or truthful portrayal. See: Samuel Hazzard Cross and Olgerd P. Sherbowitz-Wetzor. (Trans. and Eds.) "The Russian Primary Chronicle: Laurenitian text." (Mediaeval Academy of America, 1953): 38

quite late and in connection with an early treaty with Byzantium in 907, where Oleg's men ratified their agreement at a local shrine, supposedly dedicated to Perun and Volos, by swearing upon their weapons, with the clause that their weapons would turn against them if they reneged their vow.[269] A reference to a danegeld system in operation in Russia between pagans and Christians, alerts us to the existence of consecutive beliefs at this time. Yet, despite having this knowledge, classical scholars of the 18th and 19th centuries were keen to analyse everything through the narrow limitations of classicism, awarding everything a pantheon, while ignoring the implications of such a blinkered perspective. Additional obfuscations to clarity transpired in the contrived elevation of status, and in the naïve interpretation of descriptive terms as names and titles. For example, consider the primacy awarded to the three springs of creation mentioned in Völuspá. Identical water sources appear in *The Russian Primary Chronicle* alongside several other waterfalls and rivers navigated by the Rus', where they are expressed in dramatic terms that relate to degrees of ferocity: 'roaring one,' 'ever-rushing,' and 'insatiable,' thus confirming these descriptors were not unique, but were in fact commonplace terms.[270]

Literary evidence very much misrepresents the reality of that history, focussed as it is upon only the narrow period between the zenith of historical saga construction at the beginning of the 13th century, and the influences of European Romance traditions that merged within a few decades. However, the events they portray are not contemporary, nor even held in recent memory. They are in fact creative fictions based in the distorted memory of the events and peoples at least two centuries prior to their composition by Snorre Sturlusson and others. Given that we know of the former good will between Scandinavia and Russia that had already disintegrated in the 11th century, the information that entered Icelandic saga literature was at best hearsay and considerably out-dated by this time. Many names are altered or confused, and certain time-lines are not exact. For example, in the Norse sagas, Novgorod takes precedence over Kyiv, though the latter had initially been the primary city of the Rus' since the late 9th century, thus revealing a narrative set at a time when Novgorod had become the principal point of Scandinavian contact with the Eastern Slavic world. From Oleg's seizure of the city until 1169, Kyiv functioned as the capital of Kievan Rus', ruled by the Varangian Rurikid dynasty.[271]

---

269. Hazzard Cross & Sherbowitz-Wetzor, 1953: 65-66   **270.** Hazzard Cross & Sherbowitz-Wetzor, 1953: 42

THE CONTINUITY OF FOLK CULTURE 317

Most of those northern regions gradually became Slavicized. Very few of the oldest Russian cities are therefore mentioned in the sagas;[272] those that are, punctuate the stages along the recognized trade-routes (Novgorod, Polotsk, Smolensk), or at the headwaters of the Volga and its tributaries (Rostov, Murom, Suzdal), heading towards the Orient and the Black Sea. The Arabic geographer Al Biruni (973-1038) refers to the Baltic as the Varangian Sea, and the Varangians as a Swedish people dwelling on its coasts. Varangian[273] was not a term known in Russia before the latter half of the 10th century when it came into use in reference to the culturally entrenched Scandinavian warriors who served as mercenaries for the Russian princes or with the Byzantine emperors. To Russians of the last half of the 11th century, the term Varangian was indistinct from Scandinavian, just as the Rus', had been in centuries past. By the beginning of the 12th century, the term Rus', had lost all association with Scandinavia, as had Varangian, which came to reflect only the service of the Byzantine Empire particularly in Kiev after the reign of Yaroslav the Wise (1015-1054). The first datable use of the word in Norse literature occurs in the *Gísli* of the skald Einarr Skularson, delivered in 1153.

When Sviatoslav I was assassinated returning to Kyiv from a campaign against Khazaria, his sons Yaropolk I (r. 972-980), Oleg, and Vladimir fought for the crown. Oleg was killed when Yaropolk I took power. Vladimir wisely fled to Norway to the court of his relative Jarl Hákon Sigurðarson (r. c. 972/5-995) where he gathered a force of Varangians and waited for an opportunity to take the kingdom from his brother Yaropolk I (r. 972-980). Scandinavian contact with Russia was largely confined to the reigns surrounding Vladimir I (972-1015) - in whose court at Novgorod the young prince Olaf Tryggvason (King of Norway, 995-1000) grew up. Other accounts that relate to the

---

271. Ibid. Sviatoslav's successor, Yaropolk I (r. 972-980), held a conciliatory attitude towards (Greek) Orthodox Christianity, one that may have been inherited by Vladimir the Great. **272.** Those that are, include: Holmgarðr (Novgorod), Koenugaror (Kiev), Aldeigjuborg (Ladoga), Palteskja (Polotzk), Muramar (Murom), Sursdal or Surdalar (Suzdal'), Rapstofa (Rostov), Smoleskja (Smolensk), and Syrnes (probably Chernigov). **273.** Around 987, Basil II of the Byzantine Empire (r. 976-1025) sought Vladimir's aid to defend his throne. Vladimir agreed, taking Basil IIs sister Anne as his bride, a marriage approved on the condition that Vladimir must convert to Christianity. In 988, this pact resulted in the Christianization of the Kievan Rus', and the establishment of the Varangian Guard in the Byzantine Empire. Varangian is a Byzantium term that describes an elite bodyguard of Scandinavian warriors in service to the Emperor, under the Byzantium Imperial banner.

reign of Yaroslav the Wise (1015-1054) appear in the *Heimskringla*, the *Fagrskinna*, the *Morkinskinna*, and the *Eymundarpattr Hringssonar*, and are concerned mainly with the relatives and lineages of Háraldr 'Hardrada' Sigurðarson (c. 1015-1066).

According to these Norse sources Hardrada's (Old Norse: harðráði)[274] half-brother was Olaf Haraldsson (later Saint Olaf); as younger men, they had fought together at the Battle of Stiklestad.[275] Olaf's uncle, Sigurðr was an entrusted collector of taxes from the Estonians for Prince Vladimir at Novgorod. Others described in these texts are 'Hardrada's' son Magnus II (The Good), 'Hardrada's' wife Elisiv (Ellisif, or Elisaveta among Eastern Slavic people) of Kyiv (granddaughter of the Swedish king Olof Skötkonung), and daughter of the Rus' prince, Yaroslav the Wise and the Swedish princess Ingigerðr (who may have been a female relative of 'Hardrada's'), and finally, Yaroslav the Wise himself. By way of further example, Háraldr's own daughter married into the royal dynasty at Novgorod, while his other children married into European dynasties, including Henry I of France, Andrew I of Hungary and the daughter of Constantine IX. Evidently, Russian history is not so remote or isolated as many imagine, or have been led to believe, and is very much entwined with that of Europe. Elsewhere, Harald 'Gormsson' Bluetooth's son, King Svein Forkbeard (960–1014) wed Gunnhild, the widow of a former King of Sweden. She was probably a Wendish princess, daughter of King Burizlav, who may have been of Scandinavian descent. Their sons were King Harald II of Denmark and King Cnut the Great. Closely bonded ties to Europe, Frankia, England, Sweden and Russia are thusly woven into the Icelandic narratives that demonstrate the complexity of statehood, power, and shifting politics at play by the major families of these regions. Motivated entirely by the manipulation and control of taxes, tithes and tribute, trade was the key to everything, and to accomplish it, any religion that served that purpose was adopted without discrimination.

---

274. Despite the date discrepancy, many historians now favour the notion that Háraldr 'Hardrada' Sigurðarson, c. 1015-1066. (King Háraldr III of Norway from 1046-1066), was actually the widely known *Háraldr Hárfagri (Háraldr Fairhair)*, casting serious doubt in the veracity of saga-accounts of an earlier 10th century Háraldr 'Fairhair.' (Old Norse: Háraldr Hálfdanarson c. 850-60 – c. 931/2-40). See: Judith Jesch. "Norse Historical Traditions and Historia Gruffud vab Kenan: Magnus Berfoettr and Haraldr Harfagri." In *Gruffudd ap Cynan: A Collaborative Biography*. Edited by K.L. Maund (Cambridge, 1996): 117-147 See: Joan Turville-Petre. "The Genealogist and History: Ari to Snorri." In, Saga-Book XX (Viking Society for Viking Research, University College London, 1978-81): 7-23 **275.** See Appendix VI for a brief summary of Háraldr's infamous career and deeds.

BAPTISM
AND HELL-FIRE

With the failure of Vladimir's plan to unify the Rus' in a centralised official form of paganism, he quickly realised that to achieve centralisation of state and government, he would need to completely convert the population to observe one religion only, be that Christianity, Islam or Judaism. Similar resistance towards conversion to Catholic Christianity was met by Jarl Haakon in Norway and (possibly) Svein Forkbeard in Denmark. Determined to control trade and hold power within his lands, Vladimir recognised the power that lay in the domain of rival states beyond the borders of his lands that had succumbed to various monotheistic conversions. A vital condition for the mass conversion of a people, is a settled urban state, allowing churches, synagogues or mosques to provide stable focus for its religious rites, to breathe and grow - a freedom restricted or denied by the author of *The Russian Primary Chronicle*.

Obsessed with power, and driven entirely by self-interest, Vladimir invited missionaries from other countries in c. 986-7, to speak about their distinctive creeds in a meeting held in Constantinople. According to the glosses in *The Russian Primary Chronicle*, the representatives who took part in the theological dispute included a Bulgar of the Muslim faith, a Rabbi from the Khazar state, a Papal legate, and a Christian Greek philosopher from the Byzantine Empire. Each ambassador was directed to persuade Vladimir of the superiority of their religion, that is to say, which amongst them was able to show themselves to be the most lucrative for control of both state and trade. Following the advice of his tribal elders, the Boyars, Vladimir then sent his own ambassadors to the neighbouring countries to learn more before a decision could be made. Impressed by the splendour and beauty of the Greek Orthodox faith and of the St. Sofia Cathedral, Vladimir naturally succumbed to the lure of the Byzantine trade and tribute, which at that time surpassed even that of the Bulgar Muslims. The persuasion of the highest bidder, long secured already in his lands, won the day.

320 PIRATES, MERCHANTS, DEVILS & DARK DEEDS

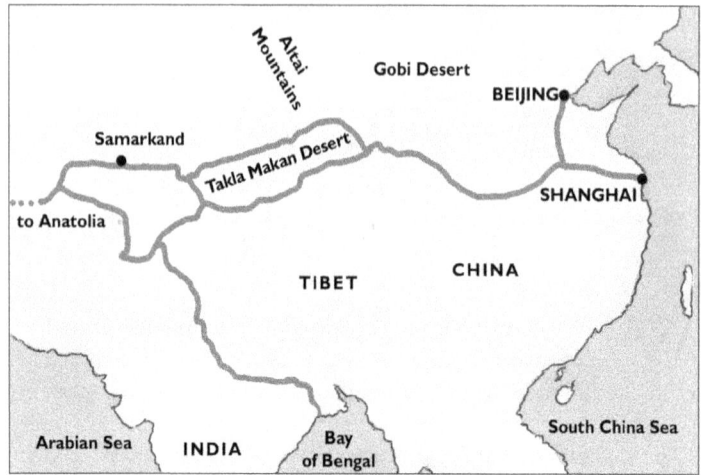

7. The Silk Road

Constantinople along with the Byzantine Empire offered without question, the most productive option at that time. It should not be forgotten however, that *The Russian Primary Chronicle* is largely an artificial narrative construct, a political work and as such, suffers from an excess of post factum addendums and revisions. Any natural or original narrative was irrevocably corrupted. Cloaked in contradiction, its fictions were composed at the behest of self-serving oligarchs who drastically filtered translations from the Old Slavic languages into a literary creation that fell under heavy influence of the Church and the State. Dates and names relating to certain events are purely speculative: "information that was not compatible was left aside, while the elements that should be there but did not exist, were invented."[276]

At the behest of the Church, Prince Vladimir destroyed the wooden statues of Slavic tutelary figures that he had himself raised just eight years earlier in his efforts to homogenise religious practises. Wooden balbals were either burnt or hacked into pieces, and the aforementioned statue only later named and known as Perun, was thrown into the Dnieper.[277] To commemorate the event, Vladimir built the first stone church of the Kievan Rus', close by another wooden church already on top of the hill and near to where the alleged heathen shrine had previously stood.[278]

The baptism of the Princess Olga (and later saint), whether

---

276. Duczko, 2004. **277**. Longsworth, 2006: 38.

BAPTISM AND HELL-FIRE 321

in Kyiv or Constantinople, occurred c.945 or 957. Then, in c.988, a notable surge occurred after Vladimir the Great, his family and the ruling elite – the Boyars – prudently accepted conversion. The entire population of Kyiv were then forcibly baptized in the river Dnieper, into the Eastern Orthodox Church, the state religion of the Byzantine Empire at that time. This so-called mass conversion and 'Baptism of Kiev' (Kyiv) recorded in *The Russian Primary Chronicle* as Vladimir's great victory over paganism, was strangely not acknowledged in the histories of the Orthodox Church who had long considered Russia theirs already. Following this, Christianisation of Russian lands occurred quickly, travelling along the waterways between Kyiv and Novgorod, consolidating the whole of Russia as it fanned outwards from this core, drawing in the numerous tribal factions and ethnicities forming a single united, state with one orthodox religion. As the line of conversions crept northwards up to Novgorod, it met with some resistance there as late as 1071, when it is recorded that Prince Gleb Sviatoslavich broke up the crowd by chopping a sorcerer in half with an axe.[279] Certain discrepancies in are evident in the contradictions that appear in varying reports, concerning not only the dates of the main conversions, but also the actual nature of those conversions, be they from localised paganisms or from one type of Christianity[280] to another official branch of it.

In reality, the Christianization of the Kievan Rus' had taken place in several stages, beginning way back in the 5th century with St Andrew,[281] continuing sporadically until around 867, when an Orthodox bishop of the Patriarch Photius of Constantinople, persuaded some of the Rus', to accept baptism.[282] Conversions progressed slowly, although by 944,[283] a sizable portion of the Kievan population were already

---

278. Lavrentevskaia Letopis, also called the "Povest Vremennykh Let." In, *Polnoe Sobranie Russkikh Letopisey (PSRL)* Vol. 1: 95-102. (Typography of Edward Prats. 1837 -) See: https://infogalactic.com/info/Complete_Collection_of_Russian_Chronicles. (Accessed 12th November 2021). **279.** Arsenii Nasonov. (Ed.) Novgorodskaia Pervaia Letopis: Starshego i mladshego izvodov, (AN SSSR, 1950): 191-96. **280.** Both would have been considered heathen **281.** According to the Church Tradition, Christianity was first brought to the territory of modern Belarus, Russia and the Ukraine, by Saint Andrew in the 5th -century North Pontic Greek colonies, both in the Crimea and on the modern Ukrainian shores of the Sea of Azov and the Black Sea, remained the main centres of Christianity in Eastern Europe for almost a thousand years. **282.** See correspondences on this topic in: Photii Patriarchae Constantinopolitani Epistulae et Amphilochia. Edited by B. Laourdas and L. G. Westerinck. (T. 1. Leipzig, 1983): 49 **283.** Photius had referred to the Christianization of the so-called Tmutarakan (or Pontic) Rus', while the Novgorod (or Northern) Rus' remained non-Christian for another century.

Christian. Despite the odd incident, conversion was largely peaceful, a feat smoothed by ministration and preaching in the native Slavic language; Saints Cyril and Methodius creation of the Cyrillic language was instrumental in this success. Lamentations by the Russian people aside, the complete Christianization of the Rus' finally and firmly allied it with the Byzantine Empire, opening up extensive trading contracts.

The Russian Primary Chronicle[284] begins in a manner not unlike *Heimskringla*, with a history of the biblical world that incorporated an extensive genealogy beginning with Noah and Adam. Leading into the flood, the ensuing turmoil and the whole journey, the narrative peaks in the year of Michael's accession as the first true prince of the Rus'.[285] Russia's position as a cultural crossroads facilitated the free-flow of cross-cultural trade between Christian Byzantium, the Muslim domination of the Volga Bulgars[286] (and others to the southeast), as well as with the Khazar converts (to Judaism and Christianity). In fact, there is strong evidence of a Russian diocese of the Byzantine church as early as 867, much earlier than previously imagined. A church dedicated to St. Ilya also existed in Kyiv during the reign of Igor, amongst whose retainers a good number were Christian.

According to the 'Russian Primary Chronicle'[287] (Povest

---

284. The earliest native sources for Russian history are the mediaeval annals. Regardless of their date and nature, practically all extant Russian chronicle texts include a generally uniform account of the period extending from the traditional origins of Rus' to the early 12th century. The idealised, highly propagandic narrative known as The Russian Primary Chronicle, or the Naclzal'naya Letopis,' is a literary expression of the prevailing political system when Kyiv was the great national and intellectual centre of the Eastern Slavs. Until the 19th century, it was habitually attributed to the monk Nestor. This view and the chronicle's authorship is now being critically reassessed. Far from being a homogeneous work, it is a compilation from several chronicle texts of greater antiquity. However, the extant chronicle is a 14th-century document that claims itself to be a copy of a 12th-century manuscript.
285. According to the RPC, the land of Rus' was first named in the year 6360 (852) when the Emperor Michael III acquired his regnal authority. However, this is the first of several factual errors. Michael's reign began a decade earlier in 842. Many other dates and events are similarly incorrect. The RPC claims that Prince Oleg of Novgorod seized Kyiv in 882, thereby uniting the northern and southern lands of the Eastern Slavs under his singular authority. The state's adoption of Christianity from the Byzantine Empire in 988, initiated the synthesis of Byzantine and Slavic cultures that defined Russian culture for the next millennium. See: http://theinfolist.com/php/HTMLGet.php?FindGo=Primary%20Chronicle (Accessed 4th August 2021)
286. The Bulgars were probably remnant Huns who remained in the east after the Goths were overthrown in 375 CE. In 482 CE, some thirty years after Attila's death, Bulgar outposts appeared on the Byzantine frontier. Bulgars were enlisted by the Emperor Zeno as allies against the Visigoths.

BAPTISM AND HELL-FIRE 323

Vremennykh Let), the much-fabled Novgorod flourished under its early rulers Rurik (c.860), Oleg (c.879) and Igor (c.913). Slavic culture was nevertheless predominant, and later rulers were completely immersed in it, adopting Slavic names (Igor's son Svyatoslav I, c. 945-78 was the first), language, customs, and artistic style (jewellery and pottery especially). Very few Scandinavian loan-words entered the Slavonic language. This level of assimilation was not unusual. Vikingr embraced the cultures they encountered on their travels, and were readily acculturalised in many of the places they settled, particularly Vinland, Normandy, Ireland, Scotland, England, and the Isle of Man. In other regions, such as Orkney, Shetland, and the Faroe Isles, their own culture was better preserved. To properly emphasise the level of Scandinavian assimilation into Slavic culture, we must look to the conflict on the Black Sea coast, between the Bulgars and the Byzantine empire. Vikingr mercenaries fought in the emperor's Varangian guard against the Bulgars and the southern Slavonic Croats, in order to curb their expansion along the eastern Adriatic coast. Conversely, the Normans, even as Vikingr descendants, were Catholic, so allied themselves with both Croats and Bulgars against Byzantium (Numerous incursions ocurred between the Normans and the Byzantine Empire from c. 1040 until 1185).

In Russia, by far the greatest external influences to its evolving culture (from architectural styles to the Kievan alphabet) was the ideology that came from Byzantium through Vladimir's adoption in 988 of Eastern Orthodox Christianity, whose tenets he favoured over Rome's. As the first Christian ruler of the Kievan Rus', Vladimir I (son of Svyatoslav I, ruled c. 978-1015), the Grand Prince of Kiev and Prince of Novgorod in 970, his conversion was founded entirely in self-serving politics however. Desirous of a dynastic marriage with a prestigious bride, he was easily persuaded to form a diplomatic alliance with the Byzantine Emperor, Basil II, in order to win his sister Anna. In return, Vladimir captured a rebellious section of the Crimea for Basil, returning to the Emperor's control. Succeeded by his sons, Svyatopolk I (1015-19) and Jaroslav 'the Wise' (1019-54), further ties were forged through them with the Holy Roman Empire and Poland. The political crisis in the Byzantine Empire had allowed Vladimir to seize Constantinople and the Crimea, marry the Emperor Basil's sister and become ruler of all Russia. Under his desperate and violent rule, the unrelenting domination of trade continued.[288]

---

287. Many academics no longer credit the composition of this chronicle with the 11th-Century Kievan monk Nestor. **288.** Hazzard-Cross and Sherbowitz-Wetzor, 1953: 93

324 PIRATES, MERCHANTS, DEVILS & DARK DEEDS

Having followed the Rus' up to their conversion and the initial trials it had generated, it is now necessary to explore further the culture and beliefs of other massively influential peoples of North-East Europe upon those of the Germanic and Scandinavian peoples -The Slavs. The Viking Age was almost over, but the raiding and plundering continued. Between the Viking Age and High Middle Ages, the Western Slavonic peoples of the southern Baltic shore (Abodrites, Rügians, Wagrians, Polabians, Liutzians and Pomeranians), commonly known as The Wends, were a highly cultured and aristocratic people, rich from trade and very closely associated with the Jómsvikings. Conflict aside, the interactions between the Wends and the Scandinavians, benefited both peoples; the latter gained knowledge of bridge-building, construction, while the former benefitted from the Scandinavian's boat-building expertise, allowing them to raid parts of Denmark, Sweden and southern Norway in turn. As we shall shortly discover, this enterprise was curtailed by the Northern Crusades. What happens there is key to understanding much of the later medieval world and the total collapse of heathenism by default, because although the conflict between east and west was partially motivated by faith (politics, trade and the acquisition of wealth and resources notwithstanding), it had never been one of paganism versus Christianity.

JÓMSBORG

According to the accounts of some medieval chroniclers, a fabled West Slavic (Polabian) cultic site that sustained the dedicated worship of Svantovit for almost three hundred years, between the 9th and 12th centuries existed on a fierce Island in the Baltic. Known as Jaromarsburg, this high citadel existed on the northeastern tip of Rügen (Cape Arkona), in the Baltic Sea. Tenuous connections are made between Jaromarsburg and the semi-legendary (semi-mythical) Vikingr stronghold known as Jómsborg.[289] For over a century towards the close of the frenetic Viking Age, the people who found sanctuary here were known as Jómsvikings. Another possible location is Wolin, a major trading centre that hosted a vibrant emporium in the early Middle Ages on an Island (of the same name) in the same region of the Baltic, which now lies in northwest Poland that once bordered the Scythian marshes. In between them lies Szczecin (Stettin), another major trading complex. The German medieval chronicler Adam of Bremen referred to a substantial port and town in this region by the Slavic name of Jumne (may also be known as Julin and Vineta). Situated near to the Oder river on the southern coast of the Baltic Sea in late Viking Age Wendland (Pomerania), Adam claimed it served Slavs, Greeks and 'Barbarians,' alike. Even so, the extent of its actual existence is yet to be agreed upon. Jómsborg appears to be a derived construction, a compound name of Germanic terms formed towards the end of the 12th century: Jómi (the place) and borg (a fortified settlement). By far the largest settlements at that time were Wolin (Wollin/Julinum) and Stettin (Szczecin), which, as Latin-based terms, are certainly distinct from Jumne in origin, if not application.[290] Comprised of around a few thousand inhabitants, these fortified settlements (proto-market towns), are perhaps better understood if

---

289. Lee M. Hollander. *The Saga of the Jomsvikings* (University of Texas Press, 1989). See also: Ólafur Halldórsson. Danish Kings and the Jomsvikings in the Greatest Saga of Óláfr Tryggvason (Viking Society for Northern Research, 2000). **290.** Alexandra Petrulevich. On the etymology of at Jómi, Jumne and Jómsborg https://www.diva-portal.org/smash/get/diva2:403702/FULLTEXT01.pdf (Accessed 16th March 2025).

we apply the Slavic term – *gord (gard in Pomeranian and Polabian language). Dedicated to trade and mercantile pursuits, these garrisoned citadels protected the stalls, craft shops, temples, churches, abbeys, markets, taverns, toll stations and even coin mints. Mentioned in the *Heimskringla*, several famous Viking Age leaders are associated with Jómsborg, including the aforementioned 10th-Century Háraldr Bluetooth (king of Denmark from c. 958 – c. 986), and the 11th-Century leader, Magnus the Good (King of Norway from 1035, and King of Denmark from 1042 until his death in 1047). After annexing Wendland, King Haraldr ('bluetooth') Gormsson is cited in Medieval Scandinavian tradition (based on the accounts in *Knýtlinga saga*, *Fagrskinna*, *Saxo's Gesta Danorum*, and *Sven Aggesen's Gesta Regum Danorum*) as the original founder of Jómsborg and for establishing a hirð in its prominent fortress, built by his elite Jómsvikings.

And there he quickly has built in his domain a fortress by the sea, exceedingly large and strongly built, which was called Jómsborg after that. There he also has built a harbour inside the fortress that three hundred longships could be berthed in at the same time, so that they were all shut within the fortress... Some parts of the fortress stood out over the sea, and structures built like that are called sea-castles, and on account of this the harbour was within the fortress.[291]

An alternative founder, a Danish jarl – Pálnatóki, is named in the *Jómsvíkinga saga*, *Óláfs saga Tryggvasonar en mesta*, and *Eyrbyggja saga*, but this substitute appears entirely political. A weak leader (Bluetooth, is replaced by a strong leader – Pálnatóki).[292] Random references to Jómsborg elsewhere in Scandinavian literature are scant, and oftentimes contradictory, and there are at least five versions of the saga of the Jómsvikings that we know of. Whatever the historical truth of these events really is, all these medieval accounts align in the notion that Jómsborg was founded as a defensive and pre-emptive Scandinavian presence for possible incursions with the Slavs. Modern studies alternatively suggest the possibility that these skilled warriors were mercenaries serving under a marauding Slavic prince.[293] This was truly a European dark age. Remember, these sagas were written hundreds of years after the alleged events took place, and at the time of writing, the more impactful memory would have been that which

---

291. *The Saga of the Jómsvikings*, translated by Alison Finlay, Þórdís Edda Jóhannesdóttir, Andrew McGillivray, edited by Svanhildur Óskarsdóttir, Emily Lethbridge, Tom Birkett, Roderick Dale, Ármann Jakobsson, and Miriam Mayburd. (De Gruyter, 2018).
292. Jakub Morawiec. "Danish Kings and the Foundation of Jómsborg." Scripta Islandica 65. 2014: 125–142.

JÓMSBORG

relates to a military conquest of Wendland by Scandinavians. What we do know for certain, is that this region of Poland ultimately became the centre of a co-ordinated attack by western Christian Kings. Prior to this event, battle controversy places Háraldr Bluetooth and his son Sweyn Forkbeard in the field of play as Danish pirates and treasure hunters seeking to benefit from the chaos of political wranglings within Scandinavia that reached across into northern Europe. Wendland's (Poland) fabulous wealth and strategic location attracted unwanted attention. "Piratical operations made their bravery famous, encouraged by the victories over neighbours; finally, they became so daring that they covered the waters of the north with the permanent destruction of sea travellers. This, like nothing else, contributed to the Danish rule."[294]

To this volatile mix we add Haakon Sigurdsson (known in Old Norse as Hákon jarl), a nobleman and ruler of Norway (975-995), who was also a vassal of the Danish and very Christian ruler, Háraldr Bluetooth. Haakon Sigurdsson maintained a firm grip on the heathen faith of his ancestors in stark defiance of his overlord's decree to embrace Christianity. This rebellious act incurred considerable conflict. While this is hinted at by Snorre in *Heimskringla*, it is far from being an historically accurate expression of events. That was not its purpose. It is largely a fantasy constructed as a literary vehicle for what culminates in the suppression of heathenism and the embrace of Christianity, a faith brought to conquer Norway by Olaf Trygvasson in 995. Nonetheless, the convoluted, meandering tale provides clues that we can follow into other supportive disciplines that aid us in our venture to build a better, and truer perspective from which to view the shifting tides of the Medieval Period. There is also an observable reverence for the warriors of old, whose steely valour is lauded as a virtue lacking in later times. Moments of nostalgia punctuate what is generally a bland, impassioned account of Norway's conversion. A small detail denotes the oath-taking procedure, whereby a man steps forward, placing one foot upon a sacred stone in the great hall (Hof) before declaring his vows and boasts to his company of fellow warriors.

At one point of the tale, it is claimed that many ships sailed from the military fortress Jómsborg (Wolin) to crush the recalcitrant Hákon jarl into submission. As a vassal of the Danish king, Hákon jarl was

---

293. Jakub Morawiec. "Danish Kings and the Foundation of Jómsborg." (*Scripta Islandica*, Volume 65, 2014) https://www.medievalists.net/2018/03/danish-kings-and-the-foundation-of-jomsborg/ (Accessed 12th February 2025). **294.** Ibid.

obliged to surrender tribute to Háraldr Bluetooth. His refusal to do so, added fuel to the smouldering unrest between these two headstrong leaders. This account features in *The Saga of the Jómsvikings*,[295] a tale that makes much of the differences in faith between the two rivals for power. In it, we are told that Hákon turns to the ancient northern gods of his people, calling upon Þorgerðr and Irpa to aid his victory over the usurpers. Desperate for victory, in true epic style akin to Greek tragedies of old, the saga claims that Hákon follows the cruel actions of Agammemnon, choosing to sacrifice a child, this time a son, Erling. It apparently worked – a huge tempest arose, pushing back the Jómsvikings in a barrage of freezing hail, piercing the bodies of men like arrows in a great naval battle that took place around 986 at an unspecified place. Its location is often cited as Hjörungavágr (off the coast of Norway), but this is a more recent and unproven association. Many Danes were slaughtered mercilessly by Hákon jarl, but it is thought his son, moved by their singular courage and gallantry in the face of death, spared some of the Jómsvikings. For a while, at least, the remaining Jómsvikings continued to enjoy their rebellious autonomy on Jómsborg, the base for their raiding exploits in the Baltic. Despite this initial defeat, however the Danes regrouped and pushed on under King Sweyn Forkbeard, who achieved his desire to control Norway around 1000, adding the English throne to his expanding northern empire.

Several Viking Age artefacts have been discovered in Wolin, yet no weapons that would indicate the presence of Norse warriors, only traders. Adam of Breman emphasised its multicultural, if not, multi-faith tolerance. "For even alien Saxons also have the right to reside there on equal terms with others, provided only that while they sojourn there they do not openly profess Christianity. In fact, all its inhabitants still blunder about in pagan rites. Otherwise, so far as morals and hospitality are concerned, a more honourable or kindlier folk cannot be found."[296] Again, Adam speaks of Christianity with the Catholic bias, and paganism with heterodox Christian bias – so we'll never know what faith they really adhered to. We can only speculate. The Jómsvikings continued to plague many coastal communities until their fortress fell in 1043, to the forces of Magnus the Good, King of Norway whose attacks on Vindland (Wendland) were savage and uncompromising.

The robbers, hemmed 'twixt death and fire,
Knew not how to escape thy ire;

---

295. The 13th-century *Jómsvíkinga Saga* relates to earlier events of the 10th to the 11th centuries. **296.** Adam of Bremen *Gesta Hammaburgensis ecclesiae Pontificum*.

JÓMSBORG

O'er Jómsborg castle's highest towers
Thy wrath the whirlwind-fire pours.
The heathen on his false gods calls,
And trembles even in their halls;
And by the light from its own flame
The king this viking-hold o'ercame.[297]

Jómsborg seems to have existed, yet its actual demise remains a mystery. "Thus the foundation of Jómsborg was preceded by armed invasions which resulted in the conquest of this part of Wendland. Consequently, it influenced the image of the settlement, which was either founded by Haraldr or Pálnatóki. It was a place profoundly military in character and it was to function as a military camp for the protection of Danish property."[298]

If it did not perish under such assaults, then it withered into obscurity, assimilated by time and tide, along with the fabled Jómsvikings who lived and supposedly fought and died there. Jómsborg was essentially a strategically strong citadel of fighting men with considerable warrior prowess, an elite brotherhood whose code centred on the blood-oath, obedience to their leader, and equity of all spoils taken. The law also forbade the presence of women, total discretion, vows of vengeance, that no arms be raised against a brother, that the ages of all warriors should be between 18 and 50, to present no fear, and amity and cooperation at all times.[299] Outside the maxims recorded in *Hávamál*, there are but few other sources that refer to the ethics, or even to the laws pertaining to warriorhood. *The Saga of the Jómsvikings* is notable in its exceptional description of the strictures of the aforementioned code that may have formed the basis for all privateering laws, or codes of conduct later drafted by pirates, who in turn, may have been the renegade inheritors of this type of mercenary brotherhood.[300]

Danish control of Wolin, initiated in the 980s, could not have lasted. In fact, it would have ended with Haraldr Gormsson's fall. His son Sveinn met too many conflicts at the very beginning of his reign to be able to mark his authority in the town.

Haraldr's achievements in Wendland, although only lasting a short time, had to be significant since they influenced the development of the Jómsborg legend in a twofold way. On the one hand, later saga authors used it to disgrace and humiliate

---

297. Snorre Sturlasson. *Heimskringla*, or The Chronicle of the Kings of Norway. **298.** Morawiec, 2014. **299.** Similar laws can be found in *Hálfs saga ok Hálfrekka*, although some individual laws from this listing reflect the laws of the hirð recorded in *Hirðskrá*. **300.** See: *Jómsvíkinga Saga* – Chapter 16 – The Laws of the Jómsvikings.

the king of Denmark. On the other hand, he was labelled conqueror of this part of Wendland and the founder of the stronghold. [...]Sveinn Úlfsson's death in 1075 turned out to be the end of Danish activity both in the Baltic region and in England. This situation started to change at the very end of the eleventh century. Eiríkr góði (1095–1103) attempted to impose his supremacy on Rügen, and he probably achieved this around 1100. He also supported Henry, the belligerent son of the Obodrite prince Gotshalk, who at that time attempted to gain the throne of Obodrites. It was just the beginning of complicated Danish-Saxon-Slavic relations that lasted until the 1160s, and ended with the establishment of Saxon domination in the whole Polabian region at the expense of both Slavic tribes and Denmark. Rulers of the latter still sought to play a bigger and more active role in Wendland.[301]

---

301. Morawiec, 2014.

THE WENDS

Looking back to a time before all these perplexing events arose, we may finally investigate the rueful foundations that instigated them. Around 500 BCE, the Polabian, or western Slavic tribes, otherwise known as Wends,[302] (Windes) who were a non-indigenous, non-homogenous people, migrated to the east Germanic region, settling on the River Oder, near to the area occupied by Saxons, displacing the Germanic Rügieri tribe on the northern promontory of Arkona. The name 'Wend' may be related to the pale-skinned peoples referred to by the Romans as *Veneti*. Medieval Scandinavians regarded those peoples as Vender – a term that referred specifically to Polabian Slavs, comprising of Rügian Slavs, Obotrites, Veleti/Lutici, and Pomeranian tribes living near the southern shore of the Baltic Sea (Vendland). A description provided in the 11th-Century German account by Adam of Bremen, and in Matthaios of Edessa, refers to the Cuman (Polovtsians) peoples as the Blond (fair, bright) Ones, which suggests some compatibility with the 'Polovtsy' people, who were also pale. Taken from the Slavic root *polje – field" (cf. Russian póle), the 'Polovtsy' suggests 'men of the field' or 'men of the Steppe.'[303] As herders and hunters, they were also skilled agriculturalists and efficient farmers. Nomadic and independent, they adapted quickly. Their engineering expertise was possibly exchanged for boat-building skills from the Scandinavians, allowing them to expand not only their trading networks of fur and fish, but also their capacity to raid cattle and trade people as slaves with the Franks and Danes.[304] In Pomerania, slaves mostly consisted of

---

302. Polabian Slavs (Wends)were formed of several tribes, including the Pomeranians east of the River Elbe in present-day northeast Germany and Poland. However, the 'Vends' were possibly a separate Finnic ethnic group. See: Mihai Dragnea. "Divine Vengeance and Human Justice in the Wendish Crusade of 1147." In, Collegium Medievale 2016: http://ojs.novus.no/index.php/CM/article/view/1366/1351 (Accessed 25th October 2019) **303.** Folban, Vallani, Valwei are terms used for the Cumans all derivatives of Proto-Germanic root *falwa- meaning 'pale' - (English 'fallow'). See: Justin Dragosani-Brantingham. "An Illustrated Introduction to the Kipchak Turks." ([1999] 2011) kipchak.com. (Accessed 29th October 2020) **304.** Eric Christiansen. *The Northern Crusades*. (Penguin Books Ltd. 1997): 287

Wendish, German or Danish peoples taken as captives of war, though not so many as other areas across Europe. Mostly, the population consisted of freemen whose subsistence depended on the fishing industry, agriculture and trade. The generation of wealth from this lush, abundant region was a prime motivator accessible to all its freemen.

After countless skirmishes with their martially adept neighbours, the Polabian Slavs developed considerable combative skills to fend off Germanic neighbours to the west and the Steppe nomads to the east. Tenacious and resilient, the Polabians managed to push out a modest, stable empire for themselves to the east during the 6th to the 7th centuries, ultimately settling half of Europe by the 8th century, including regions occupied by Germanic tribes who had emigrated there during the Migration Period. The Slavic tribes were extremely influential as they expanded throughout Europe into Asia. Encroachments onto Charlemagne's territory, caused him to establish the eastern limit of the Slavic empire at the Elbe River,[305] thus distinguishing his own initial limits for his Holy Roman Empire. It is believed that the German-Roman clash was based mainly in Slavic ethnicity and Germanic heresies.

The control later exerted by the Holy Roman Empire over the Slavic territories between the Elbe and the Oder, was initially only nominal. Pushing each other for tribute, frequent raids ocurred across the Limes Saxonicus between the (pagan) Slavs and the Christians, including the Holstein Saxons. Against such militant defiance, Charlemagne was obliged to enlist the Obotrites as allies. With their assistance, his campaign eventually subdued the rebellious Holstein Saxons.

Later however, in an ironic twist, the Polabian Slavs were largely conquered by Saxons and Danes throughout the 9th to the 11th centuries, over which time, the Frankish kings and their successors had been anxious to seize the rich land the Slavic region was renowned for. This was eventually achieved when a series of successful crusades, aided by the Saxon and Danish peoples, allowed them to annexe the Wendish 'marches,' incorporating it into the legacy of Charlemagne's Holy Roman Empire. Over time, the co-existence of Polabian Slavs led to their gradual absorption of Germanic culture, affirming their assimilation within the Holy Roman Empire.[306] This process was known as Ostsiedlung. Roman Catholic missionaries pushed hard on the Western Slavs to convert, with varying measures of success, which

---

305. Labe in Czech and Łaba in Polish. **306.** The Sorbs are the only descendants of the Polabian Slavs to have retained their identity and culture.

THE WENDS 333

marked a contrast with the Eastern Slavs who were largely disposed to Byzantium and Eastern Orthodox Christianity. During the course of the 10th century, the Ottonian dynasty and other (western) noble families encouraged the expansion of the Holy Roman Empire, eastwards, in the direction of the Wendish (West Slavic) lands. Despite this pressing intimidation, many early conversions were demonstrably cast aside in a rebellious return to former (animistic and totemic based) paganisms,[307] to the extent that many new temple complexes were erected in the West Slavic regions. I find it very interesting (and no coincidence) that this rich, fertile region is associated with thunder deities condemned by Otto.

Heady with a successful First Crusade (1096–1099) in the Holy Lands, Saxon nobles turned their attention to their Slavic neighbours early in the 12th century, whom they sought to displace with Saxon and Flemish settlers. The initiative to reclaim those lands, rich in wealth and vital resources, ultimately instigated The Northern Crusades. Mounted by bishops and nobles of the Holy Roman Empire, the initial Wendish Crusade, of 1147, saw the worst atrocities committed by Christians on other Christians. It was utterly despicable in its intent, and merciless in its execution. While many Germanic peoples from the southern regions joined the crusades in the Middle East, Saxons from the north, opted for the military campaigns against the Slavs. The Roman Catholic Church faced heresies on two fronts – (East Slavic) Orthodox Christianity and (West) Slavic paganism. Meanwhile, missionaries from Sweden and Denmark were sent to proselytise the faith in Finland. Needing firm bases from which to operate, the German archbishoprics of Bremen and Magdeburg founded further Bishoprics[308] to support these conversions. Using 11th century papal rhetoric, a Wendish Crusade was first meted by an anonymous missive, known now as The Magdeburg Letter. Composed around 1107-1110, it was a forthright appeal to greed, veiled as piety. The author of this missive boasts that:

(...) these gentiles are most wicked, but their land is the best, rich in meat, honey, corn, and birds; and if it were well cultivated none could be compared to it for the wealth of its produce. So say those who know it. And so, most renowned Saxon, French, Lorrainers, and Flemings and conquerors of the world, this is an

---

307. Polabian Slavs remained pagan. They saw Jesus as a Germanic god, so rejected his mission. **308.** King Valdemar the Great of Denmark enlisted the aid of Duke Henry the Lion of Saxony against the Slavs, so the political centre at Magdeburg was supplemented by others at Brandenburg, and Havelberg.

occasion for you to save your souls and, if you wish it, acquire the best land in which to live.[309]

This well devised lure initiated a long-lasting crusade against the Wends.[310] As apostates, the Wends were seen as a threat to Christendom, thus, justifying a crusade against them. Issued in 1147, Pope Eugenius' III papal bull (the *Divina dispensatione*), gave his full support to the Saxon initiative, allowing them to move with impunity against the Polabian Slavs (Wends). Led primarily by the Kingdom of Germany within the Holy Roman Empire, the Wendish Crusade[311] was a particularly ferocious military campaign spilling over into the Second Crusade (1147–1149).[312] Within its dictates, the Bull awarded the full remission of sins to anyone joining the just crusade against the impious Wends, thus honouring the same distinctive guarantee made by Bernard of Clairvaux[313] (a Burgundian abbot) to all other soldiers of Christ fighting elsewhere as crusaders in the Middle East. Volunteers in the crusade against the Slavs included bohemian mercenaries, but the main body of warriors in the Pope's army primarily consisted of Danes, Poles and Saxons, although the Saxon king exempted himself from participation in the crusade on ethical grounds. Therefore, the campaign was led by other leading elite Saxon families under the command of the Papal legate Anselm of Havelberg.

An astute man, Bernard of Clairvaux feared that those who participated were doing so only for the possible material gain. In an effort to persuade crusaders to focus on spiritual conversion, Bernard of Clairvaux announced: "*We prohibit completely that a truce be made for any reason with these people [Wends] either for money or tribute, until such time as, with the aid of God either their religion or their nation shall be destroyed.*"[314] Bernard's concerns were validated as the Pope's army pressed more fervently for tribute from the pagan Slavs, than it did for conversion. Of Henry the

---

309. Dragnea, 2016. **310.** Several Slavic tribes of Abrotrites, Rani, Liutizians, Wagarians, and Pomeranians who lived east of the River Elbe in present-day northeast Germany and Poland composed the people collectively known as 'Wends.' **311.** Although the Northern Crusades officially began with Pope Celestine III's call in 1195 CE, the Catholic kingdoms of Scandinavia, Poland and the Holy Roman Empire had already begun decades earlier (in 1147), to subjugate their (Slavic) heathen neighbours, the Polabian Wends, Sorbs, and Obotrites, who lived between the Elbe and Oder rivers. Campaigns were primarily led by the Swedes, but included the Saxons, Danes, and Western Poles, who collectively moved on the Finns in the 1150s during the First Crusade, Tavastia in 1249 in the Second Crusade, and Karelia in 1293 during the Third Crusade. **312.** The fall of Edessa in Syria in 1144 had rocked Christendom to the core. http://www.jstor.org/stable/24416033. (Accessed January 31, 2021)

THE WENDS

Lion's later bloody campaigns, Helmold of Bosau (c. 1120–1177) that "there was no mention of Christianity, but only of money."[315]

The rising Teutonic Order of Knights, founded during the 12th-century Holy Wars in Palestine, led the crusades into the Baltic regions to regain political control of its shipping networks. This proved to be an immensely profitable enterprise for them. German merchants further exploited the Baltic frontier, establishing trading routes along its entirety. Conflict was not new to these regions. For several centuries prior to this crusade, the Finns, Balts and Slavs who dwelt along the Baltic shores had grappled with their Saxon and Danish neighbours to the north and south for economic advantage, destroying castles and disrupting sea trade routes in their attempts to monopolise resources. What made this crusade different was its sanction by the Pope and its execution by Papal knights and armed monks, who fought vigorously as Christian warriors. The notion that the Christian army was led and fought by priests, monks and bishops, may be surprising, but they were indeed soldiers of god in the truest and fullest sense. The popular image of the peaceable monk at prayer, is wide of the historical reality; it is a false and contrived image, and one that has held back our true understandings of these and other events, not to mention their causes and consequences.

8. mounted warrior

The Self-serving local nobility had actively encouraged (through lucrative land grants for redevelopment) the resettlement by Germanic peoples of the decimated areas in order to strengthen and consolidate their own tentative positions. Relocation under the well-established Ostsiedlung process(which later peaked during the 12th to the 14th centuries), allowed the gradual absorption and assimilation of Germanic migrants into western Pomerania alongside its local Slavic population.

---

313. Although Bernard of Clairvaux (1090-1153) did not support the notion of Mary's Immaculate Conception, he was a devout champion of the Cult of Mary. His treatise on Mariology proposed that the Virgin Mary was the peoples' intercessor, the Mediatrix as the Queen of Heaven. He also believed that Mary Magdalene was the Apostle to the Apostles. Bernard's spiritual philosophy based in the principle of Sola Fide (faith alone) formed the basis for his treatise (rule and directives) composed for the Knights Templar, which soon became the ideal of all Christian nobility. Recruitment to the 'holy' cause, was stimulated by Pope Innocent III's (d.2016) shrewd dedication of the Baltic regions to the Virgin, naming them Mary's Land. **314.** Robert Bartlett. "The Conversion of a Pagan Society in The Middle Ages." *History*, 70, no.229 (1985): 185-201 **315.** Bartlett, 1985.

In accordance with Germanic tradition, tribal names reflected local place names, (e.g. Heveller from Havel, Rüjanes from Rügians). Other language, laws and customs were readily absorbed into this new admixture. Following the successful conversion of the nobility, land deeds granted by local dukes anxious to oil the wheels of the papacy, facilitated the construction of several monasteries across vast regions, depriving the ordinary people of good agricultural land. However, the nobility's acceptance of conversion to Catholicism in 1128, did not spare them from the annexation and piecemeal break-up of the Wendish states in 1147, by the greed-obsessed Holy See, who sought all acquisitions to benefit its own coffers.

The full conversion of Pomerania to Catholicism (non-heterodox Christianity) was eventually achieved by the missionary efforts first of the 11th century Otto von Bamberg,[316] and completed later by the Bishop of Absalon[317] over the course of the 12th century, primarily via the foundation of numerous monasteries, and through the Christian clergy and Christian settlers. It is claimed that despite Otto von Bamberg's extensive mission, the Rani principality of Rugia (Rügen) had remained 'pagan.' Remember, this term along with heathen was freely applied to all non-orthodox forms of Christianity, not approved by the Pope and his Catholic mission. Otto of Bamburg did not make himself a popular aggressor. Founding no less than eleven churches during his first mission, he ensured that both Szczecin and Wolin were targeted and destroyed in the Danish raids. Otto executed those who resisted his oppressive edicts against the so-called heathens he claimed were lapsing into former practises. He tore down their holy sites, many of which were actual Christian churches, though he claimed they were pagan temples, and crucified a number of priests in his inhumane purge. It is rumoured that his brutalities incurred assassination attempts, though these failed. Launched on the pretext of securing a Catholic Poland through conversion, the Northern Crusades resulted in the complete subjugation of Polabian Slavs; waves of ruthless conquests thrust the former Pomeranian peoples into vassalage and (re)Christianization as alleged former 'heathen' tribes. Countless more were transported away as slaves.

Backed by Bishop Absalon, the Danish king, Valdemar I mounted an impressive offensive against Rügen, laying siege to the fortress in the

---

316. Otto of Bamberg (1060/1061 – 1139), a German missionary and papal legate responsible for converted much of medieval Pomerania to Catholicism. **317.** Danish statesman and prelate of the Catholic Church (1128–1201). He served as the bishop of Roskilde from 1158 to 1192.

Spring of 1168, which granted Absalon (as archbishop of Roskilde), the jurisdiction he needed to rectify Otto's previous oversight. Employing tactics similar to those of the Vikingr, the Danes came in by boat, raiding along the coast, moving inland via the rivers, burning crops and hamlets along the way. Slavic people were driven from their farms as colonizing Danes and Saxons sequestered them. Slavic pirates retaliated by raiding Denmark. Measures previously implemented to protect European traders were rigorously enforced. The farms here held all the promise of Eden, making them ripe for plunder! An horrendous siege in the Arkona peninsula ended when a fire threatened to engulf the town's residents and destroy its sacred temple that housed ancestral effigies and a wooden idol supposedly of Svetovid, forcing the Rani to finally surrender. It did not save them, nor their religious effigies from the fire. Razing the temples to the ground, Bishop Absalon instructed his Danish mercenaries to ensure everything was destroyed. Former inhabitants of Rügen were forced to convert to orthodox Christianity (Catholicism). The spoils of war and Arkona's magnificent treasures, plundered by Absalon, were shared out between King Valdemar[318] and his ally, Henry the Lion. Former shrines were replaced with Roman Catholic churches throughout the region.[319] Several encampments originally intended for development as towns, were deemed unstable, and were later moved, including a Pomeranian diocese originally set up in Wolin. Wolin, formerly a major Slavic and Viking town in the Oder estuary, was also destroyed in these later Danish raids.

Complex Danish-Saxon-Slavic relations crippled on until the 1160s, when the balance of power eventually tipped in favour of Saxon control of the whole Polabian region, much to the detriment of both the Slavs and Danes who'd vied for their own dominance of this region via numerous indecisive incursions. During this complex land-grabbing enterprise, there was considerable disruption and opportunism, with much shifting of alliances (between the Pomeranians, Saxons and Danes) leading to an overall instability of these regions, as petty infighting made allies opponents, and vice versa. For example, following the Battle of Verchen in 1164, Pomeranian dukes were reduced to the status of mere vassals under the strict enforcements of Henry the Lion of Saxony. In 1168, when Valdemar's successful campaigns subjugated even the Rügian princes as vassals of Denmark, the Saxon-Danish alliance disintegrated. At this point,

---

318. King of Denmark from 1202 until his death in 1241.   **319.** After the Danes conquered the stronghold of Arkona. Valdemar allowed the Rani prince to rule as a Danish vassal. The Slavic Rani tribe had occupied the Arkona peninsula since at least the 7th century, and possibly before.

in 1169, Rügen's former autonomy shifted to the suzerainty of the Church (via the bishops of Lund), which became the inheritor of the massive land tracts of the former temple estates (whether heterodox Christian or heathen). No time was wasted in re-building programs. Further chapels appeared everywhere, making their mark upon the landscape, obliterating all signs of the former cultic sites. Upon the site of the alleged Svetovid sanctuary, the church of Altenkirchen now houses the enigmatic Priest Stone (Priesterstein) or Svantevit Stone (Svantevitstein).[320] Laid sideways, it is incorporated into the foundation of the parish church. Depicting a bearded figure bearing a large rhyton, his identity remains undecided. Sometimes Svantovit is depicted with a sword, but he was more popularly shown bearing a horn of plenty, signifying abundance, wealth and fertility, but also chieftainship and the duties of noblesse oblige. This stone image could be a medieval rendition of Svantevit as the tutelary (protective) land spirit, but it is more likely a memorial stone dedicated to one of the ancestral ruling princes after Rügen was taken. Henry the Lion's own victory was also short-lived. Compromised by corrosive internal factions, Henry fell against the campaigns initiated by the Holy Roman Emperor Frederick Barbarossa in 1181.

9. The Wends

---

320. See a drawing by Carl Schuchhardt (1859–1943) - Schuchhardt, Carl. Arkona, Rethra, Vineta, Hanz Schoetz & Co. G.M.D.H. Berlin, 1926. Berlin», 1926, Public Domain, https://commons.wikimedia.org/w/index.php?curid=36608393. See also: a photo of this stone by Lebrac – Own work, CC BY-SA 3.0, https://commons.wikimedia.org/w/index.php?curid=5182695

THE NORTHERN OR BALTIC CRUSADES

In common with many other peoples of these regions, Slavic beliefs were founded upon custom and lore, the cultural principles of ethnicity, rather than notions of supposed racial bloodlines. Ancestry was important, but related primarily to the people you were amongst, that is to say: born or adopted into.

The tribe took precedence over the family unit. The history of the former beliefs of the Slavic peoples and their resistance to conversion to (Catholicism), is written down in several minor German documents, the Icelandic *Knýtlinga saga*, and other major Latin Chronicles by learned German clergymen – Thietmar of Merseburg, Adam of Bremen in the 11th century, Helmold and Otto of Bamberg in the 12th century, and Saxo Grammaticus in the 13th century.[321] These sources typically interpret the pagan Slavic religion through their own Christian-centric perspective, frequently making comparison with the Classical religions of the Mediterranean. Rarely if ever, do they refer to those peoples already converted to non-Roman Catholic forms of Christianity. Slavs who'd settled in the Balkan Peninsula centuries earlier in the 6th to the 7th centuries, had already succumbed to Eastern Orthodox Christianity through influences from the Byzantine Empire on their southern borders.

Holding out the longest, the western Slavs finally submitted to the teachings of the Roman Catholic Church in the 12th century after their crushing defeat in the Northern Crusades. Chronicles of the time refer to the periodic lapses into apostasy throughout the previous century among the Wends (Poles) and East Slavs. Slavs from the historical region of Pomerania, namely the (West Slavic) Kashubians and Slovincians, were able to preserve important elements of their native

---

321. Other Slavic peoples are poorly documented. Writings concerning them were produced long after their conversion, appearing in the 15th century Polish Chronicle which, having no basis in their real history, is largely fantasy.

ethnicity, culture and identity. In his *Chronica Slavorum* (Chronicle of the Slavs), the 12th-century German missionary Helmold of Bosau relays his surprise in the monistic belief of the Slavic peoples he personally encountered, in a single heavenly God whose ambivalence in human affairs, led to its unique management by a host of spirits, created and deputized by him for that purpose. As distinctive as this notion is within Indo-European mythologies, similar beliefs in such all-encompassing, but aloof deific figures, would be easily recognised amongst the Uralians, the Ugrians and the Volga Finns.

The Roman Catholic kingdoms of Denmark and Sweden were long covetous of conquest along the Eastern shores of the Baltic, in fact Sweden's crusades against (Russian) Orthodox Novgorod proved to be a highly lucrative enterprise for them. Northern Lybeck, Holstein and Estonia became subject to the hegemony of Denmark under King Valdemar II's campaigns (d. 1241). In addition to Poland and the outer fringes of Russian territory, several North European Roman Catholic monarchs greedily absorbed those regions that today encompass Finland, Latvia, and Lithuania. All heathens, including eastern Orthodox Christians, suffered enforced baptisms and the ravages of military occupation. Several Popes had officially endorsed the crusades into Slavic lands that spilled over into the 13th century on the alleged pretext that so called 'heathen' Slavs threatened the stability of Christianity in Finland.[322]

The Ostsiedlung acculturation process substantially expanded the population of Pomerania, which had typically been quite modest. Monasteries and market towns thrived, especially during the later 13th century. Trading contracts administered by the incoming Germanic peoples who'd shifted their successful mercantile operations from Sweden to the newly established towns along the Baltic, ensured rich returns on their investments. With all impediments swept away, the road to profit was clear and uninhibited.

Be under no illusions, the drive behind the northern crusades was not piety but greed. The race was on for trade monopolies and the acquisition of wealth through prime agricultural land and property. Several religious wars were called crusades during the Middle Ages,

---

322. In 1221 CE, Pope Honorius III acquired this disconcerting information from the Archbishop of Uppsala. During the preparation of the Second Crusade to the Holy Land, a Papal Bull was issued supporting a crusade against the Slavs. See: James F Dunnigan and Albert A. Nofi. *Medieval Life & the Hundred Years War*. http://www.hundredyearswar.com/Books/History/1_Help_C.htm 1994. (Accessed 11th January 2021).

but others, including most of the Swedish ones, were only dubbed 'crusades' by 19th century romantic nationalist historians. Religion was used to guise avarice. Despite the drive to convert all 'heathens' (including heterodox forms of Christianity) these were never religious campaigns, though they did pretend to be. Trade was ever the trigger and catalyst for expansion, migration and settlement. Profit not theology underpinned this often-overlooked historical travesty. Beginning with the Vikingr's exploration of the New World, my research here confirms it was trade that directed the development of the mercantile world, both east and west, and the policies dependent upon it. Trade was influential in the cross-pollination of culture, language and beliefs shared by people of the pre-medieval world and the single most significant factor behind the wars and actions executed across the rapidly expanding medieval world, a premise inherited from the Neolithic and one we embrace still in the 21st century. Our world and theirs were forged by merchants and maintained by investments, bankers and backers. There is nothing new in this – there is nothing new under the sun. Whatever ideologies accompany the establishment of intrusive and oppressive trade regimes, the fundamental premise remains one of control. Everything from government to hospitality is fixed on trade. Politics, art, culture, technology, language and finally, religion, thrive or diminish on the strength of trade and commerce. Trade provides the mechanics of growth and industry. That industry alone generates all social advancements.

Trade routes link disparate regions while fostering economic growth. Trade fairs brought the merchants from northern and southern Europe together, just as it did those of the east and west. And as we have discovered, the fluid social histories of the people involved, became inexorably woven, and so nuanced, many fail to recognise the vain subtleties that underpin all aspects of culture. In such far-flung market-places, a traveller might find marten skins from Ireland, furs from Russia, linen from Flanders, tin from Cornwall, soap and fine armour from Italy, and luxurious silk and spices from India and the Orient. Everything from town planning to the building of a naval fleet was dependent upon trade. Trade oils the wheels of progress. Colonisation is now just an outdated term for the occupation (and possession) of the means to capital, i.e., the control of trade. All major civilisations have adopted it, and many continue to this day (unabated by public opinion or moral duty), under the guise of foreign aid frauds, peace-keeping missions etc., all of which amount to nothing less than self-serving enterprise.

342 PIRATES, MERCHANTS, DEVILS & DARK DEEDS

After the fall of the Roman Empire, trade in Europe suffered temporary decline. Roads fell into disrepair and commerce shrank into the local markets of small towns. Within a few hundred years this changed as new trade routes across water and land opened up as the race for trade monopolies began. Economic advantage was ever the goal. The spirituality of hearts and minds was a mere secondary consideration to power. Trade opened up the world, but the casualties of that societal shift remains unquantifiable. And so we arrive where we began, building on the foundations established by archaic barter systems that forced our ancestors to adapt, migrate, negotiate and warmonger. Thousands of years of interaction and marriage have generated the complex, shifting patterns of our mongrel dna, forming cultures that really do have more in common than we give them credit for, or perhaps care to admit. There never was a glorious isolation. Notions of separatism and exclusion are a divisive, political myth. Human nature thrives in company. Trade is the currency of evolution, and everything bends to its dictates.

 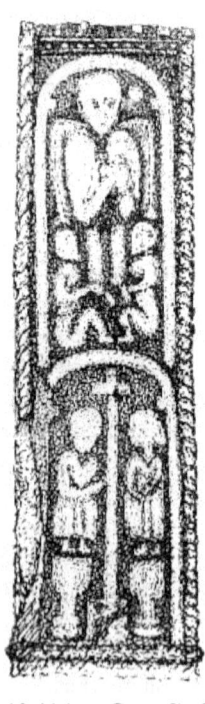 

10. Halton Cross Shaft

APPENDICES

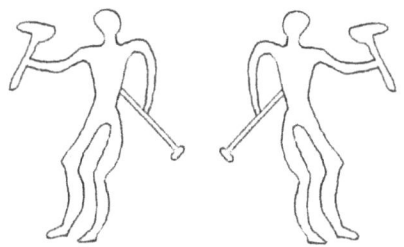

APPENDIX ONE

Appendix I: Who is the Sky Father?

An interesting correlation exists between the various names awarded to the most popular mythical figures described as sky gods. In order to identify the Scythian terms used to describe or imply deity, we first need to consider the Indo-European root form. Based on his universal archetype, *Dyḗus Ph2tḗr is generally assumed, and accepted to be the original patriarchal deity of the Indo-Europeans.

The root *dyḗus/*dyeus/*dyew/*deiwos has become the generic word for deity in several languages (i.e. Latin *deus*, Indian *deva*, Welsh *duw*, et cetera). Although the descendent form evolved from the *dyḗus/*dyeus/*dyew/*deiwos root, as the Old Iranian *daeva*, it became demoted to the demonic when Zoroaster elevated the terms *ahura* or *yazata* to represent the ultimate heavenly deific 'father.' This inverse switch may have occurred through intense religious conflict between the Scythians and the followers of Zoroaster.[323] Within the Iranian religions, other words for *"god"* that typically derive from the root *bʰagás* and *khuda*, have generated several terms that now apply to deified beings, including saints (many in modern Ossetian).

As the dominant figure, he has assumed many forms and cognates in other cultures. (i.e. Norse Týr).

    Sanskrit - Dyauspitar (Indian *Dyauṣ Pitṛ*)
    Latin - Jupiter (Iupiter)
    Greek - Zeus Pater
    Dyaus (from the Gr. *Dui*, meaning bright.) = sky (as heavenly canopy), *pitar* = father, which literally combines as 'skyfather.'

↑ is the planetary symbol for Mars. It is thought that the t-rune, being an ideographic symbol for spear, ↑ is named after Týr, the figure who appears in the Icelandic and Norwegian poems. Cognate forms (albeit reconstructed Proto-Germanic names) such as Tiwaz (*Tîwaz or *Teiwaz), features in all three rune poems. Incidents of its use find scant mention in the sagas, but in *Vinland Saga*, and in *Sigrdrífumál*, we learn how Týr -runes were carved into weapons to invoke victory in battle.[324]

Multiple Tiwaz runes

At the end of this Elder Futhark rune row inscribed on the Kylver Stone (400 CE, Gotland) we can see 8 stacked Tiwaz runes.[325] ⇑ Apparently formed of multiple stacked Tiwaz runes, this curious glyph strongly resembles a tree-like shape that appears on several other artefacts, and has been widely identified as a representation of Týr associated with Germanic and Scandinavian paganism. In my opinion, this is a mistake. These glyphs all relate to the tamgas, or sacred sigils that appear on the Sámi drums, and the artworks of many nomadic northern peoples of the arctic and sub-arctic regions. Given what we have learned of the closer interactions between northern peoples and the Sámi, this makes perfect sense.

It is often claimed that the Tiwaz rune is referred to in a stanza in *Sigrdrífumál*, a poem in the *Poetic Edda* when the Valkyrja, Sigrdrifa instructs Sigurd to carve *"victory runes"* on his sword while calling out twice the name *"Týr"* (the Tiwaz rune), to secure his victory.

---

323. Yazdan, 2020: 65-75 324. Bruce Dickins. *Runic and Historic Poems of the Old Teutonic Peoples.* (Cambridge University Press, 1915). 325. Two other examples: From 500 CE, a Scandinavian C-bracteate (Seeland-II-C) features an Elder Futhark inscription ends with three stacked Tiwaz runes. The Lindholm amulet, dated from the 2nd to the 4th century, contains three consecutive T runes, which have been interpreted as an invocation of Týr. See: Terje Spurkland. *Norwegian Runes and Runic Inscriptions.* (Boydell Press, 2005).

APPENDIX ONE 345

> Winning-runes learn,
> if thou longest to win,
> And the runes on thy sword-hilt write;
> Some on the furrow,
> and some on the flat,
> And twice shalt thou call on Týr[326]

This and similar translations (as given as above), are misleading. Týr is undoubtedly associated with victory, but only through the premise of justice; that is to say, if the cause be just, victory is assured. The implication is that the engraved sword must then only be raised for just causes. Moreover, Týr is not here associated with a sky father, nor as a patriarchal figure. Those nuances were only later absorbed into the layering of associations attributed to this archaic principle. The t-rune is referred to in several 9th to the 12th century manuscripts, where each assign different names to it. It appears as 'Ti' (*Sangallensis 270* and *Vindobonensis 795*), 'Tir' (*Cotton MS Domitian A IX*) and 'Týr' (Byrhtferth's Manuscript). Similar spellings, such as 'Tii,' are attested to in Old English. If Ti was an older name for the rune, it was later changed to Tir/Týr, (implying a celestial spirit rather than a former heathen deity) and almost certainly due to Norse Christian influence.[327]

Composed of root etymologies that infer a singular spirit, the forms used for this supposedly martial figure throughout the Roman Empire, stand in contrast to the dualistic forms found beyond the Roman Empire that suggest a twinning through descent (i.e., father to son). We find examples of this notion within English, Frisian, Icelandic and Slavic languages where two words comport the descriptor for sky-father *(Tiuw)*; vě =the plurality of personhood, and storm = wut. In his *Germania*, Tacitus informs us that ancient songs of the Germanic peoples celebrated *Tuisto* as a divine spirit, born of the earth.[328] More fascinating yet is the correlation here with the etymology of *Tuisto* that provides a possible descriptive interpretation of that name as "son of Tiu," that is to say, of the sky-father (Proto-Indo-European *Dyeus*) and an earth-goddess.[329] We can see the same formulaic approach to all Ukrainian, Wendish and other Slavic forms of *Svantovit, (Svetovid, Sveti Vid, Swantewit, Svętovit, Svatovit, Świętowit or Святовит)*.

Dyēus Ptēr, the "Shining Sky Father" - the supreme deity of the bright sky, is not at all the same as *Perkwūnos*, "The Striker" (or mighty oak spirit), who is the deity of the dark sky, of storms and thunder, rain. "Inherent in the nature of Perkwūnos is both a warrior/hero aspect (lightning) and an agricultural one (rain)."[330] And though these opposing virtues were seemingly absorbed and combined within singular deities (Zeus for example), their diverse functions suggest diverse origins. This may be the fault of mythologists and historians recording the vital animistic natures of deified elements through a western anthropomorphised and monotheistic perspective (a heavy bias and no mistake), or, it is an indication of cultural absorption and adaptation. I suspect both are ultimately responsible for

the complexities in the variant shifts and turns our once simple beliefs have taken over millennia. There is not doubt that the introduction of opposing brothers, or sons, became a means of explaining the evolving narrative regarding the nature of belief.

Furthermore, once a title is awarded, the assumption of cognate forms becomes automatic, an error so entrenched, even bringing it to our attention becomes an act of heresy. For example, the title of sky-father has been ascribed to both Óðinn and Týr, as if they are somehow similar. They are not. The

---

326. Henry Adams Bellows. (Ed.). *Sigrdrífumál*. Internet Sacred Texts Archive, 1923. https://archive.org/details/poeticedda00belluoft/mode/2up (Retrieved 3 June 2019). **327.** Marijane Osborn. "Tir as Mars in the Old English Rune Poem." In, *ANQ: A Quarterly Journal of Short Articles, Notes and Reviews*. (Taylor & Francis, 2010). **328.** *PIE for damp earth in the purest sense of animism – a divine force made manifest. See James P. Mallory and Douglas Q. Adams. *The Oxford Introduction to Proto-Indo-European and the Proto-Indo-European World*. (Oxford University Press, 2006). **329.** Mallory and Adams, 1997: Mallory and Adams, 2006. **330.** Ceisiwr Serith. *Deep Ancestors: Practising the Religion of the Proto Indo-Europeans*. (ADF Publishing, 2007)

chart below shows how vastly they differ. It also reveals their true virtue and purpose in myth and mythmaking.

Óðinn	Týr
Bi-polar [as in 'change']	Uni-polar [that is of singular focus]
Aesir	Vanir
North and East/air and fire	South and West/earth and water
Wanderer	Stability – fixed- nowl star-bright glory
Warrior – conquest and victory	Warrior – truth, honour, justice.
Deception/deceit/trickery	Honour/truth/oaths
Valfather – chooser of the slain	Binder of chaos
Master of wild beasts: wolf, raven, Horse, eagle and worm/dragon	Tamer of the beast
Fertility and harvest	Associations with the 'Thing'
Patron of skalds, poetry and mead	Binder of oaths Sacrifice & humility Religious instinct within man
Freyja taught him knowledge of runes, Séiðr and galdr	Separates heaven and earth via its imposing central column – axis mundi anima mundi/world soul

The Slavic rendering of the Germanic *Tuisco*, is *Svetovid*, whose compound name forms *Sventevith* and *Zvantewit*, are rooted in *svętъ* (meaning saint or holy), and *vit* (meaning lord, leader and victor). Because *Tuisco* represents a twinning, it seems probable that the T in *Tuisco* may represent that duality, thusly, the consonants T in *Tui*, the D in the PIE-root **Dyaus**, Dieu, S in Sius and Z in Ziu, Zeus, are consequently considered to be a symbol for a dual deity, often associated with the sky.[331] The first century BCE Roman polymath and author *Varro*, records the view suggested by his contemporary Valerius Soranus, that the Roman sky deity *IU-piter*, was looked upon as Father and Mother simultaneously: *"Jupiter*, mighty Father of kings and of gods and of all things, Mother as well of the gods, one God comprising all others."[332]

Common heritage is easily seen in the core vocabulary, in the words for both common and important things such as family relationships and numbers: *māter, and *dwo, for instance. These words have been carefully reconstructed from their descendants.[333]

---

[331]. The Germania manuscript corpus contains two primary variant readings of the name. The most frequently occurring, Tuisto, is commonly connected to the Proto-Germanic root *tvai, meaning two and its derivative *tvis, meaning twice or something duplicated (as in twin), awarding Tuisto the core meaning 'double.' Gamkrelidze and Ivanov, 1995. [332]. Saint Augustine. *The City of God Against The Pagans*. 411: 2-3 (Loeb Classical Library, 1957). [333]. Ceisiwr Serith. *Deep Ancestors: Practising the Religion of the Proto Indo-Europeans*. (ADF Publishing, 2007).

APPENDIX ONE   347

Within many sacred practises (rituals and prayers), the series of vowels *A, E, I, U, O* symbolize eternity and stability of the heavens. Comparable vowels (including runic vowels) construct titular epithets that refer to higher, abstract spirits of the sky (and also of the earth).

Calling anything "Proto-Indo-European" is a dangerous thing. The term covers thousands of years, during which large changes took place. For instance, at the beginning of the Proto-Indo European period, the language had no genders; nouns were divided into animate and inanimate classes. By the time the language was breaking up, the animate class had been split into male and female, and the inanimate had become the neuter. It can be assumed that Proto-Indo-European religion underwent equally radical changes.[334]

General guide to etymology symbols:

> — "became."

< — "comes from."

* — Reconstructed word, not found in any surviving form - it is therefore "unattested."

Proto-Indo-European ǵʰutós [335] is the earliest use of a term that bears an association with the Other, via an implied sense of the sacred. Expressed through libations, it is by default, an implication of the divine. More importantly, it is the structure and nature of sacrifice (as offerings and libations) that provides the base line for all belief systems, their attendant spirits and higher deific forms that ultimately develop into patterns of practise, and even religion.

*ǵʰutós – invoked, libated, poured as part of a liquid offering.

Etymological reconstruction from: *ǵʰew- pour, libate + *-tós.

Descendant forms occur as follows:

    Proto-Hellenic: *kʰutós
    Ancient Greek: khutós - poured
    Proto-Indo-Iranian: *jʰutás
    Proto-Indo-Aryan: *źʰutás
    Sanskrit: hutá -offered in fire, poured out
    Proto-Germanic: *gudą - god, deity
    Proto-Germanic: *gautaz m, a heiti for Óðinn (a Geat)

The Proto-Germanic reconstruction ***gautaz** appears to be a theonym derived from *gaut, a form of the Proto-Germanic verb *geutaną, meaning to pour (libations/seed), thus making the mythical ancestor Gautaz – "He who has poured (out libations/offerings)." The ethnonym that originates in this meaning is directly related to *gudą (god), *gudijô (priest), and *gutô ((a) Goth),[336] all of which are descended from the same Proto-Indo-European root as Vedic Sanskrit *hótṛ* - priest or brahmin; *hotr* – sacrifice, to libate.[337]

Descendant forms occur as follows:

    Proto-West Germanic: *Gaut
    Old English: Gēat → English: Geat (here we begin to capture the essence of a name later lost

---

334. Ibid. **335.** Gamkrelidze and Ivanov, 1995. **336.** "*guda-" See: Kroonen, 2013: 193-4 **337.** The hotr is the leading priest (Rg,veda specialist), who recites the invocations and litanies. See: "Yajamana Sutta: The Discourse on the Sacrificer." Translated & Annotated by Piya Tan. (Sa yutta Nikaya 11.16/1:233) f) *Living Word of the Buddha* SD 22 no 7 (2008) The Minding Centre https://www.themindingcentre.org 2009. See also: Gamkrelidze and Ivanov, 1995.

to hyperbole. The term relates almost directly to the function of a priest relative to ethnicity.)
Old Norse: Gautar pl, Gautr
Old Swedish: gø̄tar pl
Swedish: göt
Ancient Greek: Γοῦται pl (Goûtai), Γαῦτοι pl (Gaûtoi) → Latin: Gautae pl, Gautigothi pl.[338]

Proto-Germanic *gudą (Reconstructed) n, the one invoked, deity - *god Pronounced ɣu.ðą̃ (uther)
Etymology here is assumed via Verner's law from the earlier *guþóm and the Proto-Indo-European *ǵʰutós above. It may likewise bear an association with libations made to an idol or to the immanent presence of spirit within a burial mound.[339] Adding that revered ancestral element to the word's pronunciation, we acquire a tenuous but very intriguing correlation with how Óðinn should be pronounced, and a name that may have survived into later Arthurian legend (Uther/Uthin). Through the wide diffusion of Christianity, the originally neuter word *gudą eventually signified the concentration of the divine spirit as a being, re-formed as 'the' 'god,'[340] who was specifically masculine.[341] The nebulous divine essence had finally assumed an identity.

Proto-Germanic: ***Tīwaz** (Reconstruction)

Etymology from Proto-Indo-European *deywós (god). Possibly attested as ΤΕΙFΑ (teiva) on the Negau helmet.[342] Runic T-rune (↑) Becomes a proper noun -Týr, identified in later times with the Roman Mars.[343]

Descendant forms:

> Old English: Tīʒ (Tīġ, Tī3, Tíg), Tīp (Tīw, Tīuu, Tívv) → English: Tiw (learned)
> Old Frisian: Tii
> Old High German: Ziu, *Zīw ↑IP
> Old Norse and Icelandic: Týr, Týr Swedish: Tyr, Ti
> Gothic: *ΤΕΙΥS (*teiws)
> Proto-Germanic ↑IPFY (*Tīwaz), ↑MPFY (*Tē₂waz)

Proto-Indo-European: deywós (Reconstruction)

Etymology: Vr̥ddhi derivative of *dyew- sky, heaven; *dyew- > *diw. > nounn -*deywós m. god[344]

Descendants – [all better imply Heimdallr – as the bright/blazing light]

> Proto-Anatolian: *diu- daylight god
> Lycian: ziw
> Lydian: diwi
> Luwian: tiwaz - a sun god
> Proto-Balto-Slavic: *deiwás
> Proto-Celtic: *deiwos
> Proto-Germanic: *Tīwaz
> Proto-Indo-Iranian: *daywás
> Proto-Italic: *deiwos[345]

---

338. Kroonen, 2013: 193-4 **339.** Ibid. **340.** Alemannic and Bavarian German: Gott, German: Gott, Old Norse and Icelandic: guð, Old Swedish: guþ, Gothic: guþ. **341.** Calvert Watkins. (Ed.) *The American Heritage Dictionary of Indo-European Roots*, 2nd ed. (Houghton Mifflin Co., 2000). **342.** Tom Markey. "A Tale of Two Helmets: The Negau A and B Inscriptions", In, *Journal of Indo-European Studies*, Volume 29, Issue 1(2) (2001): 69-172. **343.** See: Oates, 2022. **344.** Gamkrelidze and Ivanov, 1995.

APPENDIX ONE 349

Proto-Germanic ansu[346] (Reconstruction) Pronunciation ɑn.suz.

Noun, *ansuz m. deity, name of the A-rune (ᚫ)

Etymology: From Proto-Indo-European *h₂émsus, from *h₂ems- to engender, beget. Compare Hittite ḫa-aš-šu-uš /ḫaššuš - king, Avestan ahu - lord, aŋhu - lord; life, existence, Sanskrit ásu - spirit, life-force, life, ásura - "godlike, powerful.

Descendants[347]

    Proto-West Germanic: *ansu, *ą̄su
    Old English: ōs
    Old Saxon: ās, ōs
    Old Norse: áss, ǫ́ss
    Icelandic: ás → Swedish: as, ås (semi-learned) → Finnish: aasa → Danish: as
    Faroese: ásur
    Norwegian: ås[348]

Proto-Germanic Þunraz (Reconstruction) Pronunciation ˈθun.rɑz

Etymology gleaned from *þunraz.

Proper noun ***Þunraz** m

This early Germanic deity may be a predecessor to a complex array of descendants, including the Old High German: *Thonar, Donar*. (Mis)Identified with the Roman deity Jupiter by way of *interpretatio germanica* in Germanic weekday names (Thursday),[349] he is otherwise identified with Hercules by way of *interpretatio romana*. Thor (*Þórr*) is a classic example of how similar cultural forms can be considered 'cognate.'

As the Slavic vessel and conduit of thunder, Perkunas, (*Perkwūnos*) bears a double-headed axe made of metal (bronze, iron) or flint. When he throws his axe, the *wágros*, it returns to him, resembling Thor's *Mjolnir*. Sometimes, like Herakles and the Daghda, his weapon is a club. There is a folk belief in Europe that the earth can't be fertile until the first thunderstorm of spring.

> The idea seems not to be only that the rain is necessary (or any rain would do), but rather that the lightning serves as a fertilizer of the earth, an electric phallus shooting out of the sky, opening it to be filled with the semen of rain. This belief fits in well with the agricultural side of Perkwūnos. He is not only the god of war; his power breaks up the cold, restricted earth, and frees the fertility hidden there. His presence at the sowing of the fields becomes clear. The ritual includes a bull sacrifice, dedicated to Perkwūnos.[350]

Descendants

    Old English: Þunor
    Middle English: Thunor
    English: Thunor
    Old Frisian: Thuner
    West Frisian: Tonger
    Old Saxon: Thunar

---

345. Donald Ringe. *From Proto-Indo-European to Proto-Germanic (A Linguistic History of English; 1).* (Oxford University Press, 2006). **346.** "*ansu-" See: Kroonen, 2013): 30 **347.** See: Kroonen, 2013): 30 **348.** Watkins, 2000. **349.** Tui, Wodan and Thor became assigned to Tuesday, Wednesday and Thursday respectively, showing not only their assimilation into western pantheonic thinking, but also, their initial distinction as deities. **350.** Serith, 2007.

Old High German: Thonar, Donar
Middle High German: Donar
German: Donar → Dutch: Donar
Old Norse: Þórr
Icelandic: Þórr
Faroese: Tórur
Norwegian: Tor
Swedish: Tor
Danish: Thor → English: Þórr[351]

Nordland is in the arctic circle, as is Troms and Finnmark

APPENDIX TWO
Influential Western-European Tribal Peoples

For around two hundred years between the 3rd to the 5th century CE, (Iron Age) Przeworsk culture thrived in hamlets of small clusters of people across the North-Eastern European region in what is now central and southern Poland. Rich grave goods, including fine weaponry, have been discovered there, indicating warriors had formed part of their social structure.[352] "Warrior burials are notable, which often include horse-gear and spurs. Some burials are exceptionally rich, overshadowing the graves of Germanic groups further west, especially after 400 CE."[353] Exceeding the wealthy graves of other, better known 5th-Century Germanic groups further to the west, several pattern-welded swords provide astonishing workman-ship, metal-work unequalled elsewhere. These enigmatic swordsmiths were plundered and conquered, first by the might of Rome, then by the barbarian Huns. "The Przeworsk people mastered and implemented the various achievements of the Celts, most importantly developing large-scale production of iron, for which they used local bog ores."[354]

Major groups of peoples who have emerged as key players throughout the bloody history of these vast regions, primarily include the following:

Marcomanni: Meaning border people. Germanic tribes with possible links to the Suebi in Southern Germany.[355]

These Germanic tribes formed a confederation with Sarmatian, Quadi, and Vandals to stave Caesar's initial attempts to occupy the borderland regions of the Roman frontier along the Rhine and Danube rivers. They failed and were eventually driven eastwards by the Roman advances. Together with the Goths, the confederations attempted to repel the Roman march on Pannonia which initiated the 2nd century Marcomannic Wars, that Marcus Aurelius triumphed over.[356] Pushing against the Roman machine, several tribes had migrated westwards. Generating a form of guerrilla warfare, they effectively bit into Roman Imperialism, that successfully reduced trade across northern Europe. Around this time, an interesting fusion took place, merging Latin with early forms of runic[357] letters that nonetheless did not surface for six more centuries, and which were then presented as the '*Marcomannic Script*.'[358]

---

351. Ibid **352.** Mallory and Adams, 1997a. **353.** A. H. Merrills. *Vandals, Romans and Berbers. New Perspectives on Late Antique North Africa.* (Ashgate, 2004): 35. **354.** Jacek Andrzejowski. "The Przeworsk Culture. A Brief Story (for the Foreigners)." In, *Worlds Apart? Contacts across the Baltic Sea in the Iron Age: Network Denmark-Poland 2005–2008.* Edited by Ulla Lund Hansen and Anna Bitner-Wróblewska. (Det Kongelige Nordiske Oldskriftselskab Panstwowe Muzeum Archeologiczne, 2010). **355.** Since the Middle Ages, various Germanic tribes living in the Netherlands are actually the Franks, Saxons and Frisians.

Alemanni: People from the (Austrian-Bavarian-Swiss) upper Rhine border regions who appeared on around 200 CE, as one of several confederations of Suebian, Germanic tribes opposing the ruthless Roman state machine.

The Alemanni established the Old High German language. Their prestigious pattern welded swords (sometimes referred to as Merovingian swords), feature heavily amongst their prized and extensive grave goods.[359]

Merovingians: were a very specific benighted Frankish dynasty who ruled Francia (a region of ancient Gaul, in addition to several Roman provinces in Raetia, and other across southern parts of Germania for almost three hundred years from the mid-5th to the mid-8th century CE.

The Merovingians were contemporaries of peoples of the Vendel Culture in the north, now Sweden, for most of this period (550 CE –w 790 CE) The Merovingians were a wealthy clan-based society of superb horse warriors who maintained Germanic cultural traditions they'd garnered from controversial mythical origins rumoured to be a fantastic sea-beast, known as a quinotaur.[360] Heirs to a vast and established iron-working industry, these "long-haired" kings wielded unprecedented power and influence in their time. As highly cultured people, their graves were a treasure-trove of pattern welded swords. The precursive Vendel period rapidly merged into the inevitable Viking Age.

APPENDIX THREE
A Vital Chronology of Eastern Tribes Peoples and the Steppe Nations/Confederacies

Archaic:
   Chorasmia 13th – 3rd centuries BCE
   Cimmerians 12th – 7th centuries BCE
   Magyars 11th century BCE – 8th century CE

Classical:
   Scythians and Sogdians 8th – 4th centuries BCE
   Saka (Sakas) 6th – 1st centuries BCE

---

356. "Marcoman(n)I" : See: Simon Hornblower; Anthony Spawforth; Esther Eidinow. (Eds.). *The Oxford Classical Dictionary* (4 ed.). (University Press, 2012). **357.** Proto-Germanic *runo we have the Germanic root run- (Gothic: runa), meaning 'secret' or 'whisper.' Runes are symbols distinct from Greek and Latin and letters. Runes are speculatively 2nd century, certainly attested on a 6th century Alamannic runestaff (as runa) and possibly (as runo) on the 4th century Einang stone. See: *runo: Vladimir Orel. *A Handbook of Germanic Etymology*. (Brill, 2003). **358.** During the Roman imperial period (1st century BCE, to the 5th century CE), increased contact between Germanic people serving as mercenaries in the Roman army resulted in a hybrid runic script that blends Elder Futhark with Anglo-Saxon futhorc. In later periods, these runes were attributed erroneously to the *Marcomanni*, possibly due to the confusion by the 8th century chroniclers of the Carolingian Empire, who accepted that origin from the *Alemanni* (Bavarian) scripts in their possession. The hybrid runes first appeared in a 9th century treatise by a benedictine monk and theologian, *Hrabanus Maurus* in his "De Inventione Litterarum," whose interest in military history led him to source his own in those earlier works. See: Hugh Chisholm. (Ed.) "Hrabanus Maurus Magnentius." In, *Encyclopædia Britannica*. Vol. 13 (11th ed.) (Cambridge Uni. Press, 2011): 842 See also: Victor Davis Hanson. *Carnage and Culture: Landmark Battles in the Rise to Western Power*. (Knopf Doubleday Publishing Group, 2007). **359.** David Edge and Alan Williams. "Some early Medieval Swords In The Wallace Collection And Elsewhere." In, *Gladius* 26(1)(2003). 191-210 DOI:10.3989/gladius.2003.50 **360.** Ian W. Wood. "Deconstructing the Merovingian Family." In, *The Construction of Communities in the Early Middle Ages: Texts, Resources and Artefacts*. Edited by Richard Corradini, Maximillian Diesenberger and Helmut Reimitz. (Brill, 2003): 149

Sarmatians 5th century BCE – 5th century CE
Bulgars 7th century BCE – 7th century CE
Transoxiana 4th century BCE – 14th century CE
Xiongnú 3rd century BCE – 2nd century CE[361]
Yuezhi 2nd century BCE –1st century CE
Tauri Wusun 1st century BCE – 6th century CE
Xianbei 1st – 3rd centuries

Migration Era: Contemporary with movements in western Europe:

Goths 3rd – 6th centuries
Huns 4th – 8th centuries
Alans 5th – 11th centuries
Avars 5th – 9th centuries plus Eurasian Avars 6th – 8th centuries
Göktürks 6th – 8th- centuries
Sabirs 6th – 8th centuries
Khazars 7th – 11th centuries
Onogurs 8th — century
Pechenegs 8th –11th centuries
Kipchaks and Cumans 11th – 13th centuries

Regions of the Steppe:

Altai Steppe, and semi-desert (Kazakhstan)
Kazakh forest Steppe (Kazakhstan, Russia)
Pontic–Caspian Steppe (Moldova, Romania, Russia, Ukraine) Selenge–Orkhon Forest Steppe (Mongolia, Russia)
South Siberian Forest Steppe (Russia)
Tian Shan foothill arid Steppe (China, Kazakhstan, Kyrgyzstan)[362]

Around the 2nd century CE, (in the Post-Hunnic era), Türkic tribes of diverse origin, namely, Altaic-Türkic, Caucasian, Iranian, and Finno-Ugric peoples, entered the Pontic-Caspian Steppe, merging together various ethnic groups into confederations. Sometime later, they encountered Slavic, Armenian, Semitic, Thracian and Anatolian Greek peoples during their Western Eurasian migrations to the Balkans. It is known that the political practises of the armies and of the ruling elite expressed a tendency to remain distinctly 'clan' oriented; this was maintained through specific origins based in mythical descent. Their divine right to rule was claimed through the imposition of such elitist beliefs.

We know that since the Palaeolithic Age at least, the Eurasian Steppe was the central locus of trade, connecting Asia and the Middle East to Europe, serving very well as the precursor of the Silk Road. It was the principle cultural, economic and political driving force through to the modern era, whence nomadic empires and tribal confederations battled for supremacy and control of its vast resources and trading networking wealth. That wealth and trade were key influential elements to the Northern traditions. Understanding these early traditions will bring fundamental context to the previously elusive origins of the peoples who migrated, traded and settled across the Scandinavian regions. Their histories are entwined mainly with those of the Scythian, Cimmerian, Sarmatian, Hunnic Empire and the Mongols, but also of the Chorasmian, Xiongnu, Xianbei, Transoxianan, Sogdianan, and finally, the of the Göktürk Khaganate.[363]

---

361. There is a firm cultural and archaeological correlation between the Iranian-speaking Central Eurasians, the Skythians (the Sakas by default) and the Xiongnú peoples. Rivers and bodies of water are intrinsic aspects of their cosmologies. **362.** https://en.wikipedia.org/wiki/Early_Slavs **363.** David Christian. *A History of Russia, Central Asia and Mongolia. Vol. I: Inner Eurasia from Prehistory to the Mongol Empire.* (Blackwell Publishing, 1998).

APPENDIX THREE 353

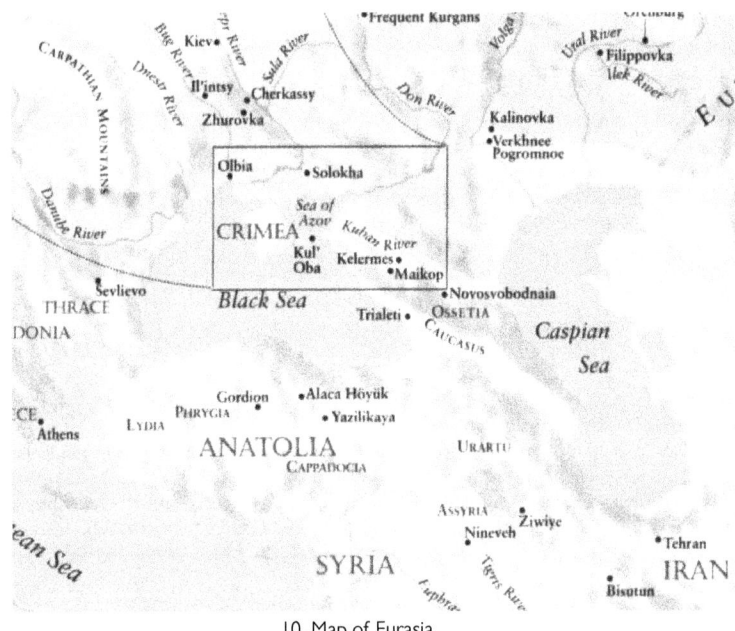

10. Map of Eurasia

Western Steppe: The Pontic-Caspian Steppe
This Steppe begins near the mouth of the Danube (extent of Roman Empire) and extends through the once heavily forested lands north-eastwards, close to Kazan, and southeast, reaching down to the southern tip of the Ural Mountains where the Black Sea area of the Caspian Steppe extends towards the Caucasus Mountains. The Crimean Peninsula on the north shore of the Black Sea extends to an interior Steppe with ports on the south coast that are linked to the Mediterranean basin cultures. Separated from the main Steppe by the mountains of Transylvania, the Great Hungarian Plain forms an island of Steppe that lies to the west.[364] A branch of this Uralic language family (Hungarian speaking peoples who had previously lived in the Steppe region),[365] settled in the Carpathian basin around 895 CE. According to the Kurgan hypothesis, the broad span of Indo-European languages originates in a shared ancestry common to the Pontic-Caspian Steppe peoples. On the cusp of pre-history, the entire Steppe population west of Dzungaria, had previously spoke Iranian languages. These were replaced by Türkic languages on the Steppe around 500 CE.[366]

Central Steppe: The Kazakh Steppe
Shared in the north with The Tarim Basin (Taklamakan) and Dzungaria, The Kazakh Steppe extends as far as the Urals. Its relative isolation and inhospitable desert regions to the north, separate it from the politics of the southern areas close to Iran, and of conflicts it shared with the peoples of Pontic and Eastern Steppes. Camels and Yaks provide transport as far west as Astrakhan. Around 3000 BCE, we find early signs of horse domestication on the Pontic-Caspian or Kazakh Steppe where they were primarily used for transportation and warfare. The evolution to mounted archery was such a slow development, the full stirrup did not arrive until sometime later, around 300 CE.

---

364. Also known as the Pannonian Steppe (Hungary, Romania, Serbia, Croatia, Slovakia, Austria, Slovenia). **365.** Now Southern Russia **366.** Christian, 1998.

*Eastern Steppe: The Grasslands of Outer Mongolia

Xinjiang is the mountainous north-western province of China, separated from the Dzungaria grasslands in the north and the arid Tarim Basin to the south, flanked in the west by the Tarbagatai Mountains and by the Mongolian Altai Mountains to its eastern borders. Extreme climatic conditions make The Tarim Basin inimical even to a nomadic population, yet wrapped around its mountainous ridges, flowing rivers provide rich irrigation for pasture and agriculture. Facilitating trade along the east-west axis, The Tarim Basin formed a rich cosmopolitan civilization in the forested centre of the Steppe, while to the north and east, a diminishing population of Siberian hunting tribes subsisted. Passing along its northern and southern edges, The Northern Silk Road crossed the mountains westwards to the Himalayas. The Tarim Basin separates Inner and Outer (Russian) Mongolia. Türkic peoples controlled the Steppe, secured healthy trade, and were able to marshal the route along The Silk Road. Inter-tribal raids appear to have been a natural feature of this region of Steppe culture. Food was scarce and conditions were harsh. Horses were swift and provided a marked advantage for the nomads who capitalised on them.[367]

Turco-Mongol states and domains by the 15th century

Asian nomads in the Russian Steppe and the adjoining steppes and deserts exerted considerable influence on Russian and Cossack culture, especially through cross-cultural contact, mostly with Slavic, Tatar-Türkic, Mongolian and Iranian people. The peoples of the Eurasian Steppes play a major role in Russia's long history, persevered in memory through the numerous folk songs of this region.[368]

Anthropology and Genetics (The Taklamakan Mummies)

Peoples of the Tarim Basin

An enigmatic group of people whose movements contributed much to proto-European culture, lived and died in the Tarim Basin,[369] where over two hundred mummies, including the exceptional 'Beauty of Xiaohe,' were found with various European-style artefacts in the Taklimakan Desert of north-western China, North of Tibet.[370] A substantial number of the mummies are 4000 years old, presenting evidence of ancient non-Chinese (Hu) inhabitants.[371] While some of the very earliest mummies are certainly typical of their Mongolian ancestry, the more abundant, recent mummies exhibit distinctly European features. Once a rich river-bed, the aridity of this inhospitable desert preserved the desiccated corpses of Siberian and European travellers to this region (who had probably already intermarried at this point). Their (Caucasian) features, the fair skin (reddish) brown hair and long noses, once belonged to people who may have participated in trade along the routes that later formed the vast Silk Road, established by their autonomous descendants.[372]

---

367. Patrick Patterson and Brian Parkinson. *Journeys in World History* I. https://pressbooks.oer.hawaii.edu/honcchist151/chapter/12-steppe-peoples-of-central-asia/ (2023). (Retrieved 15th August 2024). **368.** Paul Friedrich and Norma Diamond. (Eds.) *Encyclopaedia of World Cultures Volume 6 Russia and Eurasia China Part 1*. (New York: G.K. Hall & Co., 2016). **369.** Tarim Basin Barrow Cemetery in Xinjiang, China, is better known as the Small River Cemetery No. 5. The plateau is surrounded by a harsh mountain ridge. **370.** Currently home to China's northwest autonomous Türkic speaking Uygur people in the region of Xinjiang, also to more recent Han settlers from within the borders of China. **371.** Cultural artefacts, such as their wool clothing, along with the traded food items (cheese, wheat and millet) led to their initial misidentification as suggested traders of herders from far places, yet DNA analysis of thirteen of the oldest bodies, reveals their indigeneity via descent from a lost Ice Age Asian population. **372.** The Silk Road was an early network of trade routes (particularly of silk) connecting the East and West, via East and Southeast Asia with Persia, the Arabian Peninsula, East Africa and Southern Europe. It was initially established by the Han dynasty of 2nd century BCE to manage the trade of silk across Eurasia. The trading network itself endured up to the 15th century CE, falling only in 1453 when the Ottoman Empire closed off all trade with the West. Alongside the movement of trade goods, numerous economic, cultural, political, and religious notions had travelled freely, impacting and enriching the west, influencing science, art, music, language and technology.

APPENDIX THREE 355

Each shrivelled corpse was carefully covered in cow-hide and buried inside individual upturned boats. Rising from the sandy dune above the inhumed bodies, a forest of over two hundred wooden poles, suggests the burials were aligned to very specific animistic principles. Approximately thirteen feet tall, with flat blades, painted black and red, the staves resembled the paddle oars of a ship; some blades appear phallic, others, vulvic, leading to the assumption these were focused heavily on fertility and procreation. Life-size wooden phalluses were placed upon the bodies of the women, over their apron-like string skirts. Grave goods comprised of exquisite, hand-carved masks and beautifully woven grass baskets with bundles of ephedra, an entheogenic herb typically used ritually and as a powerful medicine. Perhaps this is a huge sacrificial site. Recent excavations of this extraordinary cemetery,[373] confirm these western travellers arrived in the autonomous region of Xinjiang, thousands of years ago, voiding the controversial claim to indigeneity by the Uygur people (who currently occupy this region) who did not actually arrive in this region in Xinjiang until sometime between the 9th and 13th centuries CE. Similarly, the Han's claim to these people as their ancestors is also voided.[374]

Some of the more recent mummies from the Tarim basin (dated to the later Iron Age), demonstrate comparable characteristics to those of the Saka,[375] Scythian, and Pazyryk cultures of the Altai Mountains of Kazakhstan and Mongolia. This is particularly evident in their garments, textiles, weapons, horse gear and animal style artworks.[376] It has been noted that several other items were very similar to European burial customs and artefacts. The Tarim Basin bodies wore scanty, intricate textiles of woven string not unlike several Bronze-Age examples of the Vinca culture of Old Europe that resemble the clothing worn by the Egtved Girl, whose burial on the peninsula of Jutland in Denmark is dated to around 1400 BCE. Their barely adequate outer clothing included, leather boots, woollen cloaks, and felt caps with feathers inserted into the brim, which closely resembled Tyrolean mountain hats.

Genetic and anthropological research into artefacts, culture and skeletal remains of archaic peoples spanning almost 1000 years up to around the 7th century CE, reveals an ethnicity among the Eurasian Steppe tribes that is very rarely ethnically homogeneous, and which in fact, typically exhibits multiple ethnicities. Later ethnic imprints are distinctly east Asian. This information is entirely compatible with the hundreds of excavated mummies in The Tarim Basin (West China) of Uygur[377] people that have Caucasoid features, and who are associated with the ancient Tocharian (Türkic) languages, an archaic Indo-European language in continuous use for approximately 3,000 years.[378]

Tests conducted upon some of the mummies by Russian Geneticists, confirm DNA markers that strongly indicate a (typically) mixed ancestry of East Asian or South Asian origin bearing additional Siberian and European genetic markers. These confirm their origin can be placed *outside* China in the ancient past.[379] Analyses of male mummies show presence of a

---

373. Rediscovered almost a hundred years ago, initial suppositions regarding the bodies are now being held to account in light of DNA analyses. **374.** Li Shuicheng. "Ancient Interactions in Eurasia and Northwest China: Revisiting J. G. Andersson's Legacy." In, *Bulletin of the Museum of Far Eastern Antiquities* 75 (2003): 9-30 (Published by the Museum of Far Eastern Antiquities). **375.** As inhabitants of the Tarim Basin and northern and eastern Eurasian Steppe, Saka (Sakas) historically relates only to the nomadic peoples of the eastern Steppe, while 'Scythian' applies only to those nomads living in the western Pontic Steppe. See: M. A. Dandamayev. "Media and Achaemenid Iran." In, *History of Civilizations of Central Asia: The Development of Sedentary and Nomadic Civilizations, 700 BCE to 250 CE.* Vol. 2. Edited by János Harmatta. Ahmad Hasan Dani, Baij Nath Puri, G. F Etemadi and Clifford Edmund Bosworth. (New Delhi: Motilal Banarsidass Publishers Private Limited, 1999): 35-64. **376.** Scytho-Siberian animal style mainly portrays excruciation of peaceful cloven-hoofed animals by predators which are mostly winged. **377.** It is possible the Uygur people may not have arrived in this region prior to the 10th century, but this is hotly disputed by the nomadic Uyghur peoples, who claim it as ancient ancestral lands. **378.** Despite its presence in the east, Tokharian seems more closely related to the *'centum'* (Latin) languages of Europe than to the *'satem'* (Sanskrit) languages of India and Iran, a distinctive articulation based on the words for 'hundred.' See: Nicholas Wademarch. *A Host of Mummies, a Forest of Secrets.* (2010) https://www.nytimes.com/2010/03/16/science/16archeo.html (Accessed 23rd November 2019) **379.** https://www.ncbi.nlm.nih.gov/pmc/articles/PMC5204334/ (Accessed 24th September 2019)

Y chromosome common to Eastern Europe, Central Asia and Siberia, but present only very rarely in China.[380] Mitochondrial DNA drawn from the female line, also reflects Siberian origins alongside two European markers. From this result, we may speculate that inter-marriage between peoples of European and Siberian tribes occurred before they entered the Tarim Basin around 4,000 years ago.

These people were probably the ancestors of the Oguric Türks. Several key nomadic Türkic tribes of Mongolia and Central Asia including the Khazars, Pechenegs and Ashlnà, eventually united to establish the first Türkic Khaganate or Göktürk Empire in the 6th century. Gradually pushing westward into Europe, their empire flourished intermittently until the mid-8th century. Of all the clans, the noble Ashinà clan were highly esteemed, and provided rulers for a number of Eurasian nomadic empires. The Steppe nomads of the Khaganate retained elements of its original animistic-shamanistic spirituality that later evolved into Tengriism, although it received missionaries of Buddhist monks, and at times, practiced a syncretic religion.[381]

As a curious aside in the continuing comparisons that occur between the historical and mythic cultures of the north and east, we are following in this research, it is worth noting the observations of several Arab writers who recorded their encounters with all the peoples of these regions through their trading expeditions. They noticed how nine clans who composed the ruling elite, each controlled a designated province. Despite being of mixed ethnicities, a distinction is made by the 10th-Century Muslim geographer al-Istakhri, between the 'White Khazars' (ak-Khazars) and the 'Black Khazars' (qara-Khazars). In keeping with a common consensus, his description of the White Khazars as an extraordinarily handsome people, with pale skin, blue eyes and auburn hair, contrasts with that of the Black Khazars, whom he states had much darker complexions and features.[382] Perhaps when considering the much garbled (and misunderstood) folklore of the Nordic people relative to the dark and bright elves (as recorded by Snorre), and to the nine regions that separate these and other peoples, we might see how obscure information relating to their geography and ethnicities (as they saw them) became transformed by myth and legend to become supranatural aspects of their cosmological literary history.

APPENDIX FOUR
Early Slavic Expansion

Nestled between the river Danube to the west and the Volga to the east, the north Pontic Steppe regions sit above the Black Sea, surrounded in the west by the Vistula and the Dnieper in the northeast. Transylvania and the North Carpathian Mountains sit to the west of the Dnieper and to the west of the Pontic Steppe. Because these regions were the equivalent of the Middle East (past and present), in terms of trade, conquest, conflict, settlements, the history is complex and fraught with subjective interpretations and at times, fantastical mythic elements.

Türkic nomads from Central Asia assumed control of the trading influence of these regions as Roman dominance here declined in the 4th century CE, which practically disappeared during the Hunnic[383] incursions that destroyed established trade centres and decimated tribal communities that depended on them. Goths were pushed to the Roman borders of the Danube, seeking refuge west into Germanic regions and south into the Crimean Peninsula.[384] Present

---

380. Friedrich and Diamond, 2016. Norma. (Eds.). **381.** Ibid. Sogdian preachers were engaged in spreading Manichaeism, Christianity (Nestorianism), and Buddhism among the animistic nomads. **382.** Thomas S. Noonan. 'The Khazar Qaghanate and its impact on the early Rus' state: the Translatio Imperii from Itil to Kiev.' In, *Nomads in the Sedentary World*. Curzon-IIAS Asian studies series. Khazanov, Anatoly M.; Wink, André (Eds.).Routledge, 2001): 76–102 **383.** Eiríkr the Vikingr, Atilla the Hun are not descriptions of their ethnicity but of their *activity as raiders*.

APPENDIX FOUR

among the Hunnic hordes, a small number of Slavs and Scythians served as allies in the form of foreign mercenaries or pressed auxiliaries, raiding the Pontic regions on horseback, staving off the colonisation of the Balkan peninsula by the Bulgars and Avars. In the following centuries, the Slavs emerged, expanding southwards into the Balkan peninsula, west into what is now Czechoslovakia, central and northwest Germany, and western Poland. During the 5th century, hillforts began to pepper the landscape in response to the continued skirmishes between the eastern Slavs and the Khazars, Bulgars and Alans near the Black Sea regions. Between the 5th to the 7th centuries CE, the Slavs colonised the lands formerly devastated by the Huns. Settling on the Oder in the 5th to the 6th centuries, Slavic culture dramatically influenced (central European) Germanic culture, absorbing it completely in the archaeological record.

Battling for supremacy and occupation of the fertile landscapes generated continual flux between these peoples into the 6th century. The Slavs were apparently superbly skilled at lightening skirmish attacks under the cloak of night. Procopius[385] describes them as Barbars, the wild people, noting with horror their ruthless cruelty and savage slaughter of prisoners. Nomadic Avars from beyond the Carpathian Mountains, advanced westwards into Germanic regions, pillaging by boat as they pushed towards the Saxon held territories of the Danube. Pillaging Thrace and Illyria, the Sclovenii ravaged Constantinople in 558 CE.[386] Then, in 567 CE, aided by the Avars, the Langobards conquered the Gepids as they pushed into Italy. Pressing the Byzantine empire to its knees, the allied forces of the Avars and the Sclovenii, dominated the 7th-Century Balkan campaigns.[387]

As a startling precursor to the later Vikingr incursions, war booty was extracted in annual raids that left the Baltic peoples terrorised, impoverished and depopulated; those who were not killed were taken as slaves. Focussing on the forest steppes of western Ukraine, the semi-nomadic Slavs extended their reach into Asia and Europe over the following centuries, cultivating huge swathes of rich, fertile land with a mouldboard plough, and item which became a significant factor in their evolving beliefs systems. Emulating the Gotho-Gepid and Byzantine artistry (but making it distinctly their own), the ancient Slavs rose from relative obscurity to major shakers and movers of these regions throughout the 5th to the 7th centuries CE. Trade developed with the Kievan Rus' and within 150 years, the Slavs had settled the Rhine, the Balkans, Southern Greece and the Adriatic, the Russian Steppes and the Black Sea.[388] Their egalitarian, tribal society shared a common language, but not a common ethnicity. As a consequence of population expansion, tribal federations developed into fledgling nation states during the 8th to the 10th centuries, established Slavic monarchies in Moravia, Bulgaria, Poland and in Russia[389] (the Kievan Rus'[390]). However, prejudicial influences from the long-settled civilizations they bordered, fragmented the once cohesive Slavic culture, and thus, the new nation states did not endure.

Sieges against Constantinople by the Slavs and others significantly delayed the process of Christianisation in Russia. Despite this, the 9th century Moravian Slavs translated the Latin bible into vernacular language. Named after the bishop Cyril (Constantinus) who created it in Bulgaria from Greek and Sarmatian languages, the Cyrillic[391] alphabet ironically induced rapid conversions through influential vernacular literature.

---

384. Vasiliev, Alexander. The Goths in the Crimea. (Cambridge Mass; Mediaeval Academy of America. 1936). **385.** Recorded mainly by Procopius and Jordanes, an enormous amount of literature preserves this complex history. Their works shed light on the events and views of their time. *The Primary Russian Chronicle* explains how the Khazars received tribute from the peoples around them. Isidore of Seville commented upon the shrinking Roman empire as Khazars and Bulgars merged with Slavic culture, united in their defeat and plunder of the former Roman empire, despite each group having been paid by Byzantines to keep the others at bay. **386.** Elisaveta Todorova. "The Greeks in the Black Sea Trade During the Late Medieval Period." *Etudes Balkaniques* Nos 3-4 (Institute for Balkan Studies with Center for Tracology - Bulgarian Academy of Sciences, 1992): 40-58 **387.** Plamen Tzvetkov. *A History of the Balkans, Vol. I.* (The Edwin Mellen Press, 1993). **388.** George Vernadsky. *Kievan Russia*. (Yale University Press, 1948). **389.** Although the Moravian cultural influence was a significant factor in the Christianization of Poland, c. 966 CE, it ocurred ultimately through the Czech–Polish alliance in preference to a Germanic alliance. **390.** Gimbutas, 1971: 80-6

358 PIRATES, MERCHANTS, DEVILS & DARK DEEDS

For over three hundred years (c. 650 CE - 965 CE),[392] the Khazarians extended their control over vast swathes of territory, reaching from the Steppe regions of the Volga-Don across to the eastern regions of the Crimea, and through to the mountainous regions of the northern Caucasus.[393] This eclectic empire was originally composed of a broad range of peoples – Iranian, proto-Mongolic, Uralic, and Palaeo-Siberian clans, all of whom were dominated by a core Türkic leadership.[394] Other nomads of the Steppe long with peoples of Sogdiana were swallowed up as they swept westwards in the 6th century.[395] It is thought that an elite West Türkic people who played a significant role in the rise of the early Khazar state, the Ashinà clan;[396] were the probable leaders of this progressive tribal confederation.

Exploiting the buffer zone regions[397] between the northern Steppe nomads of China, the Arab Caliphates of the Middle East and the emerging Kievan Rus,' the semi-nomadic, polyethnic Khazars[398] completely controlled the flow of commerce through the western marches of the Silk Road.[399] Khazar connections to a Uygur tribe within its empire (744 CE to 840 CE) are speculated as a possibility through the 'Qasar,' a term attested of splinter groups within the Göktürk confederacy, although uncertainty remains whether this represents a personal or tribal name.[400] Migrating into what would become Slavic and Islamic lands, the first peoples to leave the Steppe were eventually linked to Oghuz Khan's tribal confederation. Nevertheless, many of the Türkic and Uygur people[401] entering these regions originally practised a shamanistic based belief prior to their eventual conversion to Islam.

Religious conflicts eventually divided the nomadic Türkic Kazan Tatars. Muslim Kara-Khanid Türks, composed primarily of converted Karluks and Kazakhs, encountered considerable resistance from the animist Uygur Turks of the Altai regions, whom they branded as Infidels for their cultic practises centred upon Tengri and other spirits.[402] Scorned as 'dogs' and 'Tats,'[403] the Uygur people, along with other non-Muslim Turks, including Buddhists, were harassed for their idolatrous beliefs. Unrelenting pressure to convert, enforced their eventual submission.[404] Through marriage and cross-cultural fertilisation, the Uygur people became related to several ethnic groups including the Oghur-Bulghar, the Finns and others across central Asia as they spread westwards. Ultimately absorbed into the various dynastic Türkic khanates, the Uygur came to be known as Kashgari Türks.[405] Mongol beliefs that had once largely centred on the Tengri heaven were similarly denigrated.[406] Many of them have since converted to Islam.[407] Although it is clear that the migrations and diaspora of several nomadic Türkic speaking tribes from the Steppe regions were fundamental in the shaping of trade alliances, city-building,

---

391. It was also transferred from Bulgaria and adopted by the East Slavic languages in Kievan Rus' and evolved into the Russian alphabet and the alphabets of many other Slavic (and later non-Slavic) languages. Later, some Slavs modified it and added/excluded letters from it to better suit the needs of their own language varieties. See: Ivakhiv, 2005: 209-239 **392.** Noonan, 1999: 498 **393.** Noonan, 1999: 498 **394.** David Whittow. *The Making of Byzantium, 600-1025 C.E.*, (University of California Press, 1996): 220-223 **395.** Peter Benjamin Golden. "The Khazar Sacral Kingship." In, *Pre-modern Russia and its world: Essays in Honour of Thomas S. Noonan*. Edited by Kathryn von Reyerson, Theofanis George Stavrou and Donald, James Tracy.(Otto Harrassowitz Verlag, 2006): 79-102 **396.** The Ashinà clan whose tribal name was Tür(ü)k, appear on the scene by 552 CE. See also: Golden, 2007. **397.** Dimitri Obolensky. *Byzantium and the Slavs*. (St. Vladimir's Press, 1994). **398.** The Khazar Khaganate was composed of multi-ethnic, multi-faith peoples of the Steppe, that predominantly included, nomadic pagans, Tengrists, Jews, Christians and Muslims. See: P. B. Golden. "Khazar Studies: Achievements and Perspectives." In, *The World of the Khazars: New Perspectives. Handbook of Oriental Studies*. Vol.17. Edited by P. B. Golden, Haggai Ben-Shammai and Y. András Róna-Tas. (Brill. 2007): 7-57 **399.** A confederation of Turkic-speaking tribes that in the late 6th century CE. established a major commercial empire covering the south-eastern section of modern European Russia, southern Ukraine, Crimea and Kazakhstan. **400.** Joo-Yup Lee, 2017. **401.** See Appendices III and V. **402.** Other groups of Türkic people maintained their original animistic-shamanistic religion, some converted to Christianity, Burkhanism; Judaism (Khazars, Krymchaks, Crimean Karaites); there are also Buddhists and a small number of Zoroastrians. Several groups now support a revival of ancient traditions. Since the Soviet Union collapsed, a number of people within Central Asia revived animistic and shamanistic rituals. **403.** "Tatars" were the Türkic Steppe nobility who later formed the Russian elite, the noble warrior families that settled Siberia. **404.** Berthold Spuler. "Kirim." In, *Encyclopaedia of Islam, vol. IV. New Edition*, Bernard Lewis et. al. (Eds.) (Brill, 1978): 136-143. **405.** David Brophy. "Uygur Nation: Reform and Revolution on the Russia-China Frontier." (Harvard University Press, 2016).

ethnicity and culture of the Varangian Rus', the impact upon literary culture manifested less directly among the Norse whose contemporary Skaldic literature was much expanded in the retrospective histories of later centuries, as recalled in the sagas of those past events. The author of the Eddas made enigmatic references to the people of Turkey, and its eastern regions. I believe those references are largely misunderstood. The actual context for this curious history is more likely to relate to a pre-history that involved the movements and culture, and to some extent, language, of the peoples of the Eurasian Steppe.[408] In time, those people would leave their mark on the perception and totemic magics related to a pan-European sky deity, a figure the Scandinavian people of the 11th century CE, referred to as Óðinn.

APPENDIX FIVE
Wars and Conquests of the Türkic Kaganates

Prior to the well-documented and overwhelming events of the 14th century, there were several, very relevant concurrent Türkic dynasties that fought for control of Anatolia and the trade routes it commanded. Through the influences of trade, the following regimes contributed significantly to the accumulative culture, language, customs, magics and beliefs of the peoples who eventually settled into the Nordic lands, and who adopted their multi-ethnic aesthetics by conquest, inter-marriage, migration and trade:

   Khazar Khaganate (618 –1048 CE)
   Uygur Khaganate (744 – 840 CE)
   Ganzhou Uygur Kingdom (848 –1036 CE)
   Pecheneg Khanates (860 –1091 CE)
   Kimek confederation (743 –1035 CE)
   Oghuz Yabgu State (750 – 1055 CE)
   Cumania (1067 – 1239 CE)

Despite the extreme relevance to the shaping of Europe and the socio-religio-political events it witnessed, the formulation of Khaganates are rarely unmentioned. Yet trade, industry and even the conflict of later centuries are founded in this stringent development. The interactions between the Scandinavians during the Viking Age and the Türkic Khaganates was a significant factor in the Vikingr enterprises, and ultimately, to the developing cultures of Northern Europe, Fennoscandia and Scandinavia. We may witness some of those interactions in the heroic exploits of some of the high-profile personages lauded in literary tradition.

---

406. Charles Halperin,. *The Mongol Empire and the Golden Horde.* (Indiana University Press, 1985). **407.** Ibid. The Crimean Khanate descended from the Mongolian Golden Horde that had invaded in the 13th century. **408.** See Appendices II, III and V

APPENDIX SIX
Háraldr – King of Norway

Born circa 1015, Háraldr 'Hardrada' Sigurdsson) is renowned as the last real 'Viking.' Epitomizing the Vikingr warrior spirit, his legend boldly claims he was a charismatic, adventurous leader. His epithet "Hardrada," literally means "hard ruler," affirming his steely reputation was earned. As a youth, aged 15, he fought bravely in the Battle of Stiklestad (a battle between the Danish king Cnut the Great and Háraldr's half-brother, the later Norwegian king-saint Olav II Haraldsson – Saint Olaf). After losing, he escaped with the aid of the Earl of Orkney, Háraldr began his exile as a mercenary and military commander in the Kievan Rus' and of the Varangian Guard in the Byzantine Empire, during which time he guarded pilgrims to Jerusalem, and fought Arab pirates in the Mediterranean Sea, and in inland towns in Asia Minor (Anatolia) that had supported the pirates. He fought against other Kievan enemies and rivals such as the Chudes in Estonia, and the Byzantines, as well as the Pechenegs and other Steppe nomad people. He led campaigns against the Wends and the West Slavic people inhabiting the Baltic shore. These events occur in the sagas' wherein he was referred to as Garðaríki or Svíþjóð hin mikla. He spent some time in the town of Staraja Ladoga. Háraldr amassed sufficient wealth while serving in Constantinople to fund his claim for the crown of Norway, which he acquired and ruled as Háraldr III from 1046 to 1066 CE.

Háraldr maintained control of Norway through the use of his hirð, a private standing army composed of Norwegian lords. Háraldr strengthened the power of Norway's monarchy by enforcing of a policy that permitted only the king could retain a hirð, effectively centralising power away from local warlords. This allowed him to face down and crush several uprisings against his hefty tribute and tax demands. Despite his alleged disdain for Christianity, Háraldr advanced Christianity in Norway and many churches were built during his reign. Bishops, monks and priests were imported bishops from Kievan Rus' and the Byzantine Empire, marking a distinction in this Eastern Orthodox Christianity and that adopted by the Sweden, Denmark and the rest of Europe, of Roman Catholicism. Snorre was Catholic, and very keen to smooth over the messier aspects of Norway's previous Christian conversions. After such an auspicious life, Háraldr's attempts to claim the English throne (left vacant by the death of Edward the Confessor) were thwarted by Harold Godwinson of England at Stamford Bridge. It is claimed that Háraldr fought as a Berserkir, but was struck in the throat by an arrow and killed early in the battle, sans body armour, but with a firm grip of his sword.[409]

As a chronicler, Snorre claims a Ynglinge bloodline for Háraldr Fairhair, with whom Hardrada is now increasingly identified. "However, the lay Ynglingatal, which is Snorre's "source" and the Ynglinge bloodline's "family tree," never mentions Háraldr Fairhair even once."[410] Snorre's claims that Háraldr came from Vestfold in Eastern Norway, and that his father and mother were Halfdan the Black and Ragnhild Sigurdsdotter (of Ringerike), are not supported by other, older sources, where Háraldr's mother was Ragnhild, daughter of King Harald Goldbeard in Sogn. This may even be the result of propagandising on behalf of the 13th century Norwegian king Snorre was beholden to, that obliged him "to establish a Norwegian hereditary claim to Viken, the region around Oslo, which both the Danish and Swedish kings claimed as their area."[411]

As for contemporary events in Russia, the earliest native sources for Russian history are the mediaeval annals. Practically all extant Russian chronicle texts include, regardless of their date

---

409. See: Kelly DeVries. *The Norwegian Invasion of England in 1066.* (Boydell & Brewer Ltd.,1999): 19-49. See: Sverrir Jakobsson. "The Early Kings of Norway, the Issue of Agnatic Succession, and the Settlement of Iceland." *Viator* 47 (2016): 171-88 doi:10.1484/J.VIATOR.5.112357 https://www.brepolsonline.net/toc/viator/2016/47/3 (Accessed 27th July 2021). **410.** https://avaldsnes.info/en/informasjon/harald-harfagre/ (Accessed 10th January 2025). **411.** Ibid.

APPENDIX SIX AND SEVEN

and nature, a generally uniform account of the period extending from the traditional origins of Rus' to the early 12th century. This narrative is a literary expression of the civilization and the political system which prevailed while Kiev[412] was the great national and intellectual centre of the Eastern Slavs, and is known as *The Russian Primary Chronicle*, (The Naclzal'naya Letopis'). Until the 19th century, it was habitually attributed to the monk Nestor. This view and the chronicle's authorship is now being critically reassessed; far from being a homogeneous work, it is a compilation from several chronicle texts of greater antiquity. However, the extant chronicle is a 14th century document that claims itself to be a copy of a 12th century manuscript.

APPENDIX SEVEN
Language

Language is an effective tool for asserting social dominance amongst competing groups seeking authority and control of resources. This can be effected by a relatively small but elite population; it is less about numbers and more about primary (key) strategies. The fluidity of migration and settlement throughout Eurasia during both the prehistoric and historical eras provided a complex legacy in the distribution of languages.[413]

Despite the fact that the Komsa culture originated in southern Europe, later language structures[414] places it and the Proto-Sámi people among the Uralic, later Finno-Ugric people, which suggests that by 7500 BCE, members of the Suomusjärvi culture had travelled far enough north to influence the Komsa (culture) people, who adopted the Proto-Uralic language from them. Around 6-5000 BCE, the Uralic family of languages split into two main branches, Proto Finno-Ugric and Proto Samoyedic,[415] inculcating cultural variances in belief and spirituality aligned to those languages shifts.

Sámi languages developed on the southern side of Lake Onega and Lake Ladoga, spreading outwards from there through trade and migration, completely displacing the (Paleo-Laplandic) languages of the remnant peoples of modern-day Finland. However, those ancient languages left traces in the Sámi language that over time separated further into distinctive dialects. Since the Bronze Age, the geographical distribution of the Sámi has diverged, shifting along the coast of Finnmark and the Kola Peninsula. This movement coincides with the arrival of the Siberian genome to Estonia and Finland, and the introduction of the Finno-Ugric languages to this region.

While some linguists class this later post-Komsa Sámi language within the Finno-Ugric group, one third of the Sámi vocabulary words or terms find no parallels among other Finno-Ugric languages (spoken by the Sámi, Komi, Khanty, and Mansi). These are again, almost certainly inherited from the former archaic languages carried northwards by the peoples migrating from the Iberian Refuge. Despite sharing many features with Finnish, Estonian, Karelian (and to an extent) other languages of the Baltic-Finnic subgroup, Sámi language dialects are not closely related to any of them Nevertheless, Sámi languages and modern Uralic languages do seem to share a common ancestor, and because we know that the speakers of Finnic and Sámi languages have their roots in the middle and upper Volga region viz the Corded Ware Culture, it seems highly probable that Western Uralic

---

412. Kyiv (derived from the Ukrainian-language') instead of Kiev (derived from the Russian-language) as the name of the Ukrainian capital. **413.** The Indigenous peoples of the Eurasian Arctic and subarctic can however be grouped into four main language classes: Uralic, Manchu-Tungus, Turkic, and Paleo-Siberian. **414.** This could originally have been proto-European in basic form. **415.** Björn Collinder. *An Introduction to the Uralic Languages*. (University of California Press, 1965): 30-34

languages probably spread from the original Proto-Uralic homeland along the Volga. Uralic, later Finno-Ugric speaking people,[416] maintained extensive trading contacts (for slate and flint) in the east with other Arctic-based nomadic and hunting cultures, particularly Samoyed-speaking peoples, from whom they enriched their gene pools through inter-marriages.[417]

The Nordic-speaking peoples of Scandinavia irrefutably share varying degrees of ancestry from these cumulative migrations into the northern regions traceable through two distinct parental lineages. The mother-line informs a majority gene-pool origin in women of the second migration wave from the southeastern regions of Old Europe (as referred to by Maria Gimbutas) and Anatolia, along with a fainter layer from the first migration of Ice Age mothers. Around 3000 to 4000 years ago, a small but significant group of men from Siberia with Mongolian ancestry, migrated to the North and inter-married with women from amongst the first Ice Age hunter-gatherer populations that had survived there.[418] The father-lines similarly layer up a hefty percentage of around half of Nordic-speaking fathers who descended from the third and last wave of migrations from the Ukraine and Caucasus regions (as noted), that merged with those of previous Finnish descent. Although the latter came to be dominated though the process of acculturation, Finns and Finnish Sámi nevertheless, still speak what may be an older language form of the Finno-Ugric language family.

---

416. By the late Mesolithic, the Komsa culture people had forged links with the culture of the Volga-Oka region, and while they were ethnically dissimilar, they shared similar Proto-Uralic dialects.   **417.** Other arctic peoples speaking Samoyed languages included the Enets, Nganasan, and Selkup.   **418.** It is a (genetic) fact that generations of Sámi foremothers originated in old Europe before settling in the far north, while the majority of Sámi forefathers seem to have stayed in the eastern/Siberian regions

GLOSSARY
of cultures that have enriched and contributed to the Northern Landscape

Gravettian ca. 29000 -11000 BCE. Affecting a vast area from the Atlantic coast of the Iberian Peninsula to Siberia, this period of rapid climate change caused regional fluctuations that led to diverse subsistence strategies for many peoples. Rich in artistic innovation, it is represented best by the iconic portable artworks found in these regions.

Palaeolithic: Distinguished by the technological development of stone tools, the Old Stone Age began around c. 3.3 million years ago, and continued without change until the end of the Pleistocene, c. 9700 BCE.

Mesolithic: Throughout Europe, the Middle Stone Age spans the Upper Palaeolithic and the Neolithic from approximately 13050 BCE to 3050 BCE. Elsewhere, these times vary significantly. The Mesolithic represents the final period of hunter-gatherer cultures in Europe and the Middle East (excluding Eurasia, the arctic and subarctic regions of these land masses) lingering from the Last Glacial Maximum.

Neolithic: Beginning around 8050 BCE (in the Fertile Crescent), the Neolithic denotes a gradual shift in tool technology and culture across the world over several millennia. Referred to in some places over zealously as a 'revolution,' it wasn't; change from a largely nomadic hunter-gatherer way of life to a more settled, agrarian one was steady and sporadic. Neither was it a linear progression. Arising seemingly in disparate places, this transition is now associated with the domestication of various plant and animal species (being region specific), which the archaeological record can show originated in the geological epoch of the Holocene 11700 years ago, after the end of the last Ice Age. As a nutritional exercise, it failed, and the human diet suffered considerably, yet ironically, the sedentary lifestyle initiated an increase in fertility,[419] leading to an expansion in population.

Komsa culture ca. 10000 BCE. A Mesolithic culture named after Mount Komsa in Alta, Finnmark, of hunter-gatherers in Northern Norway. Early traces of human habitation in Scandinavia are found along the retreating ice-sheets along the western coast of what is today Norway. Following receding glaciers inland from the Arctic coast at the end of the last Ice Age (between 11000 and 8000 years BCE) the migrating peoples found new, fertile land for settlement (e.g., modern Finnmark area in the northeast, to the coast of the Kola Peninsula).[420]

Komsa culture appears to have been almost exclusively sea-oriented. Food staples were seal and fish. People were able hunters, fishermen and boat-builders. Despite early migrations, hunter-gatherer genomes remained relatively isolated from each other until about 6000 BCE, when early farmers from Asia Minor brought the trade to Europe, along with a sedentary lifestyle. Although many hunter-gatherers migrated to the north, some stayed with the farmers and intermarried. Farming started in Denmark and southern Sweden around 4000 BCE. Settlers from the more culturally developed regions of Central Europe and beyond, migrated here, introducing agriculture and their attendant nature spirits. Archaeological evidence supports this influx and merging of several different cultural groups that made their way to the core location of Sámi ancestry from 8000 to 6000 BCE. Compared to the contemporary Fosna culture of southern Norway, the stone tools and other bone-carved implements of the Komsa culture appear relatively crude, oversized

---

419. Women's menstrual cycles increased, finding a better bio-rhythm. **420.** Dr. Vincent H. Malmström. "Norway Before the Vikings" (PDF). Dartmouth College, 2012. https://web.archive.org/web/20120204235040/http://www.dartmouth.edu/~izapa/E-31.pdf (Accessed 16th May 2022).

and awkward. The Fosna tool culture and technology was evidently superior and eventually became dominant.

Fosna/Hensbacka: c. 8300 BCE - 7300 BCE. Late Palaeolithic/early Mesolithic cultures of Southern Norway are often grouped together with the Komsa culture (of Northern Norway) under the name Fosna-Hensbacka culture, despite the difference in their tool technology. The Hensbacka culture was focussed primarily along the coast of western Sweden. Rich fishing waters here secured it as the largest destination for seasonal camps in northern Europe during the Late Palaeolithic/early Mesolithic transition

The Swiderian culture: This distinctive Upper Palaeolithic/Mesolithic cultural complex c. 11000 BCE - c. 8200 BCE, developed on the sand dunes left behind by retreating glaciers in the region of modern Poland. It is thought that post-Swiderian cultures, specifically the Kunda culture of Central Russia and the Baltic zone, may derive from the seasonal migrations of Swiderian people (at the turn of Pleistocene and Holocene) when human subsistence was based on hunting reindeer.

Suomusjärvi material culture: c. 7000 BCE. The Finnish Suomusjärvi culture is a good example of the regional cultures of the Mesolithic.

Pit-Comb Ware:[421] Sometime during the Mesolithic (around 5000-3200 BCE), the material culture of both the Proto-Sámi and Proto-Finic hunter/gatherer peoples merged to create the Pit–Comb Ware culture (c. 4200 BCE, to around 2000 BCE), which then developed throughout Finland, the Baltic Sea area, Russia, the Mongolian Plateau, Liaodong Peninsula, northeastern China, and the Korean Peninsula (that also developed a shamanic culture).[422] Settlements were located at sea-shores or beside lakes; their economy was based on hunting, fishing and plant foraging. From the regions now recognised as Northern Scandinavia (Finland), down to the southern shores of the Baltic Sea and across to northwestern Russia, Pit-Comb culture was a maritime tradition that became more and more specialized in hunting seals. This cultural diffusion was characterised by small figurines of burnt clay and animal heads (moose and bear) made of stone and an abundance of petroglyphs that depict the activities of these early nomadic hunter gatherers who were not without traces of basic agriculture.[423] However, they became a strong trading tradition, dealing mainly with amber, flint, slate and asbestos. Objects made of flint and amber (pendants and other adornments) were found as grave offerings. Graves were dug at the settlements and the dead were covered with red ochre.

Artefacts from this period were found in fertile settlement sites close to good water sources throughout Finnmark (Norway), Sweden, Finland and Poland. (These regions were later absorbed by the Corded Ware horizon). Pit-Comb Ware culture is a rare but essential example whereby the innovations of pottery and farming coexisted in Europe. We know that in the Near East, farming typically appeared before pottery, and that as farming spread into Europe from the Near East, pottery-making came with it. However, in Asia, where the oldest pottery has been found, pottery developed long before farming. Their Comb Ceramic Culture reflects influences from Siberia and even China.

It seems that the spread of the Comb Ware people correlates with the diffusion of the Uralic languages, and thus an early Uralic language would have been spoken by its exponents, although an alternative view suggests that bearers of this culture spoke Finno-Ugric languages. Minor indications of a non-Uralic, non-Indo-European language initiated yet another view that the

---

421. J. P. Mallory and D. Q. Adams. "Pit-Comb Ware Culture." In, *Encyclopaedia of Indo-European Culture*. (Taylor & Francis. 1997b): 429-430. **422.** The Sámi of Fennoscandia also share a most intriguing 9000-year-old genetic ancestral connection to the Berbers of North Africa. **423.** See Appendix II

GLOSSARY 365

Comb Ware people may have spoken Palaeo-European languages. Modern scholars who have located the Proto-Uralic homeland east of the Volga, if not even beyond the Urals suggest that the great westward dispersal of the Uralic languages may actually have happened long after the demise of the Comb Ceramic culture, perhaps in the 1st millennium BCE.

Funnel (neck) beaker Culture: c. 4300-2800 BCE. Developed in north-central Europe between the lower Elbe and middle Vistula rivers, this archaeological (burial) culture was a merger of local Neolithic and Mesolithic techno-complexes that slowly replaced the Ertebolle culture (that had expanded along the Baltic coast around 7300 years ago). Grave goods included jewellery (usually amber), ceramic vessels (containing food), and flint-head axes. Around 5000 years ago in Denmark, northern Germany and southern Scandinavia, Megalithic tombs and stone passage graves with external dolmens gradually replaced the wooden-chambered graves produced at the beginning of this period.

Sharing similar burial customs to those found in central, northern, and Eastern Europe (Denmark, Holland, North Germany, Sweden, Norway, Finland, and the Fatjanovo Culture of Russia), the Funnel beaker culture's inclination for collective Megalithic graves housing collective offerings, contrasts with the individual graves (and offerings) of the Swedish-Norwegian Battle Axe/Boat (shaped) Axe culture it was contemporary with.

This popular Funnel beaker culture may even be a precursor of the Bell-beaker ceramic ware culture that spread across the western half of Europe around 4800 years ago. A Funnel beaker rock carving in Sweden depicts a sailing vessel dressed with a dragon or horse head in the bow, manned with thirteen figures. Armed with large axes, two other, possibly mythical figures, stand proudly, each sporting an erect phallus, wearing horned or elk/moose eared helmets. Similarly styled (fragile) bronze helmets found in Denmark confirm their prized status, albeit as ceremonial regalia only; they are unfit for combat. Funnel beaker burials contain a high incidence of Northwest African DNA, indicating the probability they belong to Iberian Megalithic people, whose older 6000-year-old passage graves earned them the descriptor of rock worshipers. Their megalithic tombs seem linked to the movement of celestial bodies, which may have influenced those of the later Northern cultures whom we know certainly revered the Milky Way as a sacred road for the dead.

Pitted-Ware – 3500 BCE. Descended from earlier Scandinavian Hunter-Gatherers, the people of the Pitted Ware culture were however, a genetically homogeneous and distinct population who gradually replaced the Funnel beaker culture across the coastal areas of southern Scandinavia.

Bell Beaker culture: c. 2800 to 2700 BCE. Originating in Iberia, Bell Beaker culture spread to many parts of Western and Central Europe contemporaneous with the Corded Ware culture that spread across Eastern Europe, reaching into Poland and Scandinavia but not in the British Isles. The earliest 'Maritime' Bell Beaker drinking vessel style is from Iberia, around 4800 to 4700 years ago, though there may be influences to its design from precursors in northern Africa discovered through sea faring contacts between Iberia and North Africa around 5000 years ago.

Battle Axe Culture:[424] c. 2800 BCE – c. 2300 BCE Chalcolithic (Copper Age). As another offshoot of the Corded Ware culture, Battle Axe Culture was also known as Boat Axe Culture, a name derived from the characteristic 'boat-shaped' polished flint axes found in male and female burials, though the axes are placed close to the head in male burials. In both cases, these appear to be status symbols. Other grave goods sometimes include arrowheads, weapons fashioned from antlers, amber beads, and bone chisels. Faunal remains gleaned from burials include sheep, goat and red deer. Although such burials are rare in Norway, they are abundant in Sweden, and differ from

---

424. T. Douglas Price. *Ancient Scandinavia: An Archaeological History from the First Humans to the Vikings.* (Oxford University Press, 2015).

those found in Denmark, that are generally single, flat with no barrow. Typically oriented north-south, bodies were placed in a flexed position facing towards the east.. Towards the latter end of the Battle Axe Culture, the earliest cremated remains in Scandinavia of at least six people were found, which again demonstrates close contacts with Central Europe.

Possibly formed in the area north of the Black Sea, or in the area of the Vistula and Rhine, its origins remain much debated and are far from certain. As mostly Western Steppe Herders, their ancestry was closely related to the people of the Yamna culture (or Yamnaya), which again suggests migrations from the Eurasiatic Steppes that encompassed vast swathes of Northern Europe, Central Europe and Eastern Europe. Comparable in many ways with the contemporary Beaker culture, the Battle axe culture may even have contributed to its pan-European expansion. An initial period of co-existence with people of the Pitted Ware Culture, led to the inevitable absorption circa (2300 BCE) of that culture by the people of the Battle Axe Culture, as they gradually expanded into the coastal sites of Norway they'd previously occupied (reaching as far north as the present city of Tromsø). As the (mainly) inland Battle Axe Culture of southern Scandinavia merged with the native agricultural and hunter-gatherer cultures of Northern Germany, the resulting cultural fusion (which is considered the ancestral civilization of the Germanic peoples[425]), developed into the Nordic Bronze Age. [426] Although the Sámi have been found to be genetically unrelated to people of the Pitted Ware culture, the latter are shown to be genetically continuous with the original Scandinavian Hunter-Gatherer.[427]

Despite the fact that the agricultural practices of Battle Axe Culture peoples were similar to those of its predecessor (Funnel beaker Culture), their burial practises were not. Indicating an increased emphasis on individual status, the shift away from the collective megalithic graves of the Funnel beaker culture with its multiple offerings (sacrificed animals), the Battle Axe culture instead featured prominent individual graves that contained correspondingly single offerings. As cattle herders and traders with coastal locations, they established a thriving vigorous maritime economy along the Atlantic and North Sea coastal regions of Scandinavia and the circum-Baltic areas. The vast number of widely-dispersed rock carvings of water vessels assigned to these regions are a solid testament to their seafaring cultures.

The Yamnaya culture:[428] **or the Yamna culture, 3300-2600 BCE,** also known as the Pit Grave culture or Ochre Grave culture. The peoples who carried this culture were genetically related to several late Neolithic cultures that had spread westwards throughout Europe and Central Asia (namely the Corded Ware people and the Bell Beaker culture, but including the peoples of the Sintashta, Andronovo, and Srubnaya cultures). Yamnaya material culture was remarkably similar to the Afanasevo culture of South

Siberia, which suggests they shared a common source. In fact, recent genetic studies claim that bearers of the Yamnaya (Pit-grave) culture migrated to the Central and Northern Europe in great numbers leading to a cultural fusion of elements (especially Proto-Indo-European language forms) blended from the earlier Funnel beaker culture, the Battle Axe culture and the Single Grave culture. Ultimately, from this peppering of peoples and fusion of languages in different combinations, the Germanic, Finnish, Italic, Balto-Slavic and Celtic languages were formed and dispersed in Europe during the (Chalcolithic) Copper and Bronze Ages.[429] This late Copper Age to early Bronze Age archaeological culture of the Pontic-Caspian Steppe derives from its characteristic burial tradition where the dead were placed in pit-chambers within tumuli (kurgans).★ The nomadic Yamnaya people developed quite a sophisticated society comprising of

---

425. Mallory and Adams, 1997b. **426.** Helena Malmström, et al. "The genomic ancestry of the Scandinavian Battle Axe Culture people and their relation to the broader Corded Ware horizon." In, *Proceedings of the Royal Society B. Royal Society*, 1912: 286 doi:10.1098/rspb.2019.1528. PMC 6790770. PMID 31594508 (Accessed 19th June 2022). **427.** Mallory, 2013. **428.** Mallory, 1989.

GLOSSARY 367

wheeled carts and wagons[430] that allowed them to manage large herds, an economy based upon animal husbandry, fishing, and foraging, the manufacture of ceramics, tools, and weapons, and a chiefdom system.

*Yamnaya Kurgans: First formulated as a funerary paradigm in the 1950s by Marija Gimbutas, who used the term to group together various cultures, including the Yamnaya, or Pit Grave, culture and its predecessors. The Kurgan hypothesis identifies the Proto-Indo-European homeland from which the Indo-European languages spread out throughout Europe, Eurasia and parts of Asia. It postulates that the people of a Kurgan culture in the Pontic Steppe north of the Black Sea were the most likely original speakers of the Proto-Indo-European language (PIE). Marija Gimbutas defined the Kurgan culture as composed of four successive periods, with the earliest (Kurgan I) including the Samara and Seroglazovo cultures of the Dnieper-Volga region in the Copper Age (early 4th millennium BCE). The people of these cultures were nomadic pastoralists, who, according to the model, by the early 3rd millennium BCE had expanded throughout the Pontic-Caspian Steppe and into Eastern Europe.

Where do we trace this culture from? The European gene pool is now able to identify an archaic ancestry rooted in the indigenous hunter-gatherers who entered Europe before the Ice Age, some 40,000 years ago. Significantly, around 15000 years ago, various peoples (from the regions we now know as East Asia) moved northwards to enter the American continent. Others moved north into the Siberian regions, while others looked westwards, moving rapidly through the Pontic Caspian Steppes. Eventually they arrived in the region of the Don-Volga area just north of the Caucasus, merging there with the Ice-Age hunter-gatherer descendants of Europeans and farmers from the Middle East. Around 7000 years ago, that admixture of diverse geographical and ethnic origins had formed the distinct shepherding culture known as Yamna (Yamnaya). As the first speakers of an Indo-European language,[431] we may now attribute the spread of Indo-European languages to these horse-riding metal workers. Having much in common culturally with their eastern Steppe neighbours (including Proto-Turks and Proto-Mongols), those Proto-Indo-European tribes shared agricultural innovations despite their primary nomadic and pastoral (shepherding) economies where wealth was measured according to flock fecundity. Around 5,000 years ago, Yamnaya herders entered Europe from the eastern Steppe region (present day Ukraine and Russia).

The Nordic gene pool is far more diverse than people previously imagined. Recent studies of ancient and modern genomes confirm that 50% of Y-DNA (father-to-son) lineages in Scandinavia are also shared by the majority of men living in Kazakhstan and Russia, and which derive directly from the Yamna culture peoples. The majority of mother lineages (MtDNA) together with the remaining male Y-DNA, can be traced to earlier populations rooted in prehistory prior to subsequent waves of Indo-European peoples migrating westwards several thousand years ago. Genetic markers for tallness inherited by Nordic peoples, were a common feature of the Yamna culture people. Moreover, the combination of the supposedly Nordic 'type,' fair hair, fair skin and pale coloured eyes can be attributed to early ancestral gene-pooling and admixture. Blue eyes are a European genetic anomaly, typically found in brown-haired peoples while blondeness common to the peoples of Finland and Scandinavia, derives from the Ukraine regions.

Cultural changes during the Neolithic occurred via diffusion and what is now popularly known as 'leap frogging,' whereby a strong and influential group enter a much larger populace, leave a

---

429. But not the sole source for Greek, Illyrian, Thracian and East Italic, which may be derived from Southeast Europe. See: J. P. Mallory. "The Indo-Europeanization of Atlantic Europe." In, *Celtic From the West 2: Rethinking the Bronze Age and the Arrival of Indo–European in Atlantic Europe*. Edited by J. T. Koch and B. Cunliffe. (Oxbow Books, 2013): 17-40. **430.** These seasonal mobile 'tent' structures were skins stretched over light wooden frames, placed in carts, not unlike the pioneer wagons of the wild west frontiers. **431.** In recent years, archaeological and genetic evidence parallel the initial spread of the Indo-European language family, confirming this association.

few behind and move on, dispersing cumulative cultural influences (including languages) along the way, establishing new and vibrant changes to existing cultures in large parts of Europe and southwestern Asia. In Europe, only Basque, Hungarian, Finnish, and Estonian may claim an older linguistic ancestry native to Europe that is prior to the Yamna expansion.

Corded Ware Culture. A Chalcolithic culture that ended in the early Bronze Age. Preceded by Yamnaya culture, it replaced the earlier, native, agricultural Funnel beaker culture, Narva culture and Pit-Comb Ware culture (of Finland, the Baltic regions, and the Samara Culture of Russia) while co-existing with the older, native, hunter gatherer Pitted Ware culture. Influenced by Yamna culture, the Corded Ware Culture evolved from it in northern Europe (between 2950 BCE and 2400 BCE) in a parallel manner. Encompassing a vast area of South, Central, Northern and Eastern Europe, it spread across from the river Volga in the east, to the river Rhine in the west, [432]extending into the southernmost parts of Scandinavia and Finland.

The appearance of the Corded Ware Culture in the eastern Baltic area (3000-2700 BCE) tends to be associated with the beginning of animal husbandry in this region, a phenomenon popularly linked with the migrations of peoples of Indo-Europeans ancestry. Archaeology seemingly appears to support this notion. While the culture is fairly well represented by artefacts from around the Baltic Sea basin, its domestic animal bone material (as indications of early farming) yields less certainty.

The transitional period from a hunter-gatherer lifestyle to a farming society, was initially sporadic and prolonged. It was a slow process. There was no 'Neolithic Revolution.' Change was gradual and region dependant. Similarities in the material culture across a wide area, and its origins have garnered divided opinion. Because no mass migrations have been observed, however, researchers have concluded that it was the culture itself that spread, without the people originally carrying these ideas via the leap-frogging' process. This suggests "the possibility that small pioneer groups carried farming into new areas of Europe, and that once the technique had been established, the surrounding hunter-gatherers adopted the new culture and then outnumbered the original farmers."[433] Nevertheless, Corded Ware was not a unified culture; groups within it had regionally specific subsistence strategies and economies, sharing mainly their use of pottery with corded decoration and unique stone-axes[434] in their burial practises

The collective indigenous Neolithic culture typical of 'Old Europe,' identified by its art forms, shrines and sculptures, a perished in the onslaught of a new and brutal culture of warriorhood that glorified combat. This (social and material) culture was introduced by semi-nomadic horse-riding people from the east who infiltrated the Danubian Valley and other major grasslands of the Balkans and Central Europe. "Their arrival initiated a dramatic shift in the prehistory of Europe, a change in social structure and in residence patterns, in art and in religion and it was a decisive factor in the formation of Europe's last 5000 years."[435] While bones from the Mesolithic and Early Neolithic indicate the presence of wild horse, we do not find material evidence of the domestic horse until the Late Bronze Age that. For instance, Funnel Beaker Culture sites across Europe have yielded considerable amounts of horse bone. In Denmark, many Battle-Axe (Single Grave) Culture burials and settlement sites also present bones of domestic horse. In Sweden too, horse bones have been found in megalithic graves.

Given the shared genetics we should not be surprised by the cultural similarities detected between

---

432. Also including almost all the countries and minor states of central, northern and eastern Europe. In the Late Neolithic/Early Bronze Age, it encompassed the territory of nearly the entire Balkan Peninsula, where Corded Ware mixed with other steppe elements. **433.** Lembi Lõugas, Aivar Kriiska and Liina Maldre. "New Dates For The Late Neolithic/Early Corded Ware Culture Burials And Early Husbandry In The East Baltic Region." In, *Archaeofauna* 16 (Department of History, Tartu University, 2007): 21-31 **434.** Sandra Mariët Beckerman. *Corded Ware Coastal Communities: Using ceramic analysis to reconstruct third millennium BCE societies in the Netherlands.* (Sidestone Press, 2015). **435.** Marija Gimbutas. *The Balts.* (Thames and Hudson, 1963).

GLOSSARY

peoples of the Sintashta culture, the Nordic Bronze Age and the peoples of the Rigveda, who all ultimately derived from a remigration of Central European peoples of steppe ancestry, back into the Steppe.[436]

A Basic Norwegian and Nordic chronology:

Bronze Age – 1800 – 500 BCE.
Pre-Roman Iron Age – 500 BCE–1CE
Roman Iron Age –1 – 400 CE
Migration Era – 400 – 560/570 CE
Merovingian /Vendel Period – 560/570 – 800 CE
(The transition from the Migration period
to the Merovingian period marks the division
between the early and late Iron Ages).

Viking Age – 800–1050 CE)
Early Middle Ages — 1050–1150 CE
High Middle Ages - 1150–1350 CE
Late Middle Ages – 1350–1520 CE.

---

436. Vagheesh M. Narasimhan, et al "The Formation Of Human Populations In South and Central Asia." In, *Science. American Association for the Advancement of Science* vol 365 (6457) (2019): eaat7487. doi:10.1126/science.aat7487 PMC 6822619. PMID 31488661. https://www.ncbi.nlm.nih.gov/pmc/articles/PMC6822619/ (Accessed 12th March 2024).

BIBLIOGRAPHY

PRIMARY SOURCES:

Adam von Bremen. "Gesta Danorum" *Hamburgische Kirchengeschichte*, 275-276 [Hamburg's Church History] (in Latin and German). Edited by Bernard Schmeidler. Hahnsche, 1917.

Cornelius Tacitus. "Dialogus," "Agricola," "Germania," W. Peterson and M. Hutton. The Loeb Classical Library 35, 1914.

Cornelius Tacitus, *Germania* Translated by J. G. C. Anderson. Bristol Classical Press, 1998.

Diodorus Siculus. *Library of History* Translated by C. H. Oldfather et al. Online, at http://penelope.uchicago.edu/Thayer/E/Roman/Texts/ Diodorus_Siculus/home.html

Helmold of Bosau. *The Chronicle of the Slavs* Translated by Francis J. Tschan. Columbia University Press, 1935.

Herodotus, Histories 2.60 Ed. & Trans. by G. C. Macaulay. Barnes & Noble Classics, 2004.

Hollander, Lee M. *The Saga of the Jomsvikings* University of Texas Press, 1989.

Lavrentevskaia Letopis, also called the "Povest Vremennykh Let" *Polnoe Sobranie Russkikh Letopisey* (PSRL) Vol. 1: 95-102. (Typography of Edward Prats. 1837 -) See: https://infogalactic.com/info/Complete_Collection_of_Russian_Chronicles

Norges Gamle Love Indtil 1387 Edited and Translated by R. Keyser and P. A. Munch. Christiania Grondahl, 1846-1849.

Rawlinson, George. *The History of Herodotus*, 4 vols. Edited by Jessalynn Bird, Brittany Blagburn, Anna Noone, and Marirose Osborne. New York: Tandy-Thomas Co., 1909. https://human.libretexts.org/Courses/Saint_Mary's_College_(Notre_Dame_IN)/Humanistic_Studies/Supplemental_Modules/Herodotus%3A_Racist_or_Ethnographer%3F

Saint Augustine. *The City of God Against The Pagans* 411: 2-3 Loeb Classical Library, 1957.

Snorre Sturlusson. *Sigrdrífumál*. Edited and Translated by Henry Adams Bellows. Internet Sacred Texts Archive. https://archive.org/details/poeticedda00belluoft/mode/2up (1923).

Snorre Sturlusson. *Egils saga einhenda ok Ásmundar berserkjabana* Translated by Hermann Pálsson and Paul Edwards. Penguin Books Ltd, 1976.

Heimskringla Translated by Lee Hollander. University of Texas Press, 1964.

The Prose Edda Translated by Jesse Byock. Penguin Books, 2005.

The Poetic Edda Translated by Carolyne Larrington. Oxford Uni. Press, 1999.

Noregs konunga sögur ['Heimskringla. The Kings' sagas of Norway'] Edited by Finnur Jónsson, København: Gad, 1911.

Saxo Grammaticus, *Gesta Danorum: The History of the Danes* Edited by Karsten Friis-Jensen. Translated by Peter Fisher. Vol 1 (of 2) Clarendon Press, 2015.

The Book of Settlements (Sturlubók version) Translated by Hermann Pálsson and Paul Edwards. Winnipeg: University of Manitoba Press, [1972] 2006.

The Russian Primary Chronicle: Laurentian Text. Trans. & Eds.by Samuel Hazzard Cross and Olgerd P. Sherbowitz-Wetzor. Mediaeval Academy of America, 1953.

The Saga of the Jómsvikings, translated by Alison Finlay, Þórdís Edda Jóhannesdóttir, Andrew McGillivray, edited by Svanhildur Óskarsdóttir, Emily Lethbridge, Tom Birkett, Roderick Dale, Ármann Jakobsson, and Miriam Mayburd. De Gruyter, 2018.

SECONDARY SOURCES:

Aalto, Sirpa. "Categorizing Otherness in the King's Sagas" In, *Volume 10 of Publications of the University of Eastern Finland, Dissertations in social sciences.* University of Eastern Finland, 2010.

Aalto, Sirpa., and Veli-Pekka Lehtola. "The Sámi Representations Reflecting The Multi-Ethnic North Of The Saga Literature" *Journal of Northern Studies* 11, no. 2 (2017): 7-30.

Acheraïou, A. *Questioning Hybridity, Postcolonialism and Globalization* Palgrave Macmillan, 2011.

Adamczak, Dr Kamil. "Pots Full of History." In, *Journal Proceedings of the National Academy of Sciences.* Nicolaus Copernicus University in Torun. 2023. DOI 10.1073/pnas.2310138120

Aldhouse Green, Miranda J. *An Archaeology of Images: Iconology and Cosmology in Iron Age and Roman Europe.* Routledge, 2004.

Andrzejowski, Jacek. "The Przeworsk Culture. A Brief Story (for the Foreigners)," In, *Worlds Apart? Contacts across the Baltic Sea in the Iron Age: Network Denmark-Poland 2005–2008.* Edited by Ulla Lund Hansen and Anna Bitner-Wróblewska. Det Kongelige Nordiske Oldskriftselskab Panstwowe Muzeum Archeologiczne, 2010.

Andrén, A. The Significance Of Places: The Christianization Of Scandinavia From A Spatial Point Of View" *World Archaeology* 45 (1) (2013): 27–45.

Anisimov. A.F. "Cosmological Concepts Of The People Of The North" Edited by Henry N Michael. *Studies in Siberian shamanism: Arctic Institute of North America anthropology of the North: Translations from Russian sources no. 4.* University of Toronto Press, (1963):163-176.

Anthony, D.W. *The Horse, The Wheel, and The Language: How Bronze-Age Riders from The Eurasian Steppes Shaped The Modern World* Princeton University Press, 2007.

Armstrong, T. Edward.; William Barr; Don E. Dumond; Maxwell John Dunbar; Ostenso, Ned Allen; Moira Dunbar; Tim Ingold and J. Brian Bird. "Arctic." *Encyclopaedia Britannica*, June 27, 2024. https://www.britannica.com/place/Arctic

Aruz, Joan., with Ann Farkas, Andrei Alekseev, and Elena Korolkova (Eds). *The Golden Deer of Eurasia: Scythian and Sarmatian Treasures from the Russian Steppes* Yale Uni Press, 2000.

Asheri, David, Alan Lloyd and Aldo Corcella. *A Commentary on Herodotus,* Books I-IV Oxford University Press, 2007.

Austvoll, Knut Ivar. "The Emergence of Coercive Societies in Northwestern Scandinavia During the Late Neolithic–Early Bronze Age" *Open Archaeology*, 2020. doi:10.1515/opar-2020-0100.

Barnhart, Lauren J. "The Totemic Significance Of The Deer In Iron Age Scythian And Sarmatian Cultures In Eastern Europe And Central Asia" Master's Degree, Johns Hopkins University, Maryland, 2022.

Bartlett, Robert. "Why Can the Dead Do Such Great Things?" In, *Saints and worshippers from the martyrs to the Reformation.* Princeton University Press, 2013.

Bartlett, Robert. "The Conversion of a Pagan Society in The Middle Ages" *History* 70, no. 229 (1985): 185-201. http://www.jstor.org/stable/24416033.

Baug, Irene., Wojciech Filipowiak, Øystein James Jansen and Torkil Sørlie RØhr. "Norse Whetstones in Slavic Areas—Indicators of Long-Distance Networks During the Viking Age and the Middle Ages" *Medieval Archaeology*, 68 (1) 2024: 48-71. DOI:10.1080/00766097.2024.2347751

Baumer, Cristoph. *The History of Central Asia: The Age of the Steppe Warriors* (Volume 1). I.B. Tauris, 2012.

Baumer, Cristoph. *The History of Central Asia –The History of Central Asia: The Age of Islam and the Mongols* (Volume 3). I.B. Tauris, 2016.

BIBLIOGRAPHY 373

Baldick, Julian. *Animal and Shaman: Ancient Religions of Central Asia* I.B. Tauris, 2012.

Beckerman, Sandra Mariët. *Corded Ware Coastal Communities: Using ceramic analysis to reconstruct third millennium BCE societies in the Netherlands* Leiden: Sidestone Press, 2015.

Bengtsson, L., and Johan Ling. "Scandinavia's Most Finds Associated Rock Art Site" *Adoranten* 2007: 40-50. rockartscandinavia.se, 2008.

Bengtsson, L. "To Excavate Images: Some Results From The Tanum Rock Art project 1997–2004," In, *Representations and Communications: Creating an Archaeological Matrix of Late Prehistoric Rock Art.* Edited by Å. Fredell, K. Kristiansen and F. Criado Boado. Oxbow Books, 2010.

Bergesen, Rognald. "Dutch Images of Indigenous Sámi Religion. Jan Luyken's Illustrations of Lapland" *Acta Borealia.* 32. (2015): 103-124. 10.1080/08003831.2015.1090164.

Bertilsson, Ulf. "The Rock Carvings of Northern Bohuslän: Spatial Structures and Social Symbols" *Stockholm Studies in Archaeology* 7. Stockholm University, 1987.

Berglund, Birgitta. "Recently Discovered Gievrie (South-Sámi Shaman Drums) – Contexts, Meanings and Narratives" *Acta Borealia: A Nordic Journal of Circumpolar Societies* 22 (2) (2005): 128-152. DOI: 10.1080/ 08003830500327689

Bhabha, H. K. *The Location of Culture.* Routledge,1994.

Blanchard-Wrigglesworth, E., C. M. Bitz, and M. M. Holland. "Influence Of Initial Conditions And Climate Forcing On Predicting Arctic Sea Ice" *Geophys. Res. Lett.*, 38 (2001). L18503, doi:10.1029/2011GL048807.

Bogarve, Elmer. "An Analysis Of How The Political Legitimacy Of The Sámi Peoples Is Perceived By Actors In The Indigenous Community Itself" *European Studies: Politics, Societies, and Cultures.* Bachelor's Thesis. Spring, 2022. https://www.divaportal.org/smash/get/diva2:1733289/FULLTEXT03

Buko, Andrzej. "Between Wolin and Truso: the Southern part of the Baltic Rim at the time of Rise of the Polish State (an archaeological perspective)" *The Image of the Baltic.* Edited by Michael F. Scholz; Robert Bohn; Carina Johansson. Gotland University Press, 2012.

Burton, Richard F. *Ultima Thule* vol. 1(2), or, *A Summer in Iceland* [EBook #59584]. https://www.gutenberg.org/files/59584/59584-h/59584-h.htm ([1875] 2019).

Boucherit, Gilles. "A Deer Cult in Buile Suibhne" In, *xiv Comhdháil Idirnáisiúnta Sa Léann Ceilteach Xiv. International Congress of Celtic Studies*, Maynooth, Ireland, 2011. https://hal.archives-ouvertes.fr/hal-00621072v4

Bradley, Richard. *Image and Audience. Rethinking Prehistoric Art* Oxford University Press, 2009.

Bradley, Richard., Peter Skoglund & Joakim Wehlin. "Imaginary Vessels in The Late Bronze Age Of Gotland And South Scandinavia: Ship Settings, Rock Carvings And Decorated Metalwork" *Current Swedish Archaeology* Vol 18 (2010).

Brather, Sebastian. *Archäologie der westlichen Slawen: Siedlung, Wirtschaft und Gesellschaft im früh- und hochmittelalterlichen Ostmitteleuropa*, 2nd ed., (in German) Reallexikon der Germanischen Altertumskunde, Ergänzungsband 61 De Gruyter, 2008.

Braund, David. "Greater Olbia: Ethnic, Religious, Economic, and Political Interactions in the Region of Olbia, c.600-100 BCE" In, *Classical Olbia and the Scythian World: From the Sixth Century BCE to the Second Century CE*. Edited by David Braund and S. D. Kryzhintskiy. [in Russian] Oxford University Press, 2007.

Bromwich, Rachel. Ed. and Tr. *Tri Thlws ar Ddeg Ynys Prydain* Trioedd Ynys Prydein. Cardiff: University of Wales Press, 1978; revised ed. 1991 (Critical edition of the Trioedd texts with notes, first published in 1961). Appendix III. Edited from Cardiff MS. 17, pp. 95–6, and other variants.

Brophy, David. *Uygur Nation: Reform and Revolution on the Russia-China Frontier.* Harvard University Press, 2016.

Caferzade, I., *Gobustan: Naskal'nye izobrazenija, Akademija Nauk Azerbajdzanskoj SSR*, Institut istorii, 1973.

Cavalli-Sforza, Luigi Luca; Menozzi, Paolo; Piazza, Alberto. *The History and Geography of Human Genes* Princeton University Press, 1994.

Cavalli-Sforza, Luigi Luca. (Eds.) *Genes, Peoples, and Languages* University of California Press, 2001.

Chadwick, N. Kershaw. *Poetry & Prophecy* Cambridge University Press, 1952.

Chikisheva, T. A.; Polosmak, N. V.; Zubova, Alisa. "The Burial at Ak-Alakha-3 Mound 1, Gorny Altai: New Findings1" *Archaeology Ethnology and Anthropology of Eurasia* 43(1) (2015):144-154. DOI:10.1016/j.aeae.2015.07.016 https://www.researchgate.net/publication/283858350_The_Burial_at_Ak-Alakha-3_Mound_1_Gorny_Altai_New_Findings1 (2015).

Chisholm, Hugh. (Ed.) "Hrabanus Maurus Magnentius" *Encyclopædia Britannica* Vol. 13 (11th ed.). Cambridge University Press, 1911.

Christian, David. *A History of Russia, Central Asia and Mongolia Vol. 1: Inner Eurasia from Prehistory to the Mongol Empire.* Blackwell Publishing, 1998.

BIBLIOGRAPHY 375

Christensen, Arne Emil. "Ship Graffiti: The Ship As Symbol In Prehistoric And Medieval Scandinavia" In, *A Collection of Essays: The Ship as Symbol in Prehistoric and Medieval Scandinavia*. Papers from an International Research Seminar at the Danish National Museum, Copenhagen, 5th-7th May 1994. Edited by O. Crumlin-Pedersen and B. M. Thye. National Museum of Copenhagen, 1995.

Christiansen, Eric. *The Northern Crusades* Penguin Books Ltd, 1997.

Cigán, Michal. *Priest-King of the Warriors and Witch-Queen of the Others: Cargo Cult and Witch Hunt in Indo-European Myth and Reality* 1. elektronické vydání. Brno: Masaryk University Press, 2019.

Collinder, Björn. *An Introduction to the Uralic Languages* University of California Press, 1965.

Conner, Randy P. "Enaree." In, *Cassell's Encyclopaedia of Queer Myth, Symbol, and Spirit: Gay, Lesbian, Bisexual, and Transgender Lore* Cassell, 1997.

Crumlin-Pedersen, Ole; Inger M. Bojesen-Koefoed; Athena Trakadas. *Hjortspring: a Pre-Roman Iron Age Warship In Context* Edited by Ole Crumlin-Pedersen and Athena Trakadas. Roskilde: Viking Ship Museum, 2003.

Cunliffe, Barry. *The Scythians – Nomad Warriors of the Steppe* Oxford Uni Press, 2019.

Cunliffe, Barry. (Ed.). *Prehistoric Europe: An Illustrated History* Oxford Uni Press, 1994.

Curta, Florin. *Southeastern Europe in the Middle Ages, 500-1250* Cambridge University Press, 2006.

Dandamayev, M. A. "Media and Achaemenid Iran," *History of Civilizations of Central Asia: The Development of Sedentary and Nomadic Civilizations, 700 BCE to 250 CE*. Vol. 2 Edited by János Harmatta et al. New Delhi: Motilal Banarsidass Publishers Private Limited, 1999: 35-64.

Davis-Kimball, Jeannine, Vladimir A. Bashilov, and Leonid T. Yablonsky, (Eds.) *Nomads of the Eurasian Steppes in the Early Iron Age*. Zinat Press, 1995.

Davis-Kimball, Jeannine. *Warrior Women: An Archaeologist's Search for History's Hidden Heroines* Warner Books, 2002.

Demant Hatt, Emilie., and Barbara Sjoholm. "Folktales" In, *By the Fire: Sami Folktales and Legends*. (Minneapolis; London: University of Minnesota Press, 2019): 58-67. doi:10.5749/j.ctvfjcx2d.9

de Santillana, Giorgio., and Hertha von Dechend. *Hamlets Mill* David R. Godine Inc., 1977.

Derksen, Rick. *Etymological Dictionary of the Slavic Inherited Lexicon* Leiden: Brill, 2007.

DeVries, Kelly. *The Norwegian Invasion of England in 1066* Boydell & Brewer Ltd.,1999.

Dickins, Bruce. *Runic and Historic Poems of the Old Teutonic Peoples* Cambridge University Press, 1915.

Dixon-Kennedy, Mike. *Encyclopaedia of Russian & Slavic Myth and Legend* USA: ABC-CLIO,1998.

Dolukhanov, P. M. "The Pleistocene-Holocene transition in northern Eurasia: Environmental changes and human adaptations" *Quaternary International*, Vols 41–42, (1997):181–191. doi:10.1016/S1040-6182(96)00051-1

Dolukhanov. P. M. *The Early Slavs: Eastern Europe from the Initial Settlement to the Kievan Rus'* Routledge, 2014:182

Dolgopolsky. A. *Nostraic Dictionary*. Cambridge: McDonald Institute for Archaeological Research, 2008.

Dragnea, Mihai. "Divine Vengeance and Human Justice in the Wendish Crusade of 1147 CE" In, *Collegium Medievale*. 2016: http://ojs.novus.no/index.php/CM/article/view/1366/1351

Dragosani-Brantingham, Justin. "An Illustrated Introduction to the Kipchak Turks" ([1999] 2011). www.kipchak.com.

Duczko, Wladyslaw. *Viking Rus: Studies on the Presence of Scandinavians in Eastern Europe* Brill Academic Publishers, 2004.

Dumond, D. E.; Dunbar, Moira., et al. "Arctic." In, *Encyclopedia Britannica* January 19, 2025. https://www.britannica.com/place/Arctic.

Dunnigan, James F., and Albert A Nofi. Medieval Life & the Hundred Years War 1994. http://www.hundredyearswar.com/Books/History/1_Help_C.htm

Düwel, K. *Runic Inscriptions In Eastern Europe*. Biblioteka Nauki. 2013. https://bibliotekanauki.pl

Dynda, Jiří. "The Three-Headed One at the Crossroad: A Comparative Study of the Slavic God Triglav" *Studia mythologica Slavica*. 17, (2014): 57-82. Institute of Slovenian Ethnology

Eckmann, János. "The Mamluk-Kipchak Literature" *Central Asiatic Journal* Vol. 8 (no. 4) Harrassowitz Verlag, (1963): 304-319. https://www.jstor.org/stable/i40089557

BIBLIOGRAPHY 377

Edge, David., and Alan Williams. "Some Early Medieval Wwords In The Wallace Collection And Elsewhere" *Gladius* 26(1)(2003). 191-210 DOI:10.3989/gladius.2003.50

Eliade, M. *Shamanism: Archaic Techniques of Ecstasy* Translated by Willard R Trask, Bollingen Series 76. Princeton University Press, 1964.

Ellis Davidson, H. R. *Gods and Myths of Northern Europe*, New York and London: Penguin Books,1990.

Ellis Davidson, H. R. *Roles of the Northern Goddess* New York and London: Routledge,1999.

Farkas, Ann. "Filipovka and the Art of the Steppes" In, *The Golden Deer of Eurasia*. Edited by Joan Aruz, Ann Farkas and Elisabetta Valtz Fino. Yale University Press, The Metropolitan Museum of Art, 2006.

Fjellström, P. "Cultural and Traditional Ecological Perspectives on Sámi Religion" In, *Sámi Religion*. Edited by T. Ahlbäck. Åbo, Finland: Donner Institute for Research in Religious and Cultural History, 1987.

Forostyuk, O. D. *Luhansk Religious Region* Lugansk: Svitlytsia, 2004.

Frank, Roberta. *Sex Lies And Málsháttakvaeæði: A Norse Poem From Medieval Orkney* Edited by Judith Jesch. Centre for the Study of the Viking Age. Uni. of Notts., 2004.

Friedrich, Paul., and Norma Diamond. (Eds.) *Encyclopaedia of World Cultures Volume 6 Russia and Eurasia China*, Part 1. New York: G.K. Hall & Co., 2016.

Frye, Richard N. *The Heritage of Central Asia: From Antiquity to the Turkish Expansion* Princeton: Markus Wiener, 1996.

Gamkrelidze, V. T. and V. V. Ivanov, *Indo-European and the Indo-Europeans: reconstruction and historical analysis of a Proto-language and a proto V.V. culture*. Part I: The text, J. Nichols, (Trans.) W. Winter, (Ed.) Berlin; New York: Mouton de Gruyter, 1995.

Gasparini, Evel. Communal-banquets-and-related-practices#ref533502 In, *Encyclopedia Britannica*, December 27, 2024. https://www.britannica.com/topic/Slavic-religion, 2024.

Gates, Henry Louis Jr. "Opinion – How to End the Slavery Blame-Game" In, *The New York Times*, 2010.

Geary, Patrick J. "Germanic Tradition and Royal Ideology in the Ninth Century: The Visio Karoli Magni." In, *Living with the Dead in the Middle Ages*. Ithaca, United States: Cornell University Press, 1994. doi:10.7591/9781501721632-005.

Gelling, Peter., and Hilda Ellis Davidson. *The Chariot of the Sun: and Other Rites and Symbols of the Northern Bronze Age.* London: J. M. Dent & Sons, 1969.

Gieysztor, Aleksander. *Mitologia Słowian.* Warsaw University, 1980.

Gillespie, George T. *Catalogue of Persons Named in German Heroic Literature, 700-1600: Including Named Animals and Objects and Ethnic Names.* Oxford: Oxford University, 1973.

Gimbutas, Marija. *The Balts.* London: Thames and Hudson, 1963.

The Slavs. Edited by Dr. Glyn Daniel. London: Thames and Hudson, 1971.

"Slavic Religion." In, *The Encyclopaedia of Religion.* Volume 13. Edited by Mircea Eliade. New York - London: Collier Macmillan Publishing Company, 1987.

Golden, Peter Benjamin. *Khazar Studies: An Historio-Philological Inquiry into the Origins of the Khazars.* Vol. 1, 2. Budapest: Akademia Kiado, 1980.

"An Introduction to the History of the Turkic Peoples: Ethnogenesis And State Formation in the Medieval and Early Modern Eurasia and the Middle East." *Turcologica.* Vol. 9. Wiesbaden: O. Harrassowitz, 1992.

"The Peoples of the South Russian Steppes. In, *The Cambridge History of Early Inner Asia.* Vol. 1. Edited by Denis Sinor. Cambridge University Press. [1990] 1994a.

"The Peoples of the Russian Forest Belt" In, *The Cambridge History of Early Inner Asia.* Vol. 1. Edited by Denis Sinor. Cambridge University Press. [1990] 1994b.

"The Khazar Sacral Kingship" In, *Pre-modern Russia and its world: Essays in Honour of Thomas S. Noonan.* Edited by Kathryn von Reyerson; George Theofanis Stavrou; James Donald Tracy. Otto Harrassowitz Verlag, 2006.

"The Conversion of the Khazars to Judaism" In, *The World of the Khazars: New Perspectives. Handbook of Oriental Studies.* Vol. 17. Edited by Peter B. Golden, Haggai Ben-Shammai, Y. András Róna-Tas. Brill, 2007a.

"Khazar Studies: Achievements and Perspectives" In, *The World of the Khazars: New Perspectives. Handbook of Oriental Studies.* Vol. 17. Edited by Peter B. Golden; Haggai Ben-Shammai; András Róna-Tas. Brill, 2007b.

Goldhahn, Joakim. "Sagaholm: North European Bronze Age Rock Art and Burial Ritual" Oxbow Books, 2016.

Gorbachov, Yaroslav. "What Do We Know about Chernobog and BeloBog" *Russian History*, 44 (2-3). (2017): 209-242. doi: https://doi.org/10.1163/18763316-04402011

Gramsch, Bernhard and Klaus Kloss. "Excavations near Friesack: an Early Mesolithic Marshland Site in the Northern Plain of Central Europe" In, *The Mesolithic in Europe: Papers Presented at the Third International Symposium, Edinburgh 1985*. Edited by Clive Bonsall. Edinburgh: John Donald Publishers, 1990.

Guðmundsdóttir, Aðalheiður. "Behind The Cloak, Between The Lines: Trolls And The Symbolism Of Their Clothing In Old Norse Tradition" *European Journal of Scandinavian Studies* 47, no. 2 (2017): 327-350. https://doi.org/10.1515/ejss-2017-0022

Gumilev, L. N. *Ancient Türks* Moscow: Ayris Press, [1993] 2007.

Grumeza, Ion. *The Roots of Balkanization: Eastern Europe C.E. 500–1500* University Press of America, 2010.

Gustin, I., Price, D. T., Arcini, C., Drenzel, L., & Kalmring, S. (2017). "Isotopes and Human Burials at Viking Age Birka and the Mälaren Region, East Central Sweden" *Journal of Anthropological Archaeology,* 49 (2018): 19-38. https://doi.org/10.1016/j.jaa.2017.10.002

Gwynn, Edward. (Ed. & Trans.), "Carn Furbaide" *The Metrical Dindshenchas,* Vol. 4. Dublin Institute for Advanced Studies, 1906.

Hägg, Inga. "Die Textilfunde aus dem Hafen von Haithabu." *Berichte über die ausgrabungen in Haithabu*, Bericht 20. Neumünster: Karl Wachholz Verlag, 1984. Shelagh Lewins has made available an English summary of pages 38-42 and 168-170 at https://www.shelaghlewins.com/reenactment/hedeby_apron/hedeby_apron.htm.

Hägg, Inga. "Die Tracht" *Birka II:2 Systematische Analysen der Graberfunde* Edited by Greta Arwidsson. [Systematic Analysis of the Graves Findings] Birka, Kungliga Vitterhets Historie och Antikvitets Akademien: II:2.1986

Hägg, Inga.; I. Gustin; D. T. Price; C. Arcini; L. Drenzel; S Kalmring. (2017). "Isotopes and Human Burials at Viking Age Birka and the Mälaren Region, East Central Sweden" *Journal of Anthropological Archaeology* 49 (2018): 19-38. https://doi.org/10.1016/j.jaa.2017.10.002

Halldórsson, Ólafur. *Danish Kings and the Jomsvikings in the Greatest Saga of Óláfr Tryggvason* Viking Society for Northern Research, 2000.

Halperin, Charles. *The Mongol Empire and the Golden Horde* Bloomington: Indiana University Press, 1985.

Haney, Jack, V. "Ivan, the Bull's Son" *The Complete Folktales of A. N. Afanas'ev*. 1, #137. University Press of Mississippi, 2015.

Hanson, Victor Davis. *Carnage and Culture: Landmark Battles in the Rise to Western Power* Knopf Doubleday Publishing Group, 2007.

Hasanov, Zaur. "A Reflection of the Cimmerian and Scythian Religious Rites in Archaeology" *Proceedings of the 8th International Congress on the Archaeology of the Ancient Near East*. Volume 3 University of Warsaw, 2012: 527-540.

Haugen, E., and Faarlund, Jan Terje. "Scandinavian languages" In, *Encyclopedia Britannica*, January 24, 2025. https://www.britannica.com/topic/Scandinavian-languages.

Heffron, Y. "The Material Culture of Hittite 'God-drinking" *Journal of Ancient Near Eastern Religions*. 14. (2014):164-185. 10.1163/15692124-12341261

Heissig, Walther. *The Religions of Mongolia* Translated by Geoffrey Samuel. Routledge & Kegan-Paul, 1970.

Helskog, Knut. "Selective Depictions. A Study of 3,500 Years of Rock Carvings from Arctic Norway and Their Relationship to the Sami Drums" In, *Archaeology as Long-Term History*. Edited by I. Hodder. Cambridge Uni. Press, 1987.

Hesse, Klaus. "On the History of Mongolian Shamanism in Anthropological Perspective" *Anthropos* 82, no. 4/6. (1987): 403-13. http://www.jstor.org/stable/40463470. 49

Higley, Sarah. (Trans.) *Preiddeu Annwn: The Spoils of Annwn* The Camelot Project 2007. https://d.lib.rochester.edu/camelot/text/preiddeu-annwn

Hikmet, Tanyu. *Islâmlıktan Önce Türkler'de Tek Tanrı Inancı* [The Belief of Monotheism among Pre-Islamic Turks] (in Turkish) Istanbul, Ankara Universitesi Basimevi Ankara, 1980.

Hinds, Kathryn. *Scythians and Sarmatians*. Marshall Cavendish Benchmark New York, [1962] 2010.

Hildebrand, Hans. *Svenska folket under hednatiden. Ethografisk avhandling* (in Swedish) Iwar Haeggström, 1866

Hildinger, Erik. *Warriors of the Steppe: A Military History of Central Asia, 500 B.C. to 1700 A.D.* Sarpedon, 1997.

Hornblower, Simon; Antony Spawforth; Esther Eidinow, (Eds.). *The Oxford Classical Dictionary* (4 ed.) Oxford University Press, 2012.

Hubbs, Joanna. *Mother Russia: The Feminine Myth in Russian Culture*. Indiana University Press, 1993.

Hukantaival, Sonja. "The Goat and the Cathedral – Archaeology of Folk Religion in Medieval Turku" *Mirator* 19.1(2018).

Ibragimov, T., *Rock drawings of Gobustan* (2012). Archetypes of our artistic consciousness archive.org, Open Source, ark:/13960/t85j46k15

Ignác, Jan Hanuš. *Die Wissenschaft des slawischen Mythus im Weitesten, den altpreussisch-lithauischen Mythus mitumfassenden sinne: Nach Quellen bearbeitet, sammt der Literatur der slawisch-preussisch-lithauischen Archäologie und Mythologie*. Stanislawów und Tarnow, J. Millikowski, 1842.

Ingold, Tim. (Ed.) *Key Debates in Anthropology* Routledge, 1996.

Ingold, Tim. https://www.britannica.com/place/Arctic/Political-and-environmental-issues 2024.

Irwin, John L. *The Finns and the Lapps: How they Live and Work* David & Charles, 1973.

Ivantchik, Askold I. "Une légende sur l'origine des Scythes (HDT. IV 5-7) et le problème des sources du Scythicos logos d'Hérodote" [A Legend on the Origin of the Scythians (Hdt. IV 5-7) and the problems of the sources of Herodotus's Scythicos logos]. In, *Revue des Études Grecques* [Review of Greek Studies] (in French). 112 (1) (1999): 141–192. doi:10.3406/reg.1999.4355. JSTOR 44260011

Ivantchik, Askold I. "The Funeral of Scythian Kings" *The Barbarians of Ancient Europe* – Realities and Interactions. Cambridge University Press, 2011.

Ivantchik, Askold I. "L'idéologie royale des Scythes et son expression dans la littérature et l'iconographie grecques: l'apport de la numismatique' [The Royal Ideology of the Scythians and its Expression in Greek Literature and Iconography: the Contribution of Numismatics]" In, *Dialogues d'histoire ancienne, [Dialogues of Ancient History]*. 42 (1) 2016.

Ivantchik, Askold I. "Scythians" In, *Encyclopædia Iranica*. Brill Publishers, 2018.

Ivanits, Linda J. *Russian Folk Belief* M.E. Sharpe, 1989.

Jacobson, Esther. "The Deer Goddess of Ancient Siberia: A Study in the Ecology of Belief" In, *Studies in the History of Religions*, Volume LV:91. Leiden: E. J. Brill, 1993.

Jacobson, Esther. *The Art of the Scythians - The Interpretation of Cultures at the Edge of the Hellenic World* New York: E.J. Brill, 1995.

Jacobson, Esther. "The Deer Goddess of Ancient Siberia: A Study in the Ecology of Belief" In, Ivakhiv, Adrian. "The Revival of Ukrainian Native Faith." In, *Modern Paganism in World Cultures: Comparative Perspectives*, Strmiska, Michael F. (Ed.). Santa Barbara, CA: ABC-Clio, 2005

Jacobson Tepfer, Esther. *The Hunter, the Stag, and the Mother of Animals: Image, Monument, and Landscape in Ancient North Asia* Oxford University Press, 2015.

Jacobson-Tepfer, Esther. "Deer Stones" In, *Monumental Archaeology in the Mongolian Altai*. Brill, 2023: 155–191. doi:10.1163/9789004541306_008

Jakobson, Roman. "Slavic Mythology" In, *Funk & Wagnalls Standard Dictionary of Folklore, Mythology and Legend* Volume Two J-Z. Edited by Maria Leach. Funk & Wagnalls, 1950.

Jakobsson, Sverrir. "The Early Kings of Norway, the Issue of Agnatic Succession, and the Settlement of Iceland" In, *Viator*, 47 (2016): 171-88. doi:10.1484/J.VIATOR.5.112357 https://www.brepolsonline.net/toc/viator/2016/47/3

Jakobsson, Ármann. "Beast and Man: Realism and the Occult in 'Egils Saga'" *Scandinavian Studies*, 83, no. 1 (2011): 29–44. http://www.jstor.org/stable/23075433.

Jakobsson, Ármann. "The Trollish Acts Of Þorgrímr The Witch: The Meanings Of Troll And Ergi In Medieval Iceland" In, *Saga-Book* 32 (2008): 39–68. https://www.jstor.org/stable/48610768.

Jankowiak, Marek. "Dirhams for Slaves: Investigating the Slavic Slave Trade in the Tenth Century" Paper presented at the Medieval Seminar, All Souls, Oxford, February. 2012. https://www.academia.edu/1764468/Dirhams_for_slaves._Investigating_the_Slavic_slave_trade_in_the_tenth_century.

Jazayery, M. A. "Kasravi, Ahmad (1890-1946)" In, *Encyclopaedic Historiography of the Muslim World*. Edited by N. K. Singh and A. Samiuddin. Global Vision Publishing House, 2003.

Jesch, Judith. "Norse Historical Traditions and Historia, Gruffud vab Kenan: Magnus Berfoettr and Haraldr Harfagri" In, *Gruffudd ap Cynan: A Collaborative Biography*. Edited by K.L. Maund Cambridge, 1996: 117–147

Jochens, Jenny M. "Before The Male Gaze: The Absence Of The Female Body in Old Norse" In, *Sex in the Middle Ages. A Book of Essays*. Edited by Joyce E. Salisbury. Garland,1991.

Jordan, Peter. *Material Culture and Sacred Landscape: The Anthropology of the Siberian Khanty* Walnut Creek: AltaMira Press, 2003.

Joy, Francis. *Sámi Shamanism, Cosmology and Art as Systems of Embedded Knowledge* University of Lapland, 2018.

Joy, Francis. "Sámi Shamanism Past and Present and the Desecration of the Sacred in Finland" In, *Philosophy of Law in the Arctic*, 53-60. Edited by D. Bunikowski. Lapin yliopisto, Arktinen keskus, 2016.

Kalik, Judith., and Alexander Uchitel. *Slavic Gods and Heroes* Routledge, 2018.

Kajkowski, Kamil. & Pawel Szczepanik. "The Multi-Faced So-Called Miniature Idols From The Baltic Sea Area" *Studia Mythologica Slavica* XVI, Institute of Slovenian Ethnology, (2013): 55-86. http://sms.zrc-sazu.si/pdf/16/04-sms16-kajkowski_szczepanik.pdf

Katz, D. *The Image of the Netherworld in the Sumerian Sources* CDL Press, 2003.

Kaul, Flemming. "Middle Bronze Age Long-Distance Exchange: Amber, Early Glass and Guest Friendship, Xenia" In, *Trade before Civilization: Long Distance Exchange and the Rise of Social Complexity*. Edited by J. Ling, R. J. Chacon and K. Kristiansen. Cambridge University Press, 2022.

Kincses-Nagy, Éva. *A Disappeared People and a Disappeared Language: The Cumans and the Cuman language of Hungary* Szeged University Press, 2013.

Kitov, Egor. "Revisiting the Issue of Connections Among the Nomads Social Elite from the Southern Urals According to Craniology Data from the Filippovka Kurgans" Nižnevolžskij Arheologiceskij Vestnik, 2024. DOI: https://doi.org/10.15688/nav.jvolsu.2024.1.2

Khazanov, Anatoly M. *Nomads and the Outside World* Madison, Wisconsin: University of Wisconsin Press, 1994.

Kristiansen, K. "Seafaring Voyages and Rock Art Ships." In, *The Dover Boat in Context: Society and Water Transport in Prehistoric Europe*. Edited by P. Clark. Oxbow Books, 2004.

Kohen, Elli. *History of the Byzantine Jews: A Microcosmos in the Thousand Year Empire* University Press of America, 2007.

Koch, John T.; Raimund Karl; Antone Minard; Simon Ó Faoláin. "An Atlas for Celtic Studies: Archaeology And Names In Ancient Europe And Early Medieval Ireland, Britain and Brittany" In, *Celtic Studies Publications* 12. Oxbow Books, 2007.

Kroonen, Guus. *Etymological Dictionary of Proto-Germanic* Edited by Alexander Lubotsky. Leiden Indo-European Etymological Dictionary Series II. Brill, 2013.

Kusmenko, Jurij K. "Sámi and Scandinavians in the Viking Age" *Scandinavistica Vilnensis*. (2009): 65-94. 10.15388/ScandinavisticaVilnensis.2009.2.5. Institute of Linguistic Studies, St. Petersburg, Russian Academy of Sciences.

Laestadius, Lars Levi., and Juha Pentikäinen. (Eds.). *Fragments of Lappish Mythology* K. Börje Vähämäki.(Trans.). Aspasia Books, 2002.

Lee, Richard B. and Richard Daly. (Eds.) *The Cambridge Encyclopaedia of Hunters and Gatherers.* Cambridge Uni Press,1999. DOI:10.1163/22105018-12340089

Laourdas, B. and L. G. Westerinck. (Eds.) *Photii Patriarchae Constantinopolitani Epistulae et Amphilochia*, T. 1. Leipzig, 1983.

Larrington, Carolyne. "What Does Woman Want?' Mær and munr in Skírnismál" *Alvíssmál* 1 [1992] 1993: 3-16.

Laruelle, Marlene. "Tengrism: In Search For Central Asia's Spiritual Roots" In, *Central Asia-Caucasus Analyst Bi-Weekly Briefing*, Vol. 8, no. 5. Kennan Institute, 2006.

"Lavrentevskaia Letopis, also called the 'Povest Vremennykh Let" In, *Polnoe Sobranie Russkikh Letopisey* (PSRL), Vol. 1. 95-102. (Typography of Edward Prats. 1837 -) See: https://infogalactic.com/info/Complete_Collection_of_Russian_ Chronicles.

Lindow, John. *Norse Mythology: A Guide to the Gods, Heroes, Rituals, and Beliefs* Oxford University Press, 2001.

Lombardo, A. "Enrico Dandolo" In, *Encyclopedia Britannica*, January 1, 2025. https://www.britannica.com/biography/Enrico-Dandolo.

Łowmianski, Henryk. *Religia Słowian i jej upadek, (The Religion of Slavs and its Fall)* (in Polish) Edited by Adam Mickiewicz. Warsaw: Panstwowe Wydawnictwa Naukowe, 1979.

Lee, Joo-Yup., and Shunti Kuang. "A Comparative Analysis of Chinese Historical Sources and y-dna Studies with Regard to the Early and Medieval Türkic Peoples" *Inner Asia*, 19 (2) (2017): 197-239

Lembi Lõugas; Aivar Kriiska; Liina Maldre. "New Dates For The Late Neolithic Corded Ware Culture Burials And Early Husbandry In The East Baltic Region" In, *Archaeofauna* 16, Department of History, Tartu University, 2007.

Levin, M. G., and Potapov., L. P. *The Peoples of Siberia* The University of Chicago Press, 1964.

Liddell, Henry George., and Robert Scott. 'A Greek-English Lexicon' https://www. perseus.tufts.edu/hopper/searchresults?q=ethnos (Retrieved 21st May 2024).

Liedgren, L., and I. Bergman, "Aspects of the Construction of Prehistoric Stállo-Foundations and Stállo-Buildings" In, *Acta Borealia*, 26 (1) (2009): 3–26. https://doi.org/10.1080/08003830902951516

Lincoln, Bruce. "Once again 'the Scythian' Myth Of Origins." (Herodotus 4.5-10). In, *Nordlit*, 19 2014

Ling, Johan. "War Canoes or Social Units? Human Representation in Rock-Art Ships" *European Journal of Archaeology* 15 (3) (2012).

Ling, Johan, Peter Skoglund and Ulf Bertilsson (Eds.) "Picturing the Bronze Age" In, *Swedish Rock Art Research Series*, Oxbow Books, 2015.

Linehan, Peter; Janet Laughland Nelson; Marios Costambeys. (Eds.) In, *The Medieval World* Routledge Worlds Series 10: 82-83. Routledge, 2003.

Longsworth, Philip. *Russia: The Once and Future Empire from Pre-History to Putin* St. Martin's Press, 2006.

Lødøen, T., and G. Mandt. *The Rock Art of Norway* Oxford: Windgather Press, 2010.

Lund, J. "Fragments Of A Conversion: Handling Bodies And Objects In Pagan and Christian Scandinavia ad 800–1100" *World Archaeology* 45 1 (2013): 46–63.

Lund, N. (Ed.). C. E. Fell (Trans.). *Two Voyagers At The Court Of King Alfred. The Ventures Of Ohthere And Wulfstan Together With The Description Of Northern Europe From The Old English Orosius.* William Sessions Limited, 1984.

MacDermott, Mercia. *Bulgarian Folk Customs* Jessica Kingsley Publishers, 1998.

MacFarland, Kathryn. "Religion, Ritual Behavior and Landscapes in Iron Age Central Eurasia." M.A. Thesis, 2010. https://www.Academia.Edu/8210983/Religion_Ritual_Behavior_And_Landscapes_In_Iron_Age_Central_Eurasia

Máchal, Jan. "Slavic Mythology" In, *The Mythology of all Races. III, Celtic and Slavic Mythology.* Edited by L. H. Gray. Marshall Jones Company, 1918.

Magnússon Blöndal, Ásgeir. *Íslensk orðsifjabók* [Icelandic etymological dictionary]. Reykjavík: Orðabók Háskólans, 1989.

Magnus, Bente. *Men, Gods and Masks-in Nordic Iron Age Art, Ten thousand years of folk art in the North; Nordic Iron Age Art 1* Cologne: König, 2006.

Mallory, J. P. and Douglas, Q. Adams. "Kemi Oba Culture," In, *Encyclopaedia of Indo-European Culture*, 327-8. London: Taylor & Francis, 1997a.

Malandra, W. W. "The Concept of Movement in History of Religions: A Religio-Historical Study of Reindeer in the Spiritual Life of North Eurasian Peoples" *Numen* 14, no. 1 (1967): 23–69. https://doi.org/10.2307/3269697.

Mallory, J. P. *In Search of the Indo-Europeans: Language, Archaeology, and Myth* Thames & Hudson Ltd., 1989.

Mallory, J. P. and Douglas, Q. Adams. "Pit-Comb Ware Culture" In, *Encyclopaedia of Indo-European Culture.* London: Taylor & Francis, 1997b.

Mallory, James P. and Douglas Q. Adams, Douglas Q. *The Oxford Introduction to Proto-Indo-European and the Proto-Indo-European World* Oxford University Press, 2006.

Mallory, James, P. "The Indo-Europeanization of Atlantic Europe" In, *Celtic From the West 2: Rethinking the Bronze Age and the Arrival of Indo–European in Atlantic Europe.* Edited by J. T. Koch; B. Cunliffe. Oxford: Oxbow Books, 2013.

Malmström, Helena., et al. "The Genomic Ancestry Of The Scandinavian Battle Axe Culture People And Their Relation To The Broader Corded Ware Horizon." In, *Proceedings of the Royal Society B. Royal Society.* 1912: 286 doi:10.1098/rspb.2019.1528. PMC 6790770. PMID 31594508

Malmström, Dr. Vincent H. "Norway Before the Vikings." Dartmouth College, 2012. https://web.archive.org/web/20120204235040/http://www.dartmouth.edu/~izapa/E-31.pdf

Manassero, Niccolò. "Tamgas, A Code of The Steppes" In, *Identity Marks and Writing Among The Ancient Iranians.* The Silkroad Foundation, 2013. http://www.silkroadfoundation.org/newsletter/vol11/SilkRoad_11_2013_manassero.pdf (2013).

Mannering, U. *Iconic Costumes: Scandinavian Late Iron Age Costume Iconography* Havertown: Oxbow Books, 2016.

Mathieu-Colas, Michel. "Dieux slaves et baltes."(PDF) In, *Dictionnaire des noms des divinités, France: Archive ouverte des Sciences de l'Homme et de la Société.* Centre national de la recherche scientifique, 2017. https://web.archive.org/web/20170804140911/http://www.mathieu-colas.fr/michel/Classes/Dieux_slaves_et_baltes.pdf (2017).

Matthew, S., and Kathryn A. Hain. (Eds.) *Concubines and Courtesans: Women and Slavery in Islamic History* Oxford University Press, 2017: 124-42.

Marjanic, Marjana. "The Dyadic Goddess and Duotheism in Nodilo's The Ancient Faith of the Serbs and the Croats" In, *Studia Mythologica Slavica* 6 (2015):181 DOI:10.3986/sms.v6i0.1783

Markey, Tom. "A Tale of Two Helmets: The Negau A and B Inscriptions" *Journal of Indo-European Studies*, Volume 29, Issue 1(2). (2001): 69-172

Martynov, Anatoli I. "The Solar Cult and the Tree of Life" *Arctic Anthropology,* Volume 25, Number 2. University of Wisconsin Press, 1988: 16 https://www.jstor.org/stable/i40013071

May, Timothy. "The Mongol Empire" In, *A Historical Encyclopaedia* [2 Volumes]. Santa Barbara, CA: ABC-CLIO, 2016

Mayor, Adrienne. "What Were the Griffins?" *Folklore* 104, (1&2) Taylor & Francis Group LLC 1993: 40-53

Mayor, Adrienne. *The Amazons – Lives & Legends of Warrior Women Across the Ancient World* Princeton University Press, 2014.

Mayor, Adrienne. "Amazons In The Iranian World" In, *Encyclopædia Iranica*. 2017. https://www.iranicaonline.org/articles/amazons-ii

McKay, J. G. "The Deer-Cult and the Deer-Goddess Cult of the Ancient Caledonians." *Folklore* Volume 43, (2). 1932.

McCullough, David Willis, (Ed.) *Chronicles of the Barbarians: Firsthand Accounts of Pillage and Conquest, From the Ancient World to the Fall of Constantinople* Times Books, 1998.

McCullough, Joseph A. D*ragon-slayers: From Béowulf to St. George* Osprey Publishing, 2013.

Mead, M. *Continuities in Cultural Evolution* New Haven: Yale University Press, 1964.

Melheim, Lene & Anette Sand-Eriksen. "Rock Art and Trade Networks: From Scandinavia to the Italian Alps" *Open Archaeology*. 6. (2020): 86-106. 10.1515/opar-2020-0101.

Metraux, A. "United Nations Economic and Security Council Statement by Experts on Problems of Race" *American Anthropologist* 53(1)1950.

Merrills, A. H. *Vandals, Romans and Berbers. New Perspectives on Late Antique North Africa* Ashgate, 2004.

Meredith, Jezz. "Barber's Point: a Saxon settlement in the Alde Estuary" *Saxon* 61, 2011.

Miller, Vsevolod. "Materialy dla istorii bylinnyh suzhetov" *Etnograficeskoe Obozrenie* 4. Wydawnictwo Uniwersytetu Marii Curie-Skłodowskiej, 1891: 129-31 (in Russian).

Miniaev, Sergei S., and L. M. Sakharovskaia. *Investigation of a Xiongnu Royal Tomb Complex in the Tsaraam Valley* Institute for the History of Material Culture, Russian Academy of Sciences, St. Petersburg, 2017. https://edspace.american.edu/silkroadjournal/wp-content/uploads/sites/984/2017/09/Foreign-Tribes-in-the-Xiongnu-Confederation.pdf

Mironov, Nikolaï D. et Shirokogoroff, S. M. "Sramana-Shaman: etymology of the word Shaman" In, *Journal of the North China Branch of the Royal Asiatic Society*, Vol. LV. Shangai: Royal Asiatic Society, 1924.

Montgomery, James E. "Ibn Fadllan and the Rusiyyah" *Journal of Arabic and Islamic Studies* 3, 2000. DOI: https://doi.org/10.5617/jais.4553

Moilanen, Ulla & Kirkinen, Tuija & Saari, Nelli-Johanna & Rohrlach, Adam & Krause, Johannes & Onkamo, Päivi & Salmela, Elina. (Eds.) "A Woman with a Sword? – Weapon Grave at Suontaka Vesitorninmäki, Finland" *European Journal of Archaeology* 25. (2021)10.1017/eaa.2021.30. https://www.researchgate.net/publication/353260449_A_Woman_with_a_Sword_-_Weapon_Grave_at_Suontaka_Vesitorninmaki_Finland.

Morawiec, Jakub. "Danish Kings and the Foundation of Jómsborg" *Scripta Islandica* 65. 2014: 125–142.

Mozdzioch, Sławomir; Stanisławski, Błazej.; Wiszewski, Przemysław.(Eds.) "Scandinavian culture in Medieval Poland." In, Interdisciplinary Medieval Studies Volume I. Institute of Archaeology and Ethnology of the Polish Academy of Sciences Wrocław, 2013.

Munzinger, Mark R. 2006. "The Profits of the Cross: Merchant Involvement in the Baltic Crusade (c. 1180-1230)" *Journal of Medieval History* 32 (2): 163–85. doi:10.1016/j.jmedhist.2006.04.001.

Mulk, I. M., and T. P. Bayliss-Smith. "The Representation of Sámi Cultural Identity In The Cultural Landscapes Of Northern Sweden: The Use And Misuse Of Archaeological Evidence" In, *The Archaeology and Anthropology of Landscape*. Edited by P. J. Ucko & J. Layton. Routledge, 1998.

Mulk, Inga-Maria. "Sacrificial Places and Their Meaning in Saami Society" In, *Sacred Sites, Sacred Places*. Edited by D. Carmichael, J. Hubert, B. Reeves and A. Schanche. Routledge, 1994.

Mulk, Inga-Maria., and T. P. Bayliss-Smith "Sámi Rock Engravings from the Mountains in Laponia, Northern Sweden" *Folklore*, Estonian Literary Museum Scholarly Press, 1999.

Mulk, I. M. "Laponia, Lapplands världsarv: ett natur- och kulturarv att förvaltas för framtiden" In, *Småskrifter*, Vol. 6. Ájtte, Svenskt Fjäll- och Samemuseum, 2000.

Müller-Wille, M. (Ed.) "Byzantine Presence in Viking Age Sweden – Archaeological Finds and their Interpretation" In, *Rom und Byzanz im Norden: Mission und Glaubenswechsel im Ostseeraum während der 8.-14. Jahrhun- derts; internationale Fachkonferenz der Deutschen Forschungsgemein- schaft in Verbindung mit der Akademie der Wissenschaften und der Literatur, Mainz, Kiel. 18-25th September.* Stuttgart, 1994: 291-311.

Mundal, Else. "The Relationship between Sámi and Nordic Peoples Expressed in Terms of Family Associations" *Journal of Northern Studies* 3(2) (2010): 25-37 DOI:10.36368/jns.v3i2.600

Mundal, Else. "The Perception of the Sámis and Their Religion in Old Norse Sources" *Shamanism and Northern Ecology* 36. Edited by Juha Pentikäinen. Mouton de Gruyter (1996): 97–116.

Mundal, Else. "Kontakt mellom nordisk og samisk kultur reflektert i norrøne mytar og religion" *The Sámi and the Scandinavians. Aspects of 2000 years of contact.* Edited by Juha Kusmenko Hamburg: Schriften zur Kulturwissenschaft 55 (2004): 41–53.

Namatov, Mirlan. "The Wolf Totem" *Journal of Eurasian Studies* Vol. II., Issue 2. /April-June 2010. https://tinyurl.com/y929om8h

Narasimhan, Vagheesh M. "The formation of human populations in South and Central Asia" *Science*. American Association for the Advancement of Science vol. 365 (6457) 2019: eaat7487. bioRxiv 10.1101/292581. doi:10.1126/science.aat7487. PMC 6822619. PMID 31488661. https://www.ncbi.nlm.nih.gov/pmc/articles/PMC6822619/

Nasonov, Arsennii. (Ed.) Novgorodskaia Pervaia Letopis: Starshego i mladshego izvodov, (Moscow and Leningrad: AN SSSR, (1950).

Nesheim, A. "Eastern and Western Elements In Lapp Culture." *Lapps and Norsemen in Olden Times.* Serie A, Nr. 26. Instituttet for Sammenlignende Kulturforskning, Oslo, 1967.

Noonan, Thomas S. "European Russia c.500 CE to c.1050 CE" In, *The New Cambridge Medieval History: Volume 3*, C.900-c.1024 C.E. Volume 3:485-534. Edited by T. Reuter., and R. McKitterick. Cambridge University Press, 1999.

Noonan, Thomas S. "The Khazar Qaghanate and its impact on the early Rus' state: the Translatio Imperii from Itil to Kiev" In, *Nomads in the Sedentary World.* Curzon-IIAS Asian studies series. Edited by Anatoly M Khazanov and André Wink. Routledge, 2001.

Noonan, Thomas S. "The Economy of the Khazar Khaganate" In, *The World of the Khazars: New Perspectives. Handbuch der Orientalistik: Handbook of Uralic studies.* Vol. 17. Brill. Edited by Peter B Golden, Haggai Ben-Shammai and András Róna-Tas. Brill, 2007: 207–244.

Oates, Shani. *The Search for Odinn, From Pontic Steppe to Sutton Hoo* Anathema Publishing LTD, 2022.

Obolensky, Dimitri. *Byzantium and the Slavs* St. Vladimir's Press, 1994.

Okladnikov, A. P. "Yakutia Before its Incorporation into the Russian State" *Studies in Siberian shamanism: Arctic Institute of North America anthropology of the North: Translations from Russian sources*, N°8:156. University of Toronto Press, 1970.

Ojala, Carl-Gösta. "Sámi Prehistories, The Politics of Archaeology and Identity in Northernmost Europe Occasional Papers" *Archaeology* 47. Institutionen För Arkeologi Och Antik Historia Uppsala Universitet, 2009.

Olley, Katherine Marie. "The Icelandic Hogni: The Re-imagining of a Nibelung Hero in the Eddic Tradition" *Scandinavian Studies*. 90 (2) (2018): 237–264. doi:10.5406/scanstud.90.2.0237.

Olsen, Venke. "Northern Scandinavia: A Multi-Ethnic Society Seen from an Ethnological Point-of-View" *Northern Studies* volume 23. Scottish Society for Northern Studies, 1986.

O' Keeffe. J. G. "Buile Suibhne" (The Frenzy of Suibhne) Intro by Joseph Falaky Nagy. Irish Texts Society, [1913] 1996.

O'Meadhra, U. "Viking-Age Sketches And Motif-Pieces From The Northern Earldoms" In, *The Viking Age in Caithness, Orkney and the North Atlantic*. Ed. by C. E. Batey, J. Jesch and C. D. Morris, Edinburgh Uni. Press. 1993.

O'Neill, Joseph. (Ed. & Trans.), "Cath Boinde" *Ériu* vol. 2 (1905):173-185.

Orel, Vladimir. *A Handbook of Germanic Etymology* Brill. 2003.

Osborn, Marijane. "Tir as Mars in the Old English Rune Poem" *ANQ: A Quarterly Journal of Short Articles, Notes and Reviews*. Taylor & Francis, 2010.

Pálsson, Hermann. "Úr landnorðri. Samar og ystu rætur íslenkrar menningar" [From the North-East. Sámi and the outermost roots of Icelandic culture] *Studia Islandica* 54, Reykjavík: Bókmenntafræðistofnun Háskóla Íslands,1997.

Pálsson, Hermann. "Searching for the Sámi in early Icelandic sources" *Dieðut* 1 1998: 75–83.

Pálsson, Hermann. "The Sámi people in Old Norse literature" *Nordlit* 5 1999: 29-53. https://doi.org/10.7557/13.2143.

Pálsson, Hermann. Seven Viking Romances Translated by Paul Edwards. Penguin Classics, 1985.

Partington, S. W. *The Danes in Lancashire and Yorkshire* Sherratt & Hughes, 1909. https://www.gutenberg.org/files/43910/43910-h/43910-h.htm

BIBLIOGRAPHY

Patterson, Patrick., and Brian Parkinson. *Journeys in World History I* 2023. https://pressbooks.oer.hawaii.edu/honcchist151/chapter/12-steppe-peoples-of-central-asia/

Pettazzoni, Raffaele. "Turco-Mongols and Related Peoples. The All-Knowing God" In, *Researches into Early Religion and Culture*, Rose, H. J. (Trans.) Methuen and Co.,[1955] 1956.

Pettazzoni, Raffaele. "West Slav Paganism" In, E*ssays on the History of Religions*. Brill Archive, 1967.

Petrulevich, Alexandra. *On the etymology of at Jómi, Jumne and Jómsborg* https://www.diva-portal.org/smash/get/diva2:403702/FULLTEXT01.pdf

Polomé, Edgar C. "The Slavic Gods and the Indo-European Heritage" In, *Festschrift für Nikola R. Pribic*. Edited by Wolfgang Gesemann and Helmut Schaller. Hieronymus Verlag Neuried, 1983: 545-555.

Porzig, Walter. "Die Gliederung des Indogermanischen Sprachgebiets" [The Indo-European Languages] Heidelberg: Universitätsverlag Winter, (1954).251 Paper, DM 35.

Prescott, C., and E. Walderhaug, E. "The Last Frontier? Processes of Indo-Europeanization in Northern Europe, The Norwegian Case" *Journal of Indo-European studies* 23, (1995).

Prescott, Christopher; Anette Sand-Eriksen; Knut Ivar Austvoll. "The Sea and Bronze Age Transformations" In, *Water and Power in Past Societies*. Edited by E. Holt. SUNY Press, 2018.

Price, Neil. *The Viking Way: Religion and War in Late Iron Age Scandinavia*. Uppsala University, 2002.

Price, Neil. "Dying and The Dead: Viking Age Mortuary Behaviour" In, *The Viking World*. Edited by Stefan Brink and Neil Price. Routledge, 2008: 257–73.

Price, T. Douglas. *Ancient Scandinavia: An Archaeological History from the First Humans to the Vikings* Oxford University Press, 2015.

Price, Neil; C. Hedenstierna-Jonson; T. Zachrisson; A. Kjellström; J. Storå; M. Krzewinska et al. 2019. Viking Warrior Women? Reassessing Birka Chamber Grave Bj.581. *Antiquity*, 93:181–98. https://doi.org/10.15184/aqy.2018.258

Quinn, Judy. "Mythological Motivation in Eddic Heroic Poetry: Interpreting Grottasöngr" In, *Revisiting the Poetic Edda. Essays on Old Norse Heroic Legend* Edited by Paul Acker and Carolyne Larrington. Routledge, 2013.

Radziwillowicz, Natalia. "Considering the Connections Between Scandinavia and the Southern Baltic Coast in the 10th - 11th Centuries" *Innervate*, Volume X (2016-2017): XXXX.

Rask, Rasmus. "En Udsigt over de lappiske og finiske Stammers Historie" In: *Rasmus Rask: Ausgewählte Abhandlungen* 2. Kopenhagen, 1932-3: 285–320.

Reed, Michael F. "Norwegian Stave Churches And Their Pagan Antecedents" RACAR: *Revue D'art Canadienne / Canadian Art Review* 24, no. 2 (1997): 3-13 http://www.jstor.org/stable/42631152.

Ringe, Donald. *From Proto-Indo-European to Proto-Germanic* (A Linguistic History of English; 1) Oxford University Press, 2006.

Robb, John. "People Of Stone: Stelae, Personhood And Society In Prehistoric Europe" *Journal of Archaeological Method and Theory*, Vol. 16, no. 3 (2009):162-183. DOI 10.1007/s10816-009-9066-z

Rockhill, W. W. *The Journey Of William Of Rubruck To The Eastern Parts Of The World, 1253-55, as narrated by himself, with two accounts of the earlier journey of John of Pian de Carpine* Hakluyt Society, 1900.

Rolle, Renate. *The World of the Scythians* F. G. Walls. (Trans.) Uni. of California Press,1989.

Rollinger, Robert. "Herodotus iv. Cyrus According To Herodotus" In, *Encyclopædia Iranica* https://www.iranicaonline.org/articles/herodotus-iv (2003).

Róna-Tas, Yazar András. *Hungarians and Europe In The Early Middle Ages: An Introduction To Early Hungarian History* Yayıncı Central European University Press, 1999.

Rosborn, S. *A Unique Object From Harald Bluetooth's Time?* Malmö: Pilemedia. Academia, 2015 https://www.academia.edu/9647410/A_unique_object_from_Harald_Bluetooth_s_time_2015_

Rybakov, Boris. *Yazycestvo drevney Rusi Moscow* The Academy of Sciences of the USSR, 1987.

Rydving, Håkan. "The Sámi Drums And The Religious Encounter in The 17th And 18th Centuries" *The Saami Shaman Drum*. 14 (1988): 28–51. Scripta, Instituti Donneriani Aboensis. Edited by Tore Ahlbäck and Jans Bergman, Jan. Donner Institute, Åbo, Finland, 1991. https://doi.org/10.30674/scripta.67195

Rydving, Håkan. *The End Of Drum-Time: Religious Change Among The Lule Sámi. 1670s–1740s* Almqvist & Wiksell International, 1993.

Sabatini, S., and S. Bergerbrant. (Eds.) *The Textile Revolution in Bronze Age Europe: Production, Specialisation, Consumption* Cambridge University Press, 2019.

Sagona, Antonio. *The Heritage of Eastern Turkey: from earliest settlements to Islam* AU: Macmillan Art Publishing, 2006.

Salmi, A. K; T. Äikäs; M. Fjellström; M. Spangen. "Animal Offerings At The Sámi Offering Site Of Unna Saiva - Changing religious practices and human-animal relationships" J *Anthropol Archaeol* 40 (2015): 10–22.

Salmi, A. K. "The Archaeology of Reindeer Domestication and Herding Practices in Northern Fennoscandia" *The Archaeology of Reindeer Domestication and Herding Practices in Northern Fennoscandia* 31 (2023): 617–660 https://doi.org/10.1007/s10814-022-09182-8

Sand-Eriksen, A. S. "Mjeltehaugen: Europe's northernmost Bell Beaker expression?" *New Perspectives on the Bronze Age. Proceedings of the 13th Nordic Bronze Age Symposium held in Gothenburg 9th to 13th June 2015* (7–18). Edited by S. Bergerbrant and A. Wessman. Archaeopress, 2017.

Santos, P; G. Gonzàlez-Fortes; E. Trucchi; A. Ceolin; G. Cordoni; C. Guardiano; G. Longobardi; G. Barbujani. "More Rule than Exception: Parallel Evidence of Ancient Migrations in Grammars and Genomes of Finno-Ugric Speakers" *Genes* (Basel). 11(12)(2020):1491. doi: 10.3390/genes11121491. PMID: 33322364; PMCID: PMC7763979.

Sawyer, B. and P. Sawyer. "Scandinavia enters Christian Europe" In, *Helle*, 121-42.Schanche, A 2000, Graver i ur og berg: Samisk gravskikk og religion fra forhistorisk til nyere tid, Karasjok: Davvi Girji, 2003.

Sawyer, Peter. *The Oxford Illustrated History of the Vikings* Oxford University Press, 2001.

Schmitt, Rüdiger. "Massagetae" In, *Encyclopædia Iranica*. https://www.iranicaonline.org/articles/massagetae (2018).

Sedov, Vladimir. *Tserkov Rozhdestva Bogoroditsy v Peryni: novgorodskiy variant bašneobraznogo hrama*, (in Russian) Moscow: Severny Palomnik, 2009.

Serith, Ceisiwr. *Deep Ancestors: Practising the Religion of the Proto Indo-Europeans* ADF Publishing, 2007.

Sevin, Veli. "Mystery Stelae" *Archaeology*, Volume 53, (4) 2000. https://www.jstor.org/stable/41779470.

Shepard, Jonathan. "Closer Encounters with the Byzantine World: the Rus at the Straits of Kerch" In, *Pre-Modern Russia and Its World: Essays in Honor of Thomas S. Noonan*. Edited by Kathryn L. Reyerson, Theofanis G. Stavrou and James D. Tracy. Harrassowitz Verlag, 2006: 15-77.

Shuicheng, Li. "Ancient Interactions in Eurasia and Northwest China: Revisiting J. G. Andersson's Legacy" *Bulletin of the Museum of Far Eastern Antiquities*. 75: 9-30 Published by the Museum of Far Eastern Antiquities, 2003.

Simek, Rudolf. *Dictionary of Northern Mythology* Translated and Edited by Angela Hall. D. S. Brewer, [1993] 2000.

Skutsch, Carl., and Martin Ryle. (Eds.) *Encycl. Of The World's Minorities* Routledge, 2005.

Slupecki, Leszek. "West Slavic Pagan Ritual As Described At The Beginning Of The Eleventh Century" In, *Old Norse Religion In Long-Term Perspectives: Origins, Changes, and Interactions: An international Conference in Lund, Sweden, June 3-7. 2004.* Edited by A. Andrén; K. Jennbert; C. Raudvere. Nordic Academic Press, 2006.

Stanley, Joseph F. "Negotiating Trade: Merchant Manuals and Cross-Cultural Exchange in the Medieval Mediterranean" *The Interdisciplinary Journal of Study Abroad* Volume XXX, Issue 1, Winter. Simmons College, 2018) https://files.eric.ed.gov/fulltext/EJ1168964.pdf

Stone, Alby. *The Cosmic Mill* https://www.indigogroup.co.uk/edge/cmill.htm

Storå, N. "Burial Customs of the Skolt Lapps" *Folklore Fellows Communications* 89 (2) 1971. Helsinki (Suomalainen tiedeakatemia/ Academia Scientiarum Fennica).

Storli, I. "Sami Viking Age pastoralism – or 'the fur trade paradigm' reconsidered" *Norwegian Archaeological Review* 26. (1993) 1–20.

Svestad, Asgeir. "The Impact Of Materiality On Sámi Burial Customs And Religious Concepts" *Fennoscandia Archaeol* 28 (2011): 39–56.

Svestad, Asgeir. "What happened in Neiden? On the question of reburial ethics?" *Norway Archaeol Rev* 46 (2) 2013: 194–222.

Svestad, Asgeir. "Buried in Between: Re-Interpreting the Skjoldehamn Medieval Bog Burial of Arctic Norway" *Medieval Archaeology* 65 (2)(2021): 286-321. doi:10.1080/00766097.2021.1997202.

Svestad, A. Forthcoming, "LARM Investigations in Inner Troms 2: The Guomojávrrit Region" In, *Archaeological Perspectives on Hunter-Gatherer Landscapes and Resource Management in Interior North Norway. The Guomojávrrit region.* Edited by M. Skandfer, H. P. Blankholm and B. C. Hood. 2023. doi: 10.1558/equinox.36897

Siikala, Anna Leena. "Finnish Rock Art, Animal Ceremonialism And Shamanism." *Temenos: Studies In Comparative Religion, Presented By Scholars in Denmark, Finland, Norway and Sweden,* 17. Finnish Society for the study of Comparative Religion, 1981.

BIBLIOGRAPHY

Skoglund, P. "Cosmology And Performance: Narrative Perspectives On Scandinavian Rock Art" In, *Changing Pictures: Rock Art Traditions and Visions in Northern Europe*. Edited by J. Goldhahn, I. Fuglestvedt, and A. Jones (Eds). Oxbow Books, 2010.

Sognnes, K. "Symbols in a Changing World: Rock-Art and the Transition from Hunting to Farming in mid Norway" In, *The Archaeology of Rock-Art*. Edited by C. Chippindale and P. S. C. Tacon. Cambridge, 1998.

Spuler, Berthold. *"Kirim."* In, *Encyclopaedia of Islam*, vol. IV New Edition. Edited by Bernard Lewis et. al. E.J. Brill, 1978.

Spurkland, Terje. *Norwegian Runes and Runic Inscriptions* Boydell Press, 2005.

Stalsberg, Anne. "Women As Actors in North European Viking Age Trade" In, *Social approaches to Viking Studies*. Edited by Ross Samson. Cruithne Press, 1991.

Starr, S. Frederick. *Lost Enlightenment: Central Asia's Golden Age from the Arab Conquest to Tamerlane* Princeton University Press, 2013.

Storå, N. "Burial Customs of the Skolt Lapps" *Folklore Fellows Communications* 89 (2) 1971. Helsinki (Suomalainen tiedeakatemia/ Academia Scientiarum Fennica).

Stokes, Whitley. "Cóir Anmann" (Fitness of Names) In, *Irische Text mit Wörterbuch, Dritte Serie*, 2 vols. Edited by E. Windisch and W. Stokes. Verlag Von S. Hirzel, 1897: 288-411

Stoyanov, Roman V. "On the Iconography of the Potnia Theron in the North Pontic Region" *Ancient Civilizations from Scythia to Siberia* 27 no. 1 (2021): 1-10. doi:10.1163/15700577-12341386.

Sutherland, Patricia. "The Norse and Native Norse Americans" In, *Vikings: The North Atlantic Saga*, 238-247. Edited by William W. Fitzhugh., and Elisabeth I. Ward. The Smithsonian Institution, 2000.

Tambets, K., et al. "The Western And Eastern Roots Of The Saami-The Story Of Genetic 'Outliers' Told by Mitochondrial DNA and Y Chromosomes" *Am J Hum Genet* 74(4) (2004): 661-82. doi: 10.1086/383203. Epub 2004 Mar 11. PMID: 15024688; PMCID: PMC1181943.

Taylor, Isaac. *Names and Their Histories: A Handbook of Historical Geography and Topographical Nomenclature* University of Michigan: Rivingtons. 1898.

Thodis, Konstantinos. "The Great Route 'From the Varangians to the Greeks'" https://www.academia.edu/30094727/The_Great_Route_From_the_Varangians_to_the_Greeks_

Thomas, G; A. Pluskowski; R. Gilchrist., et al. "Religious Transformations in the Middle Ages: Towards A New Archaeological Agenda" *Medieval Archaeol* 61(2) (2017): 300–29.

Turville-Petre, Joan. "The Genealogist and History: Ari to Snorri" In, *Saga-Book XX* Viking Society for Viking Research, University College London, 1978-81: 7–23

Tekin, Talât., and Irk Bitig. "The Book of Omens" In, *Turcologica 18*. Harrassowitz Verlag, 1993.

Thorvarðardóttir, Ólina. "Spirits of the Land: A Tool for Social Education" *Bookbird 37* (4) 1999: 34

Todorova, Elisaveta. "The Greeks in the Black Sea Trade During the Late Medieval Period" *Etudes Balkaniques*. Nos 3-4. Institute for Balkan Studies with Center for Tracology - Bulgarian Academy of Sciences, 1992.

Tolley, Clive. "Evidence for The Existence of a Cosmic Mill in Germanic Mythology. An Excerpt from 'The Mill In Norse And Finnish Mythology'" In, *Saga-Book for the Viking Society of Northern Research*, 24 (1994-97): 63–82. https://www.jstor.org/stable/48611731

Tolley, Clive. *Shamanism in Norse Myth and Magic, I-II*. Academia Scientiarum Fennica, 2009.

Turville-Petre, E.O.G. *Myth and Religion of the North: The Religion of Ancient Scandinavia* Greenwood Press Publishers, 1964.

Tzvetkov, Plamen. *A History of the Balkans*, Vol. 1 The Edwin Mellen Press, 1993.

Unterländer, Martina; Friso Palstra; Iosif Lazaridis., et al. "Ancestry And Demography And Descendants of Iron Age Nomads Of The Eurasian Steppe" *Nature Communications* 8: 2017. doi:10.1038/ncomms14615

Ustinova, Yulia. *The Supreme Gods of the Bosporan Kingdom: Celestial Aphrodite and the Most High God* Brill. 1999.

Ustinova, Yulia. *6 Snake-Limbed and Tendril Limbed Goddesses in the Art and Mythology of the Mediterranean and Black Sea, Scythians and Greeks: Cultural Interactions in Scythia, Athens and the Early Roman Empire (6th century BCE. – 1st century CE.)* University of Exeter Press, 2005.

Vasiliev, Alexander. *The Goths in the Crimea* Mediaeval Academy of America, 1936.

Veletskaya, N. N. "Forms of Transformation of Pagan Symbolism in the Old Believer Tradition" In, *Russian Traditional Culture: Religion, Gender and Customary Law*. Edited by Marjorie Mandelstam Balzer and Ronald Radzai. Routledge, 1992.

BIBLIOGRAPHY 397

Vernadsky, Georgy. *Kievan Rus'* Yale University Press, 1977.

Vince-Pallua, Jelka. "A Newly Discovered Figurative Representation of the Mythical Baba – "Old Baba Vukoša" in St. Mary's Church of Gracišce in Istria" In, *Sacralization of Landscape and Sacred Places*. (Proceedings of the 3rd International Scientific Conference of Mediaeval Archaeology of the Institute of Archaeology Zagreb, 2nd and 3rd June 2016). Edited by Juraj Belaj, Marijana Belaj, Siniša Krznar, Tajana Sekelj Ivancan and Tatjana Tkalcec. Zbornik Institutaza , Arheologiju, Serta Instituti Archaeologici, Knjiga Volume 10, 2018: 105-115

Vitale, Emma; Jacob A. Rasmussen, Bjarne Grønnow, Anders J. Hansen, Morten Meldgaard, Tatiana R. Feuerborn. (Eds.). "An Ethnographic Framework For Identifying Dog Sledding In The Archaeological Record" *Journal of Archaeological Science* Vol. 159, 2023. https://doi.org/10.1016/j.jas.2023.105856. https://www.sciencedirect.com/science/article/pii/S030544032300136X

Vlasov, V. G. "The Christianization of Russian Peasants" In, *Russian Traditional Culture: Religion, Gender and Customary Law*. Edited by Marjorie Balzar Mandelstam and Ronald Radzai. Routledge, 1992.

von Herberstein, Sigmund Freiherr. Notes upon Russia: Being a translation of the earliest account of that country, entitled Rerum Moscoviticarum Commentarii. 2 [1549] (the original document, translated). London: Hakluyt Society, 1852.

Wademarch, Nicholas. *A Host of Mummies, a Forest of Secrets* 2010. https://www.nytimes.com/2010/03/16/science/16archeo.html

Watkins, Calvert. (Ed.) *The American Heritage Dictionary of Indo-European Roots*, 2nd ed., Houghton Mifflin Co., 2000.

Weaver, Jace. "The Red Atlantic" *American Indian Quarterly* no 3 (2011): 418-463, 477.

Webb, Simon. *The Forgotten Slave Trade* Pen and Sword Books Ltd., 2020.

Werbart, Bozena. "Khazars or Saltovo-Majaki Culture? Prejudices about Archaeology and Ethnicity" *Current Swedish Archaeology*, Vol. 4 1996.

Westerdahl, Christer. "Boats Apart. Building and Equipping an Iron-Age and Early Medieval Ship in Northern Europe" *International Journal of Nautical Archaeology*, 37 (2007): 17-31. https://doi.org/10.1111/j.1095-9270.2007.00170.x

Whitfield, Susan. Silk, Slaves, and Stupas: Material Culture of the Silk Road University of California Press, 2018.

Whitelock, Dorothy. *The Beginnings of English Society* Penguin Books, 1963.

Whittow, David. *The Making of Byzantium, 600-1025* C.E. University of California Press, 1996.

Williams, Gareth. *Viking Camps Case Studies and Comparisons* Edited by Charlotte Hedenstierna-Jonson and Irene García Losquiño. Routledge, Taylor & Francis Group, 2023. DOI: 10.4324/9781003347682-3

Wilde, Lyn Webster. *On the Trail of the Women Warriors: The Amazons in Myth and History* St. Martin's Press, 2000.

Wickler, Stephen. "Visualizing Sámi Waterscapes in Northern Norway from an Archaeological Perspective" In, *A Circumpolar Reappraisal: The Legacy of Gutorm Gjessing (1906-1979)*. Edited by C. Westerdahl. BAR International Series 2154., 2010.

Wiklund, Professor K. B. "The Race Biology of the Swedish Lapps": With the Collaboration of the Staff of the [Swedish State] Institute [for Race Biology] and of Professor K. B. Wiklund. General survey. Prehistory. Demography. Future of the Lapps, Part 1. Edited by Herman Bernhard Lundborg., and Sten Gösta William Wahlund. Almqvist & Wiksell, 1932.

Wolf, Eric. *Europe and the People Without History* Berkeley: University of California Press, 1982.

Wood, Ian N. "Deconstructing the Merovingian Family" In, *The Construction of Communities in the Early Middle Ages: Texts, Resources and Artefacts*. Edited by Richard Corradini; Maximilian Diesenberger; Helmut Reimitz. Brill, 2003.

Yazdan, Safaee. "Scythian and Zoroastrian Earth Goddesses: A Comparative Study on Api and Armaiti" In, *Archaeology of Iran in the Historical Period*. University of Tehran Science and Humanities Series. Edited by Kamal-Aldin Niknami and Ali Hozhabri. Springer International Publishing. (2020): 65–75. doi:10.1007/978-3-030-41776-5_6

Young, R. *White Mythologies – Writing History and the West* London: Routledge, 1990.

Zachrisson, Inger. "The Sámi And Their Interaction With The Nordic Peoples" In, *The Viking World*. Edited by Stefan Brink and Neil Price. Routledge, 2008: 32–9.

Znamensky, Andrei A. "Az osiség szépsége: altáji török sámánok a szibériai regionális gondolkodásban (1860-1920)" In, *Csodaszarvas. Ostörténet, vallás és néphagyomány*. Vol. I, 128 (in Hungarian). Molnár, Ádám (Ed.) Molnár Kiadó, 2005.

Zvelebil, Marek. "The Agricultural Transition And The Origins Of Neolithic Society In Europe" *Documenta Praehistorica*. XXVIII (2001): 1-26. 10.4312/dp.28.1https://www.researchgate.net/publication/291911861_The_agricultural_transition_and_the_origins_of_Neolithic_society_in_Europe

BIBLIOGRAPHY

ONLINE SOURCES

Sophie Bergerbrant. "Revisiting the 'Egtved Girl" (2019). https://www.researchgate.net/publication/333046418_Revisiting_the_'Egtved_Girl'

Harold Alden, Shamanism and Sacred Arts in Finland – Part 2. https://www.spiritboat.ca/2014/06/shamanism-and-sacred-arts-in-finland.html

William Shakespeare, Troilus and Cressida, Clark, W. G. and Aldis Wright, W. (Eds.) The Globe Shakespeare. (New York: Nelson Doubleday Inc. 1960). https://www.litcharts.com/shakescleare/shakespeare-translations/troilus-and-cressida/act-1-scene-1

"Yajamana Sutta: The Discourse on the Sacrificer" Translated & Annotated by Piya Tan. (Sa yutta Nikaya 11.16/1:233) f) Living Word of the Buddha SD 22 no 7 (2008) The Minding Centre https://www.themindingcentre.org 2009.

Joshua J. Mark, https://www.worldhistory.org/Kievan_Rus/ (2018).

Terence Edward Armstrong. "Study and Exploration" https://www.britannica.com/place/Arctic/Political-and-environmental-issues

Society for the Protection of Monuments and Local History of the Lithuanian SSR(Lietuvos TSR paminklu apsaugos ir kraštotyros draugijos) - https://www.kernave.lt/kernaves-muziejui-90-metu/, Public Domain, https://commons.wikimedia.org/w/index.php?curid=151975270

Ole E. Henriksen, own work. Public Domain, Category: Runestones, Skåne, Sweden, https://commons.wikimedia.org/w/index.php?curid=1647531 :Sövestadstenen 1 (DR 290)

By Margoz - Own work, CC BY-SA 4.0, https://commons.wikimedia.org/w/index.php?curid=4491186

Zbruch idol photo by Simon Burchell – Own work, CC BY-SA 3.0, https://commons.wikimedia.org/w/index.php?curid=30940172

Drawing by Carl Schuchhardt (1859–1943) - Schuchhardt Carl. Hanz Schoetz & Co. G.M.D.H. Berlin. 1926, Public Domain, https://commons.wikimedia.org/w/index.php?curid=36608393

See also, a photo of this stone by Lebrac – Own work, CC BY-SA 3.0, https://commons.wikimedia.org/w/index.php?curid=5182695

Society for the Protection of Monuments and Local History of the Lithuanian SSR(Lietuvos TSR paminklu apsaugos ir kraštotyros draugijos) - https://www.kernave.lt/kernaves-muziejui-90-metu/, Public Domain,

Bernard Picart *"Cérémonies et coutumes religieuses de tous les peuples du monde."* (1724) Author: Bernard Picart (1673–1733) wikidata:Q559929 s:en:Author: Bernard Picart

The Editors of Encyclopaedia Britannica. "Danelaw" Encyclopedia Britannica, January 30, 2025. https://www.britannica.com/place/Danelaw.

"Anglo-Norman Studies XI Proceedings of the Battle Conference 1988" (Boydell & Brewer, 1989): 191 – 220. DOI: https://doi.org/10.1017/9781846151934.011 https://www.e-education.psu.edu/earth107/node/1496

https://yle.fi/uutiset/osasto/news/iron_age_dna_sheds_light_on_finns_genetic_origin/11072769i

https://www.ncbi.nlm.nih.gov/pmc/articles/PMC5204334/

https://commons.wikimedia.org/wiki/File:Bracteate_from_Funen,_Denmark_(DR_BR42).jpg

Thor's_hammer,_Skåne.jpg, Public Domain: https://commons.wikimedia.org/w/index.php?curid=11256957

https://en.wikipedia.org/wiki/Early_Slavs

https://avaldsnes.info/en/informasjon/harald-harfagre/

https://www.britannica.com/science/Holocene-Epoch/The-Pleistocene-Holocene-boundary

https://www.nytimes.com/2023/03/01/science/dna-hunter-gatherers-europe.html

https://www.labrys.net.br/labrys22/archeo/jeannine_daviskimball.htm

https://www.germanicmythology.com/original/cosmology5.html

https://www.rbth.com/history/331675-how-siberia-was-once-separate-country

https://www.etymonline.com/search?q=nifol

https://tepetelegrams.wordpress.com/2017/03/01/the-gobekli-tepe-totem-pole/

https://tourism.arctic-russia.ru/en/sights/vaygach-state-nature-reserve/

Nenets: https://www.arcticrussiatravel.com/nenets-autonomous-okrug/

Nenets: https://www.yamalpeninsulatravel.com/who-are-the-nenets/

BIBLIOGRAPHY

https://feheleyfinearts.com/sikhirtya-figures-from-siberia/

A. Sutherland. AncientPages.com https://www.ancientpages.com/2020/02/15/fenja-and-menja-sisters/

http://mcllibrary.org/DanishHistory/book9.html

https://www.historic-uk.com/.../Barbary-Pirates-English.../

https://feefhs.org/resource/russia-asrnh-staraia-ladoga

http://theinfolist.com/php/HTMLGet.php?FindGo=Primary%20Chronicle

https://www.ancientpages.com/2021/01/18/why-was-the-face-of-mysterious-ust-taseyevsky-stone-idol-suddenly-changed/

https://www.gornahoor.net/library/mcclain/BA_EPIC.pdf

https://commons.wikimedia.org/wiki/File:Kyi,_Czech,_Khoryv_and_Lubed_in_der_Radziwi%C5%82%C5%82chronik.jpg

HERITAGE: Clan of Tubal Cain
An Anthology
SHANI OATES

"In Fate and the overcoming of Fate is the true Graal, for from this, inspiration comes . . ."
ROBERT COCHRANE

Presented in prose and verse, this Clan Anthology of selected musings illustrates the poignant duty of all pilgrims in the Craft to explore and share their realisations and experiences in order to guide and shape those of others.

Drawing upon our incredible legacy, we are bound by our troth to 'pay it forward.' Thus may we ensure the survival of its three sacred tenets – Truth, Love and Beauty (that parallel those of Freemasonry – Wisdom, Strength, and Beauty) for genera to come.

Held within the lore of the folk, our insights regarding the Mysteries come direct from the source, and provide brief and thought-provoking comments on 'The Work.'

ISBN: 9781913660390

THE PEOPLE OF GODA:
Clan of Tubal Cain
SHANI OATES

Dedicated to our northern heritage, this unique work is a deeply personal and introspective insight into the mysteries of 'The People of Goda, of the Clan of Tubal Cain.' And while it is a treatise that is very much a work in progress, it offers a privileged glimpse into who and what the 'People' are. Better yet, it presents the cumulative works of former magisters of the Clan of Tubal Cain, Robert Cochrane, Evan John Jones, and Robin the dart, drawing them to a remarkable conclusion. In so doing, it constructs a dynamic template, a blueprint of their working ethos and praxes germane to the CTC Cosmology.

Asserting a very specific identity and origin, the work provides a contextual basis for emulation and adaptation, a basis from which to grow and develop, so that everyone may in turn, participate and contribute to the vitality of tradition. Peeled back, layer by layer, the very heart of our rich heritage is revealed and shared: culturally, spiritually, and magically. None of this is, nor ever should be deemed secret, but it is sacred, at least to those who cherish this precious pearl of wisdom; for it represents a way of seeing and a way of being by which everyone may 'know thyself ' and be truly blessed.

Near heretical conclusions are drawn from a hefty body of research that some may find contentious, others may see this knowledge as challenging. Many agendas have historically obfuscated the simple beauty and elegance of a system based in northern culture. It is hoped this innovative material will rekindle the needful fires of cultural enquiry in the pursuit of a life given purpose and meaning into the next generation and beyond.

ISBN: 9781913660437

INVENTING WITCHCRAFT
Aidan A. Kelly

When the first edition of this book was released, conservative Gardnerian Witches attempted to suppress it, claiming that it discredited their religion. Even though its first printing quickly sold out, the original publisher, faced with death threats and boycotts, agreed to abandon the project and no other publisher has dared to reprint it before now.

Dr. Aidan A. Kelly has thoroughly investigated the history, rituals and documents behind the evolution of modern Witchcraft and has concluded that Gerald Gardner invented Wicca as a new religion. Although Wicca claims to be a persecuted pagan religion dating from before the rise of Christianity, it draws upon controversial historical sources, modern occult practices, including those of Aleistair Crowley and the Hermetic Order of the Golden Dawn, 19th century translations of medieval grimoires and the poetry of Gardner's priestess, Doreen Valiente.

This extensively revised edition contains new research which was unavailable at the time, as well as detailed textual comparisons of Gerald Gardner's own manuscripts, magical books and rituals that could not be included in the earlier edition. It contains contributions from people who helped Gardner create modern Witchcraft and looks at the sources of his inspiration. Both liberal Wiccans and religious scholars hailed the earlier book as a classic in the new field of Pagan Studies. This revised edition is a must-have for anyone interested in Witchcraft and modern religious history.

ISBN: 9781870450584

WITCHFATHER, A LIFE OF GERALD GARDNER Vol. 1 and Vol. 2
Philip Heselton

From his birth into an old family of wealthy Liverpool merchants, through an unconventional upbringing by his flamboyant governess in the resorts of the Mediterranean and Madeira, it tells how, having taught himself to read, his life was changed by finding a book on spiritualism.

During a working life as a tea and rubber planter in Ceylon, Borneo and Malaya, he came to know the native people and was invited to their secret rituals. But it was only on his retirement to England, settling on the edge of the New Forest in Hampshire, that destiny took him firmly by the hand. Through various twists and turns involving naturist clubs and a strange esoteric theatre, he became friends with a group of people who eventually revealed their true identity – they were members of a surviving witch coven.

One evening in 1939, as the hounds of war were being unleashed, he was initiated into the "witch cult" by these people, who called themselves 'the Wica'. Gardner was overwhelmed by the experience and was determined that the witch cult should survive. This book chronicles his efforts over the remaining quarter century of his life to ensure not only that it survived but that it would become the significant player on the world religious stage that it now is – the only religion that England has ever given the world, in the words of Ronald Hutton, Professor of History at the University of Bristol, who calls it '*a very fine book: humane, intelligent, compassionate, shrewd, and based upon a colossal amount of primary research*'.

Vol. 1 ISBN: 9781870450805   Vol. 2 ISBN 9781870450799

THE WESTERN MYSTERY TRADITION
Christine Hartley

A re-issue of a classic work by a formidable priestess, pupil of Dion Fortune and working partner of Charles Seymour, F.P.D., the 'Forgotten Mage'.

Working at a time when many were turning to Eastern spirituality, Christine Hartley believed that Britain had its own mystery tradition, hidden in myth and legend and in the land itself. She had known Merlin on the inner planes, journeying with him to the Celtic Underworld and she was more than happy to show us the entrance to this realm. Drawing on folk lore and song, the legacy of Druidic culture is brought alive, providing practical guidelines for modern students of the ancient mysteries. The Western Mystery Tradition is the basis of the Western religious feeling, the foundation of our spiritual life, the matrix of religious formulae, whether we are aware of it or not.

To it we owe the inspiration and force of our spiritual life. Very much reflecting the current return to paganism in our search for the spiritual, Christine Hartley reminds us that
'*The corn is still green and the ears are ripening for the harvest.*'

ISBN: 9781870450249

THE WIZARD OF MILTON BRODIE
R.A. Gilbert

John William Brodie Innes (1848–1923) was one of the most significant players in the drama of the Golden Dawn, one of the few real scholars in the Order, and one who also maintained a fine balance between his occult pursuits and his genuine Christian faith. But his esoteric writings have been, for too long, undeservedly overlooked.

Brodie Innes wrote well and intelligently on a wide range of occult subjects, often recounting and reflecting on his own experiences, but most of his work was printed in the occult periodicals of his day –very little of it, apart from his occult fiction, appeared in book form.

This new anthology collects the best of these fugitive contributions – ranging from astrology and the Tarot to magic and witchcraft, and taking in Theosophy, folklore, hauntings, possession, prayer and a long occult novella – together with unpublished material on the Cromlech Temple. All this with the aim of bringing back Brodie Innes where he deserves to be: at the heart of the Hermetic Order of the Golden Dawn.

ISBN: 9781913660383

www.ingramcontent.com/pod-product-compliance
Lightning Source LLC
Chambersburg PA
CBHW071311150426
43191CB00007B/584